PROOF

OF

CORRUPTION

ALSO BY SETH ABRAMSON

Proof of Conspiracy
Proof of Collusion

PROOF
OF
CORRUPTION

BRIBERY, IMPEACHMENT, AND PANDEMIC
IN THE AGE OF TRUMP

SETH ABRAMSON

ST. MARTIN'S
PRESS
NEW YORK

First published in the United States by St. Martin's Press,
an imprint of St. Martin's Publishing Group

PROOF OF CORRUPTION. Copyright © 2020 by Seth Abramson. All rights reserved. Printed
in the United States of America. For information, address St. Martin's Publishing Group,
120 Broadway, New York, NY 10271.

www.stmartins.com

Designed by Steven Seighman

The Library of Congress Cataloging-in-Publication Data is available upon request.

ISBN 978-1-250-27299-7 (hardcover)
ISBN 978-1-250-27300-0 (ebook)

Our books may be purchased in bulk for promotional, educational, or business use.
Please contact your local bookseller or the Macmillan Corporate and
Premium Sales Department at 1-800-221-7945, extension 5442,
or by email at MacmillanSpecialMarkets@macmillan.com.

First Edition: 2020

10 9 8 7 6 5 4 3 2 1

for my father

CONTENTS

AUTHOR'S NOTE

The 3,250 endnotes for *Proof of Corruption* comprise 5,000 citations and run more than 300 pages. To ensure that this element of the text is link-enabled and searchable, it has been published for free online. You can find it at http://read.macmillan.com/proofofcorruptionnotes. The pages at this link are numbered as they would have been numbered had they appeared in print.

Proof of Corruption is the third in a trilogy of books about Trump's foreign policy—following *Proof of Collusion* (Simon & Schuster, 2018) and *Proof of Conspiracy* (St. Martin's Press, 2019)—so its predecessors should be regarded as prefatory material. Except as necessary, *Proof of Corruption* does not reiterate content from *Proof of Collusion* or *Proof of Conspiracy*.

PROOF

OF

CORRUPTION

THE RULE OF LAW

On February 20, 2014, Russia invaded Ukraine, a sovereign nation in eastern Europe.

In seeking to assume partial dominion over the second-largest country by land area in Europe—and the largest located entirely within the continent—Russian president Vladimir Putin had cause to apprehend a dramatic response from the United States, particularly if Democrat Hillary Clinton won the U.S. presidency in 2016.[1] If *Proof of Collusion*, the first book in the trilogy that *Proof of Corruption* concludes, detailed Putin's anti-Clinton, pro–Donald Trump interference in the 2016 election, and if the second book in the trilogy, *Proof of Conspiracy*, described attempts by Trump and Putin and their agents to partner on geopolitical schemes involving Saudi Arabia and the United Arab Emirates (UAE), the book you now hold concludes the trilogy by telling the story of how Putin came to see Trump's 2020 reelection as every bit as important to the Kremlin's global adventurism as Russia's 2016 election interference had been. It is also the story of a presidency so venal and unscrupulous that its agents sought to cooperate not only with autocrats in Russia, Ukraine, Saudi Arabia, and the UAE but also with governments around the world hostile to U.S. interests.

This is the big picture—sprawling, complex, untidy. Yet the narrative at the core of what we now call "the Ukraine scandal" is surprisingly uncomplicated. It is admirably summarized by a *New York Times* editorial calling for the impeachment of the president. "President Donald Trump abused the power of his office," wrote the *Times* editorial board in December 2019, "by strong-arming Ukraine, a vulnerable ally, holding up hundreds of millions of dollars in military aid until it agreed to help him influence the 2020 election by digging up dirt on a political rival."[2]

For those who read about the Trump-Russia scandal in *Proof of Collusion*, this fact pattern is familiar. As the *New Yorker* has written, "The Russia and Ukraine scandals are, in fact, one story. Indeed, the President's false denials in both of them capture the common themes: soliciting help from foreign interests for partisan gain, followed by obstruction of efforts to uncover what happened."[3] Just so, those who read *Proof of Conspiracy* will know that several still sparsely reported Trump scandals involving nominal U.S. allies in the Middle East also featured apparent bribery and obstruction of justice. In *Proof of Corruption*, this same coupling of offenses reappears—not just in the president's public and clandestine dealings with Ukraine, but also in his back-channel negotiations with China, Turkey, Israel, Venezuela, and even domestic political donors pushing supposed miracle drugs during the ongoing COVID-19 pandemic. These narratives confirm Trump's behavior as predictable and unchanging. The question is whether America can dynamically respond to a novel threat to its rule of law—and whether we will continue to abide the horrific losses this threat has imposed on us.

The word "corruption," applied to a U.S. presidential administration and its foreign policy, denotes a perniciously systemic penchant for four types of activity: criminal activity enumerated as impeachable by the U.S. Constitution; other criminal activity qualifying as a "high crime or misdemeanor" under the Constitution's impeachment clause; noncriminal activity that nevertheless is eligible for impeachment under the U.S. Constitution as a threat to national security or a violation of the nonstatutory "catch-all" component of the impeachment clause's "high crimes and misdemeanors" proviso; and noncriminal, nonimpeachable conduct that indicates a president is unfit to serve as a matter of ethics, conformity to democratic norms, and commitment to the rule of law. The Trump administration may be regarded as corrupt because many of its offices and departments have from January 2017 onward exhibited in abundance all four forms of malfeasance.

If the impeachment and trial of President Bill Clinton in the late 1990s ultimately focused on conduct unrelated to the president's execution of his official duties, President Trump's impeachment and trial could not have been more intimately concerned with the responsibilities of the nation's highest office and the federal statutes that ensure politicians remain faithful to voters. The criminal statutes in play in the narrative this book unfolds include the following: bribery, extortion, illegal solicitation of foreign campaign donations, obstruction of justice, wire fraud, bank fraud, conspiracy, aiding and abetting, witness tampering, making false statements to Congress or federal law enforcement, perjury, the Logan Act, and the Hatch Act. Noncriminal impeachable offenses appearing in the narrative include abuse of power, obstruction of Congress, violations of the presidential oath of office, and breaches of the Constitution's emoluments clause. Two additional offenses investigators are considering with respect to individuals discussed in this book are Foreign Agent Registration Act (FARA) crimes and money laundering.[4]

Above all, however, the question remains whether Trump is a national security risk as a result of foreign "compromise"—a term encompassing both sensational scenarios and the mundane possibility that a geopolitical enemy of the United States has so much more knowledge of the president's clandestine activities at home and abroad than Congress or the American people that the revelation of such secrets could be leveraged against him to the detriment of U.S. interests. Compromise can also occur if America's head of state has so many pecuniary conflicts of interest and countervailing motives that he cannot be trusted to uphold his oath of office, conform to the norms of international diplomacy, or put the safety and security of the United States ahead of personal avarice or ambition.

The Atlantic has written that, federal statutes and the Constitution's impeachment clause aside, what Trump and his aides, advisers, allies, agents, and associates perpetrated in Ukraine in the president's first three years in office is "a conspiracy against American democracy. Fearing that the 2016 election was a fluke in which Trump prevailed only because of a successful Russian hacking and disinformation campaign and because of a last-minute intervention on Trump's behalf by the very national security state Trump defenders supposedly loathe, Trump and his advisers sought to rig the 2020 election by forcing a foreign country to implicate the then–Democratic front-runner in a crime that did not take place. If the American people could not be trusted to choose Trump on their own, Trump would use his official powers to make the choice for them. It was, in short, a conspiracy by Trump and his advisers to keep themselves in power, the exact scenario for which the Framers of the Constitution devised the impeachment clause."[5]

Even this categorization undersells the depth and reach of the Trump administration's corruption—which bent itself not only toward the rigging of an upcoming presidential election but also toward a rewriting of the history of the last one to justify Trump's and his political party's unwillingness to protect America's electoral infrastructure. By seeking to exculpate Russia for meddling in one election and secretly coercing Ukraine to meddle in another, Trump and his inner circle created a paradigm for corrupt federal elections that risks poisoning our democracy for decades. Still worse, by launching a rhetorical war on our European allies, our intelligence agencies, federal law enforcement, our system of justice, and even the maxim that says domestic politics ends at the water's edge, Trump has threatened to burn vital components of America's superstructure to the ground if the nation does not bend to his caprice and venality. That corrupt conduct by the president and his entourage is evident in other countries around the globe besides Russia, Ukraine, Saudi Arabia, and the UAE, and that it has now manifested again during the present COVID-19 outbreak in the United States—with spectacularly destructive results—exponentially increases the national security risk posed by a historically corrupt presidency.

CHAPTER I

MANAFORT

In 2007, Trump's future campaign manager Paul Manafort partners on an $850 million real estate deal with three men: future Trump deputy campaign manager Rick Gates; a Russian oligarch considered an "ally of Vladimir Putin," Oleg Deripaska; and a Soviet-born oligarch whom federal prosecutors call a "[Russian] organized-crime member," Dmitry Firtash.[1] According to an October 2019 *Daily Beast* article, the deal involves the acquisition of New York City's Drake Hotel by "launder[ing]" Firtash's "ill-gotten" oil and gas fortune—the implication being that Manafort and Gates are participating in laundering hundreds of millions of dollars for the Russian mob.[2] Manafort and Gates's past involvement with the Russian mafia constitutes an immediate national security risk upon their hire by then-candidate Trump in March 2016. Manafort's business connection to the Russian mafia means, too, according to former CIA chief of Russia operations Steve Hall, that Manafort had been "at the very least vetted by the Russians when he worked for [former Ukrainian president Viktor] Yanukovych in Ukraine"—employment he discontinued just twenty-four months before applying to work for Trump's presidential campaign.[3]

Manafort had partnered with Deripaska and Firtash prior to 2007 as well. In 2006, according to the Associated Press (AP), Manafort signed a $10 million-a-year contract with "longtime Putin associate" Deripaska to covertly "aid Putin" in the United States; Manafort's charge was to "greatly benefit the Putin Government" via unspecified "political and economic efforts inside the United States."[4] As part of his work for Deripaska,

Manafort assisted Yanukovych in building the political might of Ukraine's pro-Kremlin "Party of Regions." As reported by NBC News, Firtash—a "top-tier comrade of Russian mobsters"—was also a "major [financial] backer of the Party of Regions."[5] Deripaska, Russia's second-richest man as of 2007, by his own public confession "do[es] not separate [himself] from the state"—meaning that he self-identifies as a Kremlin agent.[6]

In 2006, Manafort's first task for Deripaska, and therefore Putin, is, per *The Atlantic*, "to see whether there was any hope of thwarting the democratic revolution that had swept through Ukraine in late 2004."[7] The assignment bears an eerie resemblance to Manafort's efforts during the 2016 presidential campaign to damage Ukraine's reputation and retard its political progress (see chapter 5). That Manafort's chief co-conspirator in Putin and Deripaska's mid-aughts conspiracy against Ukraine, Konstantin Kilimnik—a dual Russian-Ukrainian citizen with "ties to a Russian intelligence service"—will stand accused of being Manafort's right-hand man throughout his 2016 undermining of Ukraine while working on the Trump campaign is yet another improbable coincidence.[8]

According to *The Atlantic*, after Manafort and Kilimnik's Ukrainian patron, then-president Yanukovych, is deposed by pro-democracy forces in 2014, the two men are desperate to find a way to get their Party of Regions allies back to positions of power in Ukraine. To that end, they begin seeking a mechanism to gain "lucrative access to the machinery of state" in Ukraine.[9] This mechanism arrives in the form of Donald Trump in 2016. As *The Atlantic* details, when Kilimnik flies from Ukraine to the United States just as Trump is securing the GOP nomination for president in 2016, the Russian-Ukrainian citizen tells friends he has "come to the United States for 'very significant meetings,'" and it isn't "hard for his friends to intuit what he mean[s] . . . [having] read the news reports that Paul Manafort had engineered his own comeback, procuring a top job in the Trump campaign. Just like in the good old days [in Ukraine], Manafort had summoned Kilimnik to trail after him."[10]

That the course of Manafort's contract to "aid Putin" via "political efforts inside the United States" includes his management of the 2016 Trump campaign and—critically—the many months of private Trump-Manafort political discussions following Manafort's August 2016 departure from the campaign is confirmed by U.S. media reports that Manafort told Deripaska agents in early 2016 that he would seek to use his work with Trump to "get whole" with Deripaska financially.[11]

In 2016, the same year Manafort signs a contract to advance the Kremlin's interests in the United States, he moves into the very New York City building Trump lives in—Trump Tower.[12] Manafort has already known Trump for decades when he moves into the building where Trump's office and personal residence are located; indeed, Trump was Manafort's first client when the latter began his political consulting business with future Trump presidential adviser Roger Stone in 1980.[13] While Manafort does not "own" the Trump account in 1980—that honor goes to Stone (see chapter 8)—a partner in the firm at the time will later say that Manafort would often, when Trump's account was being discussed, "dispense advice and pitch in," a practice routine enough that in short order Manafort finds himself, per his former colleague, "winning Trump's trust."[14] Manafort himself will say in 2016, somewhat cryptically, that "Donald Trump and I had some business in the 1980s."[15]

Manafort and Trump develop a sufficiently close relationship in the early to mid-1980s that when Manafort is deputy convention manager for the 1988 Republican National Convention, he issues a special invitation to Trump to come to the Louisiana Superdome to "see how a convention [i]s really run"; per *U.S. News & World Report*, "the two convened in a trailer outside the Superdome during a steamy weekday for a friendly chitchat."[16] Enough respect develops between the two men that by the time Trump taps Manafort to be a major player in his presidential campaign in March 2016, Manafort is, according to GOP operative Scott Reed, Trump's "peer, not someone Trump can bully and boss around." Manafort's daughter Andrea will refer to her father's relationship with candidate Trump as "the most dangerous friendship in America" in a text—while her sister Jessica, in another text, will write that "Dad and Trump are literally living in the same building and mom says they go up and down all day long hanging and plotting together."[17]

Trump remains a Manafort client from 1980 "through the early 1990s," notes the national-security-expert-staffed website *Just Security*, with the two men having "mutual close friends," mutual local political interests ("both Manafort and Trump were active in the New Jersey political scene in the 1990s"), mutual lobbying interests ("both men were involved in lobbying Capitol Hill on Indian gaming issues"), and mutual business interests ("[in] 2006, Manafort . . . became involved in the Manhattan real estate scene").[18] By Manafort's admission, in at least one instance he performs work directly for Trump, helping to "clear noisy airspace over Mr. Trump's Florida resort, Mar-a-Lago," per the *New York Times*.[19] According to the *Hartford Courant*, by 1993 Trump is saying publicly that he is "very loyal" to Manafort and Stone's consulting firm, which he notes has "represented him over the years."[20]

In 2001, Manafort meets and goes into business with Julius Nasso—a man who in 2003 will plead guilty to federal extortion charges—with the two associates' matchmaker being none other than Trump himself. Trump is sufficiently close to Nasso that before the latter enters into an agreement to make a film with well-known Broadway producer, real estate investor, and politician Abe Hirschfeld, he asks Trump's opinion of the man. "I checked [Hirschfeld] out with Donald Trump," Nasso told the *New York Post* in 1999, "[and] Donald said he was a nice guy."[21]

Manafort has been working primarily for and in Ukraine for two years at the time he purchases his Trump Tower condo in November 2006 for $3.675 million, the funding for which purchase therefore almost certainly comes, in part or entirely, from his millions in Kremlin-backed earnings.[22] According to *Slate*, Manafort sees and speaks to Trump in Trump Tower with some regularity from November 2006 onward, with the digital media outlet noting that "when Manafort took an apartment in Trump Tower in 2006, he would kibitz with his old client when they'd run into one another." While the subject of these informal chats is unknown, both men are at the time deeply immersed in high-end real estate, even as the contract with Deripaska that Manafort had negotiated required Manafort to, as the Associated Press describes, "influence . . . business dealings . . . inside the United States . . . to benefit President Vladimir Putin's government."[23]

In the same year that Manafort—by this time one of Ukraine's top political operatives—becomes a tenant of Trump Tower, Trump suddenly develops a powerful interest in Ukraine. As *Politico* notes, it is only eight months after Manafort and Deripaska begin discussing in mid-2005 what Manafort can do for the Kremlin via "business dealings" in the United States that Trump's children Don and Ivanka travel to Ukraine to meet face-to-face with government officials; it is in the same month, February 2006, that Trump fixer and "[Russian] mob-linked operator" Felix Sater gives Don and Ivanka a guided tour of Moscow ("at Donald Trump's request," according to the *Washington Post*) and arranges for Ivanka to not only access Putin's private office in the Kremlin but sit in his chair.[24]

Exactly how Trump's two eldest children gain direct access to Manafort's co-workers in the Ukrainian government in February 2006 is unclear, though their chief topic of discussion in Kyiv is well known: "a multimillion dollar hotel and golf course in the country."[25] The discussions Don and Ivanka have with government officials in the Ukrainian capital are serious and fruitful enough that as late as two years later, in 2008—as Trump is considering whether to run for president in 2012—Don goes back to Ukraine to meet with potential developers for the project.[26]

It is also in 2008 that Manafort creates a real estate development team, CMZ Ventures, with, among others, Brad Zackson—the longtime "right-hand man" and "exclusive broker and manager" for Donald Trump's father, Fred Trump, when the latter was running "the original Trump Organization."[27] Zackson is, per *Commercial Observer*—a New York City real estate publication launched and owned by Trump's son-in-law, Jared Kushner—a man so linked to the Trump family that he had literally "[gained] access to [New York] society's inner circle through the Trumps."[28]

Just as Manafort manages to regularly "kibitz" with Trump by living in Trump Tower, the Ukrainian political operative is able to befriend Trump's father's "right-hand man" by becoming his "neighbor in the

Hamptons"; it is Manafort's second real estate purchase putting him in the orbit of the Trumps while he is under a Kremlin-backed contract.[29] Zackson would, in the 2000s, invest in several of Manafort's business projects, even as, according to *Just Security*, the latter developed a reputation in professional and social circles as a man with "an uncanny ability to conjure investors, such as Ukrainian billionaire gas king Dmitry Firtash," according to a 2011 panegyric in Kushner's *Commercial Observer*.[30] Years later, Manafort would get hired by the 2016 Trump campaign in substantial part based on the recommendation of Jared and his wife, Ivanka.[31]

Manafort's 2008 Drake Hotel venture with Oleg Deripaska, Dmitry Firtash, and Fred Trump's fixer Brad Zackson quite nearly involved Trump himself, according to Kushner's paper. *Commercial Observer* writes that "Mr. Manafort . . . met with Ukrainian billionaire Mr. Firtash, a part owner of Eural Transgas, in Kyiv, and secured the promise of an initial $112 million for the project, but that fell apart when Mr. Firtash became distracted by an investment in troubled Bank Nadra back home. Grasping, Mr. Zackson wrote in an email in March 2009: 'I have an idea to bring [Donald] Trump in on the Drake. I think it solves a lot of issues right away.'"[32] How far the longtime Trump family friend got in connecting Ukrainian political operative Manafort, Ukrainian oligarch Firtash, Russian oligarch Deripaska, and future U.S. president Donald Trump as business partners is unknown. What is known is that after Manafort's boss Yanukovych was ousted from power (for the first time) in 2007, his successor, the reformer Yulia Tymoshenko, unsuccessfully "alleged in a lawsuit that 'Firtash used [the joint Manafort-Zackson-Firtash venture] CMZ as a front in order to hide income illegally skimmed from his natural gas company RosUkrEnergo," an outfit whose revenue comes in substantial part from the Kremlin-owned gas company, Gazprom. Tymoshenko further alleged that the "real owner" of RosUkrEnergo was infamous Russian mobster Semion Mogilevich, a man who employed Trump attorney Michael Cohen's father; allegedly made longtime Cohen friend Felix Sater one of his "main American liaisons," per the *Daily Beast*; and helped Dmitry Firtash "get his start in business," according to statements by Firtash to William Taylor, a former U.S. ambassador to Ukraine.[33] Reuters reports that RosUkrEnergo was plagued for years by accusations it was a wholly unnecessary middleman between Russian and Ukrainian gas concerns, existing only to enrich Russian and Ukrainian oligarchs at the expense of the Ukrainian government.[34] That Donald Trump quite nearly ends up in a business venture in 2009 with Zackson, Manafort, Deripaska, Firtash, Firtash's energy interests, and—indirectly—the Putin-controlled Gazprom will become relevant to his impeachment a decade hence, as the latter event has at its heart all five of those elements: Manafort, Deripaska, Firtash, Firtash's energy interests, and Gazprom (see chapters 10 and 11).

The Manafort-Firtash deal isn't Trump's only near-miss in Ukraine, nor are Manafort and Zackson the only longtime Trump Organization associates with whom Trump crosses paths in the former Soviet republic. One of the Trumps' agents in Ukraine in the mid- to late 2000s—during the years Manafort was making powerful connections there—was none other than Sater, who not only came close to closing a Trump Tower Moscow deal for Trump in 2005 but would infamously, with then-candidate Trump and Trump's attorney Michael Cohen, have Trump sign a mid-presidential campaign letter of intent on a second, Kremlin-approved Trump Tower Moscow plan in 2015.[35]

While the level of Sater's involvement in Trump's mid-aughts to mid-teens attempts to do business in Ukraine is uncertain, the Trump Organization's track record in the region at the time suggests Trump may have felt he had cause to be upset with his agents in Ukraine, Ukrainian officials and businessmen, or both. In 2006, per popular New York City real estate website *The Real Deal*, "Trump reportedly demanded $20 million to put his name on a proposed high-rise development in Moscow. Ukrainian-Russian developer Pavel Fuks met with Trump several times in 2005, and later with his daughter Ivanka and son Donald Jr. to discuss a Trump-branded tower in Moscow. . . . Fuks apparently offered the Trump Organization $10 million for the branding rights, but Trump demanded $20 million. Ultimately, no deal was reached."[36] The same year, Trump worked with another of his several real estate agents in Ukraine, Dmitry Buriak, on what he hoped would be a multimillion-dollar real estate project in the country; Buriak, like Sater, was at the time simultaneously scouting for business opportunities for Trump in Russia.[37] According to *Politico*, the deal Trump hoped to do in Ukraine—still an active negotiation in 2008, just forty-eight months before he decided to run for president in 2016—was a substantial one. Per the digital media outlet, "Yevhen Chervonenko, then the Ukraine minister of transportation, was quoted in 2005 as saying Trump's expected financial contribution [to the project] was estimated to be $500 million."[38] *Politico* reports that the Trump Organization also considered building "a hotel and yacht club in the seaside city of Yalta, which is now part of the Russian-annexed area of Crimea [in Ukraine]."[39]

While it is unclear what role, if any, Trump's well-connected tenant Paul Manafort played in the Trumps' multiple prospective deals in Ukraine and multiple trips there to advance them, *Politico* reports that "the Ukrainian government granted the [Trump] organization the right to build properties in both cities [Kyiv and Yalta]."[40] The digital media outlet adds that it is "unclear why neither project [the $500 million deal or the Fuks deal] got off the ground," an especially curious development given that some reports suggest Trump had the option to, instead of putting up $500 million of his own money in the former deal, "license [the Trump Organization's] name and receive royalties from any Ukraine project instead of owning the properties, a model [the Trump Organization] follows in many locations around the globe."[41] Whatever the basis of this or other aborted Trump business plans in Ukraine, in November 2019 the Republican counsel for the House Permanent Select Committee on Intelligence, Steve Castor, will submit, during a televised impeachment hearing, that Trump had for years harbored "genuinely deep-rooted concerns about corruption in Ukraine" stemming from his "business dealings in the region."[42] Attorney Castor does not specify which corrupt Ukrainian deals, businessmen, politicians, or political operatives Trump found himself close to in the 2000s, nor does he explain what sort of corruption could trouble a man who in 2012 called the Foreign Corrupt Practices Act—which prohibits

Americans from bribing foreign officials to advance business deals—"ridiculous" and "horrible."[43]

Indeed, there is evidence that Trump's initial interest in Ukraine was predicated upon its corruption rather than diminished by it. In the 2000s, while Buriak is running a company (DeVision) that "bills itself as one of the largest real estate businesses in Ukraine," the Ukrainian is also a vice president at Petrochemical Holding, an entity whose managing director had been convicted, not long before Trump began using Buriak as his in-country agent, for crimes committed while he was working at "Russian government-owned energy giant Gazprom."[44] The corruption at Petrochemical Holding hadn't been limited to Buriak's peers in upper management, either; according to *Politico*, Buriak himself was being investigated, around the time Trump was doing business with him, for allegedly "funnel[ing] money from Russian special services [Russian intelligence]" to political operations in a former Soviet republic.[45] That republic, Lithuania, would later issue a formal finding that Buriak "pos[ed] a threat to the interests of Lithuania"—particularly with respect to "political and electoral interference."[46]

Trump's ties to Manafort at a time the political consultant was a significant figure in a corrupt Ukrainian presidential administration also undercuts contemporary claims by Trump or his allies that corruption in Ukraine has long been a concern of the president's. Manafort's patron Yanukovych was Ukraine's prime minister for sixteen months—from August 2006 through December 2007—before his eviction from office; mere months later, Trump's son entered Ukraine to continue business negotiations his father had initiated while Yanukovych's political star was still rising.[47]

By 2008, therefore, Buriak, Manafort, and Yanukovych all had become potential political liabilities for Trump: not because of Ukraine's corruption, but because of their own, and not because Ukraine had done nothing to combat their corruption, but because it had done all it could. Indeed, Trump could not have failed to note that his business fortunes in Ukraine waned concurrent with the rise of anti-corruption forces in Kyiv, particularly in the person of reformer Yulia Tymoshenko, who was elected Ukraine's prime minister, succeeding Yanukovych, in 2007.[48]

Prior to Tymoshenko's election, the Trumps had excellent access to the government in Kyiv, with Don and Ivanka's February 2006 trip involving a meeting with Viktor Tkachuk, adviser to then–Ukrainian president Viktor Yushchenko, as well as Andriy Zaika of Ukrainian Construction Consortium, a newly formed construction company.[49] By the time of Trump Jr.'s June 2008 return trip to Kyiv, however, he was meeting only with Buriak's peer developers at DeVision—a meeting from which no deal resulted.[50] As Sater would put it in a 2008 deposition, while speaking in particular of the business opportunity the Trumps pursued in Yalta, "It didn't get to the finish line."[51]

Though *Politico* numbers at only two Trump's failures in Ukraine—one in Kyiv and one in Yalta—in fact the number is at least four. Sater testified under oath that he was looking at multiple opportunities for the Trumps in Yalta, and *Politico* distinguishes between a failed Trump Organization project involving the $60 million Euro Park hotel in Kyiv and a second project (a proposed golf club) in Koncha-Zaspa, a neighborhood in southern Kyiv.[52] These missed opportunities stand alongside a host of similarly unrealized Trump Organization projects in former Soviet republics in the 2000s and 2010s. As *Politico* notes, Trump's "broader push in the former Soviet Union never resulted in any completed properties. Trump pulled out of a deal to develop a forty-seven-story luxury tower in the Black Sea resort town of Batumi, Georgia . . . [a]nd a Trump highrise in Baku, the capital of Azerbaijan, remains unfinished."[53]

The reason Manafort still needs to "get whole" with Deripaska when he volunteers to work for Trump pro bono in 2016 is that his business dealings with the Russian oligarch since 2006 have not, in fact, been exclusively pursuant to their year-to-year contract.[54] In March 2007, Manafort and Deripaska co-founded Pericles Emerging Market Partners, a Cayman Islands–based private equity fund; it is through Pericles that Manafort, Gates, Deripaska, and Firtash aim to purchase the Drake Hotel in 2008.[55] In 2011, when Tymoshenko, by then no longer Ukraine's prime minister, unsuccessfully sues Manafort and Firtash—alleging that the Drake

Hotel deal was "a vehicle to launder illegal funds"—she is in the midst of being prosecuted by Ukraine's new presidential administration, one headed by the man she supplanted as prime minister in 2007, longtime Manafort boss Viktor Yanukovych.[56] The charges Tymoshenko faces under the Yanukovych administration are decried as "politically motivated" in statements from both the United States and the European Union, and Tymoshenko's resultant seven-year prison sentence is overturned in 2014 after a court finds that in fact she committed no crime.[57]

Whatever the full story of the Pericles and Drake Hotel projects, what is clear is that by 2011 Manafort is so deeply in debt to Deripaska for having squandered the latter's tens of millions of dollars in investments that he has no choice but to "stop[ ] responding to Deripaska's efforts to reach him."[58] Deripaska subsequently sues Manafort for business behaviors marked, according to Deripaska, by "fraud, gross negligence, blatant disloyalty, and rapacious self-dealing."[59] Yet there is reason to doubt that Manafort's only anxiety with respect to Deripaska, as he begins his work on the Trump campaign, relates to financial debts; as *The Atlantic* will report in June 2018, Manafort knew in 2016 that Deripaska had a "reputation that justifiably inspired fear, given the pattern of deaths that had followed the unlikely rise of his [business] empire in the 1990s."[60] The possibility Manafort joined Trump's campaign as a man in fear for his life is therefore due serious consideration. As *The Guardian* has reported, "Right after Manafort joined the Trump campaign in March 2016, he and Kilimnik began emailing and brainstorming about avenues to escape the Deripaska litigation threat and improve ties with the powerful oligarch."[61] Manafort's now infamous entreaty to Trump friend Thomas Barrack to help him access the businessman's presidential campaign—"I really need to get to [Trump]," Manafort had told Barrack in late February 2016—suggests the desperate straits the former power broker was facing at the time.[62]

Manafort's business associations with Dmitry Firtash in the 2000s may have been slightly less fraught than those he shared with Deripaska, but they are no less relevant today. According to *Mother Jones*, by the time of Trump's inauguration Firtash had spent "years . . . cut[ting] deals with Russia's state-owned gas company, Gazprom."[63] The question of whether the money Firtash received from Gazprom was ill-gotten—part of a long course of suspicious payments to Firtash that Russian president Vladimir Putin had orchestrated (see chapters 10 and 11)—arises not only in the 2019 Trump-Ukraine scandal but also in the most controversial component of special counsel Robert Mueller's earlier Trump-Russia investigation: the so-called Steele dossier, compiled by former MI6 Russia desk chief Christopher Steele in 2016 with indirect funding from Republican and Democratic entities.[64] Steele's MI6-derived sources alleged, in 2016, that the Kremlin had promised money from Gazprom's coffers to then-candidate Donald Trump; when the Trump-Ukraine scandal breaks in the United States in mid-2019, one of its key open questions is whether two individuals paid by the Gazprom-connected Firtash, Lev Parnas and Igor Fruman, have been illegally funneling money to Trump or pro-Trump entities—an allegation that, if true, would closely resemble the raw intelligence compiled in Steele's dossier (see chapters 3 and 11).[65]

Based on Trump and Manafort's interactions in the 1980s, 1990s, and 2000s, *Just Security* will conclude in 2017 that "Trump and Manafort have been crossing paths for decades."[66] As for how frequently the two interacted once Manafort was brought aboard the Trump campaign, the national security news outlet quotes a source "close to the [2016] Trump campaign" as saying that during the campaign Trump was "calling Manafort like 20 times a day"; *New York* magazine and the *Weekly Standard* report that "from the time Manafort joined the [2016] campaign . . . [he was] 'firmly in charge of all major aspects of Trump's campaign' and 'asserting . . . [an] active role in shaping the direction of the campaign and the candidate.'"[67] Manafort was even one of the few people in Trump's political orbit permitted to call him "Donald."[68]

These and like accounts paint the picture of a presidential candidate and campaign manager with such a long history, and enjoying such intimate in-campaign interactions, that if one of the two engaged in illicit collusive behavior—for instance, if Manafort was found, as he was by the April 2019 Mueller Report, to have transmitted in mid-campaign proprietary campaign data to Oleg Deripaska via the Russian-intelligence-linked Kilimnik—there would be good reason to imagine Trump knew of such activities at the time or learned of them eventually.[69] So it is that in January 2018, as Manafort is under federal indictment in multiple jurisdictions, NBC News reports that Trump is "telling friends and aides in private" that one of the chief reasons things are "going great for him" is that "he's decided that a key witness in the Russia probe, Paul Manafort, isn't going to 'flip' and sell him out."[70] Partly for this reason, Trump has determined that he will be able to, if need be, "crush[ ]" Robert Mueller without firing him as special counsel.[71] Left unexplained in NBC News' reporting is what element of Manafort's dealings with Trump, or Trump's knowledge of his campaign manager's dealings with Ukrainian and Russian oligarchs in the 2000s and 2010s, could be used by Manafort to harm the president.

There is, therefore, a paradox at the heart of President Trump's ongoing concern for Manafort's fate in the federal courts and the federal prison system. Trump tells reporters in June 2018 that Manafort's plethora of federal charges "has nothing to do with our [2016] campaign," even as Manafort has, over the preceding eighteen months, been regularly in secret contact with both the president and his political team regarding federal investigations of that very campaign.[72] The 2019 Ukraine scandal will bring this paradox into even higher relief, as the president spends much of 2017, 2018, and 2019 publicly fuming over investigations of Manafort—his words and demeanor indicative of a man who believes he is being personally attacked. Indeed, during the October 2019 congressional testimony of ambassador to the European Union Gordon Sondland, Rep. Devin Nunes (R-CA), a top Trump ally, implies that Trump's now-infamous May 2019 complaint about the Ukrainian government— "they tried to take me down"—referred to Manafort-related leaks to the press in the summer and fall of 2016.[73]

After Manafort's first felony convictions arrive in August 2018, Trump applauds his former campaign chief for not being willing to "make up stories" to avoid federal prison, implying that he believes one of the foremost purposes of the Manafort investigation has been to inculpate America's president in as yet unspecified federal offenses.[74] This belief may explain why, the day after Manafort's deputy Rick Gates pleads guilty in federal court—on February 23, 2018—Trump, per reporting in the *Washington Post*, "seemed anxious about the development . . . He began asking aides whether Manafort might also cooperate with the investigation and whether the former campaign chief knew of anything that could hurt him."[75] Left unanswered in this query is how Trump could be unsure whether a longtime associate could inculpate him. Likewise unanswered is the question of why, per the Mueller Report, Manafort told Gates, days before Gates flipped on the Trump campaign in February 2018, that he should instead "sit tight" because Trump agents had assured Manafort that he and Gates would be "taken care of" by Trump's people if they remained silent.[76]

Whatever its source, what Trump's anxiety over Manafort's legal difficulties underscores is how important it is to the president in 2018 and 2019 that neither American nor Ukrainian investigations of his former campaign manager put sufficient pressure on the veteran political operative that he "sells out" Trump as part of a federal cooperation deal—a "flip."[77] But it will take certain key details of the Ukraine scandal, which do not emerge until early 2020, to fully illuminate the source of the president's obsession with the Ukrainian power broker who managed his 2016 presidential campaign.

CHAPTER 2

EUROMAIDAN AND CRIMEA

In November 2013, the same month then-businessman Donald Trump is being hosted by "leading Russian businessmen," "top-of-the-government" Kremlin officials, and possibly Putin himself in Moscow as part of the 2013 Miss Universe pageant festivities, a popular uprising begins in Ukraine that is now known variously as the Ukrainian Revolution, the Euromaidan Revolution, or the Revolution of Dignity.[1] While different sources provide different estimates, between 104 and 780 Ukrainians die during the three months of protests in Kyiv's Independence Square—also known as Maidan Square—extending from November 2013 to February 2014; many of the dead are killed in Maidan Square by Ukraine's machine-gun-wielding Berkut, a special police force known as the "Black Unit," between February 18 and February 20, 2014.[2]

One result of the uprising is that certain pro-Kremlin Ukrainian politicians considered corrupt by a significant segment of the Ukrainian population, including Manafort patron Viktor Yanukovych, are forced to flee to Russia.[3] America's ambassador to Ukraine between 2016 and 2019, Marie Yovanovitch, will describe the elections that follow the events of mid- to late February 2014 in Ukraine as follows: "The Ukrainian people . . . made clear in that election that they were done with corruption, and they wanted to live a life with dignity, [an idea] called the 'Revolution of Dignity.' And what that term means for Ukrainians is that it's rule of law—that what applies to you applies to me."[4]

Future Trump campaign manager Paul Manafort is driven from the corridors of power in Ukraine precisely because he is regarded as an anathema to these principles. Following the Euromaidan Revolution, it becomes harder for Manafort and others who have profited from corruption in Ukraine to find individuals in government willing to play by the old rules—the rules that, per Yovanovitch, inspired a revolution. Indeed, Yovanovitch will testify to Congress in October 2019 that an immediate result of the revolution, besides new elections, is the "architecture . . . of a special investigative office that would be all about the crimes of corruption above a certain level of public official. And [the office] would be devoted to that. . . . [It was] kind of like an FBI, but for a particular mission. Secondly, there would be a special independent anti-corruption prosecutor [who] . . . reported to Mr. [Yuri] Lutsenko. And then there would be a special anti-corruption court. So that you would have . . . this continuum of new organizations with vetted individuals who are trained, who are handling these crimes. People who would get reasonable salaries so that they wouldn't actually be forced to go out and take bribes."[5]

The anti-corruption court referred to by Yovanovitch, the National Anti-Corruption Bureau of Ukraine (NABU), is written into law in October 2014 but not fully staffed until December 2015. During this fourteen-month period, the chief prosecutorial entity handling corruption cases in Ukraine remains the Office of the Prosecutor General of Ukraine (GPU).[6] The online newspaper *Ukrayinska Pravda*, founded by legendary Ukrainian reformer Georgy Gongadze, will describe the state of affairs between the GPU and NABU once the latter begins regularly taking on cases in early 2016 as a state of "war."[7] Ambassador Yovanovitch will tell Congress that during the Poroshenko administration "a number of cases" were brought by the GPU against Artem Sytnyk, the head of NABU, "that looked [to the U.S. embassy in Kyiv] like harassment cases"—cases intended merely to undermine Ukraine's new anti-corruption entity.[8] While the U.S. embassy in Kyiv takes the part of NABU in these conflicts—even as, beginning in 2017, Trump and his allies secretly reach out instead to GPU officials—by spring 2019 U.S. officials in Kyiv have developed grave concerns about backsliding in both the GPU and NABU.[9]

The Euromaidan Revolution throws Ukraine into sufficient civil disarray that it creates an opening for the Kremlin to do something it has long hoped to do: annex Ukraine's Crimean peninsula. *Foreign Affairs* calls Putin's February 2014 annexation of Crimea "the most consequential decision of his 16 years in power. By annexing a neighboring country's territory by force, Putin overturn[s] in a single stroke the assumptions on which the post–Cold War European order had rested."[10] Speculation about why Putin took this extraordinary step abounds in national security circles; certainly, analysts are aware that Putin has called the collapse of the Soviet Union "the greatest geopolitical catastrophe of the 20th century," a statement that implies a desire for Russia to reassert its influence among the former Soviet republics, including the European "Baltic states" Estonia, Latvia, and Lithuania—all three of which are members of the North Atlantic Treaty Organization (NATO), a "collective defense" military alliance comprising North American and European countries.[11]

According to its website, NATO is open to "any European country in a position to undertake the commitments and obligations of membership, and contribute to security in the Euro-Atlantic area."[12] In addition to the alliance's current thirty members, three "partner" countries "have declared their aspirations to NATO membership: Bosnia and Herzegovina, Georgia, and Ukraine."[13] Georgia and Ukraine have both, since 2000, been the sites of massive vote-rigging and election fraud scandals orchestrated by pro-Kremlin domestic political entities. In Georgia, the culprit was the administration of President Eduard Shevardnadze, whose rule (the *New Yorker* records) helped Georgia "approach[ ] the very top of Transparency International's corruption index"; in Ukraine, the corruption was allegedly orchestrated in significant part by a man identified as "the Kremlin's agent in Kyiv" in a *Daily Beast* interview with a senior Yanukovych administration official: future Trump campaign manager Paul Manafort.[14] The *Kyiv Post* notes that of the "scores of media articles about Manafort . . . 90 percent . . . [call Manafort] a Kremlin Trojan horse."[15]

The *Post* reports that in late November 2013 "Kremlin pressure" causes Yanukovych to back out of an agreement (the Ukraine–European Union Association Agreement) that would have moved Ukraine into political and economic association with the European Union.[16] Under the agreement, Ukraine would have moved closer, too, to coverage under the European Union's Common Security and Defense Policy—an eventuality that would pull the former Soviet republic still further from Putin's orbit. In the weeks after Yanukovych dashes Ukraine's hopes of full EU membership, pro-EU protests break out throughout the country, culminating in massive demonstrations on Maidan Square in February 2014, just as Trump's daughter Ivanka is in Moscow scouting locations for the multibillion-dollar Trump Tower Moscow her father had agreed to in principle in Moscow just days before Yanukovych—under pressure from Moscow—rejected the Ukraine–European Union Association Agreement.[17]

Per the *Kyiv Post*, Manafort family text messages discovered in 2016 suggest that, far from urging his client Yanukovych to hold fast to his decision on the agreement, future Trump campaign chairman Paul Manafort may well have taken a more nefarious tack: encouraging pro-EU protests on Maidan Square that he knew would lead to a slaughter of civilians, hoping that such an event would force Yanukovych back to the agreement and thereby permit both him and Yanukovych to remain in power.[18] As the *Post* writes, "According to a cryptic messaging exchange between Manafort's daughters . . . it was none other than the arch spin doctor [Paul Manafort] who hatched a plan to 'send those people [protestors] out and get them slaughtered' . . . [and to] 'cause th[ose] Revolts and what not . . . as a tactic to outrage the world and get focus on Ukraine.'"[19] Whether Manafort indeed believed the massacre of civilians would "generate political pressure on Yanukovych to stay with the West"—thereby saving the Kremlin puppet's presidency—or anticipated that such killings would have the opposite effect, tearing Ukraine apart and giving Putin the space needed to take whatever parts of Ukraine he wanted, is unclear.[20]

Whatever Manafort's esoteric motives, the *Post* notes that "all of them had a dollar sign. He [had] received $42 million [in] payments . . . from [Yanukovych's chief of staff Sergey] Lovochkin . . . [who] was not just a government official, but also the junior partner in business of notorious gas oligarch [Dmitry] Firtash."[21] It is in this context that—perhaps motivated by money from Firtash's business partner—Trump's future campaign manager helps stage, in early February 2014, a series of events that "triggered Ukraine . . . spiral[ing] into the mass demonstrations [on Maidan Square] two days later, and ultimately the shooting of scores of demonstrators on February 20, 2014, and the flight of Yanukovych [to Moscow]."[22]

Within hours of the massacre on Maidan Square, the *New York Times* reports, "a disinformation campaign began on social media to try to reframe the violence. Reporting by the *Washington Post* has attributed the effort to the GRU, Russia's military-intelligence agency. . . . The GRU also set up online groups that promoted Crimea's secession from Ukraine. The effort, which also used paid Facebook ads, presaged Russian interference with the 2016 presidential election in the United States."[23]

In March 2014, just weeks after the Maidan massacre, "Russian forces" annex Ukraine's Crimean peninsula, prompting, according to the BBC, the "worst East-West crisis since the Cold War"; it is, moreover, what the Brookings Institution will call a "gross" and direct violation of the 1994 Budapest Memorandum—an agreement signed by the United States and Russia that binds the latter to honoring the territorial sovereignty and by then established boundaries of Ukraine.[24] Russia's aggression constitutes an invasion of the largest nation (by land area) located entirely in Europe, an extraordinary circumstance that prompts not only the United States but also the European Union to impose "harsh sanctions" on Russia almost immediately after the annexation.[25]

One of the Kremlin-connected entities hit by sanctions is Sberbank, the Russian bank that had announced its plan to fund the Trump Tower Moscow project just a few months earlier, on November 19, 2013. During his November 2013 stay in Moscow, Trump had attended "a private meeting . . . arranged by Herman Gref, Putin's former energy minister and now chief executive of the state-owned Sberbank, Russia's biggest bank."[26] Trump therefore knows, by mid-2014, that the anti-corruption forces in Ukraine that had long stood against Yanukovych, Manafort, Lovochkin, and Firtash had now also scuttled a potential multibillion-dollar Trump Organization development deal in Moscow.

* * *

Crimea, once part of Russia, was "given" to Ukraine in 1954 by Soviet leader Nikita Khrushchev, at a time when none foresaw the dissolution of the Soviet Union and therefore the eventual movement of Crimea outside Moscow's sphere of influence.[27] Approximately the size of the U.S. state of Maryland, Crimea immediately became a semi-autonomous region of Ukraine with "strong political bonds to Ukraine—and equally strong cultural ties to Russia."[28] The fact that Crimea was, fifteen years into Putin's career as a national leader, indisputably Ukrainian geopolitically but arguably Russian culturally will form the backdrop of the scandal that leads to Trump's December 2019 impeachment.[29]

Crimea's significance to Russia goes beyond cultural affinity, however. For well over two hundred years, the Russian navy has stationed its Black Sea Fleet at Sevastopol—the Crimean peninsula's largest city—because it is one of the two warm-water ports to which Russia (a nation whose climate is frigid in the main) has access.[30] But the strategic importance of Crimea to Putin is not merely a military one; indeed, it even more powerfully presents as a matter of energy policy, as Putin's annexation of the region costs Ukraine, per the Ukrainian Energy Ministry, "80% of [its] oil and gas deposits in the Black Sea."[31] As for the U.S. interest in Ukraine, former U.S. ambassador Marie Yovanovitch will testify to Congress in October 2019 that Ukraine's territorial sovereignty is a critical national security interest for America: "Because of Ukraine's geostrategic position bordering Russia on its east, the warm waters of the oil-rich Black Sea to its south, and four NATO allies to its west, it is critical to the security of the United States that Ukraine remain free and democratic, and that it continue to resist Russian expansionism."[32]

In April 2014, Putin, emboldened by the lack of any military response to his government stealing more than 4 percent of Ukraine's territory, supplies arms and soldiers in support of "pro-Russian armed groups seiz[ing] parts of the Donetsk and Luhansk regions on the Russian border of eastern Ukraine," an act of unilateral aggression that increases the percentage of Russia's European neighbor held by the Kremlin to 7 percent of the former's total land area.[33] The Ukrainian military immediately launches operations to retake its territory.[34] Because it is facing the second-strongest military in the world according to the 2019 Firepower Index, however, Ukraine—fielder of the world's twenty-ninth-strongest military, per the index—suffers more than 13,000 casualties in the first sixty months of its war with Russia.[35] While many of the troops opposing the Ukrainian military are pro-Russian separatists or Russian irregulars, for the duration of the war NATO and Western intelligence experts will "repeatedly accuse[ ] Russia of sending heavy weapons and combat troops into eastern Ukraine to help the rebels."[36] For its part, the Kremlin will admit only that "Russian 'volunteers'" are fighting in Ukraine.[37]

By 2019, Ukraine has amassed what the *Washington Post* calls "considerable evidence" that Russian aggression in Crimea and Donbass (the latter an area comprising the Donetsk and Luhansk regions of Ukraine) is a violation of at least two international treaties, "the International Convention for the Suppression of the Financing of Terrorism and the International Convention on the Elimination of All Forms of Racial Discrimination."[38] Scholars specializing in the region's geopolitics argue that Putin's aggression in Donbass is motivated in significant part by his fear of NATO expansion, specifically the possibility that Ukraine will shortly join NATO and receive the benefit of its powerful mutual defense pact.[39] Though NATO says that its "ongoing enlargement process"—which it describes as an "open door policy" for qualifying countries—"poses no threat to any country" because it is exclusively "aimed at promoting stability and cooperation, at building a Europe whole and free, united in peace, democracy and common values," NATO has long been seen as a threat by the Kremlin regardless.[40] Putin's angst stems not merely from the fact that a powerful military alliance to which Russia does not belong—but the United States does—is located on its western doorstep, but also that in the 2000s NATO "extended its influence further into Eastern Europe by aiding revolutions against pro-Russian regimes in Georgia and Ukraine."[41] While this aid involved mostly financial investments targeted at electoral and judicial reforms, it nevertheless was seen by the Kremlin as undercutting not only its medium- and long-term military posture with respect to its neighbors but also its political influence inside several of the former Soviet republics. The fact that, in addition to three such former republics (Estonia, Latvia, and Lithuania) being full NATO members and two former Soviet republics (Georgia and Ukraine) being "aspiring" NATO members, eleven former Soviet republics are, alongside Russia itself, part of NATO's "Partnership for Peace" (Armenia, Azerbaijan, Belarus, Georgia, Kazakhstan, Kyrgyzstan, Moldova, Tajikistan, Turkmenistan, Ukraine, and Uzbekistan) means that NATO has the potential to transform dramatically Russia's capacity to influence governments and cultures it once considered within its sphere of governance.[42] Putin appears, therefore, to regard the annexation and subsequent invasion of parts of Ukraine as Russia's last best chance to exert itself militarily and politically upon the second-largest former Soviet republic.[43]

Other experts in the geopolitics of the region believe Putin partially annexed and then invaded a European nation in 2014 because Ukraine, if it joined NATO, might "evict Russia's Black Sea Fleet from its long-standing base in Sevastopol," thereby substantially weakening Russia's offensive and defense military posture.[44] Still others accuse Putin of throwing something akin to a temper tantrum after his Manafort-advised Ukrainian puppet, Yanukovych, was chased from Kyiv by the Euromaidan Revolution; in this view, Putin's policy toward Ukraine throughout 2014 was, as summarized by *Foreign Affairs*, "an impulsive decision that Putin stumbled into rather than the careful move of a strategist with geopolitical ambitions."[45]

This last phrase hints at the fourth and darkest interpretation of Russia's annexation and invasion of Ukraine: that, as *Foreign Affairs* describes it, it was "part of a Russian project," broadly classifiable as "imperialist," to "gradually recapture the former territories of the Soviet Union."[46] Such a grand design would suggest that "Putin never accepted the loss of Russian prestige that followed the end of the Cold War," according to *Foreign Affairs*, and "is determined to restore it, in part by expanding Russia's borders."[47]

Whatever Putin's motivations, *Military Times* reports that "Russian officials began arriving in the Crimean peninsula [in February 2014], shortly after the pro-Western government took power in Kyiv" following the

Euromaidan Revolution.[48] These officials were accompanied by "troops without insignia" who began "occupying crucial infrastructure including Ukrainian military bases"; it will take years for Putin to admit publicly that these unidentified troops had indeed been Russian soldiers.[49] In the face of these insignia-less but identifiably Russian forces, "Ukrainian troops largely did not put up resistance and retreated," according to *Military Times*.[50] In short order, Russian officers among the invading troops had "forced the hand of local Crimean lawmakers to pass a motion for a referendum to secede from Ukraine and join Russia. An overwhelming majority of votes cast on March 16, 2014, supported secession. Two days later, Moscow signed a declaration with self-proclaimed Crimean officials, sealing the annexation. Neither the vote nor the annexation was recognized by the United Nations."[51]

CHAPTER 3

PARNAS AND FRUMAN

Manafort "return[s] to Ukraine after Yanukovych fle[es] the country" to help his former boss's pro-Kremlin Party of Regions try to retake the Ukrainian government in the nation's October 2014 parliamentary elections.[1] In the lead-up to the elections, a picture appears on social media depicting Donald Trump alongside a Florida businessman, Lev Parnas, who was born in the 1970s in what is now Ukraine.[2]

The Trump-Parnas photograph is posted on Facebook on March 8, 2014, by a Parnas associate named Shawn Jarosovich. The post appears two days after the first Crimea-related sanctions against Russia are leveled by the Obama administration, and reappears on April 2, two weeks after the joint Kremlin-Crimean declaration of annexation.[3] Jarosovich captions the photograph—which shows Trump and the Soviet-born Parnas "shoulder to shoulder, smiling at the camera at what appears to be an outdoor nighttime event," per *Politico*—with words indicating Jarosovich believes Trump and Parnas to be friends: "the big homies!!!!!!!!!!!! for real tho."[4] Both Trump and Parnas are dressed in business casual attire in the picture; Parnas wears a royal blue collared shirt, and Trump wears a sport coat.[5] Jarosovich implies in a March 14, 2014, social media post that Lev is a friend of his who can help him "meet the donald" and "soon."[6] An analysis of Jarosovich's Facebook account by *Politico* concludes that Jarosovich and Parnas are business partners and, though the nature of their business is unclear, it appears to be both "lucrative" and involve "foreign investments"—possibly "gold[,] oil, [and] rough diamonds" via

Jarosovich's company Gabriel and Jaros Holdings, which "negotiate[s] and close[s] deals" in those three markets.[7]

In October 2019, CNN reveals that the March 7, 2014, Trump-Parnas photograph posted by Jarosovich on social media the following day was taken in Florida at a Trump National Doral golf tournament connected to an Ivanka Trump–hosted fashion show.[8] Notably, a jewelry company Ivanka co-owned at the time, Madison Avenue Diamonds (d/b/a Ivanka Trump Fine Jewelry), dealt—just like Jarosovich's Gabriel and Jaros Holdings—in gold and diamonds; the company was also allegedly part of a 2017 "scheme to cover a $100 million debt owed by an [Emirati] oil trading family to the Commercial Bank to Dubai."[9] While Ivanka has not been charged with any wrongdoing in the Ivanka Trump Fine Jewelry case, her former business partner has been sued by the Department of Justice (DOJ).[10]

By March 2014, Trump had already decided to run for president, having made the decision and announced it to his longtime friend Roger Stone on New Year's Day in 2013.[11] Because Trump was not, however, as of March 2014, a declared political candidate prone to taking selfies with prospective donors, CNN observes that the casual Trump-Parnas photograph "raises questions about whether [Parnas] had any existing relationship with [Trump]."[12] "Representatives for the Trump Organization did not respond to repeated requests for comment on the event," per CNN, and a "White House spokesperson for Jared Kushner and Ivanka Trump declined to comment."[13]

According to the *Wall Street Journal*, Parnas's Instagram account establishes him as someone with "VIP access" to Trump beginning in 2015 at the latest.[14] Parnas's Instagram feed, which begins in April 2015, features a photo with Ivana Trump, Donald Trump's first wife, as its second-ever entry. The entry's caption contains the word "TRUMPS" and identifies the event as a "Fraud Guarantee pow wow"—Fraud Guarantee being a Parnas-owned company that got its start, per its website, "shipping the first containers of freight between the United States and the former Soviet Union in the early 1990s."[15] While it is unclear how well Parnas and

Trump knew each other prior to 2015, Parnas will tell the *Washington Post* that he "sold Trump Organization condos while Trump's father, Fred, was still running the business."[16] According to the *New Yorker*, Parnas's work involved selling Trump Organization co-ops for a Brooklyn company called Kings Highway Realty beginning in 1988, when Parnas was sixteen; Parnas has noted that, "growing up in that area, you knew who Trump was, because his name was all over the place."[17] Given this timeline, the Soviet-born Parnas would have begun his work selling Trump Organization properties between eight and eighteen months after Trump made his first trip to the Soviet Union.[18]

Trump's 1987 trip to Moscow has been denominated a KGB-sponsored event by Luke Harding, a *Politico* and *Guardian* reporter. Per Harding, "The top level of the Soviet diplomatic service arranged [Trump's] 1987 Moscow visit. With assistance from the KGB. [The trip] took place while [head of the First Chief Directorate of Foreign Intelligence for the KGB, Gen. Vladimir Alexandrovich] Kryuchkov[,] was seeking to improve the KGB's operational techniques in one particular and sensitive area. The spy chief wanted KGB staff abroad to recruit more Americans."[19]

Even after Parnas moves in 1995 from New York City—the site of Trump's primary residence—to Florida, the site of Trump's secondary residence, he remains uncommonly focused on the Trump Organization, always staying at Trump properties whenever he returns to New York.[20] During these years, Parnas will later say, he "bumped into" Trump "plenty of times" at social events in the city.[21] Per a 2019 *New Yorker* feature on Parnas, Parnas's "go-to" hotel when staying in New York has long been Trump International Hotel & Tower, a building less than a mile from Trump's personal residence in Trump Tower.[22] While Parnas does not quantify for the *New Yorker* the number of "bump-ins" he had with Trump prior to Jarosovich posting a picture of the two men on Facebook in March 2014, CNN uncovers eight encounters between the two Florida businessmen between 2014 and 2019.[23] Per CNN, "photos and videos splashed across the Internet . . . paint a far more casual and familiar relationship [between Parnas and Trump] than the President has let on," including "inauguration galas, an intimate dinner, and a White House party."[24]

When Trump announces his candidacy for president in mid-June 2015, Parnas's son Aaron tells his father that "one of your friends is running for President."[25] Indeed, Parnas and his son are close enough to the Trumps that shortly after Trump launches his campaign, Aaron Parnas calls the Trump campaign to get "passes" to a Florida rally for the new GOP candidate.[26]

In short order, Lev Parnas will tell the *New Yorker*, he becomes a "regular" at Trump's rallies and "other [campaign] gatherings" as well as a donor and fundraiser for Trump.[27] His Instagram account includes an October 2015 photo of him, Aaron, and Trump; another photo, taken the same month, again places Parnas and his son with Trump at a Trump campaign event, though this time the photo is accompanied by a video of Trump speaking just a few feet from the camera.[28] After the October 2015 post, Parnas's Instagram account shows no entries for the next three years; it is unclear if any intervening posts were deleted or if Parnas simply declined to use Instagram in the interim.[29] The *Wall Street Journal* notes that Instagram entries by Parnas reappear in 2018—just as he and Igor Fruman begin making allegedly fraudulent donations to Republican candidates and groups.[30]

Parnas describes his own family, the Trumps, and other significant Trump donors as being "one big family" in the early days of the Trump campaign; in particular, Parnas becomes close to Tommy Hicks Jr., a Texas investor "close to Donald Trump, Jr." who by 2019 is co-chair of the Republican National Committee (RNC).[31] Aaron Parnas volunteers in 2016 to work for the Trump campaign in Florida, a critical battleground state.[32] The elder Parnas tells the *Washington Post* that alongside the "fundraising" he did for Trump during the campaign, he also became "very good friend[s]" with Trump campaign adviser Rudy Giuliani.[33]

It is during this period—the timeline on the company's website notwithstanding—that Parnas co-founds Fraud Guarantee Holdings, LLC in Delaware with David Correia, another Florida businessman; in 2019 Correia will become Parnas's federal co-defendant.[34] Correia, a former professional golfer, "reportedly worked with [Parnas and Fruman] while they attempted to collect documents that they said showed corruption by former Vice President Joe Biden."[35] CNN reports that Correia traveled to Ukraine with Parnas and Fruman in 2018 in order to "make the effort [to find dirt on Biden] pay off in lucrative business deals," particularly a deal to sell American liquefied national gas (LNG) to Ukraine through a pipeline in Poland.[36] The pending federal indictments against Correia include allegations that he was involved "in an effort to lobby for a marijuana business that . . . was secretly backed by a Russian businessman [Andrey Kukushkin]."[37] Correia also offered a job to a member of Trump's pre-election national security advisory committee, Walid Phares, and "used" Phares, per CNN, to "help set up a meeting in the summer of 2018 with Okba Haftar, the son of renegade Libyan general Khalifa Haftar"; Haftar was originally intended to be one of the founding members of the multinational pre-election "grand bargain"—involving covert foreign assistance to the Trump presidential campaign—discussed at great length in *Proof of Conspiracy*.[38]

Correia was also a "regular" attendee at the pro-Trump salon convened by Giuliani in 2019 in the BLT Prime restaurant at the Trump International Hotel in D.C. (see chapters 7 and 17).[39] According to CNN, the former athlete attended numerous Trump events both pre-election and post-election, and has been photographed with the president at least twice.[40] In the summer of 2019, Correia spent over a week with Dmitry Firtash in Vienna, returning to Florida in mid-August "intent on finding someone who would sell liquefied natural gas to Firtash" and considering seeking such a seller in Qatar, one of the nations alleged to have illegally funded Trump's inauguration. By fall 2019, Correia was in the UAE—a founding member of the "grand bargain"—to, he told friends, "close a deal with Firtash."[41] CNN reports that on April 1, 2019, Correia texted a friend, "It's starting"—enclosing with the text a link to a just-published column by John Solomon of *The Hill* entitled "Joe Biden's 2020 Ukrainian Nightmare."[42]

Parnas doesn't merely become close with Trump advisers and donors during the presidential campaign, but is also regularly in contact with the candidate himself. He explains to the *New Yorker* in 2019 that during the 2016 election season he "bump[ed] into ... [Trump] constantly" because he was one of a very small group of people at the core of Trump's campaign.[43] In October 2016, a few weeks before Election Day, Parnas makes an "appearance in Mr. Trump's circle at an exclusive, high-price ... fundraiser hosted by the construction magnate Robert Pereira at his home in Hillsboro Beach, Florida," an event at which Rudy Giuliani is also an attendee, according to the *Wall Street Journal*.[44] Pereira recalls seeing Parnas speaking with both Trump and Giuliani during the event.[45] At around the same time, Parnas donates approximately $100,000 to Trump and the GOP.[46]

On election night, Parnas is "invited to attend a gathering with Trump and his family" to celebrate the Republican presidential candidate's victory.[47] The gathering is Trump's invite-only election-night party at the Midtown Hilton in Manhattan; on entering the party, Parnas describes himself to a reporter as a "friend of the president-elect" who lives near Trump's Mar-a-Lago club.[48] Parnas tells the reporter, too, that an unnamed friend of his had "hosted several fundraising events for Trump" and that his friend's daughter "had traveled around the state singing on the candidate's behalf."[49] *Politico* notes that Trump's "cozy" election-night event was so selective about its guest list that the "die-hard supporters" in attendance "barely outnumbered" the media present.[50] Giuliani—a longtime Trump friend, Trump campaign adviser, and at the time the attorney for Parnas's company Fraud Guarantee—was also present at the Manhattan event, as was Felix Sater, the man who got Ivanka Trump access to Putin's personal office in the Kremlin in the 2000s and has since said he "knows" Parnas, though he does not specify in what capacity or for how long he has known him.[51]

Other attendees at what *GQ* has called a "modest" event "dominated by a large press pen and risers for camera crews" include Trump shadow national security adviser Erik Prince, 2012 GOP vice presidential nominee Sarah Palin, Fox News commentators Laura Ingraham and Jeanine Pirro, actors Joe Piscopo and Stephen Baldwin, entrepreneurs Michael Lindell (My Pillow) and John Catsimatidis Jr. (Red Apple Group), alt-right personalities Milo Yiannopoulos and Charles Johnson, GOP "mega-donors" Shalabh "Shalli" Kumar and David Koch, and Trump campaign media surrogates Scottie Nell Hughes, Katrina Pierson, and Boris Epshteyn.[52] On his way to the election-night event, Sater, according to his chauffeur, spends the drive from Long Island to New York "talking to somebody in the Russian language."[53]

Trump surrogate Hughes will say that those permitted to attend the Hilton event were individuals who "had put their necks on the line for President Trump."[54] Bruce LeVell, a party attendee and the executive director of the National Diversity Coalition for Trump, tells *GQ* that to become an invitee to the Midtown Hilton party one had to be among Trump's "really core surrogates."[55] According to France's oldest daily newspaper, *Le Figaro*, Parnas, self-identifying to one of its reporters as a "Russian [who] lives in Boca Raton, not far from Trump's second home," "arrive[s] at Trump's November 2016 election night party . . . with two other men in suits."[56] All three men "present themselves as friends of Donald Trump" and tell *Le Figaro* "they support [him] with fervor."[57] It is unclear whether either of the other two men with Parnas on election night is among Parnas's three federal co-defendants in 2019—Correia, Igor Fruman, and Andrey Kukushkin—but it is certain that Correia and Fruman were at the time Florida residents, and *Le Figaro* reports that the two well-dressed "friends of Donald Trump" with Parnas on election night were both from Florida and wore "chic pants."[58] Kukushkin, meanwhile, is known to be friends with Sater on a Russian social media site; by September 2019 he will be on the cusp of beginning a $650,000-a-year consultancy with the Trump administration's Department of Veterans Affairs.[59] As for Parnas, by 2019 he will be described in U.S. media as a "personal fixer" for Giuliani.[60]

After the election, Parnas and his new friend Giuliani begin "looking to do business together," though according to Parnas they do not have the opportunity to do so until Giuliani approaches him about "gather[ing] information in Ukraine to counter the findings of the special counsel Robert Mueller's Russia investigation."[61] By the time of this request Parnas has grown significantly closer not only with Giuliani, but also with

Trump himself. Indeed, according to the *Wall Street Journal*, Parnas and Fruman have spent Trump's presidency becoming "known by business associates [in Ukraine] for touting their connections to the Trump administration," and equally well known in the United States for their "propensity for name-dropping."[62] On social media as well as in conversations with associates, reports the *Journal*, the men "boast[ ] . . . about their close ties to American politicians, including President Trump."[63] This particular boast is startling in part because, per the *Journal*, many of Parnas's interactions with political figures and potential business associates over the years have seen him "tout[ing] his connections to Russian money"—a possible reference to his financing by Firtash and to Firtash's patronage, in turn, by Vladimir Putin (see chapter 4).[64]

Parnas and Fruman's journey into the innermost ring of President Trump's social circle continues just weeks after Election Day in 2016, when the two men contrive to be "the first two in a long line for a photo with the president-elect at a [presidential-transition period] donor thank-you event in Florida."[65] After Trump's inauguration, they initiate a course of political sponsorship that sees them "making about $1 million in [2020] campaign contributions," writes the *Journal*.[66]

In March 2018, Fruman "attend[s] a donor event . . . at Mr. Trump's Mar-a-Lago resort," and on another date is "photographed with the president."[67] It is unclear whether Parnas is with him on these occasions. The *Daily Beast* reports that, after the Mar-a-Lago event, Fruman tells the Russian-language website *ForumDaily* that he was invited to the March fundraiser because he had donated to Trump's 2016 campaign; however, per the *Daily Beast*, the Federal Election Commission (FEC) has no record of any such donation.[68] The digital media outlet ultimately discovers that some of Fruman's political giving is traceable to a home in Boca Raton owned by a "Russian-born man named Victor Imber."[69] As for Parnas, the *Daily Beast* notes the oddity of him being "involved with a financial venture [Fraud Guarantee] that is pouring huge sums into political campaigns" following Trump's inauguration, given that, among many other outstanding financial and legal imbroglios, Parnas allegedly owes $11,000 in unpaid rent to his landlord, $100,000 to a man

(Felix Vulis) who loaned him funds for Parnas's son's bris, $30,000 to a charter jet company in Florida, and over $500,000 in court-ordered restitution for "lur[ing]" a friend into investing in a film intended to star Jack Nicholson; Parnas had also recently been "work[ing] for three firms that were, after his departure, permanently expelled from the securities industry by the Financial Industry Regulatory Authority (FINRA), a private financial watchdog group."[70]

Parnas and Fruman are both on the board of a Ukrainian charity, American Friends of Anatevka, that will eventually bring Giuliani to Ukraine to become the honorary mayor of a settlement of Jewish refugees—even as the executive for the charity, Michael Kolden, says he has never met either of the two Florida businessmen.[71] A rabbi associated with the charity, Rabbi Moshe Azman, has called Parnas and Fruman the "closest assistants" of Trump's personal attorney Giuliani.[72] For his part, Parnas, on Instagram, calls Giuliani "my brother" and "one of the greatest m[e]n I know."[73] According to the *Wall Street Journal*, Parnas's Instagram features "frequent" Parnas-Giuliani stops at Trump properties around the United States, as well as pre-election trips to battleground states and multiple trips to Europe.[74]

The Republican governor of Florida, Ron DeSantis, a recipient of donations from both Parnas and Fruman, calls Parnas "a guy who was at . . . a lot of these [Republican National Committee] things, [and] was, I think, viewed as one of the top supporters of the president in Florida."[75] *Politico* will describe Parnas "hopscotch[ing] the state [of Florida] with DeSantis on a campaign trip just before" the 2018 midterm elections.[76] Observing the Parnas-DeSantis relationship, the *Tampa Bay Times* notes that it is "still unclear why [Parnas and Fruman] dropped $50,000 into DeSantis' campaign account a day before he was endorsed by Trump"—a sequence of events suggesting the two men may have had foreknowledge of Trump's plans.[77] When Parnas resumes posting on his Instagram account in June 2018, one of the first pictures posted is of him, DeSantis, and Donald Trump Jr.[78]

Parnas will eventually refer to his role in the Ukraine affair as that of "Rudy's assistant, his investigator."[79] Both Parnas and Fruman are residents, according to the *Financial Times*, of a neighborhood in North Miami known as "Little Moscow."[80]

On April 30, 2018, Parnas visits Trump at Trump International Hotel in D.C. and has his picture taken with him.[81] Parnas boasts about the event on social media, explaining, as summarized by the *Washington Post*, that he had "attended an eight-person session with Trump in Washington . . . to discuss the upcoming midterm elections."[82] Parnas's social media posts further note, as recounted by *Politico* in 2019, that he had an "incredible dinner and even better conversation."[83] Per the *Post*, the conversation included Parnas telling the president that the U.S. ambassador to Ukraine, Marie Yovanovitch, was "unfriendly to Trump's interests," to which the president responded that Yovanovitch should therefore be fired.[84] April 2018 is also, perhaps not coincidentally, the month that Rudy Giuliani—attorney for Parnas's Fraud Guarantee—formally joins Trump's legal team, a development that means both the president and Parnas can now speak to Giuliani, including on matters relating to Ukraine, under the cover of attorney-client privilege.[85]

Less than three weeks later, on May 21, 2018, Parnas posts a picture of himself, Fruman, Donald Trump Jr., and Trump Jr.'s friend (and Republican fundraiser) Tommy Hicks Jr. at a Beverly Hills restaurant with the caption "Power Breakfast!!!"[86] At some point in their eventful May, Parnas and Fruman give a $325,000 gift to America First Action, a pro-Trump super PAC, via a limited liability company that, federal prosecutors will later note, "conceal[ed] their identities."[87] In October 2019 federal prosecutors will indict Parnas and Fruman, per a *Washington Post* report, for "disguis[ing] the source" of this $325,000 donation "by giving the money in the name of Global Energy Producers (GEP), a purported liquefied natural gas company that Parnas and Fruman controlled."[88] As summarized by the *Post*, the indictment alleges that GEP was a "front used to disguise the funds' true source and that the money for the political action committee came from a 'private lending transaction between Fruman and third parties.'"[89] While the identities of these "third parties" remain unknown, the *Miami Herald* notes that Fruman has "'personal ties' to a powerful businessman in the Ukrainian port city of Odessa called 'the Grey Cardinal' who is believed to associate with organized crime figures, according to OCCRP, an international consortium of investigative journalists."[90]

In July 2018, just a matter of weeks after making his extraordinarily large donation to the Trump reelection effort, Parnas is permitted to attend a breakfast meeting with Giuliani and U.S. special representative for Ukraine negotiations Kurt Volker.[91] Volker, per his October 2019 testimony to Congress, had been asked in spring 2017 by secretary of state Rex Tillerson to serve as Trump's special representative for Ukraine negotiations, in part to help answer two key questions stemming from Russia's interference in the 2016 presidential election and Russia's conduct in the Russia-Ukraine war: "Would the administration lift sanctions against Russia?" and "Would [the administration] make some kind of grand bargain with Russia in which it would trade recognition of Russia's seizure of Ukrainian territory for some other deal in Syria or elsewhere?"[92] Volker will subsequently testify to Congress that "hanging over everyone's head [i]n the expert community is, is there some grand bargain with Russia where we throw Ukraine under the bus?"[93] Volker's testimony seems to confirm that from July 2018 onward, his work with Ukraine on Trump's behalf would have been seen by Kyiv as part of a broader effort by the Trump administration to simultaneously resolve America's tensions with Russia and tensions between Russia and Ukraine over Crimea—in both instances, problems whose solution Putin perceives to be sanctions relief.[94]

In August 2018, Parnas and Trump both travel to upstate New York for a fundraiser for Republican congresswoman Claudia Tenney.[95] At the event, Parnas takes a photograph with Trump; fundraiser attendees will subsequently tell media that "they got the impression that Trump and Parnas knew each other," and they will note further that during a question-and-answer session during the event "Trump called Parnas by his first name."[96] After the event, Trump sends Parnas a "personal note" that thanks Parnas for his "friendship."[97] By the time of Trump's note,

Parnas and Fruman have given over half a million dollars to GOP politicians and groups.[98]

On March 25, 2019, a day after attorney general William Barr publishes a summary of the Mueller Report that—contradicting the report—exonerates Trump, Trump's legal team celebrates with Parnas at the Trump International Hotel in D.C.[99] Six days later, Parnas and Fruman attend a gala event connected to the National Council of Young Israel; at the event, also attended by Rudy Giuliani, House minority leader Kevin McCarthy, Republican National Committee co-chair Tommy Hicks Jr., and former Arkansas governor Mike Huckabee, Parnas tells Josh Nass, owner of a New York–based public relations agency, that he has "'incredibly vast' connections 'in the pro-Trump apparatus, and they go all the way up to the senior-most echelons of the [Republican] party.'"[100]

In the summer of 2019, as Parnas and some of his associates are "propos[ing] to serve as middlemen in a deal to sell natural gas from the Middle East to fertilizer companies" owned by Dmitry Firtash, Parnas will also boast to friends of ties to billionaire Russian oligarch Farkhad Akhmedov, described as a "Vladimir Putin hanger-on" who appears from pictures on his Facebook feed to have visited Mar-a-Lago—for unknown reasons—between March 2 and March 8, 2017, a period during which Trump spent approximately seventy-two hours (March 3 to March 5) at the club.[101] Akhmedov has since deleted the photos he took at Mar-a-Lago, and indeed his entire Facebook profile, despite it being liked and followed by more than 10,000 people at the time it was removed.[102]

At the time Trump and Putin associate Akhmedov were both in Mar-a-Lago, Trump was less than three weeks removed from having fired his national security advisor Michael Flynn, who had had repeated contacts with Kremlin agents and even Putin himself during the 2016 campaign and presidential transition.[103] Akhmedov is so close to Putin that the Trump administration has, as part of its compliance with congressional sanctions against the Kremlin, put the oligarch on the "Putin List," a small and selective list of approximately twenty Russians considered close associates of the Russian president.[104] The *Washington Post* reports that Putin and Akhmedov are such intimates that the latter single-handedly improved relations between Putin and the nation of Turkey—a critical diplomatic role for the Parnas associate that, given Trump's subsequent appeasement of both Russia and Turkey in northern Syria, likely demands further investigation.[105] Akhmedov is also friends with Israeli-Russian oligarch Roman Abramovich, a man long known to be friends with Jared Kushner and Ivanka Trump.[106]

Through a spokesman, Akhmedov has claimed to have no ties to Parnas.[107]

After Parnas's arrest in October 2019, Trump will say of Parnas and Fruman, "I don't know them. I don't know about them. I don't know what they do."[108] He adds, "I don't know those gentlemen. . . . Maybe they were clients of Rudy. You'd have to ask Rudy, I just don't know."[109] When asked if Parnas and Fruman's business associate Giuliani is still his personal attorney, the president tells reporters, per the *Washington Post*, that he "doesn't know."[110]

Trump's denials aside, U.S. media reports the relationship between Trump and the newly indicted Parnas and Fruman far differently. The two men "worked on behalf of President Trump in Ukraine," the *New York Times* reports.[111] As for Trump's implication that Giuliani may not be his attorney, it is ignored by media as a falsehood, with outlets across the country continuing to refer to the former New York City mayor as the president's personal lawyer, in part because, vehemently and publicly, Giuliani himself does.[112] What remains unclear, however, is who is paying Giuliani besides Parnas and Fruman, or is compensating Giuliani for his representation of Trump, as Giuliani has been clear that it is not the president himself.[113] Pressed by the *Daily Beast* to explain how a high-priced attorney can travel around the world for months doing work for a client without any source of income, Giuliani responds that "the costs of his travel were covered by private clients for separate work that happened to correspond with his Ukraine portfolio. Speaking specifically about an August trip he made to Madrid to urge Andriy Yermak, a top Ukrainian official, to reinvestigate the Bidens, Giuliani said that he happened to be going to the Spanish capital already for 'business and vacation'" (see chapter 12).[114] Despite subsequently saying in early November 2019 that "the investigation I conducted concerning the 2016 Ukrainian collusion and corruption, was done solely as a defense attorney to defend my client [Trump]," Giuliani tells the *Daily Beast* in October 2019 that he did much of his Ukraine work for free "as a service to my government."[115]

Throughout Trump's presidency, the *Wall Street Journal* writes, "people in Florida political circles" have considered Parnas someone who talks freely about his "connections to politicians"; while "trying to drum up business" in Ukraine during the same period, the media outlet adds, Parnas would make clear that those connections were specifically to "Mr. Giuliani and President Trump."[116] Indeed, according to an October 2019 letter (written in Comic Sans font) sent to the House Permanent Select Committee on Intelligence by the attorney for both Parnas and Fruman at the time, John Dowd—the same attorney who represented President Trump during the period in 2018 when Trump and Giuliani were meeting with Parnas and Fruman—the latter two men in fact worked as part of Trump's legal team from "late 2018" onward.[117] As Dowd will recount in late 2019, "Messrs. Parnas and Fruman assisted Mr. Giuliani in connection with his representation of President Trump."[118] During the period Parnas and Fruman were working with Trump's legal team, Dowd recounts, they were also working with two other key members of Trump's legal advisory corps: Joseph diGenova and Victoria Toensing (see chapter 7).[119]

In December 2018, Giuliani invites Parnas to attend the funeral of former president George H. W. Bush with him. The next day, Parnas and Fruman are photographed with President Trump, Vice President Pence, and Rudy Giuliani at a Hanukkah party at the White House.[120] CNN reports that "at one point during the party that night, Parnas and Fruman slipped out of a large reception room packed with hundreds of Trump donors to have a private meeting with the President and Giuliani."[121] The secret meeting at the White House—which comes as Parnas is assisting Giuliani and Rep. Devin Nunes in making contacts with Ukrainian officials (see chapter 17)—is, per CNN, "further indication that Trump knew Parnas and Fruman, despite Trump publicly stating that he did not on the day after the two men were arrested at Dulles International Airport [in October 2019]."[122] During the December 2018 meeting, according to Parnas, not only did the president discuss Ukraine, but Trump "task[ed] him and Fruman" with a "secret mission"—one whose aim, CNN reports of Parnas's account, was to "pressure the Ukrainian government to investigate Joe Biden and his son Hunter."[123] Parnas contemporaneously relayed this news to multiple compatriots, to whom he explained that Trump had put him on a "James Bond [international intelligence] mission."[124]

From this White House meeting onward, says Parnas's now-attorney Joseph Bondy, Parnas considered himself an agent of the president of the United States. "Mr. Parnas at all times believed that he was acting only on behalf of the President," Bondy will tell media following Parnas's October 2019 indictment, "as directed by [the president's] personal attorney, Rudy Giuliani."[125] Parnas's claim is bolstered by the fact that he was loquacious about his new role—and new principal—at the time; according to a former federal prosecutor with "numerous high-level clients in Ukraine" who speaks to CNN, "Parnas told everyone in Ukraine about the White House meeting. He was adamant he was 'their guy'—that they [Trump and Giuliani] chose him to be their ambassador in Ukraine."[126]

Two months later, in February 2019, Parnas meets with Ukrainian president Petro Poroshenko to make good on his role as Trump's personal envoy to Ukraine, "extend[ing] Poroshenko an invitation for a State dinner at the White House," CNN reports, but only "if [Poroshenko] would commit to publicly opening investigations [into the Bidens] in Ukraine."[127]

* * *

An October 2019 *BuzzFeed News* investigative report offers a glimpse inside Parnas and Fruman's long partnership with Giuliani. Per the digital media outlet, during the course of the trio's cooperation "the money kept flowing" to Parnas and Fruman without cease: "There was a $1,410 charge to a Palm Beach limousine service and nearly $20,000 in expenses at Trump hotels in Washington, D.C., and New York. There were bills running to hundreds of dollars at exclusive restaurants such as Novikov in London and BLT Prime [in the Trump International Hotel] in Washington. During one of [Parnas's] many trips to the Ukrainian capital of Kyiv, there was a $657 charge at Tootsie, the popular strip club in the heart of the city. At the same time that [Parnas] was facing court judgments for hundreds of thousands in personal debts, the 47-year-old political operative was traveling like a freewheeling CEO as he met with Ukrainian prosecutors and other officials."[128] An unresolved question—of interest in no small part because of Parnas's concurrent ability, in the midst of his "freewheeling" lifestyle, to "spend[ ] hundreds of thousands of dollars on Republican causes"—is who in the United States or abroad was paying for Parnas's transatlantic lobbying activities, extravagant globe-trotting, extraordinary access to the Trumps and their inner circle, and largesse as a major GOP donor in Florida.[129] That Parnas will tell *BuzzFeed News* that he met "many times" with President Trump in the latter half of 2018 and the first half of 2019 underscores the importance of resolving this question.[130] Of aid in this task is a January 2020 federal court decision that permits Parnas to "provide documents and iPhone data to the House Intelligence Committee as it continues its impeachment inquiry," some of which documents will also become available to the public (see chapters 21 and 22).[131]

According to *BuzzFeed News*, the money Parnas and Fruman receive during their time as Trump's clandestine ambassadors in Ukraine begins flowing in May 2018, when Fruman takes out a $1.26 million mortgage on a south Florida oceanfront condo he owns and immediately gives Parnas access to the money.[132] The dispersal of the $1.26 million appears to include "$325,000 to a Trump-aligned super PAC" and "$845,000 to various companies" jointly owned by Parnas and Fruman; that this leaves well less than $100,000 for Parnas to spend on himself between May 2018 and mid-2019—a figure inconsistent with the struggling businessman's exorbitant expenditures over the same period—suggests other sources of income.[133] *BuzzFeed News* reports, for instance, on a three-week stretch in July 2019 in which Parnas spent a minimum of $25,000 on food, drink, and hotels during a whirlwind four-city international tour.[134] Cash withdrawals on a single Parnas bank card totaled almost $42,000 in 2018, the digital media outlet finds.[135] Between July 2018 and April 2019, Parnas and Fruman spend a minimum of $203,000 on either themselves, their businesses, or their efforts to track down dirt on Joe Biden and undermine Ukrainian investigations of Paul Manafort (see chapter 6).[136]

In November 2019, some of the mystery surrounding the financing of Parnas's lifestyle is resolved when CNN reports that one of Parnas's secret patrons during the course of his work for Trump and Giuliani was none other than Dmitry Firtash, who had begun lavishing Parnas with a "windfall of money" by summer 2019 at the latest; per CNN, "beginning in mid-August [2019]" Parnas's "newfound luxurious lifestyle," which was "bankrolled by Firtash," includes "around-the-clock bodyguards, two luxury SUVs for his entourage . . . at least six private charter flights . . . [and] private security guards outside of his home in Florida."[137]

In June 2019, Parnas is spotted with Rudy Giuliani in the VIP area of two consecutive Red Sox–Yankees baseball games played in London.[138] Just a few weeks later, in July 2019, Firtash hires Giuliani friends and Trump legal advisers Joe diGenova and Victoria Toensing as his new attorneys; at the same time, the Russian-mob-linked oligarch—then fighting extradition to the United States on bribery charges—hires Parnas to work as a "translator" for diGenova and Toensing.[139]

Despite these landmark dates in the early summer of 2019, it is clear that Parnas's sudden wealth manifests well before June of that year. For instance, in fall 2018 "a company owned by Parnas paid Giuliani $500,000 for consulting" (see chapter 9).[140] When asked by the *New York Times* in October 2019 whether he ever worked for Parnas's Fraud Guarantee in 2018, Giuliani will initially confirm that he did so and then attempt to retract his confession, telling the *Times* interviewer, "All I can tell you is that most of the Fraud Guarantee work, in fact the Fraud Guarantee work, which—or I should say—I can't acknowledge it's Fraud Guarantee, I don't think. I can acknowledge I gave them substantial business advice."[141] As to whether Parnas and Fruman sought out Giuliani to become their paid representative or the other way around, reports differ; several friends of Parnas and Fruman who encountered the men at the time they were trying to cut a deal with Giuliani in 2018 say the men were asking people in their social and professional circles, "Can you loan me $500K, so I can get Rudy off my back?"[142]

In December 2019, when asked if he has any business in Ukraine, Giuliani is frustratingly ambiguous: "I have no business interests in Ukraine," the former mayor replies, but adds, "I've done two business deals in Ukraine. I've sought four or five others."[143] The October 2019 revelation that the Southern District of New York has been monitoring "more than a dozen cell phones" as part of its investigations of Parnas, Fruman, and Correia suggests that federal prosecutors are now or will soon be in a position to present to a jury the nature and extent of the three defendants' contacts with Giuliani, Trump, diGenova, Toensing, the Ukrainian Firtash, Nunes, and others.[144]

Giuliani's vacillations on the subject notwithstanding, major media describes the relationship between the president's personal attorney and Parnas's Fraud Guarantee bluntly: "[Giuliani] worked with Mr. Parnas' company, Fraud Guarantee," the *New York Times* reports in October 2019, adding that "the fraud prevention and mitigation company . . . retained Mr. Giuliani."[145] Giuliani's business and political associations with Parnas notwithstanding, Trump's personal attorney has expressed views on the Ukrainian-American's patron, Firtash, that can fairly be termed scathing. In March 2019, he tells *The Hill* that Firtash "is considered to be one of the close associates of [Semion] Mogilevich, who is the head of Russian organized crime, who is Putin's best friend . . . [Firtash is] considered to be one of the high-level, Russian organized crime members or associates."[146]

Parnas's claim that he needed to pay Giuliani in response to a demand from the president's attorney is puzzling, as it is Parnas who conducts errands in Ukraine and elsewhere on Giuliani's behalf following his payment of $500,000 to the president's attorney. Given that, as MSNBC reports in November 2019, Giuliani does all his work for Trump "for free," the possibility remains that Parnas and Fruman are, from mid-2018 through mid-2019, paying for Giuliani's hunt for Biden dirt in Trump's stead and doing so using money from a foreign source; such payments, if made, would constitute an illegal campaign contribution and—if followed by official acts from the president that benefit Parnas, Fruman, or any foreign source of the duo's significant income and polit-ical donations—bribery.[147] MSNBC notes, in circumscribing the unusual pecuniary relationship between Trump and Giuliani, that in the late 1990s a federal ethics watchdog informed President Clinton that receiv-ing pro bono legal work was impermissible.[148]

As for whether Parnas and Fruman would be willing to risk receiving illicit monies from Firtash to pay Giuliani or to indirectly but illegally benefit Trump by paying Giuliani on Trump's behalf, a stunning devel-opment in December 2019 complicates the question still further: it is revealed that in September 2019, just a month before his arrest by federal law enforcement, Parnas had received $1 million from a Russian bank account later confirmed to belong to Firtash.[149] Federal prosecutors do not disclose whether Firtash was also "the source of [the] funds for [Parnas's] political donations to curry favor with state and federal officials"—funds whose illegal funneling into the United States is the subject of both Par-nas's and Fruman's indictments.[150] Nevertheless, Bloomberg News notes that "the [September 2019] payment came the same month that Parnas and Fruman received the first of two requests for documents from con-gressional committees investigating the Trump administration's actions in Ukraine. The pair initially refused to comply with the requests."[151]

At the time of their arrest, Parnas and Fruman had been seeking "to board a plane with one-way tickets to Vienna"—the city where Dmitry

Firtash was then living (see chapter 7).[152] In December 2019, CNN reports that Parnas and Fruman, as well as their co-defendants David Correia and Andrey Kukushkin, are also "under investigation for additional crimes," and that the further charges being considered by prosecutors include conspiracy, obstruction of justice, additional campaign finance violations, and money laundering.[153] As the federal prosecutions and ongoing investigations of Parnas and Fruman unfold, additional background facts regarding the two Giuliani associates are revealed, among them an allegation that Parnas twice threatened his landlord in 2008—once by holding a gun to his head—as part of a property dispute involving Parnas's condo in Trump Palace in Sunny Isles Beach, Florida, just an hour south of Mar-a-Lago.[154]

According to *Politico*, Parnas's business history reveals a man who was "often working with fraudsters and others tied to organized crime," and who at one point ran a "charity organization" aimed at "eliminat[ing] illiteracy" out of a Trump-branded property.[155] Another Parnas operation, computer gadget company EdgeTech, boasted a "high-ranking member of Russian organized crime," Nikolai Dozortsev, as one of its chief investors, with the Russian mobster holding 100,000 shares of EdgeTech stock.[156] *Politico* observes that "despite this past, when Trump mounted his run for president, Parnas had no problem entering the future president's inner circle."[157]

CHAPTER 4

SHOKIN

In February 2015, Viktor Shokin becomes prosecutor general of Ukraine. Within a matter of months, his stewardship of the nation's nascent anti-corruption campaign is in turmoil, with law enforcement raiding the homes of two of his top prosecutors in July 2015 and finding there "millions of dollars' worth of diamonds and cash"—a discovery, *USA Today* will note, that "suggest[s] the pair had been taking bribes."[1] When one of Shokin's deputies, Vitaly Kasko, initiates an investigation of what becomes known in Ukraine as the "diamond prosecutors" case, he shortly thereafter feels compelled (or is forced) to resign his post, on his way out calling Shokin's office a "hotbed of corruption" and a political "instrument."[2]

Shokin also receives significant international scrutiny for actions he takes to help—not harm, as Trump will later falsely claim—the Ukrainian natural gas company for which Joe Biden's son Hunter works, Burisma, with *USA Today* reporting that Shokin's office "stepped in to help [Mykola] Zlochevsky, the head of Burisma. British authorities had frozen $23 million in a money-laundering probe, but Shokin's office failed to send documents to British authorities needed to prosecute Zlochevsky. The case eventually unraveled and the assets were unfrozen."[3]

Significantly, Zlochevsky had been facing, as the *Washington Post* reports in May 2019, "the prospect of prosecution alongside other former officials from the toppled pro-Moscow government of Viktor Yanukovych"—suggesting that had Shokin proceeded with the Zlochevsky case, it might have harmed the Kremlin's interests or, even closer to Trump's sphere of concern, those of Yanukovych's former right-hand man, Paul Manafort.[4] Zlochevsky's former role in "Ukrainian government positions that influenced the issuing of natural gas production and exploration licenses," along with his subsequent stewardship of "one of the biggest gas producers in the nation," also risks the involvement of his case with another individual whose path has crossed with Trump's in ways potentially injurious to the president: Dmitry Firtash.[5]

According to a September 2019 MSNBC report, at the time Manafort joins the Trump campaign he "owe[s] millions of dollars" to Firtash.[6] In addition to being one of Manafort's creditors, Firtash is "rich almost beyond belief" at the time Shokin is considering prosecuting Zlochevsky—and rich, MSNBC reports, "specifically because Vladimir Putin made him so."[7] As the cable news outlet details, "One of the motherlode corruption stories of Ukraine and Russian foreign influence is that for years the Kremlin insisted their guy in Ukraine, Dmitry Firtash, would be given a cut of every cubic inch of natural gas that Russia pumped through Ukraine on its way to Europe."[8] Shokin's protection of Zlochevsky—possible only for as long as Shokin stays in his uniquely powerful position as Ukraine's prosecutor general—is consequently a significant boon to Firtash, Manafort, and Putin, inasmuch as it ensures that the business dealings of these men in and around Ukraine's energy markets remain hidden.

One of many questions Shokin's inaction on the Zlochevsky case keeps hidden from view, as it ensures that Zlochevsky's pre-Burisma handling of gas licenses in Ukraine will never receive public scrutiny, is why the Kremlin needed Firtash to act as a highly paid middleman in the transshipment of Russian gas through Ukraine. As MSNBC notes, "Firtash did not do anything to earn that money—he was . . . just the artificially installed middleman who got paid . . . billions of dollars a year in pure profit just at the Kremlin's direction. [The Kremlin was in essence saying to Ukraine,] 'You want Russian gas to transit your country? You will have Dmitry [Firtash] take a cut of all of it.'"[9] That Firtash then spent his billions in Kremlin largesse to prop up a pro-Kremlin political party in Ukraine—the Party of Regions, whose chief foreign adviser was Paul Manafort—means that Putin was indirectly, through Firtash, paying Manafort's salary. This arrangement would be consistent with Putin's interests, given Manafort's concurrent work, financed by Kremlin agent Oleg Deripaska, to advance the Russian president's cause in the United States and elsewhere.[10]

USA Today reports that "Shokin[ ] was ousted for the opposite reason Trump and his allies claim. . . . It was because Shokin wasn't pursuing corruption among the country's politicians, according to a Ukrainian official and four former American officials who specialized in Ukraine and Europe."[11] Shokin's unwillingness to prosecute corruption in Ukraine eventually became so infamous both within and without Ukraine that it resulted in public protests and international pressure to fire him from "European diplomats, the International Monetary Fund and other international organizations . . . [as well as] 'civil society organizations in Ukraine.'"[12] Shokin was ultimately removed from office by the Ukrainian parliament.[13]

Trump and his allies' claims about Shokin's firing are contradicted by the facts of the Ukrainian prosecutor's ouster in almost every particular. Whereas "Trump and his personal attorney Rudy Giuliani claim Biden [threatened to withhold aid to Ukraine] to quash Shokin's investigation into . . . Burisma Holdings, and its owner, oligarch Mykola Zlochevsky," in fact Shokin, as noted, assisted rather than hindered Zlochevsky's evasion of justice for his alleged crimes. Whereas Trump and Giuliani assert that Shokin's exercise of prosecutorial discretion sought to aid Hunter Biden by turning a blind eye to his alleged malfeasance, in fact *USA Today* reports that "Burisma Holdings was not under scrutiny at the time Joe Biden called for Shokin's ouster, according to the National Anti-Corruption Bureau of Ukraine, an independent agency set up in 2014 that has worked closely with the FBI." Whereas Trump and Giuliani contend that Hunter Biden's actions while on Burisma's board were in some unspecified way corrupt, in fact when Shokin briefly investigated Burisma it was via a probe "focused on a period before Hunter Biden joined the company."[14] Indeed, Shokin's review of Burisma's Ministry of Ecology permits considered only the period from 2010 to 2012; Hunter Biden "did not join the company until 2014," *USA Today* reports, and even Shokin's successor, a prosecutor publicly spoken of with admiration by both Trump and Giuliani named Yuri Lutsenko, will eventually admit that "there is no evidence Hunter Biden did anything wrong," saying in a statement to the press that Biden's son "did not violate" any Ukrainian laws.[15]

While Shokin's successor Lutsenko will keep the Burisma investigation in a "dormant" but not yet closed status after he becomes prosecutor general in 2016, Ambassador Marie Yovanovitch (see chapter 20) will tell Congress in October 2019 that this was not because Lutsenko intended to—or felt he had the evidence to—reopen an investigation into Burisma, but rather for strategic reasons. "It [was], frankly, [politically] useful to keep that company [Burisma] hanging on a hook," Yovanovitch will tell Congress.[16] When former Ukrainian president Petro Poroshenko is asked directly whether Biden ever requested that the Ukrainian government open or close any individual criminal cases, Poroshenko will answer that the former U.S. vice president did not.[17] In October 2019, one of Trump's foremost defenders in the U.S. Senate, Sen. Ron Johnson (R-WI), will concede that he signed a letter in February 2016 endorsing the collective view of Biden, President Obama, the European Union, and the International Monetary Fund that—as stated in the letter—"urgent reforms to the [Ukrainian] Prosecutor General's office and [Ukraine's] Judiciary" were necessary during the period Shokin was Ukraine's prosecutor general.[18]

Trump and Giuliani's claims that Hunter Biden's position at Burisma was unusual will also turn out to be false. *USA Today* reports that, according to former U.S. ambassador to Ukraine Steven Pifer, "it's not unusual for Ukrainian companies to bring on high-profile people from the West," with *USA Today* offering in support of Pifer's observation the fact that "Cofer Black, who served as [Republican president George W.] Bush's counterterrorism chief, joined Burisma's board in 2017."[19] While

Burisma may have sought in 2014 to "burnish [its] image and gain influence" by hiring Hunter Biden—an attorney, Navy veteran, adjunct professor at Georgetown University, member of the President's Advisory Board for the Catholic Charities of the Archdiocese of Washington, and board chairman at World Food Program USA—at the time Hunter's father was calling for Shokin's termination at the end of 2015 and beginning of 2016, Burisma was not only no longer under ongoing investigative scrutiny, it was already working toward "a [November 2016] settlement and a fine paid by one of the firm's accountants," per *USA Today*.[20]

The effort by Biden and much of the West to force Shokin out of office, according to former National Security Council (NSC) senior director for European affairs Charlie Kupchan, was intended to "push[ ] the Ukrainian government to clean up the corruption [in Ukraine], partly because it was that corruption that allowed Russia to manipulate the country politically and economically."[21] While Ambassador Pifer criticizes the appearance of impropriety created by Hunter Biden having joined Burisma approximately a year before his father began spearheading the Obama administration's Ukraine policy, *USA Today* reports that "the international effort to remove Shokin . . . began months before [Joe] Biden stepped into the spotlight [on Ukraine]," and was part of a massive campaign by "European and U.S. officials . . . to clean up Ukraine's corruption" and force out a prosecutor who had, according to former deputy assistant secretary of defense Mike Carpenter, "played the role of protecting the vested interest[s] in the Ukrainian system. [Shokin] never went after any corrupt individuals at all, never prosecuted any high-profile cases of corruption."[22] Indeed, by September 2015—just over seven months into Shokin's tenure—the U.S. ambassador to Ukraine at the time, Geoffrey Pyatt, was declaring in a speech in Odessa that "rather than supporting Ukraine's reforms and working to root out corruption, corrupt actors within the Prosecutor General's Office are making things worse by openly and aggressively undermining reform."[23] The next month, assistant secretary of state Victoria Nuland testified before the Senate Foreign Relations Committee that critical to Ukraine's future was imprisoning "dirty personnel" in the prosecutor general's office.[24] In June 2016, Firtash business associate and "indispensable" Putin ally Oleg Deripaska would be caught on camera by his self-identified mistress, Nastya Rybka, telling the deputy prime minister of the Russian Federation, Sergei Prikhodko, that Nuland—still aggressively seeking, in mid-2016, a cleaning up of Ukraine's prosecutor general's office—was the chief reason for the Kremlin's "bad relations with America," a startling claim that underscores how, like much else in Nuland's policy portfolio, her opposition to corruption in Ukraine likely irked the Kremlin significantly.[25] At the time of Deripaska's private, secretly recorded complaint about Nuland—one not revealed publicly until February 2018—Nuland's and others' efforts to rid the Ukrainian prosecutor general's office of corruption had just months earlier resulted in Shokin's firing.[26]

In December 2018, Lev Parnas "help[s] to connect Giuliani [via Skype] with former Ukrainian prosecutor-general Viktor Shokin," according to the *New Yorker* and *Just Security*.[27] Despite the basis for Shokin's firing being that he "was lax in pursuing corruption," when Shokin speaks to Giuliani over Skype a second time—on January 23, 2019, again at Parnas's orchestration—he will, per the *New Yorker*, "falsely" claim that "he was fired because he wanted to investigate Burisma"; Parnas will later append to this falsehood an equally false public claim that Shokin, rather than being fired by Ukraine's parliament during the Poroshenko administration, "basically stepped down . . . to save the country" from Joe Biden's wrath.[28] According to *Just Security*, the participants in Giuliani's January 2019 call with Shokin include not just Parnas but also Fruman and a man named George Boyle, "a former NYPD detective who works for Giuliani Partners."[29] Giuliani will subsequently say that he was first put in contact with Parnas by a "well-known investigator"; he does not say whether the investigator in question was Boyle.[30]

The reason Giuliani must Skype with Shokin in January 2019 rather than meet him face-to-face is that he has been unsuccessful in petitioning both the State Department and the White House—the latter in the person of Robert Blair, an aide to Trump's acting chief of staff, Mick

Mulvaney—to grant Shokin a visa so he can come to the United States and divulge information about Biden.[31] CNN will refer to Giuliani's back-channel visa request as "an attempt [by Giuliani] to directly influence the actions of the federal government."[32]

By the time of the second Giuliani-Shokin Skype conversation, it is widely known that Joe Biden plans to run for president of the United States in 2020. Moreover, every public poll shows Biden handily defeating the incumbent president. Among the national polls with published results, online surveys by Democratic firm Public Policy Polling (PPP), all conducted between March and December 2017, put Biden between 12 and 18 points ahead of Trump in a head-to-head general-election match-up; meanwhile, two additional polls—an October 2017 Emerson College poll and a January 2018 poll by CNN—return similar results, revealing a 9-point and 17-point Biden lead, respectively.[33] The only other polls conducted between January 2018 and November 2018—three PPP polls in February, March, and June 2018—give Biden leads over Trump of 9, 17, and 14 points.[34] Meanwhile, polls from PPP, Emerson, and Rasmussen between March 2017 and October 2018 show Massachusetts senator Elizabeth Warren either tied with or holding a moderate lead over Trump (up to a maximum of 11 points), and PPP polls released between June 2017 and June 2018 give Kamala Harris an even narrower margin of victory over the sitting president, with results ranging from a tie to a 6-point Harris victory.[35] That Biden poses the greatest Democratic threat to Trump's reelection in 2017 and 2018 is a fact Trump himself seems to acknowledge; in March 2018, according to the *New York Times*, he "threaten[s]" the former vice president, writing in a tweet that Biden "'would go down fast and hard' if the two men ever physically fought."[36] While Trump's warning to Biden is ostensibly a response to an earlier statement by Biden that if he'd known Trump in high school he would have "beat the hell out of him" for disrespecting women, Trump may also be unnerved by another recent incident: as the *Times* reports, Biden, amidst "talk of a possible 2020 presidential run," campaigned in early March 2018 for "a Democrat in western Pennsylvania who won a special congressional election in a district that had previously been considered Trump country. Mr. Trump campaigned for the Republican candidate who lost."[37]

A July 2018 *Axios* report confirms that Trump has been badly shaken by Biden's superior popularity in Pennsylvania, a major 2020 battle-ground state, with the digital media outlet revealing that "advisers to President Trump say Joe Biden is the Democrat he most fears running against, and that Pennsylvania is the state he worries most about flipping against him."[38] *Axios* adds that Trump is not worried about either Warren or Vermont senator Bernie Sanders, both of whom he perceives as "weak" and not "capable of appealing to his base of working class whites."[39] It is perhaps no surprise, then, that July 2018 also sees Trump musing publicly about a 2020 match-up with Biden, with the president telling CBS News that he "dream[s] about Biden" being the Democratic nominee, adding, "I'd love to have it be Biden."[40] Referring to the CBS News interview, *Axios* notes dryly that "what Trump meant was 'wouldn't.'"[41] The truth of Trump's willingness to face Biden notwithstanding, the president cer-tainly would not have been pleased with a spring 2018 poll revealing that, in the view of a plurality of Americans, Biden would indeed defeat Trump in a fistfight: according to the poll, 37 percent of Americans would bet on Biden, and only 32 percent on Trump.[42]

In September 2019, *Politico* reports that in the three months prior to Trump's now-infamous July 25, 2019, phone call with Volodymyr Zelen-sky (see chapter 28), the president suffered from "Biden mania" and was "extraordinarily preoccupied" with the former vice president, devoting an "inordinate amount of time [to] deriding" him publicly.[43] This in-cludes "more than 60 retweets bashing Biden" following the decision of the nation's largest firefighters' union to endorse Biden for president.[44] In late May 2019, Trump goes so far as to quote an enemy of the United States, Kim Jong Un, for the premise that, as Trump puts it, "Joe Biden is a low IQ individual. He probably is, based on his record. I think I agree with [Kim Jong Un] on that."[45] "By then," *Politico* observes, "news reports had surfaced about an internal, seventeen-state March polling project that showed the president losing to Biden in key Rust Belt states that were essential to his 2016 victory."[46] By mid-June, Trump will have "fired the pollsters involved" in the poll, "blaming them for leaks."[47]

On April 8, 2020, Vermont senator Bernie Sanders's suspension of his presidential campaign makes Joe Biden the presumptive nominee of the Democratic Party for the 2020 presidential election—precisely the eventuality Trump and his political team had been anticipating and preparing for since spring 2018 (see chapters 7, 9, 17, and 21).[48]

CHAPTER 5

KILIMNIK

When Viktor Yanukovych flees Ukraine in 2014, Paul Manafort's long-time assistant, Ukrainian-Russian dual citizen Konstantin Kilimnik—a man *The Atlantic* calls a "shadowy operative . . . link[ed] . . . to Russian intelligence" and *New York* magazine describes as a man U.S. officials consider "a Russian intelligence operative"—remains in Kyiv.[1] His mission is to reconstitute the Kremlin's base of political power in Kyiv, the now-fallen Party of Regions, by renaming and rebranding it. In short order, Kilimnik and his former boss at the International Republican Institute in Moscow, Sam Patten, have adopted a new leader for their new pro-Kremlin party: Serhiy Lyovochkin, who will shortly come to stand at the forefront of a post–Party of Regions political entity called the Opposition Bloc.[2] Kilimnik and Patten, both of whom will be under indictment in the United States within forty-eight months—Kilimnik for allegedly tampering with witnesses to aid the under-indictment Manafort, and Patten for acting as an unregistered foreign agent and secretly directing $50,000 from Lyovochkin to Trump's political coffers—work ardently to legitimize Lyovochkin by securing him meetings with D.C. power brokers.[3]

Trump announces his presidential run just sixteen months after Yanukovych flees Ukraine and Manafort, Kilimnik, and Patten try to pick up the pieces of the Kremlin's proxy operations in Kyiv. Whereas 2016 Democratic presidential candidate Hillary Clinton is considered hostile to the new pro-Kremlin Opposition Bloc due to her support for the Obama administration's Crimea-related sanctions against Russia, Trump is presumed to be a reliable ally; indeed, within weeks of his announcement of a presidential run, he answers a question at a public event from a subsequently convicted Kremlin agent, Maria Butina, confirming that he does not believe Russia should be sanctioned for invading Ukraine.[4]

Kilimnik's dual goals of reestablishing the Kremlin's influence in Kyiv and working with Manafort to pay off Manafort's debts to Putin ally Oleg Deripaska appear significantly closer to realization when, in late March 2016, Trump selects Manafort to be his chief agent to the 2016 Republican National Convention.[5] Manafort's hire is the result of a meeting the long-time political operative had secured a month earlier in which, according to the *Washington Post*, he told his longtime friend Thomas Barrack—also one of Trump's closest friends—"I really need to get to [Trump]."[6]

Time magazine will say of Trump's hiring of Manafort that "of all the examples of Trump's on-the-fly decisions, few are as confounding, and potentially as consequential, as his hiring of Manafort," adding that "none of the sources familiar with the details can quite agree anymore on how Trump came to decide hiring Manafort was a good idea."[7] By some accounts, Trump's purportedly "on-the-fly" decision is in fact the result of communications between Thomas Barrack and Jared Kushner—contact that comes even as both men are in secret communication with a pro-Trump Emirati official, Yousef al-Otaiba, working to augment his country's burgeoning relationship with the Kremlin.[8] Another version of Manafort's hiring sees Trump influenced by his close friend, former business associate, and intermittent political adviser Roger Stone, Manafort's consulting firm partner for many years and a man who proudly describes himself as having no scruples when it comes to politics (see chapter 8).[9] A third narrative surrounding Manafort's hire suggests that, with support not only from Barrack and Kushner but also from Donald Trump Jr., Manafort essentially forced his way onto the Trump campaign by sheer determination.[10] *Time* concludes in its October report, however, that "more than anything, it may have been that Manafort was just someone Trump knew."[11] After all, writes the magazine, Manafort had been Trump's "lobbyist" for many years, "work[ing] on projects" for Trump that included getting the New York City businessman "a deeper dock in Atlantic City so he could park a yacht," "rezoning city blocks," and "blocking Native American tribes from opening casinos that would compete with Trump properties in Atlantic City."[12] According to *Time*, Manafort and his consulting firm partners, including Stone, had "gotten results" for Trump for so many years that it's possible Trump believed the same would happen if Manafort ran his presidential campaign.[13] Whether Trump received any additional advice on the matter from Felix Sater, Michael Cohen, Michael Flynn, or friend and business associate Aras Agalarov—a Russian oligarch with major contracts with the Kremlin—is unknown.

That Trump's son-in-law, Jared Kushner, had just met Putin "friend" Dimitri Simes at the pro-Kremlin Center for the National Interest days before Manafort's hire is another potential explanation for why the former Party of Regions operative—for so long a useful tool for the Kremlin via his work with Deripaska, Yanukovych, and Kilimnik—became suddenly attractive to Kushner and Trump.[14] Simes, one of the Trump campaign's top advisers on Russia for almost the entirety of the 2016 presidential campaign—and a man *Washington Monthly* describes as "extraordinarily close to Putin"—now works as a highly paid Kremlin propagandist in Moscow.[15] Interestingly, the April 2016 Trump speech at the Mayflower Hotel in Washington that Kushner and Simes (along with Kremlin gas company lobbyist Richard Burt) spent the month of March planning was turned over to Manafort for his orchestration almost as soon as he joined the campaign, despite the fact that it had nothing to do with the convention management duties for which Manafort had ostensibly been hired.[16] Even so, *Washington Monthly* reports that "everyone in Washington, D.C. who closely follows the Russians' lobbying efforts [within the Trump campaign] assumed that the idea behind [Trump's speech at the Mayflower] came from Paul Manafort."[17] *Politico* goes so far as to observe that, at the time of Trump's Simes-hosted Mayflower speech, the event "represents the latest phase of a makeover strategy implemented by Paul Manafort. . . . That Trump would choose the Center for the National Interest [run by Simes] as the place to premier[e] his new seriousness on foreign policy has Manafort's fingerprints all over it. For Manafort and the Center have something very important in common: both have ties to the Russian regime of President Vladimir Putin."[18]

Whatever Trump's motivation for hiring Manafort, it is clear that Manafort immediately understands the utility of his new position for both himself and top Kremlin agents like Deripaska.[19] Shortly after his hire, Manafort "summon[s]" the Russian-intelligence-linked Kilimnik from Ukraine to assist him in turning his work on the Trump campaign into value for the Russian oligarch.[20] Kilimnik is still close enough to Deripaska that he arrives for at least one of his meetings with Manafort on Deripaska's personal jet, a convenience both he and Manafort had been allotted for a number of their eighteen or more reported trips to Moscow between 2005 and 2011.[21]

Kilimnik has been described by associates as "politically conservative" and "strongly Republican-leaning"; Trump's 2016 deputy campaign manager, Manafort aide Rick Gates, will baldly tell a third party that Kilimnik is, moreover, "a former Russian intelligence officer with the GRU."[22] As for Kilimnik's sense of his own role after coming to America to aid Manafort, it is succinctly described in one of the many Kilimnik-Manafort emails uncovered by federal investigators: Kilimnik's job in 2016 was to do whatever was necessary to get himself and Manafort "back to the original relationship" to Deripaska.[23] That relationship, established by the 2006 contract between Manafort and Deripaska, required Manafort to work on Putin's behalf in both Ukraine and the United States.

It remains unclear to what extent candidate Trump appreciated in 2016, or has come to appreciate since, Kilimnik's influence on his presidential campaign. That Kilimnik was in regular contact with Trump's top campaign lieutenants is certain, however. *The Guardian*, citing federal court filings by the special counsel's office, reports that "Kilimnik had numerous contacts with Gates in the weeks just before the 2016 election."[24] At the time, Gates had transitioned from serving as Trump's deputy campaign manager to playing an equally critical role as Trump's liaison to the Republican National Committee.[25] The fact that, as Bloomberg News reports, Gates "stayed in close contact with Trump's associates well after the election" further enabled Kilimnik to maintain his influence on the Trump transition and presidency many months after his longtime patron, Manafort, had been cast—at least publicly—out of Trump's inner circle.[26]

Post-campaign reporting reveals that Manafort's influence on Trump in fact never waned following his dismissal. Per a January 2019 article by Bloomberg, Manafort bragged to Gates that even in 2017—five months after leaving the Trump campaign—he "was using intermediaries to 'get people appointed in the administration.'"[27] Yet apparently Manafort did not always use intermediaries to advise Trump in the months after the election. In December 2019, CNN will report that "[telephone] conversations between Manafort and Trump continued after the President took office, long after the FBI investigation into Manafort was publicly known. They went on until lawyers for the President and Manafort insisted that they stop."[28] It is still unknown when these extraordinary contacts ceased; in any case, that it took the intervention of attorneys for Trump to stop him from speaking—or at least so conspicuously—to the presumed subject of a federal criminal investigation underscores the close relationship between the president and Manafort. Indeed, *Politico* will report that when the so-called Steele dossier was released in January 2017, Manafort was sufficiently exercised about its contents that he called the president-elect's chief of staff to discuss the "scandal" that was "now consuming Manafort and the Trump presidency."[29] According to CNN, federal law enforcement officers were wiretapping Manafort both "before and after" the 2016 election, so there remains the possibility that the substance of Manafort's interactions with the Trump campaign and Trump himself in 2016, 2017, and possibly beyond is now in the hands of the FBI; certainly, it is known that three days before the 2016 election, Steve Bannon wrote to Jared Kushner that "we need to avoid [Manafort] like the plague[.] They are going to try and say the Russians worked with wiki leaks [*sic*] to give this victory to us[.] Paul is [a] nice guy but [we] can't let word get out he is advising us."[30]

* * *

Having shared internal campaign polling data with Kilimnik during the presidential campaign, as well as secretly offering Deripaska (through Kilimnik) private briefings on Trump's thinking, Manafort would continue meeting with Kilimnik in early 2017—the same period during which he told Gates he was helping to select incoming officials in the new Trump administration.[31] These exchanges, as well as reporting by MSNBC indicating that Kremlin agent Maria Butina believed—per her private email exchanges—that the Kremlin "had a say" in the selection of Trump cabinet officials, will lead many to believe the influence of Kremlin agents like Kilimnik continued well after Trump's election.[32] As for Manafort's post-inauguration contacts with Trump himself, it should be noted that the political operative's ties to Kilimnik are so significant that during Manafort's federal trial in 2018 it is revealed that Kilimnik is "listed as the beneficial owner on some of the 31 offshore accounts that were used by Manafort in his financial scheming."[33]

Kilimnik's lasting impact on the Trump presidency is felt well beyond staffing decisions, however. As summarized by *New York* magazine in 2019, based on reports released from the FBI that year, "Trump's notion that Ukraine, not Russia, hacked Democratic [National Committee] emails" first came to Trump from Kilimnik, via Manafort, in summer 2016.[34] According to *BuzzFeed News*, Manafort is the first Trump campaign staffer to push the conspiracy theory, in June 2016 telling his deputy, Gates, that the hack of the Democratic National Committee (DNC) was "likely carried [out] by the Ukrainians, not the Russians."[35] This view was in short order echoed by Trump's top national security adviser, Michael Flynn, who had met with Putin and Putin's ambassador to the United States in the preceding seven months and would "adamant[ly]" insist to Trump that the hack could not have been carried out by Kremlin agents.[36] Why Manafort would have cared so much about placing blame on the Ukrainians—and why Flynn would have cared so much about exculpating the Kremlin—remains murky, though the prior associations of each man, including Flynn's then-active plan to partner with Russia on the building of nuclear reactors in Saudi Arabia and the United Arab Emirates, strongly suggest possible motives.[37] Whatever the thinking of the two men, Gates will tell the FBI in 2018 that "the idea that Ukraine was involved [in the DNC hack] was a theory pushed by Konstantin Kilimnik."[38] Per Gates, Kilimnik also suggested, as an apparent backup argument for the Trump campaign, that "the DNC hack could have been carried out by Russian operatives in Ukraine"—that is, pro-Kremlin Ukrainians.[39]

In December 2016, the Russian Foreign Ministry—the very entity confirmed by the Mueller Report to have sought a clandestine back channel to Trump during the 2016 primary and general election campaigns—will advance Kilimnik's seeding of a supposed Ukrainian election-meddling conspiracy in the Trump camp by, per *Politico*, publicly "charg[ing] that the Ukrainian government used the ledgers [documents discovered in Ukraine indicating illicit payments from Yanukovych to Manafort] as a political weapon. 'Ukraine seriously complicated the work of Trump's election campaign headquarters by planting information according to which Paul Manafort, Trump's campaign chairman, allegedly accepted money from Ukrainian oligarchs,' [Russian Ministry of Foreign Affairs spokeswoman] Maria Zakharova [will say] at a news briefing."[40]

Within the first ninety days of his presidency, Trump begins publicly repeating the Kilimnik-born conspiracy theory about Ukrainian election meddling, "falsely telling an Associated Press reporter that a 'Ukrainian-based' company had taken the Democratic server with the stolen emails. A few months after that Rudy Giuliani began meeting with Ukrainian officials."[41] Trump's personal attorney will eventually term Kilimnik's disinformation "what a defense lawyer always wants": the opportunity to "go prove someone else committed this crime."[42] Why Giuliani lumps his client in with the Kremlin as the chief suspect in Russia's 2015 and 2016 attacks on America's electoral infrastructure is unclear, as Trump is never accused of being behind the attacks—only Putin and various apparatuses of the Kremlin.

Whatever the president's or Giuliani's reason for believing that a criminal allegation against agents of the Kremlin was in fact an accusation against the president of the United States, Trump's professed indignation at reports of Russian election interference, and his self-described affront at the lack of investigation into supposed Ukrainian election interference, will continue well into his presidency. On October 16, 2019, Trump opines before a bank of reporters in the White House, "I still ask the FBI, 'Where is the [DNC] server? How come the FBI never got the server from the DNC? Where is the server? I want to see the server. Let's see what's on the server.' So the server, they say, is held by a company whose primary ownership individual is from Ukraine. I'd like to see the server. I think it's very important for this country to see the server.... The media never wants to see it. But I'll tell you, Republicans want to see it."[43] In the same press conference, long after Giuliani has told the media that he only ever acted in Ukraine on Trump's behalf as his attorney, Trump insists, "I don't know what [Rudy] did [in Ukraine]. I don't know. That's up to him.... You have to ask Rudy those questions, don't ask me."[44]

The very day that Trump denies knowledge of how his attorney is representing him and accuses an American-owned, California-based cybersecurity company (CrowdStrike) of being both Ukrainian and in possession of a cloud-connected server it never took possession of but merely imaged, the opening statement for the congressional testimony of Ambassador Gordon Sondland is published by NBC. In it, Sondland testifies, under penalty of perjury, that "my understanding was that the president directed Mr. Giuliani's participation" in clandestine negotiations with the Ukrainian government over potential investigations of CrowdStrike and Burisma.[45] CNN reports that Trump's conspiracy theory about CrowdStrike is "totally debunked," while *Wired*, a magazine focusing on the tech sector, calls it "demonstrably wrong."[46]

As Trump speaks to reporters in the White House about CrowdStrike, Mick Mulvaney is giving a press conference in which he confirms, per Reuters reporter Jonathan Landay, that "Trump still rejects [the] intelligence community's finding on Russia interference and believes the discredited conspiracy theory [that] Crowd[S]trike forged [the] report [that] Russia hacked the DNC servers."[47] Two days later, on October 18, Mulvaney gives another televised press conference, this time confessing that the White House participated in a quid pro quo with Ukraine.[48] When Jonathan Karl of ABC News tells Mulvaney—in response to Mulvaney's summary of the White House's official and back-channel outreach to Ukraine—"What you just described is a quid pro quo: it is 'funding will not flow [to Ukraine] unless the investigation into the Democratic server happens as well,'" Mulvaney replies, "We do that all the time."[49] As to the idea that there would be a "political influence" on U.S. foreign policy—meaning a consideration given to individual politicians' personal political fortunes in the setting of foreign policy—Mulvaney tells the assembled reporters that the country will have to "get over it."[50] Mulvaney adds that one of the three reasons Trump withheld aid to Ukraine was to ensure Ukraine was "cooperating in an ongoing investigation [of CrowdStrike] with our Department of Justice."[51] Referencing the opening statement of Sondland's congressional testimony, Mulvaney says that "he [Sondland] said something along the lines of: they [the administration] were 'trying to get the deliverable.' And the deliverable was a statement by the Ukraine [sic] about how they were going to deal with corruption. Okay? Go read his testimony if you haven't already. And what he says is, and he's right, that's absolutely ordinary course of business."[52] Contrary to Mulvaney's claims, however, when National Security Council official Tim Morrison and Trump's special representative for Ukraine Kurt Volker are asked by House Permanent Select Committee on Intelligence chairman Adam Schiff (D-CA), "Have you ever seen military aid held up because a president wanted his rival investigated?," both men answer no.[53]

During his ill-fated October 2019 press conference, Mulvaney—on the subject of whether the Kremlin-pushed CrowdStrike conspiracy theory was a consideration in Trump's withholding of aid to Russia's enemy Ukraine—says, "Did [the president] also mention to me in the past, the corruption related to the DNC server? Absolutely. No questions about that. But that's it. And that's why we held up the money."[54] When a reporter seeks to follow up on Mulvaney's response—asking, "So the demand for an investigation into the Democrats was part of the reason that [the president] ordered to withhold funding to Ukraine?"—Mulvaney replies, "The look back to what happened in 2016 certainly was part of the thing that he was worried about in corruption with that nation. And that is absolutely appropriate."[55] In response to a second follow-up from the reporter as to what Mulvaney was referring to as "absolutely appropriate" ("Withholding the funding?" asks the reporter), Mulvaney answers, "Yeah."[56]

Trump fires Mulvaney as acting chief of staff in March 2020, just thirty days after the president is acquitted, post-impeachment, by the U.S. Senate (see chapters 39 and 40).[57] The *Washington Post* describes Mulvaney as a "key" player in the Ukraine scandal who "contributed substantially to the unfolding political crisis" not only by "frequently" meeting with Gordon Sondland as the latter sought to push Ukraine for investigations of CrowdStrike and Burisma, but also by ensuring that the "details of their discussions were kept from then–National Security Advisor John Bolton and other officials who were raising internal concerns about the [White House's] hidden Ukraine agenda."[58] According to these officials, the work of the self-described "Three Amigos"—Volker, Sondland, and secretary of energy Rick Perry—"could not have proceeded . . . without Mulvaney facilitating meetings, halting the flow of aid [to Ukraine] and circumventing the national security bureaucracy."[59] When Bolton complains that the administration's Giuliani-aided clandestine negotiations with Ukraine constitute a "drug deal," Mulvaney is one of the two men—Sondland being the other—Bolton chiefly blames for the fiasco.[60]

In November 2019, when secretary of state Mike Pompeo, another central figure in the Ukraine scandal, is asked if he believes the Trump administration should investigate whether, contrary to the findings of the U.S. intelligence community, Ukraine rather than Russia hacked the DNC, he replies, "Any time there is information that indicates that any country has messed with American elections, we not only have a right but a duty to make sure we chase that down."[61]

CHAPTER 6

THE BLACK LEDGER AND THE JAVELINS

In November 2019, deputy secretary assistant of state George Kent testifies to Congress that Trump himself considers the "CrowdStrike" conspiracy theory to be almost entirely about Hillary Clinton and Joe Biden—the former the Democrats' 2016 presidential nominee, and the latter a leading 2020 Democratic contender. Trump "wanted nothing less than President Zelensky to go to [a] microphone [in 2019] and say 'investigations,' 'Biden,' and 'Clinton,'" Kent tells a joint session of three House committees. By January 2020, Trump's obsession with proving wrongdoing by Clinton will appear to have been a fruitless pursuit, as U.S. attorney John Huber wraps up a years-long, Jeff Sessions–ordered investigation of the Clinton Foundation having "found nothing worth pursuing."[1]

Trump wants more than just Clinton and Biden investigations from Zelensky, however. A third sensitive and potentially politically lucrative investigation centers on another name at the heart of the 2016 election: Paul Manafort. Approximately sixty days after Trump first publicly promotes the CrowdStrike disinformation provided to his team by Kilimnik via Manafort, his attorney Rudy Giuliani travels to Kyiv to meet with Ukrainian president Petro Poroshenko and Ukraine's new prosecutor general, Yuri Lutsenko.[2] Poroshenko is angling at the time for a visit to the White House; he ends up getting a visit in Kyiv with Giuliani instead, perhaps in part, the New Yorker intimates, because "Trump was convinced that an unproven conspiracy that had circulated on Fox News and other conservative media outlets was true: Ukraine, under Poroshenko, had intervened against him in the 2016 American Presidential campaign."[3]

The "intervention" here imagined involves Manafort and the "black ledger"—a physical ledger of alleged kickbacks paid to Manafort in Ukraine—rather than either Clinton or Biden. Indeed, within twenty-four hours of the Giuliani-Poroshenko-Lutsenko meeting, during which the three men, according to Giuliani and Poroshenko, discuss Ukraine's disadvantageous military positioning vis-à-vis Russia and its need for aid, "Lutsenko's office joins an existing investigation into the 'black ledger'"; the investigation "had previously been handled only by Ukraine's independent National Anti-Corruption Bureau."[4] After Poroshenko's decision to put the Manafort case under Lutsenko's thumb, "critics allege[ ] the new move was meant to bury the [Manafort] scandal."[5]

Just five days after this new development in Ukraine's Manafort investigations, reports emerge that Trump has agreed to meet with Poroshenko. Six days later, the two in fact meet, an event *New York* magazine calls "either a direct trade [of action in the Manafort case for a Trump-Poroshenko meeting], or an exchange of mutually-beneficial actions that coincidentally occurred in very rapid succession."[6] That Trump is still suspicious of Poroshenko at the time of his first meeting with him is suggested by the fact that, as the *New Yorker* notes, Poroshenko "failed to arrange an official White House visit," getting instead "a brief 'drop in' encounter" in June 2017 that "had been without any of the fanfare usually rolled out for visiting heads of state."[7]

Tellingly—given how events will unfold between Trump, Vice President Pence, and new Ukrainian president Volodymyr Zelensky in 2019 (see chapters 23, 25, and 33)—in the midst of this twelve-day period in 2017 in which a "trade" or "exchange" occurs between Trump and the Poroshenko administration, White House press secretary Sean Spicer briefly intimates that the Ukrainian president will only earn a meeting with Pence rather than Trump.[8] In 2019, as Giuliani is once again, in his own words, "meddling" in a Ukrainian investigation, and dangling as a reward for actions taken in Kyiv beneficial to Trump a face-to-face meeting between Trump and the Ukrainian president, Trump will in fact pull a switch and offer Ukraine's President Zelensky a meeting with Pence instead.[9] Poroshenko, asked in 2019 about his May 2017 meeting with Giuliani, will reveal that the two men discussed "political support and investment," leaving open the possibility, given his oddly precise insistence that he never spoke to "U.S. officials" about "[Ukrainian] commercial companies," that in May 2017 he had indeed been discussing that topic with Giuliani, who is not a U.S. official.[10] As for Manafort, *Politico* indicates that he was still corresponding directly with Trump through at least March 2017—ninety days before Giuliani apparently influenced a change in the status of Manafort's cases in Ukraine—and speaking to influential members of the Trump administration through at least February 2018.[11] Even if direct Trump-Manafort contacts had indeed subsided by mid-2017, subsequent evidence, in the form of text messages disclosed by a federal court, reveals that Manafort was in regular, "cozy" communication with one of Trump's top domestic policy advisers outside the administration, Sean Hannity, from at least July 2017 through June 2018—a period beginning shortly after Giuliani's trip to Kyiv to meet with Poroshenko.[12]

According to *Politico*, Manafort's ongoing conversations with Trump and his political team in 2017 and 2018 were not merely of a personal nature. Indeed, the digital media outlet reports that among the topics Manafort discussed with members of Trump's political operation were his fear that the Russia investigation could pose significant problems for those in Trump's orbit.[13] More troublingly, per *Politico*, Manafort attempted to push a new conspiracy theory about the Russia investigation into Trump's inner circle: that the Steele dossier—which addressed Manafort's alleged receipt of "kickbacks" in Ukraine and was shared with the FBI in summer 2016—"was tainted . . . by the motivations of the people who initiated it, whom he alleged were Democratic activists and donors working in cahoots with Ukrainian government officials."[14] Manafort's claim that Steele was biased against the Trumps will be significantly undercut when the *Washington Post* reports that Steele is in fact "a personal friend" of Trump's daughter Ivanka, and that indeed Trump and the Trump Organization had trusted Steele and his work sufficiently that they considered offering him a job early in the 2010s.[15]

In May 2017, *Politico* reports on a January 2017 phone call by Manafort to the White House. According to the report, Manafort speaks to Trump's chief of staff, Reince Priebus, who thereafter relays the content of the conversation to Trump. Other discussions between Manafort and top Trump advisers may likewise have been recounted for the president; of the content of such other conversations, *Politico* notes that Manafort is known to have discussed, with Trump allies other than Priebus, "the possibility of launching a countervailing investigation into efforts by Ukrainian government officials who allegedly worked in conjunction with allies of Trump's Democratic rival Hillary Clinton to damage Trump's campaign. . . . Manafort saw such an investigation as a way to distract attention from the parallel FBI and congressional Russia probes."[16]

That the sort of Ukrainian gambit Trump would be impeached for in late 2019 was conceived in January 2017 by his soon-to-be-indicted-and-convicted former campaign chief—a man confirmed by the Mueller Report to have colluded with Kremlin agents—sheds new light on Trump's dealings with Ukraine not just in 2019 but in 2017 and 2018 as well. Indeed, Manafort's perspective on the Steele dossier may well have been reflected in one of Trump's first reactions to the January 2017 publication of Steele's raw intelligence. It was "a group of [my] opponents that got together," Trump opined at the time, and "they put that crap together"; he declared that this consortium of his enemies comprised exclusively "sick people."[17] *Politico* reports that "Manafort was spotted in the part of the Trump Tower lobby that led to Trump's transition headquarters in the weeks after Trump's victory."[18] Moreover, the digital media outlet cites "three Manafort associates" as confirming that between January 2017—when the Steele dossier was released—and early spring 2017, Manafort and Trump "periodically" spoke; one source emphasized that Manafort and Trump were "still on good terms" in 2017.[19]

Manafort's ostensible complaints about Steele's dossier bear some discussion, as they in fact suggest Manafort can contest only a few of the former MI6 officer's submissions. Per *Politico*, in conversations with Trump and his team Manafort does not contest that he received payments from Yanukovych, merely that Yanukovych would not have (as Steele's dossier alleged) used the term "kickback" in describing them, and that some or all of the ledger of such payments that had surfaced may have been forged; just so, Manafort is of the opinion not that the conversations between Putin and Yanukovych described in the dossier did not happen, but merely that if they had happened, no one would have snitched about it afterward: "This stuff would never see the light of day," Manafort tells his associates.[20] In such conversations, Manafort "dispute[s] the assertion in the Steele dossier that [he] managed relations between Trump's team and the Russian leadership [in Moscow], using [Trump national security adviser Carter] Page and others as intermediaries"—but does so primarily by arguing that he's "never met Page" in person, a circumstance the dossier had not alleged.[21] None of Manafort's complaints about the dossier, as reported by *Politico*, undermine the dossier's central premise: that Manafort, indebted to and hoping to secure future benefits from pro-Kremlin persons and entities, colluded with the Kremlin while working for the Trump campaign.[22]

As for whether Manafort's collusion with Kremlin agent Kilimnik during the 2016 presidential campaign may have been by Kremlin orchestration rather than attributable to happenstance or the prior association between Manafort and Kilimnik, a May 2017 investigative report in the *New York Times* notes that "American spies collected information [in summer 2016] revealing that senior Russian intelligence and political officials were discussing how to exert influence over Donald J. Trump through his advisers. . . . The conversations focused on Paul Manafort, the Trump campaign chairman at the time, and Michael T. Flynn, a retired general who was advising Mr. Trump. . . . Both men had indirect ties to Russian officials, who appeared confident that each could be used to help shape Mr. Trump's opinions on Russia. Some Russians boasted about how well they knew Mr. Flynn. Others discussed leveraging their ties to [former Kilimnik and Manafort client] Viktor F. Yanukovych, the deposed president of Ukraine living in exile in Russia, who at one time had worked closely with Mr. Manafort."[23] That it is Manafort and Flynn who in the first instance aim to convince Trump and his campaign—the former on information from Kremlin agent Kilimnik—that the Russians could not and did not infiltrate the DNC in June 2016, and that in fact Ukraine had been responsible for the illegal intrusions, seems to corroborate the *Times* report.[24]

In view of the foregoing, Manafort's 2017 claims of being "unaware" of "any effort by Russians to influence me" strains credulity. In addition to his communications with Kilimnik about Ukraine, Manafort oversaw the Trump campaign's participation in the Republican National Convention, which included the successful squelching of a proposed GOP platform change that would have advocated the provision of lethal defensive assistance to the Ukrainian military as it fought off a Russian invasion on its eastern border. After the proposed platform plank was defeated, *Politico* reports, Kilimnik—the man Manafort once described as "my Russian brain"—"told associates in August 2016 that he helped play a role in the platform change."[25] *The Atlantic* describes Kilimnik's role in using the Trump campaign to weaken U.S. military aid for Ukraine as follows: "He bragged that he had shifted the Republican Party's platform. He claimed to have orchestrated the gutting of a proposal to arm Ukraine in its war against Russian proxies."[26]

Kilimnik has estimated, surely hyperbolically, that over the eleven years he and Manafort worked together they exchanged "millions" of emails, including discussions of both Putin and Trump. Kilimnik has also estimated, more reliably, that after 2010 he spent "'90 percent of his time' inside the [Yanukovych] presidential administration"—a regime whose figurehead, the *Times* reported, the Kremlin hoped to use to get to Manafort and thereafter Trump.[27] Kilimnik also admits to having been on Manafort's "payroll" as late as 2014; says that Manafort visited Ukraine—for what purpose is unclear—in the fall of 2015, well after Trump had launched his presidential campaign; and notes that during the 2016 presidential campaign he "briefed Manafort on Ukraine issues," though he does not disclose the compensation scheme, if any, for this course of consulting.[28]

After special counsel Robert Mueller begins his investigation of possible Trump-Russia collusion in mid-2017, Kilimnik "abruptly" leaves Kyiv for Moscow with his wife and two children.[29] As of 2018 he lives, according to *The Guardian*, "in a gated community in Khimki, the same Moscow suburb that houses the GRU [Russian military intelligence] unit accused by Mueller in an 11-count indictment in July of spearheading the hacking of Democratic emails in 2016."[30] According to the State Department, it was Giuliani's Ukrainian ally Yuri Lutsenko who "allowed Kilimnik to leave the country" despite him being under indictment in the United States.[31]

Kilimnik's personal background seems to confirm his utility to the Kremlin as a go-between with the upper echelon of the Trump campaign. As a young man, *The Atlantic* reports, Kilimnik "attended a language school run by [Russian] military intelligence"; at some point during his schooling, he received "training in military intelligence."[32] Throughout the 2000s and 2010s, the magazine adds, and even across repeated contacts with federal officials from the United States, Kilimnik was "dogged by suspicions . . . [and] hints that he might be serving another master, providing a set of surveilling eyes for Russian intelligence."[33] In a federal court filing, Mueller will go much further, referring to Kilimnik as "Person A" in an indictment and attesting in an accompanying statement of facts that Kilimnik's "ties to Russian intelligence" were "active" throughout the entirety of the 2016 presidential election.[34] The filing, among much other evidence about Kilimnik's background, leads *The Atlantic* to conclude that "Donald Trump's campaign chairman had a pawn of Russian intelligence as his indispensable alter ego"—even as Putin "friend" Dimitri Simes was among the campaign's most trusted Russia advisers.[35]

If the 2016 Republican National Convention saw a successful effort by Russian intelligence, with the assistance of Trump campaign chairman

Paul Manafort, to infiltrate the Trump campaign to the detriment of Ukraine, and if 2017 saw Trump's personal attorney Rudy Giuliani seemingly influencing Manafort-related investigations in Ukraine, 2018 will see a third attempt by Trump and his agents to address the lingering Manafort issue by negotiating behind the scenes with the Ukrainians—specifically, as in 2016, on the matter of U.S. military aid to Ukraine.

In April 2018, a few weeks after the State Department approves $47 million in Javelin anti-tank missile sales to Kyiv, President Poroshenko "halt[s] investigations by an anti-corruption prosecutor into Trump's former campaign chairman, Paul Manafort . . . in an apparent effort not to rock the boat in Washington."[36] A Ukrainian lawmaker close to President Poroshenko tells the *New York Times* at the time, "In every possible way, we will avoid irritating the top American officials."[37] The *Times* itself is unequivocal: "In Ukraine, where officials are wary of offending President Trump, four meandering cases that involve Mr. Manafort, Mr. Trump's former campaign chairman, have been effectively frozen by Ukraine's chief prosecutor. The cases are just too sensitive for a government deeply reliant on United States financial and military aid, and keenly aware of Mr. Trump's distaste for the investigation by the special counsel, Robert S. Mueller III, into possible collusion between Russia and his campaign, some lawmakers say."[38]

Per the *Times*, the State Department issued an export license for the Javelins on December 22, 2017; the Pentagon approved the sale of 210 Javelins and 35 launching units on March 2, 2018; and within a month "the order to halt investigations into Mr. Manafort came."[39] As a result of the order, a Ukrainian prosecutor with four open cases on Manafort, Serhiy Horbatyuk, is "blocked . . . from issuing subpoenas for evidence or interviewing witnesses"; Horbatyuk will subsequently say, regarding whether Poroshenko personally directed the shutting down of his investigation into Trump's former campaign manager, that in Ukraine "every president can order a prosecutor to run, walk or stand still."[40] Equally important is that the block gives Manafort new reason not to cooperate with the special counsel's office in its investigation of the Trump campaign's ties to Russia—and indeed, it is unlikely the seasoned political operative would have failed to note the apparent link between Poroshenko's leniency and the Ukrainian president's desire to appease Donald Trump. Poroshenko's intervention comes none too soon, either; the *Times* writes that "two months before Ukraine's government froze the cases, Mr. Horbatyuk reached out to Mr. Mueller's office with a formal offer to cooperate by sharing evidence and leads."[41]

His role in freezing the Manafort investigations aside, Poroshenko had also apparently done nothing to stop the man he and Giuliani had met with in 2017, Ukrainian prosecutor general Yuri Lutsenko, from letting Manafort's aide Kilimnik flee Ukraine. As the *Times* writes, "In another move seeming to hinder Mr. Mueller's investigation, Ukrainian law enforcement allowed a potential witness to possible collusion between the Trump campaign and Russia to leave for Russia, putting him out of reach for questioning."[42] When several members of Congress—including members of the Democratic leadership in the Senate—write Lutsenko and, in addition to mentioning the *Times* reporting on Manafort, ask him whether his cooperation with the Mueller probe is being restricted, he refuses to respond.[43]

The protection Poroshenko and Lutsenko provide to Manafort is, by proxy, a protection of Trump himself. The *Times* reports in May 2018 that "among the questions Mr. Mueller would like to ask Mr. Trump, according to a list provided to the president's lawyers, was: 'What knowledge did you have of any outreach by your campaign, including by Paul Manafort, to Russia about potential assistance to the campaign?'"[44] In view of the potential nexus between Mueller's work and Manafort's previous employment with the 2016 Trump campaign, David Sakvarelidze, former deputy prosecutor general of Ukraine, tells the *Times* that "Ukrainian politicians . . . concluded . . . that any help prosecuting Mr. Manafort could bring down Mr. Trump's wrath."[45] As Sakvarelidze says to the newspaper, "Can you imagine . . . that Trump writes on Twitter, 'The United States isn't going to support any corrupt post-Soviet leaders, including in Ukraine.' That would be the end of [Poroshenko]."[46]

That the Ukrainians' ongoing post-election investigations of Manafort indeed threatened the nation's odds of receiving desperately needed military aid from the United States will be underscored when, in 2019, Giuliani meets with Ukrainian parliamentarian Andriy Derkach as part of his development of a case against Joe Biden. Derkach had said in mid-2017—at a time when Giuliani was already meeting with potential Trump allies in Ukraine—that leaks in the Manafort investigation in Kyiv could "put at risk vital American aid to Ukraine," a conclusion that dovetailed with Derkach "openly oppos[ing] any Ukrainian role in aiding the special counsel's investigation."[47] When Derkach becomes a public ally of the president's personal attorney in 2019, it may suggest to his countrymen that his past analyses of what pleases or displeases the U.S. president had been broadly on the mark.[48] NBC News notes that Derkach, a former member of the Manafort-advised Party of Regions who "studied at the Russian FSB intelligence service (formerly KGB) academy in Moscow in the 1990s," eventually becomes one of Giuliani's "helpers"; indeed, in May 2020 he will leak an audiotape of private phone calls between Biden and Poroshenko that he claims to have received from unnamed "investigative journalists," according to the *Washington Post*, "us[ing] the new clips to make an array of accusations [against Biden] not proven by the tapes," which "shed relatively little new light on Biden's actions in Ukraine." Echoing the NBC assessment that Derkach is acting as a key assistant to Trump's personal attorney, the *Daily Beast* reports that Derkach has for years been using "flagrantly inaccurate information" to advance the same conspiracy theories pushed by Trump and the Kremlin—for instance, that certain Americans have helped Ukraine's state-owned gas company, Naftogaz, steal billions from the Ukrainian government, the very claim Firtash will seek to use in 2019 to oust Naftogaz's CEO and that Trump legal advisers Joe diGenova and Victoria Toensing promise Firtash they will help him pursue (see chapter 10).[49]

But Kyiv has more reasons than a hunch—or any communications between Derkach and Trump's inner circle—to believe, in late 2017, that it is staring down a potential hold on military aid over the Manafort investigations then being conducted by Ukrainian officials. According to the *Daily Beast*, future Trump acting chief of staff Mick Mulvaney, then the director of the Office of Management and Budget (OMB), at the end of 2017 "temporarily put[s] a hold on the delivery of anti-tank missiles to Ukraine."[50] It is a move that Trump would have at a minimum been aware of at the time he named Mulvaney his acting chief of staff in December 2018; while it is still unclear whether Trump himself ordered the 2017 hold on military aid to Ukraine, given the events of 2019, there is little reason to believe OMB would act to block military aid to a key U.S. ally absent presidential direction.

Mulvaney's explanation for the 2017 OMB hold further points toward the involvement of the president. Per the *Daily Beast*, the future Trump chief of staff's justification for the extraordinary maneuver was that selling Javelin anti-tank missiles to Kyiv might "upset Russia"—the sort of geopolitical determination an OMB director would not normally be thought to make on his own.[51] That former White House official Catherine Croft will testify to Congress in 2019 that Mulvaney's 2017 hold on military aid to Ukraine was "highly unusual" is another indication it would likely not have originated with Mulvaney or anyone else at OMB.[52] Indeed, in an echo of the events of mid-2019, Croft will tell Congress, according to the *Daily Beast*, that after OMB held up the sale of Javelin missiles to Ukraine in late 2017, "'all of the policy agencies' wanted the aid to go to Ukraine. . . . OMB's interest in the decision about whether to send Javelins to Ukraine was abnormal."[53]

November 2019 reporting by the *Wall Street Journal* will bolster the claim that Trump was behind the hold on military assistance to Ukraine in 2017. The *Journal* reports that the president's recurring habit of impeding relations with Ukraine "cropped up in [2017] deliberations in which he initially opposed the sale of missiles to Ukraine . . . [and] in his initial resistance to meeting Ukraine's then-president in 2017 at the White House."[54] Even when Trump relents and permits the sale of the Javelins to Kyiv, he clears the missiles for transmission to Ukraine "on the condition that they not be used in the war" with Russia, according to the *New York Times*, and opines that they might "provoke Russia" to escalate its operations in Donbass—a supplanting of President Poroshenko's assessment of appropriate Ukrainian military tactics with his own, to the clear benefit of both the Kremlin generally and its numerous tank units inside Ukraine in particular.[55]

In October 2019, *Politico* reports that Congress is investigating the 2018 Javelin sale to determine whether "the president, or his aides, may have been pressuring the Ukrainian government in exchange for political favors far earlier than previously known."[56] According to the digital media outlet, the "withholding [of] military assistance aid to Kyiv . . . and the concurrent pressure placed on Zelensky by U.S. diplomats, has led some Democrats to view the [2018] Javelin sale in a new light"; that in July 2019 Trump asks Zelensky for a "favor" immediately after Zelensky raises the notion of buying more Javelins from the United States—a follow-up on Poroshenko's 2018 purchase of such military hardware— further links the two episodes.[57] According to *Politico*, whether or not anyone in the Trump administration was explicit with Kyiv about the 2018 Javelin transaction being a quid pro quo, "sources said at the time that Trump wasn't looking to sell the Javelins to the Ukrainians for nothing. To get him on board, Trump's national security advisers emphasized that this would be a sale, not a gift . . . and Poroshenko won favor with Trump by facilitating an $80 million coal deal—the first between the U.S. and Ukraine—that was politically expedient for both leaders."[58] Moreover, "less than two months after the State Department approved the [Javelin] sale, Ukrainian Railways signed a $1 billion locomotive deal with GE Transportation, which boosted Trump's campaign promise to revitalize the U.S. rail industry."[59] These deals are finalized during the same period in which Ukraine was closing all "four [of the] anti-corruption probes into Manafort related to his consulting work for Russian-leaning former Ukrainian President Viktor Yanukovych."[60]

In spring 2020, a trove of sealed documents from Mueller's prosecution of Paul Manafort will be cleared by federal judge Amy Berman Jackson for eventual release. According to CNN, the documents would establish with precision the topics on which Manafort continued to lie to the federal government even after signing a cooperation deal. Of chief interest, per CNN, are Manafort's "lie[s] about 2017 and 2018 discussions with Kilimnik about Ukrainian policy, specifically a Ukraine 'peace plan' that would provide a 'backdoor' way for Russia to control part of Ukraine, and their interest in getting Trump's support for it."[61]

CHAPTER 7

DIGENOVA AND TOENSING

As reported by *Politico*, during the 2016 general election two attorneys, Joe DiGenova and his wife, Victoria Toensing, "work[ ] with Giuliani to help formulate some of Trump's law enforcement positions—and also advise[ ] the Republican on how to hone his attacks against Hillary Clinton during the FBI investigation into her use of a private email server."[1] Toensing, moreover, "organize[s] the pre-election release of an endorsement letter [for Trump] from 240 Reagan administration alumni."[2] DiGenova's contributions are more extraordinary: in October 2016, the former GOP congressional committee attorney—much like a man NBC News calls his "longtime friend," Rudy Giuliani—appears to aid rogue FBI agents leaking conspiracy theories about FBI director James Comey in the run-up to the 2016 election. These leaks, per DOJ inspector general Michael Horowitz, helped convince Comey and other top FBI officials to reopen the Clinton email investigation just days before the 2016 election—a decision prominent U.S. political statistician Nate Silver says cost Clinton the presidency.[3]

By 2019, diGenova and Toensing have found a new way to assist President Trump: by facilitating the transfer of large amounts of cash to a key witness in the impeachment investigation against him, Lev Parnas. Through the duo's summer 2019 representation of the Vienna-dwelling Ukrainian fugitive Dmitry Firtash, they manage to hire Parnas as an interpreter—indeed, as Parnas himself will later boast, the "best-paid interpreter in the world."[4] That Firtash does not actually need Parnas to do interpreting work for him is confirmed by Firtash's business associates, with Bloomberg News reporting that "people familiar with Firtash's business say he has plenty of translators and key aides who speak fluent English."[5]

According to CNN, Parnas meets with Firtash "several times" over the summer of 2019; the purpose and details of these meetings, and of Parnas's lucrative financial relationship with Firtash, are unclear. This ambiguity prompts CNN to report in November 2019 that Parnas and Firtash have "a much more substantial relationship than previously known."[6] What is clear is that it is spectacularly remunerative for Parnas: prior to his October arrest, he "boast[s] [to 'would-be business associates'] that his newfound luxurious lifestyle [is] bankrolled by Firtash."[7]

In the midst of Parnas enjoying the fruits of his sudden windfall, diGenova and Toensing, through their spokesman Mark Corallo—notably, also a longtime spokesman for Trump's private legal team—claim that Parnas is only being paid by Firtash for his work as an interpreter, that he had not met or otherwise known Firtash before becoming his interpreter in June 2019, and that Parnas's business partner Igor Fruman likewise has no relationship with the Ukrainian oligarch.[8] This sequence of events is belied, in the first instance, by the fact that it is Parnas who introduced diGenova and Toensing to Firtash, doing so while "specifically touting [in conversations with Firtash] their [diGenova and Toensing's] personal ties to Giuliani."[9] That diGenova has counted Trump's attorney general, William Barr, a friend for over thirty years may also be significant to Firtash's decision to hire him as counsel in his extradition battle against the DOJ, CNN reports.[10]

In October 2019, Reuters solves the mystery of Parnas's nebulous relationship with Firtash by revealing that in fact—contrary to claims by diGenova, Toensing, and Corallo—Parnas and Fruman "had been working for Firtash for several months before Parnas joined the Ukrainian mogul's legal team, and that Firtash [had] paid their expenses in the past . . . costs includ[ing] private jet charters in the United States and foreign travel to Vienna."[11] On the subject of whether there is a "business relationship" between Firtash, Parnas, and Fruman, Giuliani tells Reuters, "They could be involved in business with each other. . . . I don't know."[12] Giuliani's professed uncertainty notwithstanding, the fact that Parnas and Fruman will use Firtash's name not only to gain access to potential business investors in March 2019 but also to try to retire $1 billion in Firtash's legal obligations to Naftogaz suggests a likely business relationship between the three men—and explains why Reuters classifies Parnas and Fruman's employment by Firtash "work[ ] in an unspecified capacity for Firtash before Parnas joined the Ukrainian's legal team" (see chapter 10).[13]

The *Washington Post* will note that, beyond Firtash's energy industry associations, of interest to federal prosecutors in Chicago is whether the "Ukrainian energy mogul . . . has played a shadow role in [the] effort" to find "damaging information about Democrats."[14] Evidence to this effect will emerge in September 2019, when Firtash's legal team—a group that includes five individuals closely linked to Trump: diGenova, Toensing, Parnas, Fruman, and Corallo—files in court an affidavit from Viktor Shokin in which Shokin claims "he was fired because he was investigating then–Vice President Joe Biden's son Hunter Biden."[15] The affidavit—created, as it notes, "at the request of lawyers acting for Dmitry Firtash," specifically diGenova and Toensing—quickly makes its way into American media via another Trump legal adviser, Giuliani.[16] Given that Firtash is at the time seeking aid from the Trump administration to avoid extradition to Chicago, the Shokin affidavit appears to constitute an exchange of value between Trump and Firtash in which both ends of the transaction are arguably covered by attorney-client privilege. Indeed, the Shokin affidavit, which materially benefits Trump's reelection campaign, is acquired by diGenova and Toensing in the brief window between them being retained by Firtash in July 2019 and the document being released in September 2019. Meanwhile, as the *Washington Post* reports, shortly after Firtash retains the two self-identified Trump legal advisers for his own purposes his legal team is afforded, for the first time, a "rare face-to-face meeting with Attorney General William P. Barr and other Justice Department officials," at which meeting diGenova and Toensing are given an opportunity to "argue against the charges" Firtash faces in Chicago.[17]

Firtash's role in finding dirt on Joe Biden to aid in Trump's reelection is not limited to giving diGenova and Toensing a pending case under cover of which the two attorneys can secure an affidavit from Shokin intended to benefit the president. According to Bloomberg News, throughout the summer of 2019 "Firtash's associates began to use his broad network of Ukraine contacts to get damaging information on Biden."[18] In total, diGenova and Toensing bill Firtash at least $1 million as this clandestine investigative work is under way in Ukraine.[19] Beyond procuring a politically valuable affidavit from Shokin, however, it is unclear what work diGenova, Toensing, and their "interpreter" Parnas do to justify earning $1 million from Firtash over such a short period, given that Firtash has no demonstrated need of Parnas's services as an interpreter, and the publication of Shokin's affidavit in U.S. media by diGenova and Toensing's friend Rudy Giuliani in fact violates a promise Firtash's legal team made to Shokin that "his statement wouldn't be made public."[20]

It is despite this promise that, just over three weeks after Shokin's September 4 signing of the affidavit attempting to inculpate Biden, op-ed columnist John Solomon, a Trump ally, publishes it in *The Hill*—and yet another member of diGenova and Toensing's circle, Giuliani, is "waving it around on cable news" and "suggest[ing] he had a role in making it public" (see chapter 18).[21] As for diGenova and Toensing, their receipt of $1 million from Firtash, as well as a Fox News report revealing that "only the president knows the details" of their work with Giuliani "trying to get damaging information on Joe Biden from Ukrainian officials," sits uneasily beside concurrent Fox News reporting assuring viewers that the trio's work "dig[ging] up dirt on the Bidens in Ukraine" is being done "off the books" of the Trump administration.[22]

An even more troubling proposition is that Firtash was not merely funding Parnas and Fruman's search for dirt on Joe Biden, but seeking to donate to Trump and other Republicans directly. Bloomberg News notes that "if indeed Firtash's camp aided the Trump political machine, that could be a problem. American politicians cannot accept foreign campaign contributions, and as Special Counsel Robert Mueller's investigation has laid out, even non-monetary assistance can have a value."[23] *Politico* writes that Firtash "is coming under increasing scrutiny as a possible source of the money that Lev Parnas and Igor Fruman, two Americans from Eastern Europe, are charged with illegally funneling to the Trump campaign and GOP lawmakers."[24] One reason this scrutiny is significant is Firtash's status as a proxy for the Kremlin; indeed, in April 2018, Sen. Roger Wicker of Mississippi—a conservative Republican—will accuse Firtash of being a "direct agent" of Vladimir Putin's government.[25] Consistent with Wicker's analysis, *Time* reports that Firtash's role as a "partner to the Kremlin in the European gas trade" required the direct "approval of Russian President Vladimir Putin" (see chapters 10 and 11).[26] The magazine notes, too, Firtash's time spent "working alongside . . . American political operative Paul Manafort" during a period when Firtash was partnered with the Kremlin on gas distribution in Ukraine and Manafort was under contract with Deripaska to bolster Putin's activities outside Russia.[27]

According to a Ukrainian government official who speaks to *Politico*, Firtash's connections to Naftogaz are the oligarch's "cash cow," meaning that if Firtash provided money to Parnas and Fruman, "the money from the gas corruption scheme [Firtash ran] in Ukraine is in the U.S. political system"—money that originates from Firtash's resale, with the support of the Kremlin, of "an estimated $2 billion of natural gas provided by Naftogaz without reimbursing the [Ukrainian] state-run company" (see chapter 10).[28] Just so, if Parnas and Fruman were, as Bloomberg reports, "assisting Giuliani in his legal work for Trump" at a time when Parnas was also assisting Firtash with his legal case, it creates the profoundly problematic scenario of Parnas being at once an agent of Trump's agent and an agent of Putin's agent.[29]

Despite not being formally on Trump's legal team, Joe diGenova describes himself and his wife as "lawyers on television and in real life [for Trump]," publicly acknowledging that the two "informally advise" Trump on legal matters; Trump's formally retained legal team has said that diGenova and Toensing assist the president "in other legal matters" besides those pertaining to the special counsel's investigation into Trump campaign ties with Russia.[30] As Giuliani has described the arrangement between the three, Trump "[will] call four of five people like Joe and say, 'What do you think? So-and-so says this. Who's right?'"[31] Per Giuliani, diGenova gives Trump his professional legal opinion and advice not only by phone but also in writing, including on the topic of federal investigations relating to Russia; Giuliani, speaking with *Politico*, will implicitly put diGenova in the same category of Trump legal counsel as a formally named and retained Trump attorney, Jay Sekulow.[32] *Politico* notes that "both lawyers [diGenova and Toensing] enjoy an open line to Trump," adding that this open line is one they have used in the past to lobby for clients, including former Dick Cheney aide Scooter Libby—for whom diGenova and Toensing secured a presidential pardon in April 2018.[33] While it is unclear whether they have directly lobbied Trump as well as the DOJ on Firtash's behalf, Toensing has said in the past that she is "sure" Trump is listening to her when she gives public statements on television.[34] Giuliani and Sekulow have both admitted they "lean" on Toensing and diGenova not merely as "campaign-style surrogates" but also as "outside advisers" and consultants, even acknowledging that the two have acted as agents of the legal team by getting a "call [from the team] to respond" on cable television during particularly fraught moments in Trump's presidency.[35]

The matter of how Lev Parnas intersects with diGenova, Toensing, and Giuliani is likewise fraught. While it is known, from reporting in the *Washington Post*, that Parnas "met [Donald Trump] several times before" the New York City businessman announced his run for president, and that Parnas had come to "admire" Trump by the time he began aiding Trump's campaign in 2015, Parnas's repeated interactions with three of Trump's legal advisers at a regularly convened salon at the BLT Prime restaurant in Trump's hotel in D.C. are a significant complication in his narrative (see chapters 17 and 21).[36] Not only are Parnas and Fruman agents of Giuliani as part of the latter's work for Trump, and therefore also themselves agents of Trump, Giuliani is also, in turn, representing the two businessmen-cum-lobbyists—meaning that he is their agent as much as he is Trump's. Meanwhile, Parnas, at least, is an agent of diGenova and Toensing, even as diGenova and Toensing are acting as legal advisers to the president. Alongside Fruman, Parnas's connection to a former Trump agent, Manafort, remains murky; in October 2019, when Parnas and Fruman face a federal judge for the first time following their arrest, they are represented by Kevin Downing and Tom Zehlne—Manafort's lawyers—with Parnas later taking on an attorney, John Dowd, who previously represented Trump himself (see chapter 21).[37] As *Politico* reporter Kyle Cheney will note in 2019, if both the initial indictment against Parnas and Fruman and Dowd's subsequent letter about the two men possibly enjoying "attorney-client privilege" with the president are correct, "two people who worked on legal matters for Trump were simultaneously running a [pro-Trump] straw donor scheme on behalf of foreign interests."[38]

In April 2019, having been members of the secretive Trump International Hotel–based "BLT Prime team" with Parnas and Fruman for nearly six months, diGenova and Toensing seek, according to the *Daily Beast*, to "land . . . a quarter of a million dollars [from Ukrainian sources] to push conspiracy theories about Ukraine in the United States"—the same sort of work Manafort had been doing both on and off Trump's political team in 2016 and 2017, though at whose direction and with whose funding remain unclear.[39]

CHAPTER 8

STONE

At the trial of longtime Trump friend and adviser Roger Stone in fall 2019, the truth about Trump and his campaign's 2016 efforts to discover the contents of the hacked DNC server via overseas entities—particularly Kremlin cutout WikiLeaks—emerges. Federal prosecutors establish that "President Trump was more personally involved in his campaign's effort to obtain Democratic emails stolen by Russian operatives in 2016 than was previously known . . . [per] phone records introduced in federal court."[1] The evidence of Trump's involvement in the plot to access the contents of the DNC server is sufficiently voluminous that by November 2019 the House of Representatives will have opened an investigation into "whether President Donald Trump lied to special counsel Robert Mueller in written answers he provided in the Russia investigation," with a particular focus on the president's answers regarding WikiLeaks and Stone.[2] In order to complete its investigation, the House requires grand jury records long denied to Congress by Trump's attorney general, Bill Barr, and thereafter subjected to an extended federal court battle; a federal judge finally orders these records disclosed in March 2020, though by late spring 2020 the matter remains under appeal.[3]

In his opening statement to the Stone jury, federal prosecutor Aaron Zelinsky argues that Stone committed the crime of lying to congressional investigators from the House Permanent Select Committee on Intelligence because "the truth looked bad for Donald Trump."[4] The government's case further contends that Stone's dissembling to federal officers and other criminal behavior in the summer of 2016, fall of 2017, and early 2018 included concealing hundreds of texts and email exchanges and threatening multiple potential witnesses to his actions.[5]

The story of Trump's avarice with respect to the contents of the DNC server is a relatively straightforward one. On June 14, 2016, the day CrowdStrike announces that the DNC server has been hacked by Russians, Stone calls Trump once and Trump calls Stone two times.[6] In the ensuing two weeks, an online account used by the hackers responsible for the attack on the DNC mentions Trump by name; the same day, Stone calls Trump again.[7] Stone will later admit that he was in contact with the Russian hackers' online persona, Guccifer 2.0, though he will claim he did not know the identity of the account owner.[8]

In late July, immediately after a several-minute phone call with Trump, Stone sends a message directing an associate to "see Assange"—the founder and editor of WikiLeaks—at the Ecuadorian embassy in London, where he has taken refuge and which he is unable to leave lest he be arrested and extradited.[9] Shortly thereafter, Stone writes Manafort, his longtime business associate and now Trump's campaign chief, to tell him that he has an idea to "save" Trump's candidacy but "it ain't pretty."[10] The same month, August 2016, Stone tweets that "it will soon [be] Podesta's time in the barrel"—a prediction that accurately presages a massive data dump by WikiLeaks, six weeks later, relating to Clinton campaign chairman John Podesta.[11] During the month of August, Stone has twenty-five calls with Manafort, twenty calls with Trump's deputy campaign manager Rick Gates, two calls with Trump's campaign CEO Steve Bannon, and two calls with Trump himself.[12] Bannon, a co-founder and executive chair of the far-right media outlet *Breitbart*, will testify that throughout the general election campaign, the Trump campaign believed Stone to be its conduit to WikiLeaks.[13] Evidence from Bannon further reveals that the day after Bannon was named Trump campaign CEO in mid-August 2016, Stone wrote him a message similar to the one the longtime Trump adviser had written Manafort before the latter was fired as Trump's campaign manager. The message from Stone to Bannon read, "Trump can still win—but time is running out. Early voting begins in six weeks. I do know how to win but it ain't pretty."[14] Stone's cryptic missive is consistent with his brand; the *New York Times* calls him a "self-described dirty trickster" who once said, "The only thing worse than being talked about is not being talked about."[15]

Over the course of the summer of 2016, Trump speaks to Stone "repeatedly" by phone, according to the *New York Times*; federal prosecutors note at Stone's trial that the calls occurred "at a time when Mr. Stone was aggressively seeking to obtain the stolen [DNC] emails from Julian Assange, the founder of WikiLeaks . . . [and] the timing of their calls dovetailed with other key developments related to the theft and release of the Democratic emails."[16] Per the *New York Times*, the phone records offer a "concrete suggestion that Mr. Trump may have had a direct role in his campaign's effort to benefit from Russia's hidden hand in the election," despite his subsequent claims that he believed the hack had originated in Ukraine.[17]

As Stone and Trump keep in regular contact during the general election, a working group within the Trump campaign forms to "strategize about taking advantage of forthcoming WikiLeaks dumps," the timing of which the group believed it had an inside track on because of Stone's information.[18] The working group included Manafort and his deputy Rick Gates—both of whom were in near-constant contact with Stone, per phone records—as well as Trump senior policy adviser Stephen Miller and Trump's chief spokesman, Jason Miller.[19] According to the Associated Press's summary of court testimony by Gates, the day after the DNC hack was announced, Stone asked the Trump campaign to provide him with Jared Kushner's contact information so he could "debrief" Trump's son-in-law "about hacked emails from the Democratic National Committee."[20] Gates also testifies that at least some of Stone's contacts with Trump during the campaign were confirmably on the subject of WikiLeaks, adding that in one instance he and two Secret Service agents witnessed such a call firsthand.[21]

Stone's role as an intermediary between Trump and his campaign and WikiLeaks has long been shrouded in mystery, both because Stone's call records appear to have been redacted in the April 2019 Mueller Report and because, while he "has acknowledged trying in 2016 to contact Mr. Assange for information damaging to Hillary Clinton . . . he has denied any knowledge of Russia's role in the theft of the emails and has said he never managed to reach Mr. Assange, though he continually bragged that he had a backchannel to him."[22] During Stone's trial in November 2019, it is revealed that not only did the veteran political operative's contacts with Manafort spike dramatically in April 2016—the latter having been brought onto the Trump campaign at the very end of March—but that April was also the month Stone began "telling the campaign about WikiLeaks' plans"—despite revelation of the DNC hack being months away.[23] The revelation raises, for the first time, the possibility that Trump and his campaign became aware of Russian hacking operations months before the rest of the country. This possibility will appear to be bolstered by another key revelation arising from Stone's trial: that the day before the fact of a DNC hack was announced publicly for the first time, Stone wrote Gates a message that read, "Need guidance on many things. [C]all me."[24]

In earlier testimony before Congress, Trump's personal attorney Michael Cohen had dropped another bombshell about Stone, testifying under oath that during one Stone-Trump phone call, Stone told Trump "that he had just gotten off the phone with Julian Assange and that Mr. Assange told Mr. Stone that, within a couple of days, there would be a massive dump of emails that would damage Hillary Clinton's campaign."[25] Per Cohen, Trump replied with unambiguous enthusiasm, saying something to the effect of, "Wouldn't that be great?"[26]

In early October 2016, Stone and Trump adviser Erik Prince exchange several messages, during which conversation Stone reveals that he knows another "payload" is coming from Assange and WikiLeaks; when Prince asks Stone if he has heard this "from London"—where Assange is holed up at the Ecuadorian embassy—Stone answers in the affirmative and tells Prince he wants to move the conversation to WhatsApp, an encrypted messaging service.[27]

* * *

On November 15, 2019, Stone is convicted in federal court of seven felonies, including obstructing Congress, lying to investigators under oath,
and witness tampering.[28] It takes jurors only seven hours to convict the
former top Trump adviser on all counts. The *New York Times* reports
that "together, the charges carry a maximum prison term of 50 years."[29]
When the DOJ prosecutors working Stone's case recommend a seven- to
nine-year federal prison sentence for Trump's longtime friend and adviser, however, they are overruled by Attorney General Barr—such an
extraordinary degree of direct interference by the attorney general that
it leads all four of the lead prosecutors in the Stone prosecution to withdraw from the case.[30] Barr's intervention comes just hours after a Trump
tweet calling the DOJ sentencing recommendation "horrible and very
unfair" and declaring that the department "cannot allow this miscarriage
of justice"; the president also attacks Amy Berman Jackson, the federal
judge in the Stone case, accusing her—without evidence—of a pro-Clinton
and anti-Trump bias, and thereafter attacks one of the Stone jurors, a
civilian, accusing her of "significant bias" against his friend.[31] The DOJ
main office quickly echoes the first of Trump's two assessments, calling
its own line prosecutors' sentencing recommendation "extreme and excessive and grossly disproportionate to Stone's offenses."[32] *The Hill* reports
that, following Barr's intervention, Trump "congratulates" the attorney
general for "taking charge" of the Stone case.[33] Remarkably, the DOJ
prosecutors assigned to the Stone case had found out about Barr's inter-
cession in their work only after it was reported by Fox News.[34]

Both Trump and Barr receive criticism from congressional Republicans
over their reaction to federal prosecutors' sentencing recommendation in
the Stone case. Sen. Lisa Murkowski (R-AK) opines that the conjunction
of Trump's tweet and Barr's intervention "doesn't look right"; Sen. Susan
Collins (R-ME) says that Trump "should not have gotten involved," and
that in doing so he had done something that should "never" be done; Sen.
Lindsey Graham (R-SC) concedes that Trump's actions were inappropriate;
and Sen. Mitt Romney (R-UT) calls "unfortunate" the "appearance" that
Trump had exerted undue influence on the DOJ.[35] The White House
responds by insisting that Trump and Barr did not speak directly about

the Stone case, while also contending that the president would have had a "right" to do so as "the chief law enforcement officer in the land."[36] Trump's concurrent claim that he is not seeking to oversee federal prosecutions of his friends and subordinates is undercut shortly thereafter, when NBC News reports that "AG Barr is taking control of legal matters of interest to President Trump . . . according to multiple people familiar with the matter."[37] Any lingering doubts about Trump's intentions are removed when he tweets that he has the "legal right" to interfere in any federal criminal case he wants.[38]

The mild concern expressed by his fellow Republicans notwithstanding, Trump, emboldened by his apparent success in influencing Barr to come to the aid of Roger Stone, begins "floating the possibility of pardons for his former national security adviser Michael Flynn" as well as Stone, according to CNN.[39] Per the *New York Times*, Barr thereafter "installs an outside prosecutor" to review the sentencing recommendation in the Flynn case and the conduct of Flynn's prosecutors. The prosecutor Barr handpicks will eventually, after Flynn files motions contesting his in-court confession and conviction, move to dismiss the case against Flynn entirely—despite the fact that the former Trump national security advisor has already pleaded guilty to a felony and under oath absolved federal agents of wrongdoing in his case, a circumstance that by May 13, 2020, will see federal judge Emmet Sullivan contemplating "perjury or contempt charges" against Flynn.[40]

On February 16, 2020, over 1,100 former federal prosecutors and DOJ officials of both political parties publish an open letter demanding that Barr resign over his unprecedented interventions in cases significant to the president; three months later, following the DOJ's motion to dismiss in the Flynn case, a similar letter will be published, now signed by a bipartisan group of over 1,900 former Justice Department employees. The signees of the February letter write, "[We] strongly condemn[ ] President Trump's and Attorney General Barr's interference in the fair administration of justice," adding that "it is unheard of for the Department's top leaders to overrule line prosecutors, who are following established policies, in order to give preferential treatment to a close associate of the President, as Attorney General Barr did in the Stone case."[41] A day earlier, the *Washington Post* had reported that Trump and Barr's actions were "feeding resentment and suspicion inside the Justice Department ... [by] raising concerns among current and former officials that agency leaders are trying to please the president by reviewing and reinvestigating cases in which he is personally or politically invested."[42]

Exacerbating such concerns over the Valentine's Day weekend is Trump's reaction to DOJ's decision not to prosecute former FBI deputy director Andrew McCabe—one of the law enforcement officers responsible for the appointment of special counsel Robert Mueller. According to the *Washington Post*, the president responds by "asking [aides] for advice on whom he should fire [over the decision not to prosecute]."[43] The *Post* reports also that Trump has fumed "over the lack of criminal charges against former FBI director James B. Comey," "repeatedly complained about FBI Director Christopher A. Wray ... not do[ing] enough to ... purge the bureau of people who are disloyal to him," been "enraged" by the lack of charges against Hillary Clinton, and privately railed at DOJ's recommendation that Michael Flynn serve between zero and six months in prison for conduct that the federal judge in his case at one point likened to "treason."[44] According to the *Post*, Trump is also "insistent" that Barr designee John Durham complete his review of the Russia investigation (see chapter 35) quickly, as he "wants to be able to use whatever Durham finds as a cudgel in his re-election campaign."[45]

On February 20, Stone is sentenced to forty months in federal prison.[46]

The day before Stone receives his sentence, *The Guardian* reports on arguments made by lawyers for Julian Assange at Westminster Magistrates' Court in London asserting that "Donald Trump offered Julian Assange a pardon if he would say Russia was not involved in leaking Democratic party emails."[47] Per the allegation—which "was denied by the former Republican congressman named by the Assange legal team as a key witness"—"during a visit to London in August 2017, congressman Dana Rohrabacher told the WikiLeaks founder that 'on instructions from the president, he was offering a pardon or some other way out, if Mr. Assange . . . said Russia had nothing to do with the DNC leaks.'"[48]

Notably, Rohrabacher's "denial" of the accusation is limited in scope. The onetime California representative says that "he had made the proposal on his own initiative, and that the White House had not endorsed it."[49] According to *The Guardian*, despite White House spokeswoman Stephanie Grisham telling reporters that the president has "never spoken to [Rohrabacher] on this subject or almost any subject," Trump did "invite[ ] Rohrabacher to the White House in April 2017 after seeing the then congressman on Fox [News] defending the president," and "in September 2017, the White House confirmed that Rohrabacher had called the then chief of staff, John Kelly, to talk about a possible deal with Assange."[50] The White House insists, somewhat dubiously, that Trump's chief of staff thereafter kept from the president any information about his administration's contact with Rep. Rohrabacher on the subject of Assange.[51]

The Guardian notes that Assange's in-court claims about Trump and Rohrabacher have been ruled admissible evidence by London district judge Vanessa Baraitser.[52] Of Rohrabacher, *The Guardian* writes that "until he was voted out of office in 2018, [he] was a consistent voice in Congress in defence of Vladimir Putin's Russia, claiming to have been so close to the Russian leader that they had engaged in a drunken arm-wrestling match in the 1990s. In 2012, the FBI warned him that Russian spies were seeking to recruit him as an 'agent of influence.'"[53] Consistent with these accounts is a June 2016 audio recording unearthed by the *Washington Post* in May 2017, shortly after Rohrabacher meets with Trump at the White House. In the recording, House majority leader Kevin McCarthy (R-CA) can be heard speaking to "his fellow GOP leaders" and saying, "There's two people I think Putin pays: Rohrabacher and Trump. Swear to God."[54] The Speaker of the House of Representatives at the time, Rep. Paul Ryan (R-WI), responds to McCarthy's extraordinary statement, per *Washington Post* coverage of the incident, by "stopping the conversation from further exploring McCarthy's assertion, and [swearing] the Republicans present to secrecy."[55] As the *Post* reports, "Ryan instruct[s] his Republican lieutenants to keep the conversation private, saying: 'No leaks. . . . This is how we know we're a real family here.'"[56]

In late April 2020, nearly three dozen unsealed search warrants in the Stone case reveal not only that Stone was repeatedly in direct contact with Julian Assange in 2017—assuring Assange that he was working "at the highest level of [the federal] government" to coordinate a pardon for the WikiLeaks founder should he be extradited to the United States—but also that he was involved in efforts to collude with foreign nationals during the 2016 presidential campaign.[57] Specifically, the documents reveal that, at a time in mid-2016 when Stone was in regular telephone contact with Trump, the longtime Trump confidant sought to coordinate a face-to-face meeting between the GOP presidential candidate and a group of men *Politico* refers to as "seemingly high-ranking Israeli officials."[58] Per *Politico*, the men sought to work with Stone to transmit "damaging information held by the Turkish government" to Trump and his campaign so that it could be used as an "October surprise" against Hillary Clinton.[59]

While the Stone communications memorialized in the trove of search warrants reveal Stone "describ[ing] multiple contacts with Trump [in summer and fall 2016] and efforts to arrange meetings for him"—a degree of general-election coordination between the political operative and the GOP presidential candidate nowhere indicated in Trump's written answers to special counsel Robert Mueller—the most consequential engagement between the two men involves a "Stone associate" in Jerusalem offering to give "critical intel" to Trump at a mid-campaign meeting to which the associate plans to bring, per *Politico*, a "foreign military officer."[60] The proposed meeting, which Stone later calls a "fiasco" for unspecified reasons, is followed by Stone emailing his friend Jerome Corsi about the need to determine "what if anything Israel plans to do in Oct[ober]," as well as Stone receiving a message in which his Jerusalem contact references "the PM" and receiving "pressure" from "the PM"—a possible reference to Israel's prime minister, Benjamin Netanyahu.[61] By August 9, 2016, Stone's mysterious source in Israel has represented to Stone an "OCTOBER SURPRISE [IS] COMING!"; on October 30, 2016, the source assures Stone that he has just "met with [Donald Trump] and [is] helping" the campaign achieve "victory."[62]

On October 30, Trump was at a campaign event at The Venetian in Las Vegas, Nevada, a hotel owned by Trump mega-donor Sheldon Adelson. Trump met with the famously pro-Israel Adelson—who according to *The Guardian* has had a "long friendship" with Benjamin Netanyahu—prior to his rally at The Venetian.[63] The Stone search warrants do not indicate who else was at the Trump-Adelson meeting in Las Vegas, though it is now known that throughout the 2016 general election campaign Adelson was both donating lavishly to Trump's campaign coffers and lobbying Trump to move the U.S. embassy in Israel from Tel Aviv to Jerusalem—an official government act ultimately taken by Trump in the second year of his presidency.[64]

Perhaps as telling as the content of the Stone emails sought by federal law enforcement is their timing. The earliest emails considered relevant to the FBI's ongoing criminal inquiry into Stone are sent in February 2016, the same month that Stone's longtime business associate Paul Manafort tells Trump friend Thomas Barrack, "I really need to get to [Trump]."[65] The next tranche of emails involves exchanges in the first week of April 2016, just ten days after Paul Manafort and his deputy Rick Gates had joined the Trump campaign and—more importantly— approximately a week after Gates had met, according to the *New York Times*, "at the Mandarin Oriental hotel along the Washington waterfront with George Birnbaum, a Republican consultant [and former chief of staff to Benjamin Netanyahu] with close ties to current and former Israel government officials."[66] Beginning in May 2016, when Manafort's deputy Gates is receiving proposals from Israeli business intelligence firm Psy-Group to "create fake online identities . . . use social media manipulation . . . [and] gather intelligence" to aid Trump's presidential campaign, Manafort's longtime business partner Stone is in contact with his unnamed source in Jerusalem to both arrange a meeting between

Trump and an Israeli official—a meeting Stone's communications make clear Trump is aware of and intends to attend—and submit intelligence to the Trump campaign.[67] At one eventually scuttled July 2016 meeting with Trump, Stone's unnamed contact says he is "At St Regis With Lt General," a reference that is not explained in the unsealed search warrants but is rendered more troubling by the fact that Trump's top national security adviser at the time, Michael Flynn, is not only involved in the intelligence industry and a retired lieutenant general but someone who had in 2015, according to the Associated Press, met with Israeli officials about a controversial regional energy deal and subsequently failed to report the meetings in his federal security clearance applications.[68]

In May 2020, a *Times of Israel* report reveals that Psy-Group was, in mid-2016, "owned by a British Virgin Islands company [Protexer Limited] that is closely associated with Russia's partly state-owned Gazprombank . . . a subsidiary of the Russian-government-owned energy conglomerate Gazprom. . . . Protexer Limited only has seven or eight publicly known subsidiaries. Almost all of them are connected to Russia."[69] According to the *New York Times*, Gazprom is a "slush fund for the Kremlin's off-the-books needs," and the intelligence operation proposed to the Trump campaign by Psy-Group preelection—which Psy-Group owner Joel Zamel subsequently told Trump campaign adviser George Nader he had executed—resembled Moscow's interference operation but for the fact that it was "narrower."[70] Per the *Times*, when Zamel pitched an election interference campaign directly to Donald Trump Jr. at Trump Tower in August 2016, Trump's son responded "approvingly."[71]

In mid-May 2020, Judge Jackson, the federal judge in the Stone case, orders, in response to a Freedom of Information Act (FOIA) lawsuit filed by the *New York Times*, that the White House turn over twenty emails between OMB official Michael Duffey and Robert Blair, the latter a senior adviser to then–acting chief of staff Mick Mulvaney (see chapter 26). The emails, which relate to the Trump administration's summer 2019 hold on military aid to Ukraine, had been held back from disclosure to Congress during its fall 2019 impeachment inquiry under a claim of executive privilege.[72] As of June 2020, the nation has yet to see the emails, the unexamined contents of which were considered of sufficient interest to the House managers in President Trump's impeachment trial that they were mentioned by lead manager Adam Schiff in his February 3, 2020, closing argument—an address now known as the California congressman's "Midnight in Washington" speech.[73] In the speech Schiff says of the emails, "The Justice Department—the department that would represent 'justice'—is refusing to produce documents directly bearing on the president's decision to withhold military aid from Ukraine. The Trump administration has them, it is not turning them over, and it does not want the Senate to know [what the documents reveal] until it is too late ... even as they argued here [in the Senate] that they [a]re not covering up the president's misdeeds."[74] The DOJ's effort to withhold the documents from Congress had come in a midnight filing in federal court at the very end of the president's impeachment trial; according to the *Washington Post*, DOJ officials "acknowledge" that the emails "reveal Trump's thinking on Ukraine" during the period of time he engaged in the actions for which he was later impeached.[75]

CHAPTER 9

GIULIANI

If Rudy Giuliani spends the final month of the 2016 presidential campaign seeking to inculpate Hillary Clinton for her use of a private email server, his longtime friend Donald Trump spends the same period attempting to exculpate Russia for its mid-campaign cyberattacks on the DNC.[1] *The Atlantic* notes that during the final months of the 2016 general election Trump will variously float the possibility of "a 400 pound person," "someone living in New Jersey," "China," and "a lot of people out there" as having been responsible for the pre-election hacking and propaganda campaigns that by January 2017 had been conclusively determined by U.S. intelligence to be part of a sophisticated, Kremlin-funded information war directed by Vladimir Putin himself; the GOP candidate will even publicly speculate, just four weeks before Election Day, that "maybe there *is* no hacking."[2] At a presidential debate in October 2016—two months after Trump, his national security adviser Michael Flynn, and transition chief Chris Christie received a counterintelligence briefing by the Office of the Director of National Intelligence discussing Russian election interference—Trump will say of Clinton that, as to the DNC hack, she has "no idea whether it is Russia, China, or anybody else."[3] Notably, the day after cybersecurity firm CrowdStrike disclosed Russia's hacking of the DNC in June 2016, Trump had put forward an even more unusual public statement: "We believe it was the DNC that did the 'hacking' as a way to distract from the many issues facing their deeply flawed candidate and failed party leader. Too bad the DNC doesn't hack Hillary Clinton's 33,000 missing emails."[4] While at no point before the election does Trump publicly finger Ukraine as a possible culprit in the DNC hack, he also does not accept CrowdStrike's forensic conclusion that it was the Russians. Meanwhile, his advisers, most particularly Manafort, Flynn, and Bannon—the last of whom would suggest to the campaign that Bulgarian hackers might be responsible for the hack—urge him to look elsewhere, including Ukraine.[5]

After the election, Giuliani's investigations in Ukraine with respect to Clinton and the Bidens will commence, continuing well beyond the Trump administration's special envoy to Ukraine, Kurt Volker, "warn[ing] Giuliani against trusting the information he was receiving from Ukrainian political figures."[6] Volker will "caution Giuliani that his Ukrainian sources [a]re unreliable and that he should be careful about putting faith in their theories."[7]

Among the Ukrainian political figures Volker is speaking of is almost certainly Yuri Lutsenko, Viktor Shokin's replacement as Ukraine's prosecutor general. In January 2019, Giuliani invites Lutsenko to come to New York City for a meeting; the two had previously met in Kyiv during Giuliani's June 2017 meeting with Ukrainian president Petro Poroshenko. Lutsenko will tell the *New York Times* that as soon as he heard from Giuliani, "I understood very well what would interest them. I have 23 years in politics. I knew. I'm a political animal."[8] Lutsenko tells the *Times* that what he "understood" was that Giuliani wanted him to investigate the Bidens.[9] At the time Giuliani reached out to him, the *Times* notes, Lutsenko was "a prosecutor with no legal training and a record of using the law as a political weapon."[10] What follows Giuliani's outreach to Lutsenko is two months of contacts between Giuliani, Lutsenko, and *The Hill* columnist John Solomon to discuss the Bidens—a period that ends with Lutsenko confessing he has no information of any wrongdoing by either the former vice president or his son (see chapter 18).

According to the *Wall Street Journal*, on April 12, 2019, Victoria Toensing signs contracts agreeing to represent Lutsenko and his deputy Konstantin Kulyk "in meetings with U.S. officials about alleged 'evidence' of Ukrainian interference in the 2016 U.S. elections." It is unclear who the "U.S. officials" in question are, though *The Week* reports that—according to Lev Parnas—Toensing and attorney general William Barr are "best friends," and in April 2019 Barr was "basically on the team" convened for regular meetings by Toensing and her husband at Trump International Hotel's BLT Prime restaurant (see chapter 17).[11] The *Wall Street Journal* notes that both of Toensing's new Ukrainian clients "had previously met with Mr. Giuliani," and that on the same day she signed the Lutsenko and Kulyk contracts "Toensing was in frequent contact with Messrs. Parnas and Giuliani."[12] The *Daily Beast* reports that the contract prepared by Toensing covered other areas of representation as well, with her and her husband also agreeing to represent Lutsenko and Kulyk "in connection with recovery and return to the Ukrainian government of funds illegally embezzled from that country."[13] The intended result of the contract, therefore, is that Lutsenko and Kulyk will hand information about the CrowdStrike conspiracy theory to the Trump administration in exchange for Lutsenko and Kulyk suddenly acquiring "funds" allegedly stolen from the former's office.[14] Because the "embezzlement" cited in the diGenova-Toensing-Ukraine contract refers to allegations the U.S. government did not pay Lutsenko's office all the foreign aid it was entitled to receive, what diGenova and Toensing are promising an office of the Ukrainian government is a disbursement of U.S. government funds presumptively within Trump's sphere of influence at the same time the two Trump legal advisers are requesting foreign election interference.[15]

It remains unclear whether the diGenova-Toensing-Lutsenko-Kulyk contract was ever countersigned by its two Ukrainian parties. Regardless of its status, it is certain that in October 2019 Ukraine's State Bureau of Investigations (SBI) opened a criminal investigation into Lutsenko for alleged abuse of power; as for Kulyk, he was fired by the Ukrainian government at the end of December 2019 after failing to show up for a required review of his work.[16]

In addition to meeting with Rudy Giuliani in January 2019 in New York City and then again in February in Warsaw, Lutsenko had received from Giuliani Partners a $200,000 contract offer ostensibly aimed at helping Lutsenko "recover assets he believed had been stolen"—an offer the Ukrainian prosecutor says he refused, though his refusal may have been attributable to his intention to sign a contract under similar terms with diGenova and Toensing.[17] Giuliani contests Lutsenko's claim that he rejected Giuliani's offer, insisting that in fact it was he who rejected Lutsenko's request for representation on the grounds that it would be a conflict of interest for him as the president's personal attorney.[18] Whoever initiated the Giuliani-Lutsenko negotiations, and whatever their result, it is clear that an alternative $300,000 arrangement was at one point discussed between Giuliani Partners and Lutsenko in which the president's attorney would have represented Lutsenko's Ministry of Justice in Kyiv as a foreign agent; as the proposed contract would have also seen Giuliani receive $200,000 directly from Lutsenko—for a total of $500,000 in payments to Trump's lawyer—it is worth noting that $500,000 is the amount Parnas and Fruman are seeking to pay Giuliani for unspecified reasons in the late summer of 2019 (see chapter 9).[19] Had this $500,000 Giuliani-Lutsenko contract been signed, Giuliani would have been representing both a prospective provider and a prospective receiver of disinformation about Joe Biden, thus rendering the entirety of any such illicit exchange of information—in an echo of diGenova and Toensing's dealings with Ukrainian oligarch Dmitry Firtash—at least arguably a matter of attorney-client privilege, and therefore invisible to federal investigators.

The *Washington Post* reports that a third iteration of the Giuliani-Lutsenko contract discussed by the two men in February 2019 would have led to Lutsenko being represented by all three of Giuliani, diGenova, and Toensing. For reasons that remain unclear, by April the latter two attorneys have dropped Giuliani from their proposal to Lutsenko.[20] Lutsenko will subsequently tell the *Post* that Giuliani insisted to him that in order for the Ukrainian government to access Attorney General Barr it would have to pay two lobbyists for the privilege of their assistance: namely, diGenova and Toensing.[21]

Prior to his January meeting with Giuliani, Lutsenko prepares a document for Giuliani alleging, without evidence, crimes by Joe Biden and his son—but also, per CNN, allegations "that the Obama Administration was behind the leaking of an 'information operation aimed at discrediting P[aul] Manafort.'"[22] Just days earlier Giuliani had spoken to Viktor Shokin over Skype, during which call the former Ukrainian prosecutor general told Giuliani that Obama's ambassador to the Ukraine, Geoffrey Pyatt, advised him in passing to use "white gloves" in dealing with Burisma, a comment Shokin says he interpreted—it is unclear why—as a clear directive from Washington not to investigate Burisma in any way.[23] CNN reports that Shokin's deputy at the time the exchange with Pyatt allegedly occurred, David Sakvarelidze, has since 2015 rejected all of Shokin's claims, telling CNN that "the U.S. and its embassy in Kyiv [have] been 'very supportive . . . of all our efforts to clean up the system from the corruption, from the protectionism, from the huge corruption.'"[24] Of Shokin himself, Sakvarelidze says the former prosecutor has been, with Lutsenko, "heading the corruption, the systemic corruption . . . in Ukraine" since 2015.[25] Sakvarelidze adds, "Shokin was deeply corrupt and he had to be dismissed. Lutsenko was deeply corrupt and had to be dismissed. And because of these guys we lost five years in Ukraine, five desperate years."[26] CNN reports that another Shokin deputy, Vitaly Kasko, resigned rather than work with Shokin, disclosing to the cable news outlet, "I don't think that he's a reliable person."[27] According to Daria Kaleniuk of AntAC, an entity the U.S. State Department calls "the key Ukrainian anti-corruption NGO," "Both Shokin and Lutsenko failed to reform the prosecutors' office, and attacked actual reformers and civil society activists."[28] Of Lutsenko, Kaleniuk says, "[He] turned the [prosecutor general's] office into his personal PR office and political platform."[29]

In mid-May 2019, Lutsenko retracts his allegations against the Bidens, telling Bloomberg that "Hunter Biden did not violate any Ukrainian laws . . . we do not see any wrongdoing."[30] Several months later, two of Lutsenko's former colleagues will tell CNN that "they believe he was trying to save his own political career" by handing disinformation on Biden to Giuliani; "Lutsenko wanted an insurance policy" to guarantee he would not lose his job if his boss, Poroshenko, was not reelected, the former co-workers explain, and was hoping that "a direct line to the personal lawyer of the U.S. president . . . [would] fit the bill."[31] Lutsenko seems to admit to such a scheme in his May statement, saying of his meeting with Giuliani in January 2019, "I wanted to use the meeting with Giuliani to assure the President of the U.S. that they had a stable channel of information about Ukraine."[32]

Lutsenko's eventual retraction of his false allegations against the Bidens notwithstanding, hope among Trump's advisers for a fruitful contractual relationship with the Ukrainian prosecutor was initially high. Call records acquired by the House Permanent Select Committee on Intelligence indicate that on the day Lutsenko was to have signed a contract with diGenova and Toensing, there were multiple calls between the couple's future "translator" Lev Parnas and Rep. Devin Nunes—Parnas having previously acted as Lutsenko's intermediary to Trump's inner circle—as well as between Parnas and John Solomon at *The Hill*. At the time, Solomon was Rudy Giuliani's client as well as Lutsenko's amanuensis in U.S. media. In addition to these communications, phone records for the day reflect calls between Parnas and Giuliani, Giuliani and another Trump attorney (Jay Sekulow), and Giuliani and the White House.[33]

While the April 12 Toensing-Lutsenko contract falls through, the *Wall Street Journal* reports that on April 15 Toensing signs an agreement to represent Viktor Shokin "for the purpose of collecting evidence regarding his March 2016 firing as prosecutor general of Ukraine and the role of Vice President Biden in such firing, and presenting such evidence to U.S. and foreign authorities."[34] A telling component of both this contract and its April 12 predecessor is their timing relative to a key event on Ukraine's political calendar: they are presented to former or current Ukrainian officials approximately a week before Petro Poroshenko faces Volodymyr Zelensky in Ukraine's presidential election.[35] By seeking to cut a deal with the Poroshenko administration's two prosecutors general just prior to one of the most important days in Poroshenko's political life, diGenova and Toensing may believe they are putting themselves—and Trump—in the best position possible to extract value from top Ukrainian officials.

Poroshenko himself, if aware of the contracts, might well have believed them capable of earning him an endorsement from Trump in advance of the April 21 presidential election in Ukraine. Not only does Lev Parnas tell CNN in January 2020 that he directly offered Poroshenko Trump's endorsement in exchange for an investigation of Biden, but former U.S. ambassador to Ukraine Marie Yovanovitch will testify to Congress in October 2019, according to the *Washington Examiner*, that Lutsenko "accused Joe Biden of corruption . . . in part to convince President Trump to endorse Ukrainian President Petro Poroshenko's doomed re-election campaign."[36] "There was always a hope that President Trump would endorse President Poroshenko," Yovanovitch explains to Congress, adding that "this is something that President Poroshenko wanted."[37] Even the *Examiner*, a conservative publication generally supportive of the Trump presidency, will conclude in November 2019 that "Yovanovitch's assessment suggests that Poroshenko's team saw Giuliani, in his search for evidence against Biden, as an opportunity to salvage Poroshenko's ailing re-election bid."[38] That the Shokin contract was likewise, per the *Daily Beast*, "explicitly aimed at advancing the sorts of conspiracy theories that Trump and Giuliani have pushed about Ukraine" suggests that it too may have been informed by Poroshenko's dire political straits.[39] Just so, any plans by Trump and his inner circle to throw their lots in with Poroshenko would help to explain the U.S. president's sullen disposition toward the man—Volodymyr Zelensky—who soundly defeated Poroshenko in an election that Trump, per Parnas, contemplated directly interceding in through a surprise endorsement.

Shokin does not ultimately countersign diGenova and Toensing's proposed $125,000 deal—a contractual exchange that seemingly carried far greater benefit to Donald Trump than to Shokin himself. In July 2019, however, diGenova and Toensing finally get the Ukrainian contract they've been hunting for from Putin agent Dmitry Firtash, receiving $1 million from the infamous oligarch and international fugitive.[40] One of their first acts as Firtash's lawyers is to secure a statement from Shokin that serves the same purpose as the contract they had originally proposed to the former Ukrainian prosecutor general in April 2019: to cast aspersions against the conduct of Joe Biden in Ukraine.[41] It remains unclear whether Firtash, Parnas, Fruman, or any other party paid

Shokin for his affidavit and whether any such payment was larger than the $125,000 contract with Shokin originally contemplated by diGenova and Toensing.

That the evidence Shokin provides diGenova and Toensing about Biden is false is clear. As *Time* magazine reports, Shokin's "claims have not stood up to scrutiny," with "officials in the U.S. and Ukraine, as well as independent experts and investigative journalists, [saying] Shokin was fired because of his lax approach to fighting corruption."[42] Likewise clear is Shokin's reputation among many in Ukraine and the rest of Europe; the *Independent*, quoting Ukrainian member of parliament Yehor Soboliev, reports that Shokin's reputation positions him as "the embodiment of the post-Soviet prosecutor" who makes "an art of dumping cases while pretending to investigate."[43] The British media outlet adds that, per Soboliev, "if there is one thing Shokin never did, it is investigate."[44]

Whether diGenova and Toensing ever performed any legal work for Shokin's successor Lutsenko remains unclear. In a carefully worded statement, their spokesman Mark Corallo notes that the proposed agreement between the parties was never signed, but the *Daily Beast* writes that in late 2019 Congress made a different finding, issuing a report concluding that while "the [diGenova-Toensing-Lutsenko] retainer agreement was 'not signed by the Ukrainians . . . a spokesman for Ms. Toensing and Mr. diGenova confirmed that the firm represented Mr. Lutsenko.'"[45]

In October 2019, as the role of diGenova and Toensing in the Ukraine scandal is a topic of significant national discussion, *Mother Jones* reports that Brady Toensing, Victoria Toensing's son, "has found his way into a senior Justice Department spot that doesn't require Senate confirmation. It's unclear exactly why he was hired or what he's doing there."[46] Whatever the initial basis for Brady Toensing's hire by a federal department headed by Trump appointee William Barr—a hire that comes during a period in which Brady Toensing's mother is telling Ukrainian officials she can help them access "U.S. officials"—it appears certain that the hire helped diGenova and Toensing land Firtash as a client, and that representing Firtash facilitated their receipt (from Shokin) of Biden dirt intended to aid Trump's reelection. According to Bloomberg, Firtash "considered [it] potentially useful" to have Brady Toensing at DOJ when he made the decision to retain Brady's parents as attorneys in the summer of 2019.[47]

According to the *Wall Street Journal*, Rudy Giuliani's relationship with Trump has for years been sycophantic and grasping. The *Journal* writes that despite years of humiliating abuse from Trump in public and private, "Mr. Giuliani rarely complain[s] about such treatment, jockeying with other aides and advisers to sit next to Mr. Trump at dinner or on [a] plane. 'Rudy never wanted to be left out,' one former aide said. 'If you were ever between Rudy and the president, look out. You were going to get trampled.'"[48]

It is in this context that, following Trump's election on November 8, 2016, Giuliani found himself in a position to expect some reward from the man he had loyally advised and assisted throughout the presidential campaign. The first position in the new administration floated as a possible fit for Giuliani—floated, in fact, by Giuliani himself—was secretary of state.[49] Indeed, Giuliani had such a strong interest in managing Trump's affairs with overseas leaders that he eschewed even a role more in keeping with his legal training: attorney general.[50] According to CNN, Rick Gates ultimately tells the FBI that Giuliani "turned [the position of attorney general] down because he wanted to be Secretary of State."[51] It is unclear whether, as Trump's attorney general, Giuliani would have maintained the view he held on fraud and bribery when he was a federal prosecutor: "If you violate the law, whether it's . . . fraud or bribery . . . the overwhelming general rule is that you go to prison."[52] As of December 2019, President Trump remains an unindicted co-conspirator—on a fraud-related offense—in the Southern District of New York, the very federal jurisdiction where Giuliani once worked and established his prosecutorial ethos with respect to such charges.[53]

As for Giuliani's hopes of becoming secretary of state during the presidential transition in mid-November 2016, CNN's chief political analyst, Gloria Borger, will note that—regardless of his failure to secure the position at the time—by 2019 Giuliani had "actually" come to occupy, by dint of his responsibilities and authorizations, precisely the federal role he had hoped to be nominated for years earlier.[54] An even more striking revelation comes from Michael Wolff's January 2018 book *Fire and Fury*, which discloses that, during the presidential transition, Trump had in fact wanted Giuliani as his secretary of state—and "had in so many words offered [the job] to him"—but never followed up with a nomination "because of opposition from his inner circle," which "pushed back" on the idea.[55]

When Giuliani discovers in late November 2016 that he will not be tapped as the Trump administration's first secretary of state, he publicly withdraws his name from consideration for the post, saying during an interview with Fox News—quite presciently—that "I thought I could play a better role being on the outside [of the administration]."[56] In fact, the *New York Times* will report that Giuliani was excluded from consideration for the role of secretary of state in part because his "business ties are a major red flag," including problematic associations with the government of Qatar and "a shadowy Iranian opposition group that until 2012 was on the State Department's list of foreign terrorist organizations."[57] The latter course of overseas consulting and domestic lobbying is one Giuliani has never registered with the federal government, a possible crime that NBC News will report could cause Trump's personal attorney serious "legal woes" once his "ally" and former law partner Michael Mukasey retroactively registers as a foreign agent in September 2019 for the same work.[58]

A review of Giuliani's domestic and foreign entanglements in the decade before Trump's election reveals that in a single year, 2006, he made "124 speeches, for as much as $200,000 each, and had earned a total of $11.4 million . . . [while making] extravagant demands in return for agreeing to make a speech, including that the private plane that flew him to the engagement be a certain size."[59] One of the Giuliani clients highlighted by the *Times* exposé of his conflicts of interest is "TriGlobal Strategic Ventures, a company that aims to 'assist Western clients in furthering their business interests in the emerging economies of the former Soviet Union,'" including Ukraine.[60] The *Times* finds that TriGlobal has offices in two cities—the capital cities of Russia and Ukraine, Moscow and Kyiv—and that its business model is to provide "image consulting to Russian oligarchs and clients with deep Kremlin ties."[61] One of Tri-Global's contracts is with Transneft, an oil pipeline company owned by the Kremlin, which in 2016 is laboring under the international sanctions leveled by the United States and the European Union after Putin's annexation of Crimea and invasion of eastern Ukraine.[62] TriGlobal is therefore in a position to benefit enormously if sufficient pressure can be put on Ukraine by the Trump administration to force the European nation to sign a peace accord with the Kremlin—one that would include the elimination of crippling sanctions on Russia.

The *Times* report on TriGlobal uncovers co-founders and board members at the "image-consulting" company that include a Putin adviser; a man who boasts "strong relations" with the sort of "regional and municipal governments in Russia" hit hard by the after-effects of Western sanctions; and a man whose website says he provided "international image development and PR for Russian [and] Ukrainian companies" while working "closely" with Giuliani's company from 2008 to 2011.[63] In 2015, TriGlobal had asked Giuliani to become a consultant to the mayor of Kyiv, with the apparent aim of increasing American military aid to Ukraine.[64] Records reveal that Giuliani's consulting work also took him to Moscow in 2004, where he met with both the Russian foreign minister, Sergey Lavrov, and "other prominent Russian politicians and business executives."[65]

In October 2019, the *Washington Post* reports that Giuliani supported Trump national security advisor Michael Flynn's effort to get Trump to extradite U.S.-dwelling Turkish cleric Fethullah Gulen to Turkey, a push Flynn made in the fall of 2016 while he was secretly working as an agent of the Turkish government (see chapter 36).[66] In 2017, senior Trump administration officials will become "so concerned that Giuliani might . . . [be] paid to push Turkey's interests that . . . they confront[ ] him and ask[ ] him not to bring up Turkish issues" in meetings with the president.[67]

* * *

On January 12, 2017, technology website *Ars Technica* reports that Giuliani will be "coordinating a cybersecurity advisory group" for the new administration, even though, as the website reports, "it's not clear that Giuliani has ever had any direct experience in cybersecurity law or policy."[68] This inexperience in a field Trump wants his friend to oversee becomes evident in the coming years, which feature a series of embarrassing episodes suggesting that Giuliani only poorly understands contemporary technology, let alone the byzantine strictures of high-level cybersecurity measures: after Giuliani inexplicably texts a reporter a complex password that appears to be a personal access code for an unknown device, an event Giuliani calls a "butt dial," *Salon* writes that Giuliani's "technological gaffes have become legendary"; on another occasion, Giuliani twice "butt-dial[s]" an NBC News reporter, who hears Giuliani discussing "Joe Biden, business in Bahrain, and [Giuliani's] need for cash"; sometime thereafter Giuliani unwisely goes to an Apple Store to reset a highly sensitive password, a decision NBC News reports causes security experts to "question [Giuliani's] understanding of basic security measures"; and yet another embarrassing episode sees the attorney accidentally leaving a voicemail for a reporter in which he records himself making potentially inculpatory statements about a "fraud case."[69]

The last of these incidents leads a *Salon* reporter to a significant discovery: that Giuliani has convinced a wealthy attorney, Charles Gucciardo, to give half a million dollars to Lev Parnas's company, Fraud Guarantee. Gucciardo will later explain that "he did so because Giuliani was involved [in Fraud Guarantee], and Giuliani was 'the first name in cybersecurity.'"[70] Giuliani's role in bringing large sums of money into Parnas's since-indicted financial schemes appears to be the topic of the private conversation Giuliani accidentally left on a reporter's voicemail, in which conversation the president's attorney says to an unknown party, "You know, Charles would have a hard time with a fraud case 'cause he didn't do any due diligence"—a statement that could be used against Giuliani in a future fraud prosecution to establish his state of mind in seeking funds from Gucciardo for Parnas's operation.[71] As part of its Giuliani-Gucciardo investigation, *Salon* discovers that Giuliani's "communications director,"

Christianné Allen, is a former intern for Gucciardo as well as a current finance committee member for the Trump Victory Committee, a joint operation of the Trump campaign and the RNC.[72] The Trump Victory Committee had in 2016 been vice-chaired by Elliott Broidy, who is, as of January 2020, under a multiyear federal investigation for bribery and other federal crimes.[73] In all, Giuliani's activities paint the picture—as yet unconfirmed—of an attorney coordinating illegal campaign donations to Trump through shell companies run by Lev Parnas; it is perhaps no surprise, therefore, that in November 2019 Bloomberg reveals that among the crimes Giuliani is being scrutinized for across three federal investigations are campaign finance violations.[74] As for Gucciardo, it is notable that in 2018 he had attended a major gathering of Trump donors at the Trump International Hotel in D.C., an event that included the president, Donald Trump Jr., Lev Parnas, and Igor Fruman.[75] Either immediately before or immediately after the gathering, Gucciardo donated $50,000 to the organization sponsoring it, a pro-Trump super PAC named America First Action.[76] Gucciardo would later say that he donated the $50,000 so that he could get close to Trump while at the hotel event.[77]

A month after the America First Action fundraiser, Gucciardo will travel to Israel with Parnas, Fruman, former Arkansas governor Mike Huckabee, former Trump communications director Anthony Scaramucci, Rabbi Moshe Azman of the Anatevka settlement in Ukraine (a settlement whose honorary mayor is Rudy Giuliani), and Joseph Frager, a "longtime supporter . . . of [energy secretary] Rick Perry" who is also the vice president of the National Council of Young Israel (NCYI)—a charity to which Parnas and Fruman donate $25,000 in August 2018.[78] Per Scaramucci, Parnas and Fruman spend the trip to Israel talking about Rudy Giuliani and trying to "rope people into their game," an apparent reference to their LNG scheme involving the United States, Ukraine, and Poland (see chapters 10 and 11).[79] It is unclear whether the two men seek Frager's assistance in contacting Perry, who subsequently takes actions in Kyiv that would assist the Parnas-Fruman LNG proposal. Frager will tell *BuzzFeed News* only "that he did not 'introduce' Parnas and Fruman to Perry."[80]

During the trip to Israel, Parnas and Fruman also meet with Prime Minister Benjamin Netanyahu's son, Yair Netanyahu, and U.S. ambassador to Israel David Friedman.[81] Asked about his impressions of Parnas and Fruman while touring Israel with them, Scaramucci will tell *BuzzFeed News* that, while "friendly," the two men were "name-dropping Rudy [Giuliani] like a machine gunner"; Scaramucci, Trump's former communications director, adds that with respect to the relationship between Trump and the two Florida businessmen, "what you have to understand about Trump, despite the bombast and the big rallies, he's a fairly reclusive guy. . . . So if you're having dinner with him in the White House residence [like Parnas and Fruman did], he knows who the hell you are."[82]

Upon returning from Israel, Parnas "promise[s] to pay Mr. Giuliani $500,000" for "advice and consulting"—a payment ultimately made by Gucciardo, on behalf of Parnas's Fraud Guarantee, in two installments in September and October 2019.[83] It is unclear why Gucciardo pays Giuliani through Parnas's company, rather than directly. Gucciardo does see Giuliani face-to-face during the period over which he is making the payments—specifically, per the *New York Times*, "at a bris ceremony for Mr. Parnas' son, for whom Mr. Giuliani had agreed to serve as the godfather."[84] CNN will subsequently report that Parnas told a client of South Florida attorney Robert Stok that he was so pressed for cash he "couldn't even pay for [his] newborn son's bris"; Parnas and Fruman jointly ask Stok's client Felix Vulis, a "Russian-American natural resources magnate," if Vulis could "kick in some money for the event," which Vulis ultimately does in the amount of $100,000—a staggering figure that raises more questions about Parnas's son's bris than it answers.[85] As part of Vulis's "bris" loan, Parnas promises the energy market titan that he will "open doors" for him with Trump's attorney, Giuliani; Vice President Pence's former chief of staff, Nick Ayers; and Washington lobbyist Brian Ballard, "a Trump fundraiser from Florida who did business with Parnas."[86] *Politico* reports that by December 2019, Ballard's firm has been subpoenaed by the FBI as part of the Bureau's ongoing investigation into not just Parnas and Fruman but Rudy Giuliani himself.[87]

* * *

The behavior of Giuliani and his associates around the world—specifically while they are acting on, as Giuliani states repeatedly, Trump's behalf—becomes so troubling and destabilizing by late 2019 that one of Trump's top allies in the executive branch, attorney general William Barr, informs Trump that Giuliani is a "liability," that the president is "not being well-served by his lawyer," and that the New York attorney's actions are generating a slew of serious "concerns."[88] As questions arise about whether Giuliani is using his position as Trump's attorney to secretly lobby the president on his own or foreign clients' behalf, Giuliani will tell the *Washington Post* that "he does not need to register with the Justice Department [as a foreign agent] for his overseas clients because he does not lobby U.S. officials on their behalf."[89] According to the *Post*, however, lobbying experts say "Giuliani's private conversations with Trump about policy matters . . . could violate lobbying rules if he [is] pressing the matters on behalf of a foreign client."[90]

As of December 2019, writes *Politico*, federal prosecutors in New York are "examining Giuliani's consulting business for a bevy of potential federal crimes, including money laundering, campaign finance violations, obstruction of justice and wire fraud," even as DOJ prosecutors in Washington have "been poking around on a separate case involving at least one of Giuliani's other clients . . . Venezuelan energy executive Alejandro Betancourt López, who has been under scrutiny for possible money laundering and bribery" (see chapter 12).[91]

On November 6, 2018, Democrats stun the nation with a net gain of forty seats in the House of Representatives in the midterm elections, a result CNN calls a "blue tsunami."[92] The election enables Democrats to seize control of Congress's lower chamber, and President Trump faces, for the first time, the real prospect of being impeached over the Russia scandal. Moreover, with Democrats experiencing, per CNN, "the largest Democratic House gain since 1974," Trump has reason to fear that his reelection odds are longer than he had anticipated.[93] He finds he must take immediate action to prepare for the 2020 presidential election—and a key aspect of that preparation involves anticipating his future political opponents. Trump quickly lights upon Joe Biden as his most likely Democratic competitor in 2020; indeed, within twenty-four hours of the midterm results coming in, McClatchy DC is writing that "perhaps no contender [for the White House in 2020] will have a more outsized impact on the shape of the field" than Biden.[94] The news service reports that Biden plans to decide on a presidential run by the end of 2018—a timeline that means Trump must act quickly if he is to counter a potential Democratic juggernaut headed his way.[95]

CHAPTER 10

NAFTOGAZ

By March 2019, Lev Parnas and Igor Fruman are not only seeding Kremlin-backed, anti-Ukraine conspiracy theories in American media via Yuri Lutsenko and *The Hill* columnist John Solomon (see chapter 18), but also working diligently to interfere with the corporate operations of Ukrainian natural gas giant Naftogaz, efforts to which Giuliani and two of the "Three Amigos"—Trump's secretary of energy, Rick Perry, and his ambassador to the European Union, Gordon Sondland—will shortly become essential.

Parnas and Fruman put Ukraine's state-owned oil and gas company, Naftogaz, in their "crosshairs" because they are "pushing a scheme . . . to replace Naftogaz's chief executive officer with someone . . . more beneficial to their own business interests."[1] CNN notes that Naftogaz is "geopolitically important" due to the fact that its CEO, Andriy Kobolyev, the man Parnas and Fruman want removed from his position, has been, as Kobolyev tells the *Washington Post*, reducing Ukraine's dependence on Russian natural gas, increasing profits, and "fighting corruption" since 2014.[2] Much of Kobolyev's "fighting" has been focused on a single man: Dmitry Firtash. As the *Washington Post* describes Kobolyev's situation at Naftogaz in early 2019, "The [Ukrainian] government then was aligned with a Ukrainian oligarch [Firtash] who opposed the CEO's corruption fighting efforts."[3]

Naftogaz is a major point of focus not just for Firtash but for Vladimir Putin as well. As the *Post* reports, the company "transports billions of dollars of natural gas through and around Ukraine each year . . . [and]

is among the most valuable businesses in one of Europe's most populous and tumultuous countries."[4] Kobolyev's 2017 and 2018 efforts to end corruption within Naftogaz, cheered by U.S. ambassador to Ukraine Marie Yovanovitch, are significant not just to the company but indeed to the future of Ukraine itself. According to Thane Gustafson, senior director of research firm IHS Markit and the author of several books on the energy industry, "gas has been the single greatest source of corruption in Ukraine" since the early 1990s.[5] Amos Hochstein, the former U.S. special envoy for international energy affairs and now a member of Naftogaz's supervisory board, has lauded Kobolyev's efforts to fight corruption in the industry by calling the Naftogaz CEO "one of the most remarkable anti-corruption leaders in Ukraine."[6] Yovanovitch has called him "as clean as they come" and "fearless," a man "determined to sort of shake everything up" in a way that reduces corruption in the Ukrainian energy market.[7]

Kobolyev's efforts to fight corruption in the Ukrainian energy industry also stand to boost Ukraine's economy significantly—a prospect anathema to the Kremlin—given that in under five years Kobolyev has transformed the state-owned Naftogaz from a company "losing billions of dollars a year" to one that in 2018 "contributed 15 percent of the government's revenue, through tax and dividend payments."[8] There could, consequently, be few better targets for Putin and his agents in eastern Europe and elsewhere than Kobolyev, as ending Kobolyev's stewardship of Naftogaz would return a nation with which Russia is at war to billions in energy-market losses and a pervasive culture of corporate corruption.[9] Perhaps unsurprisingly, since taking over Naftogaz in March 2014 Kobolyev has at least once faced what he calls an "act of intimidation"—a situation the *Washington Post* describes as "an unidentified gunman fir[ing] shots just over the roof of his car, hitting his house as he was leaving on a business trip."[10]

The *Washington Post* describes the state of affairs between the Kremlin and Naftogaz baldly: because of Kobolyev's efforts, reports the *Post*, "Ukraine is now less beholden to its archrival, Russia. . . . Naftogaz under Kobolyev started buying more gas from Western suppliers, eventually eliminating all purchases from Russia, amounting to billions of dollars a year."[11] Among those largely cut out of Ukraine's energy industry schematics as a result of Kobolyev's exertions is Firtash, whose seemingly unnecessary situation in the middle of Russian-Ukrainian LNG transshipment corridors has enervated Ukraine's economy even as it has enriched the Ukrainian oligarch. That by summer 2019 Putin's proxy in Ukraine boasts many of the same allies, advisers, and agents as Donald Trump—including diGenova, Toensing, Parnas, Fruman, and, indirectly, Rudy Giuliani—means that in the third year of his presidency Trump and Putin enjoy an overlapping inner circle on the subject of Ukraine's energy market. The result is a proxy war between Kobolyev and Firtash in which America's diplomatic corps and many of the political coalitions that constitute the West are aligned with Kobolyev, while Trump, Putin, and their associates have commensurate links to Firtash.[12]

According to a 2019 interview with Kobolyev in the *Washington Post*, Firtash is "one of [Kobolyev's] primary headaches," a man who "has caused Naftogaz trouble for many years."[13] Specifically, Kobolyev accuses Firtash of using his *oblgazy*—a word denoting "companies that acquire gas from Naftogaz and sell it to [Ukrainian] households for use in heating and cooking"—to receive billions of dollars in gas from Naftogaz without compensating the state's energy giant.[14] Kobolyev claims that these non-payments are "corrupt schemes" that siphon money from Naftogaz to the *oblgazy*; the scheme is enabled by a Ukrainian regulation that requires Naftogaz to give gas to the *oblgazy* regardless of whether they have paid for it. That Firtash controls 70 percent of the *oblgazy* in Ukraine means he has enormous influence over the financial well-being of the nation's energy sector.[15] The fact that, per Kobolyev, the Ukrainian government under President Poroshenko "protected Firtash's *oblgazy* even though they were damaging Naftogaz" underscores that Ukraine's transition to the Zelensky administration in the late spring of 2019—especially given that the new president had campaigned on an anti-corruption platform—posed substantial new difficulties for Firtash.[16]

As for Naftogaz itself, it was originally "carved out of the Soviet Union's energy industry," according to the *Washington Post*, and after the fall of the Soviet Union "retained Ukraine's pipelines and began charging Russia's gas monopoly, Gazprom, to ship gas through Ukraine to customers in Western Europe"; at the same time, the company began buying gas from Russia for domestic use.[17] This explains, in substantial part, Putin's historical and ongoing interest in Naftogaz and its management.[18] Nor has the Russian president lacked mechanisms to damage or otherwise impede Naftogaz's operations. As the *Post* notes, Russian oligarchs "politically connected" to Putin are able to act as middlemen who "buy gas from Gazprom at below-market prices and resell it to Naftogaz at a big markup, pocketing large profits without adding any value."[19]

These Putin-linked middlemen had nearly sent Naftogaz into bankruptcy in 2007.[20] Two middleman-run companies, RosUkrEnergo and UkrHazEnergo, had been partially responsible for the near-bankruptcy.[21] In addition to his numerous *oblgazy*, Firtash, the perpetual middleman, owns half of RosUkrEnergo as well—meaning that between his many and varied energy industry holdings, he has the ability to manipulate the Ukrainian energy market to the point of instability. This is among the reasons that, in March 2009, U.S. ambassador to Ukraine William Taylor sends a cable to Washington describing Firtash's RosUkrEnergo as "a cash cow and a serious source of corruption and political patronage."[22]

The 2014 fall of former Ukrainian president Viktor Yanukovych—and, by extension, his political guru, Paul Manafort—was a significant blow to Firtash. As the *Post* recounts in its interview with Kobolyev, Firtash "wield[ed] great influence in Ukraine's gas industry under the pro-Russian President Viktor Yanukovych."[23] For his part, Kobolyev was installed as the chief executive of Naftogaz by the interim government that took power the month following the February 2014 Euromaidan Revolution.[24] That one of Kobolyev's first acts was, per the *Post*, "putting an end to several intermediaries that were earning unjustified profits by buying gas from Russia and selling it to Ukraine" would both underscore and presage the ongoing threat Kobolyev posed to Firtash's longtime business model.[25] While by 2014 Firtash's RosUkrEnergo "had already been sidelined," any opportunity for Firtash to seek a return to the Ukrainian energy sector's wild days—the 2000s—dissipated with Kobolyev's ascension at Naftogaz.[26]

The decline of RosUkrEnergo notwithstanding, by 2015 Kobolyev had found other ways of antagonizing Firtash's penchant for corruption within Ukraine's energy market. As the *Washington Post* details, in 2015 Naftogaz "cut off gas to two Firtash-controlled chemical factories until they agreed to pay debts of $120 million," a "standoff" that lasted four months.[27] During the stalemate, Firtash used one of his television stations, Inter, to attack Kobolyev relentlessly.[28]

In the spring of 2019 Firtash knows, as do his associates Parnas and Fruman, that a change in the composition of Naftogaz's seven-person supervisory board could ultimately lead to Kobolyev's ouster. At the time Parnas and Fruman begin working for Firtash—this being at a minimum "several months" before they introduce the oligarch to Trump legal advisers diGenova and Toensing in summer 2019, per Reuters—Naftogaz's board has several Western directors and is considered supportive of Kobolyev.[29] A shift in the composition of the board's Western contingent, or an expansion of that contingent, could change the situation quickly and dramatically, however.[30]

It is under these circumstances that, in May 2019, Trump's secretary of energy, Rick Perry, is sent to Kyiv for Zelensky's inauguration by direct order of the president, and while there hands Zelensky a list of proposed new members for Naftogaz's supervisory board.[31] The list Perry produces—at whose direction and with whose input remains unclear—includes Robert Bensh and Michael Bleyzer, "two longtime energy executives based in Perry's home state of Texas"; whether this indicates petty cronyism by Perry (acting on his own accord), a design by the Trump administration to install new board members it believes it can control, or both is unclear.[32] Not long after Zelensky is handed a paper with Bleyzer's name on it, Bleyzer and his partner Alex Cranberg land "a lucrative oil and gas exploration deal from Ukraine's government," despite "offering a bid that was lower than their only other competitor."[33]

Politico reports that Perry's intention in dealing directly with Zelensky on energy issues was to "shak[e] up Naftogaz," implying the possibility of a push for new leadership as well as additional board members.[34] Indeed, Gordon Sondland, one of the "Three Amigos" alongside Perry, will later testify to Congress that he and others in the Trump administration had been working on addressing "corporate governance issues" at Naftogaz—a seeming euphemism for the replacement of Kobolyev either directly or via the vote of a newly Trump-friendly supervisory board.[35] The reporting from *Politico* further suggests that Perry's gambit is aimed partly at Naftogaz board member Amos Hochstein, a Biden aide during the Obama administration, as a source familiar with Perry's thinking tells the outlet that in the spring of 2019 the secretary of energy "didn't feel like the [supervisory] board of Naftogaz was sufficiently high level and connected to global energy companies, so he suggested that they expand the board and bring in new higher-level, industry-connected people on an international basis."[36] When Giuliani, then a business associate of Firtash agents Parnas and Fruman, is asked whether he knows anything about Perry's efforts to reconstitute the board of Naftogaz in May 2019, he replies cryptically, "I may or may not know anything about it."[37]

While the White House has never explained why it would be seeking a change in the Naftogaz board's size or composition, Hochstein does tell the *Post* that he personally wanted to "prevent the firing of the CEO [Kobolyev]" in the spring of 2019 because any such firing would be "simply for the reason that [Kobolyev] refused to cooperate with a corrupt oligarch [Firtash]."[38] While this positions Hochstein as an opponent of Firtash and ally of Kobolyev, it is unclear how exactly Perry intended to remediate Hochstein's support for Kobolyev. *Politico* reports that Perry's actions in May 2019 were aimed at forcing Naftogaz to expand rather than restaff its supervisory board, an alteration that would dilute Hochstein's voice on the board but not eliminate it.[39] In October 2019, however, the Associated Press (AP) reports that in fact, "in a private [late May 2019] meeting with Zelensky, Perry pressed the Ukrainian president to fire members of the Naftogaz advisory board. Attendees left the meeting with the impression that Perry wanted to replace the American representative Amos Hochstein . . . with someone 'reputable in Republican circles.'"[40] This politicization of the governance of a foreign state-owned energy company takes so long to be reported in the United States, the AP implies, because there were in fact multiple meetings between Perry, Ukrainian officials, and "energy sector people" in May 2019, the second of which was not originally reported in stories covering Perry's trip to Kyiv. According to the news service, at "a second meeting during the trip, at a Kyiv hotel . . . [with] Ukrainian officials and energy sector people . . . Perry made clear that the Trump administration wanted to see the entire Naftogaz supervisory board replaced . . . [and] Perry again referenced the list of advisers that he had given Zelensky."[41] Strikingly, all three of the "Three Amigos"—Perry, Sondland, and Volker—were present in the room when Perry revealed the administration's intentions.[42] The AP's source, who requested anonymity "due to fear of retaliation, said he was floored by the American requests because [he] had always viewed the U.S. government 'as having a higher ethical standard' . . . [and] Ukrainian officials perceived Perry's push to swap out the board as circumventing [the] established process [for board selection]."[43] The composition of Naftogaz's supervisory board is of such significance to Ukraine's economy that it is normally selected by the Ukrainian president's cabinet only after substantial formal consultation with "international institutions, including the International Monetary Fund, the United States, and the European Union"—the same three entities that had worked to ensure the firing of Viktor Shokin for corruption in 2015.[44]

The *Washington Post* describes the spring 2019 activities of Lev Parnas and Igor Fruman as an "attack [against Naftogaz's CEO] by two associates of Rudolph Giuliani, President Trump's personal attorney. They wanted to install a new Naftogaz chief and secure a gas-supply deal."[45] The two Florida businessmen begin their clandestine efforts to destroy Kobolyev's career just weeks before Rick Perry, Gordon Sondland, and Kurt Volker travel to Kyiv for Zelensky's inauguration.

Sondland arrives in Kyiv as a wealthy hotelier from Portland, Oregon, who had been confirmed as Trump's ambassador to the European

Union less than a year earlier, in June 2018, after giving $1 million to Trump's inaugural fund.[46] The new ambassador will subsequently earn his $1 million back—in a sense—as in October 2019 the *Washington Post* reports that the centimillionaire is renovating his government-provided residence using $1 million in taxpayer money, a project current and former federal officials call "extravagant and unnecessary."[47]

Prior to Trump's presidency, the *Post* reports, Sondland was known for "taking on fundraising roles for the Republican National Committee."[48] He was also, by his own admission, known for something else in 2016: quid pro quos. In March 2016, Sondland told the *Portland Business Journal* that while assisting Oregon's governor in securing federal funds from the Bush administration in the 2000s, "we would make these requests [for funds] and they were done quietly. They were done with rifle precision and there was always a quid pro quo . . . it was very transactional."[49] In the interview Sondland bemoans the fact that by March 2016, Washington's penchant for discreet quid pro quos had apparently dissipated.[50] Trump would become the presumptive Republican nominee for president just a few weeks later, on May 4, 2016.[51]

Three months after Trump's inauguration, in April 2017, the new president gives Michael Cohen, Elliott Broidy, and a logistics company executive named Louis DeJoy new roles as deputy finance chairs at the RNC. At the same time, he appoints Gordon Sondland one of five regional vice chairs of finance for the Republican National Committee.[52] The result of these appointments is that within ninety days of Trump assuming the presidency, Cohen, Broidy, and Sondland number among the nine most powerful finance officials in the GOP's national bureaucratic structure.

The apparent ambition of the interwoven activities of Trump, Putin, Firtash, Parnas, Fruman, Giuliani, Perry, Sondland, and Volker—a quid pro quo involving Firtash's extradition case, changes in management at Naftogaz, and the byzantine political machinations of members of Trump's inner circle in the face of a likely 2020 presidential campaign against Joe Biden—does not seem to have been lost on Kobolyev. As the *Washington Post* notes, in the wake of the Naftogaz CEO winning a $2.6 billion arbitration case against the Kremlin-owned Gazprom—a

development that gave Firtash ally Putin even more reason to seek Kobolyev's dismissal—Naftogaz warned Washington in March 2019 that
"some Ukrainian officials were trying to take 'direct managerial control
of Naftogaz. This outcome would quickly result in the reestablishment
of corrupt schemes in the natural gas sector, redirecting funds out of the
company, away from the state budget, and into the pockets of individuals
like Dmitry Firtash.'"[53]

In early March 2019, at a time they are working in an unspecified capacity for Firtash, Parnas and Fruman meet with two men in Houston:
GOP mega-donor Harry Sargeant, who with "his wife and corporate entities tied to the family have donated at least $1.2 million to Republican
campaigns and PACs over the last 20 years, including $100,000 in June
[2019] to the Trump Victory Fund," and Andrew Favorov, the Naftogaz
senior executive Parnas and Fruman want to see supplant Kobolyev as
Naftogaz's CEO.[54] Sargeant has personal and political connections to
both the GOP and Rudy Giuliani, having "served as finance chair of
the Florida state GOP" and having given "nearly $14,000 to Giuliani's
failed 2008 presidential campaign."[55] At the meeting in Houston, Parnas, Fruman, and Sargeant tell the Ukrainian, Favorov, that they want
to "recruit him to be their partner in a new venture to export up to 100
tanker shipments a year of U.S. liquefied gas into Ukraine."[56] According
to the Associated Press, the pitch doesn't stop there. Sargeant tells Favorov that he "regularly meets with Trump at Mar-a-Lago and that the
gas-sales plan had the president's full support."[57] Parnas and Fruman
then tell Favorov—as the latter will subsequently summarize the conversation for CNN—that they "have an ability to meet and discuss Ukraine
policy with senior members of the current administration and they have
other channels of communication."[58] The two men add that their contacts
include, but are not limited to, Giuliani.[59] Favorov will later say of the
meeting in Houston, "It was the first time in my experience when two
private actors were offering or discussing . . . issues that are supposed to
be part of U.S. foreign policy."[60]

Shortly after the meeting, Favorov confides in two associates the contents of his conversation with Parnas, Fruman, and Sargeant, telling each confidant that he perceives the pitch he has just received to be a "shakedown"; one of the men to whom Favorov speaks is Dale Perry, a former business partner.[61] Favorov's concern, he explains to his two associates, is that Parnas has included in his proposal the intelligence that "Trump plan[s] to remove U.S. ambassador Marie Yovanovitch"—one of Kobolyev's biggest boosters—"and replace her with someone more open to aiding their business interests."[62] In mid-April 2019, Dale Perry becomes sufficiently concerned about what Favorov has told him that he informs two State Department officials of the Parnas-Fruman-Sargeant plot, including Suriya Jayanti, a foreign service officer focused on the energy industry and stationed with Marie Yovanovitch at the U.S. embassy in Kyiv.[63] Per a subsequent interview Perry gives to CNN, Parnas and Fruman not only insisted to Favorov that they knew Yovanovitch would be removed, but said that her removal had "already been agreed to at the highest level of the U.S. government."[64]

While Sargeant denies any involvement in a scheme to replace Kobolyev with Favorov, he admits being at the spring 2019 meeting in Texas with Parnas, Fruman, and the Naftogaz executive. Not long after the meeting he will appear in news reports regarding another alleged clandestine course of international negotiation with significant diplomatic overtones, this time in Venezuela. There, too, he appears in the orbit of both Giuliani and Parnas (see chapter 12).[65] As for Giuliani, who has tweeted in the past that Parnas and Fruman are his clients, he will admit to the Associated Press that Sargeant is a "friend"; with respect to any business dealings he may have had with him, Giuliani tells the AP that he will not discuss them.[66] Of all four men—Parnas, Fruman, Giuliani, and Sargeant—Parnas and Fruman will be the most forthcoming with the media, telling the AP through their attorney John Dowd that they indeed "approached Rick Perry to get the Energy Department on board" with replacing Kobolyev.[67] Given Parnas and Fruman's role as agents of President Trump's personal attorney, their confession raises substantially the likelihood that at the time Rick Perry traveled to Kyiv in late May 2019 with a list of proposed Naftogaz supervisory board members, both he and the man who had sent him to Kyiv—Trump—were aware of the effort afoot to replace Naftogaz's CEO.

While Giuliani is not present in Houston in March 2019 with Parnas, Fruman, Sargeant, and Favorov, just two weeks after that meeting Giuliani and Parnas meet with Healy Baumgardner, CEO of 45 Energy Group, a Houston-based energy company named in honor of Trump, America's forty-fifth president.[68] Baumgardner is "a former Trump campaign adviser who once served as deputy communications director for Giuliani's [2008] presidential campaign."[69] At the meeting, Baumgardner, Giuliani, and Parnas make a business pitch to an unnamed investor "involving gas deals in the former Soviet bloc"—though Giuliani will later claim it is Uzbekistan, not Ukraine, that is the former Soviet republic under discussion.[70] Parnas mentions his foreknowledge of Yovanovitch's imminent removal at this meeting as well.[71] Giuliani will admit, months later, that he "play[ed] a role" in getting Yovanovitch fired, and indeed that he "needed Yovanovitch out of the way"—though not, he claims, because her absence might facilitate LNG deals being sought by him or his "clients" but because, he says, "she was going to make the investigations [of Burisma and CrowdStrike] difficult for everybody."[72]

Giuliani admits to speaking with Rick Perry in late May 2019—a phone call that occurs at Trump's direction—but does not say whether Naftogaz was discussed. Instead, Giuliani says that on the call he explained to Perry "the reason" Trump wasn't "comfortable" with Zelensky; according to the *Wall Street Journal*, Giuliani told Perry that the president "blamed Ukraine for the dossier about Mr. Trump's alleged ties to Russia that was created by a former British intelligence officer . . . and asserted that Ukraine had Mrs. Clinton's email server and 'dreamed up' evidence that helped send former Trump campaign chairman Paul Manafort to prison."[73] While the question of whether Giuliani and Perry also discussed Naftogaz remains unresolved, it is clear that their conversation in late May—which Trump told Perry would center on the topic of Zelensky—comes shortly after Trump's energy secretary had met with the new Ukrainian president to try to get Naftogaz's supervisory board fired, a subject with repercussions for any energy deals being pursued by Giuliani and for the global energy market broadly writ. As the *Washington Post* has noted, Russian exports account for nearly 37 percent of all the natural gas in Europe, and billions of dollars in Russian gas is shipped to Europe via Naftogaz pipelines.[74]

According to the *Wall Street Journal*, after May 2019 the "Three Amigos" (Perry, Sondland, and Volker) continue to "stay in touch" on a number of issues, "including . . . energy issues that had come up in their meeting with the Ukrainian president" in Kyiv—this being the meeting, as reported by the Associated Press, that included significant discussion of Naftogaz.[75]

In mid-November 2019, federal prosecutors in New York—having been told by associates of Rudy Giuliani, per the *Wall Street Journal*, that Giuliani "stood to profit from [a] natural-gas project [Parnas and Fruman] pitched alongside [a] campaign for investigations of Joe Biden"—open a criminal investigation of the president's attorney.[76] The *Journal* further reveals that at several additional meetings pitching a Poland-to-Ukraine LNG pipeline—a deal that "would need the support of Ukrainian officials and a partnership with Naftogaz"—Parnas and Fruman not only had told Ukrainian officials and energy experts that their plans had the support of the Trump administration, but had conjoined their pitches and references to the president with demands for assistance with the Biden (Burisma) and Clinton (CrowdStrike) investigations.[77] The two Florida businessmen also tell the Ukrainians, according to a witness, that Giuliani is a "partner" in their proposed LNG venture; another witness tells prosecutors that the men positioned Giuliani as a possible "investor," while yet another indicates that Parnas and Fruman more broadly established that Giuliani was "involved" in their efforts.[78]

Regardless of Giuliani's status vis-à-vis any LNG schemes proposed by Parnas and Fruman, the potential for criminal conduct on Giuliani's part arises, attorneys involved in the Parnas and Fruman cases say, from the fact that "the Ukrainians understood the pipeline to be 'part of the essential package' Mr. Giuliani and his associates were pushing, often mentioned immediately after the demand for investigations."[79] According to Fiona Hill, identified by CNN as Trump's "former top Russia adviser," Ukrainian officials complained to an "American member of Naftogaz's board"—by process of elimination, almost certainly former Biden aide Hochstein—that not just Parnas and Fruman but also the president's personal attorney, Giuliani, were "pushing to change the board of Naftogaz," one of many indications that the president himself was aware of Parnas and Fruman's activities in Ukraine (see chapter 21).[80] That these activities are simultaneously tied to Dmitry Firtash, a man wanted for bribery in the United States and represented by two of Trump's legal advisers, becomes clear when the *Journal* reports that Parnas, Fruman, and Giuliani's pipeline schemes have "the backing of Dmitry Firtash."[81]

According to Trump, it is Rick Perry who asks him to call President Zelensky in July 2019, requesting that he discuss with the Ukrainian president "something about an LNG (liquefied natural gas) plant."[82] The Associated Press notes that "while it's unclear whether Trump's remark [about Perry and LNG] . . . referred specifically to [Parnas and Fruman's] behind-the-scenes maneuvering . . . involving the multibillion-dollar state gas company . . . four people with direct knowledge of the attempts to influence Naftogaz . . . [indicate] Perry playing a key role in the effort."[83] As evidence for its claim that Perry's conversation with Trump about a call with Zelensky may have involved a discussion of Naftogaz, the AP points to Parnas and Fruman "appear[ing] to have had inside knowledge of the U.S. government's plans in Ukraine. For example, they told people that Trump would replace the U.S. ambassador there months before she was actually recalled to Washington."[84] That between late 2018 and mid-2019 Parnas and Fruman were, with Giuliani, part of a group of Trump allies who met regularly at the BLT Prime restaurant at Trump International Hotel (see chapter 17) strongly suggests that the men received their foreknowledge of Trump's plans either directly from the president—during any one of their several meetings with him—or during one of their meetings with his personal attorney at Trump's D.C. hotel. As the AP observes, "During the same period [Parnas and Fruman] were pursuing the Naftogaz deal, the two were coordinating with Giuliani to set up meetings with Ukrainian government officials and push for an investigation of the Bidens."[85]

CHAPTER II

FIRTASH

In 2015, Dmitry Firtash calls "repulsive" a speech by Joe Biden urging the Ukrainian energy sector to be "competitive" and "ruled by market principles—not sweetheart deals."[1] Reuters summarizes Firtash's business record by noting that the Ukrainian oligarch "made [his] fortune selling Russian gas to the Kyiv government."[2] Firtash agent Parnas situates the Ukrainian oligarch as having the same enemies as Trump, Giuliani, and indeed Parnas himself, telling Reuters that Firtash is "the victim of a cabal . . . involved in suppressing corruption by Joe Biden and his son in Ukraine"; it's the "same people involved" in both narratives, Parnas tells Reuters, a comment that suggests others in Trump's inner circle, including other members of the BLT Prime team, may likewise believe that the situations at Naftogaz and Burisma—two Ukrainian energy giants—are entwined.[3]

Untangling Firtash's role in these connected spheres of intrigue requires disengaging, first, the related matter of to whom Firtash has made direct or indirect payments in recent years. Chief among the parties directly paid by Firtash appear to be Parnas and Fruman, whose unexplained and superficially improbable revenue streams remain an unresolved mystery. For instance, *ProPublica* finds that a company owned by Fruman, Otrada Luxury Group—whose brochure says it sells jewelry, watches, yachts, speedboats, private planes, submarines, amphibious vehicles, and high-end real estate—is officially located in a "rent-by-the-hour office" whose current occupants have never heard of either Fruman or Otrada Luxury Group.[4] Just so, while Parnas's Fraud Guarantee has paid Giuliani

$500,000 for consulting, according to the *Wall Street Journal*, like Otrada Luxury Group it appears to have no business operation or customers.[5]

Fruman sits with Parnas on the board of a nonprofit, American Friends of Anatevka, "that raises money for a Jewish refugee settlement outside Kyiv" whose honorary mayor is Rudy Giuliani.[6] According to *BuzzFeed News*, "in addition to contributions to the Anatevka project, financial documents show that Fruman and Parnas made a previously undisclosed donation of $25,000 to an affiliate of the National Council of Young Israel, a New Jersey–based nonprofit whose board included Joseph Frager, then a fundraiser for U.S. energy secretary Rick Perry. The donation was given in the same month [in summer 2018] Parnas and Fruman traveled to Israel with NCYI and Republicans such as Mike Huckabee and Anthony Scaramucci. The Giuliani associates' financial support of both charitable causes appears to have bought them access to conservative figures in the U.S. and Israel, as well as businesspeople in Ukraine. That access helped to bolster their back-channel campaign with Giuliani to try to dig up dirt on, and push conspiracy theories about, the Democratic presidential candidate and former vice president Joe Biden."[7] During their trip to Israel, Parnas and Fruman told those traveling with them, per the *Washington Post*, "We're best friends with Rudy Giuliani. We work with him on everything."[8]

ProPublica reports in November 2019 that American Friends of Anatevka is "advertising a million-dollar match for donations," even though it had less than $1,500 in income as recently as fiscal year 2017.[9] The Anatevka settlement, less than a half-hour drive west of Kyiv, not only boasts Parnas and Fruman as patrons and Rudy Giuliani as "mayor" but has a host of wealthy donors that includes, per *BuzzFeed News*, "mainly businesspeople from the former Soviet Union, includ[ing] such controversial figures as Vadim Rabinovich, a Ukrainian oligarch, 2014 presidential candidate, and lawmaker who founded a pro-Russian party with a close friend of Vladimir Putin's, and Alexander Mashkevich, a Kazakh Israeli mining billionaire whose company, Eurasian National Resources Corporation, is being investigated for corruption in the United Kingdom."[10] That Giuliani uses his connection to Anatevka as a pretext for certain of his activities in Ukraine is underscored when the former mayor cancels a May 2019 trip to the refugee settlement because he cannot meet with President Zelensky during the trip; Giuliani had been scheduled to travel to Kyiv with Victoria Toensing.[11] Instead of giving a planned speech to the Jewish refugees of Anatevka, Giuliani travels to Paris to meet Nazar Kholodnytsky, whom *BuzzFeed News* identifies as "head of Ukraine's Specialized Anti-Corruption Prosecutor's Office" and "one of the sources for Giuliani's back-channel Ukraine campaign."[12]

That Parnas and Fruman may also have used the dubiously funded Ukrainian village as a means to coordinate efforts and revenue streams connected to U.S. domestic politics is suggested by their redirection of funds intended for the settlement. Writes *BuzzFeed News*, "Parnas and Fruman made use of Giuliani's closeness to the [Anatevka] project to attempt to direct money toward [a] New York charity [linked to Anatevka], rather than toward the local [Ukrainian] fund for the Anatevka project. According to a Ukrainian businessperson who encountered Parnas and Fruman in Kyiv this year, the two men used Giuliani's planned visit to Anatevka as a selling point to drum up contributions to the project from members of the country's Jewish community. The businessperson, who spoke on condition of anonymity, said he found it strange that the two men were asking Ukrainian businesspeople to send money to the U.S.-based nonprofit."[13]

In addition to their New York–based activities for a Kyiv-based charity, Parnas and Fruman also run a company called Global Energy Producers, which in May 2018 donates $325,000 to a pro-Trump super PAC despite being an energy company that—per CNN and the federal indictments against Parnas and Fruman—had never "engaged in the [liquefied natural gas] business, and had no income or significant assets."[14] Another company, run solely by Fruman—FD Import & Export—was, by Fruman's own admission in court documents, "going out of business" when he used it to donate $300,000 to Republican political campaigns. CNN reports that from 2016 to 2019, $21 million passed through the company, much of which Fruman allegedly failed to disclose to the federal government.[15]

* * *

According to CNN, Parnas and Fruman not only mention Firtash in their March 2019 meeting with Andrew Favorov about a potential internal revolt at Naftogaz, but also tell the Naftogaz senior executive that "Firtash believed Naftogaz owed him money," was "concern[ed]" about this supposed outstanding debt, and was convinced a "new [Naftogaz] CEO could potentially make that payment"—a likely reference to Kobolyev's efforts to shut down corrupt revenue streams tied to Firtash and recover monies from Firtash's companies in court.[16] Per CNN, Favorov later told his confidant Dale Perry that the two Florida businessmen must have "had assistance" from Firtash, as Parnas and Fruman had "no prior experience in the gas business."[17]

The *Washington Post* reports that federal investigators have made plans to question Favorov directly about his interactions with Parnas and Fruman, which include not only their initial March 2019 meeting in Houston but a follow-up meeting on May 1 in Washington, just three weeks before Rick Perry sought a change in Naftogaz's supervisory board that could lead to the ouster of Kobolyev and in theory the installation of Favorov as Naftogaz's new CEO—a position Favorov has since indicated he does not want.[18]

By late November 2019, it has become clear that federal prosecutors are following the money trail left behind by Parnas and Fruman to try to determine, as CNN reports, how the two men "appeared to rise out of nowhere to become fixtures at Trump fundraisers and fixers for Giuliani's efforts in Ukraine."[19] The prosecutors issue subpoenas to the following: "Ballard Partners, a lobbying firm run by Brian Ballard, a top Trump fundraiser"; "Paul Okoloko, an executive with a Nigerian fertilizer company who lives in Florida . . . [and whom] Parnas pitched . . . to invest in Fraud Guarantee"; "Meredith O'Rourke, a prominent Florida GOP fundraiser who worked with the Trump Victory Fund"; and various "others involved with Republican campaigns."[20] CNN notes that in 2018 Ballard, at the same time that he was a foreign agent representing Turkey, paid Parnas $45,000, allegedly for "client referrals" (see chapter 36).[21]

According to CNN, "questions about whether Trump offered to restore military aid [to Ukraine] in exchange for politically beneficial investigations in Ukraine have formed the basis of the impeachment inquiry. But the parallel attempts to influence Naftogaz further illustrate the nature of the Trump administration's interactions with Ukraine, in which statecraft and diplomacy appear to be mixed up with political and business interests and which are now the focus of a federal criminal investigation."[22]

That the removal of Kobolyev as Naftogaz CEO was a topic of debate in Ukraine as well as America is clear. CNN reports that Ukraine's prime minister in early 2019, Volodymyr Groysman, an ally of then-president Petro Poroshenko, successfully put forward a resolution in early March 2019 allowing the government to hire or fire a Naftogaz CEO without input from the company's supervisory board—a seemingly esoteric move made at the same time Poroshenko was courting Trump's endorsement in the upcoming Ukrainian presidential election.[23] On May 14, some three weeks after Zelensky's resounding defeat of Poroshenko, a Ukrainian court ruled the Groysman resolution unlawful, in so doing reinitiating Firtash's need for assistance in removing Kobolyev from Naftogaz.[24] Indeed, it is only a week after Naftogaz's supervisory board regains its voice in the hiring and firing of the Naftogaz CEO that Perry hands Zelensky a list of proposed new supervisory board members.[25]

According to Richard Morningstar, chairman of the Global Energy Center at the Atlantic Council, "it's always hard to decipher Russia's intentions. . . . But an unsettled Ukrainian energy situation makes it easier for them to convince the Europeans they can't trust Ukraine to move natural gas"—a circumstance that would produce in Europe a turn toward Russia instead, likely via the new Nord Stream 2 gas pipeline connecting Russia and Germany.[26] The notion that Dmitry Firtash is doing Putin's bidding, with Trump's assistance, in weakening the Ukrainian energy sector through division, corruption, and confusion remains a startling possibility amidst the matrix of federal investigations now surrounding Giuliani, Perry, Parnas, and Fruman. Indeed, in January 2020 a former senior U.S. diplomat will tell NBC News that Firtash is "at the dead center of the greatest corruption operation in Ukraine's history," one that—in the view of both "Ukrainian anti-corruption activists and Western governments"—positions the Ukrainian billionaire as "a corrupt instrument of Russia" who is also his country's "most dangerous oligarch."[27] Per the diplomat, Firtash single-handedly "managed the flow of natural gas from Russia to Ukraine and beyond" in a way that deliberately "kept Ukraine dependent on Russia's gas supplies."[28] According to NBC's summary of comments by Swedish economist and Ukraine expert Anders Aslund, Firtash is "more a purveyor of bribes than a proper businessman"; Aslund tells NBC that the former Soviet soldier (1984 to 1986) has been "used by the Russians to buy political power in Ukraine. He's the person who has spent the most money on behalf of the Kremlin on Ukraine's politicians."[29] Multiple U.S. officials tell NBC that Firtash is "Putin's man," and that his "corrupt arrangements" in Ukraine—including those centering on his partnership with Gazprom, the Kremlin-backed gas company—are intended to further the interests of the Russian president.[30]

CHAPTER 12

TRUMP-VENEZUELA

According to the *Washington Post*, Venezuela "has signed over 49.9 percent of Citgo, its wholly owned [oil and gasoline] company in the United
States—including three Gulf Coast refineries and a countrywide web of
pipelines—as collateral to Russia's state-owned Rosneft oil behemoth for
a reported $1.5 billion . . . [and] Russian advisers are inside the Venezue-
lan government, helping direct the course of President Nicolás Maduro's
attempts to bring his failing government back from bankruptcy."[1] The
Post adds that "Venezuela's still-formidable defense force, once an exclusively U.S. client, is now equipped with Russian guns, tanks and planes,
financed with prepaid oil deliveries to Russian clients. Maduro scoffed
last year at President Trump's public threat to use the U.S. military to
bring him down, saying Venezuela, with Russian help, had turned itself
into a defensive 'fortress.'"[2] The newspaper notes that supporting Venezuela militarily "has become a geo-strategic move for Putin, who sees a
long game in gaining a stronger foothold over global energy supplies even
as he puts down a political stake in Latin America."[3]

President Trump's approach to the Maduro regime has been idiosyncratically hostile, with the administration ordering multiple rounds of
sanctions on Venezuela over the same sort of political, economic, and humanitarian scandals that go unrecognized by America's current head of
state when they occur in Pyongyang, Ankara, Beijing, Moscow, Manila,
Riyadh, or anywhere else foreign strongmen hold sway. The president
announced major new rounds of sanctions against Venezuela in August
2017, March 2018, May 2018, and August 2019—with the last of these

constituting a "total economic embargo against the country," according to CNN.[4] Moreover, in January 2019, the administration formally backed Maduro's political rival, Juan Guaidó, while continuing its policy of "repeatedly denounc[ing] Moscow's economic and military ties to [Maduro's] socialist government in Caracas," a policy in which it has been joined, per CBS News, by "more than 50 mostly Western governments."[5]

Despite all the foregoing, in spring 2018—shortly after a new round of administration sanctions are announced against Venezuela—clandestine negotiations between Trump allies and Trump's purported foe Maduro begin, according to the *Washington Post*. First, GOP mega-donor Harry Sargeant III—chief executive of a global energy company, former finance chair of the Florida GOP, regular visitor to Trump's Mar-a-Lago, and the man who allegedly worked with Lev Parnas to overthrow the leadership of Naftogaz and install a CEO more friendly to Dmitry Firtash's interests—begins publicly "encouraging negotiations to ease Maduro out of office."[6] While ostensibly aimed at provoking a transition of power to Guaidó or another Maduro alternative, subsequent revelations indicate that Sargeant's proposed negotiations have the opposite design.

As Sargeant begins to speak out on the need for "negotiations" with Maduro, Rep. Pete Sessions (R-TX)—a Trump ally and one of the coordinators of the effort to oust U.S. ambassador to Ukraine Marie Yovanovitch, the key U.S. official standing in the way of new leadership at Naftogaz (see chapter 20)—initiates a "shadow diplomatic effort, backed in part by private interests, aimed at engineering a negotiated exit to ease President Nicolás Maduro from power and reopen resource-rich Venezuela to business."[7] Sessions's effort, still ostensibly a program for transitioning power in Venezuela, is eventually joined not just by Sargeant but also by Rudy Giuliani and Lev Parnas. The result is that even as Parnas is meeting with President Trump in spring 2018 to discuss removing Yovanovitch, he and three partners in that effort are also pushing a new round of clandestine negotiations with Maduro.[8]

Sessions, who per the *Post* has known Rudy Giuliani "for three decades," begins his unofficial diplomatic work in Venezuela by visiting Maduro in Caracas in spring 2018.[9] Sessions's goals in Venezuela, as well as his background and interests, align well with Sargeant's. Sargeant is a global energy executive, and Sessions has "long been interested in Venezuela, in part because many of his Texas constituents [have] energy interests there"; Sargeant is a GOP mega-donor, and Sessions is "former chairman of the National Republican Congressional Committee"—a man whose job had for years required him to engage with GOP mega-donors.[10]

As with Giuliani's outreach to Ukraine, Sessions's outreach to Venezuela is the subject of public confusion as to who authorized it. Sessions's spokesman Matt Mackowiak tells the *Washington Post* that Sessions's trip "was coordinated with the highest levels of the U.S. State Department"—a statement suggesting that Secretary Mike Pompeo knew of the back-channel outreach to Maduro—but "people familiar with State Department officials' role" tell the *Post* that "those officials did not initiate the trip or organize or participate in Sessions' meeting with Maduro. And several U.S. officials disputed the notion that the trip was done with the government's backing."[11] Mackowiak explains the Trump administration's denial of involvement in Sessions's scheme by calling it part of a "turf battle" among officials at the State Department and the National Security Council, leaving unstated whether one or another side of any such battle includes the president himself.[12]

The *Texas Observer* describes Sessions, in 2019, as "an unwavering supporter of an embattled president"—not, therefore, someone likely to cross Trump in a "turf battle" or deal with a hostile foreign government without the president's blessing.[13] Certainly, evidence compiled during the House's 2019 impeachment inquiry establishes that Sessions believed he had, and sought to exploit, direct access to Pompeo, as attested to by his May 9, 2018, letter to the just-confirmed secretary of state urging the firing of Yovanovitch (as well as by Mackowiak's claim that "the highest levels" of the State Department supported Sessions's work in Venezuela).[14] The *Observer* notes that "Sessions is well-connected in Trumpworld. Vice President Mike Pence stumped for him on the campaign trail. Donald Trump Jr. came to the Dallas suburbs to host a fundraiser with tickets as high as $10,000. Sessions's longtime political ally Rudy Giuliani held a fundraiser in Dallas . . . for the congressman and also [to] honor Roy Bailey, a GOP mega-donor and Giuliani business associate. Bailey is a close friend of Sessions who has served as his campaign chair. He was also the finance chair for the Trump-allied super PAC America First Action in 2018, and is now the finance co-chair of Trump's presidential campaign."[15] It is America First Action to which Parnas and Fruman will donate $325,000 following their initial interaction with Sessions.[16] In turn, America First Action spends nearly as much money trying—unsuccessfully—to help Sessions defend his House seat in November 2018 as it does on any other race.[17]

Sessions's spring 2018 trip to Caracas is partially funded by Venezuelan billionaire Raúl Gorrín Belisario, who hosts Sessions in his "lavish, modernist, walled compound in a fashionable part of [Caracas]" and is shortly thereafter indicted in Florida on unrelated money laundering and bribery charges—the same two charges leveled, likewise via sealed indictments in Florida, against a Venezuelan billionaire later represented by Rudy Giuliani.[18] Like Gorrín, Giuliani's client, Alejandro Betancourt López—described by the *Washington Post* as a "Venezuelan tycoon under investigation by the Justice Department for possible money-laundering"—would during Trump's first term play host to a top Trump supporter in the midst of clandestine international negotiations: Giuliani himself, who lodges with Betancourt at the latter's "historic estate" in Spain when he goes to Madrid in August 2019 to secretly negotiate "with a top aide [Andriy Yermak] to the Ukrainian president [Zelensky] and press for political investigations sought by President Trump."[19]

In the view of the conservative *National Review*, "Giuliani's defense of Venezuelan thuggery [in the person of Betancourt] will outrage Latino voters. Venezuelan dissidents and writers have already denounced the president's lawyer on Twitter. If Trump continues to retain Giuliani's services, he will be seen as condoning corruption of the worst order. In that most crucial of swing states [Florida], this could be an underrated [2020] election story."[20] Suspicions of an organized Sessions-Giuliani scheme in Venezuela are likely to increase as it becomes more widely known that Gorrín is in fact now a co-defendant and accused co-conspirator of Giuliani's client Betancourt; just so, the January 2020 revelation that attorney general William Barr significantly deviated from DOJ convention to attend a meeting with Giuliani about Betancourt raises questions about Barr-Giuliani coordination on foreign policy that remain unanswered.[21]

Sessions returns to the United States from Caracas with a proposed Trump-Maduro deal in hand—one that, per the *Washington Post*, "U.S. officials said they worried [about]" because "the deal Sessions was floating was intended to legitimize the upcoming [May 2018 Venezuelan] election by opening up the vote to at least some opposition candidates, which could help Maduro remain in power, rather than ease him from office."[22]

In August 2018, Giuliani becomes more closely involved in what has by then begun to appear like a pro-Maduro campaign by Trump ally Sessions. As the *Washington Post* notes, Giuliani "had joined Trump's legal team months earlier," beginning "talks with individuals who were part of the back channel to Maduro. In August, Giuliani met in New York with Parnas and two American business executives with investments in Venezuela to discuss the effort."[23] This summit between Trump's personal attorney and men seeking a clandestine arrangement with a supposed Trump enemy occurs "at a favorite Giuliani hangout, the Grand Havana Room cigar bar, blocks from Trump Tower in Manhattan"—the very same establishment in which Trump campaign manager Paul Manafort had given Kremlin agent Konstantin Kilimnik proprietary Trump campaign polling data some twenty-four months earlier.[24] Per the *Post*, during the August 2018 meeting Giuliani agreed "over whiskey and cigars . . . to try to discern whether there was a way to negotiate with Maduro and perhaps reach a diplomatic solution to the political chaos and economic collapse overtaking [Venezuela]."[25]

Shortly thereafter, in September 2018, Sessions and Giuliani hold a conference call with Maduro himself.[26] During the call, the three men review, presumably for Giuliani's benefit, the deal Sessions and Maduro had agreed upon several months earlier.[27] The *Post* deems this call yet another instance—Ukraine being the primary exemplar—of Giuliani "us[ing] his private role to insert himself into foreign diplomacy, alarming administration officials confused about whose interests he was representing [in Venezuela]. . . . His freelancing has triggered concerns among White House officials that his intercessions have muddied and at times undercut official U.S. policy."[28] Senior White House officials, once informed of the conference call, will say of the president's personal attorney that they do "not know why he was involved" in foreign policy negotiations with Maduro.[29]

According to the *Post*, sometime after the September 2018 conversation between Giuliani, Maduro, and Sessions, Giuliani tells associates that "he had taken the idea of a soft landing for Maduro to [John] Bolton, the president's national security adviser."[30] The revelation that Giuliani has lobbied the federal government on behalf of a deal agreed to by Maduro himself is striking, given that Giuliani does not thereafter register as an agent of Venezuela or reveal whether he has run the idea past his most important client, Trump.[31] There is reason to doubt, however, that the president's attorney would have been willing to work so ardently on a foreign policy initiative wholly unknown to his primary client.[32]

Giuliani's 2019 representation of Betancourt remains a mystery. When the *Post* asks a former senior administration official to react to Giuliani representing a "wealthy energy executive [with a potential criminal case] before the administration while also serving as the president's personal attorney," the official responds, "You have to ask, 'Why is he doing this?'"[33]

On December 30, 2019, the Associated Press reveals that longtime Trump adviser Erik Prince is covertly involved in the Venezuela crisis as well. Prince was among those who had recommended pre-election that the Trump campaign develop "an alternative narrative" to Russia's having hacked the DNC—advice ultimately accepted by way of false accusations against Ukraine by Trump and his allies.[34] Per the AP, Prince "has been referred to the U.S. Treasury Department for possible sanctions violations tied to his recent [November 2019] trip to Venezuela for a meeting with a top aide of President Nicolas Maduro."[35] The AP notes that "the visit was flagged . . . [due to] the concern of officials in the Trump administration over what appeared to be an unauthorized diplomatic outreach to Maduro."[36] It adds that "the mere presence in Venezuela of a businessman with longstanding ties to the U.S. national security establishment prompted questions about whether he was there to open a secret back channel to Maduro on behalf of the Trump administration."[37] Much like Giuliani and Parnas, Prince has acted as a clandestine Trump administration emissary before; according to the Mueller Report, Prince, acting on Trump's behalf as an "envoy," sought to connect with top Putin lieutenant Kirill Dimitriev at a series of secret January 2017 meetings in the Seychelles.[38]

Just as Sessions will claim that the administration knew of and endorsed his secret negotiations with Maduro, a person familiar with Prince's trip to Venezuela will say he notified both the NSC and the Treasury Department prior to his visit.[39] Nevertheless, U.S. special envoy to Venezuela Elliott Abrams will inform the AP that he cannot find a single U.S. official briefed by Prince about his trip either before or after it happened.[40]

On February 6, 2020, the *Post* reports that the "U.S. embargo on Venezuelan oil" has resulted in a "clear win" for Vladimir Putin—one that is earning him upward of $1.4 billion per year in "secret deals" with the same Maduro government with whom Trump's allies, allegedly with administration approval, have been secretly negotiating.[41] The next day, CNN reports that Lev Parnas still has a "trove" of as yet unseen documentary and material evidence substantiating his claims of clandestine dealings with Trump and his inner circle, including evidence relating to Giuliani's activities in Venezuela. "The images obtained by CNN," the network notes, "are of trips that provide a peek into relationships Giuliani has not been willing to discuss, specifically work he's done for legally embattled foreign clients whose interests could intersect with his most prominent client—the President of the United States. Parnas says that the photos help show ties that Giuliani had with business and political interests in Venezuela. Asked about [a] trip [to Madrid to meet with his Venezuelan client Alejandro Betancourt López], Giuliani told CNN that he could not discuss details because it is a matter of 'national security'"—suggesting that his work in Venezuela has been on behalf of either the president or the federal government broadly writ.[42] Per CNN, Giuliani's "effort" with respect to Venezuela "bears striking similarity to how Parnas has described an effort to solve legal problems in the U.S. faced by Ukrainian oligarch Dmitry Firtash."[43]

In January 2020, the *Wall Street Journal* notes that Maduro has been aided in circumventing U.S. sanctions by Russia, Turkey, and the UAE—all countries with autocratic leaders whose fellowship Trump has long courted.[44] Critically, writes the newspaper, Trump's "reluctance to impose sanctions on Russian enterprises and others" in response to their covert maneuvers in South America has "kept Venezuela's oil and gold flowing to buyers" in Moscow, Ankara, Abu Dhabi, and Dubai—an illicit export of goods from Caracas that has been a "lifeline . . . help[ing] Mr. Maduro . . . consolidate his grip on power."[45] The *Journal* reports that while "the U.S. has warned officials in Russia, Turkey, [and] the UAE . . . about sanctions violations in private meetings . . . [it] hasn't moved to blacklist companies or individuals suspected of breaking the sanctions"—a position consistent with Trump's long-standing resistance to sanctioning or otherwise vexing any nation in which he has done or intends to do private business through the Trump Organization (see chapter 36).[46]

Vladimir Putin appears to be well aware of Trump's tendencies in this regard. In April 2020, Rosneft sells all its assets in Venezuela to the Kremlin; it is a move, according to Reuters, that means "any future U.S. sanctions on Russian-controlled oil operations in Venezuela would target the Russian government directly."[47] Reuters has often noted President Trump's hesitation in sanctioning Kremlin interests.[48]

CHAPTER 13

VOGEL AND STERN

On January 11, 2017, nine days before Trump's inauguration, an article by Ken Vogel and David Stern in *Politico* alleges that Clinton's 2016 presidential campaign had been "boosted" by the Ukrainian government.[1] In support of this claim, Vogel and Stern opine that several Ukrainian government officials aided Clinton by "publicly questioning [Trump's] fitness for office," and that these same officials "disseminated documents implicating [Paul Manafort] in corruption" in Ukraine; the dissemination at issue was part of the European country's announcement of a criminal investigation into activities that were unrelated to the 2016 U.S. presidential election but did center on Manafort.[2]

Ukraine aside, Vogel and Stern do not dwell on the history of foreign officials offering assessments of Clinton and Trump during the 2016 presidential election. For instance, as the Associated Press notes, the president of Hungary, Viktor Orban, had argued on July 23, 2016, in an address "broadcast on Hungarian media," that Donald Trump would "be the best option for Europe" (see chapter 14).[3] Orban's public endorsement of Trump's candidacy "make[s] him the first European leader in office to back Mr. Trump," according to the *Wall Street Journal*, which quotes the longtime Putin ally as announcing at a press briefing on July 26 that "the foreign policy of the Democrats is bad for Europe and deadly for Hungary. In contrast, the foreign policy of the Republicans and proclaimed by presidential candidate Trump is good for Europe and means life for Hungary."[4] According to *The Guardian*, Orban also calls "valiant" Trump's security policies—specifically, his insistence that the

United States would not necessarily join NATO in defending a European nation attacked by Russia, absent the imposition of new "conditions" on the long-standing military alliance—a position that the British media outlet notes underscores Orban's "close ties" to the Kremlin.[5] After Orban calls Trump "outstanding," the *Hungarian Free Press* observes that "no other sitting leader of a NATO member state, or of any other European country, has injected him or herself so directly into the US presidential campaign."[6]

This last observation will cease to be true in September 2016, when another leader of a NATO nation endorses Trump: Milos Zeman, of the Czech Republic, who tells a Czech newspaper that "if I were an American citizen, yes, I would vote for Donald Trump"—an endorsement immediately republished, as Zeman might have anticipated, all around the world.[7] Trump also receives an official endorsement from, among other foreign nationals, the prime minister of Cambodia, Hun Sen ("I really want Trump to win"), the president of Zimbabwe, Robert Mugabe, and the president of the Philippines, Rodrigo Duterte, as well as opposition party leaders in Serbia, the Netherlands, France, Belgium, the United Kingdom, and elsewhere.[8] There is no evidence of Trump rejecting any 2016 endorsements by foreign nationals, whether governmental or nongovernmental.

In other instances, Trump receives "soft" endorsements from foreign officials who praise him and issue no praise for his 2016 opponent, Hillary Clinton. For instance, in successive September 2019 meetings with Trump and Clinton, Egyptian president Abdel Fattah el-Sisi's preference for Trump becomes unmistakable to U.S. media, as does that of longtime Fred Trump and Kushner family friend Benjamin Netanyahu, Israel's prime minister; el-Sisi's rooting interest in the 2016 election is considered so obvious by the *Washington Post* that in October 2016 it adjudges el-Sisi even "more partial to Trump" than the candidate's family friend Netanyahu.[9]

Nevertheless, as late as November 2019 Trump surrogates will be citing Vogel and Stern's article during television appearances, particularly its finding that Ukrainian ambassador to the United States Valeriy Chaly in early August 2016 "penned an op-ed for *The Hill*, in which he chastised Trump for a confusing series of statements in which the GOP candidate at one point expressed a willingness to consider recognizing Russia's annexation of the Ukrainian territory of Crimea as legitimate."[10] While Vogel and Stern do not equate Ukrainian officials' opposition to the theft of 7 percent of Ukraine's land area by a foreign aggressor with an "endorsement" of Trump's opponent Hillary Clinton, Trump allies will subsequently accuse the Ukrainian government of "interference" with the 2016 presidential election by publicly opposing Trump's statement on Ukraine, which saw the GOP candidate arguing that "the people of Crimea . . . would rather be with Russia than [with Ukraine]."[11] That such a claim should have provoked emotional outbursts from Ukrainian nationals in the midst of a hot war with Russia—including one from an official besides Chaly, Ukrainian minister of internal affairs Arsen Avakov, who in July 2016 calls Trump a "clown" and "a dangerous misfit"—may have been inevitable rather than a sign of coordinated political activity.[12]

At the time of Chaly's August 2016 op-ed, Trump is being directly advised on Russia policy by Putin "friend" Dimitri Simes; on UAE policy by Yousef al-Otaiba, the Emirati ambassador to the United States and a top adviser to the de facto leader of the United Arab Emirates, Mohammed bin Zayed (MBZ); and on Israel policy by Ron Dermer, the Israeli ambassador to the United States.[13] By August 3, 2016, George Nader, an agent representing the interests of both MBZ and Mohammed bin Salman (MBS), the crown prince of Saudi Arabia, has come to Trump Tower to tell Trump's son that the Saudis and Emiratis will support Trump's election not just with private words of support but with private actions, too—an overture Don Jr. responds to "approvingly" and never discloses publicly; the Saudi and Emirati agent Nader thereafter becomes a "close ally" of the campaign, according to the *New York Times*, regularly meeting with members of Trump's foreign policy advisory corps, including Michael Flynn and Jared Kushner, in the weeks leading up to the 2016 presidential election.[14]

On the same day as Trump Jr.'s meeting with Saudi/Emirati emissary Nader, *Business Insider* publishes an article entitled "Here Are the Seven

Most Controversial Politicians Around the World Who Support Donald Trump."[15] On the list are such figures as Vladimir Putin, North Korean dictator Kim Jong Un, and Matteo Salvini, the leader of far-right Italian political party Lega Nord; Trump rejects none of these expressions of support.[16] Just a week before the 2016 election, the *Washington Post* will publish a similar article, entitled "The Foreign Leaders Who Are Rooting for Trump," which includes many of Trump's foreign-government endorsers and adds yet another one: Recep Tayyip Erdogan, who the *Post* says is undoubtedly "pulling for" Trump over Clinton (see chapter 36).[17]

Regarding Vogel and Stern's second allegation of a Ukrainian "boosting" of Clinton's campaign—Ukraine's domestic criminal investigation into Paul Manafort's pre-campaign activities in Ukraine—Trump will repeatedly declare that this had "nothing to do with [his] campaign" and involved a man who had only worked for him "a very short time."[18] It is unclear what harm Trump believes Manafort's legal troubles in Ukraine may have caused his successful 2016 campaign, especially as Manafort is let go by Trump on August 19, 2016—less than five days after information on the so-called black ledger that Trump will later say disrupted his presidential campaign is published by the *New York Times*.[19] Neither Trump nor his campaign is ever linked to the transactions detailed in the ledger, either in August 2016 or thereafter.

A third allegation made by Vogel and Stern is more troubling, and potentially fruitful for a Trump administration looking to deflect attention from Russian interference in the 2016 presidential election and justify the pressure put on Ukraine by Trump and his allies beginning in 2017. The two journalists' *Politico* article alleges that Ukrainian government officials "helped Clinton's allies research damaging information on Trump and his advisers."[20] Vogel and Stern identify just one such "ally," however: Alexandra Chalupa, a Ukrainian American attorney, activist, and part-time DNC consultant who had become involved in pro bono political activism in 2014—disconnected from any domestic political operation, and long before Trump announced his candidacy for president—to "research Manafort's role in [former Ukrainian president Viktor] Yanukovych's rise, as well as his ties to the pro-Russian oligarchs who funded Yanukovych's political party."[21]

That Chalupa does not discontinue this pre-campaign work after the 2016 presidential election season begins in mid-2015—doing paid consulting work for the Democratic Party during the Democratic primaries, when Trump is not yet the GOP nominee, but conducting none during the general election, when he is—is taken by Vogel and Stern as an indication of Ukrainian interference in the U.S. election, given that among Chalupa's network of sources in Kyiv and Washington are not just "investigative journalists" and "private intelligence operatives" but also Ukrainian government officials.[22]

The *Politico* duo's chief evidence of indirect aid to the Clinton campaign by Ukrainian officials is its finding that Chalupa "occasionally shared her findings [on Manafort's activities in Ukraine and Trump's ties to Russia] with officials from the DNC and Clinton's campaign."[23] However, Chalupa began discussing Manafort with the DNC in January 2016—"months before Manafort had taken any role in Trump's campaign," Vogel and Stern concede—suggesting that her interest in discussing Manafort with Democratic officials was a prophylactic against the possibility that Manafort could be used by Putin to "manipulat[e] U.S. foreign policy and elections," a service Manafort appears to have provided for the Kremlin beginning in 2006, according to the Associated Press.[24] Vogel and Stern confess that the overwhelming majority of consulting work Chalupa did for the DNC during the 2016 Democratic primary "centered on mobilizing ethnic communities—including Ukrainian-Americans," and subsequent findings by the *Washington Post* will contradict certain of Vogel and Stern's implications, with the *Post* reporting that "former Clinton campaign officials said they never received information from Chalupa," "a top [Ukrainian] embassy official denied working with reporters or with Chalupa on issues related to Trump or Manafort," "DNC officials denied that they coordinated with Chalupa on opposition research," "[Chalupa] was not a researcher for the DNC," and "DNC officials told *Politico* that the Democratic Party had been looking into Trump and his ties to Russia long before Chalupa alerted them"; the *Post* also quotes Chalupa as insisting that "the DNC never asked me to go to the Ukrainian Embassy to collect information."[25]

Even without the benefit of these subsequent clarifications and corrections, Vogel and Stern conclude in January 2017 that "there's little evidence of . . . top-down [election interference] effort by Ukraine"; that the country, even if it wished to, would be "unable to pull off an ambitious covert interference campaign in another country's election"; that Ukraine's presidential administration and stateside diplomatic corps publicly declared themselves "neutral" in the 2016 presidential race; that any Ukrainian activity that could be perceived as interfering in the 2016 U.S. presidential race was "far less concerted or centrally directed" than Russia's pro-Trump "hacking and dissemination of Democratic emails"; that a full investigation of the matter had led only to a conclusion that certain Ukrainians "appear[ed]" to "strain"—rather than break—diplomatic protocol; and that even Valeriy Chaly, who, with ambassadorial aide Oksana Shulyar, spoke to Chalupa, "wasn't particularly concerned about [Manafort's] ties to Trump" from the time of Trump's June 2015 announcement of his presidential run through late March 2016, because Chaly "didn't believe Trump stood much of a chance of winning the GOP nomination, let alone the presidency."[26]

That Chalupa's consulting work with the DNC ended in June 2016 leaves only a narrow window for her to have been simultaneously in contact with the DNC and the Ukrainian embassy at a time when Manafort was working for Trump—under ninety days—and during that period, Vogel and Stern report, the most that can be said is that "with the DNC's encouragement, Chalupa asked [Ukrainian] embassy staff to try to arrange an interview in which Poroshenko might discuss Manafort's ties to Yanukovych," a discussion separate from Manafort's involvement with Trump that the Ukrainian embassy nevertheless "declined."[27] The two *Politico* journalists note that no documents changed hands between Chalupa and the Ukrainians, with the latter doing no more than "provid[ing] guidance" if Chalupa "asked a question . . . [about who she] needed to follow up with" to learn more about domestic Ukrainian investigations of

Manafort—investigations that would have been ongoing and the subject of public journalistic inquiry and reporting on both sides of the Atlantic whether Chalupa had been in contact with the DNC and looking into the subject or not.[28] The longtime activist Chalupa aside, Vogel and Stern note that the Ukrainian embassy also answered questions from reporters who were "researching Trump, Manafort and Russia to point them in the right directions," and the two men accept Chalupa's representation that the Ukrainians "were being careful . . . very, very careful because they could not pick sides [in the election]. . . . [T]hey didn't want to get involved politically because they couldn't."[29] Just so, the *Politico* journalists note that the Ukrainians have "vehemently denied working with reporters or with Chalupa on anything related to Trump or Manafort" beyond answering baseline journalistic inquiries.[30] Indeed, the purpose of the initial meeting between Chalupa and the Ukrainian embassy was, Vogel and Stern report, "to organize a June [2016] reception at the embassy to promote Ukraine . . . [an] event highlight[ing] female Ukrainian leaders."[31]

The only evidence Vogel and Stern provide in January 2017 of a unique channel of information transfer between Ukrainian nationals and Chalupa comes from a single source: Andriy Telizhenko, a political officer in the Ukrainian embassy who worked for Ambassador Chaly's aide Oksana Shulyar.[32] Telizhenko claims Shulyar "instructed him to help Chalupa research connections between Trump, Manafort and Russia."[33] Vogel and Stern are unable to corroborate Telizhenko's claim, however, finding evidence only that on one occasion Shulyar asked Telizhenko to "provide [Chalupa] an update on an American media outlet's ongoing investigation into Manafort."[34] That American media outlet may have been Yahoo News, as Michael Isikoff, a reporter for Yahoo News, had already received information from Chalupa—information unrelated to Trump—on the basis of the latter's long-standing expertise on the subject of Manafort's pre-campaign business ventures in Ukraine.[35]

While Chalupa did allegedly communicate directly with the DNC about Trump's ties to Manafort on several occasions, Vogel and Stern unearth no evidence that these communications included information originating from Ukrainian officials, or that any information received from

Ukrainian officials was earmarked for the DNC.[36] Indeed, per Fox News, in September 2019 Ambassador Chaly will release a statement insisting that "all ideas floated by [Chalupa] were related to approaching a Member of Congress with a purpose to initiate hearings on Paul Manafort or letting an investigative journalist ask President Poroshenko a question about Mr. Manafort during [a] public talk in Washington," adding that throughout his engagements with her, he believed Chalupa to be working on "her own cause."[37] Fox News will likewise quote the Ukrainian embassy as "disput[ing] the suggestion that Chalupa sought 'dirt' on Trump, saying that she was merely concerned about the role of Manafort [in Trump's campaign] due to his previous work in [Ukraine] . . . [and] did not ask for any materials from the embassy. . . . [T]he embassy's encounter with Chalupa was 'null' and produced no further action."[38]

Vogel and Stern discover that Chalupa's most urgent communications with the DNC relate to the hacking of her emails, a crime later tied to Russian actors. Chalupa's emails end up being published by Kremlin cutout WikiLeaks, described by future Trump CIA director and secretary of state Mike Pompeo as a "hostile nonstate intelligence service."[39]

The involvement of a Kremlin-linked entity in the hacking of Chalupa's emails underscores Russian intelligence's apparent interest in using Chalupa to pin its own cyberattacks against the United States on Ukraine. As for the DNC—another victim of Russian hackers—it has maintained that Chalupa was a consultant working on outreach for the party, and not engaged in research; that she received no direction from the DNC in conducting various investigations "on her own"; and that "the party did not incorporate her findings in its dossiers" on Trump or Manafort.[40] Indeed, per Vogel and Stern, Chalupa's work during the 2016 general election (as opposed to primary season) was focused exclusively on "provid[ing] off-the-record information and guidance" to journalists as an activist rather than as a political operative.[41] That federal law enforcement considers Chalupa a victim of election interference rather than a perpetrator of it is underscored by the fact that the FBI interviewed her following the summer 2016 DNC hack only to examine her laptop and smartphone as possible evidence of equipment accessed illegally by

Russian agents.[42] Throughout the general election, Chalupa had received "alerts of state-sponsored hacking" into her Yahoo email account.[43]

On July 25, 2019, when Trump raises with new Ukrainian president Volodymyr Zelensky two specific concerns about alleged corruption in Ukraine, neither of them will relate to Chalupa (see chapter 28).

In December 2019, the *Washington Post* reports that, according to former White House officials, "almost from the moment he took office, President Trump seized on a theory that troubled his senior aides: Ukraine, he told them on many occasions, had tried to stop him from winning the White House."[44] Per these officials, Trump "grew more insistent that Ukraine worked to defeat him" almost immediately "after meeting privately in July 2017 with Russian President Vladimir Putin at the Group of 20 summit in Hamburg."[45] Trump met with Putin in Hamburg for three hours, the final hour in a separate meeting without any American observers present.[46]

In the weeks following the meeting, according to former senior administration officials, "Trump repeatedly insisted . . . that he believed Putin's assurances that Russia had not interfered in the 2016 campaign" and "told aides . . . that he believed Ukraine had interfered and tried to help Clinton win the White House."[47] While the White House issued no formal readout of the final hour of the Trump-Putin conversation in Hamburg—indeed, never voluntarily disclosed it to the press—"Trump repeatedly told one senior official that the Russian president said Ukraine sought to undermine him."[48] After his first two hours with Putin in Germany, Trump "[took] the notes [of the meeting] away from his interpreter and instruct[ed] her not to discuss what had transpired."[49]

In sum, the *Post* writes, numerous White House officials report that the president's "intense resistance to the assessment of U.S. intelligence agencies that Russia systematically interfered in the 2016 campaign— and the blame he cast instead on a rival country—[have] led many of his advisers to think that Putin himself helped spur the idea of Ukraine's culpability."[50] One official discloses to the *Post* that Trump told staff he knew Ukraine was the "real culprit" in 2016 election interference because "Putin told me."[51] The official contemporaneously reported this startling comment to two other officials, both of whom confirmed their colleague's account to the *Post*.[52]

The newspaper notes that the incident "underscores long-standing fears inside the administration about the Russian president's ability to influence Trump's views"—an ability White House officials feared Hungarian president and Putin ally Viktor Orban would have as well, with one official telling the *Post* that "we were against [any meeting between Trump and Orban] because we knew there was a good chance that [they] would bond and get along."[53] As the *Post* summarizes, Trump's advisers "worried about Orban's influence on the U.S. president."[54]

The German broadcasting company Deutsche Welle (DW) reports that Orban and Putin have a "special relationship," with "deep ties" that go beyond both being "nationalistic strongmen with a dislike for western liberalism."[55] Orban's explicit endorsement of Trump in 2016 aside, the foreign leader's public praise for Putin echoes Trump's own domestic political rhetoric, including Orban's lauding of the Russian president for having "made his country great again"; moreover, Orban has, like Trump, "strongly criticized EU sanctions against Russia," and like the Trump administration has pursued joint nuclear energy deals with Russian interests.[56]

According to DW, Orban's admiration for Putin goes beyond rhetoric, as during the course of his own presidency he has "transformed his country in a way reminiscent of Russia."[57] Just as candidate Trump answered queries about Russia's 2014 annexation of Crimea by indicating that the Kremlin should be allowed to keep the land it had taken, Orban, per DW, "repeatedly broke Russia's diplomatic isolation by welcoming Putin in Budapest after the 2014 annexation of Crimea."[58] It is perhaps little surprise, then, that according to the *Hungarian Free Press*, Budapest is the European headquarters of Russia's state intelligence service, the FSB—a successor to the KGB.[59]

* * *

In tracing the origin point of Trump's conspiracy theories about Ukraine, another landmark event is a visit by Putin to Budapest on February 2, 2017, during which the Russian president declared, "As we know, during the [2016] presidential campaign in the United States, the Ukrainian government adopted a unilateral position in favor of one candidate. More than that, certain oligarchs, certainly with the approval of the political leadership, funded this candidate, or female candidate, to be more precise."[60] According to the *Washington Post*, the oligarch to whom Putin was likely referring was Ukrainian steel magnate Viktor Pinchuk, whose nonprofit donated to the Clinton Foundation. The *Post* notes, however, that in 2015 Pinchuk also gave $150,000 to the Trump Foundation—an entity since shuttered pursuant to a New York court ruling that found it misused millions of dollars in donations.[61]

Like Putin, Trump frequently marries his denial of Russian culpability for 2016 election interference with conspiracy theories surrounding Ukraine's alleged role in the election. At a summit in Helsinki in July 2018, Trump responded to a question about whether he accepted the consensus of U.S. intelligence that Russia meddled in the 2016 election by saying, "I have President Putin; he just said it's not Russia. I will say this: I don't see why it would be." Trump immediately adds—in a reference to the DNC server he has repeatedly claimed is in Ukraine—"I really do want to see the server."[62]

Trump's public credulousness following conversations with Putin in Hamburg and Helsinki is, the *Washington Post* reports, consistent with what Trump says privately. According to a U.S. official who speaks to the *Post*, whenever Trump is confronted in private meetings with the question of Russian interference in 2016, his response is, "This is ridiculous. Everyone knows I won the election. The greatest election in the world. The Russians didn't do anything. The Ukrainians tried to do something."[63]

CHAPTER 14

ORBAN AND SOROS

A common feature of many of the conspiracy theories advanced by both the Kremlin and Rudy Giuliani is that they rely in part on unproven claims that billionaire philanthropist George Soros, a Hungarian American Jew who survived the Holocaust, is pulling the strings of far-flung attempts to undermine Trump. NBC News calls Soros "a frequent target of conspiracies about Jews controlling the world," adding that "the president's allies and other Republicans have been working to tie Soros to nefarious plots to intervene in U.S. affairs" for years.[1] As reported by NBC, when Giuliani initiates in 2018 "a successful campaign to oust Marie Yovanovitch as the U.S. ambassador to Ukraine" (see chapter 20), it is "galvanized by accusations that Yovanovitch protected Soros' efforts" to be involved in humanitarian efforts worldwide—efforts that are somehow morally wicked and politically nefarious, Trump's allies baselessly assert.[2] In September 2019, Giuliani falsely tells the *Washington Post* that Yovanovitch is "now working for Soros" since her firing by Trump; in fact, as NBC reports, she is "still a U.S. government employee."[3]

At the same time that he is spreading disinformation about Yovanovitch in the *Post*, Giuliani is telling CNN that Soros is behind a conspiracy involving the "black ledger." Giuliani alleges, without evidence, that an anti-corruption nonprofit in Ukraine called AntAC "took funding from a Soros philanthropy" and that—in repayment—AntAC decided to "fabricat[e] evidence against former Trump campaign chairman Paul Manafort" in mid-2016.[4] Giuliani adds, in an interview with Trump adviser Sean Hannity on Fox News, that unnamed Ukrainians "brought

[him] substantial [documentary] evidence of Ukrainian collusion with Hillary Clinton, the DNC, George Soros, [and] George Soros' company."[5] Giuliani does not reveal the evidence to Hannity or Fox News' viewers.

Giuliani's allegations against Soros have appeared in a John Solomon article in *The Hill* (see chapter 18), its content having been coordinated, per NBC, with Trump legal advisers Joe diGenova and Victoria Toensing.[6] In November 2019, diGenova declares on Fox News, without evidence, that Soros "wants to run Ukraine" and "controls a very large part" of not only the U.S. diplomatic corps and the contingent of FBI agents assigned by the Bureau to work on Ukraine policy, but also an unstated number of other FBI agents around the world.[7] The same month, Rep. Steve King (R-IA) tweets four pictures of Soros's son and falsely claims that he is the CIA whistleblower who reported on Trump's call with Ukrainian president Volodymyr Zelensky in July 2019 (see chapter 32).[8]

Andriy Telizhenko, the former Ukrainian embassy worker who says he was instructed to pass information on Manafort to the DNC through activist Alexandra Chalupa, claims in December 2019 that he is working with Giuliani in Ukraine to uncover unspecified new evidence in the Burisma and CrowdStrike "investigations," but that "Soros people" are "working against him."[9] He notes that some of these individuals are "former Ukrainian politicians," further advancing Giuliani's and diGenova's unproven claims that Soros's influence has infiltrated the government in Kyiv. When NBC asks Telizhenko for proof that "Soros people are trying to discredit my reputation with lies and will try to block me [from entering the U.S.]," he fails to provide any.[10]

As the author of an unsubstantiated claim that he helped the Ukrainian embassy "[coordinate] an investigation with the Hillary team on Paul Manafort with Alexandra Chalupa," Telizhenko strikes an unlikely figure, as he had ceased working for the Ukrainian embassy many weeks before Trump became the GOP nominee for president, reducing the likelihood that he was present for significant conversations in the Ukrainian embassy about Trump's prospective general election campaign against Clinton.[11] Nevertheless, following Trump's inauguration, Telizhenko communicates "extensively" with Giuliani, and in May 2019, according to the *Daily Beast*, meets Devin Nunes—about whom Telizhenko will thereafter enthusiastically gush that he is a "true patriot."[12] Telizhenko is eventually featured in a video for the far-right conspiracy website InfoWars, an appearance that leads *BuzzFeed News* to call the former Ukrainian official a "bespoke purveyor of conspiracy theories."[13]

Despite his staunch criticism of alleged Clinton-Ukraine cooperation, Telizhenko spends much of his time following his departure from the Ukrainian embassy in the very role he claims to abhor: that of a foreign national privately cooperating with an active U.S. political campaign. In early 2019, according to the *Daily Beast*, he begins "help[ing] Giuliani try to investigate matters related to American politics and Ukraine."[14] By late 2019 he is calling Giuliani a "friend" and being quoted as a reliable source in *The Hill* by staunch Trump ally John Solomon (see chapter 18).[15]

In November 2019, *BuzzFeed News* reveals that Telizhenko has been working with Giuliani on a second unsubstantiated theory regarding supposed Ukrainian election meddling. Per the digital media outlet, Telizhenko, Giuliani, and other unnamed Ukrainian nationals are "hoping to find evidence that Democratic operatives faked the hack of the Democratic National Committee's servers to frame Russia for trying to swing the 2016 election in Trump's favor and then hired the American cybersecurity firm CrowdStrike to cover it up"; *BuzzFeed News* appends to this reporting that "there is no proof, of course, that any of this happened."[16] On December 9, 2019, FBI director Christopher Wray, a Trump appointee, categorically rejects any suggestion that Ukraine interfered in the 2016 presidential election, saying that the FBI has "no information" to suggest such interference occurred.[17] Within twenty-four hours Trump has tweeted, as summarized by the *Washington Post*, that "Director Wray may not have the right attitude to fix" the FBI—an apparent threat against Wray's continued employment as FBI director.[18]

*   *   *

In 2017, Connie Mack IV, a former Republican congressman from Florida, lobbies Vice President Pence to fire one of the Trump administration's chief experts on Russia and Ukraine, Fiona Hill, doing so at the request of his client, Hungarian president Viktor Orban.[19] Orban and Mack's unsubstantiated claim is that Hill is "a Soros mole in the White House," according to Hill's later testimony to Congress.[20] Mack further alleges that Hill "attended Soros' wedding," information he said he found in a "book on the internet" whose title he "couldn't recall" and which, NBC News reports, "an internet search [does] not turn . . . up."[21] Hill denies attending Soros's wedding.[22] Undeterred, Orban's agent Mack boasts that his work is "shining 'a light on the far-reaching network of George Soros'" in an effort to "degrade his international influence."[23] According to NBC, much of Mack's information about Hill and Soros appears to have come from discredited conspiracy theory website InfoWars.[24]

On May 13, 2019, ten days before Trump instructs the "Three Amigos" to work with Giuliani to induce Zelensky to initiate investigations of Clinton and Biden (see chapter 24), Trump meets in the White House— "over the objections of top national security aides"—with Orban.[25] Trump goes "outside State Department channels to secure the meeting," according to the *New York Times*. While at the White House, Orban, "one of [Ukraine's] most virulent critics," gives Trump a "sharp assessment [of Ukraine] that bolster[s] [the president's] hostility toward the country."[26] Trump's seeming eagerness to be turned against Ukraine echoes his prior treatment of Ukrainian president Petro Poroshenko; Trump had not only snubbed Poroshenko in Washington in 2017—giving him only a "drop-in" rather than a formal visit—but also avoided him entirely at subsequent events in New York City and Switzerland, having become so hostile to Ukraine's president by December 2016, per *Politico*, that when "a delegation of Ukrainian parliamentarians allied with Poroshenko . . . traveled to Washington partly to try to make inroads with the Trump transition team, they were unable to secure a meeting."[27]

As the *Times* reports of the Trump-Orban meeting, by conversing with the Hungarian president Trump "exposed him[self] to a harsh indictment of Ukraine at a time when his personal lawyer was pressing the new government in Kyiv to provide damaging information about Democrats."[28] The *Times* observes that "Trump's suspicious view of Ukraine . . . [would] set the stage for events that led to the impeachment inquiry against him"; as important, the newspaper notes that the key sources of Trump's animus toward Ukraine are Putin, Orban, and Giuliani.[29] Per the *Times*, what Trump heard from Orban in the White House in May 2019 were "opinions he had heard from his personal lawyer, Rudolph W. Giuliani, and from President Vladimir V. Putin of Russia repeatedly over the months and years."[30]

According to deputy assistant secretary of state for European and Eurasian affairs George Kent, the president's "darkening views of Mr. Zelensky" in spring 2019—which ran counter to the assessments that would be provided to him by Volker, Perry, and Sondland in the Oval Office on May 23—were indeed in part the product of Trump's many communications with Putin.[31]

Within days of the Trump-Putin phone call and Trump-Orban White House meeting, it is "clear," the *Washington Post* reports, that Trump's conversation with Orban has "solidified" the president's already "pessimistic view" of Zelensky.[32] A former White House official will tell the *Post* that prior to the summit with Orban "everyone" at the White House agreed that under no circumstances should the Hungarian president be permitted to meet with Trump; Mulvaney had to "overrule national security officials" to facilitate the meeting.[33]

As *New York Times* coverage of the Trump-Orban meeting details, Orban "used the opportunity [on May 13] to disparage Ukraine with the president," his government having previously sought to "block important meetings for Ukraine with the European Union and NATO."[34] Mulvaney had set up Trump's joint appearance with Orban with the aid of the president's ambassador to Hungary, "an 81-year-old jewelry magnate and longtime friend of Mr. Trump's, [David] Cornstein."[35] Cornstein has said that, "knowing the president for a good 25 or 30 years . . . he would love to have the situation [in the United States] that Viktor Orban has [in Hungary], but he doesn't."[36] The *Times* describes the "situation" in Hungary as one in which Orban has "targeted nongovernmental organizations, brought most of the news media under control of his allies, undermined the independent judiciary, altered the electoral process to favor his party and sought to drive out of the country an American-chartered university founded by the billionaire George Soros"; as the autocratic Hungarian president accrues to himself sweeping new domestic powers amidst the global COVID-19 pandemic in 2020 (see chapter 42), Freedom House's annual report on democracy worldwide ("Nations in Transit") will report that Hungary has officially lost its status as a democracy as part of a "stunning democratic breakdown" sweeping the globe.[37]

The *Washington Post* writes that throughout the course of Trump's 2019 scheme to pressure Ukraine, "he was being urged to adopt a hostile view of that country by its regional adversaries, including Russian President Vladimir Putin," who, along with Orban, "reinforced his perception of Ukraine as a hopelessly corrupt country."[38] The *Post* adds that Orban and Putin "fed a dysfunctional dynamic in which White House officials struggled to persuade Trump to support the fledgling government in Kyiv"; the newspaper positions the Orban-Putin partnership as unsurprising, given that the Hungarian president has "often allied himself with the Kremlin's positions."[39] A White House official tells the *Post* that "Trump's apparent susceptibility to the arguments he hears from Putin and Orban is 'an example of the president himself under malign influence—being steered by it.'"[40] Nor are Trump's interactions with Putin in 2019 infrequent; besides the May 3 call, the president also speaks to his Russian counterpart on June 28 at a global summit in Tokyo and then again by phone on July 31, less than a week after his fateful call with Zelensky.[41]

As for Giuliani—the third Trump adviser on Ukraine, with Putin and Orban, to exhibit a marked animus toward both the former Soviet republic and George Soros—*Just Security* notes that his encompassing conspiracy theory about the 2016 election is focused as much on Soros and

Biden as it is on Clinton, CrowdStrike, Manafort, and the "black ledger."[42] Indeed, not only has Giuliani inaccurately claimed in media appearances that the information about Ukraine's Manafort investigation that made it into U.S. media during the 2016 presidential election was leaked by the partially Soros-funded Ukrainian entity AntAC, but he has also alleged, likewise without evidence, that a pending case against AntAC in Ukraine would have gone forward had Biden not engineered the firing of Viktor Shokin.[43] Per Giuliani's conspiracy theory on this latter score, the former vice president approved Shokin's replacement, Yuri Lutsenko, in part because he was assured that Lutsenko would drop the case against AntAC—an eventuality that in fact came to pass, though not, *Just Security* reports, due to any intervention by Biden.[44]

The *Daily Beast* calls Giuliani's public roping of Biden and Soros into the "black ledger" conspiracy theory "bizarre," "rambling," "flimsy," "almost entirely . . . innuendo," "vague," "reek[ing] of anti-Semitism," and—most tellingly, given that *The Hill* columnist John Solomon's employer is Jimmy Finkelstein, a longtime Trump associate—"rest[ing] largely on a March 2019 op-ed in *The Hill* written by opinion writer John Solomon."[45] Even Giuliani's claim that AntAC is "Soros-run" is false; while the anti-corruption nongovernmental organization, managed entirely by Ukrainian activists, has received some funding from Soros, its primary sources of funding are the governments of the United States, the United Kingdom, the Netherlands, the Czech Republic, and the European Union.[46] Moreover, while AntAC was indeed at one point under investigation for misusing funds, the U.S. State Department has since said it has "no concerns" that any money was misused by AntAC—and that the investigation of the anti-corruption outfit was mere "retribution" for its activities in fighting corruption in Ukraine. As the *Daily Beast* summarizes, even the current position of the Trump administration is that the probe of AntAC was a "politically motivated pursuit . . . meant to punish the good-governance group."[47]

* * *

BuzzFeed News calls Orban "an authoritarian leader . . . reviled around the world for his far-right views," and notes the irony of his use of anti-Semitic dog-whistling involving Soros to advance his political career given that he is an "old friend" of Israeli prime minister Benjamin Netanyahu and—even more strikingly—himself the recipient of Soros money. CNN reports that Orban once "received money from Soros" for his "small underground foundation Szazadveg," which published critiques of the then-government of Hungary.[48] The digital media outlet diagnoses Orban's unending rhetorical assault on Soros as a toxic, self-contradictory "stew" comprising "resentments for [Soros's] assault on communism," "allegations that [Soros] is a communist," "anti-Jewish slurs and charges [Soros] is a Nazi," and, "above all, the old mix of European anti-Semitism."[49] As for Putin, one probable motive for his anti-Soros animus is that the Hungarian "has been funding projects in Europe for decades to fight corruption and promote the transition to democracy in former Soviet states."[50]

What is less clear is the political calculus behind Trump and Giuliani's use of Soros as a bogeyman, even as the Holocaust survivor's ubiquity in the president's rhetoric remains unmistakable: indeed, Trump has situated Soros behind everything from the vocal opposition to Supreme Court nominee Brett Kavanaugh to the migrant caravan that arrived on America's southern border in late 2018, and his advisers, agents, and allies have repeatedly roped Soros into their conspiracy theories on Ukraine.[51] Regardless, it is clear that the Trump team's idiosyncratic and at times anti-Semitic rhetoric on alleged Ukrainian election meddling benefits Vladimir Putin: in November 2019, the Russian president states at a public event, per *Politico*, that "he's pleased that the 'political battles' in Washington have put on the back-burner accusations that Russia interfered in U.S. elections. 'Thank God,' he [tells] an economic forum in the Russian capital . . . 'no one is accusing us of interfering in the U.S. elections anymore; now they're accusing Ukraine.'"[52]

CHAPTER 15

LESHCHENKO

In the summer of 2016, Ukraine's independent anti-corruption agency, the National Anti-Corruption Bureau of Ukraine (NABU), reveals that it is conducting a criminal investigation of illicit payments allegedly made to Paul Manafort by the pro-Kremlin Party of Regions in the years prior to Trump's announcement of his presidential run. As the payments are recorded in a ledger NABU has in its possession, the ledger comes to be called the "black ledger," and the scandal attached to the ledger the "black ledger scandal."[1] "Less than a month and a half before it release[s] the ledgers," NABU signs "an evidence-sharing agreement with the FBI"—a synchronicity that will launch a conspiracy theory about coordination between the Bureau and NABU on the matter of Manafort's crimes.[2]

After the ledger is revealed, the *New York Times* reports on the discovery, noting that the payments to Manafort are actually only one of many focuses of a much larger and broader NABU investigation.[3] Days later, CNN reports that the FBI is also looking into Manafort in an "overlapping" inquiry.[4] The concurrence of the NABU and FBI inquiries will encourage some in the president's milieu to accuse NABU of seeding an FBI investigation of Trump's campaign chief; in December 2019, however, a report filed by DOJ inspector general Michael Horowitz discloses that Manafort was in fact being probed by the FBI well before the Bureau began its Russia investigation, and indeed for the same conduct Trump and his allies would later claim was revealed only by Ukrainian sources in summer 2016.[5] According to the Horowitz report and NBC News, Manafort was "already under investigation" as part of "an ongoing criminal investigation supervised by the Money Laundering and Asset Recovery Section in the Department's Criminal Division, concerning millions of dollars he received from the government of Ukraine."[6] The Horowitz report states that the "criminal investigation [of Manafort] was opened by the FBI's Criminal Investigative Division in January 2016, approximately two months before Manafort joined the Trump campaign as an adviser, and concerned allegations that Manafort had engaged in money laundering and tax evasion while acting as a political consultant to members of the Ukrainian government and Ukrainian politicians."[7] The report's findings suggest that the evidentiary predicate for the Manafort investigation would have been received by the FBI in 2015—possibly from Ukrainian sources, but in any case many months before any such sources could have known Manafort would be associated with Trump's presidential candidacy, an ambition Manafort first disclosed to Trump friend Thomas Barrack on the last day of February 2016.[8]

Despite the foregoing, it is clear that the Manafort family blames one party in particular for NABU "obtain[ing] the documents showing $12.7 million in cash earmarked for Manafort": Hillary Clinton.[9] When news of the ledger showing illicit payments to Manafort drops, Manafort's daughter texts a friend, "I HATE Hillary. She hired someone to do this to my family."[10] The "someone" to whom Manafort's daughter is referring is unclear, though former MI6 Russia desk chief Christopher Steele is one option, as his raw intelligence memos revealed information about alleged kickbacks to Manafort in Ukraine, and some of these memos were the result of work Steele did while being indirectly paid by the Clinton campaign and the DNC—a fact he would only learn "several months" into his contract, per the *New Yorker*.[11] As *Lawfare* has noted, "the official record supports . . . [the] allegation" made in the Steele dossier that former Ukrainian president Viktor Yanukovych "did authorize and order substantial kick-back payments to Manafort."[12]

According to reports by *Politico* and *The Intercept*, one element of the Trump camp's allegations of Ukrainian election meddling is the fact that "a former Ukrainian investigative journalist and current parliamentarian named Serhiy Leshchenko, who was elected in 2014 as part of Poroshenko's party, held a news conference [in August 2016] to highlight the ledgers, and to urge Ukrainian and American law enforcement to aggressively investigate Manafort."[13] It is unclear how the urging of a criminal investigation into crimes committed by Manafort in Ukraine prior to Trump's presidential run could be received by Trump and his inner circle as implicating the president himself—unless there is information about Trump's connection to Manafort's activities that remains unrevealed, a possibility raised when NBC News reports in January 2018 that Trump believes Manafort is uniquely able to harm him if he decides to cooperate with law enforcement.[14]

Politico describes Leshchenko as a "former" investigative journalist, while other publications, including *The Atlantic*, note that in 2016 Leshchenko was—like many politicians in Ukraine and elsewhere—not only an elected official but also a working professional in another field. Per the magazine, in 2016 Leshchenko was "an investigative journalist . . . [who] had seen colleagues [in journalism] murdered in pursuit of their stories, but he kept on writing about the rot of the system. His best pieces were triumphs of obsessive reporting that revealed the ill-gotten wealth of the political elite. That same activist fervor had propelled him into politics."[15]

Leshchenko calls a press conference to discuss the findings in Manafort's case in Ukraine "just after" Trump receives the Republican nomination for president in 2016, a fact that seems to confirm that he has been working on the Manafort story as a journalist since before Trump was the Republican Party's nominee for president.[16] That Leshchenko would become, by 2018, an informal political adviser to Zelensky, Poroshenko's political rival, underscores another fact: like many Ukrainians, Leshchenko feared Poroshenko was corruptible—a quality Trump's successful back-channel outreach to the Ukrainian president in 2017 and 2018 on the subject of Manafort would seem to confirm.[17] Despite Leshchenko's principles and professional activities predating Trump's presidential run, Giuliani will publicly brand Leshchenko an "enemy of the American president" in May 2019, implying thereby that

Leshchenko's informal advising of Zelensky is sufficient cause for President Trump to fear that the entirety of the Zelensky administration is out to get him—the same belief Trump claimed to have about the Poroshenko administration in justifying his consistent alignment with Putin on Ukraine policy.[18]

On May 23, 2019, not long after Giuliani's attack on Leshchenko, Trump tells a gathering of top aides that Ukraine is a "corrupt country" that is "full of terrible people" who "tried to take me down."[19] One result of Giuliani and Trump's misplaced ire is that, as *The Atlantic* reports, Leshchenko's "prospective job in the Zelensky administration" instantly "disappear[s]" in the "televised flash" of Giuliani putting Leshchenko on Trump's enemies list.[20] The preemptive release of Leshchenko from Zelensky's advisory corps is one of the first indications Trump's inner circle will receive that Zelensky is prepared to capitulate to Trump—and may be monitoring statements by Trump's closest associates in determining how best to do so.

Trump and Giuliani's adoption of a conspiracy theory holding the Manafort-Yanukovych ledger to be a forgery dovetails with identical claims by Russian officials.[21] The basis for this common allegation of forgery is limited to a single sentence in the Steele dossier, in which the former British spy writes that Yanukovych assured Putin there was "no documentary trail left behind which could provide clear evidence of ['kickbacks' to Manafort]."[22] While Trump will call the dossier "A COMPLETE AND TOTAL FABRICATION," "UTTER NONSENSE," "very unfair," "fake news," "unverified and Fake [and] Dirty," "dirty and discredited," "discredited and Fake," "phony and discredited," "phony and corrupt," and "fraudulent"—and will react to its publication by tweeting, "Are we living in Nazi Germany?"—he will seem to accept one of its central claims: that Manafort's former boss successfully "covered up" evidence of any felonious "kickbacks."[23] The president's reasoning on this key contention of the dossier appears to be that if Yanukovych says he covered up any evidence of kickbacks to Manafort, he must in fact have done so, making the existence of any ledger confirming the kickbacks impossible. How the president accepts this finding of the dossier without also adopting the intelligence upon which it depends—that Yanukovych "authorize[d] and order[ed] substantial kick-back payments to Manafort as alleged" in Ukraine and thereafter the United States—is unclear.[24]

On another key contention of the dossier confirmed by the special counsel's office, that Manafort "led for the Trump side" throughout the course of the collusion between the Trump campaign and Russia documented in the Mueller Report—a months-long episode marked by secret meetings, back-channel promises, and data being exchanged between Manafort and Kremlin agent Konstantin Kilimnik—the president is silent.[25]

Serhiy Leshchenko has said that his motivation in speaking publicly about the ledger in summer 2016 was to "show not only the corruption aspect, but that [Trump] is [a] pro-Russian candidate who can break the geopolitical balance in the world."[26] A *Financial Times* article summarizing Leshchenko's thinking includes an unsubstantiated claim by the Ukrainian parliamentarian that "the majority of Ukraine's politicians . . . are 'on Hillary Clinton's side.'"[27] Though Leshchenko is a member of Poroshenko's party, there is no evidence his comments are endorsed by the Poroshenko administration or even known about in advance; indeed, Poroshenko's party will contend following the comments that Leshchenko is in fact a dissenter within their ranks and not representative of their caucus.[28] By 2019, multiple top U.S. national security officials are testifying to Congress that they have seen "no evidence" Ukraine interfered with the 2016 election in any way.[29]

In their much-discussed January 2017 *Politico* article, Ken Vogel and David Stern bolster Trump and his allies via their decision to ignore Poroshenko's denials and treat Leshchenko, without evidence, as an accurate reflection of sentiment in Ukraine's government. The two men claim, quoting an anonymous "operative who has worked extensively in Ukraine, including as an adviser to Poroshenko," that "it was highly unlikely that either Leshchenko or the anti-corruption bureau [NABU] would have pushed the [ledger] issue [in 2016] without at least tacit approval from Poroshenko or his closest allies"; the fact that Trump and Giuliani have since successfully pressured Poroshenko in the opposite direction on the Manafort investigation—convincing him, via both unofficial face-to-face meetings and subtle public signals, to take over and then freeze all investigations of a man Trump believes could harm him if he "flipped"—goes unstated.[30] Meanwhile, the Poroshenko administration will continue to insist that not just by convention but by law NABU is "fully independent" of the presidential administration, a fact Trump and Giuliani will implicitly acknowledge by thereafter lobbying Poroshenko to end NABU's independence. It is a lobbying campaign that would be unnecessary if the corrupt entwining of the presidential administration and NABU that the president and his attorney seek had already been accomplished. Of likely greater concern to Trump and Giuliani in mid-2016, if they have more knowledge of Manafort's illicit activities in Ukraine than they have publicly confessed, is NABU's decision to, as noted by Vogel and Stern, sign "an evidence-sharing agreement with the FBI in late June [2016]—less than a month and a half before [NABU] released the ledgers."[31]

In October 2017, a former member of Poroshenko's political party, Boryslav Rozenblat—recently expelled from the party for allegedly soliciting a bribe, and eighteen months from being accused of vote-buying by police—files a lawsuit against both Leshchenko and the head of NABU, Artem Sytnyk.[32] The lawsuit, which repeats an allegation made publicly by Rozenblat in 2016, contends that Sytnyk and Leshchenko "leaked" documents regarding Manafort's involvement in crimes in Ukraine to the "headquarters" of "Trump's main rival in [the] 2016 elections, Hillary Clinton"—an odd contention, given that Leshchenko had in fact held a major press conference to discuss documents Rozenblat alleges were transmitted covertly.[33] In December 2018, the Kyiv Administrative District Court rules against Leshchenko, opining in its decision that Leshchenko's actions had constituted interference in "American electoral processes"; however, just months later, in July 2019, this ruling is overturned and vacated by a higher court, the Sixth Administrative Court of Appeals.[34] By the fall of 2019, some Trump allies in Congress are still citing the invalidated lower court ruling of 2018 as proof of Ukrainian meddling in the 2016 election. In fact, the view of the U.S. embassy in Kyiv, even at the time of the later-invalidated 2018 ruling, was that the decision was "politically motivated" and one that American diplomats had every intention of "stay[ing] away from."[35]

As Leshchenko is still contesting the initial ruling in the Rozenblat lawsuit in May 2019, he gets hold of an internal memo regarding Joe Biden from Ukraine prosecutor general Yuri Lutsenko's office that reveals the office has secretly already started an investigation into Biden following Lutsenko's meeting with Rudy Giuliani in January 2019.[36] On May 14, Leshchenko releases the memo to the public, explaining that "the memo had [previously] been submitted by . . . Lutsenko's team to U.S. President Donald Trump's team."[37] In the memo, Lutsenko and his agents accuse the former founder and owner of Burisma, Mykola Zlochevsky—the case against whom Lutsenko's predecessor, Viktor Shokin, had permitted to fall dormant—of "offer[ing secretary of state] John Kerry and Joe Biden a share in the distribution of profits of the holding company Burisma Group in exchange for lobbying activities and political support."[38] There is no evidence this occurred, and Lutsenko will subsequently withdraw both this allegation against Biden and the others from the memo, including false claims that Kerry secured a Burisma board seat for a friend of his stepson Christopher Heinz and that Biden single-handedly "established indirect control over the most economically attractive Ukrainian gas and oil producing assets, which led to [Biden's] receipt of unlawful benefits in especially large amounts."[39] Lutsenko's disinformation—in essence a pro-Trump mimicry of the Steele dossier, in this case one embraced by Trump even as, unlike the Steele dossier, it is being disowned by its author—further accuses Biden, falsely and without evidence, of compelling NABU to "commit illegal actions," including "prevent[ing] Ukrainian law enforcement agencies from prosecuting allies of ex-President Viktor Yanukovych and opposition politicians and businesspeople."[40] It is unknown whether Giuliani shares this information with the client for whom he has repeatedly said all his investigations in Ukraine were intended, Donald Trump; if he does, it means that Trump is aware that a component of the Ukrainian government has substantially completed an "investigation" of Joe Biden when the president explicitly asks Zelensky to do so on July 25, 2019—and that Trump likewise had this knowledge while his allies in Congress were repeatedly insisting, for many months thereafter, that no such investigation had ever been initiated.[41]

The possibility that Lutsenko's secretive early 2019 investigation of Biden may have been directly provoked by Trump's agents is bolstered by the *New York Times* in November 2019, when Giuliani agent and longtime Trump acquaintance Lev Parnas reveals to the newspaper that sometime before Zelensky's inauguration in May, he "told a representative of the incoming government that it had to announce an investigation into Mr. Trump's political rival, Joseph R. Biden Jr., and his son, or else Vice President Mike Pence would not attend the swearing-in of the new president, and the United States would freeze aid [to Ukraine]."[42] The implications of this report include the chance that when he began his investigation into Joe Biden, Lutsenko was already aware of this demand by a self-described—per Parnas's attorney at the time, John Dowd—Trump agent, and produced his dossier on Biden for Trump's team partly in response to Parnas's demand and partly in response to his January and February communications with Giuliani. The fact that Lutsenko was in contact with Parnas in both March and April 2019 stands in support of this narrative.[43]

Parnas's admission that he was threatening American aid to Ukraine by mid-May at the latest—a threat his attorney told the *Times* was made "at the direction of Mr. Giuliani," who has since said that he took no action with respect to Ukraine other than on behalf of his client, Donald Trump—means that when Zelensky got on the phone with Trump on July 25, he likely already knew what was at stake.[44] And indeed, Parnas's attorney will tell the *Times* that Parnas "believed [Giuliani] was acting under Mr. Trump's instruction" in telling him to issue a warning to the Ukrainians about military aid and investigations of Biden and CrowdStrike.[45] That Parnas will further contend, through his attorney, that he was a member of Trump's legal team and therefore may enjoy attorney-client privilege with the president underscores that in threatening Ukraine in May 2019 he believed himself to be acting as a legal agent of the White House.[46]

While Sergey Shefir, the "member of the inner circle of Mr. Zelensky" who met with Parnas and Fruman in May 2019, will later claim—after the Ukraine scandal has broken—that he "did not treat Mr. Parnas and Mr. Fruman as official representatives . . . of the U.S. government," he does not resolve the question of whether, as a top Zelensky aide sent to meet with two associates of the president's attorney, he believed Parnas and Fruman to be speaking as representatives of Donald Trump in his *personal* capacity as a politician seeking reelection.[47] In the event, the threat Parnas issues in early May is indeed carried out later in the month—through Trump's refusal to permit Pence to attend Zelensky's inauguration—thereby helping to establish for Shefir and Zelensky Parnas's bona fides as a representative of Trump's private interests.[48]

That Zelensky was aware of Parnas and Fruman's activities in Kyiv long before his inauguration is clear. *The Atlantic* writes that "of the many subjects [Zelensky] struggled to understand over the months [of the 2018–19 Ukrainian presidential campaign], Giuliani was among the most nettlesome. Since the late winter, the city's elite had been aware of the mayor's emissaries, Lev Parnas and Igor Fruman, whom he had dispatched to uncover incriminating material about Joe Biden and his son. The bumbling pair, who had won a meeting with the incumbent president, Petro Poroshenko, spoke a little too freely about their 'secret mission.'"[49]

Though the "evidence" Lutsenko has compiled on Biden by the time his memo on the former vice president is allegedly transferred to Trump's team in spring 2019 is false, Lutsenko's deputy Konstantin Kulyk, long considered "a staunch loyalist of ex-President Petro Poroshenko" and Lutsenko himself, will baldly confess to the *Kyiv Post* in May 2019 that

Lutsenko has indeed "been investigating Joe Biden"—a startling claim, given that Trump and his allies will defend against the president's impeachment in late 2019 and early 2020 by implying that no component of the executive branch of Ukraine's government ever conducted an investigation of Biden.[50] In an exemplar of such rhetoric, Rep. Jim Jordan (R-OH) will tell Fox News in November 2019 that "most importantly [to President Trump's defense], President Zelensky didn't announce, didn't start, didn't promise he was going to start any investigation to get the aid released."[51] Whether Jordan is aware of Lutsenko's early 2019 investigation of Biden at the time of his Fox News interview is unclear, though, according to Leshchenko, Trump's "team" was aware—meaning that either Trump's inner circle had chosen to keep one of Trump's closest allies in the House of Representatives in the dark or else Jordan was not being forthcoming on Fox News.[52]

One ironic element of Lutsenko's subsequently recanted investigation of Biden is that one of its key claims, that Biden and Kerry had sought to determine the board of a Ukrainian energy company, mirrors what Trump's secretary of energy Rick Perry does in fact do in handing a list of proposed Naftogaz supervisory board members to the Zelensky administration in May 2019.[53] Equally telling is that, despite claims by Trump's legal team at his January 2020 impeachment trial that the president's interest in the Bidens centered on Hunter Biden's allegedly corrupt dealings in Ukraine and not Joe Biden's position as a 2020 presidential election front-runner, the dossier Lutsenko compiles on the Bidens—ostensibly for the consumption of Trump and his allies—mentions Joe Biden nineteen times, and his son Hunter not even once.[54]

CHAPTER 16

CROWDSTRIKE, ONYSHCHENKO, AND KOLOMOISKY

After Trump meets with Putin in Hamburg in July 2017, some of his advisers begin to believe that "the president's intense resistance to the [January 2017] assessment of U.S. intelligence agencies that Russia systematically interfered in the 2016 campaign" came from "Putin himself help[ing] spur the idea of Ukraine's culpability."[1] Within ninety days of his meeting with Putin, Trump is directing Mike Pompeo, who is then CIA director, to meet with Bill Binney, "a former U.S. intelligence official who advocates a fringe theory that the hack of the Democrats during the election was an inside job and not the work of Russian intelligence."[2] Binney is, at the time of his subsequent meeting with Pompeo, a contributor to RT, a Kremlin-owned propaganda network the CIA has "recently accused of acting as a propaganda arm for Russia, with the goal of undermining confidence in American democracy."[3] As NBC News notes, "It is extremely unusual for a CIA director to meet with someone like Binney, who for years has accused U.S. intelligence agencies of subverting the constitution and violating the civil rights of Americans. . . . American officials of all political persuasions say his allegations about the NSA are false."[4]

The CrowdStrike conspiracy theory that Trump's suspicion of Ukraine alludes to holds, according to a *Washington Post* debunking of it, that "the FBI never took physical possession of the servers at the DNC that were hacked [in 2016]," and instead a "Ukrainian" cybersecurity company, CrowdStrike, did so, with a single master server remaining to this day in its possession.[5] The *Post* explains everything wrong with the president's theory: "The 'server' Trump is obsessed with is actually 140 servers, most of them cloud-based"; the servers are "not in Ukraine," but "in Washington, displayed at the DNC's offices beside a filing cabinet the Watergate burglars pried open in 1972"; "the FBI felt it was not necessary to enter the DNC's premises [in June 2016] and take custody of the affected servers, as agents were able to obtain complete copies of forensic images made by CrowdStrike, which first identified that the DNC had been hacked by Russian operatives"; "CrowdStrike co-founder Dimitri Alperovitch is a cyber and national security expert who was born in Russia and now is a U.S. citizen"; "[Alperovitch] is not Ukrainian"; and "CrowdStrike is a California company, founded in 2011 in Sunnyvale."[6] The paper adds that "special counsel Robert S. Mueller III's investigation confirmed CrowdStrike's findings" regarding the source of the DNC hack, "and even indicted 12 Russian intelligence officers in 2018 over their alleged role in the breach."[7]

Beyond conspiracy theories relating to CrowdStrike, Burisma, the "black ledger," and Alexandra Chalupa's work as a DNC consultant, the Kremlin advances several other election-year and post-election schemes to bolster the legitimacy of Trump's candidacy and subsequent presidency, distract attention from its own 2016 malfeasance, and set the table for continued interference in U.S. politics following Trump's inauguration. One such scheme involves a Trump business associate named Oleksandr Onyshchenko, who in 2016 flees Ukraine following allegations that he has embezzled $64 million from a Naftogaz subsidiary.[8] The owner of the Miss Ukraine pageant from 2009 to 2012 and a visitor to Mar-a-Lago for meetings with Trump at least twice between 2010 and 2011, Trump's acquaintance is "a former member of ousted Kremlin-backed Ukrainian President Viktor Yanukovych's Party of Regions . . . [and is] also accused by Ukraine's Security Service of treason . . . [for] allegedly helping Russian intelligence destabilize Ukraine"—allegations consistent with the Kremlin's long-standing use of Naftogaz as a money spinner.[9]

After fleeing Ukraine, Onyshchenko becomes "known in Ukraine as a vocal critic of financier George Soros and of the Obama administration ... [He also] defends former Ukrainian prosecutors Lutsenko and Viktor Shokin ... [and] echoe[s] claims made by Giuliani that the U.S. Embassy in Kyiv worked against Trump's campaign in the 2016 election, claiming evidence against former Trump campaign chairman Paul Manafort was fabricated."[10] Having publicly broadcast his support of the "black ledger" and Chalupa conspiracy theories, Onyshchenko will also peddle a Burisma conspiracy theory, "claim[ing] to have dirt on a company linked to the Bidens"; specifically, Onyshchenko will allege in November 2019 "that 'there were "official" and "unofficial" payments to the Biden family' made by Burisma and that an FBI agent 'directed the coverup of the Biden scandal [in 2015], in concert with the U.S. embassy in Kyiv, and other Deep State American government assets "in-country."'"[11]

Investigating Onyshchenko's pre-election claims regarding corruption in the Poroshenko administration, federal law enforcement will conclude, according to the *Daily Beast*, that "Onyshchenko appeared to want to share information in hopes of obtaining a visa to travel to the U.S.," and that his "allegations were widely seen in Ukraine as part of a Kremlin-orchestrated disinformation campaign meant to undermine the Ukrainian government as it sought to strengthen ties with the West."[12] After its initial meeting with Onyshchenko, the FBI will decline to meet with him further—put off, per the *Daily Beast*, by the Trump associate's "fantastic claims," which include an allegation, offered without evidence, that "Burisma had paid $10 million to Hillary Clinton's presidential campaign through 'big bags of cash' sent instead of wire transfers."[13]

The *Kyiv Post* calls Onyshchenko "a criminal suspect, wanted by anti-corruption investigators for allegedly organizing a $125-million fraud scheme in the country's natural gas sector," who "to avoid the charges, which [he] called political persecution ... left Ukraine, initially for Russia."[14] The *Post* reveals, moreover, that rather than having exposed corruption within Burisma that inculpates the Bidens, Onyshchenko is suspected by Ukrainian authorities of Burisma-related corruption himself, having inexplicably self-published "audio recordings of his conversations with [former Ukrainian president] Poroshenko. . . . In one of the recordings, he asks Poroshenko to help [Burisma founder and owner] Mykola Zlochevsky."[15] The Obama-Biden administration had, in its second term, temporarily withheld aid to Ukraine in part to ensure that an investigation of Burisma's Zlochevsky would proceed; Viktor Shokin, defended ardently by Onyshchenko in public, was fired from his post as Ukraine's prosecutor general in large part because, like Onyshchenko, he did not want to see Zlochevsky prosecuted.[16] The *Post* notes in November 2019 that Ukrainian prosecutors have now seized funds from Onyshchenko that he had squirreled away in "the Russian state-owned VTB bank—currently under EU and U.S. sanctions . . . [as well as] a branch of SEB bank in Estonia. [SEB] has reportedly been systematically used for Russian and Eastern European money laundering in recent years."[17] According to the *Kyiv Post*, which notes that Onyshchenko is publicly "a supporter of Trump," Onyshchenko's alleged crime was "coordinat[ing] a scheme that stole state funds during the extraction and sale of natural gas," an "alleged $125-million . . . fraud [that] took place during a joint venture with Ukrgazvydobuvannia, the country's largest gas extraction company and a fully-owned subsidiary of state-owned energy giant Naftogaz. According to NABU, Onyshchenko's accomplices, employees at Ukrgazvydobuvannia, allowed the sale of gas at cheap prices to intermediary companies associated with Onyshchenko, which then resold it at market prices, pocketing the difference."[18] If this is true, Onyshchenko's activities echo those of another Kremlin- and Trump-linked Ukrainian oligarch in profound legal difficulty, Dmitry Firtash, who like Onyshchenko has attempted to pass into American political discourse, both directly and through intermediaries, Kremlin-backed conspiracy theories that would bolster Trump's political standing in the United States while implicitly advocating for Putin's continued influence over the Ukrainian energy market.[19] Onyshchenko's claims—none supported by verified, let alone corroborated, evidence—include that "Vice President Biden personally cancelled [Onyshchenko's] U.S. visa."[20]

While Trump's level of familiarity with Onyshchenko, beyond their multiple meetings at Trump's property in Florida, remains unclear, it is noteworthy that during his first phone call with Volodymyr Zelensky, on April 21, 2019, Trump quickly raises his fondness for the beauty pageant contestants that emerged from Onyshchenko's Miss Ukraine operation.[21] As Trump tells the newly elected Ukrainian president, "When I owned Miss Universe, [the Miss Ukraine pageant] always had great people. Ukraine was always well represented."[22]

Shortly after the April 2019 Trump-Zelensky phone call, Lev Parnas and Igor Fruman travel to Israel to meet with longtime Zelensky ally Ihor Kolomoisky. They subsequently seek—unsuccessfully—Kolomoisky's aid in setting up a secret back channel between Trump and Zelensky, proposing Giuliani as a go-between.[23] To prove to Kolomoisky their ties to Trump, Trump Jr., and Giuliani, the two Florida businessmen use as calling cards the selfies they have taken with the three men.[24]

Kolomoisky, at the time under investigation by the FBI for financial crimes, later tells a reporter, "I told [Parnas and Fruman] I am not going to be a middleman in anybody's meetings with Zelensky. . . . Not for them, not for anybody else. They tried to say something like, 'Hey, we are serious people here. Giuliani. Trump.' They started throwing names at me."[25] During their meeting with Kolomoisky, Parnas and Fruman also tell the oligarch that they can ensure a high-level U.S. delegation will attend Zelensky's inauguration if Kolomoisky pays them a quarter of a million dollars—a request that, given Parnas and Fruman's massive donations to Republican causes, raises the possibility that Vice President Pence's attendance in Kyiv for Zelensky's inaugural events was in midspring 2019 being put up for auction by longtime GOP mega-donors who were also agents of the president.[26] Indeed, after Kolomoisky—per his subsequent claims—declines the proposal, he tells a group of friends, "This is going to end up in a bad scandal."[27] Despite Kolomoisky's denial of any intent to connect anyone he knows with Trump, he will, six months after his abortive meeting with Parnas and Fruman in Israel, hire longtime Trump attorney Marc Kasowitz to represent him.[28]

In March 2020, a *Washington Post* report reveals that the recent firing of Ukrainian prosecutor general Ruslan Ryaboshapka—the man responsible for the country's aggressive new "anti-corruption drive"—was orchestrated "by a faction in [President] Zelensky's Servant of the People party that anti-corruption crusaders and political analysts say is close to the powerful oligarch Ihor Kolomoisky."[29]

Despite Washington Republicans' dissemination of the Kremlin-connected CrowdStrike conspiracy theory on Trump's behalf, a November 2019 report finds that in fact the National Republican Congressional Committee—just like the DNC—hired CrowdStrike after it was hacked in 2016, and is still using CrowdStrike in late 2019.[30] In a similar revelation of hypocrisy, the *New York Times* reports, also in late 2019, that a Romanian businessman Giuliani has criticized Hunter Biden for working for is in fact someone for whom Giuliani himself has previously worked.[31]

According to a December 2019 *Washington Post* fact-check, there are "not enough Pinocchios [indicators of deceitful rhetoric] for Trump's CrowdStrike obsession."[32] The *Post* quotes Trump's own former homeland security adviser Thomas Bossert as saying the CrowdStrike conspiracy theory has been "completely debunked," adding that "[this] conspiracy theory has got to go. . . . If [Trump] continues to focus on that white whale, it's going to bring him down."[33]

CHAPTER 17

NUNES AND THE BLT PRIME TEAM

In July 2019, per a CNN report, Joe diGenova, Victoria Toensing, Lev Parnas, and Parnas's business associate David Correia meet with two representatives for Russian-mob-linked Ukrainian oligarch Dmitry Firtash at the Trump International Hotel in D.C. to discuss Firtash's extradition status.[1] Given that diGenova and Toensing will shortly use their legal representation of Firtash to secure an affidavit from former Ukrainian prosecutor general Viktor Shokin alleging crimes by Joe Biden, this meeting—intended to seal diGenova and Toensing as Firtash's new legal counsel—is key to Donald Trump's political future.[2]

It is not the first time diGenova, Toensing, and Parnas have congregated at the Trump International Hotel to discuss matters involving Joe Biden and Donald Trump—nor, apparently, is it even the tenth such meeting.[3] More important, many of these meetings involve at least one representative of House Permanent Select Committee on Intelligence (HPSCI) chairman Devin Nunes (who after the 2018 midterm elections becomes the ranking minority member of the committee). As summarized by *Just Security* based on a bevy of investigative reports by CNN, NBC, the *Washington Post*, CNBC, and the *Daily Beast*, "Rep. Devin Nunes (R-CA) and his top aide, Derek Harvey, have allegedly been working in part with Rudy Giuliani and his associates, including indicted businessman Lev Parnas, to get dirt from Ukraine on Joe Biden and to pursue other discredited conspiracy theories that would benefit President Donald Trump's 2020 re-election campaign."[4] CNN reports that in early 2019 "Parnas became part of what he described as a 'team' that met several times a week in a private room at the BLT [Prime] restaurant on the second floor of the Trump [International] Hotel. In addition to giving the group access to key people in Ukraine who could help their cause, Parnas translated their conversations."[5]

According to the *Washington Post*, the "regular" salon-like gatherings described by CNN are "frequently" attended by Giuliani, Parnas, Fruman, John Solomon, diGenova, and Toensing.[6] Harvey, acting as "Nunes' proxy," "sometimes" joins the group.[7] Phone records will subsequently establish that even when Harvey does not attend the meetings in person, he stays in touch with Parnas by telephone, speaking or attempting to speak to the Florida businessman on—at a minimum—February 1, February 4, February 7, and April 5, 2019.[8]

Another apparent Nunes proxy, Kashyap "Kash" Patel, will speak extensively with Giuliani on May 10, "despite the fact," the *New York Times* notes, "that Mr. Bolton, then the national security advisor [to the president], had said that no one in his office should be talking to Mr. Giuliani"; Patel had transitioned, in February 2019, from working as an aide to Nunes to joining NSC staff working on "issues involving the United Nations and other international organizations." By February 2020, Patel has become a "top adviser" in the Office of the Director of National Intelligence, according to *Politico*.[9]

The *Times* notes the oddness of a former Nunes aide speaking to the president's personal attorney not only after his boss had instructed him not to but under circumstances in which Patel "had no formal responsibility for Ukraine policy."[10] Patel's actions will raise questions from Fiona Hill, a senior Bolton aide, "about whether [Patel] was straying from his official portfolio"; when she asks Bolton aide Charles Kupperman, who will later go to federal court to avoid testifying before Congress about his actions during the Ukraine scandal, "whether Mr. Patel had assumed a role in Ukraine matters," she will "receive[ ] no answer," according to the *Times*.[11] Hill subsequently testifies to Congress, as summarized by *Washington Post* national security reporter Karoun Demirjian, that former Nunes aide Patel was so mysteriously ubiquitous in discussions of Ukraine in the White House that the president actually "thought Kash

Patel was in charge of Ukraine matters at the NSC" instead of the person who actually was, Lt. Col. Alexander Vindman—a development, the *Post* reporter writes, that "mean[s] it seemed Patel . . . was delivering Ukraine info straight to Trump."[12]

According to Joshua Geltzer, Patel's predecessor at the NSC's International Organizations and Alliances directorate, testimony that Patel was heavily involved in "passing negative information about Ukraine" to Trump suggests a "sort of activity . . . wildly outside the scope of anything a counterterrorism senior director at NSC should be spending their time on. What's more, it politicizes a piece of the NSC staff that administrations of both parties have worked for decades to keep as apolitical as possible."[13] Patel had previously helped Nunes write a memo on the Russia investigation that the DOJ termed "extraordinarily reckless" because it included, per *Politico*, "classified information and could harm ongoing investigations."[14] Patel had earlier written another memo urging Nunes to find FBI officials in contempt of Congress for nonproduction of documents, and had secretly traveled to London in 2017 to try to meet with and question former MI6 agent Christopher Steele.[15] The *New York Times* reports that by mid-2019, "White House officials began to suspect [Patel] had won Mr. Trump's ear and had effectively created a back channel to the president that could warp American policy," in part because Patel had "little expertise."[16] Officials became "alarmed" when Trump inexplicably referred to Patel, whose remit did not even tangentially include Ukraine, as one of his "top Ukraine policy specialists" and then, later, as his "Ukraine director."[17] Despite many attempts, the *New York Times* is unable to determine who hired Patel to work for the National Security Council.[18]

When phone records acquired by HPSCI in late 2019 suggest that, separate from events involving the BLT Prime team, "Nunes was in contact with . . . Mr. Parnas"—a fact that, as with Nunes's calls to Giuliani, the *Wall Street Journal* calls "highly unusual"—Nunes responds that "while he did not recall talking with Mr. Parnas, he might well have."[19] "I remember that name now because he has been indicted," Nunes tells Fox News in December 2019.[20] A Parnas attorney, Ed MacMahon, confirms for the *Journal* that "his client's conversations with Mr. Nunes in April were focused on corruption investigations in Ukraine."[21] "They weren't talking about where to find sushi in Kyiv," MacMahon remarks dryly.[22] According to another Parnas attorney, Joseph Bondy, "Devin Nunes was definitely part of an attempt to gather information about the Bidens. He was definitely involved in Ukraine. He definitely had involvement in the GOP shadow diplomacy efforts in Ukraine, contrary to his claims."[23] Oddly, despite the voluminous evidence of his own clandestine contacts with Parnas, Nunes opines to Fox News that the Florida businessman is a "criminal."[24]

CNN reports that the origins of the BLT Prime team lie much further back than March 2019, with Parnas attorney MacMahon telling the cable news channel that Parnas began communicating with Nunes in December 2018—the same month Joe Biden called himself "the most qualified person in the country to be president"—during which period Parnas "worked to put Nunes in touch with Ukrainians who could help Nunes dig up dirt on Biden and Democrats in Ukraine"; Parnas's efforts involved not just setting up calls but face-to-face meetings—culminating, per Parnas, in Nunes making a December 2018 trip to Vienna to meet with Viktor Shokin.[25] In turn, Nunes told Parnas to work with intermittent BLT Prime team member Derek Harvey on all matters relating to Ukraine.[26]

At Nunes's meeting in Vienna with Shokin, according to MacMahon, Nunes "told Shokin of the urgent need to launch investigations into Burisma, Joe and Hunter Biden, and any purported Ukrainian interference in the 2016 election."[27] If true, this account moves from March 2019 to somewhere between November 30 and December 3, 2018—the range of dates within which Nunes is said to have met with Shokin overseas—the earliest date at which top politicos in Ukraine may have known that Trump's allies in Congress were seeking new evidence against Trump's chief political rival.[28] Whether or not Nunes's movements in Europe were tracked by various European intelligence agencies generally and Ukrainian political operatives specifically, the fact of Nunes making such a trip at all is surprising. In April 2017, he had recused himself from overseeing HPSCI's Russia investigation due to possible ethics charges stemming from conduct eerily similar to what he will stand accused of in 2019: secretly acting as a conduit for sensitive, nonpublic information in an effort to aid Donald Trump's political fortunes.[29]

Equally alarming is Derek Harvey's role as Nunes's proxy on the BLT Prime team. As discussed at length in *Proof of Conspiracy*, Harvey's work in the White House in 2017 as a top aide to Trump national security advisor Michael Flynn—and his work in the West Wing for several months after Flynn's firing—centered on effectuating a multinational pre-election bargain that would have required, as one of its key components, not only the construction of new nuclear reactors across the Middle East but also the acquiescence of Ukraine to the lifting of international sanctions on Russia.[30] Harvey's involvement in attempts to pressure Ukraine in late 2018 and early 2019 thus creates a through line with a similar scheme to approach the beleaguered nation with a dubious and clandestine international agreement in the first half of 2017; whether Harvey's 2017 efforts continued after his July firing by Trump's post-Flynn national security advisor, H. R. McMaster, is unknown.[31]

A further connection between the two schemes involving Harvey comes in the person of NSC legal adviser John Eisenberg. By the end of January 2017, Eisenberg had concluded that Harvey's work in the White House on Flynn's nuclear reactor deal was illegal, just as he would ultimately, in August 2019, support a CIA whistleblower's allegations of illegal conduct in the White House—the latter a complaint that alerted the DOJ and Congress to illegal conduct causally linked to the BLT Prime team, of which Harvey was a member (see chapter 32).[32]

When CNN attempts to question Nunes in the Capitol building about his Vienna meeting and his possible connections to the secretive BLT Prime team, Nunes tells the network's on-site reporter, "I don't talk to you in this lifetime or the next lifetime. At any time. On any question."[33]

In response to a follow-up question from the reporter, Nunes replies, "To be perfectly clear, I don't acknowledge any questions from you in this lifetime or the next lifetime. I don't acknowledge any question from you ever."[34] Nunes's ire aside, CNN's disposition toward Nunes or vice versa is clearly not Nunes's chief concern in rebuffing interview overtures from the network—as he will, in November 2019, refuse to speak even to Fox News about whether he went to Vienna to meet Shokin in late 2018.[35] Nevertheless, there is evidence the 2018 Nunes-Shokin meeting occurred; according to a CNN interview with Parnas's attorney, Joseph Bondy, shortly after December 3, 2018, "Nunes told Parnas that he was conducting his own investigation into the Bidens and asked Parnas for help validating information he'd gathered from conversations with various current and former Ukrainian officials, including Shokin."[36] It is in the week after Nunes's alleged meeting with Shokin in Vienna that Parnas attends a funeral with Giuliani and a Hanukkah party with Giuliani and Trump himself.[37]

Nunes's calls to Giuliani appear to be the most extensive of the many still-unexplained communications uncovered by HPSCI. As the *Wall Street Journal* will report, "the records show that Mr. Nunes was in frequent contact with Mr. Giuliani in early April," noting particularly the calls that occurred "on April 10, three days after John Solomon, a columnist at *The Hill*, published a piece criticizing Ms. Yovanovitch and alleging wrongdoing by Mr. Biden. Mr. Solomon's claims about Mr. Biden, the former vice president who is now a presidential candidate, echoed Mr. Giuliani's calls for an investigation into Mr. Biden and his son."[38] According to AT&T phone records, Nunes and Giuliani either attempted to or successfully reached each other by phone five times on April 10 alone.[39]

Yuri Lutsenko, the source for Solomon's piece about Biden, will later retract his allegations about the former vice president, confessing that he has "no evidence of wrongdoing" by Joe Biden.[40] But that Solomon was in the first instance a member of the BLT Prime team that Nunes proxy Harvey sometimes attended, as well as the fact of Nunes's frequent calls with Giuliani, raises the prospect that Nunes assisted Giuliani and Solomon in spreading what Lutsenko now concedes was disinformation about Biden.[41] This possibility is augmented by the fact that, even as Nunes was in contact with Parnas, Parnas was in contact with Solomon. As the *Wall Street Journal* reports, "In April [2019], Mr. Solomon, the columnist, was in frequent contact with Mr. Parnas, exchanging at least 10 calls in the first week of April alone. . . . The timing of his calls with Mr. Parnas suggests that some of [the] claims [about Biden in Solomon's columns] may have been fueled by Mr. Giuliani's own associates [rather than just Lutsenko]."[42]

In late November 2019, high-ranking Democratic sources in Congress reveal that Nunes is likely to face yet another ethics investigation over his secret meeting with Shokin to develop political dirt on Joe Biden.[43] The clandestine nature of Nunes's actions is underscored when CNBC reveals that Nunes aides were planning to travel to Ukraine in spring 2019—at the height of the BLT Prime team's activities—to speak with two Ukrainian prosecutors, but cancelled the trip when they realized that Rep. Adam Schiff, HPSCI's chairman, would eventually have access to their travel records.[44] Per CNBC, Nunes's office instead asked Parnas to set up Skype meetings between Harvey and the prosecutors.[45] Parnas subsequently does so, with Harvey speaking to Lutsenko deputy Konstantin Kulyk in one March 2019 Skype session and Ukraine's chief anti-corruption prosecutor, Nazar Kholodnytsky, in another.[46] It is during this period that Kulyk's office is producing an encompassing yet false report on Joe Biden that Serhiy Leshchenko will reveal was transmitted to Trump's political operatives—a revelation that suggests one possible topic of discussion for, and outcome of, the Nunes-orchestrated Kulyk-Harvey communication in March 2019.

According to *ProPublica*, Kholodnytsky has in the past been caught on audiotape "coaching a witness to give false testimony and tipping off suspects to police raids. Kholodnytsky acknowledged the tapes were authentic, but said they were taken out of context."[47] Marie Yovanovitch, the U.S. ambassador to Ukraine at the time of the Harvey-Kholodnytsky

Skype meeting, had by then already called publicly, on March 5, for Kholodnytsky to be fired; instead, Trump fired Yovanovitch herself just over a month later (see chapter 20).[48] Kholodnytsky would later meet face-to-face with Giuliani in Paris in May 2019—a meeting neither man will thereafter be willing to discuss with the press.[49] All Kholodnytsky will say now, per *ProPublica*, is that he "had questions about the Bidens as well as the prosecution of former Trump campaign chair Paul Manafort."[50]

By September 2019—after Trump and Giuliani's scheme to pressure Zelensky into interfering in the 2020 presidential election has been uncovered—Kholodnytsky will be telling a different story on the Bidens, explaining to Novoye Vremya radio, according to a Reuters account, that "Ukraine would open an investigation into the period when Hunter Biden was involved with Burisma if there were compelling new testimony in Ukraine," but clarifying that there is not any such evidence, and that Ukrainian prosecutors cannot open such an investigation "based solely on comments currently being made in the United States."[51] Kholodnytsky reveals that not only is there "no active investigative work" related to Burisma in Ukraine, but "detectives and prosecutors do not understand what they are supposed to be investigating."[52]

In late November 2019, CNN reports that Nunes is "not required to disclose the exact details" of the trip to Europe he is confirmed to have made with three aides during Congress's 2018 post-Thanksgiving recess, a trip during which he allegedly met Shokin.[53] Parnas tells Congress that he is willing to testify under oath that Shokin told him he met with Nunes; Shokin, who cannot readily be questioned by federal law enforcement because he is in Ukraine, claims in response that he's never heard Nunes's name before.[54] Parnas thereafter reveals through his attorney, however, that Harvey confessed to him that Nunes "sequenced this trip [to Vienna] to occur after the mid-term elections yet before Congress' return to session, so that Nunes would not have to disclose the trip details to his Democrat colleagues in Congress."[55]

CHAPTER 18

SOLOMON

In July 2017, just a few weeks after the federal investigation of Russian election interference expands to include Trump as a potential target—with the special counsel considering possible obstruction of justice charges against the president—John Solomon is hired by *The Hill*.[1] Solomon, who has previously worked for the conservative *Washington Times* as well as the *Washington Post* and the Associated Press, and who by late 2019 will be working for Fox News, is the reporter-cum-editorialist who in spring 2019, according to *ProPublica*, "set[s] off the impeachment inquiry into [President Trump]" by secretly working with Trump allies to spread disinformation about Democrat Joe Biden.[2]

Shortly after his hire by *The Hill*, Solomon finds himself embroiled in a scandal involving his inclusion in a news story (written by two of his subordinates) of a statement by the executive director of a conservative organization with which he had just negotiated an advertising deal, without notice to readers of that connection.[3] Solomon's actions, *The Hill* publisher Johanna Derlega will shortly thereafter write to the media outlet's president, Richard Beckman, not only commingle commerce and journalism but "could destroy [*The Hill*]" if discovered.[4] Within six months, *The Hill* has "forced out" Derlega, according to *ProPublica*.[5]

A month later, *The Hill* quietly moves Solomon from its news division to its opinion section, while continuing to permit him to publish articles that present as breaking news.[6] When Solomon's role in the Ukraine scandal is uncovered in 2019, "many of his [by then former] co-workers" at *The Hill* will report that they are "ashamed to be associated with him," according to the *Daily Beast*.[7] Indeed, the *Washington Post* writes that more than a dozen staffers at *The Hill* formally complained about a December 2017 piece by Solomon that criticized women allegedly assaulted or harassed by Trump, a story that, the staffers insisted, per the *Daily Beast*, had deliberately "omitted . . . important context."[8] One co-worker complained in a 2018 memo not just about Solomon's partisanship but that his "stories appear to be repeatedly leaked to a close informal adviser of President Trump (Sean Hannity) ahead of their publication."[9]

That *The Hill* does not fire Solomon for these and other alleged offenses may be partly attributable to the unusually close relationship the owner of *The Hill*, Jimmy Finkelstein, has with Trump. As CNN reports in November 2019, "Finkelstein resides at the nexus of President Trump, Rudy Giuliani, and John Solomon. . . . Finkelstein was Solomon's direct supervisor at *The Hill* and created the conditions which permitted Solomon to publish his conspiratorial stories without the traditional oversight implemented at news outlets. And he has kept a watchful eye on the newspaper's coverage to ensure it is not too critical of the President."[10] The cable news outlet reports that Finkelstein has been "friends with Trump for decades"—indeed, he calls himself a "close friend" of the president—and that Finkelstein's wife is friends with Melania Trump, even as both Finkelstein and his wife are also "close" with Rudy Giuliani.[11] Giuliani, per CNN, regularly spends weekends with his girlfriend at Finkelstein's "Hamptons home."[12] CNN notes further that Solomon had been "personally hired" by Finkelstein over the objections of editors at *The Hill*.[13] The controversial mid-2017 hire comes just a few weeks after the Mueller investigation begins.[14] From the start, CNN reveals, Solomon "reported directly to Finkelstein, allowing him to bypass the outlet's normal editorial process."[15]

In March 2019, according to the *New York Times*, Giuliani "turn[s] to Mr. Solomon . . . with a cache of information he believed contained damaging details about Mr. Biden, his son, Hunter Biden, and . . . [special counsel Mueller's] investigation of Russian interference in the 2016 election."[16] Giuliani will later say that he "turned his stuff over to John Solomon" because the Justice Department was "infected" with Obama loyalists—and therefore the material he uncovered couldn't be given to any federal law enforcement agency.[17] "I had no other choice," Giuliani will tell the *Times*, calling Solomon a "watchdog of integrity" but not explaining why his sensitive and politically explosive material, if it could not go to law enforcement, also could not go to anyone in American media but a minimally supervised op-ed columnist at *The Hill*.[18] The *Times* notes that "media scholars describe the environment that has elevated Mr. Solomon's stories as an information ecosystem entirely sealed off from other news coverage."[19] The *Times* also reports that during the years-long period in which Solomon repeatedly published stories favorable to the president and agreed to publish Giuliani's material about Joe Biden, he "discussed with colleagues a proposal to create a transparency office in the Trump White House . . . colleagues believed he might have wanted to run this office" for the Trump administration.[20] It is unclear if the information transmitted by Giuliani to Solomon in March 2019 is the "Lutsenko dossier"—a discredited document the Ukrainian prosecutor general produces during the several-month period in spring 2019 that he is negotiating a potential six-figure contract with Trump's personal attorney. It is clear, however, that Lutsenko is the primary source of the false intelligence Giuliani provides to *The Hill* as part of his representation of the president.

In late March 2019, Solomon publishes an article claiming that U.S. ambassador to Ukraine Marie Yovanovitch had "privately bad-mouthed Mr. Trump" and provided to Ukrainian prosecutor general Yuri Lutsenko "a list of individuals that Mr. Lutsenko should not prosecute."[21] Lutsenko will subsequently admit that no such list ever existed, but that he had merely been asked "not to target certain [Ukrainian] politicians and activists who worked with the embassy on its anti-corruption efforts"—a roster of persons that, if it existed, would not have included American businessmen like Hunter Biden.[22] Solomon's story about Yovanovitch is amplified with surprising alacrity by Trump's son, Don Jr., who immediately advocates publicly for Yovanovitch's firing.[23] At the White House, the NSC's interagency coordinator for Ukraine, Alexander

Vindman, will see Trump Jr.'s call for Yovanovitch's firing in response to Solomon's article and determine that something "smell[s] really rotten."[24]

During the period Solomon writes his story on Yovanovitch, he is secretly in contact with not only Giuliani but the rest of the BLT Prime team, including Joe diGenova and Victoria Toensing, with whom he would share drafts of stories that used them as sources—a practice the *Times* will subsequently call building "relationships with sources . . . closer than reporters typically get with the people they cover."[25] The BLT Prime team includes, too, Lutsenko's intermediary to the group, Lev Parnas, who helps Solomon set up his interview with the Ukrainian prosecutor. According to *ProPublica*, Lutsenko's false claims about a no-prosecute list "spark[ ] a disinformation campaign alleging Joe Biden pressured Ukrainians into removing a prosecutor [Shokin] investigating a company [Burisma] because of its ties to the former vice president's son."[26] As *ProPublica* summarizes the Solomon-Lutsenko interview and the articles by Solomon that follow, they are "the starting gun that eventually set[s] off the impeachment inquiry" into the actions of President Trump with respect to Ukraine.[27] As important, they use the pretext of misconduct by Yovanovitch as an opportunity to launch a national debate about Joe Biden—who, after "months" of buzz per the *New York Times*, announces his candidacy for president on April 25, 2019, just a few weeks after Solomon's story is published.[28]

It is in March 2019, at a time Lev Parnas is already working with "his partner Igor Fruman . . . [and] the president's personal lawyer, Rudy Giuliani, to promote a story that it was Democrats and not Republicans who colluded with a foreign power in the 2016 election," that Joe diGenova and Victoria Toensing introduce Parnas to Solomon; the duo have at this point been "informally advising" President Trump on legal matters for at least nine months, even as Parnas has been working for future diGenova and Toensing client Dmitry Firtash in an "unspecified capacity" for some length of time.[29]

Parnas's role in facilitating the subsequent Solomon-Lutsenko interview—which, in assailing Joe Biden and Burisma, stands to benefit both Trump and Firtash—is a significant one, with the Soviet-born businessman assisting Solomon with pre-interviews and providing translation services even as Solomon is, in return, "shar[ing] files he obtained related to the Biden allegations" with Parnas.[30] Given that Parnas is doing legal work for Giuliani on Trump's behalf as he receives these files, and that diGenova and Toensing, who will shortly hire Parnas to work for them, are likewise advising Trump on legal matters, it is possible Parnas shares the files on Biden he receives from Solomon with Trump or his legal team—and equally possible that Trump or his lawyers were the source of the files.[31]

After Solomon publishes, with the aid of at least three members of Trump's legal team, his interview with Lutsenko and a series of follow-up columns, Giuliani, per *ProPublica*, publicly praises them.[32] The president himself does so as well, declaring that Solomon "deserve[s] a Pulitzer Prize"—without mentioning, too, that several members of his advisory corps, including his personal attorney, helped coordinate Solomon's report-like op-eds over a period of weeks and even months.[33] Solomon's interview and subsequent columns are thereafter championed by longtime Trump adviser Sean Hannity, Trump friend and onetime candidate for White House press secretary Laura Ingraham, and Fox Business Channel host Lou Dobbs; meanwhile, the opinion of the Trump administration's top State Department official on Ukraine, George Kent, is that Solomon's work—as he will later tell Congress—is, "if not entirely made up in full cloth . . . primarily non-truths and non-sequiturs."[34]

By March 2019, *The Hill* had long been concerned about Solomon's "credibility and conflicts of interest," with his peers at the media outlet raising "alarms" about his conduct as early as January or February 2018, according to *ProPublica*.[35] By the time Solomon alleges the existence of a secret "no-go" list presented to Ukrainian anti-corruption prosecutors by the Obama administration—as well as publishing Lutsenko's claim that he will be "reviving a probe into the Ukrainian natural gas company Burisma Holdings, seeking to determine whether Joe Biden, as vice president, interfered with the initial inquiry [into Burisma] to protect his son Hunter, who sat on Burisma's board"—Solomon is no longer a reporter at The Hill, as Trump's public praise of him will imply, but an opinion columnist.[36]

Lev Parnas had been present in-studio for the Solomon-Lutsenko interview, though why is unclear. Solomon, who now claims he had initially planned to use Parnas as a translator for the interview, ultimately did not end up doing so.[37] While it is diGenova and Toensing who have been most instrumental in connecting Solomon and Parnas and therefore Solomon and Lutsenko, Solomon will ultimately admit that he had first been introduced to Parnas by Pete Sessions, the Republican congressman from Texas who had by then received political donations from both Parnas and Fruman and would, shortly after the publication of the Solomon-Lutsenko interview, again urge President Trump to fire ambassador to Ukraine Marie Yovanovitch. Sessions's first exhortation on this score had come in a 2018 letter to both the White House and State Department that accused Yovanovitch of expressing "disdain" for Trump in private, an allegation the ambassador denies.[38] Despite Solomon's statement that he met Parnas through Sessions, Sessions now claims not to know Solomon.[39]

Sessions's involvement in the Solomon-Parnas association aside, all parties agree that it is Trump legal advisers diGenova and Toensing who "set up [Solomon's] first formal meeting with Parnas."[40] Solomon will claim that he sought out the assistance of diGenova and Toensing—who were also his own personal attorneys at the time—due to concerns about the ethics of reaching out to Parnas himself. According to Solomon, using diGenova and Toensing as intermediaries with Parnas offered an "extra layer of protection" to ensure that "everything was above board" and that "everybody knew about" his communications with Parnas.[41] Solomon will not explain why such precautions were necessary, nor why, in his words, he needed to be "careful" in communicating with either Parnas or Lutsenko.[42]

Solomon now describes his relationship with Parnas in early to mid-2019 as being one in which "Lev would call me and offer things he was hearing on the ground and I would look into some things."[43] As *Pro-Publica* reports, however, the two in fact worked "closely" in spring 2019, so much so that late March 2019 would see Solomon acting as a source for Parnas rather than the other way around: within a week of Parnas securing an interview with Lutsenko for Solomon, Solomon was sending "files via Dropbox to Parnas containing financial records purporting to be connected to Biden's son."[44] The source and authenticity of these files are unknown, but the result of their transmission to Parnas is an apparent quid pro quo in which Solomon provides gas-company-related dirt on the Bidens useful to a Soviet-born businessman seeking to do gas-company-related business in Ukraine, and in return receives "scoops" originating in a foreign nation that not only aid President Trump but raise Solomon's professional profile via public praise from the president.[45] Whether the "advance copy" of at least one "Ukraine-related story" that Solomon provides directly to his attorneys diGenova and Toensing ever makes its way into the hands of another diGenova and Toensing advisee, Donald Trump, is unclear.[46] Solomon will claim that at the time Parnas was assisting him with the Lutsenko interview, he didn't know the Florida businessman was "working for" Trump legal advisers Giuliani, diGenova, and Toensing "in Ukraine"—this despite the fact that the latter two attorneys were in fact Solomon's own attorneys.[47] The end result of these byzantine arrangements is that Trump legal advisers diGenova and Toensing arguably enjoyed attorney-client privilege at both ends of an apparent U.S.-Ukraine quid pro quo that had—at best—a dubious ethical and legal provenance.

According to a *Wall Street Journal* interview with Rudy Giuliani, at some point between March 22 and March 27, 2019, he broaches with his client, Trump, the subject of firing Yovanovitch. The president thereupon "remember[s] he had had a problem with her earlier," noting that he "thought she had been dismissed."[48] While it is unclear what "earlier" problem Trump is referring to, Lev Parnas had directly proposed to Trump that he fire Yovanovitch—a proposal to which Trump quickly assented—in May 2018.[49] After Giuliani raises once again the issue his business associate Parnas had raised with Trump the year before, the president's attorney receives a call from an unnamed "White House official . . . asking him to list his concerns about the ambassador again."[50]

On March 28, Giuliani provides Secretary of State Pompeo with a nine-page report detailing "allegations of impropriety against Ms. Yovanovitch, including that she was 'very close' to [Joe] Biden"; for reasons that remain unclear, Giuliani includes in his report on Yovanovitch a timeline of seemingly unrelated actions by Joe and Hunter Biden in Ukraine—the implication being that the ambassador's relationship with the former vice president would prevent her from investigating what Giuliani insists is corrupt conduct by Biden and his son.[51] After Pompeo asks Giuliani for additional documentation to prove his claims against Yovanovitch, Giuliani complains—based on what evidence is unclear—that "the president's orders to fire [Yovanovitch] were being blocked by the State Department."[52]

In October 2019, a rumor will surface that Secretary of State Pompeo may have met with Giuliani in Warsaw in February 2019—the same month and city that saw Giuliani meet with Lutsenko for the second time, after which a Solomon-Lutsenko interview was quickly arranged.[53] When a reporter for a Nashville television station asks Pompeo whether such a meeting occurred, Pompeo replies, "I don't talk about who I meet with," and he rebuffs three further attempts by his interviewer to get the question answered.[54] Shortly thereafter, Pompeo accuses the Nashville reporter of "working . . . for the DNC [Democratic National Committee]."[55]

After Yovanovitch is removed from her post in May—three months before the scheduled expiration of her term in Ukraine (see chapter 20)—Trump will claim to reporters that he doesn't know "if I recalled her or somebody recalled her," though he will add, despite this gap in his memory, that he can clearly recall that he "heard very, very bad things about her for a long period of time. Not good."[56]

A November 2019 CNN report will see Trump offering another explanation for his firing of Yovanovitch: that she allegedly refused to hang a picture of him in the U.S. embassy in Kyiv for "a year and a half or two years."[57] Per CNN, however, "there was a worldwide delay in the hanging of Trump's official picture because Trump himself didn't sit for the picture," which resulted in the U.S. embassy in Kyiv not "get[ting] the picture until late 2017"; "so it seems like Trump was at fault for the thing he was blaming Yovanovitch for," CNN concludes.[58] These and other falsehoods together constitute what State Department official David Holmes will testify before Congress was a "barrage of allegations directed at . . . a career ambassador . . . unlike anything I have seen in my professional career."[59] Just so, George Kent will testify to Congress that, as early as March 2019, he perceived Giuliani to be waging a "disinformation" campaign inside the U.S. government.[60] In a similar vein, deputy secretary of state John Sullivan will call what Giuliani and his compatriots did to Yovanovitch a "smear" campaign.[61]

The group of Giuliani associates and other Republicans connected to the smear campaign is surprisingly large. It contains not only former GOP congressman Pete Sessions, Joe diGenova, Victoria Toensing, Lev Parnas, and John Solomon, but also former GOP congressman Robert Livingston (R-LA), who, per foreign service officer Catherine Croft, "repeatedly suggested" in calls to the National Security Council that Yovanovitch be fired, insisting to the NSC—as former representative Connie Mack IV (R-FL) had earlier, on behalf of Viktor Orban—that Yovanovitch was "associated with George Soros."[62] Livingston also contacts federal officials Pompeo, Bolton, Volker, Kent, and Ulrich Brechbuhl, the State Department's counselor—as well as the president himself—to repeat his false claim.[63]

The evidence strongly suggests that Solomon's interview with Lutsenko was the proximate cause of Giuliani's renewed efforts in March 2019 to get Yovanovitch terminated. According to the *Wall Street Journal*, Yovanovitch, who first served as America's second-highest-ranking diplomat in Ukraine under Republican president George W. Bush, had "openly criticized the office of [then–Ukrainian prosecutor general] Lutsenko . . . for its poor anticorruption record."[64] A former Western diplomat in Ukraine will tell the *Journal* that "Lutsenko hated her because she pushed for reforms, especially in the judiciary sector."[65] In his televised interview with Solomon, which appeared on Hill.TV just a few days before Giuliani renewed his push to get Yovanovitch recalled, Lutsenko told the conservative opinion columnist that "from [my] first meeting with the U.S. ambassador in Kyiv, [Yovanovitch] gave me a list of people whom we should not prosecute."[66] Pompeo's State Department will never explain why it permits the recall of Yovanovitch, a puzzling decision given that, as it will tell reporters in response to Lutsenko's allegation of a "do not prosecute list," the Ukrainian prosecutor's allegation is an "outright fabrication."[67]

Yovanovitch's history in public service at the time of her termination is both bipartisan and exemplary. Despite this, *The Hill* broadcasts on March 20 the extraordinary claim—with no evidence behind it beyond Lutsenko's representations—that Yovanovitch has "embezzle[d]" taxpayer funds earmarked for Lutsenko's prosecutor general's office.[68] In fact, according to the State Department, Lutsenko had merely not received certain funds he had wanted and expected from the United States based on its past expenditures on his office; according to the State Department, nearly $4 million in aid was legally and advisedly withheld from Lutsenko because the department had determined that "the political will for genuine reform by successive Prosecutors General [had] proved lacking," leading the State Department to "exercise[ ] our fiduciary responsibility to the American taxpayer and redirect[ ] assistance to more productive projects."[69]

In April 2019, Lutsenko—seemingly confirming the State Department's assessment of his unreliability and dubious integrity—not only retracts all his allegations against both Yovanovitch and Biden but tells a Ukrainian media outlet that, as *ProPublica* summarizes the Ukrainian-language interview, "he himself was the one who asked the U.S. ambassador for the list of supposedly untouchable figures," and that in fact he had seen "no evidence of wrongdoing that would justify an investigation into Biden's son's business dealings in [Ukraine]."[70]

On February 19, 2020, *The Hill* releases a report on John Solomon's Ukraine columns. The report finds that "while Solomon's columns on Ukraine were labeled as opinion, they largely read like news stories," creating a "potential confusion between opinion and news"; *The Hill* further acknowledges that in instances in which Solomon appeared on television to discuss his work for *The Hill*—including in appearances on Fox News—he "was not typically labeled an opinion writer," an error his editors "should have" worked to correct.[71] *The Hill* also found that it had published opinion columns in which Solomon "identified" his own work as "original reporting," an oversight that "len[t] further support to an impression that the columns were more like news stories."[72] The digital media outlet concedes that "Solomon did not report to a specific management official in the newsroom, which was an unusual personnel situation."[73]

As for Solomon's sourcing, *The Hill* self-assessment notes that "in certain columns, Solomon failed to identify important details about key Ukrainian sources, including the fact that they had been indicted or were under investigation. In other cases, the sources were his own attorneys"—a fact the publication notes Solomon "did not disclose" until November 2019, months after his publication of columns that relied on diGenova and Toensing as sources.[74] The report concludes that "the true nature and extent of Parnas's role in Solomon's work remain unclear but potentially troubling."[75]

CHAPTER 19

POROSHENKO AND ARTEMENKO

In January 2017, *Politico* writes that Ukrainian president Petro Poroshenko's "rivals" are "seeking to capitalize on his dicey relationship with Trump's team," adding that "several potential Poroshenko opponents have been through Washington since the election seeking audiences of their own with Trump allies."[1] The digital media outlet reports that some of these attempts to gain access to Trump's allies have been successful.[2] It reports, moreover, that one Poroshenko critic, Yuriy Boyko, has been so set on taking advantage of the frosty Trump-Poroshenko relationship—an apparent by-product of Manafort's false mid-2016 claims of Ukrainian election-meddling—that he is "'willing to pay big . . . a shitton of money'" to "get access to Trump and his inaugural events."[3]

Boyko's fervent efforts to spend lavishly for access to Trump are particularly worthy of note, even if they do not ultimately result in the closeness with Trump allies that other Ukrainians such as Andriy Telizhenko enjoy, because of Boyko's status as a former colleague of Manafort in the Yanukovych administration. Indeed, *Politico* will reveal in January 2017 that Manafort remains a potential power broker within Trump's orbit even as Trump is being inaugurated; the digital media outlet writes that the "Poroshenko regime's standing [with Trump] is considered so dire that [Poroshenko's] allies after the election actually reached out to make amends with—and even seek assistance from—Manafort."[4]

* * *

In June 2019, a tweet by Rudy Giuliani opines about "Biden['s] bribery of [President] Poroshenko."[5] By falsely alleging that Biden and Poroshenko were co-conspirators in a felony prior to the 2016 election, Giuliani provides a likely explanation for Trump's subsequent obsession with a Ukrainian investigation of Biden above and beyond the possibility of Biden being Trump's opponent in the 2020 presidential election: that Trump has become convinced, by Giuliani and Manafort among others, that during the 2016 election Biden was in league with the same Ukrainian president—Poroshenko—who Trump says he believes also tried to assist Clinton in ascending to the presidency.

Trump's animus toward Poroshenko is damaging not only to the Ukrainian president's political standing in Ukraine, but to Ukraine itself. The *New York Times* reports that the Poroshenko administration—in power in Ukraine from June 2014 through May 2019—spent 2017, 2018, and early 2019 doing two things in particular: "desperately [seeking] American help" for Ukraine's "struggle against Russian aggression" and "exchanging political favors" with Trump as part of "an elaborate campaign to win over Mr. Trump" at a time when Trump believed "Ukraine was a nest of Hillary Clinton supporters."[6] The *Times* adds that Poroshenko's sometimes public, sometimes clandestine efforts to appease Trump were far-ranging, and "included trade deals politically expedient for Mr. Trump, meetings with Rudolph W. Giuliani, the freezing of potentially damaging criminal cases and attempts to use the former Trump campaign chairman Paul Manafort as a back channel."[7] The *Times* notes in particular a coal deal Poroshenko pushed with Trump that both was intended to aid the U.S. president politically and moved "unusually fast"; following the deal, Poroshenko hired BGR, a lobbying firm run by former RNC chairman Haley Barbour, to represent Ukraine in its approaches to the Trump administration, thereafter suggesting that Trump appoint a BGR employee, Kurt Volker, to be Trump's special envoy for "settlement talks with Russia."[8]

As for "the multiple trips that Mr. Giuliani and his staff took to Ukraine in 2017," the *Times* observes that they "offered [Poroshenko] another opportunity to influence the Trump administration."[9] Indeed, Giuliani had sufficient "special access" to Poroshenko that, despite being outside the U.S. government, he managed to secure two meetings with the Ukrainian president in 2017.[10] David Ignatius of the *Washington Post* will write that the sequence of events in June 2017 raises the question of whether there was an "implicit understanding that Poroshenko's government would curb its cooperation with the U.S. Justice Department's investigation of Manafort." Indeed, the order of events is telling: Giuliani meets with Poroshenko and Lutsenko and discusses Ukraine's military posture vis-à-vis Russia; Poroshenko takes the four ongoing Manafort investigations away from Horbatyuk and gives them to Lutsenko; Poroshenko, just days later, scores a brief meeting with Trump; and Lutsenko then spikes all four of the Manafort investigations—just as U.S. Javelin missiles are on their way to Ukraine and Mueller is seeking information from Kyiv to assist in his probe of the Trump campaign.[11] Viktor Trepak, the former deputy head of Ukraine's security service, will tell the *Kyiv Post* regarding the Giuliani-Poroshenko-Lutsenko nexus in 2017 and 2018, "It is clear for me that somebody gave an order to bury the black ledger."[12]

Giuliani is not the only Trump emissary Poroshenko meets with privately during the course of his presidency. The *Wall Street Journal* reports that in early 2019, shortly after Parnas and Fruman meet twice with Giuliani and Lutsenko—once in New York and once in Warsaw— the two Florida businessmen meet with the president of Ukraine and (once again) Lutsenko.[13] Within just a few weeks of the Parnas-Fruman-Poroshenko-Lutsenko meeting, per the *Journal*, Lutsenko will say he is "opening an investigation into alleged interference by Ukrainians in the 2016 U.S. election" and has "evidence he want[s] to present to the U.S. Justice Department related to former Vice President Joe Biden and Burisma Group."[14]

This chain of events involving Trump's inner circle and Petro Poroshenko is made more remarkable by the fact it is effectively replicated with Poroshenko's successor, Volodymyr Zelensky (see chapters 23, 24, and 28). As with Zelensky in 2019, the *Wall Street Journal* reports, Poroshenko was in 2017 worried about his political standing at home; was interested in visiting Washington, a possibility he discussed with one of Trump's intermediaries; and was told by Trump's agents that if he were to be invited to the White House for a state dinner, he would afterward need to announce certain investigations demanded by the president.[15] With Poroshenko, this announcement was to occur, per the *Journal*, by the Ukrainian president "'hav[ing] an interview' with a major news out-let . . . '[t]hen he would say [in the interview that] he would investigate meddling in 2016 and the Bidens'"—a mirror image of the Trump team's plan for Zelensky to announce investigations into Clinton and Biden during a September 2019 interview with CNN that Zelensky was pre-pared to conduct in order to win a White House visit.[16]

According to *Politico*, Andrii Artemenko, a "Ukrainian parliamentarian associated with a conservative opposition [anti-Poroshenko] party," not only "[met] with Trump's team during the [2016] campaign" but "per-sonally offered to set up similar meetings" between the campaign and at least one other Ukrainian government official—an effort the digital media outlet reports was "rebuffed" on the Ukrainian side.[17] While Ar-temenko's intention in putting himself forward in this way remains un-clear, some sense of his discussions with Trump's political operation can be found in the way he describes to *Politico* his view of the Poroshenko administration: "They were supporting Hillary Clinton's candidacy [in 2016]," he complains, adding that "they thought Hillary would win" and they "did everything from organizing meetings with the Clinton team, to publicly supporting her, to criticizing Trump."[18] If indeed Artemenko delivered a similar message to candidate Trump, directly or indirectly, during his contacts with the Trump campaign in 2016, it may help to explain, along with Giuliani and Manafort's conspiracy theorizing, the campaign's disposition toward Poroshenko—and its post-election reliance on Artemenko as a conduit to the conservative political opposition in Ukraine.

In January 2017, Artemenko is the bearer of a Russia-Ukraine "peace plan" that is at once approved by top aides to Putin and honors Trump's insistence that direct U.S. involvement in the ongoing Russia-Ukraine war be avoided—a position he first airs at a March 2016 campaign meeting convened immediately after Paul Manafort's hiring, where he demands that the Republican Party platform deny lethal defensive aid to Kyiv to avoid him having to "go to World War III [with Russia] over Ukraine."[19] Artemenko brings the Putin-approved plan to two men well inside Trump's inner circle: Trump's personal attorney, Michael Cohen, who is the president-elect's real estate agent in the Russian market and the son-in-law of a convicted Ukrainian money launderer; and Felix Sater, Trump's unofficial fixer in Moscow and a "convicted felon" with "deep ties to Russia."[20] The intended recipient of the sealed proposal Artemenko is carrying is Trump national security advisor Michael Flynn, who has had repeated contact with Kremlin agents in the preceding year.[21]

As the *New York Times* notes, the true purpose of the so-called peace plan is to "outlin[e] a way for President Trump to lift sanctions against Russia."[22] That it is a Poroshenko political opponent who has been tasked with ferrying a deal Putin has blessed sends a clear message to Trump's inner circle regarding Putin's dim view of Poroshenko; the deal arrives in the White House even as, per *Politico*, the Poroshenko administration's "outreach" to Trump is "ramping up after Trump's victory," with Poroshenko "among the first foreign leaders to call to congratulate Trump."[23] According to *Mother Jones*, later in the Poroshenko administration Artemenko will face "an inquiry by Ukrainian prosecutors into possible treason over his collaboration with Trump associates on the Russia-friendly peace plan."[24] The magazine notes that, in an echo of Giuliani's activities with respect to Joe Biden, Artemenko in 2017 "claims to have evidence of corruption that could oust [Poroshenko], his country's current pro-European president."[25]

By April 2020, Artemenko has become a "business partner" of longtime Trump adviser and donor Erik Prince (see chapter 41)—and, per *Politico*, has elected to hire Giuliani associate Andriy Derkach, who is now going by the name Andy Victor Kuchma, to "lobby Washington on his behalf regarding 'corruption.'"[26] Kuchma, who as Andriy Derkach had repeatedly accused Joe Biden of corruption in public statements, registers to lobby the U.S. government on the subject of "corruption" on "the same day that Joe Biden [becomes the] Democratic Party's presumptive nominee."[27]

CHAPTER 20

YOVANOVITCH

In May 2018, Parnas and Fruman decide that U.S. ambassador to Ukraine Marie Yovanovitch is an "obstacle to their business ventures," and begin to put "illegal donations behind their push to oust her," according to the October 2019 federal indictments against them.[1] By June 2018, Parnas and Fruman's business associate Rudy Giuliani has begun reaching out to officials in Ukraine about Yovanovitch—overtures that, Ukrainian officials will tell Yovanovitch, they "[don't] know how to understand."[2] Parnas and Fruman also donate a substantial sum to an entity linked to Rep. Pete Sessions, and convince Sessions to send a letter to the State Department demanding Yovanovitch's ouster.[3] More than just Parnas, Fruman, Giuliani, and Sessions, however, there are also, per the federal indictment against the first two men, "one or more Ukrainian government officials" who have become invested in the matter of Yovanovitch's dismissal; indeed, one of Yuri Lutsenko's deputies will tell Yovanovitch that the first meeting between Lutsenko and Giuliani in fact occurred in June 2018—a claim broadly confirmed by Joseph Pennington, then–chargé d'affaires in Kyiv for the U.S. State Department, who tells Yovanovitch in 2019 that the first Giuliani-Lutsenko meeting came in "the middle of 2018."[4]

That Yovanovitch, the U.S. ambassador in Ukraine since August 2016 and a nonpartisan public servant under six presidential administrations—four of them Republican—should be treated this way is extremely unusual.[5] Indeed, it is notable that none of the upset toward the ambassador comes from her supervisors at the State Department; in fact, in March

2019 the department asks her to extend her tour in Kyiv until August 2020.[6]

According to deputy secretary of state John Sullivan, the "concerted campaign" to remove Yovanovitch begins in the summer of 2018.[7] In fall 2019 testimony before Congress, the ambassador will attribute the campaign against her, in part, to corrupt Ukrainian officials "selling baseless conspiracy theories to anyone who would listen," adding that "someone"—Giuliani—was ultimately revealed to be "listening."[8] Subsequent evidence suggests that other, nongovernmental U.S. sources also played a significant role in Yovanovitch's firing, such as Trump legal adviser Joe diGenova; diGenova falsely claims in an interview with Fox News' Laura Ingraham shortly after the ambassador's termination that Yovanovitch "is known and reported by people [in Kyiv] to have bad-mouthed the President of the United States, Donald Trump, to have told Ukrainians not to listen to him or obey his policy because he was going to be impeached. And finally her activities have caught up with her."[9]

Yovanovitch first learns from Ukrainian officials that Giuliani is in contact with Lutsenko in November 2018. Although not a lawyer, Lutsenko had been permitted to serve as prosecutor general by a special vote of Ukraine's governing body, the Rada.[10] Per Yovanovitch, officials in Kyiv tell her in late 2018 that Giuliani and Lutsenko "had plans, and that they were going to . . . do things, including to me."[11]

Lutsenko had come into office in May 2016 with three goals, none of which involved Yovanovitch: to reform the prosecutor general's office; to prosecute a series of homicide cases stemming from the 2014 Euromaidan Revolution; and finally and most controversially, to "prosecute money laundering cases to get back the $40 billion-plus that the previous president [Yanukovych] and his cronies [a group allegedly including Paul Manafort] had absconded with" after the revolution.[12] Lutsenko's stewardship of the prosecutor general's office therefore risked, at its start, threatening a longtime associate of President Trump. In the event, Lutsenko takes no steps toward prosecuting Manafort in his nearly three and a half years in office.

* * *

In February 2019, a Ukrainian official, interior minister Arsen Avakov, tells Yovanovitch that she must "watch [her] back," as there are "two individuals from Florida, Mr. Parnas and Mr. Fruman, who [are] working with Mayor Giuliani . . . [and] they [are] interested in having a different ambassador at [the] post [in Kyiv] . . . because they want[ ] to have business dealings in Ukraine, or additional business dealings."[13] The sudden appearance of Parnas and Fruman on the diplomatic landscape in Ukraine confounds the embassy in Kyiv, Yovanovitch will later tell Congress, as "nobody at the embassy had ever met those two individuals."[14] Embassy officials later learn that the business Parnas and Fruman were hoping to do in Ukraine is, if legitimate, just the sort the embassy promotes; per Yovanovitch, an open letter she received at the time from Ukrainian energy company executive Dale Perry confirmed that Parnas and Fruman "had energy interests that they were interested in . . . [specifically] selling [American] LNG to Ukraine," and, as Yovanovitch will later tell Congress, "that's like apple pie [and] motherhood [to the embassy] . . . obviously [the embassy] would support exporting LNG to Ukraine."[15] Both the United States and Ukraine support increasing U.S. exports of LNG to Ukraine because doing so reduces Ukraine's reliance on Russia, Yovanovitch testifies.[16]

Avakov declines to meet with Giuliani in January 2019, despite Giuliani's eagerness to do so, "because of his concerns about what they [Giuliani, Parnas, and Fruman] were doing," which he considers "very dangerous" because it would see the Ukrainian government "kind of getting into U.S. politics, into U.S. domestic politics, [which] was a dangerous place for Ukraine to be."[17] Specifically, Avakov reports to Yovanovitch that Giuliani's chief interest is in "Mr. Manafort's resignation from the Trump campaign as a result [of the 'black ledger']" and "looking into . . . how did all of that come about[,] the issue of whether . . . it was Russia collusion or whether it was really Ukraine collusion" that occurred during the 2016 presidential campaign.[18] Giuliani expresses to Avakov his belief that, "looking forward to the 2020 election campaign . . . [,]

this [alleged 2016 collusion between the Democrats and Ukraine] would somehow hurt former Vice President Biden" in his bid for the White House, a sentiment that underscores that Giuliani's focus at the beginning of 2019 is not on fighting corruption in Ukraine but on amplifying his client Donald Trump's 2020 political prospects.[19]

At the time Giuliani is making his initial entreaties to Avakov and others in the Ukrainian government, President Poroshenko is polling poorly in his bid for reelection—an election he will ultimately lose, and resoundingly, to Volodymyr Zelensky in late April 2019.[20] Ambassador Yovanovitch will tell Congress that Poroshenko's cabinet officials believed in early 2019 that if they acceded to Giuliani's wishes with respect to investigations of Clinton and Biden, "there was always a hope that President Trump would endorse President Poroshenko. . . . Mr. Lutsenko was hoping that maybe, as a result of providing information that [was] of interest to Mr. Giuliani, that maybe there could be an endorsement."[21] It is unknown whether Lutsenko discusses with Giuliani the possibility of a Trump endorsement of Poroshenko when he makes a "private visit" to the United States to meet with the president's personal attorney in January 2019.[22] Ambassador Yovanovitch will later testify under oath, however, that "there was a rumor [at the U.S. embassy] in Kyiv that during the meeting between . . . Mayor Giuliani and Mr. Lutsenko in January . . . the President got on the line" and joined their conversation.[23] Yovanovitch's testimony raises the troubling possibility that the fraudulent Lutsenko dossier—the contents of which were used to oust Yovanovitch in spring 2019, justify Trump's extraordinary demands of President Zelensky in summer 2019, and bludgeon the Democratic Party's presidential nominee throughout 2020—was in fact provoked, in the first instance, by not just Giuliani but Trump himself, and under circumstances in which Lutsenko sought to pursue a contractual relationship with Giuliani in order to retrieve funds that only Trump's personal intervention could release. This scenario, the subject of the "rumor in Kyiv" testified to under oath by Yovanovitch, would likely constitute an act of impeachable bribery.

* * *

On March 5, 2019, Ambassador Yovanovitch calls for the firing of Nazar Kholodnytsky, the special anti-corruption prosecutor for NABU and someone *ProPublica* describes as one of Giuliani's "questionable friends in Ukraine"; Yovanovitch's demand is prompted by Kholodnytsky—a Lutsenko deputy—having been accused of coaching criminal suspects prior to their interrogations.[24] Yovanovitch's position angers Lutsenko but causes no upset at the State Department. Indeed, on March 7, just forty-eight hours after Yovanovitch initiates her campaign against Kholodnytsky, the department's undersecretary for political affairs, David Hale, asks her to extend her service in Kyiv through mid-2020.[25]

According to Yovanovitch, though Lutsenko begins telling "falsehoods" about her in November 2018, and exhibiting increasing hostility toward her in early 2019, the turning point in her relationship with the Ukrainian prosecutor general comes in March 2019, when Lutsenko sits for an interview with John Solomon.[26] By then, he and Yovanovitch have not met for many months, with their last communication coming "in the fall of 2018," per Yovanovitch.[27] Instead of meeting with America's ambassador in Ukraine, Lutsenko spends this time, according to Yovanovitch, saying to other U.S. officials that he wants to "set up meetings [in the United States] with the Attorney General . . . [and] with the Director of the FBI," each time averring that he has "important information for them."[28] The U.S. embassy denies these requests because, as Yovanovitch explains to Congress, "we just don't do that. . . . [W]hat we kept on encouraging him to do was to meet with the legat, the legal attaché, the FBI at the embassy. That is precisely why we have the FBI in countries overseas, to work with host country counterparts and get information."[29]

Neither Yovanovitch nor any of her staff ever learn why Lutsenko wanted only to speak to President Trump's political appointees rather than career civil servants or FBI agents who had worked for the Bureau across multiple administrations of both parties. As Yovanovitch will testify in 2019, however, Lutsenko "clearly wanted to work around the system where . . . there's less transparency, there are more opportunities to . . . kind of fiddle [with] the [U.S. diplomatic] system."[30] The problem for Lutsenko, as Yovanovitch will tell Congress, is that while he will develop ready access to Giuliani in 2018, no part of "what Mr. Giuliani was discussing and what his interests were" was "consistent" with the policy of the United States government and its State Department.[31] Indeed, Giuliani's claims about Yovanovitch and U.S. actions in Ukraine, which "shock" American diplomats in Kyiv, are considered so nakedly "political" yet "completely mysterious" by high-level embassy staffers that they won't discuss them via cables, lest the whole embassy "lose [its] credibility" by doing so.[32]

On Sunday, March 24, not long after the Lutsenko interview with *The Hill* is published, David Hale asks Yovanovitch to write him a classified email memorializing her "understanding of what was going on [with Giuliani, Parnas, and Fruman] . . . [and] why people were doing" what they were doing with respect to back-channeling the Ukrainian government.[33] Hale's request and Yovanovitch's classified response are prompted in part by a tweet from Donald Trump Jr. on March 24, in which he refers to Yovanovitch as a "joker" and implies she should be removed from office.[34] According to Yovanovitch, when "you have the President's son saying . . . we need to pull these clowns, or however he referred to me, it makes it hard to be a credible ambassador in a country."[35] Yovanovitch asks Hale to issue a public statement of support for her, but he does not do so; she speaks with acting assistant secretary Phil Reeker instead, and he informs her that the State Department cannot issue a statement because any statement it issued "could [thereafter] be undermined by the President."[36]

Shortly after Lutsenko's interview with Solomon is published in *The Hill*, there are two phone calls between Rudy Giuliani and Yovanovitch's boss, secretary of state Mike Pompeo. Between the two calls, Giuliani delivers a packet of information directly to Pompeo's hands at the State Department—a packet a whistleblower in the department subsequently hands over to Congress through the State Department's inspector general.[37] On March 29, the day after Pompeo receives the packet, he speaks to Giuliani by phone for twenty minutes; forty-eight hours later, he speaks to Nunes for twenty minutes.[38] Subsequent records releases will reveal that Pompeo and Giuliani spoke repeatedly in spring 2019, with Giuliani reaching the head of the State Department at least once through Trump's then-assistant Madeleine Westerhout.[39]

When the State Department responds, in June 2019, to two congressional inquiries about why Yovanovitch was removed from her post, the department will dissemble, falsely telling Congress that her departure was intended to "align[ ] with the presidential transition in Ukraine" while failing to note, as reported by *Foreign Policy*, that she had originally been "asked to extend her post into 2020." Moreover, as *Foreign Policy* notes, "it is not common practice for the State Department to switch its ambassadors based on a new foreign leader coming into office."[40] Other State Department emails will reveal that assistant secretary of state for legislative affairs Mary Elizabeth Taylor had asked the department to respond to the inquiries from Congress when they first arrived in April, just after Yovanovitch's firing; instead, the department waited two months to alert Congress to what Pompeo's thinking was in terminating his ambassador to Ukraine.[41]

When they are released by Congress to the public in October 2019, the documents Giuliani sent to Pompeo in March will be revealed as, per *Politico*, nothing more than "debunked conspiracy theories" and "a packet of documents containing misinformation" about Yovanovitch and Hunter Biden.[42] The packet, described as "amateurish" by one congressman who sees it, Jamie Raskin (D-MD), also "include[s] conspiracies about the origins of the Mueller investigation," according to *Politico*.[43] At least one document in the packet, writes the *Daily Beast*, is an advance copy of a John Solomon column that had been sent to Joe diGenova, Victoria Toensing, and Lev Parnas—all members, with Solomon and Giuliani, of the BLT Prime team.[44] Oddly, many of the documents in the packet have "manufactur[ed] White House logos" on them despite not being government documents or originating in the White House.[45] Giuliani has also included in his otherwise anonymously packaged submission to Pompeo "folders from a Trump-owned hotel," though whether it is the Trump International Hotel in D.C.—the home base of the BLT Prime team—or another Trump-branded property is unclear.[46]

Pompeo distributes Giuliani's disinformation to top officials at the State Department, while waiting more than a month to provide them to the department's inspector general.[47] That the course of lobbying in Ukraine Rudy Giuliani has engaged in throughout 2018 is conducted at the behest of the president, and as his agent, is certain—as it is confirmed by Giuliani himself in October 2019, when he tells the *New York Times* that federal prosecutors have "no grounds" to charge him with violations of the Foreign Agent Registration Act because "he was acting on behalf of Mr. Trump . . . when he collected the information on Ms. Yovanovitch and the others [former Vice President Joe Biden and his son Hunter] and relayed it to the American government and the news media."[48]

Despite their implicit or explicit authorization by Trump, Giuliani's allegations against Yovanovitch are considered "so outrageous" by the State Department that it does not confront Yovanovitch with them or express any concern that they may be accurate. The department remains firm in this across multiple conversations between Yovanovitch and her boss, acting assistant secretary Phil Reeker of the department's European bureau, as well as with David Hale and George Kent.[49] That the department is not convinced by Giuliani's late March packet of disinformation is underscored by the fact that on April 1, either Secretary Pompeo or someone "in his inner circle" calls Fox News' Sean Hannity—a Yovanovitch critic and, per White House officials who speak to NBC News, Trump's "shadow chief of staff"—to ask him to either provide proof of Giuliani's allegations or "stop" making them.[51] There are no reports of proof subsequently being provided by Hannity to the State Department.

In the final week of March 2019, several days after John Solomon's interview with Lutsenko and Trump Jr.'s tweet about removing Yovanovitch, the ambassador is told by Reeker that the extension of her tour until 2020 must be cancelled and a date for her departure from Ukraine set.[52] Reeker implies, however, that Yovanovitch will be able to stay on through July 4.[53]

On April 21, 2019, Volodymyr Zelensky resoundingly defeats Petro Poroshenko in the Ukrainian presidential election. The U.S. embassy in Kyiv, led by Yovanovitch, has been urging the White House to be prepared to call Zelensky for a week, knowing that a lopsided victory for the onetime comedian is imminent. However, when Trump calls Zelensky on the night of April 21, not only is Yovanovitch not on the call, she is not permitted to assist the president in preparing for the call and is given no transcript or even a readout of the call's contents.[53]

On the morning of April 24, Giuliani appears on the Fox News morning program *Fox & Friends* to tell America to "keep your eye on Ukraine."[54] He also calls the Mueller investigation a "frame-up" of Trump; says "rogue counterintelligence guys" personally "set up" former Trump national security adviser George Papadopoulos's arrest and Donald Trump Jr.'s clandestine mid-campaign meetings with Russian nationals; alleges that it was "in Ukraine [that] a lot of the dirty work was done" and that there was "collusion" and "conspiracy" between Democrats and the Ukrainians during the 2016 election; and speaks optimistically of the commencement of investigations in Ukraine into both Clinton and Biden.[55] Giuliani also expresses, at length, his outrage at Paul Manafort's treatment at the hands of the special counsel's office, opining that during the Clinton investigation "nobody tried to turn them [witnesses in the Clinton case] the way they put Manafort in jail and in solitary confinement to turn him. They used every lever at their disposal to get him. It was an enthusiastic, over-zealous, I believe unethical, group of prosecutors—some of them with a long history of lack of ethics—and they still couldn't get him. . . . So they had to throw all this garbage out, and then leave a lot of facts out."[56]

A few hours later, at 2:45 PM EST (9:45 PM in Kyiv), Yovanovitch gets a call from Carol Perez, the director general of the State Department, who tells the ambassador that "things [are] going wrong" and "off the track" and that it is resulting in "a lot of nervousness" at the White House.[57] Perez calls again at 1:00 AM Kyiv time to tell Yovanovitch that she "need[s] to be on the next plane home to Washington" because there is "a lot of concern for [her]" in D.C. and the concern relates to her "security" and her "well-being."[58] Perez indicates that the situation is sufficiently dire that the State Department cannot give her time to pack her belongings—and that once she leaves Kyiv, she will not be able to return to retrieve them.[59] The *Wall Street Journal* will subsequently confirm that what has happened in Washington is that Trump has "ordered" Yovanovitch's "removal" from her post.[60] Trump will later say that "I really don't know [Yovanovitch]. . . . I just don't know much about her" and that "I don't know if I recalled her or somebody [else] recalled her."[61]

The next night, on April 25, Trump appears on his domestic policy adviser Sean Hannity's Fox News show.[62] Hannity leads with Ukraine, referencing John Solomon's interview with Lutsenko from a month earlier.[63] Trump says that "big, big stuff" is happening in Ukraine, and references his April 21 call with Zelensky; when Hannity falsely alleges that Ukraine is "offering this evidence to the United States" that "they colluded on behalf of Hillary Clinton's campaign in 2016," Trump says that America needs to see that evidence and adds, referencing attorney general William Barr, that "I would imagine he'd want to see this [evidence]. People have been saying—this whole concept of Ukraine—they've been talking about it actually for a long time."[64] Later in the interview he adds, "I want to find out what's on that server, the DNC server. Because that's the big thing. Nobody's seen that server yet."[65] "There's no collusion [between the Trump campaign and Russia] and there's no obstruction," Trump tells Hannity, "[and] now it's time to look at the other side."[66]

When Yovanovitch returns to D.C. on April 25, she is told by Reeker that the president has wanted her gone from Ukraine "since July of 2018."[67] On April 29, deputy secretary of state John Sullivan tells Yovanovitch that, despite her recall from Kyiv, "you've done nothing wrong. . . . [I've] had to speak to ambassadors who [have] been recalled for cause before and this [i]s not that."[68] Yovanovitch's response to Sullivan, as described in her October 2019 testimony to Congress, bears repeating: "I did ask [Sullivan]," Yovanovitch testifies, "what does this mean for our foreign policy? What does it mean for our position on anticorruption? What message are we sending to the Ukrainians, [and] to the world? How [a]re we going to explain this? And what are we going to say, not only to the people at U.S. Embassy Kyiv, but more broadly to the State Department? And I told him I thought that this was a dangerous precedent—that as far as I could tell, since I didn't have any other explanation, that private interests and people who don't like a particular American ambassador . . . [had] combine[d] to find somebody who was more suitable for their interests."[69] Sullivan replies, per Yovanovitch, "[I'll] have to think about that."[70]

By early May, Yovanovitch has still received no correspondence from Secretary of State Pompeo—nor will she ever—and when she requests a meeting with Ulrich Brechbuhl, the chief intermediary between Reeker and Pompeo, Brechbuhl denies her request.[71] Meanwhile, Giuliani spends May 2019 making public allegations against her, accusing her of being "part of the efforts against the president"; in Yovanovitch's testimony to Congress, she will report that she "had no idea what he was talking about" in May 2019 and still does not.[72]

Zelensky's defeat of Petro Poroshenko on an anti-corruption platform notwithstanding, the U.S. embassy in Kyiv had adjudged the Poroshenko administration generally opposed to systemic corruption. According to Yovanovitch, "there were more reforms in Ukraine during President Poroshenko's term than, frankly, under all the preceding [four Ukrainian] presidents."[73] The U.S. embassy had also determined, however, that "as time passed, the old system [of patronage] wasn't as scared anymore [of legal liability] as they were in 2014, as they felt there was more space to pursue their own interests, [so] it became harder to pursue [anti-corruption] reforms and there was less interest [from Poroshenko]. . . . [S]o there was a kind of slowing down [in Poroshenko's anti-corruption agenda]."[74] Yovanovitch notes that the "slowing down" had begun, in fact, in 2016, just two years into Poroshenko's term, so by the time Giuliani, Parnas, and Fruman began reaching out to the Poroshenko government in 2018, there was already "a sense in the country that [Poroshenko] was attending to his own personal interests as well, and people didn't appreciate that."[75] In the view of the U.S. embassy, and contrary to the claims of Trump's agents, after his inauguration in May 2019 the new Ukrainian president "brought back again" some of the anti-corruption prosecutors and personnel who had originally come into office "in the early days after the Revolution of Dignity"—a decision that, per U.S. officials, signaled Zelensky's earnest commitment to fighting the corruption of the Poroshenko administration's later years.[76]

Zelensky immediately faces serious obstacles upon his election in late April, however. As reported by the Associated Press, within a matter of days officials at the U.S. embassy in Kyiv have been informed by Zelensky's office that the new president is "seeking advice on how to navigate the difficult position" he finds himself in, as he is "concerned President Donald Trump and associates [are] pressing him to take action that could affect the 2020 U.S. presidential race."[77] The Associated Press report confirms that one of the key Republican defenses of Trump during the fall 2019 impeachment inquiry—that at no point did Zelensky feel pressure from Trump—is untrue.[78] Indeed, on May 7 Zelensky meets with aides Andriy Yermak and Andriy Bohdan, Naftogaz CEO Andriy Kobolyev, and the sole American member of Naftogaz's supervisory board, Amos Hochstein, to "talk about political problems with the White House."[79] According to internal notes at the State Department, "Zelensky tried to mask the real purpose of his May 7 meeting . . . by saying it was about energy."[80] The AP reveals that, in fact, Zelensky and the assembled group "spent most of the three-hour discussion talking about how to navigate the insistence from Trump and his personal lawyer Rudy Giuliani for a probe [of Biden] and how to avoid becoming entangled in the American elections."[81] At least one person familiar with the May 7 meeting will tell the AP that during the discussion Zelensky "specifically cited [his] first call with Trump [on April 21, 2019] as the source of his unease."[82] It remains unclear whether, at the time of this emergency meeting in early May 2019, Zelensky was aware that Lutsenko had already acceded to Trump's and Giuliani's wishes and initiated a wide-ranging investigation of Joe Biden.

After the May 7 meeting, Hochstein briefs Suriya Jayanti and Joseph Pennington, two U.S. embassy officials. Both officials take contemporaneous notes of what Hochstein says, thereby generating documentary evidence of the early start of Trump's high-pressure campaign against Zelensky.[83] Hochstein thereafter travels to Washington to brief Yovanovitch on the pressure being applied to Zelensky by Trump associates; within a week and a half, Yovanovitch has been relieved of her duties as ambassador—a victim of the very Trump associates whose activities Hochstein had just warned her about.[84]

By May 11, the *Washington Post* reports, numerous members of Zelensky's new government, despite having not yet begun their jobs in government, already "fear[ ] they [are] being pulled into a domestic political conflict in the United States, potentially at Ukraine's expense," and are privately telling U.S. media and politicians, "Leave us out of it."[85]

CHAPTER 21

PARNAS

In January 2020, ABC News reports on an April 30, 2018, video recorded by Igor Fruman at a dinner with Trump at Trump International Hotel in Washington.[1] The dinner, an America First Action fundraising event attended by both Fruman and Lev Parnas, comes two weeks after Rudy Giuliani begins working for the president as his legal counsel but before the two Florida businessmen have become Giuliani's employees and members of Trump's legal team.[2]

While it is not until several weeks after the April 30 event that Parnas approaches Rep. Pete Sessions about lobbying Secretary of State Pompeo to have Marie Yovanovitch removed as ambassador to Ukraine—a course of advocacy that reportedly sees a letter from Sessions to Pompeo handed to Trump by Parnas at a June 2018 America First Action event—Parnas's lobbying for Yovanovitch's ouster begins at this April gathering, which includes, among five to eight others, Trump, Trump Jr., and Johnny DeStefano, a Trump political adviser.[3] Per Fruman's video recording of the event, Parnas says to Trump during the dinner, "The biggest problem [in Ukraine], I think where we need to start is, we gotta get rid of the [U.S.] ambassador. She's still left over from the Clinton administration. She's basically walking around telling everybody 'Wait, he's gonna get impeached, just wait.'"[4] In response, Trump says—per a subsequent Parnas interview, while looking at DeStefano—"Get rid of her! Get her out tomorrow. I don't care. Get her out tomorrow. Take her out. Okay? Do it."[5] According to Parnas, on three occasions thereafter Giuliani will say that Trump has ordered Yovanovitch's firing: in one instance Pompeo declines to execute the order; in another, Bolton does the same; and on a third occasion the directive fails because the president has issued it to someone unable to carry it out—his twenty-seven-year-old personal secretary, Madeleine Westerhout.[6]

Other topics of conversation at the intimate April 2018 gathering include subtopics within the ambit of the Ukraine scandal, including Javelin missiles, liquefied natural gas, and the Russia-Ukraine war.[7] During the dinner, Parnas underscores to the president that without U.S. military assistance, Ukraine will be quickly defeated by Russia—proof the president knew in early 2018 that withholding military aid to Kyiv risked disabling Ukraine's defense of its borders.[8]

On January 15, 2020, Parnas gives an interview to MSNBC that introduces substantial new information to the Ukraine investigation. In the interview, the "main lie" Parnas identifies within the Ukraine scandal is the idea "that the president didn't know what was going on. President Trump knew exactly what was going on. He was aware of all of my movements. I wouldn't do anything without the consent of Rudy Giuliani or the president. I have no reason to speak to any of these [Ukrainian] officials [otherwise]. They have no reason to speak to me. Why would President Zelensky's inner circle or Minister Avakov or all these people or President Poroshenko meet with me? Who am I? They were told to meet with me, and that's the secret that they [Trump and Giuliani] are trying to keep. I was on the ground, doing their work."[9] As to Trump's statements about not knowing Parnas or Fruman or being familiar with their work, Parnas tells MSNBC, "He lied. . . . [H]e knew exactly who we were. He knew exactly who I was especially, because I interacted with him at a lot of events. I had a lot of one-on-one conversations with him. . . . And basically I was with Rudy four or five days out of the week. I was in constant contact with them [Giuliani and the president]. I was with Rudy when he would speak to the president [by phone]."[10] Parnas notes that these latter conversations occurred frequently "during the Mueller [investigation]," and that, just as David Holmes had testified before Congress was the case during a July 26 Trump-Sondland call that Sondland made from Kyiv (see chapter 29), when Giuliani was on the phone with Trump "[I] could hear President Trump talking. . . . [The president speaks] very loudly."[11] Parnas's claims of attending several intimate gatherings with Trump and having extended one-on-one conversations with him are subsequently confirmed by additional audio and video recordings; just so, his claims of having attempted to negotiate a quid pro quo with Zelensky's agents on Trump's behalf are confirmed by handwritten notes Parnas took on Ritz-Carlton Vienna stationery at the time of Giuliani's clandestine outreach to Kyiv.[12]

Parnas tells MSNBC that not only did Trump know about "everything" Giuliani was doing in Ukraine, but also that all of it was "about Joe Biden, Hunter Biden, and . . . the Manafort stuff. The 'black ledger.' That was another thing that they were looking into. It was never about corruption."[13] "Nobody cares about Burisma or [former Burisma CEO Mykola] Zlochevsky," Parnas tells MSNBC. "The concern [from Trump and Giuliani] was always Biden and Hunter Biden."[14] Parnas echoes Lutsenko's eventual acknowledgment that Biden had done nothing wrong with respect to Ukraine, telling MSNBC that in his view Biden sought only "to protect our country and get rid of a crooked [Ukrainian] Attorney General [Shokin]."[15]

Parnas confirms that he was both Giuliani's client as well as his authorized agent in Giuliani's capacity as Trump's personal attorney. The Florida businessman tells MSNBC that he was "absolutely, yes, absolutely" working for the president, and that "absolutely, absolutely . . . each one of those [Ukrainian] officials" he spoke to in Ukraine knew he was working for the president.[16] Parnas tells MSNBC that the "first thing I did" in meetings with Ukrainians was "introduce myself" by saying, "I'm here on behalf of Rudy Giuliani and the President of the United States."[17] In some cases, Parnas says, he would put the official on speakerphone with Giuliani so that Giuliani could tell the Ukrainian official in question—in these "exact words," says Parnas—that Parnas was "speak[ing] on President Trump's behalf."[18]

Parnas confirms that he met with senior Zelensky aide Sergey Shefir in May 2019 and communicated to him a quid pro quo—military aid to Ukraine for dirt on Joe Biden—adding that he did so because he had been told by Giuliani, shortly after Giuliani met with the president at the White House, to give a "message" to Shefir and do it "in a very harsh way, not in a pleasant way." Trump's message, delivered through Parnas, was that "all aid," and indeed the entirety of U.S.-Ukraine diplomacy, would go "sour" if Zelensky didn't announce a Biden investigation and meet "several [other] demands."[19] Parnas tells MSNBC that the aid Trump wanted Zelensky to know would be withheld included Trump's political "support"—for instance, Zelensky "having a White House visit . . . [and] having all the [U.S.] dignitaries there [at his inauguration]," which Parnas variously identifies to MSNBC as being "the number one thing" and the "biggest thing" and a "key [thing]" to Zelensky post-election, even more so than financial assistance.[20]

Parnas says he delivered this message to Zelensky's senior aide in a "very stern," even "heated" way, emphasizing that certain things "need[ed] to be done."[21] Parnas had been particularly instructed to warn Shefir that Vice President Pence would not come to Zelensky's inauguration if Zelensky did not comply with Trump's demands immediately. Parnas says that after the conversation with Shefir he "relayed back" the result of the conversation to Trump and Giuliani.[22] Parnas contends that he "know[s] 100%" that Trump withheld Pence from the Zelensky inauguration as a result of Shefir and Zelensky refusing Trump's requests.[23] Parnas quotes Giuliani as saying, when informed that Zelensky would not accede to Trump's demands, "They'll see." The next day, Trump instructed Pence not to attend Zelensky's inauguration.[24]

According to Parnas, Pence "was in the loop" about his attendance at Zelensky's May inauguration being held out to Zelensky as a chit in Trump's clandestine negotiations, and Pence's subsequent September 1 trip to Poland was intended to allow Pence to discuss the topic of investigations with Zelensky directly (see chapter 33).[25] Parnas confirms that Trump's use of Hurricane Dorian as an excuse not to travel to Warsaw himself was pretextual—a ruse whose contours Giuliani revealed to him directly (see chapter 27).[26]

In his January 2020 MSNBC interview Parnas also makes the startling claim that the push to remove Yovanovitch originated with Shokin and Lutsenko.[27] In support of this extraordinary new allegation, Parnas reveals to MSNBC a text from Lutsenko; in the text, Lutsenko tells Parnas, "If you don't make a decision about [Yovanovitch]—you are bringing into question all my allegations. Including about [Biden]."[28] The *Washington Post* summarizes the full Parnas-Lutsenko exchange as "show[ing] Lutsenko urging Parnas to force out Yovanovitch in exchange for cooperation regarding Biden."[29]

Parnas also implicates energy secretary Rick Perry in Giuliani's course of back-channel negotiations with Zelensky's office, telling MSNBC that on his way to Kyiv for Zelensky's inauguration Perry contacted Giuliani to ask him "what to discuss" with Zelensky at the inauguration; Giuliani told Perry to pass the "message" to the new Ukrainian president that he needed to announce the Biden and Clinton investigations.[30] Shortly after the inauguration, Parnas explains, Perry called Giuliani and confirmed not only that the message had been passed on but that Zelensky had agreed to the investigations.[31] Giuliani subsequently "blew his lid," per Parnas, when the resulting announcement about "corruption" by Zelensky failed to mention Biden by name. "It wasn't supposed to be [a] corruption announcement," Parnas tells MSNBC, as in Giuliani's view "it ha[d] to be about Joe Biden and Hunter Biden and Burisma."[32]

In response to Parnas's allegations about Perry, MSNBC notes the curiousness of a three-day sequence of events in October 2019: on October 16, the *Wall Street Journal* revealed that Perry had spoken to Giuliani about Ukraine "at Trump's direction"; on October 17, Perry tendered his resignation to Trump, and the resignation (with a delayed departure date) was accepted by the president; and on October 18, Perry announced that he would not comply with any House subpoenas relating to his or the president's conduct with respect to Ukraine.[33]

In a CNN interview shortly after his MSNBC interview, Parnas says that Giuliani speaks with the president "several times a day" and Giuliani "wouldn't do anything without the president's order."[34] As for another attorney in Trump's orbit, Bill Barr, Parnas says that one of the key reasons "a lot of people are scared" of the president is that "Barr . . . and the Justice Department" are "on his side" and people who "don't agree with what [Trump] is doing" don't want to speak up because they "don't want to be investigated."[35]

Parnas reveals that one of the lead attorneys in Trump's impeachment trial, Jay Sekulow (see chapter 40), was also fully "in the loop" as to the Trump-Ukraine quid pro quo, and at least once stepped in to oversee a subprocess of Giuliani's work in Ukraine.[36] According to Parnas, while Sekulow "didn't agree" with what Giuliani was doing in Ukraine and "didn't want to be involved," "he knew" what was happening as it was happening.[37] Parnas notes that both Sekulow and Trump were involved in trying to get a visa for Shokin to come to the United States so that he could accuse Biden—in a proposed meeting that would have included Giuliani, Barr, and Lindsey Graham—of firing him to protect Biden's son Hunter.[38] According to MSNBC, the U.S. embassy in Kyiv, then run by Yovanovitch, had "blocked" Shokin's visa application on the grounds that the former Ukrainian attorney general was "too corrupt" to be permitted to enter the United States.[39]

If indeed the president was personally involved in the official acts required to get a special, expedited visa for Shokin to come to the United States to provide valuable political intelligence about Joe Biden, it would constitute another act of bribery under 18 U.S. Code § 201.[40]

Parnas tells MSNBC that Trump attorney John Dowd's October 2019 representation of him was orchestrated by three Trump legal advisers: Victoria Toensing, Joe diGenova, and Rudy Giuliani.[41] It is during the course of Dowd's brief representation of Parnas that, per Parnas, Dowd attempts to coerce his new client into remaining silent to protect the president; Parnas says that Dowd was, based upon his own representations, "still doing work" for the president at the time.[42] Parnas reveals, indeed, that Trump had personally approved Dowd representing Parnas.[43] The Florida businessman further recounts for MSNBC an October 2019 conversation at Dowd's home involving not just one or two but four Trump attorneys—Dowd, Sekulow, Giuliani, and Toensing (the last married, of course, to a fifth Trump attorney, Joe diGenova)—during which it was agreed that a sixth Trump attorney, Pat Cipollone, would write Congress to say Parnas had attorney-client privilege for all of his correspondence with Giuliani, Toensing, and diGenova, and therefore would not reveal any of it to Congress.[44]

Parnas further tells MSNBC that he is willing to cooperate under penalty of perjury by speaking with the FBI, Congress, or both—not just about his relationship with the president and Giuliani, but about Dmitry Firtash as well.[45] Parnas reports that while he was at a meeting with Rudy Giuliani, John Solomon, Joe diGenova, and Victoria Toensing, Solomon told him that he had received "incredible information from the Firtash camp"; Giuliani explained that the information would show that Mueller deputy Andrew Weissmann was doing "some illegal stuff" that would "blow up" the Mueller investigation.[46] "We were tasked basically with trying to establish a relationship [with Firtash]," Parnas tells MSNBC; the goal, Parnas says, was to get information from Firtash to discredit the Mueller investigation while promising the oligarch that his extradition case would "get taken care of."[47] Parnas explains that DiGenova and Toensing, by then Firtash's attorneys, were tasked with brokering the exchange—an act of bribery, if proven—as well as assisting John Solomon in getting information about the "black ledger" to Parnas and the rest of Trump's legal team.[48]

Parnas says Barr was read in on the DiGenova-Toensing-Firtash contract for legal representation, and "was involved in lots of conversations" with DiGenova and Giuliani that the latter two attorneys conducted by phone in front of Parnas.[49] Parnas adds that Barr "had to have known everything"—not only about the two attorneys' exchanges with Firtash, but also about the president's potentially illegal attempts to get dirt on Joe Biden.[50] Giuliani, Toensing, and diGenova told Parnas that they'd talked to Barr about Ukraine and that the attorney general was "on the team" with respect to getting Ukraine to start investigating Biden; per Parnas, Giuliani, Barr, diGenova, and Toensing are "best friends."[51] Notably, Trump issued Barr's early December 2018 nomination for attorney general in the midst of efforts by Barr's "best friends"—all of whom had strong connections to Trump as well—to get dirt on Biden, dirt that was to be traded for favorable extradition arrangements that Barr would be perfectly situated to deliver.[52] Parnas says House Permanent Select Committee on Intelligence chairman Devin Nunes "wanted to help out" with the president's clandestine Ukraine negotiations, but Parnas—and the BLT Prime team—were "given Harvey to deal with" instead because Nunes was facing an ethics investigation.[53] Of Nunes, Parnas says that he was "involved in getting all this stuff on Biden. . . . He knew very well . . . what was going on [in Ukraine]. He knew what was happening. He knows who I am."[54]

As Parnas begins turning over his personal communications to Congress in late 2019 and early 2020, a substantial archive of pictures linking the Florida businessman to key GOP officials is developing in the public square.[55] In just a matter of weeks, pictures emerge of Parnas with, among others, President Trump (at least nine pictures from different dates and locations), Donald Trump Jr., Eric Trump, Ivanka Trump, Trump son-in-law Jared Kushner, Trump ex-wife Ivana Trump, Vice President Pence, House minority leader Kevin McCarthy, House minority whip Steve Scalise, counselor to the president Kellyanne Conway, former attorney general Jeff Sessions, Trump impeachment trial attorney Pam Bondi, former Trump chief of staff John Kelly, Sen. Mike Braun (R-IN), top Trump ally and fundraiser Gov. Ron DeSantis (R-FL), House Ways and Means Committee chairman Kevin Brady (R-TX), Trump fundraiser Rep. Pete Sessions, and then–White House press secretary Sarah Huckabee Sanders.[56] A video of Parnas at Mar-a-Lago in December 2016, released by Parnas's attorney Joseph Bondy, reportedly shows Trump, Parnas, and Ukrainian fiscal service chief Roman Nasirov talking with several people at a social gathering; ninety days later, the "notoriously corrupt" Ukrainian tax official—a known Shokin associate—will be arrested for fraud and abuse of office via embezzlement.[57] Nasirov's criminal case, still ongoing as of 2020, pertains in part to his alleged facilitation of a tax evasion scheme by gas company oligarch and Trump associate Oleksandr Onyshchenko, who had fled Ukraine to evade justice in 2016.[58]

As evidence establishing Parnas's connection to Trump and his inner circle is being released online, Trump—referred to, in code, as "[number] 1" or the "big one" in the many Parnas texts referencing him—is again asked by reporters in the Oval Office whether he knows Parnas.[59] "I don't know him," Trump says. "I don't know Parnas. . . . I don't know him at all. Don't know what he's about. Don't know where he comes from. Know nothing about him . . . I don't even know who this man is. . . . I don't know him. . . . I know nothing about him. . . . I don't know him. I don't believe I've ever spoken to him. I don't believe I've ever spoken to him. . . . I don't know him. I never had a conversation that I remember with him."[60] The president then snaps at a reporter to be "quiet" and stop asking questions about Parnas.[61]

CHAPTER 22

HYDE

In January 2020, the House Permanent Select Committee on Intelligence releases a trove of documents regarding Lev Parnas's clandestine efforts to remove Yovanovitch from her position. The documents substantially darken the Parnas-Yovanovitch narrative. In text messages between Parnas and a man named Robert Hyde—a Republican congressional candidate from Connecticut, a former Marine, and a Trump donor—Hyde, per *Politico*, refers to Yovanovitch as a "bitch" and appears to "provide [Parnas] continual updates on [her] physical whereabouts."[1] Additional statements made by Hyde to Parnas generate concern in Congress that the State Department's emergency extraction of Yovanovitch from Ukraine, as well as Trump's subsequent statement to Zelensky that Yovanovitch would "go through some things," had to do with more than a change in her employment status.[2] Two March 2019 text messages see Hyde telling Parnas that unnamed Ukrainians would be "willing to help [with Yovanovitch] if we/you would like a price," and that these Ukrainians could be contracted with to help get "her [Yovanovitch] out"; Hyde says the sort of operation he has in mind would require his proposed contractors to first "make contact with security forces"—though it is unclear if he means Ukrainian security forces, U.S. government personnel, or unaffiliated independent contractors.[3] MSNBC reports these texts as seeming to indicate Yovanovitch will experience "physical harm or intimidation" if Parnas and Hyde strike the deal the latter is proposing. A text between Parnas and Lutsenko during the same period, in which Parnas assures the Ukrainian prosecutor general that Yovanovitch is "not getting away," provokes a similar impression among some in Congress.[4]

Upon receiving these and similarly troubling Parnas-Hyde communications, Rep. Eliot Engel (D-NY), chairman of the House Foreign Affairs Committee, sends a letter to the State Department demanding more information on the department's response to the two men having apparently "engaged in efforts to surveil and possibly threaten the safety of the United States Ambassador to Ukraine in at least the spring of 2019."[5] Engel notes that "Mr. Hyde claimed in one message to have 'a person inside,' possibly in the U.S. embassy in Kyiv, who is 'willing to help if we/you would like a price.' The strong implication from these messages is that someone with detailed knowledge of the Ambassador's whereabouts and security protocols was providing that information in real time to Mr. Hyde and Mr. Parnas. I cannot overstate the profound security risk this poses to the U.S. mission and our interests in Ukraine."[6]

Asked by MSNBC about his texts with Hyde, Parnas calls the former Marine "a weird character" and a "weird individual," adding that he met Hyde at a Trump property—indeed, the Trump International Hotel in D.C., the base of operations for the BLT Prime team.[7] Parnas tells MSNBC that Hyde was a "regular" at the hotel, and someone who knew both Kevin McCarthy and longtime Trump friend and adviser Roger Stone.[8] Parnas adds that the Trump International Hotel was a "breeding ground" for people looking for ways to support President Trump; per Parnas, "every [Trump] event" and "all the [Trump-related] meetings" were held there, and in consequence people could "hang out" and brush elbows with "everybody" from Congress who supported Trump.[9] "You would see the same people every day, all the same Congressmen that supported the president would be there, nobody else," Parnas tells MSNBC. Parnas calls Hyde a "fixture" at the hotel during the period the BLT Prime team was meeting.[10]

Parnas concedes to MSNBC that the messages he received from Hyde regarding Yovanovitch's movements were "crazy" and "disturbing" but insists that Hyde composed them while drunk.[11] Parnas's claims that he had "never seen [Hyde] not drunk," "never" believed Yovanovitch was in danger, and never took the Republican congressional candidate from Connecticut seriously are undercut, however, when it is revealed that not only had Parnas spent at least a week discussing Yovanovitch's movements with Hyde, but was open enough to Hyde as a collaborator in the plot against Yovanovitch that he called Joe Ahearn at the pro-Trump super PAC America First Action to determine if Hyde could be trusted.[12] Parnas's relationship with Ahearn was so close at the time that, per Parnas's text messages, the two corresponded on how best to direct Donald Trump Jr.'s tweets.[13] One Parnas-Ahearn conversation concerning Trump's son, held on March 20, 2019, preceded by just four days the tweet by Trump Jr. that helped propel the State Department toward recalling Yovanovitch from Kyiv: "We need more Richard Grenells [the U.S. ambassador to Germany] and less of these jokers [Yovanovitch] as ambassador," Don Jr. tweeted at the time.[14]

The details Hyde gives Parnas about Yovanovitch's security posture in Kyiv are not only incredibly detailed, but written in sober prose. One such message reads, "She's talked to three people. Her phone is off. Computer is off"; another reads, "They will let me know when she's on the move."[15] According to USA Today, "they" refers to unspecified "people" Hyde had "hired . . . in Ukraine to surveil the ambassador"; per the newspaper, Hyde had claimed to Parnas that he was "getting updates about [Yovanovitch's] whereabouts and activities" from the individuals he had retained.[16] At another point Hyde boasts to Parnas, ominously, "You can do anything in Ukraine with money . . . [was] what I was told."[17]

Photos widely distributed online in January 2020 variously show Hyde with President Trump, Ivanka Trump, Eric Trump, Vice President Pence, Roger Stone, Rudy Giuliani, Rep. Jim Jordan, and others close to the president.[18] On January 16, CNN reports that "FBI investigators went to the home and the business of Robert Hyde."[19] The results of this FBI investigation remain unknown.

The Washington Post reports in January 2020 that Hyde was "involuntarily committed to a psychiatric hospital after an incident at one of the president's resorts" in May 2019.[20] The commitment comes just seven weeks after the texts between Hyde and Parnas about surveilling Yovanovitch.[21] The incident that leads to Hyde's commitment sees the Connecticut Republican telling officers at Trump Doral in Miami that he is being "set up," is under surveillance by the Secret Service, and has had "a hit man" sent "out to get him" because of unspecified "emails he sent."[22] After what Hyde later describes as a nine-day commitment, he is released, stating thereafter in a social media post that he had "passed all medicals, physicals, [and] psych exams . . . with flying colors."[23]

In late February 2020, NBC News reports on concerns among members of the House Foreign Affairs Committee that Hyde not only is keeping records from it and misleading media as to the extent of his cooperation with Congress, but may also have destroyed some of the records he previously agreed to turn over.[24] NBC further reports that much of Hyde's information about Yovanovitch's movements in Ukraine may have come from "encrypted" text messages sent by a "Dutch Trump superfan" named Anthony de Caluwe. According to NBC, de Caluwe has a history of "masquerading as a U.S. federal law enforcement officer"—sometimes a Drug Enforcement Administration agent, sometimes a CIA agent—and, "despite saying that he had 'no connection' to Ukraine . . . was romantically involved with a Ukrainian woman, who returns regularly to her home country, at the same time in early 2019 that he sent text messages [to Hyde] about Yovanovitch's purported whereabouts in Kyiv."[25] NBC reports that de Caluwe "has posted numerous photos and pro-Trump slogans on his multiple social media accounts, projecting proximity to Trump's orbit with a constant stream of posts that depict Republican events, Trump's Washington hotel, and even a Christmas reception at the White House."[26]

CHAPTER 23

THE FIRST TRUMP-ZELENSKY CALL

On April 21, 2019, Volodymyr Zelensky is elected the sixth president of Ukraine, and receives a congratulatory phone call from President Trump.[1] During the call, Trump promises Zelensky that "at a minimum" the United States will send a "very, very high level" official to the new Ukrainian president's inauguration, a promise Trump breaks by both refusing to attend the inauguration himself and cancelling his replacement, Mike Pence; ultimately he sends Rick Perry, his secretary of energy, as the highest-ranking member of the inaugural delegation.[2] CNN will note that during the April Trump-Zelensky call "there is no mention of corruption," despite "a White House readout released on the day of the call" falsely indicating that the issue arose.[3] According to CNN, given that "Trump administration officials later claimed that corruption was a persistent issue in Ukraine that Trump was intent on rooting out," it "beg[s] the question [of] why [Trump] didn't bring it up in his first conversation with Zelensky"; the cable news outlet calls Trump's silence on an issue his defenders contend he is singularly focused on a "notable omission."[4] It adds that the "effusive . . . praise" Trump offers Zelensky in April seems to undercut the claim by one of Trump's chief congressional defenders, Rep. Jim Jordan, that Trump held up congressionally mandated aid to Ukraine for fifty-five days in the summer of 2019 because he felt he needed nearly two months to "check out this new guy . . . [to] see if he's legit."[5] In fact, writes CNN, "in the [April] phone call it looked like Trump was already convinced" of Zelensky's integrity, telling the new president, "I have many friends in Ukraine who know you and like you."[6]

Along with the ongoing impact of what the *New York Times* calls a "yearslong operation" by the Kremlin to "frame Ukraine" for Russia's 2016 election interference in the United States—a propaganda operation so successful that its key elements will become, by late 2019, Republican talking points—another possible explanation for Trump's kindness toward Zelensky in April and his comparative hostility to the new Ukrainian president by the summer of 2019 may be the status of Rudy Giuliani's Ukrainian "investigations" at the time of the two presidents' first call.[7] A few days after Trump and Zelensky speak for the first time, Trump tells Fox News, per the network's summary of his remarks, that "Attorney General William Barr is handling the 'incredible' and 'big' new revelations that Ukrainian actors apparently leaked damaging information about then-campaign chairman Paul Manafort to help Hillary Clinton's campaign."[8] By April 2019, moreover, Yuri Lutsenko's clandestine investigation of Burisma and the Bidens was well underway, and the Ukrainian prosecutor general had already spoken extensively with John Solomon—using Lev Parnas as an intermediary—about alleged Ukrainian election interference.[9] Trump was also aware on April 21 that Lutsenko had "opened a probe into the so-called 'black ledger' files that led to Manafort's abrupt departure from the Trump campaign."[10] So Trump's cautiously optimistic approach to Zelensky during the first phone call between the two men may have been, as much as anything else, a product of the president's hope that Zelensky would retain Lutsenko as his prosecutor general.

In December 2019, despite phone records establishing that Giuliani called the Office of Management and Budget during the period of Trump's hold on military aid to Ukraine—including a thirteen-minute call on August 8—a White House spokesperson will issue a statement declaring that "no one from OMB has talked to Giuliani," and an OMB spokesperson will, via email, issue the same denial.[11] The *Washington Post* reports the same month that many of Trump's calls to Giuliani in 2019 were, despite repeated warnings to the president regarding the security of his communications, "on cellphones vulnerable to monitoring by Russian and other foreign intelligence services."[12] As the *Post* notes, that Trump has "communicated regularly with Giuliani on unsecured lines" and that his actions "continue[ ] to defy the security guidance urged by his aides and followed by previous incumbents"—the latter a fact the *Post* calls "particularly remarkable given Trump's attacks on Hillary Clinton in the 2016 presidential campaign for her use of a private email account while serving as secretary of state"—"raise[s] the possibility that Moscow . . . learn[ed] about Trump's attempts to get Ukraine to investigate a political rival months before that effort was exposed by a whistleblower report" (see chapter 32).[13] One former senior aide to Trump will tell the *Post* that such unsecure calls between the president and his personal attorney "happened all the time."[14]

American officials opine to the *Washington Post* that, given that "Russia is already using its disinformation capabilities to target U.S. citizens," it would be relatively easy for the Kremlin to "enlist its own operatives in Ukraine to feed false information to Giuliani" while he was in Ukraine—information that Giuliani would then pass on to Trump under the watchful eye of additional Russian telephonic surveillance.[15] That Giuliani meets in Kyiv in December 2019 with "a Ukrainian lawmaker who studied at the KGB's academy in Moscow" only adds fuel to this grave concern about America's national security and the possibility that its president has been compromised by Russian disinformation.[16] National security experts to whom the *Post* speaks doubt neither that Giuliani was under regular Kremlin surveillance nor that such surveillance means Putin knows significantly more about conversations relevant to Trump's eventual impeachment than either Congress or the American people.[17] One former White House aide calls Trump's habitual refusal to follow national security protocols on his communications devices not just "absolutely a security issue" but a "bonanza [of free information]" for hostile foreign intelligence services like Russia's FSB.[18]

One issue in determining how frequently Trump and Giuliani spoke on the phone during the height of the activities reviewed by Congress's impeachment inquiry—the period from November 2018 through September 2019—is that none of the phone records subpoenaed by HPSCI list Trump's phone number. Instead, near-universal speculation, based on the pattern of subpoenaed calls as well as their duration and known participants, is that Trump's personal communications device is marked as "-1" in phone records. The *Post* reports that "on the day that U.S. Ambassador to Ukraine Marie Yovanovitch was told by the State Department to return to Washington, Giuliani had 11 calls with phone numbers associated with the White House . . . as well as a nearly nine-minute phone call with '-1,'" leading congressional investigators to "suspect [Trump] may be [the] person with a blocked number listed as '-1'" in Giuliani's subpoenaed phone logs.[19] Two additional reasons for this suspicion are that, per CNN, "Giuliani made several calls to numbers associated with the White House and the Office of Management and Budget during that same time frame" and a flurry of calls between Giuliani and "-1" also "came at a time when Giuliani was helping [Trump] deal with the fallout from special counsel Robert Mueller's report on Russian interference in the 2016 presidential election after a redacted version [of the report] was released."[20] Moreover, during a ninety-six-hour period that culminates in a CIA whistleblower formally filing a complaint about Trump's July 25 call with President Zelensky—a period during which the White House would have become aware of the forthcoming complaint, per timelines prepared by major media outlets—there was "a game of phone tag between the -1 phone and Mr. Giuliani. . . . Mr. Giuliani missed calls from -1 on August 8 to two of his cellphones. Mr. Giuliani then called the White House switchboard and the White House Situation Room, before connecting with -1."[21] As the *Wall Street Journal* notes, August 8 was "a day after a U.S. diplomat [Volker] texted [Giuliani] asking him to brief the president on [Giuliani's] meeting with [Zelensky aide Andriy] Yermak."[22]

If not Trump, CNN notes, another possibility for the holder of the "-1" blocked phone number is Trump's acting chief of staff and OMB director, Mick Mulvaney.[23] Neither Trump nor Mulvaney has ever spoken on the "-1" issue; however, a *Wall Street Journal* report quotes a White

House official as having conceded that the "call records for Mr. Mulvaney's cellphone didn't match the calls listed in the [HPSCI] report."[24] While congressional investigators have not yet confirmed the holder of the blocked number so frequently dialed by Giuliani, CNN reports that "the phone number '-1' also came up during the trial of former Trump adviser Roger Stone. Prosecutors showed evidence at Stone's trial that he took a call coming from a '-1' number in August 2016, and a government witness' testimony indicated it could have come from Trump."[25] With this in mind, the *New York Times* reports that "House investigators suspect that the number may belong to Mr. Trump," rather than Mulvaney, "in part because of phone records used as evidence in the criminal case against [Stone]."[26]

During the first three years of Trump's presidency, the matter of the president's phone number will come up repeatedly and never be resolved. The reasons for this are unclear, though the perpetual lack of clarity on the subject suggests a degree of anxiety within Trump's inner circle about federal investigations that may seek to determine what the president knew and when. For instance, in early December 2017—in the midst of the Mueller investigation—Trump's son Don Jr. testifies under oath that, despite speaking regularly with his father by phone for years, he cannot remember if calls from the elder Trump show up on his phone as having come from a blocked number.[27]

CHAPTER 24

ZELENSKY AND LUTSENKO

On October 4, 2018, a few weeks before Giuliani begins working with Parnas to contact Ukrainian prosecutors about Joe Biden, Bud Cummins, a former federal prosecutor from Arkansas now representing the interests of new Ukrainian prosecutor general Yuri Lutsenko and several other unnamed Ukrainians, contacts the Southern District of New York to request a meeting between Lutsenko and Manhattan U.S. attorney Geoffrey Berman.[1] CNN reports that not only had Berman held "a position on Trump's [presidential] transition team," but he was once Giuliani's law partner, and earlier in 2018 had received his U.S. attorney position following a face-to-face interview with Trump himself.[2] In his email to Berman, Cummins lays out "allegations about Hunter Biden and his work for Burisma" and accusations "that the Black Ledger was falsified."[3] After speaking with Berman by phone, Cummins sends the U.S. attorney three follow-up emails.[4]

Cummins had served as chair of Trump's 2016 campaign in Arkansas and as a Trump whip at the 2016 Republican National Convention.[5] While the former prosecutor will not reveal to reporters which Ukrainians besides Lutsenko had sought his aid in contacting Berman, he does say that they were Ukrainians who believed the "FBI in Ukraine had either wittingly or unwittingly become the pawns of the ambassador [Yovanovitch] and secretary of state [Clinton] and vice president [Biden]" and that "they [the FBI] cannot be trusted."[6]

Three and a half months after the Cummins–Southern District communication, on January 25, 2019, Ukrainian lawmaker Hlib Zahoriy and Ukrainian prosecutor Gyunduz Mamedov—the latter specializing in "cases related to the Russian-occupied region of Crimea"—meet with Rudy Giuliani, Lev Parnas, and Igor Fruman in New York City for the express purpose of introducing the three men to Lutsenko.[7] The six men meet again on the following two days as well.[8] According to NBC News, Mamedov is the man chiefly responsible for bringing Lutsenko to New York City, a trip that in short order becomes fateful: within six weeks, Lutsenko is sitting for an interview with John Solomon of *The Hill* at Parnas's orchestration and with Parnas present in the studio, giving the Ukrainian prosecutor his largest megaphone yet to spread what he ultimately concedes is disinformation about the Bidens and other alleged foes of President Trump.[9] NBC confirms that Lutsenko meets with Parnas, Fruman, and Giuliani a month and a half before his interview with *The Hill* in part to "furnish[ ] Giuliani with a range of unsupported accusations alleging wrongdoing by Biden, his son Hunter, and officials in the U.S. Embassy in Kyiv, including then-Ambassador Marie Yovanovitch."[10]

While Mamedov is the central figure in securing Lutsenko's appearance in New York with Giuliani and his associates in late January, the meeting only occurs, according to Lutsenko, because Giuliani had used Mamedov to pass an invitation to him to come to New York.[11] Given that Giuliani was at the time in the midst of a long-term contract with the city of Kharkiv in Ukraine and so would frequently travel there—and was, moreover, the honorary mayor of a Jewish settlement in Ukraine (Anatevka) that he would have had good reason to regularly travel to as well—it is unclear why Giuliani needed Lutsenko to come to the city where Giuliani's most famous client, Donald Trump, at the time maintained his primary residence.[12]

Giuliani's invitation to Lutsenko had been carried to Mamedov by Parnas and Fruman, according to Lutsenko. NBC notes that Parnas and Fruman were particularly useful intermediaries for Giuliani in dealing with Mamedov, as Mamedov "knew Giuliani's associates [Parnas and Fruman] from his time in the Ukrainian port city of Odessa. The Black Sea port city is where Fruman built up his business network in Ukraine in the 1990s and early 2000s."[13]

Giuliani's fixation with Lutsenko is of sufficient intensity that his late January meetings with the Ukrainian prosecutor are insufficient to slake his interest. Just days after Trump's attorney meets with Lutsenko three times in New York, he again exploits his access to Mamedov to arrange a meeting with the prosecutor in Warsaw, Poland.[14] While Mamedov has no known connection to Giuliani prior to meeting him in New York City in January at Parnas and Fruman's direction, NBC notes that Mamedov hails from a family "involved at senior levels in [former Soviet republic] Azerbaijan's state-run oil and gas sector, which is heavily controlled by the family of the country's president, Ilham Aliyev."[15] Aliyev had already achieved minor notoriety in the United States by virtue of his tangential involvement in the Trump-Russia investigation as the former father-in-law of Kremlin agent and Trump business associate Emin Agalarov.[16]

Whereas Mamedov's role in the January 2019 Giuliani-Lutsenko meetings was significant, Zahoriy, the Ukrainian politician, was reportedly involved only as a translator, according to Lutsenko. Why a Ukrainian translator would have been needed, given the availability of future Firtash "translators" Parnas and Fruman for the task, is unclear.[17] For his part, Zahoriy claims his presence at the Giuliani-Lutsenko meeting was sheer coincidence—the result of Lutsenko asking him to come along after the two men had had breakfast together on January 25 while Zahoriy was on an unrelated business trip.[18] Per NBC News' summary of Zahoriy's account of events, "Giuliani and Lutsenko did most of the substantive talking" at the meeting, with the non-English-speaking Mamedov as "simply an intermediary."[19]

In contradiction of the accounts given by Zahoriy and Lutsenko, Giuliani now claims, per NBC, "that it was Ukrainian prosecutors who took the initiative in bringing to him the allegations at the heart of his [Giuliani's] campaign against Biden."[20] Says Giuliani in an interview he gives with Trump adviser Sean Hannity on the latter's opinion program on Fox News, "I didn't go looking for [dirt on] Joe Biden. The Ukrainians brought me substantial evidence of Ukrainian collusion with Hillary Clinton, the DNC, George Soros, George Soros' company. They put it in my lap."[21] No one else who attends the January 2019 New York City meetings between Giuliani and Lutsenko confirms Giuliani's account; matters will subsequently be further complicated by federal prosecutors' allegation that Parnas and Fruman were simultaneously employed by both Giuliani and Lutsenko at the time of the January meetings between the latter two men.[22]

The fourth Giuliani-Lutsenko meeting takes place in Warsaw on February 12, 2019, just as Trump appointee Bill Barr assumes his position as attorney general of the United States.[23] At the meeting, which takes place at a cigar bar and includes Parnas and Fruman as well as the two principals, Giuliani asks "whether Lutsenko is ready to meet with Barr, who would be sworn in as Attorney General two days later"—suggesting that Giuliani already had reason to believe such a meeting would be possible.[24] Notably, upon taking his post Barr is immediately informed that federal investigators are tracking potentially illegal donations from Parnas and Fruman to organizations supporting Trump's reelection.[25]

On October 24, 2019, Trump's high-pressure campaign against President Zelensky reaps dividends that hark back to the first meeting between Giuliani and Lutsenko, with Zelensky naming Gyunduz Mamedov—the very man who introduced the president's attorney to Lutsenko—deputy prosecutor general of Ukraine.[26]

On May 10, 2019, Giuliani suddenly cancels a trip to Ukraine during which, the *Washington Post* reports, the president's personal attorney had been "planning to push for investigations that include [Joe] Biden's son, Hunter, and his time on the board of a Ukraine gas company."[27] Undoubtedly unnerving to Zelensky and his staff is Giuliani's claim at the time he cancelled the trip that Zelensky had selected "enemies [of Trump]" for his government—an accusation that implies U.S.-Ukrainian relations are about to worsen substantially.[28] At stake for Ukraine in its relationship with America, reports the *Post*, is whether it will receive U.S. aid "as a key deterrent preventing Russian President Vladimir Putin from encroaching further on their territory."[29] In short, the future of Ukraine—staring down five unbroken years of Russian military aggression—is tied up with U.S. military aid for the European country, a disturbing premise given that in May 2019 its newly elected president is "a comedian with no previous political experience" who is most famous for "play[ing] Ukraine's president on a popular TV show."[30] Despite Zelensky's lack of political experience, it takes him less than three weeks, per a *Washington Post* report citing Ukrainian political insiders, to ascertain that "Trump's interest in the [domestic Ukrainian] investigations" Giuliani has opined about in fact has nothing to do with corruption in the former Soviet republic, but rather is connected with "domestic U.S. matter[s]" like the upcoming 2020 presidential election.[31]

On May 20, ten days after Giuliani declares Zelensky's administration full of "enemies of the President [of the United States]," Republican senator Ron Johnson of Wisconsin attends the inauguration of the new Ukrainian president alongside U.S. envoy for Ukraine Kurt Volker, U.S. ambassador to the European Union Gordon Sondland, and secretary of energy Rick Perry, the last of whom is a late replacement—at Trump's insistence—for Vice President Mike Pence, who had previously been tapped as the president's top envoy to Zelensky's swearing-in ceremony (see chapter 33).[32] While in Kyiv, Volker informs the other three men that Giuliani has been encouraging Ukraine to open investigations into Joe and Hunter Biden; according to the *Wall Street Journal*, this is the first time Sondland, Johnson, or Perry has heard about Giuliani's activities in Ukraine.[33]

Three of the four men—Volker, Sondland, and Perry—meet with Trump upon their return to Washington. During the May 23 gathering, all three "encourage[ ] Trump to [publicly] back Zelensky"; instead, Trump "raise[s] concerns about corruption," "direct[s] them to work with Giuliani," and, according to the *Washington Post*, "refuse[s] to set a firm date for an Oval Office meeting with the newly minted Ukrainian president"—"personally reject[ing]" the "efforts to set [a meeting] up" by "U.S. officials and members of the Trump administration."[34] The *Wall Street Journal* will report in October 2019 that on May 23 "Trump told officials there [at the White House] that they needed to work with Mr. Giuliani to resolve his [Trump's] concerns [about Ukraine] before he would agree to . . . a meeting" with Zelensky.[35]

Perry quickly follows through on Trump's directive to get in touch with Giuliani. According to the *Wall Street Journal*, upon reaching Giuliani by phone, Perry hears from the president's personal lawyer "several concerns about Ukraine's alleged interference in the 2016 election," despite the fact that, per the *Journal*, these were all "concerns that haven't been substantiated."[36] Specifically, Perry tells the *Journal* that Giuliani said to him, "Look, the president is really concerned that there are people in Ukraine that tried to beat him during this [last] president election. He thinks they're corrupt and . . . that there are still people over there . . . that are absolutely corrupt."[37] While Perry does not recount Giuliani naming any individuals in Ukraine that Trump specifically considered corrupt, during the phone call between the two men the president's attorney makes a series of allegations about the 2016 election, including, reports the *Journal*, "blam[ing] Ukraine for the [Steele] dossier about Mr. Trump's alleged ties to Russia," despite there being no evidence that any of Steele's sources hailed from the Ukrainian government; "assert[ing] that Ukraine had Mrs. Clinton's email server," despite there being no evidence there is any missing Clinton server; and accusing Ukraine of "'dream[ing] up' [the] evidence that helped send former Trump campaign chairman Paul Manafort to jail," though Manafort had been convicted by a federal jury and there had been no indication that any of the information relied upon by federal prosecutors to convict him was falsified.[38] In speaking with the *Journal* in October 2019, Perry leaves open the possibility that everything Giuliani told him in justification of the president's refusal to publicly back Zelensky is "crap."[39]

According to "a former senior administration official who repeatedly discussed the issue with Trump," Trump had much more on his mind than Paul Manafort, Hillary Clinton, and Christopher Steele when he rejected U.S. officials' mid-July 2019 efforts to grant the new Ukrainian president the courtesy of a meeting at the White House.[40] Instead, the former Trump administration official reports, Trump was thinking of what Vladimir Putin would say about U.S. foreign policy toward the former Soviet republic. As reported by the *Washington Post*, the former senior administration official says that in "private conversations" Trump disclosed that he thought "what we were doing in Ukraine [with the provision of lethal defensive military assistance] was pointless and just aggravating the Russians. The president's position basically is, we should recognize the fact that the Russians should be our friends, and who cares about the Ukrainians?"[41]

CHAPTER 25

TAYLOR

According to the *New York Times*, when Volker, Sondland, and Perry meet with Trump in the White House on May 23, all three report "favorably" on new Ukrainian president Volodymyr Zelensky's character and intentions.[1] In response, the *Times* reports, Trump is "dismissive. 'They're terrible people,'" he says of Ukrainian politicians, " 'They're all corrupt and they tried to take me down.'"[2] Notable is Trump's attachment of his concern over Ukrainian corruption to "me"—that is, his own political career. According to Sondland's congressional testimony, Trump "direct[s]" the assembled group to talk to Giuliani, his personal attorney, to "address the President's concerns" about how various Ukrainian politicians had treated him following the announcement of his presidential campaign in June 2015.[3] Sondland will testify that the group asked Trump to both have a phone call with Zelensky and invite him to the White House because it was "important," and that they were "disappointed" to be told instead to contact Giuliani.[4]

Washington Post political reporter Aaron Blake contends that Sondland and the other two officials would have well understood what Giuliani wanted from Ukraine by May 23, as the preceding two weeks had seen a major national brouhaha over Giuliani's proposed trip to Ukraine to get dirt on Biden—a trip ultimately cancelled because of, the *Post* reporter notes, "outcry" from the public and media.[5] Glenn Kessler, a *Washington Post* reporter, observes that during the run-up to the May 23 meeting Trump himself had been quite vocal about Biden, complaining in an interview on May 19, just ninety-six hours before the president's meeting with Sondland, Perry, and Volker, that Biden "call[ed]" the Ukraini-ans in 2015 and said, "'Don't you dare prosecute. If you don't fire this prosecutor'—the prosecutor [who] was after his son. Then he said, 'If you fire the prosecutor, you'll be OK. And if you don't fire the prosecutor, we're not giving you $2 billion in loan guarantees,' or whatever he was supposed to give."[6]

On May 28, Trump's secretary of state, Mike Pompeo, asks former United States ambassador to Ukraine William Taylor to "return to Kyiv to lead [the U.S.] embassy" there as "Chief of Mission."[7] Before respond-ing to Pompeo's offer, Taylor seeks counsel from the recently deposed U.S. ambassador to Ukraine, Marie Yovanovitch, who urges him to accept the assignment.[8] He also seeks advice from State Department employee Kurt Volker, asking him via text about Giuliani's public crusade to use Ukraine to aid Donald Trump's 2020 reelection campaign: "I'm really struggling with the decision whether to go [to Ukraine]," Taylor writes Volker. "Can anyone hope to succeed with the Giuliani-Biden issue swirling for the next 18 months [through Election Day]? Can [Pompeo] offer any reassurance on this issue[?]"[9]

Taylor ultimately receives just such an assurance directly from Pompeo, specifically that, under Trump, "the U.S. policy of strong sup-port for Ukraine," including "strong diplomatic support along with ro-bust security, economic, and technical assistance," remains unchanged from the Obama administration.[10] Taylor will later testify to Congress that at the time of Pompeo's invitation he had already heard informa-tion about the "role of [Rudy] Giuliani [in Ukraine]" that "worried" him, and that he therefore informed Pompeo on May 28 that "if U.S. policy toward Ukraine changed," he would "not stay" in the posting.[11] Pompeo gives Taylor no indication that—as Taylor will later say he discovered— "the official foreign policy of the United States was being undercut by . . . irregular efforts led by Mr. Giuliani," and that these efforts were in fact part of an "irregular, informal channel of U.S. policy-making with re-spect to Ukraine" that "was guided by Mr. Giuliani."[12]

* * *

Taylor arrives in Kyiv on June 17, 2019, with the official title of "chargé d'affaires ad interim."[13] He cannot use the title of "ambassador" because he has not been nominated by Trump or confirmed by the Senate—a process that Trump and Pompeo avoid, in so doing avoiding congressional queries about U.S. policy in Ukraine.[14]

At the time the Trump administration taps him to serve in Ukraine, Taylor has been a public servant for more than fifty years, having first served his country as a West Point cadet, then as an infantry officer during the Vietnam War—including a stint with the world-famous 101st Airborne Division—and then in a long succession of federal jobs under both Republican and Democratic administrations, including placements with the Department of Energy, the United States Senate, the North Atlantic Treaty Organization (NATO), and finally the State Department, for which he served in Afghanistan, Iraq, Israel, and Ukraine.[15] After serving as Republican president George W. Bush's ambassador to Ukraine from 2006 to 2009, Taylor had become the executive vice president of the nonpartisan United States Institute of Peace (USIP).[16] At the time Taylor agrees to serve in President Trump's administration at Secretary of State Pompeo's invitation, he has, all told, served under every American president since 1985.[17]

As Taylor will later testify under oath before Congress, he accepts Pompeo's invitation in part because of his "particular interest in and respect for [America's] relationship with Ukraine," a country he has "stayed engaged with [since his 2006 to 2009 ambassadorship there], visiting frequently since 2013 as a board member of a small Ukrainian non-governmental organization [USIP] supporting good governance and reform."[18] As Taylor observes to Congress, the safety and security of Ukraine are of vital interest to the United States because since 2014 the European nation has been "under armed attack from Russia," for which reason U.S. military aid to Ukraine is essential to "send[ing] a signal to Ukrainians—and Russians—that we [Americans] are Ukraine's reliable strategic partner."[19] Taylor warns that "if Ukraine succeeds in breaking free of Russian influence, it [will be] possible for Europe to be whole, free, democratic, and at peace. In contrast, if Russia dominates Ukraine, Russia will again become an empire, oppressing its people, and threatening its neighbors and the rest of the world."[20] He adds that "with the annexation of Crimea in 2014 and the continued aggression in Donbass, Russia [has] violated countless treaties, ignored all commitments, and dismissed all the principles that have kept the peace and contributed to prosperity in Europe since World War II."[21]

A week after Taylor is appointed, but before he has arrived in Kyiv to take up his position as chief of mission, Rick Perry meets with Zelensky in Brussels.[22] Zelensky also meets there with Jared Kushner. Neither the content of the Zelensky-Kushner meeting nor the content of the Zelensky-Perry meeting has ever been revealed, though the *Kyiv Post* will note that a "wide range of issues" was discussed during the meetings, including "security" and "energy."[23]

Ambassador Taylor begins his service on Trump's behalf in Kyiv having spent the preceding five years advocating for the provision of "lethal defensive weapons to Ukraine in order to deter further Russian aggression" and for the strengthening of sanctions against Russia in response to its ongoing armed encroachment on European soil.[24] On his first day in Kyiv, June 17, 2019, he presents Zelensky with a letter from President Trump inviting the new Ukrainian president to the White House; Trump's letter offers no indication that such a visit is contingent upon any action by Zelensky, and therefore Taylor is given no reason to believe that Trump's invitation is anything but transparent and authentic.[25]

Taylor will report to Congress in October 2019 that Zelensky's first weeks in office positioned him as an earnest reformer committed to fighting domestic corruption. As Taylor will testify, Zelensky "appointed reformist ministers and supported long-stalled anti-corruption legislation. He took quick executive action, including opening Ukraine's High Anti-Corruption Court, which was established under the previous presidential administration but never allowed to operate. He called snap parliamentary elections—his party was so new it had no representation in the Rada [the Ukrainian parliament]—and later won an overwhelming mandate, controlling 60 percent of the seats. With his new parliamentary majority, President [Zelensky] changed the Ukrainian constitution to remove absolute immunity from Rada deputies, which had been the source of raw corruption for two decades. There was much excitement in Kyiv that this time things could be different—a new Ukraine might finally be breaking from its corrupt, post-Soviet past."[26] In short, Taylor—America's top diplomat in Ukraine in the summer of 2019—tells Congress that as the summer of 2019 began, there were no grounds for anyone in Washington to fear that Zelensky was not aggressively combatting corruption in Ukraine. He therefore sets about, in late June, working to "support Ukraine against the Russian invasion and to help it defeat corruption" via a "regular channel of U.S. policy-making [that] has consistently had strong, bipartisan support both in Congress and in all [U.S. presidential] administrations since Ukraine's independence from Russia in 1991."[27]

Taylor soon learns, however, that his superiors in the Trump administration are in fact using an "irregular" and "informal" policy-making channel to direct events in Ukraine—one that only intermittently permits itself to be seen by America's chief of mission in Kyiv.[28] This irregular operation is fronted, Taylor subsequently tells Congress, by four "well-connected" men: Volker, Sondland, Perry, and Giuliani.[29] Giuliani will later admit, in a tweet, that none of the work he did with Volker, Sondland, or Perry was on behalf of U.S. interests; in early November he tweets that "the investigation I conducted concerning 2016 Ukrainian collusion and corruption, was done solely as a defense attorney to defend my client [Trump]."[30] Noted conservative George Conway, an attorney married to senior Trump adviser Kellyanne Conway, responds to Giuliani's confession by writing on Twitter, "This tweet by itself establishes that Donald Trump committed an impeachable offense. To say that Giuliani's and Trump's pursuit of 'Ukrainian . . . corruption' was 'done solely' to protect Trump's interests establishes that Trump was not acting for the country."[31]

* * *

On June 18, 2019, the day after Taylor's arrival in Kyiv, he participates in a conference call with Volker, Sondland, Perry, and two other men: Phil Reeker, who is acting assistant secretary of state for European and Eurasian Affairs, and State Department counselor Ulrich Brechbuhl.[32] The six men decide that a meeting between Trump and Zelensky is an "agreed-upon goal."[33] In the ensuing week, however, Volker and Sondland backpedal, informing Taylor, without additional explanation or clarification, that President Trump "want[s] to hear from [Zelensky]" before granting him an Oval Office meeting.[34] By June 27, Sondland is prepared to clarify this new directive, telling Taylor, as the latter will describe it to Congress in late 2019, that President Zelensky "needed to make clear to President Trump that he, President [Zelensky], was not standing in the way of 'investigations.'"[35] At the time of the conversation, Taylor had neither received nor become aware of any information suggesting Zelensky was doing anything but encouraging rather than hindering corruption investigations in Ukraine, and indeed the Pentagon had formally confirmed as much on May 23—more than a month earlier.[36]

On June 28, shortly before a planned conference call between Taylor, Sondland, Volker, Perry, Zelensky, and a number of "regular interagency participants," Sondland tells Taylor that he wants only himself, Taylor, Volker, Perry, and Zelensky on the call.[37] Sondland adds that he "want[s] to make sure no one [is] transcribing or monitoring" the call.[38] In a pre-call check-in, Taylor learns from Volker that the latter will be meeting with Zelensky one-on-one in Toronto in ninety-six hours' time—on July 2—and that at that meeting Volker will inform Zelensky of "what [Zelensky] should do to get the White House meeting" with President Trump.[39] Taylor will tell Congress that, despite being chief of mission in Ukraine, he had no idea at this point what Sondland and Volker were doing, or by what authority, or even what lay behind Sondland's concern about call transcriptions and Volker's as yet unspoken prerequisites for endorsing a Trump-Zelensky meeting.[40] All Volker will disclose to Taylor before the June 28 call with Zelensky is that Volker, Perry, and Sondland plan to "relay that President Trump want[s] to see rule of law, transparency, but also, specifically, cooperation on investigations [from Zelensky] to 'get to the bottom of things.'"[41]

On July 10, eight days after the face-to-face Volker-Zelensky meeting in Toronto that Volker had previewed for Taylor, Volker meets at the White House with national security advisor John Bolton, Perry, Sondland, Fiona Hill, NSC interagency coordinator for Ukraine Alexander Vindman, and two Ukrainian officials: Zelensky's national security advisor, Alexander Danyliuk, and top Zelensky aide Andriy Yermak.[42] At the meeting, per Vindman, "Sondland emphasized the importance that Ukraine deliver the investigations into the 2016 election, the Bidens, and Burisma"—an account that contradicts Perry's later insistence that he was never at a meeting at which the Bidens were discussed by name.[43]

Taylor is not asked to join the July 10 White House meeting, nor is he given a readout of it until nine days later.[44] Instead, Taylor is in Kyiv on July 10, meeting with Zelensky's chief of staff, Andriy Bohdan, and a top foreign policy adviser to the Ukrainian president, Vadym Prystaiko.[45] It is at this meeting that Taylor learns for the first time—from Prystaiko—that Rudy Giuliani has informed the Zelensky administration that, as Taylor will put it, even a "phone call between the two presidents" will be "unlikely to happen" in the near term.[46] Taylor concludes in the following days that "the meeting [with Trump] President Zelensky wanted was conditioned on the investigations of Burisma and alleged Ukrainian interference in the 2016 U.S. elections," and that the vehicle by which this demand had been communicated to the Zelensky administration was the "irregular policy channel . . . guided by Mr. Giuliani."[47] Meanwhile, in a phone call on July 11, Perry tells Bolton that he had been assured at the meeting the day before that Zelensky wouldn't "prove an obstacle to any investigations into alleged corruption."[48]

When the details of the July 10 meeting that Sondland, Volker, Perry, Hill, Vindman, and Bolton had with Danyliuk and Yermak at the White House are revealed in October 2019, it will immediately become clear why Taylor wasn't invited to the meeting—or even given a timely readout of it. According to the *Washington Post*, at the meeting Danyliuk and Yermak, who "had come to the White House hoping to shore up relations with the Trump administration," are instead ambushed by Sondland in a way that stuns even John Bolton. The incident leads to "a showdown"—indeed, multiple showdowns—"between top White House officials" in the presence of their Ukrainian guests.[49]

The first confrontation comes in Bolton's office, where the group of six U.S. officials "discusse[s] the United States' desire to see Kyiv crack down on corruption."[50] To the surprise of (at a minimum) Hill, Vindman, and Bolton, Sondland suddenly "turn[s] the conversation away from ongoing corruption probes to pursuing specific investigations that were important to Trump," namely those connected to the president's and Giuliani's past Burisma- and DNC-related allegations.[51] Sondland is not subtle; Hill will later tell Congress that "in front of the Ukrainians, as I came in, [Sondland] was talking about how he had an agreement with Chief of Staff Mulvaney for a meeting with the Ukrainians [and Trump] if they [the Ukrainians] were going to go forward with investigations. And my director for Ukraine [Vindman] was looking completely alarmed."[52] Vindman is not the only one in such a state, however: the *Washington Post* reports that Sondland's line of discussion "so alarm[s]" Bolton that he "cut[s] the meeting short."[53] Thereafter, Bolton takes four steps: he directs Hill and Vindman to "monitor Sondland" but take no part in his scheme, which he calls a "drug deal"; he directs Hill to inform "the [NSC's] lawyers" about the deal; he tells peers that he believes a Trump-Zelensky call under the terms just outlined by Sondland would be a "disaster"; and he describes Rudy Giuliani to a colleague as "a hand grenade who is going to blow everybody up."[54]

After Bolton unceremoniously concludes the meeting in his office, Sondland takes Danyliuk and Yermak to the basement of the White House for a meeting in the Ward Room, a conference room used by the White House's national security team.[55] In the Ward Room, Sondland, joined by Vindman, is undeterred by Bolton's dramatic reaction to his previous comments and "emphasize[s]," according to Vindman, "the importance that Ukraine deliver the investigations into the 2016 election, the Bidens, and Burisma."[56] Vindman objects, telling Sondland that the demand he is making of the Ukrainians is "inappropriate."[57] Thereafter, Vindman and Sondland engage in an exchange so tense that eventually Sondland must "[ask] the two Ukrainian officials if they would like to step out of the meeting temporarily," per the *Post*.[58]

One reason the tension between Sondland and Vindman escalates is that shortly after the meeting begins, Fiona Hill joins it—on Bolton's explicit orders.[59] On hearing that Sondland has already begun pressuring the Ukrainians in the same fashion and on the same topic that had just led Bolton to shut down a meeting in his office, Hill "immediately echoe[s] Vindman's objections that the request [by Sondland] was counter to [U.S.] national security goals."[60] Indeed, Sondland's behavior is considered so inappropriate and contrary to NSC policy that Hill "raise[s] her voice" at Sondland and "strongly object[s]" to his demands on the Ukrainians, according to the *Post*.[61]

After the meeting in the Ward Room concludes, both Vindman and Hill proceed to the White House counsel's office to lodge a complaint with deputy White House counsel John Eisenberg (see chapter 31).[62]

On July 11, the day after Taylor's troubling meeting in Kyiv and Sondland's "inappropriate" one with Danyliuk and Yermak at the White House, Sen. Ron Johnson, who had been part of the U.S. delegation to Kyiv for Zelensky's inauguration, meets with Andriy Telizhenko in D.C. for thirty minutes to discuss, according to the *Milwaukee Journal Sentinel*, "an unsubstantiated claim that Ukraine interfered in the 2016 election," indeed the same claim Telizhenko had been shopping to Trump allies and U.S. media since at least January 2017.[63] Telizhenko also meets with Johnson's staff for five hours.[64] The former Ukrainian diplomat will later report that it was Johnson's team that initiated the meeting. "I was in Washington," Telizhenko will say, "and Senator Johnson found out I was in D.C., and [his] staff called me and wanted to do a meeting with me."[65] Why—or at whose invitation—Giuliani's Ukrainian friend is in D.C. is unknown.

As Johnson is meeting with Telizhenko, Perry is speaking with Bolton to "again [press] for the two leaders [Trump and Zelensky] to speak ahead of the parliamentary elections on July 21, stressing that a call was needed to build the relationship and help counter Russian influence in Ukraine."[66] Perry's insistence on the importance of any Trump-Zelensky call happening before July 21 underscores that senior administration officials knew Trump's refusal to speak to Zelensky was capable of having a measurable impact on Ukrainian politics, by way of causing Zelensky to appear to Ukrainian voters as being out of favor in Washington. In the event, Trump does not speak to Zelensky until four days after the elections in Ukraine.[67]

On July 18, Taylor learns from a staff person at the Office of Management and Budget that a hold has been placed on U.S. security assistance to Ukraine. The staffer says they cannot give the reason for the hold, though it is unclear to Taylor whether the staffer does not know the reason or has been told not to discuss it.[68] What is clear, however, is the source of the directive: the president of the United States. The OMB staff person tells Taylor that "her boss had instructed her not to approve any additional spending of security assistance for Ukraine until further notice . . . [and] that the directive had come from the President to the Chief of Staff [acting OMB director Mulvaney] to OMB."[69] Taylor, in his own words "astonish[ed]" by this turn of events, realizes "in an instant" that at a moment when "the Ukrainians were fighting the Russians and counted on not only the training and weapons, but also the assurance of U.S. support . . . [t]he irregular policy channel [between the White House and the Zelensky administration] was running contrary to the goals of longstanding U.S. policy."[70]

The next day, July 19, Taylor speaks to Vindman and NSC senior director for European and Russian affairs Fiona Hill to try to find out the basis for the president's extraordinary directive. He asks Hill, in particular, to detail what was discussed at the July 10 White House meeting between Bolton, Perry, Sondland, Hill, Volker, Vindman, and the two Ukrainian officials, Danyliuk and Yermak.[71] During this and other conversations between Taylor and NSC officials, the "unanimous conclusion" of all parties is that "security assistance [to Ukraine] should be resumed" and the hold placed on security assistance by the president should be "lifted."[72]

In short order, the NSC confers with the Department of Defense to ascertain whether the latter agrees with its assessment that the hold is contrary to America's national interests. Word comes back from the Pentagon in less than twenty-four hours: the hold should be lifted as soon as possible.[73] During the same period, the NSC consults with secretary of state Mike Pompeo, CIA director Gina Haspel, national security advisor Bolton, and, yet again, secretary of defense Mark Esper; the nation's top four national security officials all agree with Taylor that "the President . . . [should] release the hold."[74] Though Taylor's efforts to schedule a meeting with Pompeo, Haspel, Bolton, Esper, and the president to discuss the hold begin in late July, by mid-September 2019 Taylor has still not been able to get such a meeting onto the president's schedule. It will subsequently be revealed that Trump had quietly met twice to discuss the hold with just Pompeo, Bolton, and Esper, in both cases rejecting their pleas to lift the block on military aid to Ukraine (see chapter 26).[75] The justification for Trump not being willing to schedule a formal meeting about the hold with his top diplomat in Ukraine, as Taylor is made to understand it, is that the president's idea of "purchasing Greenland"—the world's largest island, and a part of the Kingdom of Denmark—"took up a lot of energy in the NSC."[76] In fact, by early August 2019 Trump had been repeatedly told by the Danes that Greenland was not for sale.[77]

A February 2019 report by *Axios* will reveal that—contrary to claims by the White House that the president is regularly in meetings and has a busy schedule—the president's daily schedule is in fact nearly empty, and publicly released schedules suggesting otherwise are fraudulent.[78] According to the digital media outlet, a three-month review of President Trump's schedule (a sample extending from November 2018 through February 2019) reveals that President Trump spends approximately 60 percent of his "working" hours in wholly unstructured "executive time" in his personal residence in the White House.[79] Indeed, *Axios* reveals that while Trump's public schedule places him in the Oval Office from

8:00 AM to 11:00 AM daily, in fact Trump is "never in the Oval [Office] during those hours, according to six sources with direct knowledge [of Trump's behavior]. Instead, he spends his mornings in the residence, watching TV, reading the papers, and responding to what he sees and reads by phoning aides, members of Congress, friends, administration officials and informal advisers"—the latter a category that includes, among others, Rudy Giuliani, Sean Hannity, Joe diGenova, and Victoria Toensing.[80] Per *Axios*, on some days the president spends as many as seven of the eight hours of his "workday" in his residence doing as he pleases; in some instances, reports the media outlet, Trump uses "executive time" to hide from the public and even "most West Wing staff" certain meetings "that he doesn't want . . . [aides] to know about."[81]

According to Chris Whipple, author of *The Gatekeepers: How the White House Chiefs of Staff Define Every President*, "there's almost no [historical] parallel" for Trump's highly flexible, surprisingly vacant work schedule.[82] A December 31, 2019, CNN report reveals that Trump, as of that date, had spent over 23 percent of his presidency at Trump-branded golf courses and over 30 percent of his presidency at one of his properties rather than at the White House or another federal office building.[83] In January 2020, the *Washington Post* reveals that close Trump ally Steve Mnuchin, the treasury secretary, is refusing to disclose the cost to taxpayers of Secret Service protection during Trump's trips to country clubs and Trump properties until after the 2020 election.[84] Whereas taxpayers paid $96 million for President Obama's travel over his eight-year term of office, extrapolations from the cost of a just a single month of Trump's travel ($13.6 million, according to the *Post*) suggest that in his first thirty-six months in office, Trump's unprecedented travel demands have cost American taxpayers almost half a billion dollars.[85]

During Ambassador Taylor's July 19, 2019, phone call with Fiona Hill and Alexander Vindman, Hill informs Taylor that Sondland's actions at the White House on July 10 had "confused" the Ukrainians present at the meeting.[86] Moreover, she tells Taylor that Volker has had a meeting with

Giuliani to discuss Ukraine—a meeting that to that point Volker had not disclosed to Taylor.[87] When, the next day, Taylor asks Volker about his meeting with Giuliani, the president's special envoy to Ukraine gives "no response" to the inquiry, per Taylor's subsequent congressional testimony.[88] Though Volker refuses to confirm or deny to Taylor that he has been secretly conversing about U.S. foreign policy with the president's personal attorney, he does, on July 20, inform Taylor via text that a Trump-Zelensky phone call would be taking place shortly, and that during that call the "most important" thing would be Zelensky's agreement to "say that he will help [the] investigation" into unspecified matters in Ukraine.[89]

Later in the day on July 20, Sondland tells Taylor that he has fed Zelensky a specific line that he should use in speaking to the president: according to Sondland, Zelensky has been told that he should use the phrase "I will leave no stone unturned" when speaking of "investigations" of Clinton and Biden.[90] Taylor thereafter speaks with Zelensky's national security adviser, Alexander Danyliuk, who tells Taylor that Zelensky does "not want to be used as a pawn in a U.S. re-election campaign."[91] Profoundly affected by his conversation with Danyliuk, Taylor communicates the new Ukrainian president's "concern" to Volker and Sondland on July 21. It is unclear whether either Volker or Sondland ever passes Taylor's message on to Trump.

On August 22, 2019, Taylor speaks to NSC official Tim Morrison by phone to ask whether the official U.S. policy toward Ukraine has changed. Morrison tells him that the "President doesn't want to provide any assistance [to Ukraine] at all."[92] Per the *Washington Post*, Morrison's statement to Taylor is consistent with what John Bolton is telling U.S. trade representative Robert Lighthizer at around the same time: that "President Trump probably would oppose any action that benefited the government in Kyiv."[93] Both of these statements are consistent with the subsequent congressional testimony of Lt. Col. Vindman, who tells Congress in October 2019, as summarized by the *New York Times*, that "he drafted a memorandum in mid-August [2019] that sought to try to restart security aid that was being withheld from Ukraine, but Mr. Trump refused to sign it."[94]

CHAPTER 26

ABC NEWS AND THE HOLD

On June 13, 2019, Ellen Weintraub, the chair of the Federal Election Commission, issues a public statement reminding all candidates running for federal office in 2020 that "it is illegal for any person to solicit, accept, or receive anything of value from a foreign national in connection with a U.S. election."[1] Hours earlier, ABC News had released the transcript of a recently concluded and historically startling interview with Donald Trump, in which the sitting U.S. president declared to the network's George Stephanopoulos that, in advance of the 2020 presidential election, he was willing to receive valuable information about his domestic political opponents from foreign nationals and even foreign governments.[2]

Besides falsely telling Stephanopoulos that the Mueller Report had concluded that his campaign "rebuffed" Russian nationals throughout the campaign, Trump insists to ABC News' Sunday morning anchor that "you don't" call the FBI if "information" that is "on your opponent"—even if "it's coming from Russia," as Stephanopoulos asks—comes to your political campaign.[3] After falsely telling Stephanopoulos that he has never called the FBI for any reason (the *Washington Post* notes that in fact he has done so "when he wanted its help"), Trump says that if a foreign national or government has information on your opponent, you never call the FBI because "life doesn't work that way"—adding that his own FBI director, Christopher Wray, is "wrong" to have advised politicians to act otherwise in recent sworn testimony to Congress.[4]

In all, Trump's many stunning statements to Stephanopoulos about the sort of conduct it will subsequently be revealed he was then engaged in—more robustly than was ever the case during the Russia scandal—include the following: "If somebody [from a foreign country] comes into your office with oppo[sition] research . . . with information that might be good or bad or something, but good for you, bad for your opponent, you don't call the FBI"; "You might want to listen, there's nothing wrong with listening . . . if somebody called from a country . . . [and said], 'we have information on your opponent' . . . I'd want to hear it"; and "It's not an [election] interference, [if] they [foreign nationals] have information . . . I think I'd take it."[5] The furthest Trump will go in the direction of complying with federal law as laid out by the chair of the FEC is noting to Stephanopoulos that "if I thought there was something wrong" with information received from foreign nationals—meaning, if foreign nationals conveyed to Trump information helpfully establishing that Trump's political opponent had committed a crime—"I'd go maybe to the FBI."[6]

Though the president is, at the time of the ABC News interview, many months into secretly seeking information from the Ukrainian government on a leading 2020 political opponent, he gives no indication to Stephanopoulos that this is the case, and in fact falsely indicates that his knowledge of the Mueller Report's findings might lead him to "think differently" than he had in 2016 about how to handle the receipt of information on an opponent from foreign nationals.[7] While the evidence presented during the president's January 2020 impeachment trial will confirm that his views on the matters he discussed with Stephanopoulos had remained unchanged throughout his presidency, Trump's acknowledgment to ABC News of the findings of the Mueller Report helps establish as a matter of law that he does know, post-Mueller, that soliciting or receiving information on a political opponent from another country is an illicit act.

In April 2019, Congress approves the first of two tranches of military aid to Ukraine. Following a second authorization in June, a total of $391 million will have been dedicated by Congress to the assistance of America's European ally.[8] The $391 million comes from, per the *New York*

Times, "two pots overseen by different agencies—$250 million from the Defense Department's Ukraine Security Assistance Initiative for war-fighting equipment including sniper rifles and rocket-propelled grenade launchers, and $141 million from the State Department's Foreign Military Financing Program for night-vision devices, radar systems, and additional rocket-propelled grenade launchers. The funds [are] intended to help train and equip Ukrainian forces in their fight to stave off a Russian incursion."[9]

On June 18, "the Defense Department publicly announce[s] it [will] release military aid to Ukraine," having completed "mandated checks to ensure Ukraine ha[s] made progress on corruption."[10] According to the *New York Times*, within twenty-four hours of the Pentagon's announcement Trump "ask[s] about putting a hold on security aid to Ukraine," which he will later seek to justify by terming it an anti-corruption measure—in direct contradiction to the Pentagon's June 18 finding.[11] In February 2020, just hours after the documentary record in Trump's impeachment trial is sealed—and days removed from Rep. Schiff alleging that the NSA and CIA are withholding Trump-Ukraine scandal documents "due to pressure from the White House"—DOJ will reveal that it has been blocking two dozen emails that confirm the president "was directly involved in asking about and deciding on the [Ukraine] aid as early as June."[12]

Within hours of Trump's query about a hold, Robert B. Blair, aide to Trump acting chief of staff Mick Mulvaney, has relayed the hold as an order to acting OMB head Russell Vought, telling Vought, "We need to hold [the money] up."[13] Vought, along with Blair, associate director of national security programs at OMB Michael P. Duffey, and OMB counsel Mark Paoletta, are tasked with immediately effectuating the president's wishes.[14] When, later in the day on June 19, Mark Sandy, the career civil servant at OMB in charge of dispensing Pentagon funds, asks Duffey, his supervisor, for an explanation for the hold, Duffey cannot or will not provide him one.[15] *Just Security* will publish, in January 2020, previously unreleased Pentagon emails revealing that the Defense Department "repeatedly sounded the alarm" to the White House over a "growing concern . . . that the [Ukraine aid] hold would violate the Impoundment

Control Act"—emails that confirm, too, that "no one" but Trump "supported his position" on the aid freeze, with OMB's only response to the Pentagon's objections to the hold being that it was a "clear direction from POTUS [Trump]."[16]

That Trump's request quickly passes from OMB to the Pentagon is confirmed by the fact that deputy assistant secretary of defense Laura Cooper, as she will later testify to Congress, learns that Trump wishes to issue a hold on the congressionally mandated Ukraine funds almost immediately after Trump first raises the idea on June 19.[17] Cooper correctly surmises that the aid is not yet formally blocked; indeed, on June 27 Mulvaney emails Blair, "I'm just trying to tie up some loose ends. Did we ever find out about the money for Ukraine and whether we can hold it back?"[18] Blair responds to Mulvaney that it may be possible, but Trump should "expect Congress to become unhinged" if the aid is frozen; he adds that any holdup in aid to an ally currently at war with Russia "might further fuel the narrative Mr. Trump [is] pro-Russia," in the words of the *New York Times*.[19]

As Trump's joint White House–OMB effort to block aid to Ukraine without formal notification to Congress or the aid's intended recipient proceeds, it is mostly carried out, the *Times* reports, by "political appointees . . . with personal and professional ties to Mr. Mulvaney."[20] The *Times* identifies the key complication in the secretive effort: "It was easy enough for the White House to hold up the State Department portion of the funding. Since the State Department had not yet notified Congress of its plans to release the money, all it took was making sure that the notification did not happen. Freezing the Pentagon's $250 million portion was more difficult, since the Pentagon had already certified that Ukraine had met requirements set by Congress to show that it was addressing its endemic corruption and notified lawmakers of its intent to spend the money."[21] To accomplish the latter end, Sandy must attach "a footnote to block spending that the administration had already notified Congress was ready to go," something "he had never done" in "his 12 years [at OMB]."[22] Duffey, a political appointee, later relieves Sandy, the career civil servant, of his role in dispensing the aid to Ukraine, in what the *Times* will call a "very unusual" step.[23] By the second week of August, the *Times* reports, "Mr. Duffey had taken to issuing footnotes every few days to block the Pentagon spending. Office of Management and Budget lawyers approved each one."[24]

The NSC interagency coordinator for Ukraine at the time, Alexander Vindman, begins to hear whispers of a possible hold on the military aid to Ukraine in late June. Like Cooper, Vindman understands the aid to not yet be conclusively halted.[25] When he learns, in early July, that the aid has unquestionably been blocked, he immediately communicates this information to multiple sources, including an aide to Vice President Mike Pence, Jennifer Williams—who will later testify to Congress that she told Keith Kellogg, Pence's national security advisor, of the hold— and also Laura Cooper, who will testify that on July 9 she personally briefed Pence on the hold.[26] Williams tells Congress that, in the first week of July, only OMB and the State Department, to her knowledge, were aware of the funds being blocked, testimony that seems to suggest Pompeo may have been in the loop before the NSC was; indeed, NSC official Fiona Hill will testify that as of July 10, neither she nor Bolton knew of any hold.[27] That Bolton learned of the hold on or shortly after July 15 seems certain, however, as his deputy Charles Kupperman tells NSC official Tim Morrison on approximately that date that "[Mulvaney's] office had informed OMB that it was the President's direction to hold the assistance."[28] July 15 also sees a futile effort by the Pentagon—which had less than a month earlier certified Ukraine's anti-corruption efforts as satisfactory—to "expedite delivery" of Javelin missiles to Ukraine. This failed attempt to aid the European nation suggests that Zelensky's reference during his July 25 call with Trump about being eager to buy more Javelins may have been an implicit request to Trump to allow a previously agreed-upon sale to go through.[29]

If select officials at the State Department indeed knew of the hold in early July, as Williams will eventually testify, this knowledge did not penetrate far into Pompeo's sphere of influence. Deputy assistant secretary of state George Kent will testify that he first learned of an "unofficial" hold having been issued by Mulvaney in a video conference call on July 18; the department's Ukraine specialist, Catherine Croft, will say that she knew of the hold "before" July 18 but learned on the call, with Kent, that the order for the hold had come from the president.[30] Bill Taylor, Kurt Volker, and State Department official David Holmes will also testify that they learned of the hold on July 18, with all three believing—as Gordon Sondland says he did as well—that the hold had been effectuated on that day.[31]

One reason for the abiding confusion over when Trump issued his order to block military aid to Ukraine is that different federal officials are sent different messages on the subject. According to the *Washington Post*, OMB officials waited until mid-July to "[relay] Trump's order to the State Department and the Pentagon during an interagency meeting"— while keeping it unclear whether the "order" had been acted upon, focusing instead on the president having "'concerns'" and wanting to simply determine if the money "needed to be spent."[32]

Regardless of when individual federal agencies were able to conclusively determine that the aid had been blocked, the *Post* reports that by the time of the Trump-Zelensky call on July 25, Ukraine "likely knew" the aid had been halted or was in significant danger of being halted.[33] Just so, while it is unclear when between July 10 and July 18 Bolton learned Trump wanted to halt aid to Ukraine, it is certain that in his first conversation with the president thereafter he informs Trump that the money is needed to "curb Russian aggression"—an argument that leaves the president, per the *Washington Post*, "unmoved."[34]

According to CNN, the first White House discussion of a possible aid stoppage came in early June, and was contemporaneous with Trump ordering Bolton and secretary of defense Mark Esper to conduct a "policy review" of U.S. assistance to Ukraine; deputy assistant secretary of defense Laura Cooper's subsequent congressional testimony will confirm, however, that no such NSC or Pentagon review was conducted in July, August, or September.[35] Given that Esper was one of at least two Trump administration officials ostensibly tasked with a Ukraine policy review in early June, it is unclear why a joint finding by the Pentagon and the State Department in May 2019 "certif[ying] that Ukraine 'ha[d] taken substantial action to make defense institutional reforms for the purposes of decreasing corruption'" was insufficient to preclude discussion of an additional executive branch review of Ukraine's eligibility for military aid.[36] From the moment the hold was issued, OMB insisted on its continuance "without explanation" to the Pentagon, according to Cooper's late 2019 congressional testimony.[37]

Given how the White House will subsequently handle queries on the hold from lawmakers, this interagency confusion over the timing, purpose, and finality of the aid stoppage appears to have been deliberate. The *Post* will subsequently report that "administration officials were instructed [by Mulvaney] to tell lawmakers that the delays [in sending aid to Ukraine were] part of an 'interagency process' but to give them no additional information," a "pattern" of information withholding and even misdirection that the *Post* notes will "[continue] for nearly two months."[38]

From its very start, the *New York Times* reports, the suspension of aid to Ukraine not only caused "staff members at the State and Defense Departments who work on issues related to Ukraine" to be "puzzled and alarmed" but also provoked "confusion and frustration" in Kyiv.[39] When staff members at the U.S. embassy in Kyiv learn about Giuliani's ongoing contacts with the Ukrainians, according to the *Washington Post* they "repeatedly [express] concerns" to their superiors, noting that not only "have [they] not been privy to most of the discussions" but in many instances they "only learned [about them] later from the Ukrainians," who consistently represent to U.S. embassy staff that they have no idea whether "Giuliani [is] officially speaking for the U.S. government."[40]

While sources will tell the *Wall Street Journal* that "the delay on the aid to Ukraine came as the White House was seeking to cut a broad set of foreign aid programs," the newspaper observes that Ukraine could not have been a regular part of this review, as "the administration abandoned its effort to cut those other foreign assistance programs by August 22, while the hold on the aid to Ukraine remained for several more weeks."[41]

Indeed, when Trump ultimately releases the aid to Ukraine after the revelation of the whistleblower's complaint (see chapter 32), he will contend that the release had nothing to do with the completion of any broad-based foreign aid review, but was rather due to the fact that "[Ohio Republican senator] Rob Portman and others called me and asked" for the money to be released.[42] It is later revealed by the *New York Times* that in fact Portman's call to Trump didn't come until September 11, after the president knew of the whistleblower's complaint and had many reasons besides Portman's powers of persuasion—including the president's September 9 discovery that the House was about to open an investigation into his call with Zelensky—to release the aid and insist he had always been planning to do so.[43] "I have no doubt about why the president allowed the assistance to go forward," Rep. Eliot L. Engel, Democratic chairman of the House Foreign Affairs Committee, will later say. "He got caught."[44]

The president's claim that Portman's September call was influential in his thinking on the aid to Ukraine is further undercut in the final months of 2019, when both CNN and the *New York Times* report that three of the most powerful and influential officials in the Trump administration—Pompeo, Bolton, and Esper—had urged Trump to free the aid to Ukraine both in Bedminster, New Jersey, on August 16 and in the Oval Office in late August; on August 31, Sen. Ron Johnson of Wisconsin also tried to convince Trump to release the aid.[45] Per the *Times*, in the late August White House meeting between Trump, Pompeo, Bolton, and Esper, much as in their earlier meeting in New Jersey, the nation's top military, national security, and diplomatic officials "tried but failed to convince [Trump] that releasing the aid was in [the] interests of the United States"—with Bolton unambiguously declaring release of the aid "in America's interest" and Esper telling Trump that from the Pentagon's perspective America had "gotten some really good benefits from" its "defense relationship" with Ukraine.[46]

Whether the three men knew it or not, top lawyers at OMB—Mick Mulvaney's bailiwick—were at that very moment "developing an argument . . . that Mr. Trump's role as commander in chief would simply allow him to override Congress" on the matter of foreign aid.[47]

* * *

In November 2019, John Bolton will begin saying, through his attorney, that he can testify to "many relevant meetings" at the White House that no other witness has yet discussed with Congress—a claim that draws attention to the fact that only Bolton and Esper know why Trump ordered them to initiate a "policy review" of aid to Ukraine in early June 2019 and rebuffed their urgent, national security–based entreaties to reinstate aid to Ukraine in August 2019.[48] As CNN will report with respect to the June policy review, no one has told Congress or the American people "why the President ordered the review or what was under review."[49]

Another ongoing mystery is when the Ukrainians first learned of the hold. In December 2019, the *New York Times* reports on a diplomatic cable seen by Ukraine's deputy foreign minister Olena Zerkal as early as July 22 that mentions the hold on military aid to Ukraine.[50] Zerkal says that the "Ukrainian presidential administration was copied as a recipient of the cable from the [Ukrainian] embassy in Washington."[51] The *Times* writes, "Whether senior Ukrainian officials knew of the aid freeze before the July 25 [Trump-Zelensky] phone call or not, the accounts of Ms. Zerkal and [Laura] Cooper show that the Ukrainian government was aware of the hold on aid through several critical weeks in August as United States diplomats pressed Mr. Zelensky to make a public statement on the investigations."[52] Just as troubling, given how hard Trump's defenders will lean on Zelensky's public claims that he didn't feel pressured to investigate Clinton or Biden, Zerkal will tell the *Times* that during the period Zelensky made such statements his "administration [was trying] to squelch information that could embarrass or undercut Mr. Trump," and that in service of this goal she was told to "keep silent" about her knowledge of the hold and when it began.[53]

By October 2019, Zelensky will have shifted his tone on the matter of Trump's hold on U.S. aid, telling international media, "We're at war [with Russia]. If you're our strategic partner, then you can't go blocking anything for us."[54] Subsequent testimony by Laura Cooper will confirm that Kyiv knew there was a problem with the $391 million in military aid by July 25 at the very latest, which evidence, reports NBC News, "contradicts the argument by Republicans, including Trump, that the Ukrainians had no idea of the hold this early—meaning, according to that argument, that there could not have been a quid pro quo [during the July 25 Trump-Zelensky call]."[55]

When Trump's hold is eventually discovered by reporters covering a CIA whistleblower complaint in September 2019 (see chapter 32), the president immediately provides three cover stories, according to MSNBC, none of which prove to be accurate: "I didn't delay anything"; "We want to make sure a country is honest" (a claim contradicted by revelations that the Pentagon had already certified that Ukraine had met anti-corruption benchmarks); and "Those funds were paid, they were fully paid. . . . [M]y complaint has always been . . . I'll continue to withhold until such time as Europe and other nations contribute to Ukraine, because they're not doing it"—a claim contradicted by Trump's own actions, as he does not, in the event, wait to release U.S. aid to Ukraine until other nations increase the volume of their assistance.[56]

Shortly after the Ukraine scandal breaks in September, it is discovered that Trump's hold on military aid to Ukraine was in fact illegal, as it violated both the Impoundment Control Act (ICA) and OMB's statutory apportionment authority; still worse, it is discovered that Trump's OMB was explicitly told that the president's hold was illegal, but proceeded with it anyway.[57] Indeed, reporting by the *New York Times* in November 2019 reveals that Mulvaney sent emails in August 2019, long after the hold had been issued, seeking a formal legal justification for Trump's actions. Per the *Washington Post*, the emails, once discovered, "reveal extensive efforts to generate an after-the-fact justification" for the hold.[58] While an OMB spokesperson will later claim that the hold was legal provided it was done pursuant to a "temporary" ongoing "policy review," it is not clear that any such review was active after August 22.[59] The resignation of two OMB officials in protest of the ongoing hold, reported by the *New York Times*, will undercut the agency's claim that not only was the hold legal but there was internal "consensus" about its legality.[60]

According to OMB official Mark Sandy's testimony to Congress, at least one of the two OMB employees who resigned in summer 2019, an official in the OMB's legal office, believed the president's hold violated the ICA.[61] Per Sandy, the other employee likewise "expressed some frustrations about not understanding the reason for the hold."[62] Reporting from the *Post* confirms that even an internal OMB legal advisory opinion on the hold argued that it was legal only for "a short period of time."[63] That OMB believed an indefinite hold was illegal is confirmed when, at the end of the first week of September 2019, OMB quietly releases $141 million of the $391 million in withheld aid—without Trump's permission—on the basis of an internal "legal finding made earlier in the year."[64] Ultimately, the rest of the aid is held for a total of fifty-five days; Trump releases it on September 11, two weeks after he is briefed on a whistleblower's complaint about his dealings with Ukraine and just forty-eight hours before HPSCI—whose ranking member is Trump adviser Devin Nunes—issues a subpoena to acting director of national intelligence Robert Maguire to produce the complaint, an event the White House would have had reason to believe would lead to the complaint becoming public.[65] At the time the funds are released, the White House instructs State Department employees to "play down the release of the money" and take a "'nothing to see here'" approach to Trump's reversal of the hold.[66]

In December 2019, a *Wall Street Journal* report confirms that belief in the illegality of the hold was so pervasive at OMB that the White House had to shift authority for the dispersal of aid to Ukraine to a political appointee—and away from career public servants—because "career budget staff members questioned the legality of delaying the funds."[67] As the *Journal* reports, "Career civil servants put an initial hold on the aid, [but political appointee] Michael Duffey, associate director of national security programs in OMB, was given the authority for continuing to keep the aid on hold after the career staff began raising their concerns to political officials at OMB. . . . Mr. Duffey also began overseeing the process for approving and releasing funds, called apportionment, for other foreign aid and defense accounts."[68] The *Journal* calls Duffey's reassignment "unusual," as it is usually career OMB staff with "years, and sometimes decades, of technical knowledge of the funding process [who] have historically overseen the routine [apportionment] process."[69] Even as Duffey is overseeing the possibly illegal hold at OMB, the Pentagon is conducting its own internal review of the OMB decision after getting "repeatedly stonewalled" by the agency on the question of why the hold has been leveled.[70] The Pentagon ultimately determines that Trump's blocking of congressionally mandated military assistance to Ukraine was indeed illegal.[71]

CHAPTER 27

SONDLAND AND POMPEO

In November 2019, Gordon Sondland testifies publicly before Congress that he both learned of the hold on military aid to Ukraine on July 18, 2019, and that he believed the hold to have begun on that date.[1] Of Mike Pompeo, Sondland testifies that the secretary of state was "in the loop" on Trump's machinations in Ukraine from the beginning, even as Pompeo himself, per *Politico*, will insist "he knew little or nothing about how Trump's personal lawyer, Rudy Giuliani, sought to tie White House cooperation to Ukrainian investigations of Democrats."[2]

Sondland's testimony also includes the ambassador to the European Union's observation that, from the time of his own first involvement with the matter of investigations in Ukraine in spring 2019, the scheme to pressure Zelensky into announcing probes of the president's political rivals "kept getting more insidious"; he concedes to Congress that Trump's demands were "improper" and may well have been illegal.[3]

A detailed analysis by *Politico* of various witnesses' testimony on the timing and extent of Pompeo's knowledge of Giuliani's activities will find, in November 2019, that "there's no doubt Pompeo knew about efforts by Giuliani, who is not a U.S. government employee, to influence U.S. policy toward Ukraine. What's not clear is how seriously Pompeo took the president's attorney and the possibility that his activities could diverge from official U.S. policy."[4] Per the digital media outlet, besides Sondland testifying that Pompeo was "greenlighting" his own activities in Ukraine, the ambassador also testifies that Pompeo once acknowledged to him directly that the State Department was aware of Giuliani's clandestine activities in Kyiv, opining, "Yes, it's something we have to deal with."[5] State Department special envoy Kurt Volker—later "pushed out" of his job by Pompeo—will likewise tell Congress that he directly engaged with Pompeo on the matter of Giuliani's efforts in Ukraine.[6] *Politico* finds that when "U.S. diplomats weren't talking directly to Pompeo about Ukraine-related concerns, they often spoke with Ulrich Brechbuhl, the State Department counselor and longtime friend of Pompeo who serves as a conduit to the busy secretary."[7]

Call records indicate that Pompeo was in contact with Giuliani by phone twice in March 2019, and according to Volker, Pompeo spoke with Giuliani once in September 2019.[8] Giuliani's mission was directed by the president, Volker says, adding, "[W]ould Giuliani stop doing what he's doing because the secretary of State calls him? I'd be surprised."[9] During private congressional testimony in October 2019, Sondland concurs with Volker on both the source of Giuliani's marching orders and Giuliani's resultant recalcitrance: Pompeo "would have 'hit a brick wall when it came to getting rid of Giuliani,'" Sondland concludes.[10] While not addressing whether Pompeo could have thwarted Giuliani's efforts had he cared to, NSC official Tim Morrison will testify that he and Bolton were upset that Pompeo took no steps to rein in Sondland, who had informed Morrison that he was both acting on Trump's orders in his dealings with the Ukrainians and was regularly in touch with the president as to that matter in particular.[11] Morrison will testify that he personally confirmed that Sondland was telling the truth about having, per *Politico*, "direct access" to the president.[12]

Whatever the difficulty of Pompeo's position, Sondland is clear in his testimony to Congress, according to the *Washington Post* and *New York Times*, that "Pompeo knew, and approved, plans to have Ukraine commit to probes" of Biden and Clinton, and that Sondland "kept [Pompeo] updated" on his efforts, with Sondland at one point even showing Congress an email he sent to Pompeo through a senior Pompeo assistant, Lisa Kenna, that detailed the proposed Zelensky statement on Biden and Clinton investigations.[13] Of not just Pompeo but also Bolton and President Trump himself Sondland will testify, under oath, "They knew what we were doing [with the Ukrainians] and why."[14] Despite Sondland's testimony that he spoke regularly with Trump—including both before and after the president's July 25 call with Zelensky—after the whistleblower complaint is made public Trump, who had previously called Sondland a "great American," will say, "I hardly know the gentleman."[15]

On July 19, 2019, six days before Trump's fateful July 25 call with Zelensky, Sondland takes two important steps: he introduces Rudy Giuliani to Zelensky aide Andriy Yermak, and he briefs Zelensky directly on Trump's sub rosa Ukraine policy, afterward telling Volker and Taylor, "I [spoke] directly to Zelensky and gave him a full briefing. He's got it."[16] As the *Washington Post* will subsequently report, "it" refers to Trump's attempts to "lock down Zelensky's promise to launch an investigation into the 2016 election and into a natural-gas company that previously employed former vice president Joe Biden's son Hunter. Hanging in the air was a potential meeting between Trump and Zelensky that the Ukrainian president badly wanted."[17]

July 19 also sees Volker meet with Giuliani over breakfast to "tee[ ] up [Rudy's] call w[ith] Yermak," with Trump's special envoy noting that in the upcoming Giuliani-Yermak exchange, "most [important] is for Zelensky to say that he will help investigation"—an apparent reference to either the Burisma or CrowdStrike investigation.[18] That it is more likely the Burisma (Biden-related) investigation is indicated by a text from Taylor to Sondland and Volker sent two days later, in which Taylor notes that "President Zelensky is sensitive about Ukraine being taken seriously, not merely as an instrument in Washington domestic, re-election politics."[19] Taylor will eventually recount to Congress an exchange Volker once had with Yermak in which Volker told the Zelensky aide, "It would be a good idea not to investigate President Poroshenko, the previous [Ukrainian] President," to which Yermak replied, per separate testimony by deputy assistant secretary of state George Kent, "What, you mean the type of investigations you're pushing for us to do on Biden and Clinton?"[20]

On July 22, 2019, three days before the Trump-Zelensky call, Volker tells Sondland and Taylor that the recent Giuliani-Yermak call was "great" and that Giuliani is "now advocating [with Trump] for [the] phone call" between Trump and Zelensky that Sondland, Taylor, and Volker have long been hoping will occur.[21] Volker's implication is that Giuliani and Trump will be in direct contact with each other about any promises Yermak made on Zelensky's behalf while speaking to Giuliani; indeed, on July 25, just before the Trump-Zelensky phone call that Giuliani is now thought to be "advocating" for, Volker writes Sondland and Taylor a seeming confirmation that all three men are responding to cues directly from the Oval Office, telling his peers that he has just "heard from [the] White House [that] assuming President [Zelensky] convinces Trump he will investigate [and] 'get to the bottom of what happened' in 2016, we will nail down [a] date for [a] visit to Washington."[22]

Immediately after the July 25 Trump-Zelensky call, Yermak writes Volker to say that "Trump proposed [that Zelensky] . . . choose any convenient dates" for a White House visit, and that President Zelensky subsequently "chose 20, 21, 22 September for the White House visit"—the implication being that Zelensky had indeed done enough to convince Trump that he would investigate Biden and Clinton to earn a White House visit with Trump.[23] By fifteen days after the call, however, Sondland is texting Volker that "potus [Trump] really wants the deliverable."[24] Subsequent text messages in the same conversation confirm that the "deliverable" is a "draft statement" announcing the Biden and Clinton investigations.[25] Giuliani thereafter assists Sondland and Volker in drafting a statement for Zelensky to deliver publicly.[26]

On August 10, Yermak tells Volker that "once we have a date [for the White House visit], [Zelensky] will call for a press briefing, announcing [the] upcoming [Washington] visit and outlining [a] vision for the reboot of [the] US-Ukraine relationship, including among other things Burisma and election meddling in investigations."[27] On August 13, Volker and Sondland agree on draft language for Zelensky's statement, which they then send to Yermak.[28]

An analysis by *Politico* of the role its own reporting played at key moments in the Ukraine scandal finds that "one day after [*Politico*] revealed that military assistance aid was being withheld, Trump cancelled his trip to Poland where he was expected to meet with Zelensky, citing a need to remain in the U.S. to monitor an impending hurricane. One day later, Taylor . . . ask[ed] Sondland a pointed question following revelations that the aid [had] been frozen: 'Are we now saying that security assistance and [a] WH meeting are conditioned on investigations?' Sondland then suggest[ed] moving the conversation offline."[29]

As for the hurricane whose severity allegedly justified Trump skipping a trip to Warsaw during which he would have been compelled to confront Zelensky, Trump will—in a bizarre, even surreal episode—days later publicly present what the *Washington Post* calls a "doctored hurricane chart" in a seeming effort to convince Americans he had reason to believe Hurricane Dorian would strike three states (Florida, Georgia, and Alabama) rather than two (Florida and Georgia).[30] To make his case to the American people, Trump uses a black Sharpie to rewrite a professionally printed National Hurricane Center "cone of uncertainty" map, an act that "outrage[s] and panic[s]" scientists at the National Oceanic and Atmospheric Administration (NOAA).[31] In January 2020, a *New York Times* report will reveal that NOAA was "pressured" by the White House to confirm the accuracy of Trump's hastily altered map and his concurrent "false statements" about the hurricane—and that "NOAA officials knew full well that the map Mr. Trump presented [the public] had been altered, even as days later the agency issued an unsigned statement essentially chastising . . . forecasters for having contradicted the president."[32]

On August 30, Sondland tells Sen. Johnson that the suspended military aid will "go to Ukraine after the country appoint[s] a prosecutor to investigate the 2016 election," a confession that the aid is linked to an investigation demanded by Trump that causes Johnson, by his own later admission, to "wince" when he hears it.[33] In October, Johnson will tell far-right conservative radio host Mark Levin that he learned in late August that what Trump's unofficial diplomatic team had "in the works" was insisting that "President Zelensky would have to do something [on the investigations demanded by Trump] in order to really free up that [military] support" for Ukraine's defense against Russian incursions on its eastern border.[34] Johnson makes clear in another interview that he had heard this information directly from Trump, with the *Milwaukee Journal Sentinel* reporting that "Johnson said Trump said he was considering withholding the aid because of alleged corruption involving the 2016 election."[35] The *Washington Post* reports that these comments constitute Johnson "confirm[ing] a Trump-Ukraine quid pro quo."[36]

During a phone call with Trump on August 31, Johnson asks the president whether he will grant him, as a U.S. senator, "the authority to tell Zelensky that the U.S. aid [is] coming"; Trump flatly refuses the request.[37] Johnson will later say of his call with Trump that the president "specifically cited concerns about the 2016 election" in speaking of military aid to Ukraine.[38] During a "combative" October 6 appearance on NBC News to discuss his by then controversial August call with Trump, Johnson concedes that "what [Trump] wants is . . . an accounting of what happened in 2016. . . . Who set him up? Did things spring from Ukraine? The president told me repeatedly in the May 23rd Oval Office visit, [and] on the phone on [August] 31st, [that] the reason he had very legitimate concerns and reservations about Ukraine is, first, corruption, generalized. And then specifically about what kind of interference [there was] in the 2016 election."[39]

Neither Johnson nor Trump will ever cite any other corruption cases or investigations in Ukraine—besides potential Burisma and Crowd-Strike probes—that would give rise to Trump having a "generalized" concern about corruption in Ukraine. Sen. Chris Murphy (D-CT), speaking of a September 2019 trip to Ukraine with Johnson, discloses to the *Washington Post* that "Zelensky's 'entire' administration [is] concerned 'that the [military] aid that was being cut off to Ukraine by the president was a consequence for their unwillingness, at the time, to investigate the Bidens."[40] Murphy tells the *Post* that he heard this not only from "numerous Ukrainian officials" but also "directly" from President Zelensky.[41]

CHAPTER 28

THE SECOND TRUMP-ZELENSKY CALL

On the morning of July 25, 2019, shortly before speaking with Volody-myr Zelensky by phone, Trump has a discussion with his ambassador to the European Union, Gordon Sondland.[1] Six days earlier, Sondland had sent a message to Zelensky through one of the Ukrainian politician's aides; the message underscored for Zelensky that it would be in his best interest to offer Trump "assurances to run a fully transparent inves-tigation" of the CrowdStrike and Burisma conspiracy theories and to convince the American president that the Ukrainian government would "turn over every stone" in conducting such investigations.[2] Indeed, Sond-land had gone further still in his communications with the Ukraini-ans, insisting, according to the December 2019 House Permanent Select Committee on Intelligence report on the Ukraine scandal, that "the public announcement of these investigations [by Zelensky] was a prereq-uisite for the coveted White House meeting with President Trump" that Zelensky had sought since his first phone call with Trump, on the day of his election in April 2019.[3]

But it is not only Trump whom Sondland speaks to in the immediate run-up to the president's July 25 call with Zelensky. As detailed by *The Hill*, a *Wall Street Journal* investigation finds that the ambassador "kept top officials in the Trump administration updated on efforts to persuade Ukraine to launch an investigation into former Vice President Joe Biden ahead of Trump's much-publicized July call with the country's presi-dent . . . including acting White House chief of staff Mick Mulvaney and Energy Secretary Rick Perry, via email."[4]

Prior to his call with Zelensky, Trump is briefed extensively by the National Security Council with "talking points . . . based on official U.S. policy."[5] The talking points encourage the president to discuss broad anti-corruption reforms in Ukraine, long "a pillar of American foreign policy in the country."[6] Christopher Anderson, an assistant to Kurt Volker, will later confirm in testimony to Congress that "individual investigations [of U.S. citizens] were not part of" America's anti-corruption policy in Ukraine.[7]

When the contents of Trump's call with Zelensky are later revealed in U.S. media, the *Washington Post* will note that "the timing of Trump's attempt to pressure Zelensky made it all the more extraordinary. One day earlier, former special counsel Robert S. Mueller III had, in halting testimony before Congress, essentially ended any prospect that Trump would face impeachment for his campaign's ties to Russia in 2016 or alleged efforts to obstruct the investigation into election interference that followed."[8]

The inciting event in Trump's eventual impeachment for soliciting foreign election interference therefore comes less than twenty-four hours after an investigation of possible prior attempts by Trump to solicit or aid foreign election interference had been unable to—on the evidence available to investigators—establish such crimes beyond a reasonable doubt. As the *Post* writes, "The Russia 'cloud' that Trump [had] so frequently railed against had finally been lifted. And yet, within hours, he was exposing himself to new allegations of collusion, this time not with Russia, but with neighboring Ukraine."[9]

The *Wall Street Journal* reports that shortly before the July 25 Trump-Zelensky call, Trump national security advisor John Bolton "argued with the president that any disruption in [military] aid [to Ukraine] would leave Kyiv and the rest of Europe vulnerable to Russian aggression. One White House aide said that the argument became heated on Mr. Bolton's side. After the call, advocates for the aid within the White House and on Capitol Hill pushed for the president to reconsider."[10]

* * *

Trump's call with Zelensky lasts approximately thirty minutes. A memo describing a portion of the call—by some reckonings, as little as ten minutes and forty seconds of its half-hour duration—is later released to the public following a CIA whistleblower complaint describing the call as a national security threat.[11] The memo released by the White House is not a contemporaneous transcript; not only does it not appear to reproduce a thirty-minute conversation, but also, as the *Washington Post* will report, "odd markings [and] ellipses fuel doubts" about the memo's accuracy and completeness.[12] Nevertheless, Trump will falsely tell the public that the memo is in fact a "transcript" that reflects a "word-for-word, comma-for-comma" reproduction of the call's content.[13] The president's claim contradicts an earlier White House admission that the memo was "not a verbatim transcription but rather a summary."[14] After he receives more than a month of criticism for his erroneous description of the memo, Trump concedes, in November 2019, that the memo only "basically" comprises what happened during his conversation with Zelensky.[15]

According to "current and former U.S. officials" who speak to the *Washington Post* in early October, the White House's initial admission that the memo is incomplete is accurate. As the officials report to the *Post*, "several elements [of the memo] . . . indicate that the document may have been handled in an unusual way. Those include the use of ellipses— punctuation indicating that information has been deleted for clarity or other reasons—that traditionally have not appeared in summaries of presidential calls with foreign leaders."[16] The *Post* observes that in two instances ellipses appear in the memo at moments when Trump is speaking to Zelensky about CrowdStrike.[17] Ellipses appear yet again when Trump is speaking to Zelensky about another conspiracy theory the Kremlin has propounded and that President Trump wants the Ukrainian government to investigate: the allegation that "Democratic presidential candidate Joseph Biden had, while vice president, demanded the removal of a prosecutor looking to investigate Biden's son Hunter."[18] When the *Post* asks the White House to explain the ellipses, it refuses, pointing to an earlier statement suggesting that ellipses are used in transcripts of presidential calls when a speaker is "trailing off" or "paus[ing]"—a claim that current and former U.S. officials say is false, as in such instances those transcribing a presidential call with a foreign leader write "[inaudible]" instead.[19] According to the *New York Times*, one of the ellipses whose usage the White House neither explains nor justifies replaces a statement by Trump to Zelensky that there are multiple "tapes of Biden" speaking about Shokin that Zelensky should hear.[20] It is unclear what tapes Trump is referring to, when he has heard them, who has provided them to him, or what—if the tapes indeed exist—they contain. The White House's still unexplained redactions from the Trump-Zelensky call memo leave these questions unanswered.

According to the *Washington Post*, "the memorandum of Trump's call with Zelensky appears remarkably different in speed and content from the full transcripts of calls between President Trump and foreign leaders the *Washington Post* obtained in 2017."[21] Whereas prior transcripts acquired by the *Post* averaged between 100 and 135 words per minute, the Trump-Zelensky call—as released to the public—included only 65 words per minute, leading the *Post* to conclude that "the rough transcript of the Zelensky call includes about half the number of words that would be expected if the call had proceeded at the same or similar pace as the previous [Trump] calls [to foreign leaders]."[22] The possibility that the Zelensky call contained far fewer words than is typical for a Trump conversation because of the use of translators is diminished substantially by the fact that Zelensky speaks English and a prior call reviewed by the *Post*—a conversation between Trump and Mexican president Enrique Peña Nieto—included over a hundred words per minute despite both men speaking through interpreters.[23]

A review of the White House memo summarizing the July 25 Trump-Zelensky call reveals that for its duration Trump declines to conform to the NSC summary of official U.S. policy toward Ukraine provided to him, "deviat[ing] significantly" from the prepared script, according to the December 2019 HPSCI report.[24] In response to President Zelensky quickly raising the matter of U.S. military assistance to his country—an easily anticipated topic, given Ukraine's ongoing war with Russia—Trump undermines America's official foreign policy position by not confirming that the United States will continue assisting Ukraine in its defense against Russian aggression. Indeed, after Zelensky thanks the United States for its "great support [of Ukraine] in the area of defense" and informs President Trump of his government's intention to shortly purchase additional Javelin anti-tank missiles from the Pentagon, Trump's immediate response is, "I would like you to do us a favor though."[25] Trump goes on to ask, still without confirming U.S. support for Ukraine's defense of its borders, that Zelensky use his presidential powers to "find out what happened . . . [with] CrowdStrike" during the 2016 presidential election and "look into" the activities of "[Joe] Biden's son [Hunter]" and whether "Biden stopped the prosecution" of the Ukrainian company on whose corporate board his son Hunter served.[26]

Trump's first statement to Zelensky following the call's early diplomatic niceties is telling. He reminds Zelensky that "we do a lot for Ukraine"; "we spend a lot of effort and a lot of time [on Ukraine] . . . much more than the European countries are doing"; "the United States has been very very good to Ukraine"; and (a second time) "the United States has been very very good to Ukraine."[27] But the president also sounds a significant note of caution in his monologue, with Trump warning Zelensky that in his opinion "things are happening [in Ukraine] that are not good," and that these events are occurring under circumstances in which Trump "wouldn't say" the U.S.-Ukraine relationship is "reciprocal."[28]

Zelensky, having been well prepared for the call by his team's backchannel contacts with Giuliani and Sondland and Volker, appears to take his cue at this point, telling Trump that he is "absolutely right . . . not only 100%, but actually 1000%," and lauds America for being "a much bigger partner [for Ukraine] than the European Union," for which Zelensky says he is "grateful" because "the United States is doing quite a lot for Ukraine. Much more than the European Union."[29] Having thus established Ukraine as being in America's debt, Zelensky turns to his country's foremost priority—its defense against ongoing Kremlin aggression in

Crimea and along its eastern border—doing so in a way that unmistakably signals a willingness to cut a deal with Trump if need be. "I would also like to thank you for your great support in the area of defense," Zelensky tells Trump, adding that Ukraine is "ready to continue to cooperate for the next steps, specifically we are almost ready to buy more Javelins [anti-tank missiles] from the United States for defense purposes."[30] While Zelensky does not clarify what he means by "cooperate," his words leave an opening for Trump to describe the "favor" that would establish such "cooperation" between the two nations and return the U.S.-Ukraine relationship—in Trump's view—to a "reciprocal" status.

President Zelensky would likely have been briefed, prior to the call, on Trump's history of opposing the provision to Ukraine of the sort of lethal defensive assistance the Ukrainian leader was requesting. For instance, during the 2016 presidential campaign Trump's top political operatives had engaged in clandestine efforts—efforts for which Kremlin agent Konstantin Kilimnik would later take credit—to remove from the Republican platform any mention of providing lethal defensive assistance to Ukraine.[31] According to a GOP delegate at the 2016 Republican National Convention in Cleveland, Diana Denman, "Trump aide J. D. Gordon said at the Republican Convention in 2016 that Trump directed him [Gordon] to support" the "water[ing] down [of] support for U.S. assistance to Ukraine," and the directive from candidate Trump successfully "weaken[ed] that position in the official [GOP] platform."[32]

When, in July 2019, facing mysterious difficulties and delays in securing his last shipment of Javelins, Zelensky asks Trump to reverse the position on lethal aid to Ukraine that he has had since the day longtime Kremlin agent Paul Manafort joined his presidential campaign in March 2016, Trump introduces the idea of Ukraine doing the United States a "favor"—more particularly, a favor the president says is connected to what "our country has been through" and the possibility (or accusation) that "Ukraine knows a lot about it."[33] Trump thereafter makes three specific requests of Zelensky in response to the latter's offer of "cooperation" in exchange for Javelin missiles: first, Trump tells Zelensky that "I would like you to find out what happened with this whole situation with

Ukraine, they say CrowdStrike [ellipses in original] I guess you have one of your wealthy people [ellipses in original] the server, they say Ukraine has it"; second, he implies he wants Zelensky to make staffing changes in his anti-corruption operation, opining to the Ukrainian president, seemingly with respect to the "not good" events he says occurred during the 2016 presidential election, that "there are a lot of things that went on, the whole situation. I think you're surrounding yourself with some of the same people"; and third, Trump requests that Zelensky's government cooperate with attorney general William Barr, who in mid-April 2019 had opened, per the *Washington Times*, an investigation into "the Justice Department's move to use the Foreign Intelligence Surveillance Act, or FISA, to obtain a secret wiretap warrant on a Trump campaign figure and other department decisions surrounding the Republican Party's presidential nominee."[34] Trump tells Zelensky that "I would like to have the Attorney General call you or your people and I would like you to get to the bottom of it. . . . [T]hat whole nonsense ended with a very poor performance by a man named Robert Mueller, an incompetent performance, but they say a lot of it started with Ukraine. Whatever you can do, it's very important that you do it if that's possible."[35] Trump does not say who "they" are, though Kremlin agents Konstantin Kilimnik and—via his long-running contract with Oleg Deripaska—Paul Manafort are known to have propounded the idea that "a lot of [the Trump-Russia] scandal started with Ukraine." In making his demands of Zelensky, the president makes no reference to the United States selling any Javelin missiles to its beleaguered European ally.

Zelensky's reaction to Trump's three requests is unambiguous. In response to Trump's statement that Zelensky's cooperation is "very important," Zelensky replies, "Yes it is very important for me and everything that you just mentioned earlier. For me as a President, it is very important and we are open for any future cooperation. We are ready to open a new page on cooperation in relations between the United States and Ukraine."[36] Zelensky's reference to a "new page" simultaneously distinguishes his administration from Poroshenko's—which had fired at least one prosecutor, Shokin, whom Trump and Giuliani favored—as well as referencing the state of U.S.-Ukraine relations under the Obama administration, which had implicitly and in some cases explicitly supported corruption investigations that Trump would later oppose, most notably the Manafort investigation.

But Zelensky's assurances to Trump in response to the U.S. president's three requests go well beyond mere platitudes about "cooperation," even if Zelensky does reference "cooperating" with Trump five times over the course of a relatively short phone call.[37] The new Ukrainian president also addresses Trump's concerns about Ukrainian anti-corruption personnel, noting that "I just recalled our ambassador from [the] United States and he will be replaced by a very competent and very experienced ambassador who will work hard on making sure that our two nations are getting closer. . . . [I] assure you once again that you have nobody but friends around us. I will make sure I surround myself with the best and most experienced people."[38] As for cooperating with Trump's unofficial and clandestine investigations of the 2016 election, Zelensky assures the president that "my assistants spoke with Mr. Giuliani just recently and we are hoping very much that Mr. Giuliani will be able to travel to Ukraine and we will meet once he comes to Ukraine."[39] With respect to Trump's request that the Ukrainians investigate CrowdStrike, Zelensky says, "In addition to that investigation, I guarantee as the President of Ukraine that all the investigations will be done openly and candidly. That I can assure you."[40]

By the conclusion of Zelensky's litany of promises—all made in response to Trump's request for a "favor" to rebalance a U.S.-Ukraine relationship he deemed not "reciprocal"—Zelensky has spoken to every node in Trump's matrix of demands. Nevertheless, Trump refuses to relent in his pursuit of getting as many concessions from the Ukrainian as possible. In the president's longest monologue of the evening, he confronts Zelensky with a barrage of complaints and additional, highly specific demands. After telling Zelensky it is "good" that he has committed to the CrowdStrike investigation, Trump, pressing his advantage, launches into a lengthy complaint that blossoms into a new "ask": "I heard you had a prosecutor who was very good and he was shut down and that's really unfair. A lot of people are talking about that, the way they shut your very good prosecutor down and you had some very bad people involved. Mr. Giuliani is a highly respected man. He was the mayor of New York City, a great mayor, and I would like him to call you. I will ask him to call you along with the Attorney General. Rudy very much knows what's happening and he is a very capable guy. If you could speak with him that would be great. The former ambassador from the United States, the woman, was bad news and the people she was dealing with in the Ukraine were bad news so I just want to let you know that. The other thing, there's a lot of talk about Biden's son, that Biden stopped the prosecution and a lot of people want to find out about that so whatever you can do with the Attorney General would be great. Biden went around bragging that he stopped the prosecution so if you can look into it [ellipses in original] It sounds horrible to me."[41]

Notwithstanding that there is no evidence to support Trump's claims about either Joe Biden or his son Hunter, even more striking is Trump's certainty that Attorney General Barr is willing to investigate not only alleged election interference by the Ukrainians in 2016 but also a very different topic: whether Trump's chief political rival should see his political career unceremoniously destroyed by a scandal originating in Ukraine. Trump will never explain, nor will Barr, why Trump was certain his attorney general would be as willing to investigate Joe and Hunter Biden as he would the 2015 origins of the U.S. intelligence community's Russia investigation. A possible answer to this question may be found, however, in Trump's unusual insistence, as reported by the *Washington Post* on May 11, 2019, that it would be "'appropriate'" for him "to talk to [Barr] about opening an investigation . . . into Joe Biden, the current front-runner for the Democratic presidential nomination"; Trump's statement comes just days after Barr "stumble[s]" in sworn testimony before Congress on the question of whether "the president or anyone in the White House [had] ever asked or suggested that [he] open an investigation" during his tenure as attorney general—a question from Sen. Kamala Harris (D-CA) that Barr so conspicuously seeks to evade and dissemble on that the legal and national security experts of *Just Security* will later say he should be charged with perjury.[42]

Other elements of the Trump-Zelensky phone call are nearly as concerning as those relating to Clinton and Biden. For instance, Trump seems at one point to threaten his own former ambassador, Marie Yovanovitch, telling Zelensky that even after her firing she is "going to go through some things"; he also refers to Lutsenko as a "very good" and "very fair" prosecutor, despite his documented corruption as prosecutor general of Ukraine and the fact that, by July 25, he had publicly acknowledged that all of his prior public statements about Joe and Hunter Biden were false.[43]

A White House official who listens in on the July Trump-Zelensky call as part of their official duties will subsequently describe the thirty-minute conversation to an eventual CIA whistleblower as "crazy," "frightening," and "completely lacking in substance relating to national security"—as opposed to Trump's own personal interests.[44] According to the subsequent whistleblower account, the official appears "visibly shaken" while detailing what Trump and Zelensky discussed.[45] The conversation between the White House official and the whistleblower occurs mere hours after the call; according to an ABC News report on a two-page memo the whistleblower writes within minutes of hearing from the official, "at least one aide to the president feared that Trump's own words in the call were damning."[46] The memo, subsequently provided to both the CIA's top lawyer and the Intelligence Community Inspector General (ICIG), is soon found by the latter to be, in its totality, "credible" and of "urgent concern" to America's national security.[47]

But it isn't only a single White House official who responds with horror to Trump's actions on July 25. According to an October 2019 CNN report, "aides to Trump scramble[ ] in the aftermath of his July 25 phone call with Ukraine's leader to both alert lawyers of their concerns and to contain the damage. Unsettled aides also immediately [begin] quizzing each other about whether they should alert senior officials [to what Trump had done]."[48] When reports come flooding in to the White House Counsel's Office, the lawyers there, according to CNN, "aware of the tumult, initially believe[ ] it [can] be contained within the walls of the White House."[49] According to the whistleblower's complaint, this containment effort sees lawyers and officials scramble to secrete all notes regarding the phone call in a highly classified NSC server that would not normally be used to house unclassified material like the content of the Trump-Zelensky call; the *Washington Post* writes that the move "is at odds with long-standing White House protocol."[50]

The White House's handling of the rough transcript of the Trump-Zelensky call is seen as suspicious by White House veterans and other former U.S. officials. The *Washington Post* remarks that the memo developed from the rough transcript "is unusual for lacking a tracking number that would normally indicate it had been circulated to senior subject experts and the national security adviser's office for review and edits . . . [and because] the document additionally carries classification markings that Situation Room staffers do not normally add when they create a word-for-word transcript."[51] One former U.S. official who handles the document as part of their official duties will say that their first reaction on seeing it was, "This didn't go through the normal process."[52] Another former U.S. official "familiar with the creation of records of calls of foreign leaders" with whom the *Post* speaks insists that the document had to be an "edited summary," as given its structure and manner of circulation "the one that was released [to the public] is not the [transcript] the Situation Room created. That's just not possible."[53]

Lt. Col. Alexander Vindman, the National Security Council expert in charge of the interagency process on Ukraine, will later tell Congress that there is "no doubt" the Trump-Zelensky call featured a quid pro quo involving military aid to Ukraine and investigations of Trump's political rivals.[54] Similar testimony will be heard from acting U.S. ambassador to Ukraine William Taylor, who tells Congress that it was his "clear understanding" in the latter half of the summer of 2019 that, as summarized by the *Washington Post*, "U.S. military aid [to Ukraine] would not be sent until that country pursued investigations that could politically benefit President Trump."[55]

While the full list of those who listen in on the Trump-Zelensky call is unknown, it is certain that it includes Vindman; secretary of state Mike Pompeo; Keith Kellogg, national security advisor to Vice President Mike Pence; Charles Kupperman, deputy to Trump's national security advisor, John Bolton; Robert Blair, an assistant to President Trump and a senior adviser to acting chief of staff Mick Mulvaney; Tim Morrison, an adviser on Russia and Europe to the National Security Council; Jennifer Williams, an adviser on Russia and Europe to Pence, who will tell Congress Trump's statements to Zelensky were "unusual and inappropriate"; and various other "White House staffers working in the secure, soundproof Situation Room in the West Wing basement," a group that includes unnamed individuals "from the NSC and the office of the Vice President," according to the Associated Press and Vindman's congressional testimony.[56] The Associated Press will report that "dozens" of people were listening to the Trump-Zelensky call as it happened.[57]

In his fall 2019 testimony before Congress, Vindman will say that among the errors in the call memo that he unsuccessfully sought to correct is the deliberate exclusion of the word "Burisma" from a document President Trump had told the media and voters was "word-for-word."[58] The word's omission from the memo is significant because it obscures part of the Trump-Zelensky quid pro quo revealed by the call; when Zelensky assures Trump that Ukraine's incoming prosecutor general "will look into the situation, specifically to the company that you mentioned in this issue . . . we will take care of that and will work on the investigation of the case," it is not clear what "company" he means—though the fact that it is subsequently revealed that the company is Burisma underscores that Trump is asking Zelensky to criminally investigate his political rival Joe Biden, and Zelensky is agreeing to do so.[59]

What is clear even at the time of the call memo's release, however, is that Zelensky's assurances to Trump about conducting an investigation of the then-unnamed "company" are quickly met with three commensurate assurances by Trump: first, Trump tells Zelensky, "I will have Mr. Giuliani give you a call"; second, he informs the Ukrainian president that "I am also going to have Attorney General Barr call"; and third— and most telling—Trump implies that Zelensky's assurances will in some unstated way aid Ukraine's finances, saying, "Your economy is going to get better and better I predict. You have a lot of assets. It's a great country."[60] The significance of Trump's reference to Ukraine's future prospects, particularly at the conclusion of a conversation in which Ukraine is seeking U.S. assistance, could not have been missed by Zelensky, who closes his negotiation with Trump by requesting a face-to-face meeting in Washington, floating the possibility of a meeting in Warsaw on September 1, and implying that Ukraine wants to purchase more American energy— the latter a topic of particular interest to Giuliani agents Parnas and Fruman, who have long sought to increase American energy exports to Ukraine.[61] Using the promise of energy market deals to convince Trump to release aid to Ukraine is of course also something Zelensky's predecessor, Petro Poroshenko, had done successfully on several occasions.

Zelensky will make good on this last overture within a matter of months, with the Trump administration announcing in fall 2019 that it is "working to try and organize a visit by senior Ukrainian officials to tour American liquefied natural gas production facilities . . . for the purpose of solidifying a trade relationship between the two countries for the export of liquefied natural gas through Poland"—precisely the project Trump donors Parnas and Fruman had been pushing in Ukraine, alongside their work on Trump's behalf, during the summer of 2019.[62] Zelensky will also, within ninety days of his call with Trump, make "sweeping changes to Ukraine's top law enforcement agency . . . [that] derail a series of long-running criminal investigations, including two related to U.S. President Donald Trump's former campaign chairman, Paul Manafort."[63]

Within ninety minutes of the call's conclusion, Trump appointees act, per *The Guardian*, to formally and conclusively block the already congressionally approved military aid to Ukraine, with Trump appointee Michael Duffey "[moving] quickly after the call, behind the scenes," to convey the official word from the West Wing that the aid is to be frozen.[64] Duffey moves not only quickly, but with secrecy: his email to budget officials demanding the hold be leveled reads, "Given the sensitive nature of the request, I appreciate your keeping that information closely held to those who need to know to execute direction [of the hold]."[65] When news of Duffey's email hits U.S. media months later, in December 2019, Vice President Pence's chief of staff, Marc Short, will call the timing of the email—less than two hours after Trump ended his telephone call with Zelensky—"a coincidence."[66]

Politico notes that the Trump-Zelensky call "reduced the survival of Ukraine to a bargaining chip in an utterly petty pursuit; embroiled Volodymyr Zelensky, the Ukrainian president, in scandal and undercut his ability to defend the interests of his nation; and weakened the clout of U.S. leadership on Ukraine, the region and beyond. The biggest beneficiary of this latest Trump-derived scandal is the Kremlin."[67]

CHAPTER 29

SONDLAND AND GIULIANI

On July 26, the day after the second Trump-Zelensky call, Ambassador Sondland meets with Andriy Yermak one-on-one in Kyiv. State Department official David Holmes tries to attend the meeting as well, but is prevented from doing so by Sondland. Following the conversation between Sondland and Yermak, Sondland goes to lunch with Holmes and Suriya Jayanti; at lunch, the ambassador places a call to President Trump on his cellphone that both Holmes and Jayanti can overhear.[1] During the call, which Sondland does not reveal to Congress in his initial fall 2019 testimony, Trump speaks so loudly that Holmes is able to hear both ends of the early portion of the conversation; according to Holmes's subsequent congressional testimony, during their call Sondland told the president that Zelensky "loves your ass," earning the reply from Trump, "So he's going to do the investigation?"—a query to which Sondland responds, "He's gonna do it. President Zelensky will do anything you ask him to do."[2] When reporters ask Trump about this call in mid-November 2019, he denies having had any such conversation with Sondland, saying, "I know nothing about that. I've never heard it. Not even a little bit."[3]

After the conclusion of the Sondland-Trump call, Holmes, per his subsequent testimony, asks the ambassador "if it was true that the President did not give a shit about Ukraine. Ambassador Sondland agreed that the President did not give a shit about Ukraine."[4] When Holmes presses Sondland for the reason Trump does "not give a shit about Ukraine," Sondland replies that "the president only cares about the 'big stuff'"; when Holmes points out that "big stuff" is in fact happening in the European nation on NATO's eastern border, for instance a war with Russia, Sondland clarifies that he means "'big stuff' that benefits the President, like the 'Biden investigation' that Mr. Giuliani was pushing."[5] Though Republicans on the House Permanent Select Committee on Intelligence will question Holmes's account—of which Holmes swears under oath he has a "clear recollection"—NBC News will undermine their attack on Holmes's character by noting that, along with undertaking a long career in public service, "In 2014, [Holmes] won the American Foreign Service Association's William R. Rivkin Award for Constructive Dissent, which honors a midcareer foreign service officer for intellectual courage in speaking up."[6]

National security and foreign policy experts will say that the Trump-Sondland call on July 26 was "likely intercepted by [the] Russians," given that neither Sondland nor Trump took any precautions to have a secure, nonpublic conversation about U.S. foreign policy in an active war zone.[7] One such expert, former U.S. ambassador to Russia Michael McFaul, will tell the Associated Press that Sondland "making a phone call from Kyiv to the president of the United States means that not just the Russian intelligence services will be on the call, but a whole lot of other people, too."[8] According to the *Washington Post*, the consensus among former federal officials after the phone call is revealed is that it was a "stunning breach of security."[9] In mid-October 2019, the *New York Times* quotes an ex–White House adviser as having told federal investigators that upon his hire Sondland was "a potential national security risk because he was so unprepared for his job."[10]

Later in the day on July 26, Sondland gives an interview with Ukrainian media in which he says that he "had a wonderful hour-long meeting with President Zelensky that followed on the heels of his telephone call yesterday with President Trump," adding that during his post-call meeting with Zelensky he discussed with the Ukrainian leader the content of his communication with Trump the day before.[11] In another interview the same day, Sondland tells Radio Liberty that the United States will increase support for Ukraine if Zelensky undertakes certain actions he has "promised" the Trump administration he will pursue.[12] When Sondland is asked by his interviewer to name the actions in question, Sondland demurs, insisting simply that there is a "long list."[13]

On August 2, eight days after the Trump-Zelensky call, Rudy Giuliani meets in Madrid with Yermak, with the Trump attorney's aim being to "spell[ ] out two specific cases he believe[s] Ukraine should pursue"; the Giuliani-Yermak conversation is the one Trump had demanded of Zelensky on July 25.[14] The only two corruption cases in Ukraine that Giuliani expresses any interest in during his conversation with Yermak are "a probe of a Ukrainian gas tycoon who had Biden's son Hunter on his board" and "an allegation that Democrats colluded with Ukraine to release information on former Trump campaign chairman Paul Manafort during the 2016 election."[15] Also attending the Giuliani-Yermak meeting in Madrid is Lev Parnas, a fact the *Daily Beast* reports "indicates that [Parnas] may have significant visibility into Giuliani's efforts to pressure Kyiv to investigate a company linked to one of President Donald Trump's political rivals."[16] Further evidence in support of this conclusion arrives in the form of a report by ABC News that Parnas has supplied Congress with "audio, video and photos that include Giuliani and Trump."[17] When the *Daily Beast* contacts Giuliani to ask about Firtash "translator" Parnas's attendance at his meeting with President Zelensky's top aide in Madrid, Giuliani tells the digital media outlet to "tell [the public] Firtash had nothing to do with this."[18] Gordon Sondland will subsequently testify that the demands Giuliani makes of Zelensky via Yermak in Madrid "were a quid pro quo for arranging a White House visit for President Zelensky."[19]

According to the *Washington Post*, Giuliani's meeting in Madrid with Yermak is one of at least five conversations he has with the Zelensky adviser in 2019—all, according to Giuliani, in his capacity as an advocate for Trump's personal interests, not in connection with Trump's role as commander in chief.[20] Giuliani will tell the *Post* that he had "no idea" that his client, Trump, was reviewing aid to Ukraine at the time of his meeting with Yermak in Spain, noting only that he left the early August meeting "with the impression that the Ukrainians would pursue the cases he [had] pushed them to take up."[21]

Giuliani's reference to Manafort while speaking to Yermak in Madrid is particularly noteworthy, as Trump, in his call with Zelensky, had, at least per the White House's rough transcript, been unwilling to mention his former campaign manager by name. It is unclear whether Trump's agent Sondland raises the Manafort matter with Zelensky when the two speak on July 26.[22] According to an interview Giuliani will later give to the *Washington Post*, on August 2 he told Yermak that "your country owes it to us and to your country to find out what really happened" with respect to both Burisma and the public revelation of Paul Manafort's activities in Ukraine; having been told what Ukraine "owes" the United States in exchange for the "very very good" treatment of Ukraine Trump had spoken of with Zelensky on July 25, Yermak "indicate[s] that the Ukrainians [are] open to pursuing the investigations" and makes a "plea" to Giuliani to let Zelensky meet face-to-face with Trump to "signal to Russia . . . Washington's support for Ukraine."[23] Giuliani tells the *Post* that the discussion of the Biden and Manafort investigations, as well as Zelensky's request for a White House meeting, were part of a "whole package" he discussed with Yermak in Madrid—a metaphor consistent with the quid pro quo of a "package" deal.[24] Giuliani also tells the *Post* that "he has kept the president informed of his efforts in Ukraine for months," and that all of his efforts have been focused on advancing the "narrow interest" of "benefit[ing]" Trump.[25] Whether or not Trump has kept Giuliani apprised of his thinking on military aid to Ukraine, Giuliani's insistence that he kept Trump informed of his own efforts to force Zelensky to conduct investigations of Trump's political rivals means that, at a minimum, Trump was aware of both ends of the quid pro quo.

As for Giuliani, he confesses to the *Post* that in conducting clandestine errands for Trump in Ukraine "his goal is to make sure Biden [doesn't] become president without having to answer for" his actions.[26] "What I'm saying to [Biden]," Giuliani had previously told the *Post* in a

May 2019 interview, is "[y]ou're not getting from here to the presidency without answering these questions."[27] Giuliani adds that "I'm going to make sure that nothing scuttles the investigation that I want."[28] According to the *Post*, Giuliani had "declined" in May "to say whether he was acting at Trump's request or whether he had briefed the president. He said 'most of it' was of his own volition, but that the president wanted to get to the 'truth.'"[29] It is only later that Giuliani concedes to the newspaper that "he has kept the president informed of his efforts in Ukraine for months."[30]

Because one of the key questions Giuliani wants answered, per the *Post*, is about Paul Manafort—"whether Democrats colluded with Ukrainian authorities during the 2016 election to put out information damaging to Manafort"—it is useful to consider Trump's history of denying any close association with a man in whose fate he has become so invested.[31] Trump has insisted he knew nothing of Manafort sharing proprietary campaign data with Konstantin Kilimnik, a Manafort associate who, writes the *Washington Post*, "the FBI has said has ties to Russian intelligence"; nevertheless, the president expresses no upset at the transmission of data his campaign owned to a Kremlin agent, telling ABC News' George Stephanopoulos in June 2019, "What difference does polling information make? It doesn't matter. He was maybe trying to do something for an account or something. Who knows?"[32]

In June 2018—five months after Trump began privately opining to friends that Manafort could cause him serious difficulty if he "flipped" and cooperated with federal prosecutors—the president falsely tells reporters that his former campaign manager "ha[d] nothing to do with our campaign" and "Manafort worked for me for a very short period of time . . . a very short period of time."[33] In fact, Manafort has known Trump for decades and advised him as a presidential candidate for well over a year, from March 2016 through the spring of 2017. Moreover, not only did Manafort almost immediately take over the Trump campaign after joining it in late March 2016, becoming its de facto leader by early

April, but after he left the campaign five months later he continued his contacts not just with Trump but with Trump's top advisers as well; according to a December 2018 CNN report, Manafort stayed in touch with the presidential transition team and top administration officials for a minimum of fifteen months after he and the campaign parted ways.[34] That Manafort was a significant member of Trump's constellation of advisers from March 2016 through at least February 2018, a period of twenty-three months—rather than the "49 days" Trump will publicly contend—may help explain why in 2018 and 2019 Giuliani worked feverishly to prove that nefarious Ukrainian operators had done Manafort wrong.[35] That Manafort will lie to federal agents about his contacts with Trump administration officials during this period, even though doing so violates his federal cooperation deal and places him in jeopardy of spending additional years or even decades in prison, suggests that the subject of Manafort's clandestine contacts with Trump's inner circle was at a minimum controversial and at the extreme connected to criminal activity.[36] National Public Radio, connecting these dots as well as the fact that "Mueller's office asked Manafort to affirm that Trump was aware of the much-dissected meeting in June 2016 involving a delegation of Russians and Manafort, Trump's son and Trump's son-in-law," concludes the following: "If Trump authorized that [June 2016] meeting or simply knew about it beforehand, that would be important evidence in the investigation into whether anyone in his campaign conspired with the Russian attack on the [2016] election. Trump has denied knowing anything at the time about the meeting or, more broadly, about Russia's campaign of active measures."[37]

If Trump can prove—or compellingly intimate—that Manafort's October 2017 arrest was a by-product of Democratic collusion with the Ukrainian government, he arguably legitimizes the prospective pardoning of the now-incarcerated federal convict and thereby ensures his continued silence. Indeed, in November 2018, just weeks after Giuliani concedes he has begun a campaign to investigate Manafort's investigators, NPR reports that Trump has decided "a pardon for ex–campaign chairman Paul Manafort is not 'off the table,'" coming to this conclusion after

"Manafort's lawyer . . . briefed Trump's lawyers on his [Manafort's] testimony in the Russia investigation."[38] This late 2018 revelation invites two equally plausible conclusions: first, that Giuliani's efforts on Manafort's behalf, which begin shortly after a conference among Manafort's and Trump's attorneys, were a reward for Manafort, who, according to government prosecutors, "lied about five major issues"—including "contacts with the Trump administration"—to federal law enforcement; second, that Trump chose to put a Manafort pardon on the table as soon as Manafort's attorneys convinced the president's legal team that Manafort had remained quiet about whatever information Trump feared his former campaign manager would disclose to the FBI.[39] Certainly, many media outlets have written about Trump's secretive joint-defense agreement with Manafort—which existed at a time when the president was falsely saying he "didn't know Manafort well"—with *The Atlantic* noting that the agreement not only allowed "their legal teams to share information" but stood the chance of "help[ing] the president's former campaign chairman angle for a pardon."[40]

During the course of Trump's joint-defense agreement with Manafort, his primary contact with Manafort's defense team is Rudy Giuliani.[41] Giuliani's contact with Manafort continues well after the latter is convicted of numerous federal felonies; in the summer and fall of 2019, as the key events of the Ukraine scandal are unfolding in the United States and Ukraine, Giuliani "consult[s] several times with Manafort through the federal prisoner's lawyer"—seeking, per the *Washington Post*, information that would exculpate Manafort by proving the "black ledger" that indirectly led to his conviction and imprisonment was a fake.[42] While the Giuliani-Manafort consultations do not put Giuliani in the position of effectively joining a legal team alongside Manafort and his lawyers, as had the Trump-Manafort joint-defense agreement, Giuliani will concede to the *Post* that he and Manafort share what the newspaper will summarize as "[a] relationship . . . [that] stems from a shared interest in a narrative."[43] This narrative is, the *Post* reports, the sum and substance of the defense Manafort's legal team began "promoting as early as 2017: that the Ukrainian government separately interfered in the 2016 campaign on behalf of Clinton through the activities of a Ukrainian American contract worker for the DNC."[44] It is unclear why Manafort would remain invested in the disputation of this "narrative" following his federal convictions and the imposition of a lengthy prison sentence on him; indeed, the clearest implication in Giuliani's ongoing dealings with Manafort is that both Manafort and Trump perceive an ongoing threat to their interests—legal, financial, or otherwise—emanating from Ukraine, Russia, ongoing federal criminal investigations in the United States, or all three of these. Alternatively, Manafort may see in Giuliani's requests for information an implicit or explicit quid pro quo in which his own benefit from the exchange is a presidential pardon.

Giuliani and Manafort's theory that the so-called black ledger was the basis for Ukraine opening an investigation of Manafort during the 2016 election is without merit. As the *Post* notes, the FBI "already had a case open against Manafort before the 2016 campaign, having interviewed him twice about his work in Ukraine in 2013 and 2014" and having begun wiretapping him in 2014—a year before Trump had even announced his candidacy for president.[45] Moreover, not only did the federal prosecutors who tried Manafort never introduce the "black ledger" as evidence but the document went unmentioned at both Manafort's trial and sentencing for having laundered money in Ukraine.[46]

In December 2019, new reports released by the FBI reveal "how much former Trump campaign chairman Paul Manafort was coaxing his aide Gates not to flip" and cooperate with federal law enforcement.[47] They reveal, moreover, that not only did Manafort at one point tell Gates he had received an "email of support" from Trump's son-in-law Kushner, but Trump himself had directly admonished his former campaign chief to "stay strong" during a conference call originally intended to be between Manafort and Trump's attorneys.[48]

According to Manafort, during a period of contact with Trump's attorneys—and an alleged exhortation from the president himself—the longtime political operative told Gates, "I've covered you at the White

House"; Manafort also "told Gates about two pots of money—legal defense funds—including one that [he] and Gates could benefit from as they fought their charges [and that he had] discussed . . . with [Trump attorney John] Dowd."[49]

According to Lev Parnas, Dowd will subsequently engage in similar conduct yet again, participating in clandestine efforts to shut down federal cooperation by former Trump agents by, in October 2019, urging his new client Parnas to "sacrifice himself for [the] president."[50] Parnas says that Dowd visited him in jail and told him to "be a good boy," with Parnas later recalling for MSNBC that "John Dowd, instead of comforting me and trying to calm me down and telling me I'm going to be okay . . . started talking to me like a drill sergeant."[51] Parnas adds, "They tried to keep me quiet."[52] In January 2020, Parnas's new attorney, Joseph Bondy, releases documentary evidence confirming that Dowd was secretly communicating about Parnas with Trump's legal team—including Giuliani, diGenova, Toensing, future Trump impeachment attorneys Jay Sekulow and Jane Raskin, Giuliani's own attorney Jon Sale, and even Paul Manafort's attorney Kevin Downing—at a minimum up until the day before Parnas's arrest.[53]

CHAPTER 30

TRUMP-CHINA

Trump's fortunes as a businessman trying to do business in China change dramatically as soon as he launches his presidential campaign in June 2015. This development is not entirely unexpected; indeed, as recounted in the Mueller Report, during the 2016 presidential campaign Trump would tell his attorney and fixer Michael Cohen that he viewed his candidacy as an "infomercial" for the Trump Organization and Trump-branded properties.[1]

Before businessman Trump became candidate Trump, opportunities to bring the Trump brand to China had been virtually nonexistent. In 2008, Trump had tried unsuccessfully to work with China's Evergrande Group to "develop an office complex" there; in 2012, Trump had unsuccessfully sought to partner with the State Grid Corporation of China "to develop a property in Beijing."[2] Trump had slightly more success with Chinese businessmen living and working stateside. The Center for American Progress (CAP) notes that in 2008 the Chinese Communist Party–owned Industrial and Commercial Bank of China (ICBC) had "signed a lease for the 20th floor of Trump Tower in New York City," a contract that by 2012 had made the ICBC the tower's "biggest office tenant" and the one "paying more than any other major tenant in Trump Tower . . . per square foot"; in 2012, Trump received a $950 million loan from "four lenders, including the state-owned Bank of China," to "hold[ ] 30 percent ownership of an office building in Manhattan, at 1290 Avenue of the Americas."[3] The highly lucrative ICBC lease, which for years gave a Chinese government–owned entity unprecedented access to a building Trump himself was living in, came up for renegotiation in October 2019—the very month Trump would ask the Chinese Communist Party to assist him in investigating the Bidens' activities in China.[4] According to *Forbes*, Trump earns at least $2 million a year from the ICBC lease.[5]

Shortly after Trump launches his political career in 2015, the Trump Organization's ambitions in China exponentially increase in size, scope, and audacity. Trump's July 2015 financial disclosure—unverified by regulators, and therefore possibly incomplete—reveals that Trump is the president of eight companies that are, as underscored by the CAP, "related to potential business in China": THC China Development LLC, THC China Development Management Corporation, THC China Technical Services LLC, THC China Technical Services Manager Corporation, THC Services Shenzhen LLC, THC Services Shenzhen Member Corporation, THC Shenzhen Hotel Manager LLC, and THC Shenzhen Hotel Manager Member Corporation.[6] In 2016, as Trump is one of only two Americans (alongside Hillary Clinton) with any probability of becoming president, the *New York Times* reports that the CEO of Trump Hotels, Eric Danziger, has announced at a Hong Kong hospitality conference that Trump Hotels plans to open "20 or 30 luxury hotels in China" and that it is "confident" it will be able to do so.[7]

One immediate result of Danziger's pre-election announcement is that it preserves for Trump the ability to declare during the presidential transition—as he indeed does on December 12, 2016—that while he is president the Trump Organization will do "no new deals" either at home or abroad.[8] Because Trump Hotels' China expansion has already been publicly announced with a high degree of confidence, it arguably permits President Trump to contend that, whether or not any Trump Hotels deals with China have been formalized, the infiltration of his hotel brand into the staggeringly large Chinese market has been pre-cleared. The *Washington Post* will note in December 2016 precisely how much is at stake in any such pre-clearance argument: "If Trump Hotels goes ahead with its efforts to expand to China," the paper writes, "it could hugely complicate one of the most important foreign policy relationships Trump will have to negotiate during his presidency. And the suspicion that Trump as president might be trying to badger China or butter it up to promote his business there risks coloring perceptions of his every move in regard to Beijing."[9]

Trump knows, as he ascends to the presidency, that developing leverage over the Chinese government—or, alternately, a reputation for providing it with political favors—is essential to doing business in China. Liu Xuemei, vice president of New World Development's Huamei Real Estate Development, has told the *Post* that "if your relationship with China isn't good, there's no way your papers and permits will be approved. The Chinese government is hard to deal with, so buildings are hard to build."[10] Trump's already steep climb into the Chinese market is even greater than it would otherwise be, however, for reasons beyond the political or logistical; as Liao Jun, vice president of Vanke Oriental Properties, explains to the *Washington Post* in late 2016, in China "people trust hotels like Marriott and Sheraton . . . they still think of Trump Hotels as a bit sketchy and unheard of."[11]

That Trump is willing to burden U.S.-China relations to make friends in a place he hopes to do business has been clear from the start, though this inclination becomes evident first in Taiwan, a Chinese "state" whose independent status remains in dispute. In October 2016, just a few days before Eric Danziger announces an aggressive pre-election push for a share of the Chinese hotel market, a Trump Organization representative is in Taiwan on unspecified organization business.[12] A hint of what this business may be arrives later, in December 2016, when it is reported by the *Washington Post* that "someone professing to represent [the Trump Organization] had held talks with the mayor of Taoyuan [in Taiwan] in September about an airport development project."[13]

That the Trump brand would make a significant play for Taiwanese business was presaged in March 2013—just four months after Trump decided to run for president, according to a timeline provided by Trump aide Sam Nunberg—when the Trump Hotel Collection had opened its first-ever office in Asia, a ten-person operation in Shanghai. Todd G. Wynne-Parry, a senior vice president of global hotel development and acquisitions at the Trump Organization, would announce at the time that Trump Hotels had "identified Greater China as our top priority among high-potential emerging markets" ("Greater China" being a politically acceptable umbrella term for China, Hong Kong, and Taiwan).[14]

In the two months leading up to Election Day in 2016, Trump and his daughter Ivanka apply for eighteen trademarks in China.[15] In the first sixteen days after Trump's inauguration, Ivanka applies for six more Chinese trademarks.[16] In April 2017, on the same day Ivanka and her father meet with Chinese president Xi Jinping, Ivanka is awarded three trademarks by Beijing.[17] In May 2018—the same month that President Trump, per the *New York Times*, "vow[s] to find a way to prevent a major Chinese telecommunications company from going bust, even though the company has a history of violating American limits on doing business with [sanctioned] countries"—Ivanka Trump receives six trademarks she had applied for just fourteen months earlier, as well as one she had applied for in May 2016.[18] Charles Feng, head of the intellectual property division at the law firm East & Concord Partners, tells the *Times* that Ivanka's time from trademark application to receipt of trademark is, for China, considered "very fast."[19]

The seven Trump trademarks China announces in May 2018 come "just before and after" Trump's announcement about ZTE, the Chinese telecommunications company about which the Chinese government is experiencing significant anxiety and which by March 2020 will be under federal investigation, according to *The Hill*, for allegedly "paying bribes to foreign officials."[20] Forty-eight hours after Trump makes his ZTE announcement, an Indonesian company called MNC Group, "which is partnering with the Trump Organization to build a six-star hotel and golf course in Indonesia," signs a deal with "an arm of the Metallurgical Corporation of China, a state-owned construction company, to build a theme park next door to the planned Trump properties."[21] *ProPublica* reports that the Trump Organization deal in Indonesia is worth $425 million, to be paid by the China Export and Credit Insurance Corporation.[22]

By the end of May 2018, Ivanka Trump has been awarded thirty-four trademarks in China in total—trademarks, the *New York Times* observes, that "allow her to capitalize on her brand in the world's second-largest economy."[23] Per the *Times*, the Trumps' significant accrual of trademarks in China "raises questions about whether Chinese officials are giving the Trump family extra consideration that they otherwise might not get."[24] Calling the family's May 2018 trademark windfall "remarkable timing," the newspaper adds that it prompts "familiar questions" about why it is that "as Mr. Trump contends with Beijing on issues like security and trade, his family and the company that bears his name are trying to make money off their brand in China's flush and potentially promising market."[25] Indeed, by May 2018 Trump holds over a hundred trademarks in China himself, separate and distinct from Ivanka's thirty-four.[26] And the *Times* notes that Ivanka's husband, Jared Kushner, has since entering the White House "courted state-connected investors in China . . . [which is] in Mr. Kushner's government [policy] portfolio—to bail out the [Kushner Companies'] headquarters at 666 Fifth Avenue in Manhattan"; Kushner's behind-the-scenes contacts with the Chinese, CNBC reports, include a "secretive" meeting with "private equity investors" Kushner "convened" in China in November 2017—with the help of reported Putin girlfriend Wendi Deng Murdoch—that the president's son-in-law kept off all official "White House or State Department agendas" for reasons that remain unclear.[27]

One group Kushner approaches about Kushner Companies, Anbang Insurance Group—a "shadowy" company CAP notes has "very close ties to the Chinese government"—receives a request from the Kushners' family business to "undertake a joint venture to redevelop the Fifth Avenue property" via a $4 billion deal.[28] According to CAP, even after Kushner steps down from his family business he is still "a beneficiary of much of the business through his trusts."[29] In addition, over a period beginning just a few weeks before Trump's announcement of his presidential run and ending just a few days before Election Day, Kushner had raised $50 million from Chinese nationals via an expedited visa scheme connected to a Trump-branded tower in New Jersey, a windfall that would have underscored to both Kushner Companies and the Trump Organization, partners in the New Jersey project, how much money each stood to gain from keeping the Chinese government happy.[30] Incredibly, Trump will later justify soliciting foreign election assistance from the Ukrainian government by falsely accusing Joe Biden's son of doing through his father exactly what Trump's son-in-law had apparently done in his own right with the power granted to him by Trump: seeking to do business with a nation that was in his government policy portfolio at the time.

As soon as a vote of the U.S. Electoral College makes Trump president, the newly elected president's prospective business relationship with Taiwanese nationals becomes an unusual and troubling complication in his foreign policy in East Asia. On December 2, 2016, just weeks after Election Day, Trump speaks to Taiwan's leader, Tsai Ing-wen, by phone, in what the *New York Times* calls "an affront to China."[31] The call immediately endangers U.S.-China relations, with the *Times* calling it "a striking break with nearly four decades of diplomatic practice that could precipitate a major rift with China even before Mr. Trump takes office."[32] No president had spoken to a Taiwanese leader since the United States broke diplomatic ties with Taiwan in 1979.[33]

Trump makes the extraordinary decision to reach out to Taiwan—to discuss, among other topics, "economic development"—by himself, per the *New York Times*; Obama administration officials are not told about Trump's call until after it has occurred.[34] *The Atlantic* will write of the Trump-Taiwan call that "the president of the United States breached decades of international protocol created to preserve a precarious balance of power. That decision raised not only the possibility that Trump was blundering into a potential international incident but also that he may have done so in part out of consideration for his business prospects."[35]

When Trump reverses his long-held position on Taiwan's independence in mid-February 2017, less than a month after his inauguration, instead endorsing the "One China" policy insisted upon by Beijing, the

Chinese government within "a few days" awards him what the Associated Press calls "a valuable new trademark."[36] A week later, the Trump Organization sells a $15.8 million penthouse in Trump Park Avenue to Chinese American business executive Xiao Yan Chen, who "has been directly linked to a front group for Chinese military intelligence."[37] Chen runs Global Alliance Associates (GAA), whose business model might well have caught Trump's attention: per its website, GAA utilizes its "extensive network of relationships with the highest levels of government officials [in Beijing] . . . to facilitate [foreign companies'] immediate, efficient and skillful access into the Chinese market place."[38]

Between February 27—just days after the Xiao Yan Chen sale—and March 6, Beijing awards Trump preliminary approval for thirty-eight new trademarks.[39] *The Atlantic* writes shortly thereafter that "each subsequent [trademark] ruling in [Trump's] favor . . . serve[s] to remind Trump of the personal profits he could reap by improving his own personal relations with China, even if doing so leaves the American people worse off."[40] Meanwhile, Trump's controversial handling of the question of Taiwan post-election has confirmed for him that to the extent he can establish with Beijing that he holds leverage over the Chinese government as the U.S. president, it ultimately redounds to his pecuniary benefit. It is a lesson that his subsequent executive actions on U.S. trade policy—notwithstanding the significant pain they cause America's economy, workers, and consumers—will underscore he has learned well.

In June 2019, Trump makes perhaps his most controversial phone call to China yet, raising, per a CNN summary, "Biden's political prospects" in a conversation with Chinese president Xi Jinping in which Trump also "[tells] Xi he would remain quiet on Hong Kong protests as [U.S.-China] trade talks progressed."[41] Whether it is Trump's commingling of his personal political prospects with discussion of U.S. foreign policy or another reason, the White House decides to hide the reconstructed transcript of the Trump-Xi call. According to CNN, the transcript is moved to a "highly secure server"—a foretaste of what the White House will do with the transcript of the July 25 Trump-Zelensky call that leads to Trump becoming only the third president in U.S. history to be impeached.[42]

On September 24, 2019, Trump attorney Rudy Giuliani alleges, during an extraordinary Fox News interview—and without regard to Jared Kushner's prior efforts to extract billions from China while working on U.S.-China policy—that "the Bidens got $1.5 billion from China, which had to be a deliberate act, on the part of China, to buy the vice presidency. It cost a lot of money to buy it. They didn't invest in [Hunter Biden's] hedge fund because it made money. It made no money. The Chinese are not stupid. They don't spend their money for no reason. There's only one reason the Chinese spent that money: to buy Joe Biden's office. That office doesn't belong to him—it belongs to the people of the United States, and if a president can't vindicate that, then it's a sad day for America. I am proud of my president, because he's trying to clean up a swamp that is much worse than the American people realize."[43] Giuliani's comments prompt a question from his Fox News interviewer about why Giuliani rather than the FBI is conducting investigations overseas for Trump, to which Giuliani responds, "I'm defending him, he's my client"; Giuliani does not explain why Trump needs to be "defended" over Hunter Biden's business activities in China, or what accusations of illicit conduct in China the president himself might face that would make early preparations for a counterattack necessary.[44]

In an interview with Martha McCallum of Fox News ten days later, on October 4, Giuliani is asked the same question. He responds, "My mission is to defend my client in the best traditions of the legal profession. . . . It's in the best interest of my client to unravel the corruption in the Ukraine [sic] which involve[s] mostly collusion in the [2016] election."[45] When McCallum asks Giuliani how he was representing Trump by looking into Biden in March 2019, Giuliani says of Biden, who announced his candidacy after many months of public speculation in April 2019, "How would I have known . . . back then [in March 2019] he was going to run?"[46] Giuliani also adds a new explanation for his conduct, telling McCallum that he had to do what he did because "there was no Bill Barr when I did it"—meaning that only a Barr-led DOJ could be trusted by the president and his legal counsel to investigate Joe Biden.[47] Yet even this explanation raises new questions, as Barr had in fact been confirmed by the Senate on February 14, 2019, while Giuliani's activities in Ukraine on Trump's behalf extended well into August 2019.[48] Giuliani—who in August 2019 had been working with Volker and Sondland on a statement for Zelensky to give about investigating the Bidens in Ukraine—falsely tells McCallum that "I ended the investigation [into Biden's activities in Ukraine] in March [2019]."[49]

Giuliani provides further evidence of a garbled investigative timeline when he travels to Ukraine in early December 2019 to continue his investigation of Biden, making the trip nearly a year after Barr's confirmation. A spokeswoman for the president's attorney calls the trip a "secret assignment" for "the sole purpose of proving his client's [Trump's] innocence," though as to what charges or potential charges is unclear.[50] House Judiciary Committee chairman Jerrold Nadler (D-NY) will call Giuliani's trip on Trump's behalf to extract dirt on Biden from former Ukrainian government officials a "crime in progress."[51]

Precisely thirty seconds before Trump publicly asks China to investigate Joe Biden in early October 2019, he says the following about his ongoing trade negotiations with the Chinese government: "If they don't do what we want, we have tremendous, tremendous power."[52] Thereafter, Trump says all of the following, having just urged Ukraine to launch a "major investigation into the Bidens": "China should start an investigation into the Bidens, because what happened in China is just about as bad as what happened with Ukraine"; "I think Biden is going down ... [and] you may very well find that there are many other countries that [the Bidens] scammed, just like they scammed China and Ukraine"; and "China for so many years has had a sweetheart deal where China rips off the USA— because they deal [with people like] Biden."[53] Trump adds that while he has not brought up the prospect of investigating the Bidens with Chinese president Xi Jinping—a claim that cannot be verified, given that the president has hidden the transcript of his prior discussion about Biden with Xi on a secure server—he might well do so in the future. "I haven't [raised it]," Trump tells reporters, "but it's certainly something we can start thinking about because I'm sure that President Xi does not like being under that kind of scrutiny where billions of dollars is taken out of his country by a guy [Hunter Biden] that just got kicked out of the Navy. He got kicked out of the Navy. All of a sudden he's getting billions of dollars. You know what they call that? They call that a payoff."[54]

While the *Washington Post* will report that "it's not clear exactly what Trump is alleging here, nor has it been when Trump has previously invoked China while talking about the Bidens," it will add that, "more than [Trump's] request to Ukraine, this one has the potential for a really corrupt appearance . . . [because] Trump is currently engaged in a trade war with China."[55] The *Post* notes that not only does Trump have "significant leverage" over China, but it is leverage that he himself generated by launching a significant economic conflict with America's chief geopolitical rival—a trade war that has brutalized U.S. manufacturing, agriculture, and small business.[56] "China could very logically now believe that further escalations [in the trade war] might be tied to whether it takes the actions Trump wants. Any future decisions could be colored accordingly," writes the *Post*.[57] The newspaper imagines a situation in which information about Hunter Biden's business interests becomes public via an uncertain source, and shortly thereafter Trump ends his trade war with China—with American voters having no way to know if the two events are related, or indeed whether Trump has put numberless Americans through prolonged economic degradation either to gain an advantage in his own and his family's personal business dealings with Beijing or to advance his political career.[58]

Following Trump's request that China investigate the Bidens, the *Post* quotes Larry Noble, the Federal Election Commission's former general counsel, as observing, "I don't think it is credible that Trump has some other reason for seeking foreign investigations of Biden other than to help his 2020 campaign. It is the only context in which Biden is relevant to Trump."[59] The *Post* concludes that, following the Mueller Report and Trump's awareness of it, and the Ukraine imbroglio and Trump's awareness of the consequences it produced for both him and the nation, with China "it's hard to argue that (a) Trump wasn't aware that soliciting help from a foreign power was problematic, (b) there's no or little value in what Trump is soliciting and, of course, (c) that Trump isn't soliciting electoral help."[60] The conclusion reached by the *Post* is that none of the reasons why Trump's son Don "wasn't charged" by Mueller for his controversial June 2016 meeting at Trump Tower with Russian nationals could apply to Trump's solicitation of aid from Beijing.[61] Chuck Todd of NBC offers an even starker response to Trump's entreaty to Xi Jinping, saying on-air on *Meet the Press*, "I don't say this lightly, but let's be frank: a national nightmare is upon us. The basic rules of our democracy are under attack, from the president."[62]

In October 2019, a *New York Times* survey of "ten former White House chiefs of staff under Presidents Ronald Reagan, Bush, Clinton, George W. Bush and Barack Obama [finds] that none recalled any circumstance under which the White House had solicited or accepted political help from other countries," with all ten of the survey subjects saying "they would have considered the very idea [of soliciting foreign political aid] out of bounds."[63]

Shortly after Trump's remarks about a Chinese investigation of the Bidens, Secretary of State Pompeo is asked "whether other countries [besides Ukraine] . . . might be pressured to help the American president," to which Pompeo responds, "This is what we do," adding that it is "totally right."[64] "Nations work together," he says, "and they say, 'Boy, goodness gracious, if you can help me with X, we'll help you achieve Y.'"[65] Several weeks later, he goes further, insisting that the July 25 Trump-Zelensky call, including Trump's invitation for foreign involvement in a prospective investigation involving his political rival, was "consistent" with administration policy.[66] Trump's former national security advisor John Bolton will publicly demur from Pompeo's assessment, declaring darkly that America's "national security priorities" are "under attack from within"; in summer 2020, Bolton's White House memoir will reveal that in June 2019 Trump directly "plead[ed] with Xi to ensure he'd win [reelection in November]."[67]

Asked about Trump's China comments, Vice President Pence goes further than Pompeo in condoning them, even echoing Trump's call for foreign investigations by telling reporters that "the American people have a right to know if the vice president of the United States, or his family, profited from his position"—a stance he does not take with respect to the Trumps and their business dealings in China and elsewhere.[68] Whatever their motivation or intent, Pence's comments, like Trump's own, seem, in their particularity to Biden, to preclude any subsequent claims by either Trump or his vice president that they are only concerned about corruption broadly writ in Ukraine and China. Just so, Pompeo's public statements on possible clandestine negotiations between Trump and China over Biden dirt intimate that Trump and his administration—as will be alleged during the president's January 2020 impeachment trial—do not distinguish between a policy quid pro quo undertaken in the interests of U.S. national security and a quid pro quo intended to advance the personal interests of a U.S. president.

Much like Pence, Ukraine scandal witness and Trump ally Sen. Ron Johnson tells reporters, according to *The Hill*, that "there was no misconduct in Trump's call . . . for China to investigate Biden and his son"; Johnson states that "if there's potential criminal activity, the President of the United States is our chief law enforcement officer. We have proper agreements with countries to investigate potential crimes so I don't think there's anything improper about doing that."[69] Johnson does not cite any other investigations of U.S. citizens that the president is seeking abroad, whether in China, Ukraine, or elsewhere. When Johnson is asked, in the same interview in which he discusses a possible Chinese investigation of the Bidens, about Trump's solicitation of similar election aid from Volodymyr Zelensky on July 25, he responds that "it's Trump being Trump."[70] Meanwhile, the *Washington Post* terms Trump's call for China to investigate his potential 2020 presidential campaign rival the president's "most brazen [request] yet"—as well as "the most problematic."[71]

* * *

While Trump's and Pence's statements give the impression that the Trump administration hasn't yet formally raised the Bidens with the Chinese either publicly or via a back channel, a day after Trump's controversial statements his trade adviser, Peter Navarro, refuses to answer a direct question from CNN about whether he has discussed the Bidens as part of his trade negotiations with China.[72] Navarro will also refuse to address—or contest—prior reporting from CNN that in fact, despite his claims of the day before, Trump had already discussed Biden with Chinese president Xi Jinping in a June call that also involved trade negotiations and a promise by Trump not to discuss ongoing protests in Hong Kong in public.[73] A visibly angry Navarro goes so far as to call questions about the summer 2019 Trump-Xi call and Trump's public solicitation of election aid from China "hectoring," an "interrogation," and "witch hunt, part two"—an unexpectedly testy reply that echoes the Trump team's defensiveness over both Russia and Ukraine.[74] When he is asked if he himself has had, in the midst of trade negotiations with the Chinese, "contacts with Chinese officials" in Beijing on the subject of investigating Joe Biden, Navarro makes an unexplained reference to private conversations at the White House: "I will never talk about what happens inside the White House."[75]

China's response to Trump's entreaty is a comforting one: "[China] will not interfere in the internal affairs of the U.S."[76] This position is undercut, however, by February 2018 reporting that China is one of four countries that has discussed attempting to secretly manipulate the Trump administration by "influencing [Jared] Kushner to their advantage" and "taking advantage of his complex business arrangements . . . and lack of foreign policy experience"—a clandestine strategy that also appears applicable to the president, whose volume of Chinese interests is commensurate with or greater than Kushner's.[77] Indeed, that the Chinese government is looking for what the *Washington Post* terms "leverage" over one of the top foreign policy advisers in the Trump administration underscores that the ruling class in Beijing is by no means above appealing to Trump's venality via the promise of personal benefits.[78]

On October 10, 2019, a *Daily Beast* report confirms that those skeptical of the Chinese government had good reason to doubt that Beijing would honor its agreement to not offer illegal election assistance to President Trump. Per the digital media outlet, Trump adviser Michael Pillsbury confesses on October 9 that "China handed him intelligence on Hunter Biden in the same week Donald Trump publicly urged Beijing to investigate Joe Biden's son."[79] Pillsbury says he got the information on a trip to China, but does not reveal whether he was sent on the trip by the president, who had previously called Pillsbury "probably the leading authority on China."[80] Asked by the *Financial Times* for specifics of what he received, Pillsbury replies, "I got quite a bit of background on Hunter Biden from the Chinese"; per the *Financial Times*, the information "relate[s] to a $1.5bn payment from the Bank of China"—a figure, the British media outlet writes, that "matches the amount that Mr. Trump last week claimed Hunter Biden received from China."[81]

The revelation that the Chinese government has handed over intelligence on Hunter Biden to the Trump administration in response to Trump's request that they do so comes a day after Pillsbury reveals to the Fox Business Network (FBN), according to *Daily Beast* reporting, that he "raised the issue of the Bidens"—not just Hunter Biden, but Joe Biden as well—"during [a] trip to China"; as the *Daily Beast* observes of a McClatchy interview Pillsbury gives the day after his FBN interview, Pillsbury "declined to say whether he was instructed to raise the issue [of the Bidens] by the president."[82] After the Trump adviser's statement about receiving intelligence on the Bidens from the Chinese government goes viral, he attempts to deny, during a C-SPAN interview, that he ever told the *Financial Times* he'd received such intelligence. The *Times* thereafter tweets out an email exchange with Pillsbury "confirming," per the *Daily Beast*, that Pillsbury had indeed "claimed he had [received such intelligence]."[83]

* * *

On October 4, 2019, while speaking of his pleas for aid from both China and Ukraine, Trump says, "This is not about politics. This is about corruption. And if you look and you read our Constitution and many other things, I have an obligation to look at corruption. I have an actual obligation and a duty."[84] The same day, CNBC notes that the White House was asked by a reporter to "provide examples of any times President Trump has asked foreign leaders for corruption investigations that were not about his political opponents"; the White House does not provide any.[85] The same day, the *Washington Post* reports that "Trump's calls with foreign leaders have long worried aides, leaving some 'genuinely horrified.'"[86] The *Post* notes that in the first two-plus years of his presidency, White House staff repeatedly "fretted that Trump came across ill-informed in some calls, and even oafish. In a conversation with China's Xi, Trump repeated numerous times how much he liked a kind of chocolate cake."[87] More important, staff worried that "Trump preferred to make calls from the residence"—a practice that "frustrated some NSC staff and West Wing aides" because it meant they were not "on hand to give the president real-time advice" while he was speaking with foreign leaders.[88] This privacy would also have afforded Trump the time and space to raise topics of personal interest to him without the knowledge of even his most intimate advisers.[89]

The reaction of D.C. Republicans to Trump's outreach to China underscores why Trump might feel motivated to try to keep hidden much of his correspondence with foreign leaders, including Xi Jinping. In response to Trump's solicitation of a Biden investigation by Beijing, Sen. Susan Collins calls Trump's actions "completely inappropriate," adding that Trump made a "big mistake by asking China to get involved in investigating a political opponent."[90] Sen. Lindsey Graham calls Trump's public entreaty to the Chinese "stupid."[91] Sen. Marco Rubio (R-FL) declares it "wrong."[92] Sen. Ted Cruz (R-TX), asked by CBS whether Trump's request of the Chinese government was "appropriate," answers, "Of course not."[93] Sen. Lamar Alexander (R-TN) echoes Cruz, calling Trump's conversations with foreign governments on the topic of Joe Biden "inappropriate."[94] Sen. Rob Portman (R-OH) says of the July 25

Trump-Zelensky call—in a statement with significant implications for Trump's dealings with Beijing as well—that "the president should not have raised the Biden issue on that call, period. It's not appropriate for a president to engage a foreign government in an investigation of a political opponent."[95] Other Republicans, including Rep. Jim Jordan and Sen. Roy Blunt (R-MO), contend that Trump's October 2019 comments with respect to the Bidens, Ukraine, and China were intended as a joke—even though they evinced no outward indication of humor.[96]

Sen. Mitt Romney calls the president's conduct "wrong and appalling."[97] The senator tweets that "it strains credulity to suggest that [Trump's statement urging China to investigate Biden] is anything other than politically motivated"; Trump responds by tweeting that the 2012 Republican presidential candidate is a "pompous 'ass'" and demands his immediate impeachment from the U.S. Senate using the hashtag #IMPEACHMITTROMNEY.[98]

That China understands Trump's transactional nature—with respect to dirt on Joe Biden and his family or anything else—is clear. In November 2019, the *Washington Post* reports that "China hopes Trump will be reelected" because, according to Long Yongtu, a "former vice minister of foreign trade," the president is "easy to read."[99] According to a "politically connected person in Beijing" quoted by the *Post*, "Trump is a businessman. We can just pay him money and the problems will be solved. As long as we have money, we can buy him. That's the reason why we prefer him to Democrats."[100] In late October 2019, according to reporting by *The Hill*, FBI director Christopher Wray issues a public warning that China is expected to "explore disinformation efforts" in the 2020 presidential election.[101] Given Beijing's reported preference for the current occupant of the White House, there is reason to believe that any such disinformation efforts will be aimed at aiding Trump's reelection.

CHAPTER 31

VINDMAN

On October 31, 2019, *Politico* reports that Trump is "rewarding senators who have his back on impeachment" with access to his vast fundraising network—"lur[ing] GOP senators on impeachment with cold cash," the digital media outlet opines—and excluding from such largesse Republicans who do not co-sign "a Republican-backed resolution condemning the [impeachment] inquiry as 'unprecedented and undemocratic.'"[1] As Scott Reed, "a top Republican political strategist and former executive director of the Republican National Committee," boasts to *Politico*, Trump "has the ability to turn on the money spigot like no one else."[2] "It is the president's party now," Reed adds.[3]

Trump's iron grip over the Republican Party was evident in the immediate aftermath of his July 25 phone call with Zelensky as well. Within minutes of the call's conclusion, one of the White House officials concerned about its content, Lt. Col. Alexander Vindman, "rushe[s]" to the office of White House lawyer John Eisenberg because, according to the *Washington Post*, he is deeply "unsettled" and "disturbed" by hearing the president applying "pressure" to Zelensky to "investigate his political rivals."[4] According to the *Post*, Vindman is joined in Eisenberg's office by his twin brother, Yevgeny Vindman, an ethics attorney on the National Security Council, and Michael Ellis, a deputy legal adviser to the National Security Council.[5] At the meeting between the Vindmans, Ellis,

312 | SETH ABRAMSON

and Eisenberg, Alexander Vindman, reading directly from his notes of
the Trump-Zelensky call, tells Eisenberg that what has just happened is
"wrong."[6] Eisenberg has by this time been deputy White House counsel
for national security issues for over two and a half years—since Trump's
first day in office—working first for Don McGahn and thereafter for
Pat Cipollone; he formerly served in the Justice Department during the
George W. Bush administration.[7]

Eisenberg's response to Vindman's extraordinary news is to order
"the transcript's removal to a system known as NICE, for NSC Intelligence Collaboration Environment, which is normally reserved for codeword-level intelligence programs and top-secret sources and methods";
the move to a restricted-access server is one "other officials have said
is at odds with long-standing White House protocol."[8] Eisenberg makes
this decision even though—or perhaps because—well before July 25 he
had become "familiar," according to the *Washington Post*, "with concerns
among White House officials about the administration's attempts to
pressure Ukraine for political purposes."[9] Eisenberg's decision consequently hides from public revelation or censure not only the president's
wrongdoing, but also his own decision not to report a course of conduct
he has been aware of for some time. Indeed, Vindman has already come
to Eisenberg at least once before with an identical complaint: according
to the *Post*, both Vindman "and another senior official" raised the issue
of improper pressure being placed on Ukraine after the July 10 meeting
at the White House during which Sondland "pushed two Ukrainian
officials to investigate Trump's political rivals."[10] The second "senior official," according to *Politico*, was Vindman's boss Fiona Hill—who was
complaining to Eisenberg "at the instruction of then–National Security
Advisor John Bolton," per the digital media outlet.[11]

In addition to the removal of the rough transcript of the July 25 call
to a classified server, someone—it is not clear whether it is Eisenberg
or another White House official—is so concerned about the call that
they give "an order . . . to not distribute the reconstructed transcript of
Mr. Trump's call electronically, as would be typical. Instead, copies [are]
printed out and hand delivered to a select group."[12]

* * *

Eisenberg's decision to hide the rough transcript is made after he has "recorded Vindman's complaints in notes on a yellow legal pad" and "conferred" with Ellis.[13] According to the *Washington Post*, "former Trump national security officials [say] it [is] unheard of to store presidential calls with foreign leaders on the NICE system but that Eisenberg had moved at least one other transcript of a Trump phone call there."[14] *Politico* will report in September 2019 that, in the view of many national security experts, Eisenberg's actions constituted a "stark departure from how the [NICE] server is normally used and how memos of the president's exchanges are typically handled," with the digital media outlet adding that the deputy White House counsel's pattern of behavior has "surprised former White House and National Security officials who say the NSC's codeword-level system is specifically designed to protect highly sensitive compartmented intelligence matters."[15] According to Larry Pfeiffer, CIA chief of staff under George W. Bush, in prior administrations the NICE archive would "never be used to protect or 'lock down' politically sensitive material or to protect the president or senior officials from embarrassment."[16] Even a former Trump National Security Council official will acknowledge to *Politico* that "it would be unusual" to secrete transcripts of any kind into the code-word system, and that storing transcripts in this way is "probably not done frequently."[17]

Nevertheless, the *Politico* report reveals that nonstandard transmissions of White House transcripts to the NICE archive became commonplace "after 2017 . . . [when] the White House began to restrict the number of officials who had access to the transcripts [of presidential calls to foreign leaders]. One former Trump administration official confirmed that the White House started placing transcripts into the codeword system" shortly after the contents of two of Trump's calls were reported by the *Washington Post* in August 2017.[18] According to CNBC, two particularly noteworthy presidential relationships obscured as a result of the "severely restricted distribution of memos detailing President Donald Trump's calls with foreign leaders" include the president's communications with

Russia's Vladimir Putin and Saudi Arabia's Mohammed bin Salman—two of the six architects of the six-nation Red Sea Conspiracy that developed in the fall of 2015 (see *Proof of Conspiracy*).[19] CNBC notes that "the contents of the restricted calls with Putin and bin Salman are unknown. But Trump's relationship with both leaders has been controversial, given Russia's attack on the 2016 U.S. election on Trump's behalf and Saudi Arabia's human rights violations, including the state-sponsored murder of a *Washington Post* journalist."[20]

Eisenberg does not merely orchestrate the burying of the Trump-Zelensky call transcript, however—he also warns Alexander Vindman never to speak of the call again.[21] According to *Politico*, the admonition comes several days after Eisenberg and Ellis's July 25 meeting with the Vindman brothers. Alexander Vindman will later testify to Congress that Eisenberg's warning affected his work, as "it was [his] job to coordinate the interagency process with regard to Ukraine policy," and that policy was, after July 25, clearly under the influence of Trump's recent statements to Zelensky.[22]

In late October 2019, CNN reports that the NSC's top Russia and Europe adviser, Tim Morrison, "was involved [alongside Eisenberg and Ellis] with discussions after the [July 25] call about how to handle the transcript."[23] *Politico* will observe that Eisenberg has a "legendary reputation for secrecy," one that makes it unclear whether he "took [Vindman's] concerns up the chain to his boss in the White House counsel's office, Pat Cipollone."[24] According to a former NSC colleague of Eisenberg's who speaks with *Politico* in fall 2019, Eisenberg was "distrustful of information flows to everywhere else in the [White House]. . . . [H]e was . . . incredibly conscious of trying to restrict conversations to only those that he really, really, really felt needed to know."[25]

On September 25, "under mounting political pressure," according to the *Washington Post*, Trump will release the rough "transcript" of his July 25 call with Zelensky—but will do so only after the document has been edited to remove certain potentially problematic words and phrases, including a reference to Burisma.[26]

* * *

The *Washington Post* has identified a minimum of eight public confirmations of a quid pro quo between Trump and Ukraine that appeared either before, during, or after the July 25 Trump-Zelensky call: (1) Vindman's testimony, during an October 29, 2019, closed deposition, that "Sondland started to speak [on July 10, 2019] about Ukraine delivering specific investigations to secure the meeting with the president. . . . [He] emphasized the importance that Ukraine deliver the investigations into the 2016 election, the Bidens, and Burisma"; (2) Ambassador Taylor's testimony that during a September 1, 2019, call with Tim Morrison, Morrison "describe[d] a conversation Ambassador Sondland had with Mr. Yermak at [a meeting in] Warsaw . . . Sondland told Mr. Yermak that the security assistance money would not come until President Zelensky committed to pursue the Burisma investigation"; (3) Sondland's subsequent statement to Taylor that "he had made a mistake by earlier telling the Ukrainian officials . . . that a White House meeting with President Zelensky was dependent on a public announcement of investigations [when] in fact, Ambassador Sondland said, 'everything' was dependent on such an announcement, including security assistance"; (4) Morrison's testimony that, as to Taylor's testimony regarding the two officials' September 1 call, "I can confirm that the substance of his statement, as it relates to conversations he and I had, is accurate"; (5) a statement by U.S. senator Ron Johnson to the *Wall Street Journal* in which Johnson told the *Journal* that, according to Sondland, if Ukraine would "get to the bottom of what happened in 2016—if President Trump has that confidence, then he'll release the military spending," a confession of a quid pro quo that Johnson said he "winced" at, thinking, "Oh, God. I don't want to see those two things combined"; (6) Sondland's House testimony, as conveyed by the *Wall Street Journal*, that "he believed Ukraine agreeing to open investigations into Burisma Group . . . and into alleged 2016 election interference was a condition for a White House meeting between Mr. Trump and Ukrainian President Volodymyr Zelensky," and his later acknowledgment, in response to a question from "a lawmaker [about] whether that arrangement was a quid pro quo," that while "he wasn't a lawyer . . . he believed the answer was 'yes'"; (7) Sen. Johnson's statement to the *Milwaukee Journal Sentinel* that "the president was very consistent on why he was considering [continuing to hold the aid]. . . . [I]t was corruption, overall, generalized—but yeah, no doubt about it, what happened in 2016"; and (8) acting chief of staff Mulvaney's statement at a fall 2019 press conference that the president "mention[ed] to me . . . that the corruption related to the DNC server" was a reason to block aid to Ukraine, and that that was part of the reason "why we held up the money. . . . The look back to what happened in 2016 certainly was part of the thing that he was worried about in corruption with that nation."[27]

On February 11, 2020, the *New York Times* reports that Trump is using "threatening terms" to urge the U.S. military to discipline Alexander Vindman over his decision to report Trump's July 25 call with Zelensky to the White House counsel's office.[28] On February 19, Trump "ousts" from his job John Rood, a man Bloomberg identifies as "a top Defense Department official who advised against cutting off U.S. military aid to Ukraine" and "was involved in certifying to Congress that Ukraine was eligible to receive $250 million in security assistance."[29] Less than two weeks later, Trump withdraws his nomination for acting Pentagon comptroller Elaine McCusker to take on the role as a permanent position; according to *The Hill*, during the president's freeze on aid to Ukraine "McCusker expressed concerns about the legality of withholding the funds."[30] The next day, Trump promotes the man who worked with Eisenberg and Morrison to secrete the July 25 call transcript in the NICE archive, Michael Ellis, to senior director for intelligence on the National Security Council. As the Associated Press notes upon his sudden promotion, Ellis, who had previously been counsel to the House Permanent Select Committee on Intelligence under Devin Nunes, made the news in 2017 for being one of "two NSC officials . . . [who] helped House intelligence committee Chairman Devin Nunes view secret [NSC] reports."[31]

* * *

Trump's efforts to remove from government any officials who have opposed his wishes in the past or might do so in the future continue into 2020. In mid-April 2020, two Republican senators, James Lankford of Oklahoma and Rob Portman of Ohio, write the White House urging the president to, according to a *Politico* summary, "nominate permanent officials . . . instead of relying on temporary fill-ins that circumvent the Senate's traditional confirmation process."[32] Per *Politico*, the Republican duo's letter "tacitly warn[s] that [Trump] has threatened the[ ] independence [of U.S. inspectors general]," pursuing hiring and firing schemes that "undermine" the very notion of an executive branch watchdog.[33] Evidence of the digital media outlet's contention is legion: according to CBS News, over just six weeks in April and May 2020, Trump removed five inspectors general from their positions, including the independent auditors of the U.S. intelligence community, the Pentagon, the State Department, the Department of Health and Human Services (the department in charge of COVID-19 response), and the Transportation Department (the department whose inspector general is a member of the Pandemic Response Accountability Committee).[34] ABC News reports that "three of the . . . dismissals were late-night firings on a Friday," adding information that suggests the removals of the following four inspectors general in particular were deeply troubling: Steve Linick, the inspector general of the State Department, who was removed at secretary of state Mike Pompeo's request after "open[ing] an investigation looking into whether . . . Pompeo had misused staff for personal errands . . . [and] investigating Trump's use of emergency authority to supply weapons to Saudi Arabia in 2019"; Christi Grimm, the inspector general of the Department of Health and Human Services, who had aided in "the release of a report that identified critical shortages of medical supplies and staff as the coronavirus pandemic gripped the globe" (see chapter 42); Glenn Fine, the inspector general for the Defense Department, who "had been appointed to lead a committee overseeing the use of $2 trillion in coronavirus relief funds"; and Michael Atkinson, the intelligence community's inspector general, whose "communications to Congress about a whistleblower complaint helped initiate the Ukraine impeachment inquiry against the president."[35]

CHAPTER 32

THE WHISTLEBLOWER

In early August, 2019, a "CIA officer who was detailed to the National Security Council at one point" has a "colleague" convey his concerns about the July 25 phone call between President Trump and Ukrainian president Volodymyr Zelensky to the top attorney at the CIA.[1] After the would-be whistleblower becomes "concerned about how that initial avenue for airing his allegations through the CIA was unfolding," the officer, per the *New York Times*, "approache[s] a House Intelligence Committee aide with his concerns."[2] The information given to the aide, "some" of which is passed on to HPSCI chairman Adam Schiff, is "vague," per the *Times*, and the aide does not reveal the whistleblower's identity to Schiff; the CIA officer is told, consistent with long-standing HPSCI practice in whistleblower cases, to contact the inspector general for the U.S. intelligence community.[3]

Meanwhile, at the CIA, the prospective whistleblower's complaint "eventually reache[s] the spy agency's top lawyer," CIA general counsel Courtney Simmons Elwood.[4] Elwood is "told there [a]re concerns about the president's conduct on a call with a foreign leader, but not which leader," and decides to call deputy White House counsel John Eisenberg in part because she is "told that others at the National Security Council share[ ] the [whistleblower's] concerns."[5] It is unclear whether Eisenberg has by this time alerted Elwood to his prior relegation of the Trump-Zelensky rough transcript to the National Security Council's NICE archive.

According to NBC News, Eisenberg and Elwood, "after consulting with others at their respective agencies and learning more details about the complaint," agree to jointly call John Demers, the Justice Department's top national security lawyer.[6] By the time he agrees to call Demers with Elwood, Eisenberg has—because of his conversations either with Elwood or with other officials at the White House—decided that "the [whistleblower] allegations merit[ ] examination by the DOJ."[7] The Elwood-Eisenberg-Demers call occurs on August 14; Attorney General Barr is made aware of the call shortly thereafter.[8]

According to NBC, Elwood considers her joint August 14 call to the DOJ with a deputy White House counsel "to be a criminal referral to the Justice Department about the whistleblower's allegations that President Donald Trump abused his office in pressuring the Ukrainian president."[9] NBC reports that Elwood's "move . . . meant she and other senior officials had concluded a potential crime had been committed."[10] NBC observes that, whether or not Eisenberg was one of these "other senior officials," Elwood herself was, in calling Demers, "acting under rules that a report must occur if there is a reasonable basis to the allegations, defined as 'facts and circumstances . . . that would cause a person of reasonable caution to believe that a crime has been, is being, or will be committed.'"[11]

On August 15, the day after his call with Elwood and Eisenberg, Demers reads the "[rough] transcript of the July 25 call"; it is unclear if it is Eisenberg who assists Demers in locating and retrieving the document from its storage on the NICE system or if Demers does so himself.[12]

As it is reviewing the Elwood-Eisenberg referral, DOJ receives a second criminal referral on the same matter, this time from Michael Atkinson, the inspector general for the intelligence community (ICIG).[13] Atkinson's referral is the result of the whistleblower having been encouraged to contact the ICIG by a "staff member on the House Intelligence Committee" concurrently with the whistleblower contacting Elwood through a colleague at the CIA.[14] The whistleblower, confirmed by NBC News to be male, ultimately files his complaint with the ICIG on August 12, two days before Elwood and Eisenberg call Demers and on the deadline—per "powerful Pentagon budget official" Elaine McCusker—for $61 million of the frozen aid to Ukraine to be sent before it is lost.[15] August 12 is also one of the days on which the president orally affirms he wants the aid freeze maintained; it is not clear whether the president knows at the time—or would be concerned, if he did—about McCusker's warning that Ukraine is about to permanently lose $61 million in critical U.S. financial assistance.[16]

The whistleblower complaint filed on August 12 details, according to the *New York Times*, "Mr. Trump's campaign to solicit foreign election interference that could benefit him politically."[17]

At the end of August, the DOJ receives a third criminal referral regarding the Trump-Zelensky call, this time from the acting director of national intelligence, Joseph Maguire.[18] Maguire's referral is partially in response to the DOJ Office of Legal Counsel (OLC) opinion written following the office's contact with Atkinson; the OLC opinion had deemed Atkinson's initial referral not to be an "urgent concern" under statutory reporting provisions—citing reasons that subsequently come under substantial scrutiny—even as, per reporting in the *New York Times*, the DOJ would thereafter inform Maguire that Trump's actions could "result in a criminal referral."[19] As with the Elwood referral and the Atkinson referral, the DOJ takes no steps to investigate Maguire's referral beyond a pre-investigation legal analysis of a single term ("thing of value") in 52 U.S. Code § 30121, the federal statute prohibiting the solicitation of foreign campaign donations.[20] It is unclear whether the author of the OLC memo, assistant attorney general Steven A. Engel, agrees with the department's decision not to act on either the Atkinson or Maguire referrals.

The step taken by DOJ in response to the Atkinson referral—namely, to conduct a cursory 52 U.S. Code § 30121 analysis—had not been taken upon DOJ's receipt of the Elwood referral, an unexplained failure that retroactively bolsters the whistleblower's decision to turn to Atkinson rather than relying on Elwood. DOJ later explains its inaction in response to the Elwood referral by opining that it was communicated telephonically, and that it was therefore "unclear"—even though Elwood was acting in concert with the deputy White House counsel for national security affairs—"whether Elwood was making a criminal referral."[21] Moreover, DOJ will later claim that it felt Elwood's statements on the Trump-Zelensky phone call across two contacts, one on August 14 and one thereafter, were "vague"; it is a claim Elwood will subsequently reject, with NBC noting that she was "acting under rules set forth in a memo governing how intelligence agencies should report allegations of federal crimes."[22]

The Justice Department's decision to ignore Elwood's criminal referral notwithstanding, its dismissal of Atkinson's criminal referral is notably alacritous. This second denial is, according to NBC, "purely" based on "an analysis of whether the president committed a campaign finance law violation."[23] Per subsequent statements by the DOJ, it considered only 52 U.S. Code § 30121 in reviewing Atkinson's referral because "it was the only statute mentioned in the whistleblower's complaint [included by Atkinson in his filing]."[24] This confession suggests that DOJ did not pursue Elwood's criminal referral even gesturally, as officials there will later tell NBC that, with respect to her referral, "the issue of campaign finance law was not part of their deliberations."[25]

In October, NBC conclusively determines that Barr's department rejected Elwood's criminal referral outlining a potential national security breach exclusively because it "needed to be in writing" and wasn't.[26]

That the "analysis" DOJ conducts following its receipt of the whistleblower's complaint and Atkinson's accompanying ICIG criminal referral includes no formal criminal investigation is striking. According to Berit Berger, a former federal prosecutor who is now director of Columbia University's Center for the Advancement of Public Integrity, the DOJ "didn't do any of the sort of bread-and-butter type investigatory steps that would flush out what potential crimes [in addition to campaign finance law violations] may have been committed. I don't understand the rationale for that . . . it's just so contrary to how normal prosecutors work. We have started investigations on far less [than what the whistleblower and Atkinson submitted]."[27] Indeed, per NBC, "former federal prosecutors contend that the conduct" outlined by the whistleblower and Atkinson could easily "have fit other criminal statutes, including those involving extortion, bribery, conflict of interest or fraud, that might apply to the president or those close to him."[28]

As for the federal statute criminalizing solicitation of foreign campaign donations, the DOJ concludes that President Trump would not be receiving a "thing of value" if he successfully persuaded the Ukrainian president to open a criminal investigation into his chief Democratic rival for the presidency of the United States; this finding comes despite the fact that, in their July 2019 contract negotiations with Dmitry Firtash, Trump legal advisers Joe diGenova and Victoria Toensing had already put a minimum value on their transmission of Firtash's purported dirt on Biden to U.S. officials: $1 million.[29]

On the strength of its pre-investigation analysis excluding opposition research as a "thing of value" to politicians, the DOJ chooses not to, per NBC, "examin[e] . . . documents or interview[ ] . . . witnesses to the [Trump-Zelensky] phone call, participants in the White House decision to withhold military funding from Ukraine, the president's lawyer, Rudy Giuliani," or "Ukrainian officials who were the target of Trump's and Giuliani's entreaties."[30] Moreover, DOJ does not consider any "text messages . . . in which diplomats appear to suggest there was a linkage between aid [to Ukraine] and Ukraine's willingness to investigate a case involving Joe Biden."[31]

Under 18 U.S. Code § 201, it is a federal felony punishable by up to fifteen years in prison and possible permanent disqualification from federal office for President Trump to, "directly or indirectly," "corruptly seek anything of value in return for being influenced in the performance of any official act," with "anything of value" being defined in the federal bribery statute as anything that can be considered to have a "market value."[32] Given that Trump, by September 11, 2019, will have withheld $391 million in military aid to Ukraine for nearly two months in response to Ukraine's refusal to open an investigation into either Burisma or the DNC server hacked by the Russians in 2016, the "market value" set by the White House for such investigations would seem to be $391 million; meanwhile, the official acts Trump's agents have variously implicitly and explicitly promised Zelensky include a call with Trump, a meeting at the White House, the release of $391 million in pre-authorized military aid to Ukraine, and the future sale of the Javelin missiles Zelensky was requesting of the United States in the moments before Trump said to him, on July 25, "I would like you to do us a favor though."

Common Cause, a Republican-founded but nonpartisan advocacy organization focused on government reform, proposes its own "value" analysis: according to a complaint Common Cause files with the Justice Department and the Federal Election Commission in October 2019, summarized by NBC News following an interview with Common Cause's vice president of policy and litigation, "it wouldn't have been difficult for the [DOJ] to determine how much money Ukraine would have spent in an investigation of Joe Biden and his son. That would give them a dollar amount to show that Trump solicited 'something of value'" under either 52 U.S. Code § 30121 (Contributions and Donations by Foreign Nationals) or 18 U.S. Code § 201 (Bribery).[33]

Establishing that a politician is acting for his own benefit rather than the benefit of his constituents is sufficient to establish "corrupt" intent under all of these statutes, and the flexibility of 18 U.S. Code § 201 with respect to both "direct" and "indirect" entreaties to third parties arguably criminalizes both the Trump-Zelensky phone call of July 25 and any preceding or subsequent efforts made on Trump's behalf and with Trump's knowledge by Giuliani, Sondland, Volker, Perry, Parnas, Fruman, diGenova, Toensing, or any other designated Trump agent. When the head of DOJ's criminal division, Brian Benczkowski, convenes with "career lawyers at the public integrity section" in mid-August 2019, however, 18 U.S. Code § 201 is neither considered nor discussed. Even when Benczkowski's discussions of the July 25 phone call expand to include, per NBC, "the [DOJ] national security division and the Office of Legal Counsel," 18 U.S. Code § 201 is ignored.[34]

Benczkowski ultimately makes the decision "not to open an investigation." DOJ will not now say whether there was any dissent at the time from the Public Integrity Section, the National Security Division, or the OLC lawyers with whom Benczkowski conferred, noting only that the "relevant components of the department" agreed that even a sprawling, internationally broadcast, foreign-government-run criminal investigation of a president's chief political rival has no legally recognizable "value" in the context of a presidential campaign—indeed, has less cognizable, quantifiable value than a $1 contribution from a small donor.[35]

Despite this assessment by the DOJ that the "dirt" Trump requested is either unquantifiably valuable or confirmably worthless, an October 2019 *BuzzFeed News* report reveals that in fact the Department of Justice has in the past called (variously) "sex, information, and worthless stock . . . things of value."[36] Moreover, as Ryan Goodman, the editor-in-chief of *Just Security*, will report, the Mueller investigation, conducted under the auspices of the DOJ and FBI, had just weeks before Benczkowski's determination concluded that the phrase "thing of value" encompasses such things as "reports," "candidate-related opposition research . . . [including] derogatory information about an opponent," and various other "intangibles," including "information" broadly defined; by this definition, Ukraine's prosecutor general, Yuri Lutsenko, had already provided Trump's personal attorney Rudy Giuliani with a significant "thing of value" in the spring of 2019, when he reportedly handed over a detailed—if false—report on the Bidens' activities in Ukraine.[37] Per Goodman's analysis, the Mueller Report goes so far as to identify as a "thing of value" anything "defined broadly to include the value which the defendant subjectively attaches" to it.[38] That Trump in July 2019 perceives the CrowdStrike and Burisma investigations as a thing of substantial value to him is uncontested—as is the fact that, by October 2019, the FBI has contacted the whistleblower to potentially use him as a witness in a criminal investigation now being undertaken by the Bureau.[39]

In defending Benczkowski's decision not to open an investigation into the president's conduct, DOJ spokeswoman Kerri Kupec will state that Benczkowski considered the "facts" before making his determination—a statement that raises the question of how facts can be gathered in the absence of an investigation. In response to Benczkowski's significantly attenuated decision-making process, former federal prosecutor Chuck Rosenberg will opine that the DOJ's criminal division chief was "not by any stretch of the imagination limited to the [ICIG] referral . . . [and] in fact . . . [had an] obligation to look more deeply and more broadly"; Berger, the former federal prosecutor, will add that, according to the standard operating procedures at the DOJ, "when you get a criminal referral, you don't go into it saying, 'This is the criminal violation and now I'm going to see if the facts prove it.' You start with the facts and the evidence and then you see what potential crimes those facts support. It seems backwards to say, 'We are going to look at this just as a campaign finance violation and oops, we don't see it—case closed.'"[40]

According to an interview NBC News conducts with Berger, "in a case in which a government official is allegedly using his office for personal gain, and pressuring someone to extract a favor, the bribery and extortion statutes are usually considered. The Foreign Corrupt Practices Act [FCPA], which prohibits bribery of foreign officials, may also . . . [be] implicated."[41] Just a matter of months before making his final decision to run for the White House, and long after the point in 2011 when Trump "first started thinking seriously about [a 2016 bid for] the presidency," according to longtime aide Sam Nunberg, Trump had told CNBC that the FCPA is "ridiculous" and a "horrible law" that should be "changed."[42] In mid-January 2020, *The Hill* reports that Trump—even in the midst of an impeachment trial that could reveal he has violated the FCPA—is "exploring making changes to [the] global anti-bribery law" in response to "complaints" from the sort of U.S. company the FCPA "bars . . . from paying bribes to secure contracts abroad."[43]

While neither of the two relevant divisions within the DOJ—Criminal (including the Public Integrity Section) or National Security—conducts an investigation upon receiving the CIA whistleblower's complaint, nor does the Office of Legal Counsel (under the supervision of the assistant attorney general), ICIG Atkinson takes a different tack, conducting a significant preliminary investigation before passing the whistleblower's complaint on to the DOJ with his own annotations. Atkinson interviews multiple witnesses and investigates the whistleblower's background and ability to perceive the events described in the complaint before eventually concluding, according to the *New York Times*, that the complaint is "credible" and that "there [is] reason to believe that the president might have illegally solicited a foreign campaign contribution—and that his potential misconduct create[s] a national security risk."[44]

Atkinson also makes a legal finding: that the complaint represents an "urgent concern," a determination that requires him to find that the acting director of national intelligence, Joseph Maguire, has an "operational responsibility to prevent election interference"; in subsequently refusing to act on the complaint, the Office of Legal Counsel concludes, in a September 2019 memo, that the United States' acting director of national intelligence bears no responsibility for ensuring that foreign powers do not conduct domestic hacking, propaganda, or intelligence campaigns that interfere with a U.S. election—a ruling that would have given the director of national intelligence under President Obama no role in collecting information on the pro-Trump Kremlin cyberattack that disrupted the 2016 election.[45]

Engel, the author of the OLC memo, argues, in addition to his unusual interpretation of U.S. intelligence responsibilities, that the whistleblower's complaint does not constitute an "urgent concern" because the whistleblower had at some point exhibited "unspecified indications" of an "arguable" political bias.[46] By comparison, Atkinson, while noting in his report that the whistleblower may have favored a candidate other than Trump in the 2020 presidential election, underscores that any such bias could be regarded only as "arguable" and by no means as a terminal flaw in the complaint.[47] As for the final finding Atkinson makes in favor of his informing Congress of the whistleblower's complaint—that Trump's actions might expose the president himself "to serious national security and counterintelligence risks"—Engel's September 3 memo does not address such concerns, instead opining that "the President is not a member of the intelligence community" even though the nation's Director of National Intelligence reports directly to him.[48]

Reaction to the whistleblower complaint among units of the Trump administration outside DOJ is immediate and dramatic—and favorable to the complaint. According to NBC, "multiple senior government officials appointed by Trump [find] the whistleblower's complaints credible, troubling, and worthy of further inquiry," reaching this conclusion "soon after" the July 25 Trump-Zelensky call.[49] As these senior government officials reach their own conclusions on the matter, the White House continues stonewalling attempts by Congress to view the complaint.[50]

On September 30, *The Hill* reports that the White House is "trying to find out" the whistleblower's identity, even though the whistleblower statute does not provide for the White House receiving this information and the whistleblower's attorneys have already said publicly, per Reuters, that "efforts to identify their client 'will place that individual and their family at risk of serious harm.'"[51] Heedless of this warning, Trump's son Don Jr. tweets out the alleged name of the whistleblower in late September.[52] Simultaneously, Devin Nunes aide Derek Harvey is, per the *Daily Beast*, "providing conservative politicians and journalists with information—and misinformation—about the anonymous whistleblower ... [including] notes for House Republicans identifying the whistleblower's name. . . . The purpose of the notes, one source said, is to get the whistleblower's name into the record of the proceedings" of the House Permanent Select Committee on Intelligence.[53] As Trump Jr. and Harvey are disseminating the alleged name of the whistleblower, Kremlin-controlled television networks in Russia begin doing the same.[54]

CHAPTER 33

PENCE

On September 1, 2019, Vice President Pence travels to Warsaw for an event commemorating the eightieth anniversary of the beginning of World War II.[1] While in Warsaw, Pence meets with Zelensky; Gordon Sondland is also present at the meeting.[2] Prior to the Pence-Zelensky meeting, Sondland tells Pence that he has "concerns that the delay in [military] aid [has] become tied to the issue of investigations."[3] Pence does not ask Sondland to explain what he means by "delay," "aid," or "investigations," seeming to well understand what the president's ambassador to the European Union is discussing. According to Sondland's November 2019 congressional testimony, in response to his updating of Pence on Trump's demand for specific investigations from Zelensky, the vice president "nod[s]" in what Sondland describes as "sort of a duly noted" way.[4] Pence's chief of staff—likely aware of how much damage such an exchange could be to the vice president if corroborated—will accuse Sondland of lying under oath, insisting that Pence "never had a conversation with Gordon Sondland about investigating the Bidens, Burisma, or the conditional release of financial aid to Ukraine based upon potential investigations."[5] Pence himself does not comment on Sondland's testimony. In January 2020, Lev Parnas will tell MSNBC and CNN, in two successive interviews, that Pence was aware Trump was conditioning certain official acts on the Ukrainians' announcement of an investigation of the Bidens—what Parnas calls a "quid pro quo"—by mid-May 2019 at the latest, stating that Pence was "in the loop" and "couldn't have not known," at another point adding that "of course [Pence] knew" about the quid pro quo.[6]

On the day of Pence's arrival in Warsaw, Ambassador Taylor texts Sondland and Trump special envoy Kurt Volker to ask, "Are we now saying that security assistance and [a] White House meeting are conditioned on investigations?"[7] Whereas Taylor had been deliberately kept apart from the effort to erect such a quid pro quo, the same does not, apparently, hold true for the vice president, who, per the *Washington Post* in October 2019, had by early September "repeatedly" been involved by Trump "in efforts to exert pressure on the leader of Ukraine."[8] The *Post* includes in its itemization of such involvement Trump's late April 2019 directive to Pence to attend Zelensky's inauguration in his stead at a time "when Ukraine's new leader was seeking recognition and support from Washington"; the president's subsequent withdrawal of that order on May 13; and the way Trump "used" Pence, in Warsaw, to "tell Zelensky that U.S. aid was still being withheld while demanding more aggressive action on corruption . . . [at a time] the Ukrainians probably understood action on corruption to include the investigation of former vice president Joe Biden and his son Hunter Biden."[9] Despite this reporting by the *Post*, and claims by Parnas that the Ukrainians' rejection of his Giuliani-orchestrated demand for investigations of Biden led directly to Trump withdrawing Pence from Zelensky's inauguration, Pence's spokespeople will continue to claim throughout the fall 2019 congressional impeachment inquiry that the vice president was "unaware of Trump's efforts to press Zelensky for damaging information about Biden and his son" until September 17, 2019.[10]

In fact, the *Washington Post* reports, even if Pence had not been "in the loop," despite Parnas's claim, numerous public indications of pressure being exerted on Zelensky by Trump would have been evident to Pence well before September 17, including "the abrupt removal of the U.S. ambassador to Kyiv [in spring 2019]," "visible efforts . . . by Giuliani to insert himself in the U.S.-Ukraine relationship," "alarms being raised inside the White House even before the emergence of the extraordinary whistleblower complaint," and, "most significantly, [the fact that] one of Pence's top advisers was on the July 25 [Trump-Zelensky] call and the vice president should have had access to the transcript within hours."[11] Indeed, as summarized by CNN, Pence's aide Jennifer Williams tells Congress in mid-November 2019 that she "flagged news articles to the vice president about Rudy Giuliani's dealings in Ukraine," including a May 28, 2019, interview Giuliani had given in Ukraine in which, according to her testimony, Giuliani "referenced particular investigations that he would like to see the Ukrainians undertake"; Williams tells Congress that the investigations Giuliani said he wanted in the May 28 interview "related to the 2016 election, and what role, if any, Ukraine may have played in that, as well as looking into the situation with former Vice President Biden's son and Burisma."[12] Williams also testifies not only that Pence's briefing book the day of the July 25 Trump-Zelensky call had a transcript of the call in it, but that in her estimation the transcript detailed a call that was "unusual as compared to other [Trump] discussions with foreign leaders"—testimony that suggests Pence would have found it noteworthy at the time, or at a minimum would have been advised by his staff that certain material in his briefing book required special attention.[13]

USA Today reports that at the time of Yovanovitch's firing, months before the July 25 call, Pence would have had reason to inquire with the president about his intentions toward Ukraine after "Pence's office was in the preliminary planning stages to send the vice president to Zelensky's May [2019] inauguration when [Pence's aide Jennifer Williams] was told by an assistant to Pence's chief of staff that Trump didn't want Pence to go"—and, moreover, from the fact that no one in either the NSC or the vice president's office "knew the reason behind that direction [from the president]," a particularly odd one given that the as yet unscheduled inauguration could not have conflicted with any prior event on Pence's calendar.[14]

That Trump's withholding of Pence from Zelensky's inauguration was a significant political punishment of the new Ukrainian leader is confirmed by The Atlantic, which reports that Zelensky "desperately wanted

Vice President Mike Pence to attend his inauguration, because Joe Biden had graced his predecessor's ceremony."[15] When Trump "thwarts" Zelensky's "desire" (as *The Atlantic* terms it), it undermines the new president's legitimacy in a way that weakens him politically on the very first day of his presidency.[16]

For Pence to have remained unaware of the content of the July 25 Trump-Zelensky call until September 17 would therefore have required extraordinary withholding from him by members of his staff, as well as his own refusal to review the transcript of a critical exchange between President Trump and a new world leader whose nation was at war with Russia. This may explain why Pence aides do not say that Pence hadn't read the transcript of the July 25 call at the time he traveled to Warsaw in September 2019, but rather, according to the *Washington Post*, float an alternative narrative: that Pence may have in fact read the transcript, but did so "without having . . . fully registered" any element of it.[17] Even this somewhat attenuated explanation of Pence's muddled understanding of U.S.-Ukraine geopolitics will be contested by Williams's congressional testimony, which details how "before the end of the day [July 25] . . . my colleagues who helped prepare the Vice President's briefing book received a hard copy of the transcript from the White House Situation Room to include in that book. . . . [W]e wanted to make sure the Vice President got it."[18] Moreover, the *Post* adds, if Pence had failed to register Yovanovitch's May 2019 firing, the sudden order from the president that he not attend Zelensky's inauguration, Giuliani's highly unusual public declarations, alarms raised within the White House about the extraordinary hold on aid to Ukraine, updates from his own staff on the July 25 call, the readily available transcript of that call, and even his own briefing book's summary of the call, he still "would have received the detailed notes of the president's call" in the "briefing materials he took with him to Warsaw [on September 1]"—sixteen days before his office now claims the vice president learned of Trump's push for investigations of his political rivals.[19] That Pence had at least two of his representatives on the July 25 call, both Williams and her immediate supervisor—Pence's national security advisor, retired Lt. Gen. Keith Kellogg—and that another

Pence aide now insists Pence was not "poorly prepared for his [September 1] meeting with Zelensky" only adds to the confusion about what Vice President Pence knew and when.[20] Indeed, the same Pence staffer who tells the *Post* that Pence was well prepared for his meeting in Warsaw will "point[ ] to the eventual outcome [of the event]—that the Trump administration ultimately released the aid to Ukraine—as a sign of a productive meeting," an unusual boast inasmuch as it implies that the topic of the September 1 Pence-Zelensky meeting was indeed Trump's ongoing withholding of previously authorized military aid to a European ally of the United States.[21]

Reviewing the public record and timeline of events, Greg Sargent of the *Washington Post* concludes that though "Vice President Pence's aides are making the spectacularly implausible suggestion that, even as President Trump repeatedly directed him to place pressure on Ukraine, Pence had no earthly idea it had anything to do with Trump's private agenda of getting Ukraine to smear Joe Biden," "the evidence [is] that Pence knew exactly what he had been enlisted to do," as "before Pence did any of those things [with respect to the Ukrainians], Trump's lawyer, Rudy Giuliani, [had] repeatedly said he wanted Ukraine to investigate—i.e., fabricate smears against—Biden, on Trump's behalf."[22] Sargent adds that "Trump himself said publicly that Biden's activities in Ukraine merited scrutiny. News reports spelled out exactly what Giuliani and Trump wanted, in detail."[23]

The Pence camp's insistence that the vice president had no knowledge of the Bidens' relevance to Trump-Zelensky negotiations until September 17 is difficult to credit for more reasons than these, however. On September 2, the day after the Pence-Zelensky meeting in Warsaw, Pence is asked at a press conference for "an update on Ukrainian security aid money," and specifically whether he "discuss[ed] Joe Biden at all" during his meeting with Zelensky.[24] Before Pence can respond, the reporter presses him further, insisting that Pence "assure Ukraine that the hold-up of that money has absolutely nothing to do with efforts, including by Rudy Giuliani, to try to dig up dirt on the Biden family."[25] As had been the case with his response to Sondland the day before, Pence exhibits no surprise at the question or its premise, offering, in a 416-word response, that while he did not discuss Biden with Zelensky, he did discuss in "great detail" both "America's support for Ukraine and the upcoming decision the President will make on the latest tranche of financial support."[26] Pence adds that, in addition to discussing these topics, he had been asked by the president to talk to Zelensky about "the progress that he's making on a broad range of areas" because, "as President Trump had me make clear, we have great concerns about issues of corruption.... [I] told [Zelensky] that I would carry back to President Trump the progress that he and his administration in Ukraine are making on dealing with corruption in their country."[27]

After Pence nods in response to Sondland's September 1 statement to him that "aid [has] become tied to the issue of investigations," and after the vice president meets with Zelensky, Sondland tells top Zelensky aide Andriy Yermak, in a "brief pull-aside conversation," that "resumption of U.S. aid would likely not occur until Ukraine provided the public anti-corruption statement that we [Sondland, Volker, and Ukrainian officials] had been discussing for many weeks."[28] Perhaps understanding the gravity of this conversation, Sondland excludes it from his October 17, 2019, closed-door testimony to several House committees, revealing it only in a November 4, 2019, supplemental declaration to Congress.[29] While Sondland testifies that, as of September 1, it was unclear if Trump would be satisfied by Zelensky's prosecutor general making an announcement of new investigations into CrowdStrike and Burisma, the ambassador concedes that "soon thereafter" he "came to understand," from either Volker or Giuliani, that Zelensky would in fact have to make such a statement himself.[30]

In October 2019, several unnamed federal officials tell the *Washington Post* that during his September 1 meeting with Zelensky "Pence's emphasis on corruption probably would have been interpreted by Zelensky as 'code' for" conducting inquiries into "[Joe] Biden or the dormant probe of Burisma, the company for which his son had served as a board member."[31] In subsequent congressional testimony, both NSC official Fiona Hill and State Department official David Holmes echo this sentiment, "unequivocally" telling Congress, according to the *New York Times*, that "President Trump's mentions of Burisma were 'code' for investigating the Bidens and that anyone working on Ukraine would know that, in part because [Trump's attorney] Rudy Giuliani made the link 'publicly, repeatedly' on TV."[32]

On September 18—seventeen days after Pence's meeting with Zelensky in Warsaw, and the day the *Washington Post* reveals the existence of a whistleblower complaint regarding the July 25 Trump-Zelensky call— Vice President Pence speaks to Zelensky by phone.[33] Two months later, Pence staffer Jennifer Williams will attempt to testify in open session before Congress about "additional information" regarding the September 18 Pence-Zelensky call that "review[ing] certain materials . . . cause[d] her to recall," only to be told by the vice president's office, per *The Hill*, that "the new information was classified."[34]

After Williams's additional classified testimony about Pence's knowledge of the administration's dealings with Ukraine, HPSCI chairman Adam Schiff issues a public statement saying, as summarized by the *Washington Post*, that "Pence's office may have purposefully misled [HPSCI] about [the] contents of his [September 18] Zelensky call," and that its blocking of Williams's public testimony is an attempt to obstruct the revelation of evidence that is—in Schiff's words—"directly relevant" to the impeachment inquiry.[35] When HPSCI tries to follow up on Williams's subsequent "classified written submission [to Congress] regarding the call," Pence's office will say that it can't comply with congressional requests to declassify the call because it is confused by them; "the Office of the Vice President does not even know what [HPSCI] wants declassified," a Pence spokeswoman says at the time.[36] This obtuse response runs counter to Pence's November 2019 claim that he has "no objection

at all to releasing further details about [his September 18] call with Zelensky," a concession that is followed by the White House counsel's office
refusing to release a transcript of the call to Congress.[37] On October 9,
when Pence is asked several times if he knew of Trump's demand that
Ukraine investigate the Bidens at the time that demand was being made,
he dodges the questions.[38]

Six days later, as reported by *USA Today*, Pence "refuse[s] to turn over
documents requested by House Democrats as part of their impeachment
inquiry," telling Congress through his attorney that "the purported 'impeachment inquiry' has been designed and implemented in a manner
that calls into question your commitment to fundamental fairness and
due process rights."[39] Pence's attorney, as Pence had effectively done a
week earlier, directs Congress to "discuss[ ] with the White House Counsel's Office . . . compliance with constitutionally mandated procedures."[40]

After three weeks pass without the release of any of the documents
requested by Congress, including the September 18 Pence-Zelensky call
transcript, NBC reports that the reason for the delay as to the latter document is an "internal debate [that] has divided White House officials over
whether releasing the [transcript of the September 18 Pence-Zelensky]
call would help or hurt their flailing efforts to counter accusations that
President Donald Trump held up military aid to pressure Ukrainian
President Volodymyr Zelensky to investigate his political rivals."[41] Per
NBC's reporting, there are concerns within the White House that the
September 18 transcript could "fuel[ ] the impeachment inquiry rather
than tamp it down."[42] Not long after NBC publishes its report, the White
House counsel's office refuses to declassify Jennifer Williams's supple-
mental congressional testimony, which had offered the hope of shedding
new light on the Pence-Zelensky call.[43]

One piece of evidence suggesting Pence and Zelensky may have discussed
more than Zelensky's gratitude for America's friendship and the logistics
of an upcoming United Nations event (as an initial *Washington Post* report
on the September 18 call had it) is found in the November 2019 revelation

that Zelensky had been on the verge of giving an interview with CNN to "announce an investigation into Trump's political rivals" the week of the Pence-Zelensky call.[44] The possibility that Pence was tasked, on September 18, with promising Zelensky a meeting with Trump at the United Nations if he agreed to do the CNN interview cannot be discounted.

According to Fareed Zakaria, Zelensky's would-be CNN interviewer, CNN "had been negotiating with President Zelensky and his office for a while, for months, to try to get an interview with him," but after major revelations about the whistleblower report were published in the *Washington Post* on September 18, "it became clear . . . that the interview was off."[45] An October 2019 *New York Times* report will reveal that during the period in September when Zelensky appeared poised to give a CNN interview, Sondland, Volker, and Giuliani had already prepared a statement for him to give about investigating the Bidens and CrowdStrike; it is unclear if the three Americans intended Zelensky to give the statement on-air or as a separate press release synchronized with his CNN appearance.[46] In either case, a call from Pence to Zelensky on September 18 would have been well timed to revisit the issue.

According to the *New York Times*, by early August 2019 the Ukrainians had prepared a draft of a potential Zelensky statement for Sondland, Volker, and Giuliani to review, upon which review Giuliani declared that the statement didn't go far enough, as it didn't explicitly reference Burisma or the 2016 election.[47] With respect to the subsequent draft—revised to be far more explicit—that Trump's agents sent to the Ukrainians in response, the *Times* reports, "The Ukrainians never released the [revised] statement. But if they had, Mr. Trump's aides would have effectively pressured a foreign government to give credence to allegations intended to undercut one of the Democratic Party's leading 2020 president candidates . . . without leaving Mr. Trump's fingerprints on it."[47] Per the *Times*, the CNN interview Zelensky nearly conducted—an interview "Trump wanted"—as well as the revised statement, which the "White House request[ed]" Zelensky issue on-air, together would have signaled that Zelensky and his government "had decided to capitulate to President Trump's demands to publicly announce investigations against his political enemies."[48] It appears that only the release of the whistleblower's complaint prevented Trump and his agents from getting what they wanted out of Zelensky—a fact that may explain the president's seemingly perpetual anger at the anonymous CIA officer behind the complaint.

According to CNN, "almost all of Zelensky's aides"—a group that includes several men who spoke directly to Trump allies—"supported the planned announcement [of investigations] on [Fareed Zakaria's CNN] show. . . . They agreed that American military aid and diplomatic support during upcoming peace talks were worth the risk of seeming to support Trump in the American political process."[49] Zelensky aide Andriy Yermak had, by September 18, spent weeks drafting a statement suitable for Zelensky to give on CNN or issue as a press release in mid-September. Per CNN, a *New York Times* report reveals that Yermak "hashed out wording with then-US Special Envoy to Ukraine Kurt Volker," and that the public statement would have been aimed at "discredit[ing] Joe Biden."[50] According to his October 2019 congressional deposition, Volker knew that any reference to "Burisma" in Yermak's proposed statement would be code for "Joe Biden"; in describing to Congress his insistence, met by Yermak's grudging acceptance, that Zelensky mention Burisma by name, Volker testifies that he had initially been worried that any mention of the Ukrainian company would constitute the Ukrainian government "interfering in [the] 2020 elections" in the United States.[51]

Trump ultimately releases the $391 million in aid to Kyiv less than three weeks before it is slated to disappear from the federal budget due to the end of the fiscal year. Even so, Trump's actions punish Ukraine to the tune of $35 million—as the White House, intentionally or otherwise, fails to get that amount of the promised $391 million to Ukraine by October 1.[52] Even after Congress reappropriates the missing $35 million, by mid-December Kyiv is still missing $20 million in promised military aid.[53]

* * *

When HPSCI releases its report on impeachment on December 3, 2019, *USA Today* reports that, according to the just-released document, "Vice President Mike Pence is among the top officials culpable in President Donald Trump's efforts to bend U.S. foreign policy for personal gain."[54] The HPSCI report provides substantial evidence that Pence was among a group of top White House officials who "were either knowledgeable of or active participants in an effort to extract from a foreign nation the personal political benefits sought by the President," and that Pence aided this effort by not producing "a single document" requested by Congress.[55]

On December 11, 2019, Pence's office issues its final statement on document production to the House of Representatives, saying that it will under no circumstances release any information from the vice president's call with President Zelensky.[56]

CHAPTER 34

SEPTEMBER

One of the chief components of President Trump's defense to the fall 2019 House impeachment inquiry is a conversation he allegedly had with Gordon Sondland on September 9, 2019. Per Sondland's congressional testimony, on this date the ambassador called the president to ask an "open-ended question" about "what [Trump] wanted from Ukraine," to which Trump allegedly replied, "Nothing."[1] Subsequent evidence will establish, however, that Sondland's testimony as to both the timing of the call and its content is suspect; the House Permanent Select Committee on Intelligence report notes that "a call on September 9 [rather than September 7] . . . would have occurred in the middle of the night . . . [and] is at odds with the weight of the evidence and not backed up by any records the White House was willing to provide to Ambassador Sondland."[2] The report observes that "Ambassador [William] Taylor and Mr. [Tim] Morrison, relying on their contemporaneous notes, testified that the call between Ambassador Sondland and President Trump occurred on September 7, which is further confirmed by Ambassador Sondland's own text message on September 8 in which he wrote that he had [had] 'multiple convos' with President Zelensky and President Trump."[3]

As CNN reports regarding Morrison's congressional testimony, "a top National Security Council official testified Thursday that he was told President Donald Trump wanted a top Ukrainian official to announce an investigation that would help the President politically before U.S. security aid to Ukraine would be released, corroborating a key part of U.S. diplomat Bill Taylor's testimony that's central to the Democrats' impeachment inquiry."[4] Of Sondland's description to him of the ambassador's September 7 call with Trump, Morrison tells Congress, per CNN, that "Sondland told him the President would release the aid if the Ukrainian prosecutor general announced an investigation"—a confirmation of the quid pro quo that in December 2019 makes up the sum and substance of the first article of impeachment against Trump (see chapters 39 and 40).[5]

Questions about the timing of the Trump-Sondland call ultimately produce even more questions about Sondland's description of its content. According to *Politico*, "Sondland [eventually] hedged his testimony . . . noting that he may have been mistaken about when the call occurred. An analysis by *Just Security* posits that the call actually took place on September 7, and is the same call in which Trump demanded to Sondland that Zelensky publicly announce investigations into the Bidens and alleged Ukrainian interference in the 2016 election"—a call *Just Security* somewhat facetiously denominates the "no quid pro quo call," adding that it incriminates, rather than exculpates, the president.[6] Sondland's initial account of the call had indeed seen Trump not only saying that he wanted "nothing" from Ukraine but angrily insisting, "I want no quid pro quo"; it now appears that if any such comment was in fact made by the president, it was merely his self-exculpating response to media reports alleging a "quid pro quo" rather than a spontaneous profession of innocent intent. As the *Post* will later report, not only has the White House "not located a record in its switchboard logs of a call between Trump and Sondland on September 9," but there is, instead, "evidence of another call between Trump and Sondland that occurred a few days earlier—one with a very different thrust, in which the president made clear that he wanted his Ukrainian counterpart to personally announce investigations into Trump's political opponents."[7]

In late November 2019 the *Washington Post* reports that "the president's argument that the [early September] call proves he was not seeking favors from Ukraine is undercut by the timing: At the end of August, White House lawyers had briefed Trump on the existence of a whistleblower complaint describing the administration's pressure campaign on Ukraine and the possibility that Trump abused his power. . . . By early September, the president had also begun to confront public questions about why U.S. aid to Ukraine was stalled. So if Trump did tell Sondland flatly that he wanted 'no quid pro quo,' he did so knowing there was growing scrutiny of his posture toward Ukraine."[8]

When Sondland relays the content of his early September call with Trump to Morrison, the latter gets a "sinking" feeling because, as he later testifies to Congress, "I . . . did not think it was a good idea for [Zelensky] to . . . involve himself in our politics."[9] He subsequently reports the call to "NSC lawyers" in the White House.[10] That Morrison would have been unnerved by the content of the September 7 Trump-Sondland call is underscored by Sondland's second attempt to describe its content to Congress, in which, according to the HPSCI impeachment report, he says—contradicting his earlier testimony—that "the President told him that President Zelensky should go to a microphone and announce the investigations, and that he should want to do so."[11]

On September 9, Ambassador Taylor texts Sondland and Volker, "I think it's crazy to withhold security assistance for help with a political campaign."[12] Sondland disappears from the conversation for nearly five hours, during which time he calls Trump, according to the *Wall Street Journal*. When he rejoins the conversation with Taylor, he offers the chief of mission in Ukraine a message that clears Trump of wrongdoing; it will later be discovered that Trump had dictated the message to Sondland.[13] Of the text he had secretly written for Sondland the president will later falsely say that it was merely a text he "saw" that "nullified everything" in the Democratic allegations against him.[14] Sondland's Trump-dictated denial of a quid pro quo with Zelensky also contains a request to Taylor that "we stop the back and forth by text."[15]

Taylor's impression of how matters stand between Trump and Zelensky on September 9 is consistent with text messages sent between Volker and Sondland in mid-August. On August 13, Volker had sent Sondland a proposed statement for Zelensky to offer publicly. The statement read:

"Special attention should be paid to the problem of interference in the political processes of the United States, especially with the alleged involvement of some Ukrainian politicians. I want to declare that this is unacceptable. We intend to initiate and complete a transparent and unbiased investigation of all available facts and episodes, including those involving Burisma and the 2016 U.S. elections, which in turn will prevent the recurrence of this problem in the future."[16] Four days later, in response to a revised draft of the statement supplied by the Ukrainians, Sondland writes to Volker, "Do we still want [Zelensky] to give us an unequivocal draft with 2016 [the CrowdStrike investigation] and Boresma [Burisma]?," to which Volker replies, "That's the clear message so far."[17]

When Trump finally releases the military aid to Ukraine on September 11, 2019, Republican senators on the Senate Appropriations Committee put out, within twenty-four hours, a cover story for Trump's withholding of the assistance: according to the *Washington Post*, the new GOP position is that Trump was just "explor[ing] whether Zelensky, the country's new president, was pro-Russian or pro-Western"—implying that Trump's concern was for the protection of American interests and the frustration of the Kremlin's, when indeed the president's effort had aimed to use corruptly initiated Ukrainian criminal investigations to exculpate the Kremlin and undermine U.S. intelligence assessments.[18]

Prior to the Ukraine military aid's September 11 release, the White House had cycled through a litany of explanations for its delay, including, according to the *New York Times*, claims that the White House was unsure of the "effectiveness of the aid" or whether it was "in the best interest of foreign policy" and the submission that the hold was part of a comprehensive review of "corruption in Ukraine"—though it was not.[19] Nine days earlier, in Warsaw, Vice President Pence had offered his own spin, telling reporters that "the president wants to be assured that those [$391 million in] resources are truly making their way to the kind of investments that will contribute to security and stability in Ukraine."[20] In fact, the president had never expressed any doubt that military aid to Ukraine was being used consistently with its earmarking; indeed, the day after Pence's remarks his acting chief of staff would receive a letter from a bipartisan group of U.S. senators confirming for the White House, Pentagon, and State Department that the aid to Kyiv was "vital to the long term viability of the Ukrainian military [and was helping it] fend off the Kremlin's continued onslaughts within its territory."[21]

According to the *New York Times*, even Trump's grudging September 11 release of the aid comes only after "Senator Lindsey Graham of South Carolina inform[s] the White House that he plan[s] to support an amendment by Senator Richard J. Durbin, Democrat of Illinois, that would block [new] Pentagon spending to ensure that the Ukraine funds [are] released."[22] Graham, despite being a top Trump ally in the Senate, will later contest the president's spreading of Kremlin conspiracy theories about Ukraine, announcing that he is "1,000% confident" that Russia, not Ukraine, meddled in the 2016 presidential election.[23] In December 2019, Sen. Angus King (I-ME) will tell CNN that as a senator he has "sat through 25 hearings, briefings, meetings, probably more, on the question of what happened in 2016. In none of those meetings was there ever a hint, a breath, a suggestion, a word that somehow Ukraine was involved in the 2016 election. . . . [I]t was Russia."[24] The same month, CNN reports that the Republican-controlled Senate Intelligence Committee had probed, in October 2017, "possible Ukraine interference in the 2016 election and found nothing worth pursuing."[25] Not only had the GOP-led committee considered the CrowdStrike issue, per CNN— even meeting with CrowdStrike president Shawn Henry—it had also met with Alexandra Chalupa for a "more-than-two-hour meeting covering a range of subjects . . . [and] Chalupa was never called back before the committee and investigators considered the matter closed."[26] With respect to allegations that certain Ukrainian officials may have developed a rooting interest for Clinton following Trump's proposal that Russia keep 7 percent of Ukraine's territory without penalty, CNN reports that "officials in the Ukrainian government publicly criticiz[ing] Trump and support[ing] Clinton . . . [is something] intelligence and national security officials widely do not consider to be 'interference' in an election."[27]

* * *

In late September, Trump terms his July 25 conversation with President Zelensky a "perfect phone call" during which—nevertheless—"it doesn't matter what I discussed," and insists that any criticism of the call is part of a Democratic "witch hunt."[28] In short order, Trump is publicly reiterating his problematic late July demand for an investigation of Biden. "The one who's got the problem is Biden," Trump tells the press on September 23. "What Biden did is a disgrace. What his son did is a disgrace. The son took money from Ukraine. The son took money from China—a lot of money from China."[29] In another public appearance on the same day, Trump submits that pressuring Ukraine to investigate Biden would have been acceptable had it happened, even as he insists that it did not. According to *The Hill*, Trump tells a press gathering, "There was no pressure put on them whatsoever. I put no pressure on them whatsoever. I could have. I think it would probably—possibly—have been okay if I did."[30] Meanwhile, Trump compares Biden's actions to a capital offense, insisting that "Joe Biden and his son are corrupt. If a Republican ever did what Joe Biden did—if a Republican ever said what Joe Biden said—they'd be getting the electric chair by right now."[31] Trump will return regularly to his claim, as summarized by the *New York Times*, that "there would be nothing wrong with linking American funding for Ukraine . . . to a corruption inquiry about Mr. Biden and his family."[32] Asked whether he in fact had just linked the two, Trump responds, "No, I didn't—I didn't do it," then adds, "[But] why would you give money to a country that you think is corrupt?"[33]

As Trump is railing publicly against the Bidens on September 23, events critical to the question of corruption in Ukraine are unfolding half a world away in Austria, as Joe diGenova and Victoria Toensing are agreeing—after many weeks of negotiations—to formally represent Ukrainian fugitive Dmitry Firtash.[34] In representing Firtash, diGenova and Toensing, members of Trump's legal advisory corps, are trying to keep U.S. government prosecutors from putting on trial for public corruption a man who, as Bloomberg News reports, "Mueller's team [approached] for information about Manafort," as Manafort "did business with Firtash before he was chairman of Trump's campaign in the summer of 2016."[35] It is unclear what damaging information Firtash might offer federal prosecutors about Manafort—or Trump—if diGenova and Toensing cannot keep him from being put on trial in the United States.

CHAPTER 35

BARR, DURHAM, AND HOROWITZ

In late September 2019, the *New York Times* reports that the DOJ official named by Attorney General Barr "to review the origins of the counterintelligence investigation into Mr. Trump's [2016] campaign, John H. Durham, is looking into the role of Ukraine, among other countries."[1] The DOJ tells the *Times* that "while the attorney general has yet to contact Ukraine in connection with this investigation, certain Ukrainians who are not members of the government have volunteered information to Mr. Durham, which he is evaluating."[2] As part of his assistance of Durham's investigation, Barr conferences privately overseas with foreign leaders and intelligence services, receiving Trump's help in scheduling certain of his meetings.[3] Meanwhile, Lindsey Graham writes a letter to the prime ministers of Australia, Italy, and Britain, opining that U.S. intelligence used a "deeply flawed dossier filled with hearsay" during the 2016 election and urging them to cooperate with Barr.[4]

In October 2019, as he is seeking the Italian government's cooperation with Barr, Trump welcomes the Italian president to the White House—an honor he still will not have afforded Zelensky by early 2020.[5] As for the United Kingdom, the *Independent* reports on November 1 that "UK intelligence officials [are] shaken by [the] Trump administration's requests for help with [Durham's] counter-impeachment inquiry," with one British official saying, "It is like nothing we have come across before, they are basically asking, in quite robust terms, for help in doing a hatchet job on their own intelligence services."[6]

The full scope of the Durham-Barr investigation, and therefore its

potential effect on the 2020 general election campaign, remains unknown, though on October 24, 2019, the *New York Times* reports that
the investigation has become a criminal investigation—a development
the *Times* says "is likely to open the attorney general to accusations that
he is trying to deliver a political victory for President Trump."[7] Indeed,
by late October, Sen. John Cornyn (R-TX) had already "made waves,"
per *The Hill*, by declaring, in an apparent reference to the Durham-Barr
investigation, that "the Trump Justice Department is investigating foreign government influence, VP Biden conflicts of interest, and possible
corruption."[8]

The Durham-Barr probe comes under additional scrutiny when it
is revealed by *Politico* that "in the five months since Attorney General
William Barr tapped Durham to investigate the origins of the Russia
probe . . . he has not requested interviews with any of the FBI or DOJ
employees who were directly involved in, or knew about, the opening
of the Russia investigation in 2016. . . . The omission raises questions
about what, exactly, Durham—alongside Attorney General Barr—has
been investigating."[9] According to the digital media outlet, Barr's theory of the case in the Durham probe is that the CIA, under former
director John Brennan's leadership, was secretly engaged in a rogue
operation to prevent Trump's election, and tricked the FBI into participating in the scheme.[10] In fact, as reported in *The Guardian*, from late
2015 through the summer of 2016 no fewer than seven allied intelligence
agencies—including entities in France, Germany, the United Kingdom,
the Netherlands, Australia, Estonia, and Poland—sent information to
U.S. intelligence officials establishing that individuals in Trump's "inner circle" were meeting secretly in overseas locations with "Russian
intelligence operatives."[11] Nevertheless, Barr opts, per NBC News, to
use "accusations made by George Papadopoulos"—the Trump campaign
adviser sentenced to prison in September 2018 for lying to federal law
enforcement—to support his conspiracy theory about 2016 election interference by the CIA.[12]

* * *

On Wednesday, October 9—the day before Lev Parnas is scheduled to appear before the House Committee on Oversight and Reform, the House Committee on Foreign Affairs, and the House Permanent Select Committee on Intelligence, and forty-eight hours before Igor Fruman is expected to speak to the same three congressional panels—Barr unexpectedly travels to New York to meet with prosecutors from the Southern and Eastern Districts of New York.[13] Subsequent reporting will reveal that Barr has been "aware of the [FBI] investigation into Parnas and Fruman since shortly after he came into office in February [2019]."[14] No reason for Barr's trip to New York is ever given by the DOJ.[15]

As Barr is meeting with New York prosecutors, his longtime friend Rudy Giuliani is at Trump International Hotel in D.C. having lunch with Parnas and Fruman, according to the *Wall Street Journal*.[16] Asked by the *Washington Post*—following Parnas's and Fruman's arrest that evening—what his business had been with the two Soviet-born businessmen, Giuliani will say only that Parnas and Fruman had "helped [him] find" certain "former Ukrainian government officials."[17]

Prior to the news breaking of Parnas's and Fruman's Wednesday night arrest at Dulles, Giuliani tells *The Atlantic* that he is planning to travel to Vienna on Thursday.[18] On Thursday morning—with news of his business associates' arrest still not public—Giuliani tells the *Wall Street Journal* that Parnas and Fruman are, like him, planning to travel to Vienna, though, per reporting in the *Daily Beast*, Giuliani's contention is that "the three [will] be in the same city" but will "do no business with one another."[19] Instead, Giuliani tells the *Journal*, the three men only plan to meet up again after Parnas and Fruman return to the United States, a claim seemingly nullified by the subsequent revelation that Parnas and Fruman had one-way tickets to Vienna.[20] Once Giuliani learns that his associates have been arrested by the FBI, he refuses to comment further on either their or his own trip to Austria.[21] CNN soon reports that Parnas and Fruman were headed to Vienna to "help with a planned interview [scheduled for] the next day [with Viktor] Shokin"; the interview was to have been conducted, CNN reveals, by Trump adviser Sean Hannity.[22]

* * *

In December 2019, the *Washington Post* reports that Durham "[cannot] offer evidence to the Justice Department's Inspector General to support the suspicions of some conservatives that the [Russia] case was a setup by American intelligence."[23] After DOJ inspector general Michael Horowitz releases his report on the origins of the Mueller investigation on December 9, 2019—a report that finds no evidence of political bias at the FBI, and also that the so-called Steele dossier played no role in forming a factual predicate for the Russia investigation—Barr takes what *Vox* calls the "unusual" step of attacking the very institution that he leads.[24] In response to news of the report's conclusions, Barr privately tells "conservative allies" that his department's duly appointed inspector general "won't be the last word" on the Russia probe.[25]

Barr's criticism of former MI6 Russia desk chief Christopher Steele as being a source of biased intelligence against candidate Trump is undercut when a *Washington Post* report reveals, in early December, that not only is Steele "a personal friend of Trump's daughter Ivanka," but during the period from 2010 to 2012 he had even discussed the possibility of doing consulting work for the Trump Organization.[26]

While Inspector General Horowitz's report finds no political bias in the conduct of the Russia investigation, when it is released in December 2019 the report does identify seventeen inaccuracies across nine months' worth of Foreign Intelligence Surveillance Act (FISA) warrant applications in the Russia investigation; all of the warrants involve Trump campaign adviser Carter Page, who had, prior to the 2016 presidential election, described himself as an "informal adviser" to the Kremlin, and after the election had withheld evidence about both private pre-election meetings with Kremlin officials in Moscow and his disclosures of those meetings to the Trump campaign.[27] While Horowitz will observe in the seventeen FISA-warrant errors "significant omissions and inaccurate information"—including about whether Page had been a CIA source between 2008 and 2013—the *New York Times* will compare these seventeen errors in the years-long Russia investigation to the seventy-five FISA-warrant errors the DOJ had previously uncovered in a single 2000 self-audit.[28]

In response to the inspector general's report, Barr gives an interview to NBC News that unnerves many. In it, he contends that in 2016 the Obama administration—not Russia—was the "greatest danger" to American democracy, going on to contradict Horowitz's report by insisting that the Trump campaign was "clearly spied upon" and accusing the FBI of possibly acting in "bad faith" in its investigation of Trump-Russia ties.[29] Of the 2016 Trump campaign's 272 clandestine, unreported, and in many instances unprecedented contacts and meetings with Kremlin agents in the United States and abroad, Barr will demur from any criticism, insisting that "presidential campaigns are frequently in contact with foreign persons."[30] Moving "well beyond" any criticisms of the Mueller investigation contained in Horowitz's report, Barr calls the special counsel's investigation "bogus" and "completely baseless" and falsely asserts that Mueller's report—which drew no conclusions on the matter of "collusion," finding only that a Trump-Russia hacking conspiracy could not be proven under the U.S. justice system's highest burden of proof, "beyond a reasonable doubt"—failed to find "any" evidence of "collusion."[31]

In subsequent testimony before Congress about his report, Horowitz discusses the October 2016 leak of sensitive investigative information by rogue agents in the FBI's New York field office to Rudy Giuliani, indicating that the DOJ is "very concerned" about these offenses.[32] Indeed, Horowitz's investigation turns up what Pulitzer Prize–winning journalist James Stewart will call "hotbeds of anti-Clinton hostility" in the FBI's Manhattan office, with Horowitz noting, per the *New York Times*, that field agents working in the city "leaked regularly to right-wing media sources [claims] that the bureau was turning a blind eye to what [the agents] saw as Clinton's criminality."[33] Horowitz finds a trove of anti-Clinton messages exchanged between FBI agents during the presidential election, including exhortations to agents working on the Clinton email case, by their peers, to "finally . . . get that bitch" and "get her."[34] As the *Washington Post* explains, "The Russia investigation . . . isn't the only thing the FBI did that raised eyebrows during the 2016 election; so too did [FBI director] Comey's announcement of newly discovered Clinton emails a week and a half before the election. Clinton and others continue to blame that for her narrow loss. At issue . . . for Horowitz is Comey's indication that part of the reason for the announcement was because of leaks from the FBI's New York field office."[35]

In his testimony, Horowitz acknowledges a number of "contacts" between FBI agents in New York City and either journalists or the Trump campaign, saying that his office had found "violat[ions] of FBI policy" and had "some investigations ongoing" in response to the evidence it had collected.[36] When pressed in November 2019 about his repeated claims in October 2016 that he was speaking to "active" and "current" FBI agents about the Clinton email investigation, Giuliani offers a new explanation for his statements: "[When] I use[d] the word 'active' and 'current,'" Giuliani explains, "I mean[t] they [the FBI agents I spoke with] are not old men, they can still do things."[37] Giuliani tells *The Guardian* thereafter that "in the security business" it is widely understood that the words "active" and "current," when used with regard to law enforcement officials, mean physically active and in good health.[38] Assuming Giuliani has given or will give the same explanation to Horowitz or his investigators, the president's personal attorney is at risk of violating a federal felony statute, 18 U.S. Code § 1001, which punishes with up to five years in federal prison each instance of lying to federal law enforcement officers.[39]

In February 2020, the *New York Times* reports that "Trump administration officials investigating the government's response to Russia's election interference in 2016 appear to be hunting for a basis to accuse Obama-era intelligence officials of hiding evidence or manipulating analysis about Moscow's covert operation"—and have continued their search for such a basis despite "officials from the FBI and National Security Agency" having "told Mr. Durham and his investigators that such an interpretation is wrong and based on a misunderstanding of how the intelligence community functions."[40] The *Times* notes that "Mr. Durham's questioning is certain to add to accusations that Mr. Trump is using the Justice Department to go after his perceived enemies."[41]

On March 31, 2020, Inspector General Horowitz releases the results of a far more encompassing internal audit of FISA applications—one not tied to any review of the FBI's pre- or post-election Russia investigations—and reports, per NPR, that in fact, far from being uniquely present in FBI investigations of Donald Trump, there are "widespread problems with the bureau's handling of national security surveillance warrants [that go] beyond the recent highly charged case of former Trump campaign adviser Carter Page."[42] Indeed, according to his report on recent non-Trump-related FISA applications, Horowitz finds "apparent errors or inadequately supported facts in all of the 25 applications . . . reviewed."[43] The findings by the Justice Department's chief watchdog significantly undercut Attorney General Barr's theory that the 2016 Trump presidential campaign was specially targeted for FISA malfeasance by unnamed actors within federal law enforcement—a persistent if wholly unsubstantiated "deep-state" conspiracy theory that has become, especially in the run-up to the 2020 presidential election, a hobbyhorse for the president and his congressional allies.

CHAPTER 36

TRUMP-TURKEY

In 2012, Trump and his daughter Ivanka travel to Turkey for the open-ing of Trump Towers Istanbul.[1] The development, which consists of two conjoined towers, is one of just nine Trump Towers–branded construc-tions worldwide; the Trump Organization boasts, as reported by NBC, that Trump Towers Istanbul is "the organization's first and only office and residential tower in Europe."[2] During the trip to open the towers for business, Trump and Ivanka meet with Turkish president Recep Tayyip Erdogan; Ivanka had previously traveled to Turkey to meet with the Trump Organization's business partners there in 2009, 2010, and 2012.[3] Trump will describe his licensing deal in Istanbul as a "conflict of inter-est" that will impact his dealings with Turkey as president.[4] Trump's con-fession of a "conflict of interest" comes during a 2015 Breitbart interview with the man who will later become his campaign CEO, Steve Bannon.[5] Trump acknowledges the conflict in response to a question about how as president he would "prosecut[e] the war [against ISIS]," "partner" with Turkey in prosecuting the war, and regard Turkey as a "reliable" ally.[6]

Erdogan weaponizes Trump's self-confessed "conflict of interest" well before the businessman becomes president. In 2016, the Turkish presi-dent threatens to strike Trump's name from his Trump-branded towers in Istanbul in response to candidate Trump's proposal of a travel ban aimed at Muslim countries.[7] Erdogan is sufficiently enraged at Trump over the ban that, according to the *Wall Street Journal*, he publicly declares his 2012 decision to attend the opening of Trump Towers Istanbul "a mistake."[8]

Newsweek reporting suggests that Trump is in a position to track the health of his business interests in Turkey by monitoring Erdogan's reaction to his foreign policy, with the media outlet noting that the "pressure [on Trump caused by the travel ban] eased after Trump expressed support for Erdogan's wide-ranging crackdown against political opponents follow[ing] a failed coup in 2016."[9] In 2019, when Trump greenlights a Turkish invasion of Syria against the admonitions of both the Republican establishment and his own top advisers, *Fast Company* will report that many "question[ ] whether Trump might have deeper motives, including economic ones," observing that between 2014 and 2018 it appears Trump has brought in between $3.2 million and $17 million as a result of his licensing deal in Istanbul.[10] A *New York Times* estimate sets Trump's seven-year profit from Trump Towers Istanbul far higher, at somewhere between $15.5 million and $44 million.[11] *Mother Jones* terms the Turkish towers a "massive conflict of interest" whose influence on Trump's foreign policy the president has already presaged, "admitt[ing] that his business interests in the country would make it difficult for him to deal with Turkey with a clear mind [as president]."[12] Indeed, as the magazine notes, Trump refers to his project in Istanbul as a "major, major" one, and brags about how "tremendously successful" it has been for the Trump Organization.[13]

The details of Trump's "major, major" deal in Turkey are just as troubling as its fundamentals. Trump's partner in the deal is Turkish "magnate" Aydin Dogan, who *Mother Jones* notes "has been described as the single largest payer of taxes in Turkey."[14] More important, Dogan is "in step with the strongman [Erdogan]" politically, putting Trump in a difficult position, the magazine notes, whenever his views are not aligned with the Turkish president's.[15] Indeed, during the international imbroglio over Trump's 2016 "Muslim ban" proposal, it is not only Erdogan who publicly complains, but Dogan, too.[16]

In May 2017, Erdogan visits the White House. While he is in Washington, his agents "violently attack[ ] protesters outside the Turkish ambassador's residence—shoving past local police officers to do so. Video will show Erdogan calmly watching the attack from his car."[17] The assaults by Erdogan's bodyguards on American police officers result in a stunning 397–0 vote of condemnation in the U.S. House of Representatives; Trump alone refuses to condemn the attacks, even calling Erdogan "a very good friend" several months later and giving him "very high marks" for his management of Turkish affairs.[18] In November 2019, it is revealed that Erdogan's men didn't just push past D.C. police officers; in fact, several of the Turkish president's bodyguards assaulted members of the U.S. Secret Service as well.[19] Ultimately, a report by the Metropolitan Police Department (MPD), summarized by *The Hill*, finds that "more than a dozen" Turkish security officials "instigat[ed] violence" during the episode outside the Turkish ambassador's residence.[20] Charges will ultimately be dropped against most, and all Erdogan's men flee the United States before any of them can be arrested.[21] According to *The Hill*, victims of the Turkish attack in Washington include "women and elderly men," "two Diplomatic Security special agents, six U.S. Secret Service officers, and one MPD officer"—many of whom sustain multiple injuries, with at least one requiring hospitalization.[22] At one point, according to a law enforcement report described by *The Hill*, "seven Turkish security officials jumped out of the diplomatic convoy . . . to attack a lone, female protester."[23] The violent clashes at the Turkish ambassador's residence now stand as an early, microcosmic indication of Trump's willingness to abide Turkish violence against U.S. interests without public condemnation.

In the weeks leading up to the May 2017 Trump-Erdogan meeting and the violence that surrounds it, Trump "explore[s] whether the U.S. could cut off taxpayer funding for a network of charter schools affiliated with a political opponent of [Erdogan]" named Fethullah Gulen, who is living in Pennsylvania; information on the possibility had been explicitly "sought for the president," according to Bloomberg News.[24] For reasons that will soon become clear, "one of the people who [takes] an interest in the matter" is Trump's soon-to-be personal attorney, Rudy Giuliani, who just months earlier had met with Erdogan in Turkey.[25]

As the Ukraine scandal unfolds in mid-2019, a connection between the White House's request to consider closing Gulen's U.S. schools and the president's demand that Ukraine investigate Joe Biden becomes clear: in both instances, Giuliani is involved in a secret, pseudo-governmental investigation targeting someone Trump and his allies might reasonably consider a political rival. As Bloomberg reports in 2019, "the White House suggested [in early 2017] that the Education Department could investigate whether Gulen was laundering money through the schools, or could argue that the schools' ties to Gulen—a Muslim cleric—amounted to a religious affiliation and meant they couldn't receive federal funding. But the Education Department pushed back against both approaches. Department aides told the White House that the government would be seen as hypocritical and discriminatory if it continued to support Christian schools while punishing schools affiliated with Islam. Many officials in the department were particularly disturbed by the conversations because cutting funding would also deny resources to schools largely attended by low-income children."[26] Bloomberg notes that during the investigation of Gulen's schools, Giuliani was simultaneously "attempting to work out a diplomatic deal" connected to his work in Turkey and involving himself in the administration's official review of a federal policy related to that work—a conflict of interest offering additional echoes of the Ukraine scandal.[27] Indeed, Giuliani even passed along to secretary of state Rex Tillerson a pamphlet he had acquired during the personal investigation he had conducted into the Turkish cleric's schools—conduct identical to his handling of personal investigative documents relating to Ukraine, some of which he passed on to secretary of state Mike Pompeo in spring 2019.[28] A key difference between the two clandestine campaigns, however, is that whereas the latter sought only to harm Trump's chief political rival, the former arguably, according to a Bloomberg source, "extend[ed] to trying to limit the educational opportunities available to American children"—a much wider harm, and one pursued to damage a U.S.-dwelling political opponent of an intermittent foreign ally.[29]

* * *

Had Trump divested himself of his business entanglements upon taking office, there would be less cause to question whether his dealings with Erdogan and the Turkish government are motivated by patriotism or venality—his top adviser Roger Stone's past efforts to secure illegal election aid from Turkey, in the form of intelligence about Trump's political rivals, notwithstanding. As *Mother Jones* notes, "When he ran for office, Trump said he would handle conflicts of interest . . . by turning over his businesses to his children. He didn't. Instead, he simply stepped away from the daily operations of his business empire, but he retains full ownership of almost all of the assets, including the licensing company that collects royalties from [his Turkish business partner Aydin] Dogan."[30] As NBC News explains, the "Trump family's multitude of continuing business entities and interests . . . [are] separated from the president—at least on paper—by the trust that now controls them. But the president is the beneficiary of that trust and two of his children have roles in it."[31]

Trump Towers is only the most visible element of Trump's self-confessed "conflict of interest" in Turkey, however. In October 2019, NBC reports on a pending federal lawsuit initiated by 215 members of Congress that alleges Trump is "at least a partial owner of 119 business ventures in Turkey."[32] Per a major investigative report on Trump's conflicts of interest with Turkey by NBC, "the Turks are also the top patrons of any country at Trump properties worldwide. So there are a lot of business connections there. And Ivanka Trump is also close to some of these [Turkish] business partners. One of them, the one who is close to Erdogan, [Dogan son-in-law] Mehmet [Ali] Yalcindag, also attended Trump's victory party in Manhattan [on Election Day in 2016]. They are that close."[33]

According to NBC, Yalcindag has conceded that he is a "close friend of Trump and his family," while the president has termed the Trumps' relationship with Dogan and his family in Turkey a "great, great friendship," calling them "beyond [business] partners."[34] Yalcindag will eventually become the president of the Turkish-American Business Council (TAIK); in May 2017, days after Erdogan's visit to the White House, and at the height of the Turkish president's lobbying of President Trump over two major geopolitical issues—the extradition of Gulen to Ankara from Pennsylvania and the release of a Turkish businessman from U.S. custody—TAIK holds a "three-day conference inside the Trump International Hotel in Washington, an event attended by U.S. government notables including Commerce Secretary Wilbur Ross."[35] In 2018, Yalcindag publicly "express[es] confidence that Trump would ultimately sympathize with Turkey's approach to foreign policy," telling a group of reporters that "U.S. President Donald Trump thinks regional problems should be resolved by regional actors. In this regard, the U.S. should see what is happening on Turkey's borders from the point of view of its strategic ally, Turkey."[36]

Trump's 2016 support for Erdogan comes despite the fact that, post-coup, Erdogan had "locked up thousands of people . . . including many who had nothing to do with [the coup]."[37] As candidate Trump expresses support for Erdogan, so too does his campaign's top national security adviser, Michael Flynn, who pens a pro-Erdogan op-ed in *The Hill*; Flynn is at the time in the midst of a secret $530,000 consulting contract with Turkey—despite having failed to register with the federal government as a foreign lobbyist, as required by law.[38] Echoing his adviser Flynn, after the coup Trump takes the position, per NBC, that "the U.S. shouldn't criticize Erdogan" for what Human Rights Watch will describe, again per NBC reporting, as a campaign of "taking over dozens of television and radio stations and arresting reporters."[39] Instead of condemnation, Trump issues a public statement giving Erdogan "great credit . . . for turning [the coup] around."[40]

Soon, however, Fethullah Gulen—the Pennsylvania-dwelling Turkish cleric who, according to the *Washington Post*, Erdogan "blame[s]" for the coup—becomes a significant complication for Trump's ongoing relationship with the Turkish government.[41] During the same period Flynn is receiving more than half a million dollars from Turkey and advising Trump on foreign policy and national security, he "reportedly," says the *Post*, "raise[s] the idea of surreptitiously extraditing Gulen to Turkey—in essence, kidnapping him."[42] According to *The Guardian*, the conspiracy that Flynn allegedly goes on to participate in would have involved kidnapping Gulen and "fly[ing] him to an island prison in Turkey in return for

$15 million"; the planning for the scheme involves multiple meetings between Flynn and several Americans and Turks, including one December 2016 gathering at "a prohibition-era New York speakeasy patronized by Trump."[43] By then, Trump had already "named Flynn his national security advisor," and the retired general was "playing a central role in [Trump's presidential] transition."[44] *The Guardian* notes that, as a Trump transition official, Flynn was potentially open to bribery charges for his role in the plot; while Trump's knowledge of Flynn's illicit activities remains unclear, when they ultimately come to light the president offers no condemnation of his former adviser, only praise.[45]

As Flynn is allegedly plotting with the Turks during the presidential transition period, NBC reports—quoting from the congressional lawsuit against Trump for violating the U.S. Constitution's emoluments clause—that "foreign diplomats . . . [from] Turkey" received "a sales pitch about [Trump's] newest hotel," the Trump International Hotel in D.C.[46] "Four events related to the Turkish government" are subsequently held there, including at least one event that included "two advisers to Erdogan and the [Turkish] ministers of trade, defense and treasury."[47]

In March 2017, just before Rudy Giuliani begins working on Trump's behalf—purportedly for free—to convince Ukrainian president Petro Poroshenko to take over the Manafort investigation from NABU, the former New York City mayor takes on a new client: Turkish and Iranian citizen Reza Zarrab, a trader who at the time "held embarrassing and politically damaging information about Erdogan and other top Turkish officials in [Erdogan's] government."[48] The *New York Times*, citing federal investigators, reports that Erdogan and his son-in-law, Turkish finance minister Berat Albayrak, "personally approved" a Turkey-Iran "sanctions-evasion scheme" involving Zarrab—doing so, incredibly, "even after officials in the United States had arrested [Zarrab]."[49] It is telling that Erdogan believed, according to the *Times* report, that he could, without consequence, "publicly dismiss[ ] the sanctions on Iran [under Trump] as American policy that was not binding on Turkey."[50]

Concerned that Zarrab might reveal sensitive details about the Turkish government to federal law enforcement while incarcerated in the United States for "orchestrating a multibillion-dollar conspiracy to evade U.S. sanctions against Iran," Erdogan spends the spring and summer of 2017—a period during which Zarrab's attorney Giuliani is negotiating with the Ukrainians on Trump's behalf—"repeatedly lobb[ying] Trump to release Zarrab" to Turkey.[51] In 2017 and 2018, Albayrak successfully lobbies Trump's treasury secretary, Steve Mnuchin, to delay action against the state-owned Turkish bank, Halkbank, which had allegedly been involved in the sanctions-evasion scheme.[52] In late 2019, *The Hill* reports on a Treasury Department finding that during the course of Albayrak's lobbying of Mnuchin, Trump personally "asked multiple federal agencies to address . . . Erdogan's 'concerns' that Turkey's state-owned bank would be under threat of U.S. sanctions."[53] According to *The Hill*, the revelation "is the first public U.S. admission of Trump directing Cabinet officials, in this case in Treasury and the Department of Justice, to involve themselves with Erdogan's concerns around Halkbank. . . . It also raises questions about how Trump's personal relationships and business dealings influence his foreign policy decisions, at a time when his dealings with Ukraine are under scrutiny as part of a formal impeachment inquiry led by House Democrats."[54]

Trump's behind-the-scenes efforts on Erdogan's behalf also raise questions about why, in late June 2019, Attorney General Barr offers Erdogan a fine over Halkbank's illicit activities instead of an indictment.[55] Erdogan refuses Barr's lenient offer, after which the DOJ indicts Halkbank—even as Mnuchin's Treasury Department, per the *New York Times*, continues to "not impose penalties" on the bank.[56] That the actions of both Barr and Mnuchin have come at Trump's direction now seems clear; Bloomberg News reports in late 2019 that Trump "ordered" Barr and Mnuchin to review their approach to Halkbank.[57] Bloomberg calls Trump's actions an "unusual intervention" in an "active federal investigation," noting in particular, regarding Barr's involvement in the Manhattan-based prosecution of Halkbank, that the attorney general had represented to Turkish officials that he would try to "reach a deal" with prosecutors in Manhattan to help Halkbank avoid a trial.[58] Bloomberg will later observe that Trump's and Barr's actions, as well as a lack of clarity on the timeline for Halkbank's indictment, "rais[e] questions about whether [the Halkbank indictment] was set aside until it became politically expedient for the Trump administration to unseal it"—an observation that implies the original sealing of the indictment, too, was politically motivated.[59] Bloomberg's recitation of its attempts to get a comment from the Trump administration on the Halkbank case underscores how politically sensitive Trump's team considers it: "Justice Department officials declined to comment when asked about Barr's efforts, and the Treasury Department declined to comment on Mnuchin's role. The White House declined to comment, and the State Department declined to discuss the part Pompeo played. Bolton declined to comment."[60]

Giuliani had been lobbying Trump on Zarrab and Halkbank as far back as 2017. At the time, Giuliani was also following in the by then fired Flynn's footsteps in lobbying Trump to extradite Gulen to Turkey. According to former White House officials who speak to the *Washington Post*, "the former New York mayor brought up Gulen so frequently with Trump during visits to the White House that one former official described the subject as Giuliani's 'hobby horse.' He was so focused on the issue—'it was all Gulen,' recalled a second former official—that White House aides worried that Giuliani was making the case on behalf of the Turkish government."[61] That Giuliani's interest in Gulen was linked to his representation of Zarrab is clear, for, as the *Post* reports, "Erdogan blamed Gulen for helping bring to light a wide-ranging scheme to help Iran evade international sanctions by laundering money through sales of gold—a plan in which Erdogan was eventually implicated" along with Zarrab.[62] CNN reports that during one political rally, Erdogan both called Gulen a "terrorist" and announced his support for a "reintroduction of the death penalty" in Turkey.[63] For President Trump and his allies, then, the clear choice in dealing with Erdogan has been between rewarding his corrupt efforts to circumvent U.S. and international sanctions on Tehran and acknowledging Gulen's valiant anti-corruption efforts by safeguarding him; Trump, Giuliani, and Flynn have all chosen the former option, as has the father of Trump personal attorney Marc Mukasey—former U.S. attorney general Michael Mukasey—who in June 2017 takes on Zarrab's case as co-counsel alongside Giuliani, despite a court seeing "potential conflicts of interest" in the representation.[64]

U.S. officials are so concerned that Giuliani is, alongside Erdogan, lobbying Trump directly for Zarrab's release that "at one point in 2017, they confront[ ] [Giuliani] and ask him not to bring up Turkish issues when he [meets] with the president."[65] As for Flynn, in addition to writing a pro-Erdogan op-ed in late 2016, he also lobbies Trump on the Gulen issue from late 2016 through early 2017.[66] In February 2017, following Flynn's firing by Trump, Giuliani flies to Turkey to speak directly with Erdogan about Gulen and Zarrab.[67] Lobbying experts will tell the *Washington Post* that even if Giuliani is not lobbying on behalf of Ankara in 2017, he is nevertheless lobbying on behalf of a foreign principal whose release from U.S. custody the Turkish government also desires—a circumstance that may trigger his requirement to register as a foreign agent or else face federal criminal charges.[68] That Trump works to extradite Gulen throughout 2017, at a time when Flynn, who had long worked for the same purpose, is cooperating with federal law enforcement in an investigation involving the 2016 Trump campaign, underscores the ambiguity surrounding Trump's motives with respect to Turkey in the first year of his presidency.

As for how Trump responds to Giuliani's, Flynn's, and Mukasey's pro-Erdogan entreaties, the *Washington Post* reports that at one point in 2017, "with Giuliani and [Michael] Mukasey in the room, Trump reportedly asked secretary of state Rex Tillerson to try to get the Justice Department to drop the case against Zarrab. The president also suggested [Tillerson] speak to Giuliani about the case. Tillerson refused."[69] MSNBC anchor Chris Hayes has argued that Trump's attempt to use the State Department to interfere with a DOJ investigation to benefit his personal attorney is, "if true . . . also a high crime" under the U.S. Constitution—as well as yet another echo of the 2019 Ukraine scandal.[70]

* * *

According to the *Washington Post,* in Turkey, as in Ukraine, Trump appears for all purposes to be "following Giuliani's lead." The newspaper reports that "Trump asked [his advisers] frequently about why Gulen couldn't be turned over to Turkey, referring to Erdogan as 'my friend.'"[71] But more than just asking questions on the subject, Trump militates for Gulen's rendition despite being told that the case against him in Turkey does not meet U.S. evidentiary standards for extradition. The *Post* reports that Trump "repeatedly wanted to [extradite Gulen], but . . . advisers were appalled [and] blocked [it]. Aides worried Giuliani was doing Turkey's bidding."[72] One White House official tells the *Post* that it seemed that some in the White House simply wanted to "do a solid for Erdogan."[73] That the president himself is willing to appease corruption, and even punish anti-corruption efforts, for the sake of a "friend" is clear—even as "administration officials are overwhelmingly opposed to the idea and [telling] the president that the move could violate the legal process and damage him politically."[74] As for Giuliani, when the *Washington Post* asks whether he ever advocated for Gulen's extradition—conduct confirmed by many former White House officials—he replies that the allegation "sounds wacky."[75]

That Halkbank did what it is alleged to have done—helped undermine the very Iran sanctions that Trump has publicly not only supported but sought to augment—is clear. The *Post* notes that "a high-ranking official with the bank has already been convicted on related charges, after testimony from . . . gold trader [Zarrab], who was an apparent mastermind of the effort."[76] Even so, when top Trump Senate ally Lindsey Graham accidentally speaks to a Russian hoaxer pretending to be Turkey's minister of defense in August 2019, he assures the "minister" that as to the case "involving the Turkish bank . . . [Trump] does not want that case to hurt our relationship. He mentioned that twice."[77] The *Post* calls Graham's words "telling" because the comment comes "during Graham's second conversation with the Russian/fake Turkish official, after Graham claims to have spoken with Trump about their first conversation. It's only after having spoken with Trump that the bank case comes up, and it's the only new issue introduced by Graham in the second call."[78]

In the event, there is indeed evidence that the Trump administration had originally stalled action against Halkbank to keep Erdogan appeased. Per the *Washington Post*, it is just six days after Trump warns Erdogan against invading Syria in early October 2019—and Erdogan ignores the president's warning—that "the Justice Department announce[s] criminal charges against Halkbank."[79] Bloomberg News reports that, prior to the indictment, Trump had "told Erdogan that [Attorney General] Barr and [Treasury Secretary] Mnuchin would handle his pleas to avoid charges against Halkbank over sanctions evasion."[80]

Even before Erdogan's invasion of Syria in October 2019, there are other reasons to suspect that Trump's foreign policy with respect to Turkey is compromised. In mid-April 2019, Trump allows Turkish officials to use Trump International Hotel in D.C. for their Annual Conference on U.S.-Turkey Relations.[81] The lucrative gathering at the Trump property— which, combined with Turkish officials' 2017 gathering at the same site for the same purpose, generates "hundreds of thousands of dollars" for Trump's hotel, according to the *New York Times*—is addressed by Jared Kushner, among others; attendees include "at least three ministers in Turkey's government," "a senior advisor to [Erdogan]," and Trump's family friend and business associate, Mehmet Ali Yalcindag. On the second day of the conference, the featured speaker at the event, Turkey's finance minister, Berat Albayrak—Erdogan's son-in-law—is invited to meet with the president at the White House.[82] Per U.S. media outlet *Courthouse News*, Albayrak was "implicated (but never charged) in the Reza Zarrab case."[83] The conference thereby acts as an opportunity for Trump to meet with an Erdogan agent and Zarrab associate just four and a half months before Turkey announces its intention of invading Syria. The meeting at the White House is not a low-key affair, either; present at the event, besides Erdogan's son-in-law, Trump's son-in-law, and Trump himself, is Treasury Secretary Mnuchin—"whose agency," *Courthouse News* notes, "had probed Zarrab and Halkbank."[84]

According to the *New York Times*, Kushner, Albayrak, and Yalcindag are, taken together, a "back channel" between Trump and Erdogan comprising "a trio of sons-in-law."[85] While it is unknown how frequently Trump uses this back channel, the *Times* notes that, Albayrak aside, Trump sees Yalcindag "socially" three to four times a year.[86] Immediately after Trump's election, Erdogan had ensured his own ongoing exploitation of the Trump-Yalcindag relationship by "nam[ing] Mr. Yalcindag to a new role as chairman of a state-run business group that lobbies Washington on behalf of Ankara."[87] The *Times* adds that the state-run business group's "previous chairman, Ekim Alptekin, had run afoul of American prosecutors by paying more than $500,000 to the consulting firm of the retired Lt. Gen. Michael T. Flynn, who went on to become Mr. Trump's first national security advisor."[88] Alptekin remains at large overseas, beyond the reach of U.S. law enforcement. His association with Flynn will return to relevance with the April 2020 release of certain investigative documents in the Roger Stone case, which reveal a cryptic Turkish-Israeli plot to interfere in the 2016 presidential election on Trump's behalf that involves Stone, Israeli officials, proposed covert meetings with Trump in New York City, Turkish intelligence, an unstated anti-Clinton "October surprise," and an unnamed "Lieutenant General"—a strange confluence of data points that suggests the possible involvement of Flynn, a retired lieutenant general and intelligence expert whose dealings with Alptekin pre-election saw the two men working simultaneously for Turkish and Israeli interests and thereafter dissembling about their engagements.[89]

The *New York Times* calls Trump's three-man back channel to Erdogan an "often-unseen connection" between the Turkish and American presidents that enables "private dialogue" and "backdoor diplomacy."[90] Per the *Times*, Trump's former national security advisor John Bolton will cite Trump's relationship with Erdogan as an instance of him "confus[ing] personal relationships with national relationships," noting in a November 2019 speech Trump's "reluctance to confront Mr. Erdogan by imposing sanctions on Turkey."[91] According to NBC, Bolton suggests in the speech that Trump's "approach to U.S. policy on Turkey is motivated by his personal or financial interests."[92]

During the Annual Conference on U.S.-Turkey Relations in mid-April 2019, "Kushner summon[s] Mr. Albayrak to an impromptu meeting in the Oval Office, where Mr. Albayrak successfully presse[s] Mr. Trump to hold back the sanctions against Turkey for buying Russian weapons"—a victory for both Erdogan and Putin.[93] Albayrak will later say of the Oval Office meeting that Trump showed an "understanding perspective" on the matter of Turkey purchasing Russian missiles, and that this perspective was the product of "Mr. Trump's fondness, love and real warm feelings both toward Turkey and our president [Erdogan]."[94] Nor could Trump have failed to see the value of expressing such warmth toward Albayrak himself; the *New York Times* reports that in Turkey Erdogan's son-in-law wields so much influence that he is considered by many in Ankara to be the nation's "shadow premier."[95]

Several months later, in summer 2019, when, according to NBC News, "Republican senators [seek] to punish Turkey . . . for its purchase of a Russian missile defense system by pushing the president to impose congressionally mandated sanctions, Trump invite[s] them to a White House meeting to ask for 'flexibility' in dealing with the issue. Those sanctions have not been implemented."[96] A spokesman for Erdogan will reveal that during the April 2019 meeting with Albayrak, Trump had agreed to use "the power that he has to intervene" on the issue of sanctions and prevent them.[97] The Russian missile confrontation thus sees Trump at once taking a position advantageous to the Kremlin and creating the appearance of blocking a congressionally mandated action to finesse a personal and business relationship with a hostile foreign leader—a juxtaposition of personal and political interests that not only is evident in the Ukraine scandal as well but will, by July 2019, see Trump falsely declaring that Erdogan "was not allowed" by President Obama to buy American-made Patriot missiles rather than Russian missiles, and that Trump must therefore permit Turkey's purchase of Russian arms to go forward.[98] As the *New York Times* reports, Trump is merely "repeating Mr. Erdogan's rationale" for the purchase.[99]

Perhaps no incident in Trump's presidency better illustrates the dangers of his clandestine intertwining of his personal interests and U.S. foreign policy than his disastrous withdrawal of U.S. forces from Syria in the fall of 2019.

In late August 2019, Erdogan warns Trump that if he doesn't sign on quickly to a "safe zone" plan developed by Erdogan to push Syrian Kurds twenty miles away from Turkey's southern border, Turkey will invade Syria. Under the plan, Turkey would establish and control a strip of Syrian land along the latter country's northern border and evict from it all Syrian Kurds.[100] Erdogan threatens to launch an invasion of Syria in a matter of "weeks" if Trump does not capitulate to his demands.[101] Weeks later, as the Trump administration is still considering this ultimatum, Erdogan asks Jared Kushner to come to Turkey to meet with his son-in-law Albayrak to discuss—per *New York Times* reporting—"trade."[102] Kushner sets up and joins an "official five-day trip to Turkey ... by [the] commerce secretary, Wilbur Ross"; the trip creates the appearance of the Trump administration being willing to agree to Erdogan's military demands in northern Syria if the Turkish strongman will agree to favorable trade terms—or other arrangements—with the Trump administration.[103] The resultant Kushner-Ross plan for "expanded trade" with Turkey is oddly timed, as "lawmakers in Washington [are] calling [in September 2019] for economic sanctions in response to Turkey's purchase of Russian weapons."[104]

Secretary Ross does little while in Turkey to dispel concerns about the Trump administration's motives—and suspicions that Trump is willing to place economics above human rights considerations in northern Syria. Per Ross's public remarks in Ankara, in the midst of Erdogan's ultimatum on the Kurds the administration is focused on crafting "an open and constructive discussion about the importance and complexity of [the U.S.-Turkey] commercial relationship. Today," Ross opines, "there are 1,700 U.S. companies operating in Turkey, with many of America's most iconic brands committed to producing their products here in Turkey."[105] Left unsaid is that one of these "iconic brands" is Trump's own. Ross's address seems to presage Trump's October greenlighting of a Turkish invasion of Syria, with the secretary remarking of the U.S. trade delegation that "we are here to promote our mutual commercial interests and strengthen the ties that have developed over the decades between our two great nations. . . . Our commercial partnership has transcended the inevitable ups-and-downs of our geo-political alliance, and it is instrumental to our continued engagement with the Turkish government."[106]

After Trump takes no action in September 2019 to come to terms with Erdogan on Syria, the Turkish president announces, per *Newsweek*, that Turkey is "planning to invade Syria," and "reinforce[s] his army units at the Syria-Turkish border."[107] A call between the two leaders ensues, during which, according to an NSC official who listens in, Trump gets "out-negotiated" and then "rolled" by Erdogan: the president agrees to withdraw U.S. troops from Syria, per the official, "only . . . to make it look like we are getting something—but we are not getting something. The U.S. national security has entered a state of increasing danger for decades to come because the president has no spine and that's the bottom line."[108] The *New York Times* notes that early October 2019 is the second time—the first being December 2018—that Trump has "surprised his own advisers by agreeing during phone calls with Mr. Erdogan to pull United States troops from northern Syria . . . clearing the way for Turkish forces to attack an American-backed militia there."[109] CNN will subsequently report that the second of these two calls with Erdogan constituted Trump's "go-ahead" or "green light" for Turkey to invade Syria.[110]

On October 7, Turkey begins bombing northern Syria in preparation for its invasion.[111] As U.S. forces withdraw from observation posts at Tel

Abyad and Ras al Ain, "Kurdish forces indicate," according to *The Hill*, "that they might start talks with Russia or the government of Syrian President Bashar Assad to fill [the] security vacuum."[112] Another immediate result of the invasion, CNN reports, is the Syrian Democratic Forces (SDF) "suspending military operations against ISIS in northern Syria"—operations long considered critical to U.S. national security—to avoid attacks from the oncoming Turkish invasion force.[113] As the SDF stands down, a humanitarian crisis takes shape: according to CNN, the number of displaced persons resulting from the Trump-Erdogan pact is likely to exceed 300,000.[114]

The reaction to Trump's decision to withdraw troops from Syria is immediate, bipartisan, and scathing. U.S. officials tell Fox News that the Pentagon considers itself to have been "completely blindsided."[115] Senate majority leader Mitch McConnell (R-KY) opines that "a precipitous withdrawal of U.S. forces from Syria would only benefit Russia, Iran, and the Assad regime."[116] Top Trump Senate ally Lindsey Graham calls the situation a "complete and utter national security disaster in the making" and "the biggest blunder of [Trump's] presidency," accusing the administration of lying about its justification for withdrawing troops and saying that its "biggest lie" is Trump's claim—concurrent to his announcement of the U.S. withdrawal—that ISIS has been defeated.[117] Sen. Liz Cheney (R-WY) calls news of Trump's withdrawal decision "sickening," adding that with "Turkish troops preparing to invade Syria from the north, Russian-backed forces from the south, [and] ISIS fighters attacking Raqqa," it is "impossible to understand why Donald Trump is leaving America's allies to be slaughtered and enabling the return of ISIS."[118] Sen. Rubio accuses Trump of "cut[ting a] deal with Erdogan allowing him to wipe [the Kurds] out," adding that the deal would cause "damage to our reputation and national interest" in a way that will be both "extraordinary and long lasting."[119] House minority leader Kevin McCarthy issues a statement saying that the Turkish attack enabled by Trump's decision to withdraw troops from Syria "threatens to halt momentum against ISIS, directly assaults our [SDF] partners, and could give the likes of al-Qaeda and Iran new footholds in the region."[120] Rep. Adam Kinzinger (R-IL), a member of the House Foreign Affairs Committee, tells CNN that Trump's decision is "disgusting" and "sickening."[121]

As reported by CNN, Sen. Graham and a Democratic Senate colleague, Maryland's Chris Van Hollen, quickly introduce a plan to "place immediate sanctions on senior Turkish government officials, ban all U.S. military business and military transactions with Turkey, and immediately activate 2017 sanctions on the country until Ankara stops its operations against the Kurds."[122] Members of a bipartisan congressional delegation who had been overseas at the time of Trump's announcement "quickly cobble[ ] together a joint statement as they wait[ ] in customs at Dulles International Airport," sitting "on a bench at baggage claim to write it," according to the Associated Press.[123]

The response Trump receives from current and former U.S. soldiers is every bit as striking as the response from Congress. Trump's secretary of defense, Mark Esper, whose department had just days earlier downplayed any chance of a U.S. withdrawal, posts, then deletes, a tweet insisting that the Pentagon "does not endorse a Turkish operation in Northern Syria . . . [and will] reiterate to Turkey the possible destabilizing consequences of potential actions to Turkey, the region, and beyond."[124] The former top U.S. general in the Middle East, Gen. Joseph Votel, "lambast[s]" Trump's decision, writing in *The Atlantic* that "the abrupt policy decision to seemingly abandon our Kurdish partners could not come at a worse time. The decision was made without consulting U.S. allies or senior U.S. military leadership and threatens to affect future partnerships at precisely the time we need them most."[125] Retired Marine general John Allen tells CNN that "there is blood on Trump's hands for abandoning our Kurdish allies," adding that the disaster that followed Trump's announcement was "completely foreseeable" and Trump's actions had "greenlighted it."[126] Former Trump national security advisor H. R. McMaster observes during a public event, per *Politico*, that the Syria withdrawal may "push the [SDF] to ally with Russia or Syrian dictator Bashar Al Assad"; McMaster adds that because the majority-Kurdish SDF controls "65 to 70 percent of Syria's oil reserves," abandoning them means that Putin and Assad—who want that oil "really badly"—could be in a position to take control of it.[127] Brad Bowman, a fifteen-year military veteran and senior director of the Center on Military and Political Power at the Foundation for Defense of Democracies, calls the Turkish invasion of Syria "a sickening and shameful moment in U.S. history and I put that at the foot of the President."[128] Bowman adds, "We are breaking faith with the Kurds. The SDF did everything we asked them to do. This will have ramifications for every individual [U.S.] soldier, every squad, every platoon operating in a dangerous place trying to earn the trust of their [foreign] partners."[129] President Trump's former special envoy on countering ISIS, Brett McGurk, writes on Twitter that "Donald Trump is not a Commander-in-Chief. He makes impulsive decisions with no knowledge or deliberation. He sends military personnel into harm's way with no backing. He blusters and then leaves our allies exposed when adversaries call his bluff or he confronts a hard phone call."[130]

It is not just Trump's decision that leaves many rattled, but the manner in which it was made. *Politico* reports that Trump neither spoke to nor even texted his longtime ally Lindsey Graham—a key figure on the Senate Committee on Foreign Relations—before making his decision.[131] *The Hill* reports on congressional testimony by the Trump administration's special envoy for Syria, James Jeffrey, in which Jeffrey concedes to Graham's Senate committee that he was "not on [the] phone call between Trump and . . . Erdogan that preceded Trump's decision."[132] Jeffrey also admits that, despite being Trump's top adviser in Syria, neither he nor Trump "know where [the ISIS fighters] are" who escaped in Syria as a result of Trump's decision; his comments "directly contradict" those of the president, who had earlier on the same day stated that the escaped fighters had "largely been recaptured."[133] In fact, as the *New York Times* will report, of sixty-two "high value" ISIS detainees in northern Syria, Trump's troop withdrawal announcement costs the United States and its allies sixty of them, with it now being "too late" for any to be recaptured.[134] The *Times* adds that whereas the United States and its allies previously had custody of 11,000 ISIS captives in total in northern Syria, the number of mid-withdrawal escapees is presently unknown.[135] When a CNN op-ed, reacting to Trump's false claims on recaptured ISIS detainees, concludes that "Trump's lies on Syria [a]re jaw-dropping," Sen. Sheldon Whitehouse (D-RI) responds on Twitter, "A senior official from a friendly government told me that Trump has handed the Mideast over to Putin, and that it will be decades to repair the damage done to American interests."[136] Indeed, by mid-October Russia has announced that it is now patrolling the territory vacated by the U.S. military at Trump's command; a viral video released shortly after the U.S. withdrawal shows the Russians taking over an American airstrip.[137]

Long-range consequences aside, one of the most immediate results of the Turkish invasion of Syria is that American soldiers come under fire from Turkish forces. On October 11, the Pentagon confirms that U.S. troops in Syria "came under artillery fire from Turkish positions," forcing U.S. military command to "demand[ ] that Turkey avoid actions" that would require American troops to take "immediate defensive action."[138] The Pentagon says the shelling occurred even though it was directed at "an area known by the Turks to have U.S. forces present."[139] Still worse, per a CNN report, "the U.S. does not believe the Turkish shelling near U.S. troops posted near Kobani was an accident, and that it was likely designed to chase the U.S. from the area"—a claim that, if true, means one of America's NATO allies has deliberately aimed hostile fire at U.S. forces even as America's president is capitulating unconditionally to that ally's demands.[140]

Without having had any forewarning of the need to withdraw, U.S. forces find themselves underprepared for removing themselves from the area. The *Washington Post* reports that certain evacuation maneuvers run the risk of "marooning" other U.S. units in the middle of an active war zone.[141] The Associated Press writes of a situation on the ground that is "deteriorating rapidly," one whose immediate result is that "U.S. troops are at risk of being isolated, unable to travel without 'high risk' of armed confrontation with Turkey-backed forces."[142] In a public statement, Sen. Rubio describes an even grimmer scene, contending that it is not only Turkish forces that are threatening the American withdrawal, but indeed soldiers in the region with more nakedly nefarious intent. "U.S. troops are at serious risk of being cut off and of coming under attack by enemy fighters," Rubio writes.[143]

A second, seemingly equally foreseeable aftereffect of Trump's decision—given the history of animosity between the Turks and the SDF, with the latter considered a terrorist organization by the Turkish government—is a wave of atrocities committed against Kurdish civilians by Turkish soldiers. According to an MSNBC legal analyst, local journalists on the ground in northern Syria "report that a Kurdish politician, a 35-year-old woman, was raped and stoned to death by advancing Turkish forces."[144] Shortly thereafter, the Pentagon confirms that Turkish forces "appear to be" committing war crimes against Kurdish civilians and unarmed prisoners, acknowledging "footage appearing to show the summary execution of Kurdish captives."[145] The *Washington Post* reports on a "gruesome and explicit" video showing "Turkish-allied Syrian fighters pumping bursts of automatic fire into the body of a bound man lying on the side of a desert road as a gunman shouts to his comrades to take his phone and film him doing the shooting. Another trembling, handcuffed man crouches on the opposite side of the road as the shooting erupts. 'Kill them,' one man is heard shouting."[146] In another video reported on by the *Post*, Turkish-backed fighters "crowd[ ] around a black, bullet-riddled SUV that had apparently come under a hail of gunfire before being forced to stop. The fighters step over the body of a man in civilian clothing to reach inside the vehicle. 'Another fleeing pig has been liquidated by the hands of the National Army,' one of the fighters says as the others clamor to be filmed."[147] A female left alive in the car, per the video, will be "found later in a nearby morgue."[148] When the woman's body is identified as that of Kurdish politician Hevrin Khalaf, secretary general of the Future Party of Syria—believed to be the same woman reportedly raped and stoned to death by foreign invaders—a Turkish newspaper "trumpet[s] Khalaf's killing as a 'successful operation,'" crowing about how she was "neutralized."[149] According to the Syrian Observatory for Human Rights, in a separate incident following the invasion "nine civilians were executed . . . at the roadblock to the south of the town of Tal Abyad," a claim that receives some corroboration in "photos and videos posted by the Ahrar al-Sharqiya rebel group, which was apparently among those involved in staffing the roadblock"; the photos and videos "show captured men surrounded by fighters on the side of the road."[150] Sen. Rubio tweets of Turkish forces "filming themselves beheading Kurds."[151]

At the time of the initial invasion, Trump had vowed to take measures against Turkey if it engaged in any "unforced or unnecessary fighting."[152] But the president will quickly break his pledge, despite the "chaos and bloodletting" that kills "scores of people" in the first days of the invasion, per the *New York Times*.[153] Instead of taking action to prevent post-invasion Turkish war crimes, Trump agrees to drop sanctions on Turkey shortly after the invasion, calling it a "great outcome."[154]

According to the Associated Press, "hundreds" of ISIS fighters escape from a single location during the invasion, a development for which U.S. ally Australia, based on on-scene observations, blames Turkey.[155] Sen. Rubio shortly thereafter publishes a statement confirming that 700 ISIS supporters have escaped from U.S.-ally captivity in a single Kurdish-held city; his statement is subsequently confirmed by Kurdish news, which reports that "at least 785 people with links to ISIS" escaped custody from a single lockup on October 13, 2019.[156]

NBC News reports that across northern Syria, the SDF had in fact been guarding "tens of thousands" of ISIS prisoners; by January, no fewer than 5,000 ISIS prisoners will be missing from just one locally reported head count in the area.[157] In a sign of the incoherence of Trump's withdrawal decision, the U.S. military announces on October 19 that—having just pulled out of areas where thousands of ISIS fighters were once kept, and are now free—it will send all its Syria-based forces "to western Iraq . . . to conduct operations against [ISIS] to prevent a resurgence in that country."[158] The redeployment of American forces in Syria to another Middle Eastern theater comes as Trump is falsely telling U.S. voters that the troops withdrawn in Syria are coming home.[159] These mixed messages from the president and the Pentagon only worsen over time, with the latter announcing, just two days after its declaration of an imminent redeployment to Iraq, that in fact it will be leaving some troops in Syria after all—rendering moot Trump's chief public justification for his precipitous withdrawal from northern Syria, which is that it would result in U.S. forces there returning home.[160]

Another foreseeable result of the Turkish invasion is a significant strategic victory for Russia. As the *New York Times* reports, shortly after the invasion, lacking any other option following the withdrawal of U.S. forces, "Kurdish forces long allied with the United States in Syria announce[ ] a new deal . . . with the government in Damascus, a sworn enemy of Washington that is backed by Russia, as Turkish troops moved deeper into their territory. . . . The sudden shift marked a major turning point in Syria's long war. For five years, United States policy relied on collaborating with the Kurdish-led forces both to fight the Islamic State and to limit the influence of Iran and Russia, which support the Syrian government, with a goal of maintaining some leverage over any future settlement of the conflict. . . . [A]fter Mr. Trump abruptly abandoned that approach, American leverage appeared all but gone."[161] Leaving Russia and its allies in control of large swaths of Syria means giving a free hand to Russian war crimes in the region; as the *Times* reports in October, "thousands of previously unheard Russian Air Force communications in Syria" reveal that during a single twelve-hour period, the Russians "bombed four hospitals" in Syria.[162]

According to the *Washington Post*, Russia's and Assad's strategic victory in Syria is likely countrywide and permanent. As the *Post* details, the Kurds "strik[ing a] deal to bring Assad's troops back into Kurdish areas" has the immediate effect of "dimming [the] prospect of further U.S. presence in Syria."[163]

President Trump's hastily announced withdrawal also results in a series of public humiliations for the United States. Following U.S. soldiers' evacuation of northern Syria, the U.S. Air Force is compelled to use two F-15 jets to blow up American installations, munitions, and matériel so they won't fall into the hands of the Russians, armed militias hostile to the United States, or terrorist groups.[164] As U.S. troops are withdrawing, their former allies the Kurds "pelt [them] . . . with potatoes," according to *Vice*.[165] A video by the Kurdish Hawar News Agency, reported on by *Vice*, shows American soldiers "being confronted by a hostile crowd, which bombarded the withdrawing forces with vegetables and insults."[166] A U.S. soldier in Syria will tell a Fox News reporter during the evacuation, "I am ashamed for the first time in my career."[167] Another soldier, an officer, tells the *New York Times*, "They [the Kurds] trusted us and we broke that trust. It's a stain on the American conscience."[168] The *Washington Post*, summarizing numerous interviews with U.S. soldiers who currently serve or formerly served in Syria, reports that "the calamity on the ground in Syria has wrought angry reactions from service members like few other recent foreign policy decisions. Troops have reacted viscerally in interviews and on social media despite Defense Department restrictions on them expressing political opinions."[169]

America's Kurdish allies are indeed blindsided by the Trump-Erdogan pact. When Gen. Mazloum Abdi, the SDF commander, is asked about Trump's decision to exit Syria and permit a Turkish invasion, he tells NBC that "the people who fought with [America] against international terrorism, against ISIS, are under risk right now and they are facing a big battle alone," adding later, to *Foreign Policy*, that the Americans have a "role in stopping [Turkey's] actions" and "their efforts are not sufficient."[170] Responding to Trump's handling of the Turkey-SDF conflict, former CIA chief of Russian operations Steve Hall will tell CNN that it has been a "veritable buffet of horribleness."[171] The *New York Times* comments that "Trump has repeatedly promised to end what he calls America's 'endless wars.' However, [he] is not so much ending wars, as he is moving troops from one conflict to another."[172] The newspaper adds that "Mr. Trump's pullout has handed the Islamic State its biggest win in more than four years and greatly improved its prospects. . . . It has lifted the morale of fighters in [ISIS] affiliates as far away as Libya and Nigeria."[173]

* * *

As the fallout from Trump's pullout unfolds, MSNBC reports that "this is the first time . . . that you have the president making a major national security decision, where lives are being put at risk, where he has admitted that he has a major business conflict of interest. . . . [Trump Towers Istanbul] are not just some part of his portfolio . . . [but] the [Trump Organization's] crown jewel in Europe. . . . The Trump Organization considers this a major investment. [Trump's] friends in Turkey, who are tied to Erdogan, invested $400 million in these towers. He personally was paid $10 million in order to have his name put on it."[174] *Politico* reports that after the withdrawal, "lawmakers, and even President Trump's own staff, are questioning whether his business deals are influencing U.S. foreign policy."[175]

During a tense White House meeting on October 16, Speaker of the House Nancy Pelosi issues what the *Washington Post* calls a "staggering accusation" against the president in a moment that is captured by a photographer. As the *Post* describes the face-to-face confrontation, which ends with Pelosi quickly departing the White House, "Why, [Pelosi] asked, did [Trump] withdraw U.S. troops from Syria—a geopolitical calculation that allowed a toehold in northern Syria for Russian President Vladimir Putin? Why, she asked with lawmakers and aides watching and a White House photographer snapping away, do 'all roads lead to Putin'?"[176] When a more robust accounting of the event is later reported by the *Post*, Pelosi's full statement to the president before excusing herself from her meeting with him will become, for many, a dire summary of Trump's presidency: "With you, all roads lead to Putin," the Speaker tells the president.[177]

That Trump's actions are a windfall for Russia is made even more evident when Erdogan meets with Putin on October 22, an event that seems to underscore that Russia may now be the sole superpower in this part of the Middle East.[178] As the *Washington Post* writes, both the meeting and the agreement on future Turkish-Russian collaboration it produces "cement Russian President Vladimir Putin's preeminent role in Syria as U.S. troops depart and America's influence wanes."[179] Putin adds further injury to America's standing in the Middle East by choosing in the midst of the Syria crisis to visit—for the first time in a decade— two other nations whose leaders have long considered Russia an emerging superpower in the Middle East: Saudi Arabia and the United Arab Emirates.[180] As the *Post* notes, these meetings "emphasiz[e] not only coordination between three of the biggest oil producers in the world but also Moscow's growing influence in the Middle East."[181]

Once Erdogan has established his desired "safe zone" in Syria— functionally an extension of Turkey's territory by approximately 5,500 square miles—he informs Trump that he is willing to make permanent a previously agreed-upon cease-fire that Turkey had not, in the event, honored; it is a conveniently timed "concession" that results in Trump immediately lifting all remaining sanctions on Ankara.[182] Within a week, however, the House of Representatives has passed new sanctions on Turkey by a bipartisan vote of 403–16.[183] Just 15 House Republicans oppose the bill, while 176 support it—a significant "rebuke" of Trump, per media accounts.[184]

Trump's reaction to the universal condemnation with which his Syria withdrawal announcement is met leaves many political observers gravely concerned. As Erdogan's brutal invasion of northern Syria and longtime U.S. forward positions in the area is unfolding, Trump warns Turkey, in a public statement summarized by the *Washington Post*, that there will be "devastating economic consequences if the Turkish government takes any steps" that displease the president; Trump specifically promises retaliation against Turkey if it engages in any behaviors "that I, in my great and unmatched wisdom, consider to be off-limits."[185] Trump adds that if the country displeases him, he "will totally destroy and obliterate the Economy of Turkey," something he boasts he has "done before."[186]

It is Trump's comments about the Kurds and Turks that strike many as bordering on the obscene, however—and contribute to, as CNN reports, "members of President Trump's own party . . . [being] privately alarmed at his demeanor . . . and his apparent lack of understanding of the consequences of his Syria policy."[187] Justifying his decision to permit the Turks to attack the SDF despite 11,000 Kurdish fighters having died assisting the United States in fighting ISIS, Trump says of the Kurds, "They didn't help us in the second World War."[188] He adds that the Kurds only aided America's fight against ISIS for the sake of "their land" and because they "were paid massive amounts of money and equipment to do so."[189] At another post-invasion press conference, Trump calls the Kurds "no angels" and says that their situation vis-à-vis Turkey has "nothing to do with us," despite having previously called them—before his "friend" Erdogan invaded their territory—"great people," "incredible fighters," and "wonderful, warm, intelligent allies"; Trump will later contradict U.S. officials and official U.S. policy by declaring that American troops are in Syria "only for [the] oil."[190] Trump's D.C. hotel even cancels a "prayer event" scheduled to occur there under the auspices of a Christian aid group after it is revealed that the intent of the event organizers had been to pray for Kurdish refugees.[191] At yet another press conference in mid-October, Trump calls the PKK, a Kurdish political and military organization based in Turkey, "more of a terrorist threat, in many ways, than ISIS."[192] Trump ally Lindsey Graham tweets in the midst of Trump's relentless attack on the Kurds that "the statements by President Trump about Turkey's invasion being of no concern to us . . . completely undercut Vice President Pence and Secretary Pompeo's ability to end the conflict."[193]

Trump's comments on the PKK in particular risk a significant break from standing U.S. policy. Per the Middle East Policy Council, America has "supported" the People's Protection Units (YPG)—the Syrian branch of the PKK—on the basis of it being "the most effective force on the ground in combatting ISIS"; despite Turkish pressure, the United States has long rejected calls to cease both financial and military support for YPG.[194] By railing against PKK broadly writ, Trump risks tarring the very fighters who have stood side by side with America against ISIS, and doing so purely to endorse Erdogan's self-interested geopolitical rhetoric.

Indeed, Erdogan has in the past executed offensives against the PKK and YPG simultaneously.[195]

Many of Trump's other public remarks during the crisis in Syria leave analysts and allies alike befuddled. When Trump is asked if he's worried that dangerous ISIS detainees have escaped from SDF-managed prisons in northern Syria, Trump responds that it doesn't matter because "they're going to be escaping to Europe" rather than the United States.[196] Trump thereafter tells Fox News that he is not overly concerned about the Turks attacking the Kurds because "they have been fighting with the Kurds for many years, for centuries. . . . It's like . . . [the way] some people go to lunch."[197] In another particularly troubling episode following the Turkish invasion, Trump, per CNN, "appear[s] to confirm that U.S. nuclear weapons are being housed at Incirlik Air Base in Turkey, making him the first U.S. official to publicly acknowledge" a circumstance never before discussed by either the U.S. government or NATO.[198]

On October 17—after Erdogan has, to all appearances, completed his military objective in invading Syria—Vice President Pence announces that the United States has reached a deal with Turkey to temporarily suspend its military offensive.[199] The same day, Sen. McConnell announces, according to Bloomberg News, that "he would like the chamber to take up a resolution rebuking President Trump on w[ith]drawing from Syria that is tougher than the one that cleared [the] House y[ester]day on a 354–60 vote."[200] In calling, in his words, for "something stronger," McConnell may be registering the depth and breadth of the calumny being heaped on the United States for Trump's actions, including the Pence-negotiated suspension of military activities. As NBC reports on the day Erdogan ends his military operations in northern Syria, "experts are already saying the U.S. just granted Erdogan everything he wanted all along, including exclusive rights to patrol the safe zone by air. They are calling this a total capitulation [to Erdogan]."[201] A senior Turkish official subsequently confirms this assessment, telling CNN, "We got exactly what we wanted [from Pence]" and "[our] military operation paid off."[202] NBC reports that according to the "fine print" of Pence's cease-fire, Erdogan "gets Syrian Kurd land he's wanted for years. Kurdish fighters have to disarm and get out. Russia gains influence. ISIS does what it wants. Trump cancels sanctions on Turkey. [It's the] Art of the [D]eal . . . [i]f you are Erdogan."[203]

When McConnell ultimately introduces his measure, its contents suggest that the president is no longer trusted with foreign policy even by members of his own party, with CNN reporting that the GOP-sponsored bill would "tie the hands of the commander-in-chief by requiring the President to report to Congress that ISIS and al Qaeda have been defeated 'before initiating any further significant withdrawal' of U.S. troops from the region."[204]

Despite the Pence-negotiated cease-fire constituting a "total capitulation" to Erdogan by Trump, the *Washington Post* reports that Turkey breaks even this conspicuously lopsided deal almost instantly, with "fighting continu[ing] in [a] Syrian border town despite [the] Turkish agreement to halt [its] offensive."[205] The *Post* adds that, Pence's and Trump's statements notwithstanding, the United States and Turkey had not even "come away from their negotiations with the same understanding of what they had agreed to in signing the vaguely written deal."[206] Whatever the parties understand about the deal, however, the *Post* unambiguously declares it "a stunning victory for Erdogan" that involves only a 120-hour delay in his expansionist ambitions in northern Syria.[207] Indeed, the *Post* reveals that Turkey is permitted to extend its sphere of control 20 miles into Syria and for a length of the border stretching for 275 miles, per a statement by Erdogan on the size of the "safe zone" that the Turkish president says the United States "did not say anything negative" about during negotiations.[208] While U.S. officials disagree with Erdogan's characterization of the safe zone, and also on whether Turkey agreed to take no military action against the city of Kobani, they quickly discover that, without any troops in the area or any remaining leverage in the country, there is no means for America to enforce its will. Indeed, a summary by U.S. defense policy news website *Defense One* notes that just forty-eight hours into the ceasefire Gen. Abdi, the SDF commander, informs reporters that "Turkey is continuing its assault into northern Syria and blocking the SDF's attempts to withdraw"; the general adds, "I would like to inform the American public that . . . this is leading to . . . ethnic cleansing in front of the American administration."[209] According to the Kurdish general, "What is becoming clear now is that Erdogan is not listening to Trump and is not abiding by his commitment to him. I am asking President Trump right now to fulfill his promise to us and stop this war."[210] Shortly after Gen. Abdi's statement is issued, NBC News reports that "U.S. officials tell [NBC that an] alarm bell [is] ringing among diplomats in D.C. that the U.S. could one day be held responsible for Crimes Against Humanity for ethnic cleansing of Syrian Kurds by opening the door to it, watching it, encouraging it[—with] Trump's tweets and statements[—]and not stopping it."[211]

According to the *New York Times*, the Trump administration was aware of the troop movements Turkey was using during the cease-fire to continue to attack the Kurds, with "a U.S. official with direct knowledge of events" telling the *Times* that the United States knew "Turkey transported Arab militiamen from one part of Syria west of Manbij into Turkey, to then cross back into Syria alongside the Turkish military in order to fight Kurds."[212] Such information could ultimately be used in a prosecution of both Trump and his administration for crimes against humanity.[213]

Despite Trump's "total capitulation" to Erdogan and the growing evidence of Turkish war crimes against the Kurds, following the cease-fire Trump announces, "It's a great day for the Kurds. It's really a great day for civilization. It's a great day for civilization. So I just want to thank everybody."[214] Seemingly as a means of justifying his inability to prevent the invasion or its attendant war crimes, Trump says at another event the same day, regarding what he calls a "pause" in the hostilities, "Sometimes you have to let them fight a little while. . . . Sometimes you have to let them fight. Like two kids in a lot, you got to let them fight. Then you pull them apart."[215] Of reports of massive Kurdish casualties along the Turkey-Syria border, Trump says, "They [Turkey] had to have it cleaned out."[216]

* * *

Another notable slight of the president at Erdogan's hands comes when Trump sends the Turkish president a highly unusual letter urging him to restrain himself in invading Syria. "Don't be a tough guy," Trump writes Erdogan, "Don't be a fool!"[217] Elsewhere in the letter—shortly before insisting that Erdogan will be deemed "the devil" by history "if good things don't happen"—Trump writes, "Let's work out a good deal! You don't want to be responsible for slaughtering thousands of people, and I don't want to be responsible for destroying the Turkish economy—and I will."[218]

Trump also makes a comment that profoundly concerns those tracking the president's many conflicts of interest, telling Erdogan that he has "worked hard to solve some of your problems"; Trump offers no additional details or explanation for the remark.[219] The *Washington Post* interprets the line as referring to Trump's efforts to push the extradition of Fethullah Gulen, to forestall prosecution of Halkbank, to "hold[ ] back on new sanctions" against Turkey, and to "drop[ ] charges against Erdogan's bodyguards" following the 2017 attacks in D.C. at the Turkish ambassador's residence—all actions whose benefit to U.S. national security or interests is unclear.[220] Indeed, the *Daily Beast* will report in December 2019 that despite Halkbank having "played a role in a multi-billion-dollar scheme to move billions to Iran," the president is inexplicably having his administration "make[ ] the case against sanctioning" the Turkish state-owned entity.[221] Not long after Trump seeks to block any sanctions against Turkey arising from the Iran-Turkey scandal—a decision that also profoundly benefits the Iranians—the president tells reporters, in reference to the recent suppression of anti-government protests in Iran, that the Iranian government "is killing perhaps thousands and thousands of people right now as we speak."[222]

What Erdogan does with Trump's letter to him, reports the BBC, underscores the ill repute into which the Trump-Turkey scandal brings the United States: the Turkish president throws the U.S. president's letter in the trash.[223] Despite having not yet gotten any response to his missive, and despite Erdogan's orchestration of atrocities in northern Syria, Trump invites him to the White House over significant objection from his own party.[224] The invitation, following Erdogan's apparent commission of war crimes in Syria, is just the sort of goodwill gesture Trump has with-held from Ukraine's anti-corruption crusader Volodymyr Zelensky for months. As the *Washington Post* reports in December 2019, since Trump's aides first promised Zelensky a White House visit in summer 2019, "a dozen other leaders [have] got[ten] one instead."[225]

During his subsequent visit to Washington, Erdogan will, while meet-ing with a group of GOP senators, use an iPad to show "a propaganda video casting the Kurds in a negative light"; one Republican who sees the video calls it "surreal" and "straight propaganda."[226] At Trump and Erdogan's subsequent joint press conference, Trump declares himself a "big fan" of the Turkish president, adding that he thinks Erdogan has "a great relationship with the Kurds."[227]

Hours after Erdogan leaves the Oval Office, the White House demands that Lindsey Graham block a resolution in the Senate that would formally recognize Turkey's genocide of Armenians in the twentieth century.[228] Ac-cording to *Axios*, the measure, had it passed, "would have infuriated Erdo-gan."[229] Though Graham will later contend that he blocked the measure only because Erdogan was still in Washington, when the resolution comes to the floor of the Senate again ten days later, the White House again demands that a GOP senator—this time Sen. David Perdue of Georgia—block it.[230]

On December 17, 2019, the Trump administration strongly intimates, in contradiction of a bipartisan resolution from both houses of Congress, that Turkey did not commit genocide against the Armenians in the twen-tieth century.[231]

On January 30, 2020, the State Department announces that—partly due to the "setback" of Turkey's invasion of Syria—it is "seeing ISIS come back as an insurgency, as a terrorist operation, with some 14,000 to 18,000 terrorists between Syria and Iraq."[232]

CHAPTER 37

TRUMP AND ZELENSKY

Trump's efforts to persuade the Ukrainians to investigate a potential 2020 political opponent, Joe Biden, are ultimately successful—even beyond the report on Biden allegedly given to Trump's agents by Yuri Lutsenko in spring 2019. In October 2019, President Zelensky announces that his government will "happily" investigate Trump's claims about Biden, as well as the president's allegations that it was Ukraine, not Russia, that interfered in the 2016 election.[1] The Ukrainian president even agrees to use whatever information Trump passes to him as the basis for his investigation, announcing that "when the U.S. [government] says, 'Yes, there was meddling [in the 2016 election],' I say, 'Please pass details and we will find [the meddling]. We will be happy to investigate."[2]

In response to Zelensky's statements, the Associated Press reports that the Ukrainian president is trying—in "encourag[ing] U.S. and Ukrainian prosecutors to discuss investigating a gas company linked to the son of Trump's Democratic rival Joe Biden, although no one has produced evidence of criminal wrongdoing by the former U.S. vice president or his son"—to "ensure Ukraine has continued support no matter who wins the [2020] presidential election."[3] Zelensky's comments follow an early October 2019 announcement by Ukraine's top prosecutor, as reported by the AP, that "his office would review several cases related to the owner of the gas company where Hunter Biden sat on the board," a decision to which Zelensky appends an invitation for U.S. prosecutors (presumably to be selected by Attorney General Barr) to "cooperate" with Ukrainian attorneys on the investigation.[4]

* * *

In a briefing to lawmakers in the fall of 2019, U.S. intelligence officials disclose, according to *The Hill*, "that Russia engaged in an effort to frame Kyiv for its election interference."[5] NBC News likewise reports that after Fiona Hill's congressional testimony, senators are told in a closed-door briefing that the "effort to frame Ukraine for the Russian meddling of 2016" had been "a Russian intelligence propaganda campaign."[6] Despite this, several GOP senators, in advance of Trump's impeachment trial, inaccurately state that Ukraine meddled in the 2016 presidential election. Among these senators are John Kennedy (R-LA), who calls such meddling "a fact" and "well-documented" and insists Poroshenko "actively worked for Secretary Clinton," and Sen. Ted Cruz, who alleges there is "considerable" evidence that Ukraine "blatantly interfered" in the 2016 election.[7]

On October 4, Trump tweets, "As President I have an obligation to end CORRUPTION, even if that means requesting the help of a foreign country or countries. It is done all the time. This has NOTHING to do with politics or a political campaign against the Bidens. This does have to do with their corruption!"[8] Nevertheless, under intense questioning from the White House press corps, the administration is unable to name any instances in which the president attempted to combat corruption anywhere but Ukraine, or even in Ukraine within any company or pursuant to any scenario not directly associated with his own personal political interest. When Trump is asked to name an instance of him investigating corruption abroad by someone who is not a political opponent, he responds, "You know, we would have to look."[9] CNN reports, in response to Trump's tweet and his statements on the South Lawn of the White House, that "he [wants] to make this about corruption rather than about his political rival Joe Biden. . . . [D]ozens of times today . . . [he] insist[ed] that this was about corruption and not about politics. But when he was asked about what other corruption investigations he has asked other countries to launch, he could not name any others but the one involving Joe Biden in Ukraine."[10]

Trump's comments on the South Lawn come just days after his decision to retweet a prominent supporter, Pastor Robert Jeffress, who had used his social media feed to raise the specter of a second civil war in the United States. Specifically, Jeffress had opined that "if the Democrats are successful in removing the President from office . . . it will cause a Civil War like fracture in this Nation from which our Country will never recover."[11] Trump's retweet prompts a longtime *Washington Post* columnist to assert in the headline of an op-ed, "Trump Threatened 'Civil War.'"[12] As if to erase any doubt about his intentions, Trump tweets, the day after his retweet of Jeffress, that Adam Schiff should be "arrest[ed] for treason" for inaccurately paraphrasing the July 25 Trump-Zelensky call during a House committee hearing; the president's tweet is consistent with his subsequent January 2020 declaration that every "cop, politician, [and] government official" involved in the Russia or Ukraine investigations should "be in jail for treason (and more)" for having participated in the "CRIME OF THE CENTURY, far bigger and more sinister than Watergate!"[13] In October 2019, a close congressional ally of the president, Rep. Louie Gohmert (R-TX), will, echoing Jeffress, raise the prospect of armed conflict in the United States if Congress persists in investigating the president, saying that even an impeachment inquiry—whether or not a vote on impeachment ever occurs—could "push this country to a civil war."[14]

Days after accusing Schiff of treason, Trump tells staff members during a speech at the United States Mission to the United Nations that the White House source for the whistleblower's complaint is "close to a spy," adding—in a reference to the death penalty, which can be imposed upon conviction for treason against the United States—"You know what we used to do in the old days when we were smart with spies and treason, right? We used to handle it a little differently than we do now."[15] The same day, the *Washington Post* editorial board announces that, in its view, a quid pro quo involving previously authorized military aid to Ukraine and a White House visit for Volodymyr Zelensky aside, the transcript of the Trump-Zelensky call also "contained at least a hint that Mr. Trump was linking the 'favor' he wanted [from Zelensky] to [future] arms sales," adding that subsequently released text messages exchanged between U.S. diplomats and a Ukrainian official "definitively show that not only did the Trump administration seek to extract Ukrainian promises of political probes in exchange for a summit meeting, but also [that] they spent weeks negotiating the deal both before and after the Trump-Zelensky phone call." The *Post* editorial board concludes that Trump's course of conduct toward Ukraine amounted to "a blatant act of corruption."[16]

In October 2019, Trump orders a "significant staff cut" at the National Security Council shortly after tweeting an unsubstantiated claim that the Ukraine-scandal whistleblower is "a CIA official who was at the NSC under [President] Obama."[17] *Politico*, quoting Bloomberg journalists Jennifer Jacobs and Justin Sink, will term the NSC cut "substantial."[18] Less than ninety days later, on December 13, 2019, the Trump White House announces another national-security-related cut: this time, in the number of people who are permitted to listen to the president's calls with foreign leaders.[19]

CHAPTER 38

TRUMP-IRAN

In November 2019, Israeli prosecutors reveal that Trump's top ally in the Middle East, Israeli president Benjamin Netanyahu, faces impending indictments for fraud, breach of trust, and bribery; in a related case, the State Prosecutor's Office in Jerusalem announces that Netanyahu's personal attorney will face charges of money laundering.[1] The next month, Secretary of State Pompeo and Jared Kushner meet in Portugal with Netanyahu, who tells international media before the meeting—at a time when he would benefit from a distraction from his own political strife—that "Iran's aggression is growing but its empire is tottering. And I say, 'let's make it totter even further.'"[2]

On December 27, 2019, a rocket attack on an Iraqi military base near Kirkuk kills American civilian contractor Nawres Hamid, a linguist for Valiant Integrated Services LLC. The *New York Times* reports that it is "not clear who was responsible for the attack."[3] The attack also wounds several U.S. soldiers and Iraqi personnel.[4] According to the *Times*, the attack was, despite its results, routine in many respects. "Starting last fall [2019]," the *Times* reports, "Iranian-backed militias launched rockets at Iraqi bases that house American troops, shattering nerves more than doing much damage. So when rockets smashed into the K1 military base near Kirkuk on December 27 . . . the only surprise was the casualties."[5] Indeed, Kataib Hezbollah, the group Trump would later blame for the K1 incident, "had fired at least five other rocket attacks on bases with Americans in the previous months without deadly results."[6]

The possibility that local militias such as Kataib Hezbollah had deliberately been avoiding U.S. casualties is eventually confirmed, according to the *Times*, when "American intelligence officials monitoring communications between Kataib Hezbollah and . . . [the] Islamic Revolutionary Guard Corps learn[ ] that the Iranians wanted to keep the pressure on the Americans [in fall 2019] but had not intended to escalate the low-level conflict. The [December 27] rockets landed in a place and at a time when American and Iraqi personnel normally were not there and it was only by unlucky chance that Mr. Hamid was killed."[7]

These circumstances—and the Trump administration's inability to definitively attach responsibility to the K1 attack—notwithstanding, within twenty-four hours of Hamid's death Trump has both decided the attack was conducted by Kataib Hezbollah and ordered a significant retaliatory strike that hits five targets in two countries, resulting in twenty-five dead militia fighters and at least fifty more injured.[8] Iran quickly decides that the death of twenty-five of its allies is "out of proportion" to the death of one American; it responds, however, not with strikes on U.S. forces but "protests outside the American Embassy in Baghdad."[9] While the protests are "violent" in tone and result in the "breach[ing] [of] the compound's outer wall," they cause no casualties.[10] Indeed, despite Trump's deadly, large-scale attack on Iranian assets, pro-Iranian protestors in Baghdad "[do] not enter the main [U.S.] embassy buildings" and "later with[draw] from the compound," limiting themselves to "chanting," "throwing rocks," "plant[ing] militia flags," "climb[ing] on . . . adjacent buildings," "covering the [outer embassy] walls with graffiti," setting several remote embassy "outbuildings" on fire, and "demanding that the United States withdraw its forces from Iraq."[11]

Trump's response to the protest—which, the *Times* reports, makes him anxious about a repeat of the 2012 Benghazi attacks he used to wound Hillary Clinton politically during the 2016 presidential election—is a tweet: "Iran will be held fully responsible for lives lost, or damage incurred, at any of our facilities. They will pay a very BIG PRICE! This is not a Warning, it is a Threat. Happy New Year!"[12] The *Times* later reveals that Trump had already "ordered more than 100 Marines to rush to Baghdad from Kuwait," intending the fresh troops to "secure the embassy" and obey "one clear order: If protestors enter[ ] the compound, kill them."[13] That the Marines Trump sends have been cleared by the president to do extreme violence to protestors, whether armed or unarmed, rather than merely act as peacekeepers, and that Trump has spread this news to his inner circle, appears to be confirmed when Trump's son Eric responds to the new deployment by announcing on social media, in a subsequently deleted tweet, that the United States is "[a]bout to open up a big ol' can of whoop ass."[14] Trump's order to kill even unarmed trespassers is—for reasons that remain unclear but may be guessed at—never followed, with a number of protestors subsequently "breaching the compound's outer wall" without being killed.[15] Instead, notes the *Times*, the Marines "use[ ] nonlethal weapons like tear gas to disperse protestors" and, despite Trump's potentially illegal order, "the siege end[s] without bloodshed."[16]

Forty-eight hours later, on January 2, after deploying an additional 750 U.S. troops to the region, Trump delivers on his tweeted "Threat" by retaliating for the protestors' property damage with the assassination of Gen. Qasem Soleimani—a man the *Times* calls "the most important person in Iran after Ayatollah Khamenei."[17] The Trump-authorized strike also kills nine "officials from Iraqi militias," including a popular commander named Abu Mahdi al-Muhandis.[18] Such an attack, say experts, would only be legal in the face of an "imminent" threat to U.S. interests; intelligence officials will later tell the *Times* that Trump ordered the attack despite "not hav[ing] enough concrete information to describe . . . [the Soleimani] threat as 'imminent.'"[19] After Secretary Pompeo alleges publicly that Soleimani was positioning himself to kill "hundreds" of Americans, intelligence officials tell the *Times* that "they had no specific intelligence suggesting that," either.[20]

In February 2020, the reason for Soleimani's presence in Iraq on the day of his death will be revealed by Iraqi prime minister Adel Abdul Mahdi: the Iranian general was carrying Iran's response to a "Saudi offer to reduce tensions [with Iran]." It is a message that, if delivered, might have frustrated the geopolitical designs of any elements within the United States, Israel, or Saudi Arabia supporting what Israeli prime minister Benjamin Netanyahu has called the "common goal" of a "war" with Iran.[21]

In early January, however, the Pentagon justifies the Soleimani killing by declaring that the general had been "actively developing plans to attack American diplomats and service members in Iraq and throughout the region."[22] President Trump follows this statement with the claim that his assassination of the second-most-important man in Iran was intended to "stop a war."[23] Meanwhile, media response is decidedly circumspect, with the *Times* writing of the January 2 operation that because Soleimani was "a commanding general of a sovereign government," the decision to kill him was a deviation from convention. "[T]he last time the United States killed a major military leader in a foreign country," the newspaper writes, "was during World War II, when the American military shot down the plane carrying the Japanese admiral Isoroku Yamamoto."[24] The *Times* concludes that Trump's decision to kill Soleimani was consequently "the riskiest move made by the United States since the invasion of Iraq in 2003."[25]

Israel's intelligence agency, Mossad, had begun speaking publicly about killing Soleimani just weeks before Trump's decision to do so, a fact that returns to the forefront of U.S. media when *Salon* reports that "Israeli Prime Minister Bibi Netanyahu, under indictment for criminal charges, was the first and only national leader to support Trump's action, while claiming that Trump acted entirely on his own."[26] Netanyahu's claim is belied, however, when the *Times of Israel* reveals that he was "briefed . . . ahead of time about [Trump's] plans," including a late December communication on the subject, a January 1 pre-assassination call between Pompeo and Netanyahu, and a cryptic January 2 tweet from Netanyahu about "very, very dramatic things" about to happen just hours before Soleimani's killing; the *Jerusalem Post* adds that Netanyahu, a longtime friend of both the Trump and Kushner families, received a clear political "boost" from the killing as he faced both criminal charges and a reelection battle.[27] With NPR reporting that Trump's decision to kill Soleimani was made on December 31 at the earliest, and the *Los Angeles Times* reporting on January 3 that Israel had known of the coming attack for "a few days," the likelihood that Trump coordinated with Netanyahu on a targeted international killing of uncertain legality is high.

In May 2020, additional evidence of a course of collusion between Trump and Netanyahu will emerge, as it is revealed that the Israeli business intelligence firm Psy-Group—whose work for the 2016 Trump presidential campaign was the result of an introduction arranged by former Netanyahu chief of staff George Birnbaum—has been found by the *Times of Israel* to have spent much of 2017 "allegedly harass[ing] pro-democracy activists in Ukraine," specifically the very group that Trump and Giuliani had been seeking to discredit since Trump's election: AntAC. Per the *Times*, "troubling questions [remain] about who a firm staffed by ex-Israeli intel officers was working for" in Kyiv; while the investigation of that question continues, it is clear that Psy-Group's actions in Ukraine (which include the production and dissemination of fake news reports) dovetail with Trump agents' efforts there, and that any covert intelligence activities bolstering Trump's reelection rhetoric in the United States would be pleasing to Netanyahu as well.[28]

Any Trump-Netanyahu coordination on the matter of Soleimani's January 2020 assassination notwithstanding, the killing of the Iranian general fulfills a previously articulated Israeli military objective synchronous with a geopolitical vision long supported by the Sunni leaders of Saudi Arabia and the UAE: the collapse of the Iranian regime.[29] It is these same three Trump allies—Netanyahu of Israel, Mohammed bin Salman of Saudi Arabia (MBS), and Mohammed bin Zayed of the United Arab Emirates (MBZ)—with whom Pompeo speaks about Iran on December 31, 2019, the day Trump decides to kill Soleimani.[30] Moreover, just ninety-six hours after the assassination, Trump meets in the Oval Office with Prince Khalid bin Salman, the Saudi vice minister of defense and a younger brother of MBS. The White House keeps the meeting off Trump's public schedule and never provides media with any notice or readout of the conversation.[31] Indeed, the secrecy of the meeting between Trump and bin Salman is so noteworthy that the White House Correspondents' Association (WHCA) publicly decries it.[32] Bin Salman later admits to passing a message from MBS to Trump, and Trump subsequently concedes that he and bin Salman discussed the Iran situation.[33]

Days after the Soleimani strike, the *Washington Post* reports that, just as Mossad had begun openly discussing assassinating Soleimani in October 2019, Pompeo—Trump's intermediary to Netanyahu in the hours before the January 2 operation that resulted in Soleimani's death—"first spoke with Trump about killing Soleimani months [earlier]."[34] After the attack, the *Post* writes, Pompeo "held back-to-back phone calls with his counterparts around the globe but . . . received a chilly reception from European allies, many of whom fear[ed] that the attack put[ ] their embassies in Iran and Iraq in jeopardy and . . . eliminated the chance to keep a lid on Iran's nuclear program."[35]

On January 3, the day after the strike on Soleimani, Trump significantly augments the Pentagon's after-action threat assessment by announcing that Soleimani had been plotting "imminent" attacks on "American diplomats and military personnel"—attacks so imminent, the president claims, that Soleimani was in fact "terminated" while "in the act" of carrying out these "sinister" plots against American forces.[36] Shortly thereafter, Joint Chiefs of Staff chairman Mark Milley, Trump national security advisor Robert O'Brien, and Secretary of State Pompeo echo Trump's assessment. The *New York Times* will observe, however, that the details provided by Milley, O'Brien, and Pompeo "did not describe any threats that were different from what American officials say General Soleimani had been orchestrating for years."[37] Nevertheless, the three men, per the *Daily Beast*, "claim[ ] that killing Soleimani was designed to block Iranian plans to kill 'hundreds' or even thousands of Americans in the Mideast," a scheme by Tehran that the digital media outlet notes would be a "massive escalation from the recent attack patterns of Iran and its regional proxies."[38] O'Brien tells reporters that the legal authority to kill Soleimani arises from the eighteen-year-old Authorization for Use of Military Force (AUMF) that was passed by Congress after the September 11, 2001, terrorist attacks and was intended to combat Iraqi president Saddam Hussein's tyrannical regime.[39] Meanwhile, other U.S. officials tell conservative think-tank experts that the administration had "exquisite intelligence" regarding "a plot to strike Americans in Iraq, Syria and Lebanon," and boast that the killing of Soleimani "disrupted" the plans—while declining to describe them in detail.[40]

Two immediate results of Trump's decision to assassinate Soleimani on Iraqi soil are the "State Department urg[ing] American citizens to leave Iraq immediately" and the *Times* reporting that the Iraqi parliament will "consider a measure to expel all United States forces from the country for the first time since 2003."[41] After the parliament "pass[es] a nonbinding resolution calling for foreign troops to withdraw" from Iraq, the U.S. military is forced to prepare itself for an emergency withdrawal on short notice—just as it had in northern Syria weeks earlier.[42]

A third consequence of Trump's decision on Soleimani comes seventy-two hours after the general's death, when Iran announces it will suspend its adherence to the limits imposed on its nuclear program by the 2015 nuclear deal it signed with Britain, France, Germany, Russia, China, and (before Trump's unilateral withdrawal from the agreement in May 2018) the United States.[43] A day later, the Trump administration stops up to 200 Iranian Americans at the Canadian border, many of them U.S. citizens, subjecting them not just to "hours" of detention but also to interrogations "about the current situation in Iraq and Iran."[44] CNN legal analyst and former FBI agent Asha Rangappa comments on Twitter, following news of the detentions, that "the Non-Detention Act (passed [in 1971] in the aftermath of [World War II] Japanese internment) prohibits the detention of U.S. citizens without congressional authorization."[45]

* * *

Trump's purpose in killing Soleimani is hotly debated, with the *Daily Beast* quoting Jarrett Blanc, an Iran expert and former State Department official, as saying that Iran's Quds Force did not rely on Soleimani to operate, and that therefore "the idea that the Quds Force had attacks in the works and now it doesn't because [Soleimani] is dead is obviously false. It's not clear why killing Soleimani changes the threat profile."[46] The *New York Times* notes "questions about the attack's timing and whether it was meant to deflect attention from the president's expected impeachment trial," adding in other reporting that prior U.S. presidents had all come to the same conclusion: killing Soleimani was simply "too provocative" a move to be in America's national interest.[47] CNN reports that "for Trump . . . the decision [to kill Soleimani] reflected a more immediate victory. . . . [I]t changed the subject, however briefly, from his impeachment."[48]

Given its dire and immediate consequences—including, per the *Wall Street Journal*, forcing U.S. troops to "pause[ ] counter–Islamic State operations with Iraqi forces" to "concentrate on protecting themselves"—the strike faces continued scrutiny in the weeks following Soleimani's death.[49] This scrutiny is marked by a series of startling revelations about the attack's real motivations. The *Journal* reveals that after the strike Trump "told associates he was under pressure to deal with General Soleimani from GOP senators he views as important supporters in his coming impeachment trial in the Senate"; per *New York* magazine, the *Journal* report positions Trump as having committed a "grave dereliction of duty," adding that even a "straightforward read of [the *Journal*] reporting is that Trump has confessed to a grave and even impeachable abuse of his power as commander-in-chief."[50]

Trump's impeachment-focused explanation for the Soleimani assassination is subsequently called into question, however. The *New York Times*, which calls the Soleimani attack "the most perilous chapter so far in President Trump's three years in office," reports that the president's claim that Sen. Tom Cotton (R-AR) had demanded the January 2 strike could not have been accurate, as the two men "had not spoken about Iran since before Christmas," and Trump's decision to kill Soleimani was made on December 31 at the earliest.[51]

The *Times* further observes that while "Trump boasted that he had taken out an American enemy," the "confusion" caused by his actions led to "a Ukrainian civilian passenger jet . . . [being] destroyed by an Iranian missile, killing 176 people."[52] As to whether this deadly "confusion" can be tied to information coming from Trump or his immediate political circle, it is worth observing that in the hour before the Ukrainian airliner was downed, top Trump adviser Sean Hannity was on his internationally televised Fox News program announcing that "if you work in an Iranian refinery, you might want to get a new job—I'd start *now* . . . [because Iran's] three major refineries could soon go up in flames. Their illicit nuclear sites may finally be annihilated. And the mullahs of Iran, well, they may want to . . . keep a watchful eye on the sky tonight as they look from their bunkers, where I'm sure they are hiding. Powerful U.S. military forces . . . are in position tonight. We can report that six B-52 bombers are on the way to the region. Multiple carrier groups are already within striking distance. And, in a show of force, 52 of the world's most advanced aircraft, the F-35, launch[ed] in succession at a U.S. military base. Because of the escalating aggression from this rogue terrorist regime in Iran, the United States is prepared . . . for conflict."[53] Hannity does not reveal the source for his report on America's imminent military plans; it has been noted before, however, that Hannity and Trump speak "several times a day."[54] The *Arizona Republic* subsequently calls the Trump adviser's false claims—all coming during an hour of peak tension between the United States and Iran—"threats" against the Iranian regime.[55]

In February 2020, the *Daily Beast* will report on an internal Fox News document accusing Hannity, John Solomon, Rudy Giuliani, Victoria Toensing, and Joe diGenova of regularly spreading disinformation on its air.[56]

* * *

Another criticism the Trump administration faces over the Soleimani strike relates to a post-strike briefing given to the Senate by Pompeo and Esper. After the briefing, the two Trump officials demand that senators not make any public comments about anything they have heard, even if the information in question is already publicly available.[57] Republican senator Mike Lee of Utah calls the admonition and the presentation it is part of "insulting."[58] Briefing attendees become even more concerned when Trump alleges that Soleimani had been planning to "blow up our embassy [in Iraq]"—an allegation that Pompeo and Esper had never mentioned in addressing members of Congress.[59] Nevertheless, Pompeo subsequently augments the president's allegation by insisting that "Soleimani was actively planning new attacks and he was looking very seriously at our embassies and not just the embassy in Baghdad."[60] Trump thereafter doubles down on Pompeo's startling new disclosure, declaring in an interview that "I can reveal that . . . it probably would've been four embassies [struck by Soleimani]," a claim not only never thereafter substantiated but subsequently denied outright by Esper—who seeks to justify Trump's comments by insisting that the president was only presenting his untutored opinion rather than, as his words imported, a "revelation" founded on processed intelligence.[61] Esper concedes that he personally "saw no evidence Iran [had] targeted four embassies," leading the New York Times to call the administration's justification for the extraordinary attack on Soleimani "ever-evolving"—even as the event it seeks to find a justification for is one that had "led [the U.S.] to the brink of war."[62]

In an interview with NBC, Trump national security advisor Robert O'Brien appears to falsely substantiate the president's baseless claims, "declin[ing] to say what, if any, measures [the] U.S. took to protect [the] three other embassies Trump says were threatened" to avoid "tip[ping] [America's] hand to adversaries"—a statement that falsely implies U.S. embassies were indeed under imminent threat from Soleimani.[63]

On January 10, the Associated Press reveals that Trump attempted a second assassination on the same night as the Soleimani attack, but hid it from U.S. media and voters.[64] The unsuccessful attack against Islamic Revolutionary Guard Corps commander Abdul Reza Shahlai is both mysterious and troubling in part because its most immediate beneficiary is Saudi Arabia. Shahlai had in 2011 "direct[ed] a plot to assassinate the Saudi ambassador in Washington," and at the time of the January 2020 attempt on his life was nowhere near U.S. forces but rather in Yemen, where Saudi Arabia has interceded militarily in a Yemeni civil war.[65] The *Washington Post* reports that the Shahlai revelation means "Trump's deceptions [about the Soleimani strike] were deeper than we thought," adding that "Shahlai is operating in Yemen, meaning the conflict he is waging at the moment is less against the United States than against Saudi Arabia."[66] Multiple Democrats in Congress imply, as summarized by the *Post*, that the Trump administration is engaged in a "wider effort that's mostly being concealed from Congress"—with the implication being that the Soleimani and Shahlai attacks could be part of preparation for a broader campaign against Iran in coordination with Israel, Saudi Arabia, and the UAE.[67]

The possibility that Trump is planning to use U.S. military assets to aid Saudi Arabia—despite no imminent threat to America from Iran—is only underscored when, on January 11, Trump boasts that "we're sending more [troops] to Saudi Arabia, and Saudi Arabia is paying us for it . . . they're paying us. They've already deposited $1 billion in the bank."[68] According to a Fox News interview with Trump, the president's view is that "we have a very good relationship with Saudi Arabia. [So] I said, listen, you're a very rich country. You want more troops? I'm going to send them to you, but you've got to pay us."[69] In fact, as CNN reveals on January 14, 2020, Trump's claim that MBS has already paid $1 billion for U.S. troops to act as mercenaries abroad is untrue, with Pentagon officials unable to find any evidence of such a payment. CNN later discovers a December 2019 payment by Saudi Arabia to the Pentagon in the amount of $500 million, but it remains unclear if the payment had been intended to cover past deployments or the new deployment Trump discussed in his interview with Fox News. Regardless, by late May 2020 Trump, Pompeo, and Jared Kushner are, according to a *Daily Beast* report, "prep[aring a] new weapons sale to Saudi Arabia"—despite the Saudis' apparent nonpayment for prior U.S. munitions transfers and the Senate having "rejected weapons sales to the Saudis" on a bipartisan basis following a "highly contentious $8 billion sale in 2019."[70]

Perhaps the most troubling revelation in the immediate aftermath of the Soleimani assassination, however, is a CNN report revealing that Erik Prince, a top national security adviser to both Trump and MBZ—the latter the leader of Saudi Arabia's closest ally, the United Arab Emirates, a key partner in the Saudis' war in Yemen against Iranian proxies—had in September 2015 advised the Trump campaign in writing that "[the fact] that Soleimani and his ilk are not already DEAD is a national disgrace for America."[71] The Prince memo, sent to Steve Bannon, was thereafter given to Michael Flynn, who had just days earlier become Trump's top national security adviser; Prince subsequently was granted a meeting with Flynn.[72] Less than a year later, Prince would attend a meeting at Trump Tower with Donald Trump Jr. at which he and George Nader, acting as emissaries from Saudi Arabia and the UAE, offered the Trump campaign illicit pre-election assistance.[73] Just two and a half months after this—a week before the 2016 presidential election—Trump would meet secretly at his "private residence" with Saudi crown prince Mohammed bin Salman himself, a summit Trump and his political team keep secret from U.S. voters until its discovery via a Freedom of Information Act request in January 2020.[74] There has as yet been no reporting on what the two men discussed, or on what—if any—agreements they may have made.

On January 4, forty-eight hours after the Soleimani assassination, former CIA director Michael Morell tells CBS News that the result of Trump's decision will be "dead civilian Americans," adding that "at a time and place of their choosing, [Iran is] going to conduct a terrorist strike that kills a senior American official. . . . That's why the Bush administration and the Obama administration chose not to do something like this."[75] The *New York Times* reports that "the American assassination of [Soleimani] may make it impossible for American forces to stay in Iraq . . . [and] could ease an ISIS comeback"; Trump's decision, the *Times* adds, is therefore a "two-for-one victory" for ISIS.[76] In a separate report, the *Times* reveals that "top Pentagon officials were stunned" when Trump chose to kill Soleimani.[77] Per the *Times*, the officials had put the option of assassinating Soleimani on the table for Trump "mainly to make other options seem reasonable."[78]

Administration claims of an "imminent" attack have largely fallen apart by January 4.[79] While continuing to insist Trump had "clear and unambiguous" intelligence about "plotting" by Soleimani, Gen. Milley concedes that he cannot say if an attack was "days," "weeks," or even "months" away.[80] Pompeo offers Fox News a simultaneously more dire and more vague assessment of the threat posed by Soleimani, upgrading the single "imminent" attack the administration had warned of to "a series of imminent attacks"—even as he confesses that "we don't know precisely when and we don't know precisely where" any of the attacks would have occurred.[81] Another U.S. official, speaking to the *Times* on condition of anonymity, reports that the intelligence Trump had on December 30, at the beginning of the seventy-two-hour window in which he made the decision to assassinate Soleimani, suggested "a normal Monday in the Middle East" and "business as usual," without anything out of the ordinary to justify a historic shift in U.S. foreign policy.[82] CNN will report that the evidence of any short- or medium-term threat from Soleimani was so disputed by Trump's top advisers that they believed they would need to "work behind the scenes to develop a legal argument [for the strike] before the operation was carried out."[83] The cable news network notes, too, Gen. Milley's implicit acknowledgment that killing Soleimani had not in fact prevented any attack, as he tells reporters following the Iranian general's death that the supposedly upcoming "attacks [associated with Soleimani] could still happen."[84]

January 4 sees "two [Iranian] rocket attacks near Iraqi bases that host American troops," according to the *New York Times*, as well as reports from "American spy agencies . . . that Iranian ballistic missile units across the country [have] gone to a heightened state of readiness."[85] Receiving this intelligence, Trump decides to escalate tensions considerably, not just sending 3,500 more troops to the Middle East—"one of the largest rapid deployments in decades," the *Times* notes—but also threatening to commit war crimes against Iran, specifically the destruction of Iranian cultural sites, if Iran responds with force to Soleimani's assassination. "Let this [tweet] serve as a WARNING," Trump writes on Twitter on January 4, "that if Iran strikes any Americans, or American assets, we have targeted 52 Iranian sites (representing the 52 American hostages taken by Iran many years ago), some at a very high level & important to Iran & the Iranian culture, and those targets, and Iran itself, WILL BE HIT VERY FAST AND VERY HARD."[86] Any U.S. soldier agreeing to carry out Trump's retaliatory strikes would face prosecution under the War Crimes Act, 18 U.S. Code § 2441, which carries a maximum penalty of execution by lethal injection.[87]

After Trump is informed that his proposed retaliation against Iran constitutes a war crime, he continues to insist, as summarized by the Associated Press, that Iranian cultural sites are "fair game."[88]

On January 7, Iran launches two missile attacks at Iraqi military bases hosting U.S. servicemembers.[89] The result of the attacks, which include the firing of over a dozen missiles, is 109 U.S. casualties, per Department of Defense guidelines defining a "casualty" as "any person who is lost to the organization by reason of having been declared beleaguered, besieged, captured, dead, diseased, detained, duty status whereabouts unknown, injured, ill, interned, missing, missing in action or wounded"; on January 7, all of the U.S. casualties are soldiers who have suffered traumatic brain injuries as a result of the Iranian attack.[90] Several Pentagon officials will tell CNN that the casualty count is "likely to continue to change," noting that "approximately 200" soldiers "were in the blast zone at the time of the attack."[91] Confronted by reporters over his and the Pentagon's initial claim that there had been "no casualties" in the twin missile strikes of January 7, Trump refers to as "headaches" the scores of traumatic brain injuries suffered by U.S. soldiers.[92] Per CNN, Trump calls traumatic brain injury "not very serious," and adds that "he does not consider potential brain injuries to be as serious" as "physical combat wounds."[93] The president adds that he would consider a soldier's injuries "bad" only if the soldier had "no legs and . . . no arms," and stands by his statement the day after the missile strike that "no Americans were harmed in last night's attack by the Iranian regime. We suffered no casualties."[94]

On January 9, the House votes 224–194 to limit Trump's ability to take additional military action against Iran.[95] On January 13, Trump declares that "it doesn't really matter" if Soleimani posed an "imminent" threat, a statement he augments days later by noting that Soleimani was "saying bad things" about the United States—the inference being that the man's rhetoric required both his death and the risk of an imminent war with Iran, whether or not the general's words portended an immediate danger to U.S. interests.[96] "How much of this shit do we have to listen to?" Trump fumes to a room full of GOP mega-donors on January 18. "How much are we going to listen to?"[97] At the same fundraising event, Trump boasts about adding trillions to the deficit by building up America's military might. "Who the hell cares about the budget?" he tells his financial supporters.[98] Covering the event, the *Washington Post* writes, "For most of President Barack Obama's time in office, Republicans seemed to care very much about the budget, making fears around the national debt and deficit their top talking point. They've backed off those concerns under Trump."[99]

By January 13, just ten days after the Soleimani assassination, the Trump administration has abandoned claims of an imminent threat in favor of what Attorney General Barr and Secretary of State Pompeo now call "a larger strategy of deterrence."[100] Barr, the nation's top law enforcement official, calls the "imminence" standard—which determines the legality of a unilateral foreign military strike—a "red herring."[101] Barr opines that as long as Trump knew there was "a campaign that involves repeated attacks on American targets," "I don't think there's a requirement frankly for, you know, knowing the exact time and place of the next attack."[102] Barr reveals to the media that DOJ was consulted about the strikes beforehand and had concluded it "was [not] a close call" because the president had "numerous different bases" to assassinate Soleimani.[103]

Two days later, the administration abruptly cancels four classified congressional briefings intended to explain to Congress its bases for the Soleimani attack, providing, per CNN, "little or no explanation for doing so."[104] On February 7, the administration cancels yet another key congressional briefing tied to Iran: the annual Worldwide Threats briefing given to the House Permanent Select Committee on Intelligence, run by Adam Schiff. *Politico* reports that the cancellation is intended to avoid "provoking Trump's ire."[105]

The same day that the Worldwide Threats briefing is abruptly cancelled, the *New York Times* releases a bombshell report, revealing that "it is unlikely that the [Iran-backed] militia the United States blamed for the [initial December 27] attack, Kataib Hezbollah, carried it out."[106] Per the *Times*, not only has Kataib Hezbollah "not had a presence in Kirkuk Province since 2014," but the area is in fact "hostile territory for Shiite militia like Kataib Hezbollah" because it is "notorious for attacks by the Islamic State, a Sunni terrorist group" hostile to Shiites.[107] Indeed, belying the fact that it was never blamed by Trump for the December missile strike that killed an American contractor, the Islamic State "had carried out three attacks relatively close to the base in the 10 days before the attack," and "Iraqi intelligence officials sent reports to the Americans in November and December warning that ISIS intended to target K-1"— the very base that was struck on December 27.[108] Moreover, the retrofitted civilian vehicle used in the December 27 attack, a Kia pickup truck, was "found . . . less than 1,000 feet from the site of an ISIS execution."[109] An eyewitness to events leading up to the attack, a local political official, reported seeing a truck "barely a mile from the launch site" shortly before the strike on K1; the truck was coming from "territory friendly to the Islamic State."[110] Consistent with all of this evidence, writes the *Times*, is the fact that "Kataib Hezbollah has denied responsibility for the attack."[111]

Abu Ali al-Basri, the director general of Iraqi intelligence and counterterrorism, will tell the *Times*, per its summary of the conversation, that "the United States did not consult Iraq before carrying out the December 29 counterattacks on Kataib Hezbollah. 'They did not ask for my analysis of what happened in Kirkuk and neither did they share any of their information,' he said. 'Usually, they would do both.'"[112]

In mid-January 2020, NBC News releases a major investigative report revealing that Trump had in fact first authorized the killing of Soleimani in June 2019, just days after the president signed a new defense pact with the United Arab Emirates.[113] NBC reports that "the timing . . . could undermine the Trump administration's stated justification for ordering the U.S. drone strike that killed Soleimani."[114] *Washington Post* columnist Greg Sargent writes that these "new details about [the] Soleimani killing further undercut Trump's lies."[115] When the administration sends a report to Congress on the Soleimani assassination in mid-February 2020, it makes no mention of any "imminent" attack by the Iranian general.[116]

On February 13, 2020, the U.S. Senate passes a bipartisan war powers resolution that, according to an Associated Press summary of its particulars, "says Trump must win approval from Congress before engaging in further military action against Iran."[117] The AP notes that "Trump is expected to veto the war powers resolution if it reaches his desk"—adding that this was precisely the fate of a similar measure the Senate passed in 2019, once again on a bipartisan basis, with respect to Trump's coordination of "U.S. involvement with the Saudi-led war in Yemen."[118]

The day after the Iran resolution passes the Senate, the *New York Times* summarizes a new congressional filing by the White House as conceding that "President Trump authorized the strike last month that killed Iran's most important general to respond to attacks that had already taken place and deter future ones."[119] The *Times* reports that the filing "contradict[s] the president's claim that he acted in response to an imminent threat."[120]

CHAPTER 39

THE IMPEACHMENT

The president's attempts to impede the impeachment inquiry the House of Representatives opens in late September 2019 are far-ranging and draconian. When the White House can block witnesses altogether, it seeks to do so; when it cannot, it tries to limit what individual witnesses can say.[1] Trump compares impeachment to a "lynching," tweets that it is "BULLSHIT," and claims that the impeachment inquiry has "treated [him] worse than anybody's been treated from a legal standpoint in the history of the United States."[2] He calls Adam Schiff a "low life," "shifty," and "dishonest"; says that the California representative should resign from Congress; falsely accuses him of "help[ing] write" the whistleblower complaint that precipitated Congress's fall 2019 impeachment inquiry; terms Schiff's rough paraphrase of the July 25 Trump-Zelensky call during a House committee hearing "illegal"; insists Schiff be "looked at . . . for treason," a death-penalty-eligible federal crime; and says that he wants the congressman to face justice of the "much tougher than [American]" sort that people do "in Guatemala," an apparent reference to summary execution that Schiff takes as a "threat."[3] Trump also threatens to fire the inspector general for the intelligence community, Michael Atkinson, who had determined the whistleblower's complaint was "credible" and on that basis reported it to Congress. The president will ultimately fire Atkinson in early April 2020, an act of retribution CNN calls "the latest case of the Trump administration removing officials who took part in the President's impeachment."[4]

As the fall 2019 impeachment inquiry moves into its second and third months, Trump and his aides begin their course of retaliation against civil servants who testify during the impeachment inquiry by "moving [them] out of their White House jobs."[5] As for the anonymous whistleblower, Trump implies at a rally that he or she could be considered a "spy," even as his legal adviser Joe diGenova calls whistleblowers "suicide bombers" and accuses the Democrats of both "sedition" and "regicide"—the latter a monarchistic as well as hyperbolic analogy that positions Trump as a king.[6]

An in-depth analysis of the whistleblower's complaint conducted by CNN in October 2019 will reveal that, contrary to Trump's repeated claims that the complaint is a "fraud," "con," "scam," and "hoax," all fourteen of the complaint's "key allegations" about the July 25 Trump-Zelensky call have been in short order proven correct.[7] The *Washington Post* calls the anonymously authored complaint "overwhelmingly substantiated—by the sworn testimony of administration officials, the inadvertent admissions of Trump's acting chief of staff and, most important, the president's own words."[8] Indeed, *PolitiFact* will name Trump's claim that the whistleblower complaint got the Trump-Zelensky call "almost completely wrong" its 2019 "Lie of the Year."[9]

Trump's anger at House Speaker Nancy Pelosi as the impeachment inquiry unfolds is as intense as diGenova's at whistleblowers and the Democratic Party. Trump at one point in fall 2019 tweets that Pelosi has committed "treason" and demands that she be "impeached."[10] In an effort to undermine the Pelosi-led inquiry, Trump contacts Attorney General Barr to ask him to declare that no laws were broken during his July 25 call with Zelensky; it is a request the usually compliant Barr rejects.[11] When the president sees Ambassador Yovanovitch testifying in the midst of the inquiry, he tweets an intimidating message to her, leading Fox News' Bret Baier to declare that with his ill-advised tweet Trump was, with respect to "witness tampering or intimidation," "adding an article of impeachment [in] real-time."[12] Yovanovitch, questioned by Schiff about the tweet just minutes after it is published—while she is still testifying before Congress—refers to the president's words as "very intimidating."[13]

As the impeachment vote in the House draws near—and therefore, too, a post-impeachment trial in the Senate—Trump "lash[es] out at GOP senators he sees as disloyal," calling Senate majority leader Mitch McConnell "as often as three times a day" and "telling McConnell he will amplify attacks on those Republicans who criticize him."[14] CNN observes that among the many immediate results of Trump's threats is the "House GOP disregard[ing] expert warnings that [a] debunked Ukraine theory [Crowd-Strike] helps Russia," with most Republicans in the House "unwilling to break from the President—even on a matter that national security experts warn could help Russia in its efforts to undermine Ukraine."[15]

At one point during the impeachment inquiry Trump gains "advance knowledge [of]," gives his "blessing" to, and "support[s]," along with House GOP leadership, a small group of House Republicans "storming" a Sensitive Compartmented Information Facility (SCIF) inside the Capitol building in order to gain access to a meeting. The Trump allies—some of them committing a federal crime by carrying an unauthorized cellphone into a SCIF—disrupt testimony by Pentagon official Laura Cooper in a "standoff" that lasts five hours and involves Trump's compatriots "[blowing] past police officers," "shouting," and "loudly denouncing . . . impeachment."[16] "In reality," *Politico* reports, despite the House Republicans' claims that they were interrupting a secret proceeding, "nearly a quarter of the House GOP conference already ha[d] full access to the depositions [being taken in the SCIF] through their membership on one of the three panels leading the impeachment inquiry."[17] The Trump-condoned action requires that the nonpartisan security director of the House Permanent Select Committee on Intelligence summon the House sergeant-at-arms.[18]

President Trump is not the only member of his family to seek to stir up mob anger at the impeachment inquiry. In mid-October 2019—as the investigation into whether Trump solicited foreign bribes unfolds in Congress—a "Lock him up!" chant begins at a Trump rally after Trump's son Eric accuses former vice president Joe Biden, without evidence, of embezzlement and "crookedness."[19] Meanwhile, two staunch Trump allies in the Senate, Senate Finance Committee chairman Sen. Chuck Grassley (R-IA) and Senate Homeland Security Committee chairman Ron Johnson, are using the beginning of the impeachment inquiry as an opportunity to call for a DOJ investigation of possible collusion between Hillary Clinton and Ukraine.[20] A similarly incongruous event had occurred in the House of Representatives in late September, when a group of Republicans opposed to Trump's impeachment for inviting a foreign power to interfere in a presidential election had insisted that Rep. Schiff be formally censured by the House for loosely paraphrasing, for rhetorical effect, a rough transcript of the July 25 Trump-Zelensky call.[21] In a sign of the lower chamber's intensely divided membership, 218 House Democrats vote to table the censure proposal in late October, while 185 Republicans—94 percent of the 197-strong Republican caucus in the House—vote to formally censure the HPSCI chairman. All of the 185 Republicans voting in favor of the resolution subsequently vote against impeaching the president.[22]

During the course of the impeachment inquiry, House Republicans and other Trump allies put forward six potential defenses of the president, all of which the *Washington Post* calls "dishonest and bad": (1) that "quid pro quos happen all the time," an argument that elides the fact that Trump is accused of seeking a quid pro not in service of U.S. interests but "corruptly," that is, for his own personal benefit; (2) that those who aided Trump's scheme "didn't know [the] Burisma [investigation] was about the Bidens," despite one of the chief architects of the scheme, Rudy Giuliani, discussing this publicly on repeated occasions, and Trump's own reference to Biden during his July 25 call with President Zelensky; (3) that "the whistleblower has been proved wrong," when in fact, as the *Post* reports, the whistleblower's complaint got "almost all of the key details about [the Trump-Zelensky call] correct"; (4) that "Trump isn't getting due process in the House inquiry," a complaint that sidesteps the fact that due process is not required in an impeachment inquiry because it is a noncriminal pre-trial investigative process; (5) that "abuse of power is not a crime," even though impeachment does not require a statutory crime, the articles of impeachment that ultimately issue from the House do indeed make out a prima facie case of criminal conduct, and abuse of power has been regarded as a constitutional "crime" under the Constitution's impeachment clause in every impeachment of a U.S. president; and finally (6) that "Ukraine didn't know about the frozen military aid"—a claim belied by major-media reporting, which reveals that Zelensky likely knew of the hold on military aid to Ukraine by the time of his July 2019 call with Trump.[23]

By early February 2020, the *Washington Post* will have identified thirty additional GOP defenses of Trump, including that "Trump is incapable of a quid pro quo" due to his own incompetence; that Trump's calls for foreign assistance in investigating Clinton and Biden were intended as political humor and therefore were "not serious"; that "the whistleblower is part of the 'deep state'"; that "impeachment is a coup d'état"; that "it's the media's fault"; and that everything is "moving too quickly."[24]

In December 2019, the House of Representatives brings forward two articles of impeachment against Donald Trump: one for abuse of power and one for contempt of Congress.[25] The former article lays out all the elements of a bribery charge under 18 U.S. Code § 201.[26] The federal bribery statute prohibits, in 18 U.S. Code § 201(b)(2)(A), "a public official, directly or indirectly, corruptly seeking anything of value personally in return for being influenced in the performance of any official act"; this language mirrors the first article of impeachment against President Trump, which accuses the president of "soliciting the Government of Ukraine to publicly announce investigations that would benefit his re-election, harm the election prospects of a political opponent, and influence the 2020 United States Presidential election to his advantage. President Trump also sought to pressure the Government of Ukraine to take these steps by conditioning official United States Government acts of significant value to Ukraine on its public announcement of the investigations ... [and] engaged in this scheme ... for corrupt purposes in pursuit of personal political benefit."[27]

By establishing in its first article of impeachment all the elements of bribery—a "public official," "directly," "corruptly," "seeking something of value personally," "in return for being influenced in an official act"—the House of Representatives announces perhaps the most serious charge ever formally leveled by Congress against an American president. Moreover, the article alleges that Trump's solicitation of a bribe from the Ukrainian president "compromised the national security of the United States and undermined the integrity of the United States democratic process."[28] As for its several-page factual predicate, the article details Trump's withholding from the Ukrainian government, with "corrupt" intent, both a White House visit and $391 million in military aid "to obtain an improper personal political benefit" through the announcement by Ukraine of investigations into the Burisma and CrowdStrike conspiracy theories.[29]

The second article of impeachment accuses Trump of a "violation of his constitutional oath faithfully to ... execute the office of President of the United States and, to the best of his ability, preserve, protect, and defend the Constitution of the United States," as well as a "violation of his constitutional duty to take care that the laws be faithfully executed," by "direct[ing] the unprecedented, categorical, and indiscriminate defiance of subpoenas issued by the House of Representatives pursuant to its [constitutional] 'sole Power of Impeachment.'"[30] The article goes on to accuse Trump of abusing his powers, subverting the Constitution, and "assum[ing] to himself functions and judgments necessary to the exercise of the 'sole Power of Impeachment' vested by the Constitution in the House of Representatives."[31] The factual predicate for the article is straightforward, having previously been laid out in the HPSCI report that preceded the articles: "President Trump ordered federal agencies and officials to disregard all voluntary requests for documents [during the impeachment inquiry] and defy all duly authorized subpoenas for records," as well as "direct[ing] all federal officials in the Executive Branch not to testify [before Congress]—even when compelled."[32] Just as the first article makes out a statutory bribery case under the constitutional heading of "abuse of power," the second article makes out an obstruction of justice case within the constitutional offense of "obstruction of Congress"; 18 U.S. Code § 1505 makes punishable by up to five years in federal prison the act of "corruptly impeding any investigation by any [congressional] committee"—exactly what the second article of impeachment against the president alleges.[33]

Trump's defense against the allegations—that he merely sought to fight corruption broadly writ in Ukraine—will by the time of the House's impeachment vote in December 2019 have been undercut by two revelations in major media over the preceding fall: first, that "in a letter sent to four congressional committees in May [2019] . . . undersecretary of defense for policy John Rood informed lawmakers that he 'certified that the Government of Ukraine has taken substantial actions to make defense institutional reforms for the purposes of decreasing corruption [and] increasing accountability,'" after which certification the president's ire toward Ukraine reached new heights, rather than subsiding; second, an October 2019 *Washington Post* report revealing that "the Trump administration has sought repeatedly to cut foreign aid programs tasked with combatting corruption in Ukraine and elsewhere overseas, White House budget documents show, despite recent claims from President Trump and his administration that they have been singularly concerned with fighting corruption in Ukraine."[34]

According to the House Permanent Select Committee on Intelligence, Trump is "the first President in the history of the United States to seek to completely obstruct an impeachment inquiry undertaken by the House of Representatives under Article I of the Constitution, which vests the House with the 'sole Power of Impeachment.'"[35] Advocates for the second article of impeachment will underscore that while the president may have been constitutionally permitted to, in the first instance, argue that certain privileged documents are not subject to congressional subpoena even during an impeachment inquiry, and that certain executive branch testimony compelled by Congress during the impeachment process may require modest curtailment via the omission of certain privileged White House communications, achieving this result would have required the president and his legal team to formally raise narrowly tailored assertions of privilege in response to specific evidentiary requests from Congress. As Trump instead elects to issue categorical orders that no documents or testimony should be provided to Congress by anyone in the branch of the federal government he leads, he becomes, on December 18, 2019, just the second president in American history—the first being Andrew Johnson in 1868—to be impeached for either abuse of power or obstruction of Congress, and the first to face an article of impeachment laying out the elements of an allegation of bribery.[36] According to a former federal prosecutor writing in the *Washington Post*, Trump may also be guilty—given the orders he gave to Volker and Sondland—of a criminal violation of the Hatch Act, which prohibits any person, including the president, from "commanding, coercing, or attempting to command, or coerce, any employee of the Federal Government . . . to engage in . . . any political activity"; each violation of the act is a felony punishable by up to three years in prison.[37]

According to *Politico*, it is only for political reasons that the House of Representatives does not seek to impeach President Trump for any conduct described in the April 2019 report filed by special counsel Robert Mueller. In the days leading up to the introduction of articles of impeachment, the dozen Democratic members of Congress "most vulnerable" to losing their 2020 reelection campaigns due to the conservative bent of their districts tell Speaker Pelosi, according to *Politico*, to "keep impeachment focused only on the Ukraine scandal."[38] At a meeting of the House Democratic leadership in early December, the chairman of the House Judiciary Committee (Jerrold Nadler of New York), the House majority leader (Steny Hoyer of Maryland), and the House majority whip (Jim Clyburn of South Carolina) all lobby Pelosi for an article of impeachment for obstruction of justice based on the Mueller Report; the chairman of the House Permanent Select Committee on Intelligence (Adam Schiff of California) offers instead a view consistent with Speaker Pelosi's own "long-held private belief that the caucus should take a narrower focus" for strategic reasons.[39]

That Rep. Schiff believes the Mueller Report to have in fact contained evidence of impeachable offenses is certain. As he tells *The Atlantic* in July 2019, "The Russians interfered in a presidential election to help Donald Trump," and the president "knew it was going on, welcomed it, and then lied about it and covered it up. . . . [T]hose actions and his actions since continue to put us at risk, because it encourages the Russians to get involved again."[40] The Mueller Report had exposed, said Schiff, "evidence of collusion in plain sight"—indeed, what "most Americans view as quintessential collusion with a foreign adversary"— adding that just because the presently available evidence "didn't meet the requirements of the criminal law doesn't make it any less corrupt."[41] As for Pelosi, she had told reporters, following Mueller's congressional testimony on his report, that her position was what "[it] has always been: whatever decision we make in that regard [on impeachment] would have to be done with our strongest possible hand, and we still have some outstanding matters [with respect to material and testimonial evidence] in the courts. It's about the Congress, the Constitution and the courts. And we are fighting the president in the courts."[42] The week that the House Judiciary Committee passes articles of impeachment, a Fox News poll finds that "53% of voters say Trump abused his power, 48% say he obstructed Congress, and 45% think that he committed bribery. Sixty percent of voters say it is generally wrong for Trump to ask leaders of foreign countries to investigate political rivals."[43]

The two articles of impeachment Democrats bring against Trump in December 2019 both make implicit reference to the Mueller Report and the Russia investigation broadly writ. In laying out the elements of a bribery case in an article of impeachment alleging abuse of power, House

Democrats add toward the conclusion of the article that "these actions were consistent with President Trump's previous invitations of foreign interference in United States elections"—a reference to Trump's public solicitation of Russian interference in the 2016 presidential election.[44] As the *New York Times* had reported in July 2018, "Trump invited the Russians to hack Clinton"; moreover, it was clear his invitation was a solicitation to provide him with a personal political benefit, and to do so at a time when he was prospectively offering the Kremlin the official act of opposing all sanctions on Russia over its annexation of Ukrainian territory, should he win the presidency.[45]

As for the obstruction of Congress article, it includes the following reference to the Mueller investigation: "These actions [Trump's acts of obstruction] were consistent with President Trump's previous efforts to undermine United States Government investigations into foreign interference in United States elections."[46] Indeed, the Mueller Report had, per the Associated Press, referred "ten instances of possible obstruction" by Trump to Congress for consideration in impeachment proceedings.[47] Moreover, the report had accused Trump and his aides, allies, agents, associates, and advisers of "sometimes provid[ing] information that was false or incomplete" and "delet[ing] relevant communications or communicat[ing] during the relevant period using applications that feature encryption or that do not provide for long-term retention of data or communications records. In such cases," Mueller wrote in his report, "the [Special Counsel's] Office was not able to corroborate witness statements through comparison to contemporaneous communications or fully question witnesses about statements that appeared inconsistent with other known facts."[48]

Just days prior to the introduction of the articles of impeachment, the HPSCI report had noted that not only did Trump issue orders to executive branch employees that ran contrary to law and the Constitution, but employees who testified before Congress despite Trump's admonition not to do so were subjected, by Trump, to a "brazen effort to publicly attack and intimidate" them.[49] By comparison, even President Richard Nixon, who voluntarily resigned the U.S. presidency in 1974 to avoid his imminent impeachment by the House of Representatives, instructed his employees to "appear voluntarily when requested" by Congress and "answer fully all proper questions."[50] Just so, not only did Nixon, unlike Trump, orchestrate substantial document production by the White House to Congress during the course of his impeachment inquiry, but he even agreed to give the House "more than 30 transcripts of White House recordings and notes from meetings with the President"—material that arguably could have been subject to a claim of executive privilege.[51] Nixon's ultimate refusal to turn over certain additional recordings and full, unedited records led to the House Judiciary Committee approving an article of impeachment for obstruction, which decision precipitated Nixon's resignation.[52]

Throughout the impeachment process in the House of Representatives, which lasts from September 24 through December 18, 2019, Trump's public statements are historically idiosyncratic. At one point after the whistleblower's report appears in major media, Trump declares, "We're fighting all the subpoenas," and he announces, counterfactually, that "I have an Article II . . . right to do whatever I want as president."[53] On September 26, Trump declaims, again counterfactually, that under the U.S. Constitution Congress is not "allowed" to impeach him, and that in his opinion there "should be a way of stopping [an impeachment]—maybe legally, through the courts."[54] As recorded in HPSCI's impeachment report, on October 8, 2019, the White House counsel's office "confirms that President Trump [had] directed his entire Administration not to cooperate with the House's impeachment inquiry"; White House counsel Pat Cipollone tells Congress that "President Trump cannot permit his Administration to participate in this partisan inquiry under these circumstances."[55] After October 8, according to HPSCI, "not a single document . . . [is] produced by the White House" as part of the committee's impeachment investigation, nor is there any document production from "the Office of the Vice President, the Office of Management and Budget, the Department of State, the Department of Defense, or the

Department of Energy," despite "71 specific, individualized requests or demands for records in their possession, custody, or control."[56] Trump even extends his nonproduction and no-testimony orders to include, as the December 2019 HPSCI report notes, "former officials no longer employed by the federal government."[57] Former officials refusing to comply with congressional subpoenas under White House instruction include former national security advisor John Bolton, former deputy assistant to the president for national security affairs Charles Kupperman, and (by December) former secretary of energy Rick Perry, who had resigned his office in October, effective December 1.[58]

Trump's intimidation of the more than a dozen executive branch officials who defy his directive not to testify before Congress is persistent, striking, and effective. According to the HPSCI report, he "issue[s] threats, openly discuss[es] possible retaliation, [makes] insinuations about their character and patriotism, and subject[s] them to mockery and derision. . . . The President's attacks were broadcast to millions of Americans—including witnesses' families, friends, and coworkers."[59] One predictable result is that several career public servants who testify before Congress in a way that displeases the president receive, in short order, a significant volume of death threats. Fiona Hill, Alexander Vindman, and law partners Bradley Moss and Mark Zaid (the last of these four being one of the attorneys for the anonymous CIA whistleblower) all report getting victimized in this way subsequent to being publicly attacked by the president.[60] Vindman in particular has to have his "security . . . monitored by the Army after he share[s] concerns about the safety of his family."[61]

At the State Department, Secretary Pompeo "force[s] out" Volker, according to the *Daily Beast*—despite Volker being "[Pompeo's] own Ukraine rep"—in order to help Trump "squash" the Ukraine scandal.[62] And Ambassador Taylor is asked to leave his post in Kyiv just days before Pompeo is due to visit the Ukrainian capital.[63] Per the *Wall Street Journal*, the timing of Taylor's firing "allow[s] Mr. Pompeo to avoid meeting or being photographed with an ambassador who has drawn President Trump's ire for his testimony in the congressional impeachment inquiry."[64]

As for the whistleblower, the HPSCI report recounts that "in more than 100 public statements about the whistleblower over a period of just two months, the President [has] publicly questioned the whistleblower's motives, disputed the accuracy of the whistleblower's account, and encouraged others to reveal the whistleblower's identity. Most chillingly, the President issued a threat against the whistleblower and those who provided information to the whistleblower regarding the President's misconduct, suggesting that they could face the death penalty for treason."[65] In early November, Trump urges reporters to reveal the whistleblower's name, insisting it would do "the public a service."[66]

Just prior to his impeachment, Trump sends a six-page letter to Speaker of the House Nancy Pelosi under penalty of a federal crime for lying to Congress for any misstatement. In the letter, Trump departs from his usual narrative by declining to say that there was no quid pro quo in his dealings with Ukraine; instead, he opts to quote Gordon Sondland saying so in a text message that Trump had secretly dictated to him, thereby arguably avoiding criminal liability for making the claim himself.[67] The letter, termed "rambling" by the *New York Times*, is historically extraordinary, and sees the president—who had in 2008 called for the impeachment of President George W. Bush for "lies"—arguing that the articles of impeachment against him, despite outlining the constitutional offenses of abuse of power and obstruction of Congress, are invalid because "they include no crimes, no misdemeanors, and no offenses whatsoever."[68] Trump goes on to express the opinion that House Democrats are "violating your oaths of office," "breaking your allegiance to the Constitution," "declaring open war on American Democracy," "display[ing] unfettered contempt for America's founding," "offending the Founding Fathers," "offending Americans of faith," "misquot[ing], mischaracteriz[ing], and fraudulently misrepresent[ing]" the July 25 Zelensky call, "falsely accusing me of doing what Joe Biden has admitted he actually did," "develop[ing] a full-fledged case of what many in the media call Trump Derangement Syndrome," "view[ing] democracy as your enemy," and "attempt[ing] to undo the election of 2016 and steal the election of 2020"—this last an observation the president punctuates with an exclamation point.[69] The letter, which all told includes eight exclamation points and receives widespread condemnation in the press as unpresidential, includes phrases like "you have found NOTHING!" and numerous false claims, including debunked allegations that the FBI used "spies" to monitor the 2016 Trump campaign, that impeachment is an "illegal, partisan attempted coup," and that special counsel Robert Mueller's office was staffed by "18 angry Democrat [sic] prosecutors."[70]

On December 13, 2019, the House Judiciary Committee passes the two articles of impeachment against Donald Trump by a party-line vote of 23–17, making President Trump the fourth president in U.S. history to face such a vote by the committee.[71] Over the next five days, at least a dozen newspaper editorial boards endorse Trump's impeachment, including those of the *New York Times*, the *Washington Post*, the *Los Angeles Times*, the *Boston Globe*, the *Chicago Sun-Times*, the *Philadelphia Inquirer*, the *San Francisco Chronicle*, the *Orlando Sentinel*, the *Salt Lake Tribune*, *USA Today*, the *Tampa Bay Times*, and the *Honolulu Star-Advertiser*.[72] Two other papers, the *St. Louis Post-Dispatch* and the *Connecticut Post*, conclude that Trump should either resign or, if he refuses, be impeached.[73] The editorial boards of the *Detroit News* and the *Chicago Tribune* argue for Trump to be censured by Congress rather than impeached.[74] The editorial board of one newspaper—the *Wall Street Journal*—announces that it opposes both censure and impeachment, though it adds, "We don't condone Mr. Trump's mention of Joe Biden in his call to Ukraine's President, which was far from perfect and reflects his often bad judgment."[75] Several major newspapers, including the *Arizona Republic*, the *Cincinnati Inquirer*, the *Columbus Dispatch*, the *Dallas Morning News*, and the *Houston Chronicle*, decline to stake out any position on impeachment prior to the House vote on the two pending articles, though some issue clear statements about the president's conduct, with the editorial board of the *Arizona Republic* calling Trump "dangerously reckless" and the *Houston Chronicle* editorial board supporting the opening of an impeachment inquiry in late July 2019, many weeks prior to its eventual initiation in September.[76]

In the days before the scheduled impeachment vote in the full House, a small number of Republicans break from their congressional colleagues to indicate that they are willing to consider—if not ready to commit to—censuring Trump, including Rep. Steve Chabot of Ohio, Sen. Pat Roberts of Kansas, and Sen. Lamar Alexander of Tennessee.[77]

On December 16, forty-eight hours before the final vote on impeachment, the House Judiciary Committee publishes a 169-page report alleging that President Trump committed "multiple federal crimes," including bribery, wire fraud, and obstruction of justice.[78] A separate analysis by the blog *Lawfare* will come to similar conclusions, including that Sondland's congressional testimony was the legal equivalent of an accusation of bribery against the president.[79]

On December 18, the House of Representatives votes on the two articles of impeachment against President Trump, passing the abuse of power article by a vote of 230–197 (with one representative, Hawaii Democrat Tulsi Gabbard, voting "present") and the obstruction of Congress article by a vote of 229–198 (with Gabbard again voting "present").[80] Trump thereby becomes just the third U.S. president ever to be impeached.[81] On the eve of his impeachment, Trump is asked by a reporter whether he takes any responsibility for the upcoming vote in the House. "No," Trump responds. "I don't take any. Zero, to put it mildly."[82]

While media coverage in December 2019 will observe that no Republicans voted in favor of Trump's impeachment and that the votes against the president's impeachment came from both parties, the reality of the historic event is more complicated. One independent representative, Justin Amash of Michigan, votes with the Democrats; as CNN reports, "when Justin Amash became the only congressional Republican to back impeachment [in July 2019] . . . he was essentially chased out of the party."[83] Meanwhile, according the *New York Times*, one of only three House Democrats to vote against impeachment, Jeff Van Drew of New Jersey, had told his staff the week before the vote—one day after a decisive face-to-face meeting with President Trump—that he would be leaving the Democratic Party to join the House Republican caucus. Per *The Hill*, after making the decision to switch parties during his meeting with the president, Van Drew "waits" to announce the switch until after he has cast his vote on impeachment as a Democrat.[84] The day after the vote, Trump meets for a second time face-to-face with Van Drew at the White House—with reporters present—and the day after that the president pledges his support for Van Drew's reelection and urges other Republicans to donate money to him.[85]

Rep. Amash's decision to vote in favor of Trump's impeachment, made while he was and believed he would remain a Republican, coupled with Van Drew's decision—only after deciding to leave the Democratic Party— to vote against the president's impeachment, complicates any analysis of how bipartisan the House tally for and against Trump's impeachment finally was. What can be said for certain is that in the lead-up to the December 18 vote there is one member of the Republican caucus who decides to vote for impeachment, and three members of the Democratic caucus who decide to vote against it.

One of the most vocal opponents of Trump's impeachment is Russian president Vladimir Putin, who—"echo[ing] Republican talking points," as the *New York Times* puts it—declares the day after Trump's impeachment that "one party that lost the elections, the Democrats, is now trying to find new ways [to win] by accusing Trump of collusion with Russia. But then it turns out there was no collusion, this can't be the basis for the impeachment. Now they came up with some pressure on Ukraine."[86] *Mother Jones* will observe in November 2019 that, with respect to Putin and Trump's simultaneous promulgation of "conspiracy theories about Ukraine interfering in the 2016 election," "the convergence of the two leaders' views on Ukraine is . . . notable."[87]

On the same day Putin's views on Trump's impeachment are revealed, Trump's views on the potential impeachment of a previous Republican president—George W. Bush—resurface. As CNN reports on December 18, in late 2008 Trump had told the cable news network that while the Clinton impeachment was "nonsense," it would have been "a wonderful thing" if the Democrats had impeached President Bush for his deceit on matters of foreign policy.[88] Facing down the prospect of his own impeachment in 2019, Trump will do an about-face, telling a crowd of reporters outside the White House in May that "to me, it's a dirty word, the word 'impeach.' It's a dirty, filthy, disgusting word."[89] On the same day that Trump's 2008 interview with CNN is republished, a 2016 tweet by his son Don Jr. goes viral; it reads, "Dear Clintons, You know what's deplorable? Being Impeached!!!"[90]

Several days after the impeachment, House attorneys "open [the] door to more articles of impeachment" as part of an oral argument in federal court.[91] The case before the court is whether former White House counsel Don McGahn—a witness to several of the ten incidents of alleged obstruction of justice detailed in the Mueller Report—can be forced to testify before Congress.[92]

As Trump is facing impeachment in the House in December 2019, Rudy Giuliani is in Ukraine, having "arriv[ed] with his shady band of conspiracy theorists," per *BuzzFeed News*.[93] The digital media outlet reports that Giuliani is "on a mission to 'destroy' the Democrats' impeachment narrative via a documentary series on the vehemently pro-Trump One America News (OAN) Network. But judging by the questionable cast of Ukrainian characters he's meeting, whatever information he manages to dig up is likely to be extremely dubious."[94] Giuliani returns from Ukraine on a "private jet that costs $3,300 per hour," the outlet reports, as well as noting, more startlingly, that the jet is owned by Ukrainian American billionaire Alexander Rovt—a Trump donor who's "done business in the past with Dmitry Firtash."[95]

News of Giuliani enjoying largesse from a business associate of the Kremlin-connected Firtash comes the same week federal prosecutors reveal that one of Firtash's lawyers has secretly "loaned" Lev Parnas (who is under indictment) $1 million through Parnas's wife, Svetlana.[96] As for Rovt, a company for which he provides financial backing, Spruce Capital, had previously given a $3.5 million mortgage "loan" to Paul Manafort almost immediately after Manafort's dismissal from the Trump campaign in August 2016—a time when Manafort's silence about his recent meetings with Kremlin agent Konstantin Kilimnik to transmit proprietary campaign data to the Russian-intelligence-linked businessman was paramount.[97] NBC calls Spruce Capital's failure to properly record the Manafort loan "highly unusual"; moreover, Manafort had left his name and signature off all the loan documents, used a shell company to execute the agreement, never filed mandatory paperwork detailing a repayment plan, never paid taxes on the transaction, and worked with Spruce's co-founder Joshua Crane to complete the deal.[98] In addition to receiving financial backing from Rovt via Spruce, Crane has in the past "partnered with Donald Trump on real estate deals," specifically as "a developer of Trump hotel projects."[99] The *Wall Street Journal* reports that as Giuliani's Rovt-provided private jet was taxiing to its gate upon its return to the United States, Trump called Giuliani to ask him, "What did you get?"[100]

Giuliani's receipt of an in-kind travel benefit from a close associate of Kremlin agent Firtash and Trump campaign manager Paul Manafort comes as the former New York City mayor is tweeting out some unusual allegations against President Obama. Specifically, Giuliani accuses the former president, without evidence, of money laundering, misuse of government funds, bribery, extortion, and collusion with a foreign power—coincidentally, the exact roster of offenses for which his client Trump stands accused in the media and by legal experts.[101] Giuliani's flurry of tweets also accuses former ambassador Yovanovitch of multiple perjuries and obstruction of justice, former vice president Joe Biden of money laundering, and someone (it is not clear who) of attempting to murder former Ukrainian prosecutor Viktor Shokin, with the president's personal attorney claiming without further explanation that Shokin was "poisoned, died twice, and was revived."[102]

Giuliani's odd public statements regarding Obama, Biden, Yovano-vitch, and Shokin are in keeping with another, even more cryptic series of statements the president's attorney had made the month before. In the latter half of November 2019 Giuliani had discussed, on television and Twitter and in at least one phone interview, that he had "insurance"—he at one point said "very, very good insurance"—in the event Trump decided "to throw [him] under the bus."[103] When the comments create an uproar in U.S. media, Giuliani adds to the confusion by explaining that the insurance policy that would protect him against being betrayed by the president comprises "files in my safe about the Biden Family's 4 decade monetizing of his office"—an alleged archive of inculpatory information that, if it existed, would profoundly benefit the president's political career and would therefore seem a poor insurance policy against the president's betrayal of his longtime friend and attorney.[104] Giuliani assures the public that his file on Biden will "appear immediately" if he should mysteriously "disappear."[105]

Trump aside, Giuliani will say, of possible legal repercussions for his actions in Ukraine, that federal prosecutors would be "idiots" and "out of their minds" if they were to investigate his clandestine work in Kyiv. "If they're investigating me, they're assholes," Giuliani tells *New York* magazine in a December 2019 interview. "They're absolutely assholes if they're investigating me."[106] Giuliani's admonitions notwithstanding, according to *Vanity Fair* Giuliani is presently the subject of three federal investigations over his activities in Ukraine: one investigation by federal prosecutors for "potential campaign-finance violations and failure to register as a foreign agent" and "possible charges for conspiracy or violating laws against bribing foreign officials," and two additional investigations constituting "a counterintelligence investigation as well as a criminal investigation into Giuliani's business relationship with Lev Parnas and Igor Fruman."[107] Per CNN, the counterintelligence investigation is focused on "whether a foreign influence operation was trying to take advantage of Giuliani's business ties in Ukraine and with wealthy foreigners to make inroads with the White House."[108] As for the criminal investigation of Giuliani, it is said to be connected to a still "widen[ing]," post-indictment investigation of Parnas and Fruman, which has come to "include records of extravagant spending at Trump hotels and millions of dollars in financial transfers," as well as the question of "whether other people, including foreign nationals, were trying to influence the top levels of government and impact the 2020 presidential campaign."[109] The investigation of "activities surrounding Rudy Giuliani's back-channel campaign in Ukraine," notes *BuzzFeed News*, "has extended beyond campaign finance violations . . . and may examine more serious financial crimes," including "money laundering and fraud."[110]

In late November, Trump appears to do precisely what Giuliani had feared—"throw [him] under the bus"—by telling former Fox News host Bill O'Reilly that he in fact never sent his personal attorney to Ukraine.[111] The claim contradicts Trump's statement to Zelensky on July 25 that he wanted the Ukrainian leader to "speak to [Rudy]" and that "I will ask him to call you," after which (in keeping with Zelensky's July 25 remark to Trump that "we are hoping very much that Mr. Giuliani will be able to travel to Ukraine and we will meet once he comes to Ukraine") the former New York City mayor became deeply involved in back-channel negotiations with Zelensky aide Andriy Yermak over a White House visit for Zelensky, military aid for Ukraine, and Biden and Clinton investigations for Trump.[112]

In the same week that Trump disclaims any knowledge of Giuliani's activities in Ukraine, he appears to do the same with respect to Gordon Sondland, the other Trump adviser who had been in touch with him about Ukraine on the day of his call to Zelensky and on repeated occasions thereafter. On November 20, the day of Sondland's public congressional testimony, Trump declares of the man he appointed to be his ambassador to the European Union, "I don't know him very well. I have not spoken to him much. This is not a man I know well. . . . I don't know him well."[113] On the same day, Giuliani—whether at Trump's directive or otherwise—similarly distances himself from Sondland, tweeting a claim that "I never met [Sondland] and had very few calls with him, mostly with Volker."[114] Giuliani emphasizes his view that Sondland's congressional testimony constitutes "speculat[ion] based on VERY little contact" with Giuliani himself.[115] Giuliani also tweets that "I have NO financial interests in Ukraine, NONE!"[116]

During his December 2019 trip overseas to film a documentary with OAN, Giuliani travels to Hungary—home of Trump and Putin ally Viktor Orban—meeting there with Lutsenko before traveling on to Kyiv to meet with Shokin and Lutsenko's deputy Kulyk.[117] When the *New York Times* asks Giuliani whether he has kept Trump apprised of his movements in Budapest and Kyiv, the president's attorney refuses to answer, though Trump himself will say that "[Giuliani] says he has a lot of good information" during the trip and "I hear he's found plenty."[118]

One of the men Giuliani meets in Ukraine in December 2019 is Andriy Derkach, the Ukrainian lawmaker who is "working to build a corruption case against Hunter Biden."[119] Given that any such case would necessarily include Trump's chief domestic political rival as a key witness, Giuliani's contact with Derkach constitutes an additional attempt to work directly with elements of the Ukrainian government to influence the 2020 presidential election.[120] Derkach is a former member of Manafort and Yanukovych's pro-Kremlin Party of Regions, and, in addition to attending "Dzerzhinsky Higher School of the KGB in Moscow," he is "the son of a KGB officer."[121] A day prior to Giuliani's arrival in Kyiv, Derkach seeks to make contact with Lindsey Graham, Devin Nunes, and Trump's acting chief of staff, Mick Mulvaney; his aim, according to the *Washington Post*, is to encourage the three Trump advisers' "participation" in his activities relating to the Bidens.[122]

Though the *Washington Post* reports that "analysts have dismissed Derkach as spreading disinformation to support the [Burisma conspiracy] theory . . . promoted by Trump allies," a review of the former Ukrainian lawmaker's history reveals new indications that Trump and the Kremlin's efforts to spread pro-Russia, anti-Ukraine conspiracy theories date back years. Specifically, the *Post* notes that "Derkach has previously led calls to investigate the Bidens and alleged Ukrainian interference in the 2016 U.S. elections. In 2017, he wrote a letter to the Ukrainian prosecutor general's office, demanding an investigation into alleged interference in the elections by Ukrainian officials to hamper Trump's campaign."[123] Derkach's 2017 letter urging the U.S. government to investigate the Kremlin's conspiracy theories about the 2016 presidential campaign was sent just "one day before Trump called on the U.S. attorney general's office . . . to investigate 'Ukrainian efforts to sabotage the Trump campaign.'"[124]

Dan Eberhart, "a prominent Republican donor and Trump supporter," will say of Giuliani's December 2019 trip to Ukraine, per the *Washington Post*, that "the fact that Giuliani is back in Ukraine is like a murder suspect returning to the crime scene to live-stream themselves moon dancing. . . . It's brazen on a galactic level."[125] As for Giuliani's traveling companion—the far-right media outlet OAN—at least one of its journalists is paid by the Kremlin, according to the *Daily Beast*, which observes that "stories broadcast by the Trump-endorsed One America News Network sometimes look like outtakes from a Kremlin trolling operation," such as a "wholly fabricated" segment on Hillary Clinton allegedly "funding," according to a report filed by OAN employee Kristian Brunovich Rouz, "bricks, hammers, bats, and chains" for the left-wing movement Antifa.[126] OAN is also found by the *Daily Beast* to have aired multiple "debunked" stories about George Soros, as well as audio and video rife with "Kremlin propaganda" and content that is "dedicated to conspiracy theories and fake news, and . . . overtly supportive of Russia's global agenda."[127] The digital media outlet quotes former FBI agent Clint Watts's premise that OAN is "a merger between Russian state-sponsored propaganda and American conservative media."[128]

While overseas with the Kremlin-friendly OAN, Giuliani issues a threat against future U.S. aid to Russia's enemy Ukraine, tweeting, per the *Washington Post*, that "U.S. assistance to Ukraine on anti-corruption reforms could face a 'major obstacle' until the 'conversation about corruption in Ukraine' is resolved" by acknowledging allegedly "'compelling' evidence of criminal misdeeds by [Joe] Biden."[129]

CHAPTER 40

THE TRIAL

On December 3, 2019, Trump speaks publicly about his desire not only to have a post-impeachment trial in the Senate, but also to have a number of his aides testify in the proceedings. "I want them to testify," the president tells reporters, "but I want them to testify in the Senate, where they'll get a fair trial."[1] Less than six weeks later, Trump castigates the Senate for agreeing to hold a trial at all, tweeting, "Many believe that by the Senate giving credence to a trial based on the . . . Impeachment Hoax, rather than an outright dismissal, it gives the partisan Democrat Witch Hunt credibility that it otherwise does not have. I agree!"[2] CBS News, after speaking with a Trump confidant, reports that certain Republican senators were warned pre-trial that if you "vote against the president . . . your head will be on a pike."[3]

After five days of "procedural moves," the impeachment trial of President Trump begins in earnest in the U.S. Senate on January 21, 2020—with a key unresolved question being whether the trial schedule proposed by Senate majority leader Mitch McConnell will permit senators to intelligently follow House managers' presentation of their case. The schedule McConnell develops, which he does not reveal publicly until shortly before it is to be voted on by the Senate, grants both House managers and the president's legal counsel twenty-four hours of opening argument—but only forty-eight hours within which to complete it.[4] The resulting trial calendar, which would see trial coverage beginning at 1:00 PM and ending at 3:00 AM or later each day, prompts the hashtag #MidnightMitch to trend on Twitter; more important, it sparks pushback from within the fifty-three-member Senate GOP caucus.[5]

Even after the two sides' opening arguments are extended from four days total to six days, significant questions arise about whether Republican members of the Senate are prepared to fulfill their oaths to act as impartial jurors. Within a day of the trial beginning, Sen. Rand Paul (R-KY) announces that there are already forty-five Republican votes—85 percent of the GOP caucus in the Senate—to immediately dismiss the articles of impeachment without hearing any arguments, calling any witnesses, or reviewing any documentary evidence.[6]

Among Trump's attorneys for the impeachment trial are Eric Herschmann, whose law firm (Kasowitz Benson Torres) is at the time of the trial representing Ukrainian oligarch Ihor Kolomoisky, a man the *New Republic* reports has been "plying tales about Biden in order to erase what may well be the largest money-laundering case the U.S. has ever seen." Herschmann, whose firm arguably faces a conflict of interest in representing both Trump and Kolomoisky—as the latter is a witness in the very case Herschmann is trying—is specifically tasked with lecturing Congress on Hunter Biden's alleged conflicts of interest in Ukraine.[7] Another Trump attorney, Pam Bondi, is likewise tasked with lecturing Congress on the corruption of the Bidens. Per *The Hill*, however, Bondi herself has faced serious allegations of corruption, having "requested and received money from Trump as her office was considering whether to join the New York [legal] action [against Trump University]"; the media outlet calls such a request for cash donations by a prosecutor from a potential defendant not just "inappropriate" but "something [Trump] clearly knew [was inappropriate] when he signed his Foundation's $25,000 check to support Bondi."[8] The attorney on Trump's legal team tasked with arguing that Democrats are trivializing impeachment is Kenneth Starr, the independent counsel who led the charge to impeach Democratic president Bill Clinton for abuse of power following his affair with a White House intern—and whose late-in-life conversion to opposing a Republican president being impeached for the very same offense on the grounds that impeachment requires a statutory crime had in August 2019 led *Esquire* to call his public statements on the matter "the most incredible hypocrisy in the history of cable news."[9] Trump attorney Mike Purpura, charged with establishing that the president did not engage in a quid pro quo, gives an hour-long presentation on the topic to the Senate on Monday, January 27, 2019—less than a day after a report on John Bolton's unpublished book manuscript confirms that, per the president's former national security advisor, Trump outlined a quid pro quo to Bolton directly and explicitly.[10]

The Trump attorney tasked with further advancing Starr's argument that impeachment requires articles with statutory offenses in their titles is Alan Dershowitz, who like Starr had taken the opposite position during Clinton's trial in 1999.[11] The two men also jointly represented serial child sex offender and longtime Trump friend Jeffrey Epstein in the 2000s; when Gawker investigated the ex-convict Epstein's "black book" for "keeping track of his friends and associates" in 2015, it was found to have "two addresses, 14 phone numbers, and an emergency contact" for Trump.[12] Like Dershowitz and Starr, another Trump attorney, Robert Ray, has lately reversed his position on whether abuse of power and obstruction constitute "high crimes and misdemeanors"; Ray was the independent counsel for the Whitewater investigation of the Clintons in the late 1990s and early 2000s, during which case he took the view that both abuse of power and obstruction are impeachable offenses.[13]

Two Trump impeachment attorneys, Jay Sekulow and Pat Cipollone, face accusations of improperly representing the president while they are witnesses in his case, with the former also facing persistent accusations of corruption. The Associated Press reports that "charities" have "steered $65 million to Trump lawyer Sekulow and [his] family"; these charities include the nonprofit Christian legal advocacy group the American Center for Law and Justice (ACLJ), where Sekulow is "chief counsel" along with five other ACLJ attorneys who are "named . . . as members of Trump's defense team"—even though federal law bars the ACLJ from "engaging in partisan political activities."[14] Per the Associated Press, "10 years of tax returns for the ACLJ and other charities tied to Sekulow" reveal that "from 2008 to 2017, the most recent year [of tax returns] available . . . more than $65 million in charitable funds were paid to Sekulow, his wife, his sons, his brother, his sister-in-law, his nephew and [for-profit] corporations they own."[15]

Allegations of corruption aside, in the months leading up to Trump's impeachment trial both federally indicted Trump agent Lev Parnas and federally convicted Trump agent Michael Cohen allege that Sekulow is an eyewitness to material facts in the Russia and Ukraine investigations—facts that are arguably not covered by attorney-client privilege. Parnas reports that Sekulow worked with four of Trump's other attorneys to provide Parnas with a sixth Trump attorney, John Dowd, as counsel; Parnas alleges that from the beginning of Dowd's representation of him the Trump lawyer worked to silence him rather than zealously advocate for his interests. Meanwhile, Cohen accuses Sekulow of urging him to amend his congressional testimony to withhold key evidence from Congress.[16]

Nor is the other co-lead defense counsel at Trump's impeachment trial, White House counsel Pat Cipollone, free of accusations of a conflict of interest. House Democrats seek his recusal from the trial on its second day, arguing that Cipollone—who is not the president's personal counsel but represents the Office of the Presidency—is a "material witness" to controversial actions and deliberations by Trump that arguably fall well outside the scope of his official duties as president.[17]

The only Trump impeachment attorneys not the subject of some controversy during the impeachment trial are Jane Raskin and Patrick Philbin.[18] Five other Trump attorneys or members of Trump's legal team—Giuliani, diGenova, Toensing, Parnas, and Fruman—cannot represent him or do work on his behalf during his impeachment trial because they are either key witnesses in ongoing federal criminal investigations connected to the Ukraine scandal or under federal indictment; Giuliani, however, does make a public offer, in late December 2019, to "try the case" for Trump before the Senate, including conducting unspecified "demonstrations" for the senators.[19] Two former Trump attorneys, Dowd and Kasowitz, arguably cannot represent Trump at his impeachment because of conflicts of interest centering on their involvement with two witnesses (Parnas and Kolomoisky, respectively) in the Ukraine investigation. Nor can Trump readily be represented by Trump Organization attorneys Alan Garten or Alan Futerfas, as both are, at the time of Trump's impeachment, significant witnesses in at least one ongoing federal investigation.[20] As for longtime Trump attorney Michael Cohen, he is imprisoned at the time of his former client's impeachment trial.[21]

With only two cameras permitted in the Senate chamber—both controlled by the Senate itself—the public comes to rely on on-site media to describe the scene inside the Senate chamber.[22] Reporters' eyewitness accounts reveal that some Republican senators spend their time as jurors playing with fidget spinners (Burr of North Carolina, Cotton of Arkansas); reading unrelated books (Blackburn of Tennessee, Cornyn of Texas); smuggling banned wearable tech into the room (Cornyn); doodling sketches of the U.S. Capitol (Paul of Kentucky); playing crossword puzzles (Paul); impermissibly leaving the chamber when the chief justice refuses to out a federal whistleblower on camera (Paul); chatting with other senators, contrary to Senate trial rules (Cotton, Ernst of Iowa, Sasse of Nebraska, Scott of South Carolina, Perdue of Georgia, Cassidy of Louisiana); trying unsuccessfully to chew tobacco until reprimanded by the Senate sergeant at arms (Sasse); giving interviews to Fox News from a remote location while the trial is in session (Blackburn); or sleeping (Risch of Idaho and a "few" others, according to Fox News).[23] As the New York Times notes, "cameras were primarily trained on those speaking at the podium, which allowed some members to rest their eyes out of view."[24]

As the impeachment trial is in the midst of opening arguments, a former top aide to Republican president George W. Bush, Michael Gerson, writes in the Washington Post that "watching Republican senators complain that there is 'nothing new' in the case made by House impeachment managers, while they are actively opposing the introduction of new evidence and new testimony, is confirmation of [their] barefaced bad faith."[25] He adds that Republican senators "aren't serving the country" and, "having decided that no amount of evidence would be sufficient for conviction, they realize that the presentation of a full and compelling case would convict them of servility and institutional surrender. So a quick and dirty Senate trial is the best way to limit the exposure of their malpractice."[26]

Not only is there an effort by GOP jurors to shorten the trial by opposing witnesses and additional evidence post-argument, but they try as well to shorten their own service as jurors. Media reports establish that many Republican senators are not—despite Senate rules requiring it—present in the Senate chamber for large portions of the trial, with *Politico* noting that at one point twenty-four GOP senators (45 percent of the GOP caucus) were absent.[27] As noted by *Law & Crime*, McConnell and Senate minority leader Chuck Schumer (D-NY) had issued a joint letter to all senators prior to the trial ordering both caucuses to "plan to be in attendance at all times during the proceedings" and to "remain in their seats at all times they are on the Senate floor during the impeachment proceedings."[28] Despite this admonition, Republican senator John Barrasso of Wyoming acknowledges, per the *Wall Street Journal*, that "Republican senators . . . ha[ve] left the chamber for long periods of time."[29] Less than three hours into House Democrats' three days of opening arguments, Barrasso announces on MSNBC that the trial is a "political stunt" whose sole aim is to "overturn[ ] the last election . . . [and] the next one, too."[30] Jim Risch of Idaho tells the *Wall Street Journal* that some Republicans who left their seats and their role as jurors in contravention of Senate rules may have had "an inclination to visit with a friend [outside the chamber] about an issue."[31]

According to Reuters, on day two of opening arguments in the nation's third-ever impeachment trial, the first Republican leaves his seat after twenty minutes.[32] While on occasion Democrats likewise leave their seats—with Reuters singling out Bennet of Colorado, Sanders of Vermont, and Klobuchar of Minnesota, all Democrats then in the midst of presidential runs—by and large the tallies taken by reporters consistently show a sizable percentage of the GOP caucus, along with a smaller number of Democratic senators, absent from their seats as Democratic

House managers lay out their case.[33] One Reuters assessment counts twenty-two absent Republicans and nine absent Democrats; *Yahoo News* journalist Jon Ward counts twelve Republicans and zero Democrats absent from the chamber at another point in the trial; CNN captures a moment at which there are fifteen empty Republican seats and eleven empty Democratic seats; and the New York *Daily News*, the most persistent observer of senators' comings and goings, finds, as summarized by *Law & Crime*, that "a large bloc of Republican Senators . . . skipped large portions of [day one of opening arguments in] the impeachment trial, flouting Senate rules requiring them to remain in their seats at all times during the proceedings."[34] Much like the *Daily News*, *Politico* notes that those senators who leave the room entirely for long periods—rather than merely their seats—are overwhelmingly Republican, with "nearly all" Democrats present in the chamber during an extended observation by the digital media outlet.[35] Likewise, CNN notes that, based on its various counts, "most [of the empty seats] were on the Republican side."[36] One count conducted by the *Daily News* registers twenty-one out-of-seat GOP senators—40 percent of the GOP caucus—and just two Democrats, with "most" of the twenty-one Republicans out of the room altogether.[37]

Of the fifty-three Republican senators sitting as jurors in the impeachment trial, at least four—Portman of Ohio, Johnson of Wisconsin, Graham of South Carolina, and Braun of Indiana—are potential eyewitnesses in the case. None of the four recuse themselves from service as jurors, and every majority vote throughout the trial, including votes on the admission of witnesses and documents, goes the president's way by a sufficiently narrow margin that the recusal of these senators would have led to a different result.[38] Lev Parnas opines, in an MSNBC interview at the Capitol during the impeachment trial, that in his own experience, "Trumpworld is like a cult, and a lot of these [GOP] senators are in the cult."[39] Indeed, another GOP juror, Sen. McConnell, faces allegations that his public pre-trial promise to be partial to the president and to coordinate with him throughout the trial renders him ineligible to serve as a juror.[40] After McConnell successfully closes the evidentiary record in the impeachment trial without the admission of any new witnesses or documents, the *Wall Street Journal* reveals that "McConnell's office . . . advised the president's legal team throughout the process on which arguments were important to be made on the floor to resonate with certain undecided senators"; the revelation prompts NYU law professor, *Just Security* editor, and former special counsel to the general counsel of the Defense Department Ryan Goodman to declare the impeachment trial a "mistrial."[41]

During the first few days of the trial, Trump is in Davos, Switzerland, at the annual World Economic Forum. While there, he brags about having successfully withheld subpoenaed documents from the House during the impeachment inquiry. "We have all the material," Trump says at a press conference at the forum. "They don't have the material."[42] As soon as Trump returns from Switzerland, he sets a personal record for most tweets in a day, publishing 142 in total on January 22, 2020.[43] Shortly thereafter, Trump undertakes a series of official acts that risk the appearance of attempting to influence his impeachment trial, including sending Mike Pompeo for a friendly photo op with Zelensky in Ukraine—while still withholding a White House invitation from the Ukrainian president— and announcing unexpectedly an Israeli-Palestinian peace "deal" that the *New York Times* calls the "hardest to take seriously" of any such plan ever announced by a U.S. president.[44] Days later, the *Washington Post* reports on the White House's intention of "keeping Ukraine aid intact in [its] new budget, a big departure from past efforts to slash assistance."[45] The administration also announces—in another seeming bid to portray itself as friendly to Ukraine and tough on Russia—that it will "issue[ ] new sanctions related to Russia's takeover of Crimea."[46]

Of Trump's proposed Israeli-Palestinian peace deal, the *Times* writes that it "seem[s] nothing more than a cynical attempt at a diversion by two politicians in trouble [Trump and Netanyahu], a sop to their right-wing bases as each leader vies for re-election—Mr. Netanyahu in early March, Mr. Trump in November. A chorus of analysts declared the deal dead on arrival and worse, an American abdication of any mediating role [between

Israel and the Palestinians] in the future."[47] Indeed, just a day before the plan's hasty rollout, the Palestinian Authority cuts all diplomatic ties with both Israel and the United States, with the Palestinian prime minister announcing that the Trump-Netanyahu proposal is simply "a plan to finish off the Palestinian cause."[48]

As the impeachment trial continues, polling shows strong support for the calling of witnesses and some sort of punishment for the president. A Pew poll taken from January 6 through January 19 finds that 51 percent of Americans support Trump's removal from office, and that nearly a third of Republicans deem Trump to have been a lawbreaker while in office; a Quinnipiac poll reports that 75 percent of American voters want to see witnesses in the impeachment trial; and a *Politico*–Morning Consult poll reveals that 57 percent of American voters oppose Trump using executive privilege to block witnesses from appearing.[49] After the completion of the House managers' case, a Fox News poll taken during the course of the managers' presentation—from January 19 through January 22—reveals that 50 percent of Americans want to see the president convicted by the Senate and removed from office.[50]

The trial comprises just over eighty hours of debate, including a day of rules debates, six days of opening arguments, a two-day question-and-answer period, and a debate over the admission of witnesses and documents.[51] The Associated Press, citing "many of the nation's TV executives," calls the event—marked by arguments stripped of witnesses or evidence—"not ready for prime time."[52] One exception is an extraordinary presentation by Trump attorney Alan Dershowitz, whose defense of the president echoes disgraced former president Richard Nixon's infamous post-resignation insistence that "when the president does it . . . that means it is not illegal."[53] According to Dershowitz, because "every public official . . . believes that his election is in the public interest," and because a president cannot be impeached for an official act they subjectively believe advances the "public interest," if a president "does something that he believes will help him get elected . . . that cannot be the kind of quid pro quo that results in impeachment."[54] Dershowitz's argument results in his being "excoriated" by his "former colleagues, students and fellow lawyers," who "warn [that his argument] essentially renders the impeachment process meaningless."[55] Indeed, as the impeachment trial unfolds, the *Washington Post* editorial board declares that Trump's defense is "designed to destroy [the] guardrails on presidential power," that the trial itself is a "truncated" and "rigg[ed]" event that is a "perversion of justice," and that Republicans' successful effort to massage the process to ensure an acquittal will "gravely damage the only mechanism the Constitution provides for checking a rogue president."[56]

In the midst of the Trump defense team's three-day opening argument, the *New York Times* releases a bombshell report summarizing sections of a soon-to-be-published book by John Bolton.[57] According to the *Times*, Bolton's forthcoming book will make the following key submissions: that in August 2019, Trump directly confessed to Bolton a quid pro quo involving military aid to Ukraine and the announcement of investigations into Biden and Clinton by the Ukrainians; that Trump intended to continue the aid freeze for as long as was necessary to obtain dirt on Biden; and that Bolton had revealed Trump's plot to Attorney General Barr when he first learned about it—a claim Barr will deny but refuses to speak about further.[58] *Vanity Fair* builds upon the *Times* report by emphasizing that after Bolton expressed concerns to Barr about Trump "granting favors" to two autocrats his company does substantial business with—Xi Jinping of China and Recep Erdogan of Turkey—"Barr allegedly echoed [those concerns by] . . . suggesting the president was exercising 'undue influence over what would typically be independent [federal] inquiries' into companies in Turkey and China."[59] According to Bolton's account, summarized by the *New York Times*, "Barr singled out Trump's conversations with Mr. Xi about Chinese telecommunications firm ZTE," the sanctions against which Trump lifted in 2018 "over objections from his own advisers and Republican lawmakers." Barr also mentioned Trump's remarks to Erdogan that year "about the investigation of . . . state-owned bank [Halkbank] . . . on fraud and money-laundering charges."[60] In February 2020, CNN will report that,

Barr's statements to Bolton in the first half of 2019 notwithstanding, the attorney general had in fact been working behind the scenes on Trump's behalf to end the Halkbank case altogether.[61] Per CNN, "Barr personally spearheaded an effort [in 2019] to negotiate a settlement with the bank that would have allowed it to sidestep an indictment after Turkey's President, Recep Tayyip Erdogan, pressed Trump in a bid to avoid charges."[62]

Politico reports that the Bolton revelations "rock" the impeachment trial and so "throw[ ] [Republicans] off balance" that their responses to the *Times* reporting are "scattered" and "all-over-the-map."[63] "If Bolton's claims are substantiated," the digital media outlet writes—a circumstance that would first require Republicans to allow Bolton to testify before them—"they would deal a major blow to one of the White House's core defenses in the trial: that no witness has firsthand knowledge of Trump linking Ukraine aid to his desire for investigations of his political rivals."[64]

Just days after its first report on Bolton's unreleased book, the *Times* publishes a second major revelation from the text, disclosing that in "early May [2019]" Trump held a meeting with Bolton, Mulvaney, and Cipollone at which he gave Bolton an "instruction" to "help with his pressure campaign to extract damaging information on Democrats from Ukrainian officials."[65] Per the *Times*, Bolton's book establishes that both Mulvaney and Trump's lead attorney throughout the impeachment trial, Cipollone, are "early witnesses in the effort that they have sought to distance the president from."[66] The early May 2019 Trump-Bolton-Mulvaney-Cipollone meeting also situates Zelensky's May 7 emergency meeting in Kyiv about how to handle pressure from Trump in the middle of a critical two-week period in which Giuliani announces plans to travel to Ukraine to "meddl[e] in an investigation" (May 9) and then sends a letter directly to Zelensky on May 10—"with [Trump's] knowledge and consent," the attorney writes in the letter—asking for a face-to-face meeting "in my capacity as personal counsel to President Trump . . . not as [counsel to the] President of the United States."[67]

Concurrent to these *New York Times* articles on Bolton, Rep. Eliot Engel, the Democratic chairman of the House Foreign Relations Committee, reveals that Bolton approached him in late September 2019 to urge him to "look into the recall of Ambassador Marie Yovanovitch. He strongly implied that something improper had occurred around her removal as our top diplomat in Kyiv."[68]

As the *New York Times* is publishing details about Bolton's forthcoming book, Joseph Bondy, Lev Parnas's attorney, informs Congress that Parnas can testify under oath to facts about Trump, Giuliani, and others within Trump's inner circle that he would also "corroborate[ ] by physical evidence, including text messages, phone records, documentary evidence, and travel records."[69] These facts include, per Bondy's letter to Congress, proof that Trump, Pence, Pompeo, Barr, Graham, Perry, Nunes, Harvey, Solomon, Giuliani, diGenova, Toensing, and "others" were all in the loop on a months-long plot to establish a "quid pro quo" with Zelensky in which Trump "demand[ed] public announcements of anti-corruption proceedings regarding the 2016 election and the Bidens in exchange for American financial aid."[70] The GOP-led Senate does not respond to Bondy's letter.

On January 30, the day before he sent his letter to the Senate, Bondy had released a new videotape of Parnas meeting with Trump, this time at Mar-a-Lago in April 2018. In the video, Republican National Committee chairwoman Ronna McDaniel welcomes both Parnas and Fruman to Trump's country club with, as *Politico* terms it, "a level of familiarity."[71] According to CNN, Rep. Pete Sessions is also at the mid-April dinner; Sessions was at the time part of Parnas's and Fruman's efforts to lobby Trump to fire Yovanovitch.[72]

After all but two GOP senators vote to block any witnesses or documents from being introduced during the trial—even persons and evidence unavailable to Congress until after the House's mid-December 2019 impeachment vote—Senate Republicans issue a series of head-scratching declamations. Sen. Marco Rubio confesses that Trump's actions "meet" the "standard of impeachment," but says he will vote to acquit the president anyway because it is not "in the best interest of the country" to remove Trump from office, as it would make his supporters angry and lead to allegations of a "coup d'état"—albeit ones whose reasonableness Rubio does not endeavor to defend.[73] CNN calls Rubio's reasoning "mind-blowing," "stunning," and a "reminder of the knots ambitious Republicans are tying themselves in to avoid outraging the President while also trying to keep themselves credible with the broader Republican electorate."[74] Sen. Lisa Murkowski declares that there can be "no fair trial in the Senate"—and decides, therefore, to vote to block both parties from subpoenaing witnesses or documents, conventional hallmarks of a fair trial in the U.S. justice system.[75] Following closing arguments, Murkowski calls Trump's behavior "shameful" and "wrong."[76]

Sen. Rob Portman announces, during the trial's final week, that Trump's actions were "wrong and inappropriate"—and, by accusing Trump of simultaneously "asking a foreign country to investigate a potential political opponent" and "delay[ing] . . . aid to Ukraine," seems to confirm a quid pro quo—but nevertheless votes to acquit on February 5, arguing that the impeachment clause is differentially operative when "early voting has already begun in some states in the presidential primaries."[77] Sen. Chuck Grassley says of Trump's actions that the president was indeed "going after" Biden, which was "not something that should have been done" and resulted in Trump "needlessly inviting a lot of controversy."[78] Meanwhile, Iowa's junior senator, Joni Ernst, calls Trump's actions "wrong" and "something [she] wouldn't have done"; she adds that the president's self-described "perfect" call with Zelensky was "not . . . perfect."[79] Sen. Susan Collins calls Trump's mention of Biden to Zelensky "wrong," and likewise calls his request for Ukraine to investigate Biden "wrong," adding that the latter request was "improper" and "demonstrated very poor judgment."[80] Sen. Lamar Alexander concedes that the House has proven, through a "mountain of overwhelming evidence," that the "president withheld United States aid, at least in part, to pressure Ukraine to investigate the Bidens," and Alexander refers to this withholding as both "inappropriate" and an official act that "undermines the principle of equal justice under the law"; he later adds that Trump's actions "cross[ed] the line," constituting an "offense" that had been sufficiently "proved."[81] Sen. Ben Sasse, reacting to Alexander's statements, tells reporters that "Lamar speaks for lots and lots of us [in the GOP Senate caucus]."[82] Nevertheless, Rubio, Murkowski, Portman, Grassley, Ernst, Collins, Sasse, and Alexander all eventually vote to acquit the president on both articles of impeachment. Collins will explain her vote by saying she believes "the president has learned" a "pretty big lesson" and would without a doubt be "much more cautious" about seeking foreign assistance in the future.[83]

In February 2020, the *Washington Post* reports that the Republican Party privately put a poll in the field, prior to the Senate vote on whether to allow witnesses at Trump's impeachment trial, to determine if acquitting the president—including acquitting him without calling any witnesses—would harm vulnerable GOP senators. Per the *Post*, the results of the poll allowed Republican jurors to be "confident that voters were paying little attention" to their potentially controversial decisions.[84]

After the conclusion of the evidence at the impeachment trial, an NBC/*Wall Street Journal* poll reveals that a majority of Americans believe Trump both abused his office and obstructed Congress.[85] Even the chief legal analyst for conservative cable news network Fox News, Andrew Napolitano, announces during the trial that Trump should be convicted of the charges against him and removed from office because the evidence before the Senate is "ample and uncontradicted," adding that "though the House chose delicately not to accuse the president of specific crimes, there is enough evidence here to do so."[86] A similar finding comes—on the first day of the impeachment trial—from a surprising source: the nonpartisan Government Accountability Office, which announces, as summarized by Fox News, that "Trump's request [of Zelensky] for a favor was a violation of law because only Congress can impose conditions on government expenditures. So, when the president did that, he usurped Congress's role and acted unlawfully."[87] Former Trump chief of staff John Kelly will tell a New Jersey reporter during the final week of the trial that GOP senators are "leav[ing] themselves open to a lot of criticism"—specifically to the charge that they conducted only "half a trial."[88] And even a staunch Trump ally, Bill Barr, inadvertently harms the president's cause when in mid-trial a 2018 memo written by the now attorney general reveals that he believes—contrary to what many Senate Republicans are saying as the president's impeachment trial unfolds—that "abuse of power" is indeed an impeachable offense; shortly thereafter, Barr's DOJ discloses, in a federal court filing, that it likewise considers obstruction of Congress via a refusal to comply with subpoenas an impeachable offense.[89]

Kelly's words, Barr's memo, and Bolton's bombshell revelations notwithstanding, ten days after *Vox* calls the president's defense a "blizzard of lies," the Senate objects to the calling of witnesses by a vote of 51–49 and thereafter acquits Trump 52–48 on the abuse of power article and 53–47 on the obstruction of Congress article.[90] The final tally on the abuse of power article features a historic vote from Republican Mitt Romney, who becomes the first-ever senator to vote for the removal of a president of his own party.[91] Trump's son Don Jr. immediately calls for Romney to be expelled from the GOP.[92]

During the course of the impeachment trial, the *Washington Post* had warned that an acquittal would "confirm to Mr. Trump that he is free to solicit foreign interference in the 2020 election and to withhold congressionally appropriated aid to induce such interference," and that he "can press foreign leaders to launch a criminal investigation of any American citizen he designates, even in the absence of a preexisting U.S. probe, or any evidence."[93] The view of the *Post* will eventually be echoed, after the trial, by the Republican governor of Vermont, Phil Scott, who announces within twenty-four hours of the Senate verdict that he believes Trump "abused his powers," adding that "I don't believe that he should be in office"; Scott is the first Republican executive branch official to issue such a declaration.[94] Asked by MSNBC to summarize the state of the U.S. Constitution, rule of law, and American democracy at the conclusion of Trump's impeachment trial, Pulitzer Prize–winning historian Jon Meacham replies that the result of Senate Republicans' acquittal of their party leader is that Trump is now "functionally a monarch" rather than a president.[95]

Within minutes of the verdict, *Just Security* publishes a detailed analysis of GOP senators' comments on the trial, concluding that, the official vote on the two articles of impeachment notwithstanding, senators' public statements following the evidentiary portion of the trial suggest that a majority of the Senate—fifty-three senators—considered Trump "guilty on the facts."[96]

At a prayer breakfast the day after the acquittal, Trump opines, with Nancy Pelosi sitting several feet away, that he has been the victim of "dishonest and corrupt people" who have "done everything possible to . . . badly hurt our nation," adding—in a clear reference to Sen. Romney, who had cited his sworn oath before God as a partial explanation for his historic vote to convict the president of abuse of power—"I don't like people who use their faith as justification for doing what they know is wrong."[97] Trump further declares that America is "in a fight" over "religion" that is seeing religion "under siege"; he promises the assembled crowd that his administration is "going to protect Christianity."[98] Hours later, Trump attorney Jenna Ellis, explicitly referencing Trump's prayer breakfast comments, confirms that he was positioning the impeachment fight as a religious war. Ellis says of the impeachment process, "The Democrats are trying to undermine the American system of government. This was literally a battle between good . . . [and] evil."[99]

Shortly after the prayer breakfast, Trump gives a lengthy address from the White House. During his remarks, he contends that he has never in his life intentionally done anything wrong, and alleges that an "evil" network of government conspirators began targeting him the day he announced his candidacy in 2015.[100] Trump refers to Robert Mueller's special counsel's office, as well as the FBI agents who participated in the pre-election "Crossfire Hurricane" investigation of ties between the 2016 Trump campaign and Russia, as "dirty cops," "leakers," and "liars"—despite a finding by Inspector General Horowitz that there was no political bias in any component of the Russia investigation, either pre-election or post-election.[101] Trump observes that those involved in the joint DOJ-FBI investigation of his campaign from 2016 to 2019, as well as any Democratic members of the House involved in his impeachment, should be "in jail for a long time."[102]

Days later, when asked by a member of the White House press corps whether, as previously suggested by Sens. Collins and Portman, he had "learned a lesson" from his impeachment, Trump dismisses the idea out of hand, declaring that all he has learned is "that the Democrats are crooked—they've got a lot of crooked things going—that they're vicious, [and] that they shouldn't have brought impeachment."[103]

Republican senators spend the days immediately after the acquittal trying to make it more difficult for Trump to be held accountable in the future, with Rick Scott (R-FL) proposing a constitutional amendment to raise the threshold for a House impeachment from a majority vote to a three-fifths vote.[104] Meanwhile, a group of sixteen Republican senators pushes for a rules change that would allow the Senate to begin an impeachment trial without having yet formally received any articles of impeachment from the House of Representatives, and moreover to allow any senator to move to dismiss articles of impeachment—whether yet received by the Senate or not—immediately upon a successful impeachment vote in the House.[105]

A similar effort to protect Trump from any future repercussions for his actions begins simultaneously at the Department of Justice, where Attorney General Barr formally approves—on the day Trump is acquitted—a new DOJ regulation prohibiting the department from investigating a presidential candidate without the attorney general's express permission.[106] Barr's new edict is a broad one, covering both criminal and counterintelligence investigations; both presidential and vice presidential candidates; senior campaign staff and advisers not formally part of a political campaign; political operatives and mere "donors"; and "preliminary" investigations as well as "full" investigations.[107] In short, Barr prohibits even the consideration of a future investigation—at least without his prior authorization—of any Trump donor, family member, campaign staffer, adviser, or running mate.[108] Barr even prohibits FBI investigations of "illegal contributions, donations, or expenditures by foreign nationals to a presidential or congressional campaign" unless and until the FBI has notified and consulted with "relevant leaders" at the DOJ, a requirement that ensures Barr will quickly learn of any investigation that could possibly impact the president's reelection campaign.[109] Barr's announcement comes the same week that Rudy Giuliani announces he will be "ramping up" his investigations of Joe Biden—which announcement Barr meets with an agreement to receive at the Department of Justice any evidence Giuliani develops.[110] Indeed, Barr's interest in facilitating precisely the sort of investigation of a Democratic presidential candidate he has just attempted to foreclose in the case of President Trump is of sufficient intensity that he establishes a special "intake process" by which the DOJ will triage foreign-born Biden dirt brought to it by Giuliani.[111]

On the same day as Giuliani's announcement of a renewed push to investigate Joe Biden, Trump's Treasury Department complies with a series of wide-ranging, just-issued requests from GOP senators to provide Congress with "highly sensitive and closely held" records involving Biden and his son.[112] Meanwhile, Adam Schiff announces that former Trump national security advisor John Bolton—who had volunteered to testify before the GOP-led Senate during Trump's impeachment trial—is now refusing to provide the Democratic-led House with an affidavit outlining what his testimony would have been.[113]

On February 7, 2020, Trump executes what the *Washington Post*, MSNBC, the *Daily Beast*, and others will call the "Friday Night Massacre": the sudden firing from their government jobs of two impeachment witnesses—Alexander Vindman and Gordon Sondland—as well as Vindman's twin brother, Yevgeny, also a National Security Council official.[114] Don Jr.

publicly confirms that his father's firing of the three men is retribution for Vindman and Sondland complying with congressional subpoenas, writing on Twitter, "Allow me a moment to thank—and this may be a bit of a surprise—Adam Schiff. Were it not for his crack investigation skills, Donald Trump might have had a tougher time unearthing who all needed to be fired. Thanks, Adam!"[115] Trump thereafter echoes his son's statement, calling Vindman "very insubordinate" for testifying before Congress pursuant to a federal subpoena.[116]

CHAPTER 41

THE AFTERMATH

That the president's mid- and post-impeachment actions continue to have dire consequences for Ukraine—still America's most important eastern European ally—is clear. As Ukraine and Russia begin peace talks in Paris in December 2019, observers worry that Trump's actions have left Zelensky with "no clear American diplomatic backing," which would force him to "make concessions to Moscow."[1] The *New York Times* reports that Trump's team privately told Zelensky that Trump would either release a public message of support for the Ukrainian president on Twitter prior to his peace talks with Putin or issue a public invite to the White House; instead, Trump tweets 100 times on the day of the peace negotiations and never offers Zelensky a Washington visit or words of encouragement.[2] The *Daily Beast* reports that "Russian state-television programs constantly reiterate that Trump doesn't care about Ukraine and gave Putin no reasons to even contemplate concessions . . . in Paris."[3] *Politico* reports that "U.S. policy toward Ukraine is in shambles, with officials in Kyiv now wondering who they can trust in Washington."[4]

Meanwhile, Ihor Kolomoisky, the Ukrainian oligarch who shares a personal attorney with Donald Trump, "alarm[s]" the political class in Kyiv in December when he "suggest[s] that Ukraine should swivel toward [cooperation with] Russia amid the chaos in Ukraine policy in the United States."[5] That Kasowitz, who "helped [Trump] coordinate his response to the U.S. special counsel's Russia investigation," should now be aiding a Ukrainian seeking to return Ukraine to Putin's sphere of influence is deeply troubling.[6] Kolomoisky, the fourth-richest man in Ukraine, has a reputation in his country that includes, per *The Atlantic*, two allegations he denies: that he is responsible for "ordering contract killings," and that he is the "shadow leader" of Ukraine during the Zelensky presidency.[7] Per the *Times*, Kolomoisky's advice to Zelensky is that "the European Union and NATO will never take in Ukraine," whereas "Russia would love to bring us into a new Warsaw Pact."[8] The *Times* further reports that Kolomoisky has said that "if he were Ukraine's president, he would proceed with the investigations sought by Mr. Trump," and that if a Democrat wins the White House in 2020 and—in the oligarch's words— "they get smart with us, we'll go to Russia. Russian tanks will be stationed near Krakow and Warsaw. . . . NATO will be soiling its pants and buying Pampers [diapers]."[9] While Kolomoisky's threat against NATO is unnerving, so too is Trump's November 2019 "move to substantially cut [the U.S.] contribution to NATO's relatively small collective budget," and his concurrent false claim that the European Union was "established to hurt the United States."[10] *Newsweek* reports that Trump is privately telling allies that America is "getting raped" by NATO financially and is "push[ing] to exit the alliance"—an event that, if it comes to pass, will constitute perhaps the most significant geopolitical victory of Vladimir Putin's thirty-year political career.[11]

In December 2019, MSNBC reports that an IRS whistleblower attempting to report irregularities at the agency with respect to its handling of the president's tax returns has been threatened by a Trump administration official with the possibility of arrest—an act of witness intimidation that, if proven, could constitute serious and possibly criminal misconduct.[12] The MSNBC report follows on the heels of a *ProPublica* exposé revealing "major inconsistencies" in what few Trump tax documents have made it into the public sphere, with the digital media outlet concluding that for a long time "the president's businesses [have] made themselves appear more profitable to lenders and less profitable to tax officials," a practice *ProPublica* reports constitutes "fraud."[13] Weeks later, *ProPublica* finds "more discrepancies" in Trump's tax records, this time pertaining to Trump

Tower itself; the data "show the president's company report[ing] different numbers—higher ones to lenders, lower ones to tax officials—for Trump's signature building."[14] Another scandal arising in the same month sees a short-lived attempt by Trump to move the annual G7 conference to his own property, Trump National Doral Miami, a gambit Fox News' chief legal analyst, Andrew Napolitano, calls "about as direct and profound a violation of the Emoluments Clause as one could create."[15] During the course of the Doral-G7 imbroglio, Trump declares the Constitution's emoluments clause "phony."[16]

The Trump administration's handling of whistleblowers is again called into question when, in December 2019, the National Infrastructure Advisory Council (NIAC) informs the public that cyberthreats to critical infrastructure pose an "existential threat to [American] continuity of government, economic stability, social order, and national security" and, even more alarmingly, that a "catastrophic cyber attack on the United States is imminent."[17] Despite the warning, neither the president nor Republicans in the Senate permit any election security bills to pass through Congress.[18] Indeed, in December 2019, a lone GOP senator, Mike Crapo of Idaho, single-handedly blocks "legislation meant to prevent Russia and other countries from interfering in [U.S.] elections"; in February 2020, the Senate GOP collectively blocks three more election security bills.[19]

Lingering questions remain about Trump's relationship with crown prince Mohammed bin Salman of Saudi Arabia, one of the several nations that sought to offer the Trump campaign illicit election assistance in 2016. In October 2019, the *Washington Post* reports that the encrypted-messaging service WhatsApp has accused an Israeli cybersurveillance firm connected to MBS's Saudi government, NSO Group, of helping governments hack more than a hundred people worldwide—including journalists and human rights activists.[20] Soon after, two reports are released, one by the United Nations and one by a private consulting company, establishing that MBS had the phone of a top Trump "political enemy," Amazon CEO Jeff Bezos, hacked.[21] As fears of pro-Trump interference by the Saudis in the 2020 election grow—augmented by the fall 2019 DOJ indictment of two Twitter employees for spying for MBS's court "by accessing the company's information on [Saudi] dissidents who use the platform"—Trump announces that, his repeated promises to bring U.S. troops home notwithstanding, he will send "a fresh wave of troops to help defend the [Saudi] kingdom."[22]

As MBS continues to exert his power within the United States, another top Trump ally, Vladimir Putin, is devising legislation to facilitate his assumption of a permanent role as the "supreme leader" of Russia, a revelation that comes contemporaneously with, per CNN, "the entire Russian government resigning"; meanwhile, Putin and Trump's ally in Hungary, president Viktor Orban, will receive "absolute power"—the "power to rule by decree indefinitely," per *Business Insider*—after the COVID-19 outbreak hits the European nation in late March 2020 (see chapter 42).[23]

Instead of distancing himself from Putin, Trump draws the architect of pro-Trump election interference in 2016 closer, announcing in October 2019 that he has agreed to "gradually start[ ] . . . resum[ing] cooperation on cybersecurity" with the Kremlin—a development so closely linked to and beneficial for Russian intelligence that it is announced in Russia by the man within the Kremlin's state security service whom the *Daily Beast* calls "Putin's top spy."[24] Trump's decision to advance new U.S.-Kremlin collaborations on cybersecurity comes even as Bloomberg News reports that a firm linked to longtime Manafort associate and (per the *Financial Times*) Putin "money launderer" Oleg Deripaska has been raided by federal investigators as part of a previously unannounced criminal probe; according to Bloomberg, the investigation is a money laundering probe that "grew out of Robert Mueller's work."[25] Even as federal law enforcement closes in on Deripaska, however, Trump's treasury secretary, Steve Mnuchin, is inexplicably dragging his feet on imposing required new sanctions against the Russian oligarch. When, in February 2020, the sanctions remain unimposed, the *Daily Beast* reports that "the two months of inaction ha[ve] stirred suspicions of political interference in the sanctions process."[26] Mnuchin's solicitousness comes as fears grow that Barr is systematically shutting down more than twenty Trump-related criminal investigations spawned by special counsel Robert Mueller's work between 2017 and 2019.[27] Concerns that Trump's still-murky ties to Russia may never be properly investigated are only augmented when the *Daily Beast* reports in December 2019 that Trump is fighting "an aggressive new package of sanctions on Russia" with a twenty-two-page letter of condemnation, even as he "threaten[s] to veto [a] government funding bill if [a] Ukraine aid requirement is included"—the proviso Trump finds objectionable being one that mandates that "future military aid for Ukraine . . . be released quickly."[28]

In November 2019, the Trump administration asks longtime Trump adviser and donor Erik Prince to purchase a Ukrainian aerospace manufacturer, Motor Sich, purportedly to keep the company away from Chinese investors.[29] As Prince's Frontier Services Group is a Beijing-based private security contractor with substantial Chinese government contracts—indeed, its largest shareholder is a Chinese state-controlled investment fund—it is unclear how his purchase of Motor Sich would, as the administration contends, keep the company clear of Chinese influence.[30]

According to the *Wall Street Journal*, if Chinese government-backed entities acquire Motor Sich, it would allow the Chinese to master a certain "heavy-lift" aeronautical technology that America does not want its geopolitical rival either to acquire or to convey to one of China's top allies in the sharing of military technology—Russia—and which successive presidential administrations have spent "30 years" trying to keep closely held within the United States.[31] The newspaper notes, too, that "a Motor Sich sale to China would doom Ukraine's efforts to join the North Atlantic Treaty Organization and the European Union," a revelation underscoring a second reason the Kremlin might want a Ukraine-China Motor Sich deal to go through.[32] Per the *Journal*, future cooperation between China and Russia on heavy-lift technology is almost certain: "Russia's state incubator for high-tech industrial civilian and military products

[has] announced a pending joint venture with the Chinese to manufacture a heavy-lift helicopter with the ability to transport armored vehicles
and artillery."[33]

That Erik Prince has had his eye on Ukraine for some time is clear.
The *Journal* reports that the mercenary company executive traveled to
Ukraine at least nine times between Trump's November 2013 trip to
Moscow and the end of 2019; whether any of these trips helped inform or
evolve Trump's relationship with the Kremlin or the president's insistent
focus on investigations of Clinton and Biden in Ukraine is unknown.[34]
According to the *Journal*, the Ukrainian company Prince is considering
acquiring, Motor Sich, is "the successor to a linchpin in the Soviet's
Union's defense industry," and "for years supplied engines for the bulk
of the Russian military's helicopter fleet"—a business model that ended
with Russia's invasion of Ukraine in 2014, and one that by all accounts
Putin would like to reestablish.[35] The sale of Motor Sich to either "a
group of companies, including Beijing Skyrizon Aviation," or Prince's
Chinese-government-linked holding company, could therefore aid Russia
in acquiring military technology that it cost itself with its actions in
Crimea.

The Trump administration's interest in the Motor Sich deal will be
underscored in February 2020, when it is revealed that Trump is still
withholding $30 million in military equipment earmarked for Ukraine—
though in this case the withholding is of "guns and ammunition" for
which Kyiv has already paid.[36] *BuzzFeed News* reports that, in an echo of
the 2019 Ukraine scandal, Ukraine has "no idea why" it is being denied
the American war-fighting equipment it paid for, though one Ukrainian
official tells the digital media outlet that the freeze "could be because
the U.S. wants Ukraine's anti-monopoly committee to decide in its favor
[by cancelling] . . . the pending sale of Motor Sich, a strategic aerospace
company, to a Chinese firm" rather than other potential bidders, such as
Prince.[37] Whatever the cause of the new arms freeze, its effect is to make
it more likely that Ukraine sells Motor Sich to a reliable campaign donor
and longtime "informal adviser" to Donald Trump.[38] Were Prince to
thereafter make a larger than usual donation to Trump's 2020 reelection

campaign, it would be nearly impossible to clearly designate the donation an illegal kickback from any Motor Sich deal facilitated by the White House. In any case, Barr's February 2020 edict regarding campaign finance investigations of active presidential candidates makes it highly unlikely that the FBI or DOJ would receive authorization to investigate Prince or any other 2020 Trump donor.

Trump's February 2020 firing of Alexander Vindman—much like his firing of John Bolton in September 2019—deprives the federal government of one of its most vocal opponents to the sale of Motor Sich to the Chinese government or a Chinese-government-backed entity.[39] Trump therefore finds himself in the midst of a piece of international business intrigue whose resolution is almost certain to benefit at least one of two top allies: Erik Prince or Vladimir Putin.

In March 2020, the *New York Times* reports that Prince "has in recent years helped recruit former American and British spies for secretive intelligence-gathering operations that included infiltrating Democratic congressional campaigns, labor organizations and other groups considered hostile to the Trump agenda."[40] "Whether any Trump administration officials or advisers to the president were involved in the operations . . . is unclear," writes the *Times*.[41]

In December 2019, the *Washington Post* reports that Trump has promised Saudi Arabia's MBS—in a call that left White House aides "genuinely horrified"—that he would help Saudi Arabia enter the G7, a policy priority Trump has not publicly disclosed and that would likely receive near-universal pushback following the Saudi ruler's orchestration of a *Washington Post* journalist's assassination.[42] At approximately the same time, a highly public Trump promise—to eschew his $400,000 presidential salary—reenters the news, as it is revealed that the billionaire's golfing trips to Mar-a-Lago have in just thirty-six months cost American taxpayers $118 million, or the equivalent of 296 years' worth of presidential salaries.[43] In January 2020, the *Post* reports that treasury secretary Steve Mnuchin is hiding from American voters the full cost to taxpayers of Trump's unprecedented travel to and from Trump-branded golf courses and other properties he owns.[44] Prior to winning election, Trump had insisted that he would "rarely leave the White House" and would aggressively limit his travel to cut down on the expenses charged to taxpayers.[45]

In February 2020, Trump is accused of another "quid pro quo"—this time in a scheme confined to the United States. *Politico* reports that Trump has apparently chosen "to link his administration's policies toward New York to a demand that the state drop investigations and lawsuits related to his administration as well as his personal business and finances."[46] Citing, on the one hand, Trump administration policies on "Global Entry and other 'trusted traveler' programs" that "allow New Yorkers faster border crossings and shorter airport lines," and on the other subpoenas from New York attorney general Letitia James for Trump's financial records and "multiple [state] inquiries about the Trump Organization's business practices," *Politico* notes that "Trump's linkage of the investigations and lawsuits to his national security-related decisions involving New York immediately call[ ] back to House Democrats' warning [during the impeachment trial] that Trump . . . could leverage federal resources to coerce states to take actions that benefit him personally or politically."[47]

As was the case during the Ukraine scandal, Trump's own tweets become potential evidence against him. Hours before meeting with New York governor Andrew Cuomo at the White House, Trump tweets that Cuomo "must understand that National Security far exceeds politics. New York must stop all of its unnecessary lawsuits and harassment, start cleaning itself up, and lowering taxes," adding that the key for Gov. Cuomo and New York is to learn to "build relationships"—an apparent euphemism for the implementation of a quid pro quo on matters of concern to the president that causes the *Daily Beast* to conclude, "Trump's New York shakedown shows he'll never get out of the gutter. [He] again confessed out loud, demanding New York 'stop all of its unnecessary lawsuits and harassment.' He does not, of course, mean of undocumented immigrants. He means of him."⁴⁸

CNN reports that the end of his impeachment trial has unburdened Trump of much of his caution on the subject of quid pro quos. As the cable news outlet writes on February 13, "Emboldened after his impeachment acquittal, President Trump now openly admits to sending his attorney Rudy Giuliani to Ukraine to find damaging information about his political opponents, even though he strongly denied it during the impeachment inquiry."⁴⁹ The same day as the CNN report, the president declares that he may end the practice of letting administration officials listen to his phone calls with other world leaders.⁵⁰

When, in late February 2020, "a classified briefing to House members" reveals, according to the *New York Times*, that "Russia [is] interfering in the 2020 [presidential] campaign to try to get President Trump reelected," the president's response is to be "angered" that the briefing took place—because "Democrats would use it against him."⁵¹ Indeed, Trump is so angry about the briefing, per NBC News, that he "force[s] out" his acting director of national intelligence, Joseph Maguire, simply for having let it occur.⁵² Quoting a former intelligence official, NBC reports that, in the wake of Maguire's departure, the Office of the Director of National Intelligence is "nearing a meltdown."⁵³ Writing of Maguire's ouster in the *Washington Post*, retired Navy admiral William McRaven declares that "as Americans, we should be frightened—deeply afraid for the future of the nation."⁵⁴

CHAPTER 42

COVID-19

Between January and August 2019, Trump's Department of Health and Human Services (HHS), headed by Alex Azar, runs a simulation—code-named Crimson Contagion—in which a "respiratory virus [that] began in China . . . [is] quickly spread around the world by air travelers . . . [with] high fevers."[1] Upon its conclusion in August 2019, the Crimson Contagion simulation registers 110 million infected Americans, 7.7 million hospitalizations, and 586,000 fatalities.[2] A month later, White House economists working with the NSC produce a study "that warn[s] a pandemic disease could kill a half million Americans and devastate the [U.S.] economy."[3] The Crimson Contagion report and the economists' paper are follow-ups on the Pandemic Influenza Plan, developed and released by the White House in December 2017; by mid-April 2020, *Politico* will report Trump has "failed" to abide by the plan, missing "nearly all" of the pandemic-response goals established by the document.[4]

According to the *New York Times*, the "sobering" Crimson Contagion data, which circulates within the Trump administration in October 2019, "[drives] home just how underfunded, underprepared and uncoordinated the federal government would be for a life-or-death battle with a virus for which no treatment existed."[5] Nevertheless, after the COVID-19 outbreak begins in the United States, President Trump will falsely declare that "nobody knew there would be a pandemic or epidemic of this proportion" and "nobody ever thought of numbers like this."[6] In fact, writes the *New York Times* in March 2020, "his own administration had already modeled a similar pandemic and understood its potential trajectory" and "accurately predicted the very types of problems Mr. Trump is now scrambling belatedly to address."[7] In addition to ignoring the lessons of the Crimson Contagion report and the work product of economists contracted by the White House, Trump also, per *Politico*, "ignore[s]" a sixty-nine-page 2016 National Security Council document, "Playbook for High-Consequence Emerging Infectious Disease Threats and Biological Incidents," that "provide[s] a step by step list of priorities" in a pandemic.[8]

The White House's disconnect from the NSC throughout the COVID-19 outbreak is partially attributable to Trump. In April 2018, the president had fired homeland security adviser Tom Bossert, who according to the *Washington Post* "had called for a comprehensive biodefense strategy against pandemics"; weeks later, the administration "eliminat[ed]" the job of Trump's global health security team director, Rear Adm. Timothy Ziemer, and disbanded Ziemer's entire team.[9]

On November 16, 2019, in the United States—November 17 in China—a fifty-five-year-old resident of China's Hubei province is put "under medical surveillance" for an unexplained ailment, according to *The Guardian*.[10] The British media outlet reports that, according to nonpublic medical surveillance data held by the Chinese government, this man "could have been the first person to contract COVID-19."[11] The virus is believed to have originated in the Huanan "wet market," a wildlife emporium in the city of Wuhan that sells—among other exotic species—"foxes, wolf cubs, civets, turtles, and snakes."[12]

Per *The Guardian*, while Beijing will report to the World Health Organization (WHO) that its "first confirmed [COVID-19] case . . . [was] diagnosed on December 8," there is evidence to suggest that U.S. intelligence was aware of the approximately two dozen cases of the novel coronavirus recorded in Hubei province in November 2019, including that of the man in Hubei who may or may not have become the pandemic's "patient zero" on November 16/17.[13] The *South China Morning Post* reports that while "interviews with whistle-blowers from the [Chinese] medical community suggest Chinese doctors only realized they were dealing with a new disease in late December [2019]," it is "possible that there were reported [COVID-19] cases dating back even earlier than [November 16/17]."[14] This possibility appears to be confirmed by a *Business Insider* report on "a research paper from infectious-disease researchers in China" that finds "a surprising trend on the Chinese social-media platform WeChat: Usage of keywords related to the new coronavirus spiked more than two weeks before officials confirmed the first cases . . . [including] in posts and searches on WeChat . . . [beginning on] November 17."[15] That a "spike" in such searches comes in mid-November 2019 suggests that WeChat search logs including terms relating to a new illness may have begun appearing on Chinese social media at the beginning of November or even earlier.

It will be discovered in spring 2020 that a woman in San Jose, California, who became "unusually sick" in late January and died on February 6, had COVID-19 but no recent travel history linking her to China; this further suggests that the initial outbreak of the virus in China may have been earlier than the December timeframe memorialized in Beijing's official report to the WHO.[16] Dr. Jeffrey V. Smith, a Santa Clara, California, county executive and medical doctor, will tell the *New York Times* that Patricia Dowd's death from COVID-19 on February 6 means the novel coronavirus "was probably around [in California] unrecognized for quite some time."[17] Santa Clara County's public health officer, Sara Cody, adds, per *Politico*, that "we had community transmission probably to a significant degree far earlier than we had known."[18] These reassessments of the pandemic timeline are bolstered by the May 2020 discovery in France of a COVID-19 patient without a reported history of travel to China who was admitted for emergency care on December 27, 2019. Even more startling is a mid-May report by NBC News detailing X-rays of two French patients with "symptoms consistent with the novel coronavirus" taken on November 16 and November 18, 2019—a bombshell discovery that NBC says "if confirmed . . . is evidence that the [SARS-CoV-2] virus was spreading in Europe . . . well before COVID-19, the disease caused by the coronavirus, had been officially identified in China."[19] According to CNN, a peer-reviewed British study conducted at

University College London also "found genetic evidence that supports suspicions the virus was infecting people in Europe, the U.S. and elsewhere weeks or even months before the first official cases were reported in January and February [2020]"; consistent with this analysis, in May 2020 the AP finds that medical data from Seattle places the virus stateside in December 2019. Yet even these startling findings are eclipsed by a June 2020 bombshell report from ABC News, which reveals that, per satellite imagery analyzed as part of a Harvard Medical School study, so many cars were outside five major Wuhan hospitals in late September and October 2019 that it "suggest[s] the novel coronavirus may have been present and spreading through central China long before the outbreak was first reported to the world."[20]

In November 2019, eighteen months after Trump disbands Adm. Ziemer's pandemic-response team, "U.S. spy agencies . . . [begin] tracking the rise of [a] novel coronavirus," according to CNN.[21] The intelligence gathered provides "multiple early warnings about the potential severity" of the eventual COVID-19 pandemic.[22] The *Times of Israel* will confirm the CNN report, revealing that "the U.S. intelligence community became aware of the emerging disease in Wuhan in the second week of [November 2019]" and immediately "drew up a classified document" on the potential threat—a fact the Israeli media outlet learned on the basis of the document having been shared by at least one U.S. intelligence agency with both NATO and the Israel Defense Forces after the Trump White House indicated, per the *Times of Israel*, that for unexplained reasons it was "not interested" in the information.[23] The *Times* further reports that, Beijing's since-uncovered nonpublic medical surveillance information on a November 17 presumed coronavirus case notwithstanding, government documentation "on the disease outbreak was not in the public domain [between November 8 and November 14] . . . [and such information] was known only apparently to the Chinese government" and to U.S. intelligence agencies.[24] While the Israeli outlet confirms that "U.S. intelligence informed the Trump administration" of its discovery, the exact date of this intelligence transmission in November remains unknown.[25]

What is known, according to ABC News, is that by "late November" a National Center for Medical Intelligence (NCMI) report had warned the White House that "a contagion was sweeping through China's Wuhan region, changing the patterns of life and business and posing a threat to the population," with the NCMI concluding that the contagion "could be a cataclysmic event."[26] ABC adds that the report was "briefed multiple times" in November to "the Defense Intelligence Agency, the Pentagon's Joint Staff and the White House."[27] All told, the picture presented by CNN, *Business Insider*, the *South China Morning Post*, the *Times of Israel*, and ABC News is of U.S. military intelligence repeatedly passing urgent warnings to the Trump White House between November 9 and the end of November about a virus causing cold- or flu-like symptoms that may have been present in China beginning in September 2019.

On November 16, 2019, as President Trump is exhibiting cold-like symptoms, he is unexpectedly—and without any explanation to the public, either at the time or since—rushed to a U.S. military hospital, Walter Reed National Military Medical Center.[28] Hours after the unscheduled visit, during which Trump's blood is drawn and tested for unknown reasons, White House press secretary Stephanie Grisham tells U.S. media that the president had decided to complete the first portion of his annual physical exam after the sudden discovery that he had a "free weekend" to do so.[29] Within forty-eight hours, however, Grisham's claim has been contradicted not only by Grisham herself—who comes to categorize the visit as a "checkup," per CNN, making "no mention of it being part of Trump's 'annual physical'"—but also by one of Trump's doctors, Sean Conley, who calls the visit a "routine, planned interim checkup as part of the regular, primary preventative care [the president] receives throughout the year."[30] The next day, November 19, Trump reverts to Grisham's original categorization of his trip to Walter Reed, calling it part of a "very routine physical" scheduled to be completed in January 2020.[31]

CNN will refer to the White House's explanations for the trip as "shifting," quoting former vice president Dick Cheney's longtime cardiologist, Dr. Jonathan Reiner, as being "very skeptical" of the administration's claims about the reason for Trump's sudden trip to a military hospital. "The President has a physician with him every day and access to 24/7/360 care," Reiner tells CNN after being, per the media outlet, "in touch with the White House . . . about Trump's visit" to Walter Reed. "I have no doubt he was taken to Walter Reed to do something specific and separate from 'a quick exam and some bloodwork.' All that can be done at the White House."[32] According to the cable news network, Vice President Pence's former physician, Dr. Jennifer Peña, shares Dr. Reiner's skepticism, calling the "interim checkup" and "annual physical" characterizations provided by the White House "very" distinct from each other.[33] CNN adds that "multiple sources and experts have said that the President's trip to Walter Reed was abnormal or outside of the protocol for routine visits to Walter Reed," with the *Washington Post* adding that "it is unusual for a president to undergo a physical exam in multiple stages months apart."[34] Indeed, even the president's attire for his unscheduled November 16 hospital visit is unusual, with *HuffPost* noting that "the president normally wears a suit and tie for most events, including visits to Walter Reed, but that Saturday [November 16] he wore an open-collared shirt and jacket as he climbed into the SUV, carrying a thick packet of papers under one arm."[35]

Whatever the reason for Trump's unscheduled visit to a military facility— and the secrecy, procedural idiosyncrasies, and apparent deceit that accompanied and followed it—it is clear that the need for the visit caught the White House by surprise. As reported by *HuffPost*, Trump's past trips to Walter Reed were announced in advance via his daily schedule and were made using Marine One, the presidential helicopter; that Trump's team not only eschews Marine One but does not even "arrange with local law enforcement to shut down the roads to traffic along the route to isolate the president's limousine as much as possible" underscores that the decision to take the president to the nation's foremost military hospital was a sudden one.[36] The digital media outlet adds that the White House uses on-site doctors for "routine tests" and George Washington University Hospital for "serious medical issue[s]," so Trump and the "thick packet of papers" he took with him to Walter Reed apparently needed to go specifically to a military site.[37] Whether Trump is carrying his own documents rather than handing them off to an aide because of classification markings on the materials is unknown; what is clear is that, unlike every other medical exam Trump undergoes during his presidency, following the president's mysterious November 2019 visit to Walter Reed no briefing is given to the press by his doctors.[38] *Slate* reports that not only were medical staff at Walter Reed "not given advance notice" that the president would be coming to the facility, but Trump's visit was "followed by a multi-day absence from the public eye" the digital media outlet calls "highly unusual for a sitting president undergoing a routine checkup, which is what the White House claimed had prompted the visit."[39]

While it is now widely known that the Trump White House received new military intelligence on a dangerous emerging virus sometime during the same three-week period in November 2019 Trump was suddenly rushed to a military hospital, less well known is that Trump was suffering medical symptoms at the time that might have—following his and his national security team's apparent receipt of such intelligence—caused significant concern at the White House. According to the *Washington Post*, shortly before he went to Walter Reed Trump was, according to multiple eyewitnesses, "hoarse" and had "signs of a cold," with a "subdued and raspy voice" that was manifest during a critical public appearance with Turkish president Recep Erdogan.[40] As the *Post* reports, "A common cold would normally not be enough to prompt a visit to Walter Reed because the White House has adequate equipment and facilities to treat most minor illnesses and conduct routine tests. More comprehensive testing can be performed at Walter Reed."[41] The newspaper adds that "the White House Medical Unit has the ability to perform many medical procedures on-site, including most that can be done in outpatient settings."[42] The *Post* quotes renowned cardiologist Dr. John Sotos as remarking, "The most informative question to ask . . . [is] what is available at Walter Reed that is not available in the West Wing medical unit?"[43] A partial answer to this question, according to a summary of comments by Dr. Peña to the *Post*, is that "because [Walter Reed] is a military base, it is more secure, and officials are better able to maintain privacy than at a hospital open to the public."[44] *Business Insider* notes that the Emerging Infectious Diseases Branch at the Walter Reed Army Institute of Research—located four miles from Walter Reed National Military Medical Center—is now one of the Pentagon's frontline operations "involved in conducting research on a possible coronavirus vaccine."[45]

Suspicion that Trump has not been forthcoming about the reason for his trip to Walter Reed is heightened when he skips the January completion of his allegedly two-stage 2020 physical—a physical the president purportedly decided to begin on short notice, months early, and while suffering from a cold. Indeed, by mid-March 2020 Trump is still, according to the *New York Times*, being "vague about when he plans to complete his annual physical," having told reporters in early March, "I'm so busy, I can't do it"; NBC News reports that as late as the end of May, "Trump hasn't completed his physical . . . [and] [t]he White House won't say why."[46] On March 14, when what is represented as Trump's first COVID-19 test comes back negative, the *New York Times* observes that "experts [have] noted . . . that [Mr. Trump] has still never released any details on an unscheduled [November 2019] trip to Walter Reed National Military Medical Center."[47]

By "early to mid-December [2019]," according to CNN, "Chinese social media and even state-controlled media had begun providing public clues about the struggle to contain a respiratory illness that at the time was being compared to SARS [Severe Acute Respiratory Syndrome]. . . . Beijing officially notified the World Health Organization of an outbreak of a pneumonia of unknown cause on December 31."[48] The *Washington Post* reports that the U.S. Centers for Disease Control and Prevention (CDC) knew of China's report to the WHO the day it was filed, and contacted HHS to discuss the outbreak within twenty-four hours; by January 3, Alex Azar had instructed his chief of staff to brief the NSC, telling him, according to the *New York Times*, "This is a very big deal."[49] Reporting by the *Post* further establishes that, November 2019 missives from the U.S. intelligence community aside, the Trump administration didn't need to wait for formal notice of a virus outbreak from the WHO on December 31, as, according to the newspaper, "more than a dozen U.S. researchers, physicians and public health experts, many of them from the Centers for Disease Control and Prevention, were working full time at the Geneva headquarters of the World Health Organization as the novel coronavirus emerged late last year [in 2019] and transmitted real-time information about its discovery and spread in China to the Trump administration"; moreover, by the end of December, Trump's trade representatives in China had already approved the addition of a "force majeure" clause to Trump's "vaunted trade deal [with Beijing]," which "create[d] an exit path for the entire agreement"—contractual language so "rare in trade agreements," per the *Huffington Post*, that according to the analysis of an "informal advisor close to the White House" it "should have been seen as another warning sign about the coronavirus outbreak."[50]

Armed with this information from American specialists working at the WHO in Geneva, foreign WHO officials, and multiple U.S. intelligence agencies, by January 7 HHS has "begun convening an intra-agency task force" led by, among others, Azar and Dr. Anthony Fauci, director of the National Institute of Allergy and Infectious Diseases (NIAID).[51] The next day, according to a *Washington Post* report, "the CDC issues its first public warning about the outbreak in China," advising Americans in China to take "precautions" if traveling to the city of Wuhan in Hubei province.[52] By January 14, the assistant secretary for preparedness and response at HHS, Dr. Robert Kadlec, has "instructed subordinates to draw up contingency plans for enforcing the Defense Production Act [DPA], a measure that enables the government to compel private companies to produce equipment or devices critical to the country's security."[53] President Trump will not implement the DPA for another seventy-nine days, however, nor execute restrictions on air travel from China for another nineteen days—despite the CDC having begun "monitoring major airports for passengers arriving from China" on January 17.[54]

At least six weeks after the White House's first receipt of intelligence reports on COVID-19 from U.S. military sources, Trump's January 3, 2020, daily briefing formally includes for the first time "information the U.S. intelligence community had gathered about the [coronavirus] contagion in China and the potential it had to spread."[55] According to the *Washington Post*, "warnings" about the virus thereafter appear, at a minimum, in "more than a dozen classified briefings prepared for President Trump in January and February, months during which he continued to play down the [virus] threat."[56] These briefings, per the *Post*, go so far as to "[make] clear that China was suppressing information about the contagion's transmissibility and lethal toll, and raised the prospect of dire political and economic consequences . . . reflect[ing] a level of attention [from U.S. intelligence] comparable to periods when analysts have been tracking active terrorism threats, overseas conflicts or other rapidly developing security issues."[57]

Despite these clear and urgent warnings, three months later Trump will falsely claim, per CNN, that "he only learned about the seriousness of the coronavirus 'just prior' to enacting U.S. travel restrictions on China that took effect February 2."[58] In fact, international warnings in the final two months of 2019 notwithstanding, reports in the *Washington Post* and *Wall Street Journal* reveal that White House advisers spent the month of January trying not only to convince the president to take the new virus threat seriously, but in particular "to take on China more directly."[59] The *Post* reports, however, that despite the seriousness of the situation being repeatedly communicated to the president, Azar "couldn't get through to Trump to speak with him about the virus until January 18."[60] *Politico* reporter Dan Diamond explains to NPR in March that even Azar's January 18 phone conversation with Trump happens only after the secretary "push[es] past resistance from the president's political aides," with Diamond identifying Kellyanne Conway as one Trump aide who exhibited "skepticism . . . that this was something that needed to be a presidential priority."[61] Diamond adds that Trump himself was also a significant obstacle to Azar's mission to initiate an aggressive response to the virus threat: "[Trump] did not push to do additional aggressive [coronavirus] testing . . . and that's partly because more testing might have led to more cases being discovered . . . and the president had made clear [that] the lower the numbers on coronavirus, the better for the president, the better for his potential re-election this fall."[62] Indeed, on March 6, as the *Grand Princess* cruise ship—beset by a coronavirus outbreak—is waiting to dock in San Francisco, Trump tells reporters, "I'd rather have the people stay [on the ship]. . . . I would rather [that] because I like the numbers being where they are. I don't need to have the numbers double because of one ship that wasn't our fault."[63] Though Trump promises Americans on March 6 that "anybody who wants a [COVID-19] test gets a test," by early May 2020 Dr. Fauci is still predicting that such a circumstance is several weeks away.[64]

When Azar finally gets Trump on the phone to discuss the novel coronavirus on January 18, "the president interject[s] to ask about vaping and . . . flavored vaping products," per the *Washington Post*.[65] Azar will tell associates that during the call the president frames him as an "alarmist" with respect to the outbreak.[66] It is unknown whether this scolding by the president influences Azar's assistant secretary Robert Kadlec when, according to the *Washington Post*, a U.S. company contacts HHS on January 22 to offer to make "an additional 1.7 million N95 [face] masks a week"; per the *Post*, Kadlec leaves the company "with the clear impression that there was little immediate interest in [its] offer," and even months later the company—which self-describes as the "last major domestic [U.S.] mask company"—will tell the *Post* that not only did the government "not take [it] up on [its offer] . . . [but] even today [May 9, 2020], production lines that could be making more than 7 million masks a month sit dormant."[67]

The president's recalcitrance notwithstanding, by January 27, 2020, even top White House aides were telling Trump's acting chief of staff, Mick Mulvaney, that "the administration needed to take the virus seriously or it could cost the president his re-election, and that dealing with the virus was likely to dominate life in the United States for many months."[68] The *Post* reports that, despite this warning—and the fact that Mulvaney subsequently "began convening more regular [West Wing] meetings" on the subject—Trump remained "dismissive" of the coronavirus threat, reasoning that despite the near-absence of COVID-19 testing in the United States, the problem was not significant because "he did not believe the virus had spread widely throughout the United States."[69]

Throughout January 2020, per the *Washington Post*, U.S. intelligence agencies' "classified warnings" to the Trump White House about the novel coronavirus were "ominous" and formed "a constant flow of reporting," one that repeatedly underscored for Trump and his administration both that "Chinese officials appeared to be minimizing the severity of the outbreak" and that the virus "showed the characteristics of a globe-encircling pandemic that could require governments to take swift actions to contain it."[70] Instead, writes the *Post*, Trump brushed off the findings of the intelligence community and "continued publicly and privately to play down the threat the virus posed to Americans."[71]

On January 29, Trump's director of trade and manufacturing policy, Peter Navarro, circulates a memo within the White House that, as summarized by CNN, "warn[s] the White House that the coronavirus pandemic could cost trillions of dollars."[72] *Axios* reports that the Navarro memo also predicts "the novel coronavirus could take more than half a million American lives" and advises Trump to issue a ban on all travel to the United States from China.[73]

Despite this urgent private warning, Navarro publicly states—in a press gaggle less than a month after he circulates his memo—that Americans have "nothing to worry about" with respect to the coronavirus.[74] Trump will subsequently say of Navarro's memo, "I haven't seen [it]," "It [doesn't] matter whether I saw [it] or not," "[Navarro] told certain people on the [White House] staff, but it didn't matter," and "I don't remember it . . . being discussed, [but] we had a meeting [in late January] where there were a lot of people"; the *New York Times* later reveals that, "despite Mr. Trump's denial . . . he was told at the time about a January 29 memo produced by his trade adviser, Peter Navarro, laying out in striking detail the potential risks of a coronavirus pandemic."[75]

On January 31, Trump announces what he terms a "ban" on travel to the United States from China, though in fact the order is not—as he will repeatedly insist—a shutting down of all U.S.-China travel, as Navarro had recommended, but a scheme with at least eleven key loopholes, per a *Washington Post* analysis.[76] Trump had initially been "skeptical" about international travel restrictions because, as the *Post* will report, he feared they would "provok[e]" China; as if to underscore the president's aversion to displeasing Chinese president Xi Jinping, the day after his travel order takes effect, he boasts during his State of the Union speech that his administration is "coordinating with the Chinese government and working together on the coronavirus outbreak in China"—a claim he retracts when Americans begin dying from the virus in large numbers.[77] The president's anxiety on this score mirrors his prior discomfort with providing military aid to U.S. ally Ukraine, which he warned aides in 2019 could "provoke" the Kremlin. Trump will later say, falsely, that his executive order on China "basically did what the [Navarro] memo said"—shut down all incoming flights—when in fact, as Azar later concedes, the order was "incremental."[78]

The *New York Times* writes in April 2020 that the Navarro memo was a "direct warning" that "circulated at a key moment among top administration officials," as it "starkly warned Trump administration officials . . . that the coronavirus crisis could . . . put millions of Americans at risk of illness or death" and "came during a period when Mr. Trump was playing down the risks to the United States."[79] The language of the memo, the *Times* notes, was unambiguous, warning of the "elevat[ed] risk" of a "full-blown pandemic, imperiling the lives of millions of Americans," and insisting that the "risk of a worst-case pandemic scenario should not be overlooked."[80]

After Trump's executive order on travel from China takes effect in early February—nearly two weeks, the *Washington Post* reports, after the CDC "announced the first travel-related case of novel coronavirus in the United States"—its loopholes permit "nearly 40,000" people to "arrive[ ] in the United States on direct flights from China" between its full first day of implementation (February 3) and April 7, a figure the president will later seek to obscure by euphemistically calling it a "small number" in a Fox Business interview.[81] The *New York Times* notes that these tens of thousands of domestic arrivals are met with only "spotty screening" at U.S. airports.[82] The *Times* determines that if Trump had immediately reacted to China's December 31 WHO notice with a blanket prohibition on all flights from China, it might have prevented "at least 430,000 people" from coming to the United States from the beleaguered Asian nation; Dr. Fauci will later reveal that he and others on the White House's Coronavirus Task Force tried to convince the president to go beyond travel restrictions and "shut[ ] things down" domestically in February, but "pushback" kept federal "social-distancing" guidelines from being issued until March 16.[83]

Unlike most nations that impose travel orders post-outbreak—nations that, per the *Post*, nearly universally "impose[ ]...[their] restrictions immediately"—the United States under Trump waits more than two days for its first post-outbreak travel "ban" to take effect, by which time it is the thirty-ninth country to impose such a restriction, or fifty-first if travel orders slightly less sweeping than Trump's are included.[84] The president is not, therefore, as he will repeatedly claim, "a very, very early" adopter of international travel restrictions in response to the COVID-19 threat.[85]

Just so, the president's claim that his decision had been roundly opposed by Democrats, including his 2020 general election opponent Joe Biden, is false. As the *Post* notes, a pre-order accusation by Biden that Trump has for years routinely exhibited "hysterical xenophobia" is not, as the Trump 2020 presidential campaign will subsequently allege in ads, a comment on Trump's executive order.[86] Moreover, Biden will later speak approvingly of the idea of "banning all travel from Europe," noting that while such bans cannot stop a virus from being transmitted, they "may slow it."[87] In mid-February 2020, as a Food and Drug Administration-approved coronavirus test developed by the CDC is being revealed as unreliable—a development that will delay widespread testing in the United States for weeks—COVID-19 begins circulating in New York City, which shortly becomes the global epicenter of the coronavirus outbreak.[88] A *New York Times* report will reveal that community transmission in the New York City area began several days after Trump's self-declared "cutting off" of travel from China, and that the "majority" of travelers who brought the virus to the city came from Europe rather than Asia.[89] Consequently, by the time Trump makes the decision on March 11 to restrict travel from Europe, it is too late for his order to significantly slow the spread of the virus stateside.[90] The *Times* further notes that the "spread of the virus [in New York in February] . . . might have been detected if aggressive testing programs had been put in place," a reference to exactly the sort of testing regimen the president had rejected when it was proposed to him by Azar in mid-January.[91] Even the president's order on travel from Europe is profoundly flawed, with loopholes that include, per *Politico*, the "exempt[ing] [of] nations where three Trump-owned golf resorts are located."[92] Travel to the United States from these European countries—the United Kingdom and Ireland—is not terminated until the end of the day on March 16.[93]

Throughout the devastating course of the COVID-19 outbreak in the United States, Trump dispenses misinformation about the outbreak and his response to it during daily televised press conferences. The president's February 10 claim that "a lot of people think that [COVID-19] goes away in April with the heat" is eventually rejected—in April, as the virus is killing tens of thousands of Americans—by a letter from the National Academy of Sciences, which reveals, as reported by CNN, that "even under maximum temperature and humidity conditions, the virus spread[s] 'exponentially,' with every infected person spreading it to nearly two other people on average."[94]

On January 22, Trump tells CNBC that he is "not at all" worried about coronavirus becoming a "pandemic," calling the virus "totally under control"; on January 30, he says, "We think [the epidemic] is going to have a very good ending. . . . So that I can assure you"; on February 2, he tells his longtime domestic policy adviser Sean Hannity during a televised interview that "we pretty much shut [the coronavirus] down"; on February 10, he declares that "the virus is going to be fine"; on February 14—at a time when virtually no coronavirus testing is being conducted in the United States—Trump says that America is "in very good shape" with respect to the virus because only a "very small number of people in the country [have it] . . . like around 12"; on February 19, the president says of COVID-19, "I think it's going to work out fine"; and on February 24, he tweets that "the Coronavirus is very much under control in the USA," adding that "[the] Stock Market [is] starting to look very good to me!"[95]

Two days later, the president responds to senior CDC official Nancy Messonnier's February 25 comment to reporters that the coronavirus would cause "severe" disruption to life in the United States by, according to the *Washington Post*, "shout[ing]" at Azar over the phone that Messonnier is "spooking the stock market."[96] The *Wall Street Journal* will report in April that during Trump's February 26 call with Azar, the president threatened to fire Messonnier; according to *Business Insider*, Messonnier's comment not only "led to Azar's role being diminished" by Trump—a punishment for Messonnier "[breaking] from the administration's otherwise optimistic messaging on the coronavirus"—but also "effectively killed any efforts to persuade Trump to take decisive action to mitigate the virus."[97] Trump's punishment of Azar comes despite the secretary's agreement to "fix some of the damage" allegedly caused by Messonnier, something Azar attempts to do by falsely declaring in a February 26 press conference that the virus has been "contained."[98]

As *Business Insider* notes, "three crucial weeks" passed between Trump "sidelin[ing] [Azar] in favor of Vice President Mike Pence" on February 27 and Trump's announcement of "nationwide stay-at-home and social-distancing measures on March 16"—a period of forced transition from HHS control of the federal government's pandemic response to White House control, during which U.S. COVID-19 cases skyrocketed from 15 to more than 4,200. According to a May 2020 study by Columbia University, had Trump initiated social-distancing measures under Azar's leadership on March 2—rather than putting Pence in Azar's pandemic-response role and, only after the completion of that bureaucratic handover, implementing national guidelines for effective social distancing—a staggering 82 percent of all COVID-19 cases and 84 percent of all COVID-19 deaths could have been prevented. As of June 1, 2020, these "preventable" infection and fatality figures stand at approximately 1.5 million coronavirus infections and 89,000 fatalities.[99]

*   *   *

The *New York Times* reports that the Trump administration's response to the COVID-19 pandemic has been "marked by a raging internal debate about how far to go in telling Americans the truth," and that Trump "especially" has confronted U.S. officials with "resistance and doubt" whenever they have sought to be candid in public.[100] The president's history of false and misleading statements post-outbreak substantiates the *Times* analysis. On February 26, when confirmed U.S. coronavirus cases stand at approximately sixty, Trump declares at a press briefing that "within a couple of days, it's going to be down to close to zero," adding that "there's a chance that [the virus] won't spread"; the next day he tells reporters, "It's going to disappear one day . . . like a miracle."[101] On February 28—despite the lack of any drop in active cases since the first confirmed U.S. case on January 20, nearly forty days earlier—Trump insists that "almost everybody that we see [who has the virus] is getting better, and it could be everybody, soon."[102] The same day, the president claims that critiques of his administration's coronavirus response are part of a "new hoax" being perpetrated by the Democratic Party.[103] Three days later, at a time when media reports peg the earliest possible date for full deployment of a COVID-19 vaccine at mid-2021, the president falsely assures his supporters at a rally that "they're going to have vaccines, I think, relatively soon."[104]

On March 4, when the number of confirmed cases of COVID-19 in the United States is 149, the president tells an interviewer that "hundreds of thousands" of Americans with the disease are "get[ting] better" by "going to work"—a fabrication that risks encouraging asymptomatic or even symptomatic COVID-19 patients to go back to work rather than stay home, as medical experts have universally advised.[105] On March 10, a day on which there are nearly 1,000 confirmed COVID-19 cases nationwide, Trump's statements remain idiosyncratically aloof. "It's really working out," the president says at a public appearance on that date, adding that "a lot of good things are going to happen."[106] By March 15, when there are 3,500 active cases in the United States, the president has returned to a trope he first deployed fifty-three days earlier, insisting his administration has "tremendous control" over the virus.[107]

On March 13, during a press briefing in the White House Rose Garden, the president confirms what he had previously given many Americans reason to suspect: "No, I don't take responsibility at all," he says, referring to criticism of the "lag in testing" his administration has thus far been unable to remedy.[108] Seventy-two hours later, he rates his own response to the coronavirus a "10 [out of 10]."[109] All told, reports CNN, the president makes at least thirty-three significant false claims about the outbreak—along with at least fourteen "misleading" ones—in just the first two weeks of March 2020.[110] According to *Politico*, the president's misstatements often involve hard data, with Trump dramatically miscasting everything from the number of COVID-19 cases in the United States to the number of coronavirus tests scheduled to be available by mid-March; according to the digital media outlet, one consistent feature of Trump's "misleading numbers" is that they are intended to "downplay" the impact of the outbreak. Indeed, a *Washington Post* analysis reveals that when there were four confirmed COVID-19 cases in the United States, Trump said there was only one; when there were eight cases, he said five; when there were thirty-four, he said twelve; when there were 185, he said 15. Just so, when there were forty-two COVID-19 fatalities nationwide, the president said there were none; when there were forty-eight, he said there was one; when there were ninety-four, he said there were eleven; when there were 136, he said 26. The president's seemingly ubiquitous predictions of a relatively modest final COVID-19 death toll also reflect dramatic undercounts; at various points the president publicly offers final death-toll projections of 50,000, 55,000, 60,000, 65,000, 70,000, 75,000, and 80,000—abandoning his futile guessing only when the national death toll approaches 100,000, at which point he takes the opposite tack and begins boasting that "act[ing] the way [his administration] did" saved America from experiencing as many as 2.5 million COVID-19 deaths.[111]

Politico notes that from late January through early March, the president "behind the scenes, and . . . increasingly in public . . . undermine[s] his administration's own efforts to fight the coronavirus outbreak—resisting attempts to plan for worst-case scenarios, overturning a public-health plan upon request from political allies and repeating only the warnings that he [chooses] to hear."[112] *Politico* adds that one reason Alex Azar was originally "discouraged" from speaking to the president in January was that Trump dislikes bad news; he "rewards those underlings who tell him what he wants to hear while shunning those who deliver bad news."[113]

In March, Trump begins using his daily press briefings to recommend the drug hydroxychloroquine as a treatment for COVID-19, despite, the Associated Press reports, it having been "yet to be determined effective or safe for the virus" and—per the *New York Times*—there being "little evidence" it ever will be.[114] Equally important, the president's recommendation "runs counter to what his own health experts say."[115]

In early April, the nonprofit, nonpartisan organization Citizens for Responsibility and Ethics in Washington reveals that "a Pharma-funded group tied to a top Trump donor has been pushing Trump to approve the use of hydroxychloroquine for treating COVID-19."[116] The donor, Bernard Marcus, is co-founder of the Job Creators Network, a "conservative dark money nonprofit . . . calling on Trump to 'cut the red tape' and immediately make hydroxychloroquine available to treat patients"; Marcus not only spent more than $7 million to elect Trump in 2016, but by April 2020 has announced "plans to spend part of his fortune to help re-elect Trump."[117] Shortly after the Marcus revelation, the *New York Times* reports that "Mr. Trump himself has a small personal financial interest in Sanofi, the French drugmaker that makes Plaquenil, the brand-name version of hydroxychloroquine," adding that after weeks of the president pushing the drug his "assertiveness in pressing the case [for it] . . . has raised questions about his motives."[118] Subsequent reporting by *Market-Watch* reveals that Trump "look[s] to have more than . . . [a] modest sum invested in Sanofi."[119]

On March 23, just five days into what will become a weeks-long hydroxychloroquine push by Trump, an Arizona man not sick with

COVID-19—but hoping to protect himself from becoming so—dies from taking chloroquine phosphate without a prescription.[120] His wife, interviewed by NBC News after being hospitalized for her own ingestion of the drug, says, "We saw Trump on TV—every channel—[and] all of his buddies and that this was safe. Trump kept saying it was basically pretty much a cure."[121] She adds, "Don't believe anything that the President says and his people because they don't know what they're talking about."[122] Two weeks later, "data released by France's drug safety agency" includes information on "43 cases of heart incidents linked to [coronavirus patients taking] hydroxychloroquine, underscoring the risk of providing unproven treatments to COVID-19 patients."[123] On April 21, a study reveals that the combination of hydroxychloroquine and the antibiotic azithromycin is linked to increased mortality in COVID-19 patients, and shows no indications of any therapeutic benefit.[124] The National Institute of Allergy and Infectious Diseases immediately issues a statement "recommend[ing] against" the drug combination, which NPR notes has been "promoted by Trump"—indeed, the president had a month earlier described it as having a "real chance to be one of the biggest game changers in the history of medicine."[125] Following Trump's initial proposal of the potentially dangerous hydroxychloroquine-azithromycin combination, prescriptions for the drugs "jumped by 46 times the average."[126] On May 10, the Associated Press reports that there is evidence—in the form of bulk drug orders—that the Trump administration is still secretly administering hydroxychloroquine and azithromycin to veterans in Department of Veterans Affairs (VA) facilities.[127]

According to *Wired*, Larry Brilliant, "the epidemiologist who helped eradicate smallpox," has called the "advice from the President of the United States for the first 12 weeks" of the COVID-19 pandemic "the most irresponsible act of an elected official that I've ever witnessed in my lifetime"; Brilliant adds that "all we got were lies."[128]

Throughout the early months of the COVID-19 outbreak, a number of Trump's political and media surrogates make statements about the virus as inaccurate as the president's. One Trump surrogate whose dubious statements about the virus in January and February 2020 are notable, Trump 2020 campaign press secretary Kayleigh McEnany, says on Fox News on February 25 that "we will not see diseases like the coronavirus come here [to the United States] . . . and isn't that refreshing when contrasting it with the awful presidency of President Obama?"[129] McEnany is promoted to the position of White House press secretary six weeks later.[130] The same day as McEnany's statement on Fox News, top Trump economic adviser Larry Kudlow, the director of the National Economic Council, tells a CNBC interviewer, "We have contained this [virus], I won't say 'airtight' but pretty close to 'airtight.'"[131] On March 8, at a time when the United States has more than 500 confirmed cases of COVID-19—and a sufficient lack of testing to suggest that the real number is far higher—Trump's secretary of housing and urban development, Dr. Ben Carson, responds to a question from ABC News about the president's insistence on holding political rallies amidst the outbreak by saying that there is "no reason" for Trump supporters not to congregate for such events.[132] In early April, as confirmed U.S. COVID-19 cases are at 211,000—with a death toll of 4,600—Trump congressional ally Devin Nunes demands that the U.S. economy be reopened and children returned to school, calling the strict social-distancing measures recommended by the CDC "overkill"; Nunes issues his demand, the *Washington Post* notes, "amid projections that more than 2 million Americans could die if strict social distancing measures are relaxed."[133]

The failures of the Trump administration during the COVID-19 outbreak are of such scope and scale that they frustrate and astonish government officials, journalists, and experts in several relevant disciplines. David Begnaud of CBS News reports that the White House is, instead of following established disaster management protocols, selling "critical supplies" to "commercial distributors" rather than the states—creating Firtash-like middlemen with no natural place in the supply chain who "sell [supplies] to the states" even as, Begnaud writes, "the states . . .

are begging for [government] help."[134] After Trump puts his son-in-law, Jared Kushner, in charge of what *Vanity Fair* calls a "shadow" coronavirus task force, individuals involved in the official response team tell the magazine "they don't know who is in charge"; Kushner's emergence as a key figure in the federal government's pandemic response operations is complicated when he erroneously claims that the Strategic National Stockpile (SNS) of supplies for public health emergencies is "our [the federal government's] stockpile. It's not supposed to be states' stockpiles that they then use."[135] After several major-media reports highlight the language of the Strategic National Stockpile's website—which says the stockpile's purpose is to ensure "that the right medicines and supplies get to those who need them most" whenever "state, local, tribal, and territorial responders request federal assistance to support their [emergency] response efforts"—the White House quietly changes the language of the website overnight to conform to Kushner's inaccurate claim.[136]

When Sen. Cory Gardner (R-CO) asks the HHS inspector general to investigate whether "mismanagement" by the Trump administration has "led to a shortage of working ventilators or other critical supplies or equipment [in the SNS]," an Associated Press investigative report underscores his concerns by finding that "after the first alarms sounded in early January that an outbreak of a novel coronavirus in China might ignite a global pandemic, the Trump administration squandered nearly two months that could have been used to bolster the federal stockpile of critically needed medical supplies and equipment. A review of federal purchasing contracts . . . shows federal agencies largely waited until mid-March to begin placing bulk orders of N95 respirator masks, mechanical ventilators and other equipment needed by front-line health care workers."[137]

In early April, *USA Today* reveals that as the president was refusing to apply the Defense Production Act in January and February 2020, U.S. companies were selling "more than $17.5 million worth of face masks, more than $13.6 million in surgical garments and more than $27.2 million in ventilators to China."[138] During the same period, the State Department donated "nearly 17.8 tons of . . . medical supplies" to

China, "including masks, gowns, gauze, respirators, and other vital materials."[139] When the administration finally accepts that medical supplies are in such shortage in the United States that it must seek them out overseas, its phoned request for aid to the government of Thailand is met with "puzzled voices" because, as *Politico* reports, "a U.S. shipment of the same supplies, the second of two so far, was already on its way to Bangkok."[140]

The Dow Jones Industrial Average ends the first quarter of 2020 down 23.2 percent, "its worst quarter since 1987," according to the Associated Press.[141] The performance includes a 2,997-point drop in the Dow on March 16, "its worst point-drop in history."[142] More history is made when trading on the New York Stock Exchange (NYSE) is halted automatically—via an "emergency circuit breaker" intended to protect against a cataclysmic market collapse—three times in just two weeks.[143] By April 9, real unemployment in the United States is at 14.7 percent, its highest level since before World War II.[144] While a $2 trillion stimulus bill passed by Congress in late March offers some hope of relief, a Bankrate survey reveals that of the 67 percent of Americans who expect to receive a stimulus check as a result of the bill, nearly a third say the money "won't sustain their financial well-being for even a month."[145]

In late March, the *Washington Post* publishes a lengthy report on the Trump administration's pandemic response, concluding that a major culprit behind the president's delay in responding decisively and effectively to the outbreak was his "relationship with China's President Xi Jinping, whom Trump believed was providing him with reliable information about how the virus was spreading in China—despite reports from intelligence agencies that Chinese officials were not being candid about the true scale of the crisis."[146] The *Post* adds that even after the president's top advisers told him that Xi's government was lying to him about both China's COVID-19 infection rates and its death toll, "Trump publicly praised [China's] response" to the epidemic.[147] Indeed, despite China relaying to U.S. officials on January 14 the conspicuous mistruth that it had observed "no clear evidence of human-to-human [coronavirus] transmission"—a claim already contradicted by U.S. intelligence reports emerging from Wuhan in November 2019 and media and NGO reports produced in late December—ten days later, on January 24, Trump assures U.S. voters that "it will all work out well" with the coronavirus because "China has been working very hard to contain [it]" and has shown "transparency" in its efforts.[148] Trump goes on to thank President Xi "on behalf of the American People."[149]

The *Post* retrospective on the first few months of the COVID-19 outbreak concludes that "it may never be known how many thousands of deaths, or millions of infections, might have been prevented with a response that was more coherent, urgent and effective"; the newspaper does, however, make an effort at estimating the former figure, producing a "Trump Death Clock" whose algorithm attributes to "President Trump and his team's reckless handling of the coronavirus pandemic" a minimum of 61,100 U.S. COVID-19 fatalities as of May 28, 2020.[150] More broadly, the *Post* opines that "Trump's dismissive depictions of the virus" directly resulted in Republican voters "in distressingly large numbers refusing to change travel plans, follow 'social distancing' guidelines, stock up on supplies or otherwise take the coronavirus threat seriously."[151] The newspaper adds that Trump's actions have contributed to an "alter[ation] [in] the international standing of the United States, damaging and diminishing its reputation as a global leader in times of extraordinary adversity."[152] It remains unclear what connection may exist between Trump receiving nonpublic information on the Biden family from the Chinese government in mid-October 2019—along with any expectation he may have had that more aid would be forthcoming from Beijing throughout the 2020 campaign—and the president's otherwise inexplicable unwillingness to react robustly and publicly to Xi Jinping's perfidy on the matter of the novel coronavirus until the spring of 2020.

* * *

On the morning of April 11, 2020, the United States reaches what CNN calls a "grim milestone," passing Italy as the global epicenter for coronavirus fatalities. The cable news outlet reports that "New York State alone has more [COVID-19] cases than any . . . country."[153] Just hours later, the nation passes yet another tragic marker: after the federal government declares a state of emergency in Wyoming, all fifty U.S. states are under such a declaration for the first time in American history.[154] April 11 also sees the release of a major investigative report by the *New York Times* revealing that—despite having received months of briefings on the staggering COVID-19 death toll that would result in the United States in the absence of physical distancing measures—Trump has privately and repeatedly proposed that the virus be allowed to "wash over" America in order to preserve the economy.[155]

By mid-April, Trump is calling on residents of the Democratic-led states of Michigan, Minnesota, and Virginia—particularly those residents deeply invested in their constitutional right to bear arms—to "liberate" their states by protesting stay-at-home orders with mass violation of these strictures. According to a column in the *Washington Post* by former acting U.S. assistant attorney general for national security Mary McCord, Trump's exhortations on Twitter are "at least [a] tacit encouragement to citizens to take up arms against duly elected state officials of the party opposite his own," and under federal law may constitute "calling for insurrection."[156]

As of May 28, 2020, the United States ranks first in the world in total COVID-19 infections—with more than four times as many cases as the second-most-infected country, Brazil—as well as first in total deaths, with over 65,000 more deaths than the second-hardest-hit country in terms of COVID-19 fatalities, the United Kingdom.[157] Even if the analysis adjusts for population, the United States ranks ninth worldwide in the per capita death toll among nations with more than a hundred COVID-19 deaths.[158] Meanwhile, America ranks thirty-fourth in per capita testing.[159] With respect to antibody testing in particular, the *New York Times* reports that Trump's Food and Drug Administration (FDA) is "under fire from scientists and Congress for allowing wildly inaccurate coronavirus antibody tests to proliferate."[160]

While the data indicates that by the end of May 2020, 1.83 million Americans have been infected with the novel coronavirus and well over 100,000 have died from it, major-media reporting confirms that the official U.S. death toll from COVID-19 is, throughout the evolution of the outbreak, a dramatic undercount.[161] The *New York Times* reports that in New York City alone the official COVID-19 death toll in early May—even after numerous post-dated modifications in April—may still undercount deaths by 4,300. A subsequent *Times* assessment of "[year-over-year] excess deaths" likely attributable to COVID-19 in New Jersey, Michigan, Massachusetts, Illinois, Maryland, and Colorado reveals that an additional 4,700 deaths from the virus may not have been officially counted in these six states.[162] Moreover, CNN, citing the national public health group Well Being Trust, observes that the final death toll from the pandemic arguably must include deaths indirectly caused by the virus, given that "as many as 75,000 Americans could die because of drug or alcohol misuse and suicide as a result of the coronavirus pandemic."[163] Worse still, a mid-May *Washington Post* investigative report, presaging even more dire assessments by Columbia University, finds that at least 51,338 of the nation's COVID-19 deaths "can . . . be attributed to the administration's delay [in responding to the pandemic] between March 2 and March 16."[164] The Institute for Health Metrics and Evaluation (IHME) at the University of Washington, using a model long favored by the White House, announces on May 28 that the U.S. death toll from COVID-19 is likely to be 132,000 by August 4, 2020; even so, CNN reports in mid-May that "Trump and some of his aides have begun questioning whether deaths are being over-counted," with the cable news outlet calling the president's effort to "sow[ ] distrust in the institutions and data which underpin his coronavirus response" part of a scheme "designed to advance national reopening efforts that Trump believes will revive the economy and with it his reelection prospects."[165]

* * *

COVID-19 has proven itself to be more readily contagious than many Americans anticipated. CNN reports that droplets exhaled by someone who is COVID-19 positive can travel as far as twelve feet and hang in the air for eight minutes, while the *New York Times* reports that the latter figure could be as high as fourteen minutes.[166] Other studies return significantly more troubling results: according to a *New England Journal of Medicine* study reported on by *The Economist*, the novel coronavirus can "linger in the air for hours and on some materials for days"; an MIT study reported on by *USA Today* finds that in some instances the virus can travel up to twenty-seven feet from the mouth of an infected person, a finding broadly echoed by a May 27 CNN report declaring that, according to expert commentary published in the journal *Science*, "Six feet of distance may not be enough to prevent coronavirus transmission . . . the world needs to take airborne transmission of the virus seriously."[167] The *Daily Beast* reports in early May on a "new mutant coronavirus even more contagious than the original," noting that, according to a Los Alamos National Laboratory study, "the new strain can spread faster and make people vulnerable to a second infection after their first. . . . [It] originated in Europe at some point in February [2020], but quickly spread to the East Coast of the United States and has since become the dominant coronavirus strain around the world."[168] The ascendance of this new strain unfolds concurrently with a terrifying development in New York City, where after months of conventional wisdom suggesting the novel coronavirus is relatively harmless to small children, more than 100 COVID-19-positive young people are identified as having potentially life-threatening symptoms including, per CNN, "persistent fever, toxic shock syndrome and features similar to Kawasaki disease"—a dangerous and sometimes deadly swelling of artery walls.[169] Days later, several additional states report cases of "pediatric multisystem inflammatory syndrome" similar to those in New York City.[170] The perceived danger and contagiousness of the virus expands again on May 8, when a Chinese study of recovering COVID-19 patients produces evidence that the virus may be sexually transmittable through semen.[171]

Despite these harrowing facts, and the United States' globally idiosyncratic death toll from COVID-19, in early May the White House declares that it will not allow the nation's top infectious-disease expert, Dr. Fauci, to testify before Congress about the pandemic—nor will it permit any member of Trump's Coronavirus Task Force to do so.[172] Though this decision is subsequently revised to allow testimony in the GOP-led Senate, Dr. Fauci's eventual testimony to a Senate panel—harshly criticized by Trump after the fact—underlines the sort of information the White House would have preferred he not disclose. "If you think that we have [the virus] completely under control," Fauci tells senators, "we don't. When you look at the dynamics of new cases, even though some [states' infection rates] are coming down, the [overall] curve looks flat with some slight coming down. . . . [Heading in] the right direction does not mean we have, by any means, total control of this outbreak."[173] According to the *New York Times*, Fauci's message to the Senate is that the United States will experience "needless suffering and death" if it opens up again to regular commerce and social interaction on the sort of rapid timeframe long encouraged by the president.[174]

It is not only Dr. Fauci's public health prognosis that Trump is ignoring, however. In early May, the president once again ignores the findings of his intelligence agencies by announcing—without providing evidence of his claim, or citing any sources—that, as CNN will summarize, "he's seen evidence [the novel] coronavirus originated in [a] Chinese lab."[175] Secretary of State Pompeo at first seeks to bolster Trump's assertion by saying there is "enormous evidence" of the coronavirus being man-made, but backs off his assertion after days of intense questioning by reporters.[176] Trump's unsubstantiated claim, which implies that the coronavirus might have originally been intended as a Chinese bioweapon, is followed in short order by a report revealing that Chinese intelligence has told President Xi, per Reuters, that "Beijing faces a rising wave of hostility in the wake of the coronavirus outbreak that could tip relations with the United States into confrontation . . . [including] a worst-case scenario . . . [of] armed confrontation between the two global powers."[177]

Trump's startling claims about the origins of the novel coronavirus come less than twenty-four hours after a CBS News report revealing that, according to a modeling study from the Center for Infectious Disease Research and Policy at the University of Minnesota, the novel coronavirus "likely won't be contained for two years" and "70 percent of people need to be immune [to it] to bring the virus to a halt."[178] On the same day as Trump's apparently false claim that the coronavirus was man-made, CNN reports that one American died of COVID-19 every forty-four seconds in April—and Trump announces his intention, according to CBS, to replace the acting inspector general for HHS, Christi Grimm, who had previously "released a report detailing shortages of testing and personal protective equipment (PPE) in hospitals responding to the coronavirus pandemic."[179] The report had angered the president, who called it "wrong" without offering any evidence to contest its findings.[180]

Beginning in late April, single-site outbreaks of COVID-19 become commonplace, as do local and statewide outbreaks traceably linked to the Trump administration's public push for America to "reopen" whether or not federal guidelines for reopening have been met. In Iowa, 730 workers at a single pork processing plant—nearly 60 percent of the plant's workforce—test positive for the coronavirus by May 6, a larger number of infections than 109 of the world's 195 countries have seen as of that date; on the day the plant fully reopens after a two-week closure, total on-site COVID-19 cases reach 1,031.[181] In Wisconsin, after Democratic Party attempts to postpone the state's presidential primaries are opposed by Republican legislators and the state's conservative-majority supreme court, CNN reports that "at least 52" Wisconsin voters contracted COVID-19 during the subsequent live vote; it remains unknown how many hundreds or thousands of second-, third-, and subsequent-level coronavirus infections these fifty-two individuals produced in the weeks following the April 7 primary.[182] In one particularly troubling incident in Washington State, 87 percent of a choir contingent—fifty-three people—were infected by the coronavirus after a single early March choir practice with a member who had cold-like symptoms and did not realize they had been infected; two choir members died.[183]

A number of states with Republican governors permit businesses to reopen with conditions in late April and early May, despite these states having not yet met federal guidelines recommending fourteen straight days of declining infections before any statewide reopening. Indeed, Texas sees its worst daily death toll, and one of its worst-ever days for new infections, on the same day that its Republican governor, Greg Abbott, allows the state's stay-at-home order to lapse.[184] In Arizona, a state led by Republican governor Doug Ducey, the "biggest single-day increase in coronavirus cases" comes "as the state continue[s] its reopening process."[185]

The virus's economic toll is as staggering as its cost in human suffering. On April 20, 2020, global oil prices go negative for the first time in history.[186] On May 9, a front-page headline in the *New York Times* announces, "U.S. Unemployment Is Worst Since Depression"—a reference to the Great Depression, which lasted from 1929 to 1939.[187] In late April, Nobel Prize–winning economist Joseph Stiglitz tells *The Guardian*, "If you leave it to Donald Trump and Mitch McConnell, we [America] will have a Great Depression. If we had the right policy structure in place we could avoid it easily."[188] Bloomberg News confirms Stiglitz's analysis, noting on the same day as the economist's prediction that "current forecasts are for the [U.S.] unemployment rate to reach 20 percent this month. Some predict it could go as high as 30 percent this year. That would eclipse even the Great Depression in severity."[189] Per Bloomberg, among those emphasizing the possibility of a 30 percent unemployment rate by the end of 2020 is Federal Reserve Bank of St. Louis president James Bullard.[190] A May 11 assessment by the Transportation Security Administration reveals, per CNN, that year-over-year air travel is down 92 percent.[191] CNN reports that "American grocery store price tags are soaring because COVID-19 has disrupted the food supply chain."[192] And in what the Associated Press calls an "ominous" sign, Neiman Marcus, a department store, becomes in early May the second major U.S. retailer— after J.Crew—to declare bankruptcy amidst the nationwide business closures necessitated by the pandemic; it is followed by department store chain J. C. Penney and the rental-car company Hertz, shortly thereafter.[193]

Politico calls the nation's April 2020 jobs report definitive proof that "coronavirus lockdowns delivered the swiftest and hardest punch to the economy in U.S. history."[194]

This staggering economic data aside, late April and early May also see the emergence of new evidence of the novel coronavirus's hardiness and lethality. French researchers announce their discovery that, contra Trump's untutored speculation, SARS-CoV-2—the formal name for the novel coronavirus—can survive in high temperatures; 140-degree Fahrenheit temperatures cannot readily destroy the virus, per the French study, and even 197.6-degree heat takes fifteen minutes to kill the virus.[195] In late April, the CDC adds six new indicators to its catalogue of COVID-19 symptoms, which now includes fever, cough, shortness of breath, headache, persistent pain or pressure in the chest, sore throat, muscle pain, shaking, chills, confusion, loss of taste or smell, bluish lips or face, inability to arouse, diarrhea, skin rash, red eyes, runny nose, and fatigue; other less common but still widely observed symptoms, according to the *Washington Post*, include strokes, blood clots, pinkeye, vomiting, arrhythmias, kidney damage, and a purple rash on the extremities that becomes known as "Covid toes" or "Covid fingers."[196] Worryingly, some coronavirus patients continue to experience symptoms long after they begin testing negative for the virus; one such individual, a woman in Massachusetts, tells NBC News that she has had a fever nearly every day for fifty days and has begun to wonder if her condition is "permanent."[197] Bloomberg News reports that "virus survivors could suffer severe health effects for years."[198] The World Health Organization releases a related finding indicating that even individuals who previously had COVID-19 but have since recovered completely may not have gained the benefit of long-term immunity to the virus; the organization announces that while such people may enjoy "some level of protection" against a second infection, "we don't know yet . . . the level of protection or how long it will last."[199]

In view of the foregoing, it is little surprise that sentiment in the United States runs strongly against the inaction of the Trump administration. According to an NBC News/*Wall Street Journal* poll taken in

late April, 65 percent of Americans believe that Trump did not take the threat of the novel coronavirus "seriously enough at the beginning," and per a concurrent NPR/Marist poll, 55 percent of Americans disapprove of Trump's handling of the pandemic.[200] According to two other late April polls—one taken by the Harvard CAPS/Harris operation, the other by Politico/Morning Consult—nearly 60 percent of Americans say that the country should have shut down earlier than it did, and 81 percent of Americans agree that the nation should "continue to social distance for as long as is needed to curb the spread of coronavirus, even if it means continued damage to the economy."[201] Only 10 percent of Americans disagree with the latter premise.[202] It is also in late April that the percentage of Americans who have "high levels of trust in what the president is telling the public [about COVID-19]" drops to just 23 percent, according to the Associated Press.[203] By mid-May, 58 percent of Americans are telling CNN pollsters that "the government is not doing enough to prevent a second wave [of the virus] later [in 2020]."[204]

Remarkably, Trump administration policy throughout spring 2020 reflects the views of the 10 percent of Americans who want to risk a worsening of the COVID-19 outbreak to preserve the economy—as well as the views of a president increasingly detached from both the facts and even the vocal fringe of "economy-first" Americans. On April 20, Trump makes the extraordinary claim that, despite his many televised political rallies across the nation in February and March, he has not left the White House in "months" in recognition of the seriousness of the coronavirus threat; six days later, the president expands on his already fallacious statement, insisting on Twitter that he hasn't left the White House in "many" months.[205] On April 24, Trump, as reported by the Washington Post, offers the "dangerous suggestion that injecting bleach or other household disinfectants into the body might cure people of the novel coronavirus," a sentiment that quickly results in experts' "universal rejection of the president's hypothesis . . . [and] urgent bulletins . . . including from inside Trump's own administration . . . warning the public of [the] potentially lethal dangers" of the president's proposal.[206] Trump's former FDA commissioner, Scott Gottlieb, tells CNBC, of the proposal, that "there's absolutely no circumstance under which that's appropriate and it can cause death and very adverse outcomes."[207] At least two states—Michigan and Maryland—report that "emergency hotlines in their states saw increases in [poison control] calls after President Trump suggested disinfectants be investigated as a treatment for COVID-19"; nationwide data will reveal 3,609 "reported cases of accidental poisonings from household disinfectants" in April 2020, up from the typical April figure of around 1,650, and 966 cases between May 1 and May 10, up from 573 cases during the same period in 2019.[208] When asked by the White House press corps whether he takes any responsibility for such spikes, Trump answers, "No, I don't," and insists that he "can't imagine why" the spikes have occurred.[209]

The same day the president makes untutored comments about the purported therapeutic qualities of injected disinfectants, he declares publicly his belief that perhaps "a very powerful light" beamed into the body could kill the coronavirus.[210] According to NBC News, Trump's baseless speculation regarding disinfectants and ultraviolet beams being miracle cures for COVID-19 mirrors, with significant specificity, coronavirus disinformation being spread by adherents to the "QAnon" conspiracy theory. Per NBC, "QAnon adherents falsely believe Donald Trump is secretly running a military operation to rid the government of satanic, child-eating cannibals, and many QAnon followers believe those same people are responsible for the virus."[211] On May 5, 2020, NBC will reveal that Trump's selection to run the U.S. intelligence community, Rep. John Ratcliffe (R-TX), follows on social media a number of Twitter accounts "promoting the infamous QAnon conspiracy theory claiming that the world is run by a cabal of Democratic pedophile cannibals—a set of beliefs ruled by the FBI to be a potential source of domestic terrorism."[212] "In Ratcliffe's Twitter feed," NBC reports, "there are accounts that portray Trump as a messianic figure ready to use our military and intelligence agencies to rid the nation of top Democrats."[213] *Just Security* reports that Trump himself is guilty of both the "endorsement and amplification of conspiracy theories and theorists such as QAnon," including "retweet[ing] QAnon supporters . . . dozens of times," and doing so in a way, according to the *Washington Post*, that causes QAnon adherents to be "overjoyed . . . believing it's evidence he supports their movement."[214]

The president's spread of misinformation during the COVID-19 crisis is matched by a bout of inexplicable nonfeasance as well. Despite saying in early May 2020 that reopening the country mid-pandemic is safe because "we're going to practice social distancing" and "we're going to be washing hands . . . [and] a lot of the things that we've learned to do over the last period of time," when Trump travels to an Arizona mask-making facility the same week, he neither keeps six feet from his hosts, as recommended by the CDC, nor wears a face mask—despite signage in the facility indicating that doing so is mandatory.[215] The result, per Reuters coverage, is infelicitous video footage of Trump walking maskless through a Honeywell plant that produces N95 masks—flaunting safety guidelines he has promoted for others—while a cover of Paul McCartney's song "Live and Let Die" blares over a loudspeaker.[216] According to the *New York Times*, the White House reveals, on the same day, that it will "shut down" its Coronavirus Task Force "around the end of May" and "replace [it] with an unspecified new advisory body . . . focus[ed] on safety and reopening the country."[217] In mid-May, the White House announces that "officials [are] to wear masks at all times inside the West Wing," a directive that excludes one person—President Trump—despite contemporaneous *Politico* polling indicating that 70 percent of Americans (including 82 percent of Democrats, 70 percent of independents, and 58 percent of Republicans) want Trump to wear a face mask along with the rest of the country.[218]

On May 5, Dr. Rick Bright, former director of the Biomedical Advanced Research and Development Authority (BARDA) at HHS, files a formal whistleblower complaint alleging that his removal from his post in April was retaliation for, among other items, opposing the awarding of inappropriate pandemic-related contracts to "companies with political connections to the administration" and seeking an aggressive response to the pandemic from the Trump administration in January—to which efforts he reports he "encountered opposition" from his superiors, including Secretary Azar.[219] In sum, the Associated Press reports, Dr. Bright alleges that "the Trump administration failed to prepare for the onslaught of the coronavirus, then sought a quick fix by trying to rush an unproven drug to patients," and that it "reassigned him to a lesser role because he resisted political pressure to allow widespread use of hydroxychloroquine, a malaria drug pushed by President Donald Trump. He said the Trump administration wanted to 'flood' hot spots in New York and New Jersey with the drug."[220] Per the AP, Dr. Bright says "his superiors repeatedly rejected his warnings that the virus would spread in the U.S., missing an early opportunity to stock up on protective masks for first responders"; Bright's complaint further accuses Azar of being "intent on downplaying this catastrophic event" and HHS assistant secretary for preparedness and response Robert Kadlec of insisting, against all the available evidence, that "the United States would be able to contain the virus and keep it out."[221] Bright also contends that HHS falsely "publicly represented not only that COVID-19 was not an imminent threat, but also that HHS already had all the masks it would need"—despite the fact that, by his own expert assessment and that of experts outside HHS, the Trump administration had, in its more than three years of governance, stockpiled only 8.6 percent of the masks needed to defend America in the event of a pandemic on the scale of COVID-19.[222]

At the same time that Bright makes his complaint, a bombshell report in the *Washington Post* alleges that a team led by Jared Kushner that was "responsible for [procuring] PPE [personal protective equipment] had little success in helping the government secure such equipment, in part because none of [Kushner's] team members had significant experience in health care, procurement or supply-chain operations."[223] Worse still, a complaint from a volunteer within Kushner's operation—whose accuracy is confirmed for the *Post* by six administration officials—alleges, per the newspaper, that "supply-chain volunteers were instructed to fast-track protective equipment leads from 'VIPs,' including conservative journalists friendly to the White House."[224] And the *Post* reveals yet another deeply troubling component of Kushner's operation: that "about 30 percent of 'key supplies,' including masks, in the national stockpile of emergency medical equipment went toward standing up a separate Kushner-led effort to establish drive-through testing sites nationwide," adding that while Kushner "had originally promised thousands of testing sites . . . only 78 materialized; the [national] stockpile was used to supply 44 of those [78 sites] over five to 10 days."[225] According to a summary of the complaint by the *Post*, Kushner's team "had trouble developing manufacturer relationships and making inroads with brokers . . . in part because they were using personal email accounts, rather than official government email addresses"; while it is unclear why a federal government pandemic response team would eschew the use of government email accounts, one possible reason—consistent with Kushner's and his wife Ivanka Trump's own long-standing practices—would be to conduct official government business over private channels that cannot be subjected to a Freedom of Information Act request or congressional oversight.[226]

Dr. Bright's whistleblower complaint—which, like the complaint about Kushner's team reported on by the *Post*, focuses in part on federal attempts to secure face masks for first responders—goes beyond well PPE acquisition, however. Bright reports that he worked with Peter Navarro on an early February memo urging the Trump administration to "start this week to fast track vaccine development with appropriate funding"; instead, the *Daily Beast* reports, Azar's assistant Kadlec "criticized [Bright and Navarro's] insistence that the U.S. start working on vaccines at the outset of the COVID pandemic, stating that the focus should be on therapies [like hydroxychloroquine] because vaccines would take too long to develop."[227] Kadlec and Azar would hold the line on this position for two months, a decision that not only set back the search for a COVID-19 vaccine significantly but also, Bright's complaint now implies, may have been aimed at appeasing Trump donors.[228] Implicit in Bright's accusation is that decisions made by Trump and his team that stood to enrich

Trump donors could ultimately lead to substantially increased donations from these entities and their affiliates to Trump's 2020 reelection campaign.

On April 26, former FDA commissioner Scott Gottlieb confirms that Bright's demotion will "set us [the United States] back," implying that the removal of a "very effective . . . vaccine expert" from BARDA could delay work on a vaccine.[229] On May 8, the *Washington Post* reports that there are "'reasonable grounds' to believe [Bright] was removed from his post . . . for retaliatory reasons," according to the federal government's Office of Special Counsel—which, per the *Post*, intends to recommend Bright's reinstatement as the nation's vaccine chief while his whistleblower complaint is investigated. The office shortly thereafter finds a "substantial likelihood of wrongdoing" in Bright's removal.[230]

On May 15, 2020, the *Washington Post* reports that the national COVID-19 death toll is "almost certainly" lower than the real figure, as COVID-19 fatalities are "being left out of the official count" because of "widespread lack of access to testing in the early weeks of the U.S. outbreak," "people with respiratory illnesses [dying] without being counted," "some people [dying] at home or in overburdened nursing homes . . . not being tested," "postmortem testing by medical examiners [varying] widely across the country," and "some people who have the virus test[ing] negative."[231] Indeed, by early April the CDC had already announced, with respect to the rapidly increasing number of COVID-19 fatalities in the U.S., that "we know . . . it is an underestimation."[232]

By mid-May, thirty-four members of the Secret Service have been infected by COVID-19, and a member of the Joint Chiefs of Staff— Air Force general Joseph Lengyel—has tested positive for COVID-19 while waiting at the White House for a planned meeting with President Trump.[233] Even more striking, COVID-19 is inside the West Wing of the White House and in close proximity to Trump and his family, with CNN reporting that one of President Trump's personal valets—a soldier among those "responsible for the President's food and beverage [service]"—has been infected by the virus, as have Vice President Mike Pence's press secretary, Katie Miller (married to senior adviser to the president Stephen Miller), and a personal assistant to Ivanka Trump.[234] *Newsweek* reports that "Trump had been in close contact with the valet" as recently as seventy-two hours prior to the revelation of the staffer's positive COVID-19 test.[235] NBC reports that, per witnesses, Trump became "lava-level mad" when he learned his valet had the virus—a reaction that both calls into question White House national security and public health protocols and undermines the president's case to reopen America to regular business.[236] Despite the president's rage, and the fact that the precautions and testing available to a president significantly exceed anything available to the general public, by mid-May there is no indication that the ability of COVID-19 to penetrate the White House has tempered Trump's eagerness to reopen America in mid-pandemic. Per NBC, Trump's tirade against his staff following the revelations about his valet had featured the president accusing his team of not "doing all it can to protect him"—a sentiment often voiced by the president's critics with respect to the administration, but also a foreshadowing of the May 13 revelation that, per a New York University study, the SARS-CoV-2 tests in use at the White House in spring 2020 (touted by Trump as "highly accurate" during a Rose Garden press conference) miss almost half of all infections.[237]

Asked by the White House press corps about the safety measures available to Trump at the White House, White House press secretary Kayleigh McEnany touts the availability of "contact tracing" to members of the Trump administration, a pandemic response mechanism not only not yet publicly available in May 2020 but not even mentioned in a CDC report on reopening precautions that is leaked to media the same day as McEnany's statement.[238] Despite its modest expectations for the safety measures to be made available to average Americans returning to work mid-pandemic, the Trump administration "buries" the seventeen-page CDC report, deeming it too restrictive on businesses and telling its authors that it will "never see the light of day."[239] The Associated Press subsequently reports that "the decision to shelve detailed advice from the nation's top disease control experts for reopening communities during the coronavirus pandemic came from the highest levels of the White House," adding that it was only "after the AP reported . . . that the guidance document had been buried . . . [that] the Trump administration ordered key parts of it to be fast-tracked for approval."[240]

During an event with GOP lawmakers shortly after learning that the vice president's press secretary had tested positive for the coronavirus, Trump declares that "the whole concept of [virus] tests isn't great"—a strange remark he does not explain.[241] The odds of the president and vice president getting infected by the coronavirus seem to increase substantially after the *Washington Post* reports that, in the wake of the spate of infections at the top levels of the Trump administration, "White House staffers were encouraged to come into the office by their superiors" and "aides who travel with President Trump and Vice President Pence . . . [were told] not [to] stay out for 14 days, the recommended time frame to quarantine once exposed to the virus."[242] According to a "former security official familiar with White House security planning during past administrations" who speaks to the *Washington Post*, the president has "tried to minimize this threat from day one. It's the only way he can laugh in the face of this disease. If he backtracks now . . . it will contradict the red meat he's feeding to his base constantly. This is the first health crisis that has been politicized."[243]

Trump's politicization of the crisis is one that personalizes rather than globalizes it. CNN reports that "the United States—usually at the head of the table helping to coordinate in global crises—has declined to take a seat at virtual international meetings convened by the World Health Organization and the European Union to coordinate work on potentially lifesaving vaccines. Former world leaders warn that the Trump administration risks alienating allies by politicizing the deadly pandemic. . . . The administration's decision to halt funding for the WHO, the world body best positioned to coordinate the global response to the raging pandemic, has appalled global health officials."[244] By early May, *The Hill* is reporting that "world leaders [have] fall[en] short of funding goal[s] for a coronavirus vaccine" in large part because the Trump administration and Putin's Kremlin "noticeably refuse to participate" in raising funds.[245] Meanwhile, per *Politico*, Democrats in Congress, led by Speaker of the House Nancy Pelosi, allege that the freeze in aid to the WHO "is illegal and violates the same federal spending laws as the Ukraine aid freeze that partly prompted [Trump's impeachment]."[246]

By May 10, 2020, Vice President Pence, the CDC director, the FDA director, and Dr. Fauci—four top members of Trump's Coronavirus Task Force—are in varying degrees of self-quarantine after contact at the White House with individuals positive for the virus. Another recent quarantine entrant, owing to a positive coronavirus test among his staff, is Sen. Lamar Alexander, the chairman of the U.S. Senate's Health, Education, Labor and Pensions Committee and the fourth GOP senator to enter self-quarantine.[247] As the number of high-profile Republicans in quarantine steadily grows, White House economic adviser Kevin Hassett admits in an interview with *Politico* that working at the White House has become "scary."[248]

By May 11, forty-seven U.S. states have in some way eased social-distancing restrictions in accordance with Trump's ambition to fully re-open America to business, despite the fact that it is still the case that not one state has met federal guidelines indicating that, along with wide-spread diagnostic testing and contact tracing—two pandemic-response mainstays unavailable in America in mid-May 2020—a jurisdiction should see a "14-day drop in [new COVID-19] cases to reopen."[249] One state, Missouri, sees its largest-ever number of new infections on the day it reopens for business.[250] As restrictions are being lifted, 71 percent of Americans tell UCLA pollsters that "they are worried that the restrictions are being lifted too quickly," and public health officials, according to the *Washington Post*, "warn [that] a deadly [COVID-19] surge may follow [the reopening]."[251] Sen. Alexander concurs with this majority and departs from the president's narrative—which has come to include the counterfactual claim that "we have prevailed" over the virus and ensured enough tests for those who need them—by declaring, on May 7, that the United States will need "millions more tests" in order to safely reopen.[252]

Both the American public's and Alexander's assessments are consistent with the findings of a model developed by the Massachusetts Institute of Technology (MIT), which had determined in late April that "any immediate or near-term relaxation or reversal of quarantine measures currently in place would lead to an 'exponential explosion' in the number of infections."[253] A joint Harvard-MIT study had concurrently found that the planned premature reopening in just a single Republican-led state—Georgia—could cause between 600 and 1,314 additional deaths in the seven weeks between April 28 and June 15.[254] The warnings from Harvard and MIT, public health officials nationwide, and even an unreleased spring 2020 federal report finding that reopening America could lead to 200,000 new infections daily and 3,000 new deaths daily in June 2020 are ignored as Trump continues his push to jump-start the U.S. economy.[255] As a CNN analysis in May 2020 concludes, Trump "knows the price of the haunting bargain required to reopen the country—tens of thousands more lives [lost] in a pandemic that is getting worse not better. It's one he now appears ready to pay, if not explain to the American people, at a moment of national trial that his administration has constantly underplayed."[256] The reason for Trump's willingness to trade untold lives for an improved economy, per the cable news network, is his desire to "dwell in the universe that is most conducive to his political hopes" no matter how many Americans die in service of that dream.[257]

In mid-May 2020, the chief scientist for the World Health Organization predicts that it will take four to five years for the world to contain SARS-CoV-2 and that the virus may never be fully eradicated.[258] Dr. Bright tells Congress on May 14 that the typical timeframe for the development of a new vaccine is ten years, and that the Trump administration has no plan for a vaccine supply chain in the event a vaccine is found. He notes that a vaccine for SARS-CoV-2 would be ready for deployment in mid- to late 2021 only if the vaccine development process were to unfold "perfectly" in a way it never has before, that any such vaccine would not be FDA-approved, and that it would only be available for deployment on an emergency basis.[259] Asked in May—nine days before Bright's whistleblower testimony—what the historically deadly COVID-19 pandemic has taught him, Trump answers, "That I was right."[260]

In the final weeks of spring 2020, as the COVID-19 death toll in the U.S. breaches 100,000 and Trump's poll numbers against Joe Biden remain stagnant, the president's behavior degenerates to a level of instability that appears to threaten public health, public safety, and public order. Though studies indicate that wearing a face mask could reduce the chance of COVID-19 transmission by as much as 75 percent, Trump declares that mask-wearing is merely a "politically correct" gesture and refuses to don one himself; one CNN report from a beach in Gulf Shores, Alabama—a state whose COVID-19 infection data is "going the wrong way" and "trending up," according to the cable news outlet—finds that among hundreds of beachgoers, not one is wearing a mask, and some cite the president's example for not doing so.[261] "[I]f [Trump's] not wearing a mask, I'm not gonna wear a mask. If he's not worried, I'm not worried," says one man.[262] CNN also encounters limited enforcement of social-distancing guidelines—in some cases no enforcement at all—both on beaches and in local restaurants in Gulf Shores.[263] CNN's report is deeply troubling in view of a mid-May study published in the health care journal *Health Affairs* that reveals, according to a summary by *The Hill*, that "areas that don't practice social distancing face up to 35 times more potential cases of COVID-19 per capita than those that do."[264]

Eschewing the wearing of a face mask comes to be so associated with support for President Trump that, according to the *Washington Post*, businesses around the country begin banning customers who seek to keep themselves—and others—from contracting the novel coronavirus by putting a cloth covering over their faces.[265] The nation's new epidemic of avoiding basic safety measures to combat the worldwide COVID-19 outbreak comes in the face of the nation's top expert on infectious diseases, Dr. Fauci, declaring unambiguously that wearing a face mask when around others is "[what] you should be doing."[266] On

May 23, the Republican governor of North Dakota, Doug Burgum, becomes emotional while pleading with the residents of his state to wear face masks in public or at a minimum not harass those who do. "Either it's ideological or political or something, around 'mask versus no mask.' This is, I would say, a senseless dividing line. . . . If someone is wearing a mask, they're not doing it to represent what political party they're in or what candidates they support, they might be doing it because they've got a five-year-old child who's been going through cancer treatments."[267] Meanwhile, as CNN recounts, the president's position on face masks continues to be that "it's not my thing" and "I don't see it [happening] for myself," statements in the same seemingly nihilistic vein as the president's mid-May 2020 contention that testing Americans for COVID-19 is "overrated."[268] Trump's suddenly dim view of coronavirus testing comes as he is under fire for calling "great" an Abbott Laboratories "rapid coronavirus test" that shortly after his endorsement is preliminarily found to return false negatives in up to 48 percent of cases.[269]

In late May, Dr. Fauci becomes the first Trump administration official to conclusively state that hydroxychloroquine is not an effective COVID-19 treatment—an announcement whose importance to public health and safety increases significantly after President Trump announces, on May 18, 2020, that he is taking the drug.[270] The president's announcement shocks even top aides at the White House, coming as it does at a time when only 11 percent of Americans say they would take hydroxychloroquine to treat or prevent COVID-19—and as WHO is dropping hydroxychloroquine from its COVID-19 studies, citing its manifest dangerousness for COVID-19 patients.[271] Trump's surprise revelation draws "immediate criticism from a range of medical experts," according to the *New York Times*, which quotes experts as "warn[ing] not just of the dangers [Trump's taking of the drug] pose[s] for the president's health but also of the example it set[s]."[272] When Trump thereafter releases a note from his doctor, Sean Conley, that he implies confirms his prescription for hydroxychloroquine, confusion results—as the letter does not state that Trump has been prescribed the drug, only that he and Conley have had "numerous discussions" about hydroxychloroquine and together "concluded [that] the potential benefit from treatment outweighed the relative risks."[273] Asked by a reporter about a study on hydroxychloroquine from Trump's own administration—one of many studies revealing the dangers of hydroxychloroquine when used by COVID-19 patients—Trump calls the National Institutes of Health (NIH) paper a "Trump enemy statement" and falsely claims that it is "the only bad survey" on the potentially lethal complications arising from contraindicated hydroxychloroquine use.[274] Of HHS whistleblower Rick Bright, whose formal complaint about the administration's pandemic response included significant concerns about the administration's motives in pushing hydroxychloroquine, Trump will say that whistleblowers like Bright "cause[ ] great injustice and harm."[275]

The *New Yorker* writes that Trump's public statements "have taken an even darker, more manic, and more mendacious turn" as he "struggles to manage the convergence of a massive public-health crisis and a simultaneous economic collapse while running for reelection," a circumstance that leads the co-author of Trump's bestselling book *The Art of the Deal*, Tony Schwartz, to say of the man he once ghostwrote for, "His obsession with domination and power have prompted Trump to tell lies more promiscuously than ever since he became President, and to engage in ever more unfounded and aggressive responses aimed at anyone he perceives stands in his way."[276] Indeed, the *New Yorker* reports that, according to the *Washington Post*, Trump lied or misled Americans six times a day on average in 2017, sixteen times a day in 2018, twenty-two times a day in 2019, and by mid-2020 is on pace to tweet mistruths "nearly four times" as often as he did in using Twitter during his first year in office.[277]

The president's dishonesty and aggression increasingly play out in conflicts with persons and entities not normally imagined as being the focus of a U.S. president's ire. After Twitter appends a fact-checking link to two Trump tweets, the president announces that "if it [Twitter] were able to be legally shut down" by executive order, he would do so.[278] The statement leads *New York Times* reporter Maggie Haberman to write with seeming astonishment, "In the same [public] event where the president said Twitter is inappropriately cracking down on free speech, he says he would be willing to shut down Twitter if he could."[279] Trump ultimately settles for an executive order seeking to strip U.S. social media platforms of the civil-liability shields granted them by Section 230 of the Communications Decency Act—a move constituting an attack on America's cultural infrastructure that is explicitly prompted by Trump's anger at being fact-checked. In a clear reference to his own situation, Trump's order opines that "Twitter now selectively decides to place a warning label on certain tweets in a manner that clearly reflects political bias. Twitter seems never to have placed such a label on another politician's tweet [besides mine]."[280]

In launching a full-scale offensive against the concept of mail-in voting in late May, Trump's anger and fear at the prospect of a loss in the 2020 election are on display, with the president writing to his more than 80 million Twitter followers, "MAIL-IN VOTING WILL LEAD TO MASSIVE FRAUD AND ABUSE. IT WILL ALSO LEAD TO THE END OF OUR GREAT REPUBLICAN PARTY. WE CAN NEVER LET THIS TRAGEDY BEFALL OUR NATION."[281] Trump's baseless contention that a mid-pandemic national election with large-scale mail-in balloting would be "a free for all on cheating, forgery and the theft of [b]allots"—with the president insisting that "whoever cheated the most would win"—risks either delegitimizing the 2020 election results or providing significant rhetorical cover for the Trump campaign to engage in the sort of activities described by the president while falsely associating them with the Biden campaign.[282]

When the state of Michigan announces its intention to send absentee ballots to all its registered voters in advance of election day in November—an effort to keep citizens safe during a pandemic that precludes large indoor gatherings in places such as polling sites—Trump threatens to withhold federal funding from the state, possibly even COVID-19 emergency relief funding, if it does so.[283] The president's extraordinary statement, as well as being a potential violation of the federal bribery statute, also risks a violation of 18 U.S.C. § 598, which prohibits, in relevant part, "us[ing] any part of any appropriation made by Congress for . . . relief . . . for the purpose of interfering with . . . any individual in the exercise of his right to vote at any election."[284] Each count of 18 U.S.C. § 598 charged is punishable by up to a year in federal prison.[285]

When reporters ask the president, four times, to tell Americans both what is illegal about Michigan sending absentee ballots to registered voters and what federal funding in particular he would withhold from the state in response, he "dodge[s]" the questions every time, according to *Washington Post* editor JM Rieger.[286] Questions about Trump's response to Michigan's attempts to protect its citizens from COVID-19 infection come on the worst day for COVID-19 infections worldwide; the WHO announces, on May 20, that more than 106,000 people—overwhelmingly citizens of the United States, Russia, Brazil, and India—have contracted the virus in the last 24 hours.[287] Nevertheless, the president doubles down on his attacks on Michigan by thereafter telling the state of Nevada that it too would be acting "illegal[ly]" if it sends out "vote by mail ballots" to its voters, and that doing so would both "creat[e] a great Voter Fraud scenario for the State and the U.S." and possibly result in him "hold[ing] up funds to the State."[288]

On May 29, 2020, Trump announces the United States' immediate withdrawal from the World Health Organization, a decision, per *Politico*, that is "quickly panned by health experts, who claimed it would set back global efforts to defeat a novel virus that's already killed more than 360,000 people [worldwide] and sickened nearly 6 million."[289] The digital media outlet adds that the "severing [of] ties with WHO . . . [is] cheered by Trump's base, which is distrustful of international bodies."[290]

That Trump's pandemic response is inextricably entwined with his reelection campaign is underscored when the president, facing, per *Politico*, "waning confidence in the administration's coronavirus response among key religious groups"—including "a staggering decline in the president's favorability among white evangelicals and white Catholics"—declares that houses of worship are "essential places" providing "essential services" and therefore must be exempted from all statewide stay-at-home orders.[291] The declaration is accompanied by a claim, made under what legal authority is unclear, that if state governors do not immediately bend to his wishes on reopening places of worship he will "override" their authority, a threat that could quickly lead to a constitutional crisis over federalism and states' rights.[292] That Trump's concern about his mid-pandemic poll numbers is warranted is clear; the *Washington Post* reports on May 19 that the president's "coronavirus poll numbers"—data gauging public sentiment about his handling of the pandemic—are lower than those of forty-nine of fifty state governors, with the fiftieth governor (Georgia's Republican governor, Brian Kemp) tied with Trump as the most-disapproved-of jurisdiction-wide executive branch official with respect to COVID-19 response.[293]

On May 29, 2020, a Trump tweet warning, in the midst of protests against police brutality in Minneapolis following the death of unarmed forgery suspect George Floyd, that "when the looting starts, the shooting starts"—a 1960s quote from a racist Miami police chief—is considered so dangerous by Twitter that it is placed behind a warning message that indicates the president's statement is "glorifying violence."[294] The *Washington Post* reports that the tweet is part of a new pattern of "conspicuous allusions to violence" in Trump's public statements.[295]

Nevertheless, Trump's most startling actions, as the COVID-19 outbreak grips the nation in late spring 2020, continue to relate to the virus, its spread, federal efforts to combat it, and the effect of the pandemic on the U.S. economy. On May 26, the day U.S. COVID-19 deaths hit 100,000, Trump issues no statement to mark the occasion, instead implying, in a tweet, that no more Americans will die of the virus—a sentiment expressed via a mathematical equation that indicates 100,000 "will be the number" of COVID-19 deaths by the end of the pandemic.[296] The strange tweet comes just a week after the president's declaration that America's world-leading number of COVID-19 patients was a "badge of honor" because it meant "our testing is better" than any other nation's— even though, at the time of the president's statement, the U.S. still ranks thirty-fourth in per-capita testing.[297]

The instability injected into American culture by Trump in May 2020 comes in the context of the core facts of the COVID-19 pandemic taking a strikingly dark turn in the final four weeks of spring. The *Washington Post* reports that "coronavirus may never go away, even with a vaccine."[298] One reason for this, the Associated Press reveals, is that slightly more than half of Americans are either uncertain whether they will take a COVID-19 vaccine if one is developed or are already set on not doing so.[299] In a related AP poll, the news organization finds that nearly half of Americans say social-distancing restrictions in their communities should not be lifted until a COVID-19 vaccine is found—an eventuality that could be, according to U.S. vaccine chief Rick Bright, many years away.[300]

These startling revelations come as CNN reveals that "doctors are increasingly reporting that they cannot find evidence of COVID-19 infection until they perform" tests that "take[ ] a sample from deeper in the respiratory system" than a typical swab test allows; the implication of the CNN report is that common COVID-19 testing methods may be systematically undercounting how many Americans have the virus, a significant complication for national efforts to establish a "contact tracing" scheme covering all infected individuals.[301] A similarly troubling development, also reported by CNN, is that antibody tests aimed at finding out which Americans previously had COVID-19—including asymptomatically— have been found to be inaccurate "up to half the time."[302] Meanwhile, the *Washington Post* reports that conclusive evidence of a new and significant dividing line between the seriousness of the novel coronavirus and the common flu has been found: scientific proof that COVID-19, unlike the flu, "attacks the lining of blood vessels" in the lungs, producing "widespread damage to blood vessels and [causing] the presence of blood clots that would not be expected in a respiratory disease."[303] According to CNN, new research on COVID-19 published in May reveals that "the new coronavirus can infect organs throughout the body, including lungs, throat, heart, liver, brain, kidneys and the intestines."[304]

* * *

A study of thirty nations published by *Politico* finds that the U.S. ranks twenty-fourth in "health and economic outcomes" during the COVID-19 pandemic.[305] As troubling as this overall assessment is, an even more concerning analysis by NBC News reveals that a number of U.S. states seeking to hurriedly reopen businesses in May 2020 are responsible for "COVID-19 data cover-ups" that involve "making public misleading statistics or concealing information related to the coronavirus outbreak."[306] The Associated Press summarizes these findings as evidence that states may be "bungling or even deliberately fudging the statistics to make the virus appear more under control than it is."[307] The *New York Times* reports that premature reopenings, according to experts, "could mean thousands of new deaths"; indeed, one research paper, published in the journal *Health Affairs*, speaks to the possible impact of too-hasty statewide reopening edicts by noting, per the *Times*, that "the number of confirmed cases in the United States, which reached a million at the end of April, would have been closer to 35 million without the restaurant closures and stay-at-home orders that began in mid-March"—meaning, according to one of the study's authors, that "just because it hasn't been a catastrophe yet in your state, doesn't mean it doesn't have the potential to be."[308] As unnerving as this dire warning is, a May 2020 *Business Insider* report reframes it in even more harrowing terms, revealing that "roughly half the Twitter accounts pushing to 'reopen America' are bots," and moreover that "It's unclear who's behind the surge in bot activity or whether they're originating from the U.S. or abroad."[309]

According to the *Washington Post*, "The Trump administration mishandled the initial distribution of the only approved coronavirus medication, delaying treatment to some critically ill patients with COVID-19, the disease caused by the virus, according to nine current and former senior administration officials. The first tranche of 607,000 vials of the antiviral medication remdesivir, donated to the government by drugmaker Gilead Sciences, was distributed in early May—in some cases to the wrong hospitals, to hospitals with no intensive care units and therefore no eligible patients, and to facilities without the needed refrigeration to store it."[310] *Yahoo News* reports that, despite 560 confirmed cases of COVID-19 within the Transportation Security Administration, as of mid-May 2020 "there is no [federally mandated] requirement for masks" on U.S. domestic flights, and "no coronavirus screening procedures for domestic air travelers."[311] A Trump administration failing of similarly inexplicable scope comes into view at the end of May 2020, when it is revealed that the administration is still treating COVID-19 patients who are military veterans with the potentially deadly drug hydroxychloroquine. While the Department of Veterans Affairs indicates it is in the process of "ratcheting down" use of the drug, it is unclear why any veterans—at one point, more than 400—were receiving the non-FDA-approved treatment, let alone why use of it did not immediately cease once reporting of its dangers became ubiquitous nationwide.[312]

Ten days after Fed Chairman Jerome Powell announces that, as summarized by CNBC, America's "GDP could shrink more than 30%" in the second quarter of 2020, the White House announces that—for the first time in nearly a half century—the federal government will not release a midsummer economic projection for the U.S. economy.[313]

Trump's running commentary on domestic events during the COVID-19 pandemic obscures deeply troubling events abroad. On May 22, CNN reports that "Mike Pompeo pushed State Department officials to find a way to justify the emergency declaration that he had already decided to implement an order to fast-track the $8 billion arms sale to Saudi Arabia last year—stunning career diplomats."[314] According to *Politico*, Pompeo's actions required him to "disregard[ ] the advice of high-level officials at the State Department, Pentagon, and within the intelligence community"; the secretary of state's efforts to "circumvent congressional review of billions of dollars in arms sales" was "under investigation by a government watchdog who was fired . . . at Pompeo's urging," the digital media outlet adds.[315]

The *Washington Post* reports that Pompeo's reaction to being accused of engineering the firing of a man investigating his actions is extraordinary, and per the newspaper "basically boil[s] down to this: It couldn't possibly have been retaliation, because I didn't know what he was investigating. Except then Pompeo acknowledged that he might well have known that he was under investigation."[316] Indeed, the *New York Times* reports that Pompeo had already answered written questions about the proposed Saudi arms deal sent to him by State Department inspector general Steve Linick at the time of Linick's firing, giving the lie to Pompeo's claim that when he pushed for Linick's ouster he had no reason to fear repercussions from his clandestine dealings with MBS and the Saudis.[317] Pompeo will claim, instead—without evidence or explanation—that Linick was fired for "undermining" the State Department.[318]

According to the *Washington Post*, on May 18, 2020, Donald Trump's son Eric "claims coronavirus is a Democratic hoax" and insists that it will "magically . . . go away" the day after the November 2020 election.[319] On the day Trump's middle son calls COVID-19 a hoax, the number of American dead from the coronavirus outbreak reaches 90,000.[320]

Within the Trump administration, May also sees a new push to, as a CNN analysis describes it, "deflect blame" for the death toll from COVID-19 onto a new group: Americans themselves.[321] The same day that Eric Trump calls the novel coronavirus a "Democratic hoax," Alex Azar points to the "unhealthy comorbidities" of "individuals in our communities," particularly "minority communities," as being a major contributor to the COVID-19 death toll.[322] Per CNN, Azar's statement echoes one made concurrently by Peter Navarro, in which the Trump trade adviser "add[s] the government's own Centers for Disease Control and Prevention to its list of scapegoats alongside China and the Obama administration."[323]

When Trump is asked by a reporter, in late May, "What would you have done differently [in] facing this [coronavirus] crisis?" he responds, "Well, nothing."[324]

THE UNREST AND THE ELECTION

In sworn testimony on February 27, 2019—two months before reporting to a federal prison—Trump's longtime friend, attorney, and fixer Michael Cohen told the House Committee on Oversight and Reform that, "given my experience working for Mr. Trump, I fear that if he loses the election in 2020, there will never be a peaceful transition of power."[1] Doubts about the president's willingness to admit defeat should he be bested by his general election opponent—former vice president Joe Biden—notwithstanding, a chief concern heading into November 2020 is that even before the COVID-19 outbreak in the United States, "only half of Americans [said] they believe the [2020] vote will be conducted openly and fairly."[2]

If the novel coronavirus scourging America becomes a "seasonal" occurrence—as is now "inevitable," according to NIAID director Dr. Anthony Fauci—a continuation or worsening of the present 2020 COVID-19 outbreak, coupled with difficulties in building the infrastructure necessary for nationwide mail-in balloting by November, could lead to election chaos.[3] Low live-voting turnout, prompted by fears of coronavirus transmission at polling sites, could simultaneously bolster the reelection odds of a president whose handling of the COVID-19 pandemic a clear majority of Americans has disapproved of and delegitimize any victory that he and his party might manufacture through direct or indirect voter suppression.[4] That Joe Biden will be President Trump's Democratic opponent means that the complex, interweaving narratives this book has detailed will become part of what will surely be one of the most confusing, dispiriting, and nasty general election campaigns our nation has ever seen. That the nastiness of the campaign is bound to be historic is already established by May 2020, when—with the Democratic and Republican national conventions, and thus the formal beginning of the 2020 general election campaign, still months away—Donald Trump retweets a video that says, "The only good Democrat is a dead Democrat."[5]

Just so, Trump's spring 2020 confession that he opposes widespread mail-in balloting because it would produce "levels of voting that if [Republicans] ever agreed to it, you'd never have a Republican elected in this country again" underscores how frantically disputatious the fight over conducting a safe and orderly presidential election will be.[6] Trump's position on mail-in voting persists despite a May 2020 *USA Today*/Suffolk poll revealing that Americans "overwhelmingly support [Democrats'] vote-by-mail push," with 65 percent of respondents favoring mail-in voting instead of live voting amidst the nation's worst public health crisis in a century.[7] As the growing divide between Trump's partisan rhetoric on mail-in voting and Americans' voting-method preferences becomes clear, the Associated Press reports that the "partisan debate over allowing more Americans to cast ballots by mail during the coronavirus pandemic is provoking online disinformation and conspiracy theories that could undermine trust in this year's election results"; much of the disinformation is spread by Trump himself, who uses his popular Twitter account to make so many false claims about mail-in voting that Twitter must for the first time ever append a link to two of his tweets providing readers with accurate information on the subject. The president's reaction to Twitter's enforcement of its Terms of Service is epic in scale, with Trump threatening to shut down the social media platform altogether and then announcing the next day an executive order that seeks, instead, to strip not only Twitter but other social media websites of their federally legislated tort-liability shield.[8]

Trump's partisan justification for his recalcitrance on mail-in balloting is called "false" by the *New York Times*.[9] According to the president, not only should Republicans "fight very hard when it comes to state wide mail-in voting . . . [because] for whatever reason, [it] doesn't work out well for Republicans," but also because "[with] mail ballots, they cheat. . . . Mail ballots are very dangerous for this country because of cheaters. They go collect them. They are fraudulent in many cases."[10] In fact, as the *Times* reports, "studies have shown that all forms of voting fraud are extremely rare in the United States. A national study in 2016 found few credible allegations of fraudulent voting. A panel that Mr. Trump charged with investigating election corruption found no real evidence of fraud before he disbanded it in 2018."[11] Moreover, the *Times* writes, "states that vote entirely by mail see little fraud"; indeed, according to Judd Choate, director of elections in one of America's five vote-by-mail states, Colorado, "There's just very little evidence that there is more than a handful of fraudulent (vote-by-mail) cases across the country in a given election cycle."[12]

This data—and the dangers of COVID-19—notwithstanding, in April 2020 the GOP announces a nationwide, multimillion-dollar legal campaign to ensure that the overwhelming majority of Americans must vote in person in November 2020.[13] The moral force of the Republican argument to encourage large congregations of Americans during a possible "second-wave" virus outbreak in fall 2020 is undermined by the fact that, per the *Times*, "the president, vice president, and cabinet members have voted by mail recently," as well as the fact that Trump's CDC director, Robert Redfield, has publicly warned that "there's a possibility that the assault of the virus on our nation next winter will actually be even more difficult" than the ongoing spring 2020 outbreak.[14] Dr. Rick Bright warns Congress on May 14 that a second-wave COVID-19 outbreak in fall 2020 could herald "the darkest winter in modern history" and "caus[e] unprecedented illness and fatalities."[15]

Trump's partisan views on mail-in balloting gain immediate nationwide relevance when he receives a "dire warning" on April 10 that the United States Postal Service will become insolvent in September; it may therefore be unable to fully and properly aid any mid-outbreak vote-by-mail election. On April 11, Trump rejects the Postal Service's plea for a bailout.[16]

* * *

It is clear that Trump and his allies in Congress intend to spend the 2020 presidential campaign probing Hunter Biden's dealings in China (which were substantially less involved, long-standing, and legally fraught than the dealings in China of Trump and his family) and Joe Biden's alleged pre-inauguration role in investigating the 2016 Trump campaign. It is equally clear that these investigations are pretextual: an effort to punish the president's enemies, muddy the waters of both past and potential future Trump bribery investigations, and enhance Trump's chances of defeating Biden in November 2020. In announcing a congressional investigation of Joe Biden's role in "unmasking" Michael Flynn's December 2016 phone call with Russian ambassador Sergey Kislyak, Trump ally and U.S. senator Rand Paul says, "It [the investigation] goes to the heart of what type of person would . . . [Joe Biden] be in leading the country and in charge of . . . the intelligence community power," adding—apparently without irony, despite the recent articles of impeachment against Trump and his own vote to acquit the president—that "Vice President Biden is guilty of using government to go after a political opponent."[17] Just so, when Ukraine-scandal witness and U.S. senator Ron Johnson, alongside Sen. Chuck Grassley, announces in February 2020 the intention to seek Hunter Biden's foreign travel records, the Republican duo's terse, six-sentence announcement references Joe Biden directly or indirectly three times.[18]

If Trump wins in November, his historically corrupt administration endures. If he does not—and even if he leaves office with uncharacteristic dignity and humility—the country he leaves behind will be little like the country he inherited. He has deeded to the nation that gave him all he has a genus of destructive egotism and performative callousness that will continue to degrade America's political and juridical culture for decades. He has called even Republicans who oppose him "human scum," and has argued in federal court, through his attorneys, that "even if [he] were to shoot someone on Manhattan's 5th Avenue . . . authorities could not prosecute [him] or do anything about it."[19] In May 2020 Trump and his attorneys solidify their startlingly authoritarian doctrine of absolute presidential authority by declaring before the Supreme Court that Trump is entitled to "temporary presidential immunity," which CNN summarizes as "mean[ing] that Trump . . . couldn't be investigated or prosecuted while holding the office of President. No subpoenas, no testimony, no indictments."[20]

Such diction and ideations from a nation's leader cannot help but degenerate America's rule of law, democratic institutions, and public discourse. Indeed, few Americans were surprised when the former Navy SEAL who supervised the raid that killed Osama bin Laden, Adm. William McRaven, announced that America was "under attack from the president," and revealed further that a retired general of his acquaintance had told him that "Trump is destroying the Republic."[21] Hearing Adm. McRaven's assessment, Americans can draw little comfort from the precedent—and lesson—provided by Trump's ally and seeming role model Viktor Orban. As the autocratic Hungarian president acquires for himself sweeping new domestic powers amidst the global COVID-19 pandemic, Freedom House's annual report on democracy worldwide, "Nations in Transit," reports that Hungary has officially lost its status as a democracy, part of a "stunning democratic breakdown" sweeping the globe.[22]

While many of the stories of Trump administration corruption playing out in the spring of 2020 have little to do with Ukraine, the themes evident in Trump's dealings there and elsewhere—including China, Iran, Syria, Turkey, Venezuela, Saudi Arabia, the United Arab Emirates, and, of course, Russia—remain at the forefront of Trump's presidency: a president drawn to corrupt autocrats abroad; clandestine diplomacy conducted in place of conventional diplomacy, often as a means of obscuring impure motives and suspect directives intended to undercut long-standing U.S. foreign policy; and a penchant for hiding damning evidence and information from American voters—or, just as often, simply lying to them outright.

In January 2020, the *Wall Street Journal* reports that "allies of President Trump are pursuing an effort to acquire [OAN]," the right-wing cable network most responsible for pushing Kremlin conspiracy theories targeting Joe Biden.[23] In early May, *Vanity Fair* reports that the would-be OAN purchasers are "aligned with Donald Trump Jr.," raising the specter of a president and his family directly or indirectly controlling a major-media organ in the lead-up to a presidential election for the first time in modern American history.[24] In late April, Trump becomes the first candidate for the Oval Office to knowingly publish a "deepfake" when he retweets a heavily manipulated video of Joe Biden's face; it is unclear whether the use of such a machination—which *The Atlantic* notes most Americans had "assumed . . . would [only] be deployed by some anonymous, hostile non-state actor, as a no-return-address, high-tech sabotage of democracy"—presages additional uses of the tactic by Trump and his reelection campaign in the summer and fall of 2020.[25]

It is no longer possible to determine, or even guess, what the "bottom" is for the president and his political team. In mid-pandemic, the president vetoes Congress's attempts to rein in his power to make war on Iran; nominates a major donor to run the United States Postal Service amidst his push to curtail mail-in voting; cheers publicly as his hand-picked attorney general moves to dismiss all federal criminal charges against former White House national security advisor Michael Flynn, despite the fact that Flynn has already confessed to his crimes under oath and absolved the FBI and DOJ (on the record) of any misconduct against him; falsely accuses a top MSNBC anchor, Joe Scarborough, of murder; and redirects military funds from the deterrence of Kremlin aggression in eastern Europe to the effort to build his southern border wall.[26] Trump's actions, long divorced from convention and propriety, increasingly appear divorced from sense as well—and it is certain that during his 2020 reelection campaign he will add substantially to the "19,127 false or misleading claims" he has already told American voters while president, per a spring 2020 *Washington Post* count.[27]

It is with all this context that in mid-May the president and his supporters unleash a bizarre, multi-platform attack—via the president's Twitter feed, Fox News, and right-wing blogs and social media accounts— indicating that the Trump administration will seek investigation and possible prosecution of former Obama administration officials for allegedly masterminding, in 2016, a preemptive coup of the Trump presidency.[28] The president's baseless claim, hashtagged on Twitter as "Obamagate," is spectacularly dangerous to our democracy, culture, and rule of law.

An open question, through November, will be who has advised the Trump reelection campaign to proceed with this and other similarly explosive political strategies. According to a May 2020 ABC News report, "the Department of Homeland Security and FBI warned states earlier this year that Russia could look to interfere in the 2020 U.S. elections by covertly advising political candidates and campaigns."[29] If past is precedent—and there is no evidence it won't be—the candidate the Kremlin seeks to illegally aid in 2020 will again be Donald Trump.

If it is clear that not only Putin but autocrats in China, Saudi Arabia, the United Arab Emirates, Hungary, Israel, Egypt, and Turkey would like to weaken America for their own competitive advantage and to render it more pliable to—and less able to counter—their aggressive geopolitical maneuvers abroad, it is equally clear that Trump's lack of commitment to rule of law and America's foundational democratic principles is innate to his character. As summer 2020 begins, there is no clearer indication that Trump constitutes a homegrown threat to the nation's core values than his reaction to the death of unarmed Minnesota man George Floyd at the hands of police officers on May 25, 2020.[30]

Floyd—a forty-six-year-old Minneapolis resident who is positive for COVID-19 and suspected only of paying for a pack of cigarettes with a counterfeit $20 bill—is killed during his arrest, with officer Derek Chauvin putting his knee on the prone Floyd's neck for eight minutes and forty-six seconds and thereby severely restricting his ability to breathe.[31] Chauvin will subsequently be fired from the Minneapolis Police Department and charged with second-degree murder, while the three officers who assisted him in arresting Floyd will, following their own firings, be charged with aiding and abetting second-degree murder.[32]

Floyd's death, captured on video by a bystander, is harrowing. After it is played and replayed on American television and social media for a full news cycle, and is augmented by further video capturing the events preceding the arrest—with both videos confirming not only that Floyd was not resisting arrest, but that he spent his final minutes begging officers to let him breathe and crying out for his deceased mother—weeks of national and international protests ensue.[33]

Their historic scope and moral rectitude aside, the protests do as much as any event during Trump's presidency to underscore not only the danger the president poses to America's rule of law in 2020 but how grave a continuing threat he could pose to American democracy if he is not defeated at the polls in November. Indeed, it is telling that on June 3 the president tweets a description of the anti-police-brutality protestors that categorizes them as "killers, terrorists, arsonists, anarchists, thugs, hoodlums, looters, ANTIFA [anti-fascists]," and "others . . . [who are] very bad for our Country."[34] In the event any doubt remains that Trump is describing the nation's largest and most widespread anti-racist protests in over a half century as being orchestrated and participated in by violent criminals exclusively, the president thereafter retweets a claim by far-right commentator Buck Sexton that the overwhelmingly peaceful protests are in fact "American carnage" and "lawless," with Sexton adding that "these aren't protests—they're riots."[35]

The facts on the ground notwithstanding, from the very beginning of the civil unrest that follows George Floyd's death, the president positions the protests as domestic terrorism warranting the most draconian of government interventions. Trump falsely attributes the public demonstrations to clandestine machinations by "antifa," a diffuse and inchoate anti-fascist movement that the president repeatedly miscasts as a well-coordinated paramilitary organization committed to—somewhat paradoxically—domestic and international anarchy. That the protests are with only rare exception nonviolent, and arise in more than 2,000 cities and towns across America and in major metropolitan areas around the world, appears not to influence the president's thinking about them, their participants, or their purpose.[36]

One effect of Trump's misleading rhetoric about the protests is mass panic within certain U.S. communities, inasmuch as the president convinces some Americans that antifa radicals are poised to infiltrate and destroy their way of life. The *Washington Post* reports that fears of a "leftist incursion"—which it correctly identifies as an "online myth"—encourage "armed white vigilantes [to] line Idaho streets" and "fuel[] militant reactions" in many other states as well.[37] The *Post* notes that the armed vigilantes in Idaho and elsewhere say "they mobilized out of concern about rioting and looting by antifa, a movement that Trump has blamed for violence nationwide. Trump's claims have drawn support from his attorney general, William P. Barr, who pointed to the role of 'anarchistic and far-left extremists' [in the protests] without yet offering evidence of such involvement."[38] The *Detroit News* reports that "in the days since President Donald Trump blamed antifa activists for an eruption of violence at protests over police killings of black people, social media has lit up with false rumors that the far-left-leaning group is transporting people to wreak havoc on small cities across America."[39] In one particularly chilling incident recounted in detail by CNN, a caravan of armed Oregonians stalks a family on a camping vacation because it baselessly suspects them of transporting antifa radicals in their vehicle.[40] Oregon also plays host to a Black Lives Matter protest in Klamath Falls to which "hundreds of . . . mostly white" residents show up "wearing military fatigues and bulletproof vests, with blue bands tied around their arms."[41] Per NBC News, these white residents—none of whom participate in the town's anti-racism/anti-police-brutality protest—all "seemed to be carrying something: flags, baseball bats, hammers and axes. But mostly, they carried guns. They said they came with shotguns, rifles, and pistols to protect their downtown businesses from outsiders. They had heard that antifa [anti-fascists], paid by billionaire philanthropist George Soros, were being bused in from neighboring cities, hellbent on razing their idyllic town."[42]

In fact, the *New York Times* reveals in mid-June 2020 that "none of the people charged with serious federal crimes amidst the unrest following the killing of George Floyd have been linked so far to antifa, despite claims by President Trump," adding that "federal arrests show no sign that antifa plotted [the] protests."[43] Despite this publicly available arrest data, the *Times* writes, "[Barr] has blamed antifa for orchestrating the mass protests"; as the attorney general asserts without evidence, echoing political rhetoric emanating from the president and his 2020 reelection campaign, "There is clearly some high degree of organization involved at some of these events and [we are seeing] coordinated tactics . . . some of which relates to antifa."[44] National Public Radio notes that of the first fifty-one cases brought by DOJ related to the protests, "the single instance in which an extremist group is mentioned in court documents is a case against three Nevada men. Federal prosecutors allege the trio belong to the right-wing Boogaloo movement that wants to bring about a civil war."[45] Nevertheless, Barr seeks to bolster Trump's May 31 claim—unsustainable in statute or by any existing legal authority—that "the United States of America will be designating ANTIFA as a Terrorist Organization," announcing that DOJ and the FBI will use their Joint Terrorism Task Force model to "identify, apprehend and prosecute anyone who uses the guise of protest to incite violence and violate federal laws."[46]

Asked to explain a degree of righteous indignation manifesting in civil unrest the likes of which the country hasn't seen in more than a half-century, Trump tells Harris Faulkner of Fox News that "you could call them protests, [or] you could call them riots."[47] When Faulkner asks Trump what he thinks the protestors want, he replies—referring to the protests in the past tense, though they are ongoing—that "you had protesting for different reasons," including people who "just didn't know" what they were protesting.[48] While the president allows that "perhaps" some people felt they had a reason to protest, and acknowledges that Floyd's death was a "terrible" event that caused some Americans to want to protest after seeing it on television, he also claims to have repeatedly watched interviews with protestors who "weren't able to say" what they were doing at a public demonstration and exhibited no awareness of where they were or why they were there. "A lot of them were really there because they were following the crowd," Trump tells Faulkner.[49] Of those protestors who, after witnessing Floyd's death, determined it to be emblematic of systemic racism in American policing, and representative of a mindset engrained in uniformed law enforcement officers as a result of their training and workplace culture, Trump contends that "they [the protestors] don't know [or] maybe they don't think about it that much," because "police aren't like that."[50]

On June 1, Trump instigates one of the most distressing events in recent American history when—after days of being criticized for sheltering in the White House bunker during a protest event in D.C. on May 29—he seeks to project courage by risking a four-minute public walk from the White House to St. John's Episcopal Church in Lafayette Square.[51] In order for Trump to make the trip by foot without encountering protestors, the square and a portion of H Street NW must be cleared of a large crowd of civilians, who at the time are engaged in nonviolent protest; law enforcement does so, with dramatic force, following orders given by Barr. As the Associated Press reports, the sizable force under Barr's command—though it is unclear by what authority he commands them— uses "tear gas and rubber bullets [to] clear[] peaceful protestors from the park in front of the White House."[52]

This attack on nonviolent demonstrators is captured on live television via a split-screen shot as the president is speaking from the White House Rose Garden. Several minutes before the president declares, "I am your president of law and order and an ally of all peaceful protesters," one component of Barr's forces—riot-gear-clad federal officers hailing from the Secret Service, U.S. Park Police, D.C. National Guard, and Bureau of Prisons Special Operations Response Team—begin gassing, shoving, and firing rubber-pellet grenades at protestors not far from where the president is addressing U.S. media and the nation.[53] Once the protestors are cleared, Trump and a group of his top advisers walk to St. John's, where the president stands silently for a three-minute photo op while holding up a Bible backward and upside-down; his only substantive comment to reporters while at the church has him clarifying that the Bible is not his.[54]

That the president's awkwardly staged photo op had been preplanned, if only haphazardly, seems clear. Earlier in the day, on a conference call with the nation's governors, Trump had harangued the state-level executives over their responses to the anti-police-brutality protests, saying, "Most of you are weak. It's like a war. And we will end it fast. Be tough. You have to dominate. If you don't dominate, you're wasting your time."[55] Barr will subsequently claim that there was "no correlation" between the photo op and his forces' violent clearing of Lafayette Square; it is a claim so extraordinary, and seemingly disproven by major-media reporting of the two events' tight synchronization, that Democratic senator Kamala Harris of California shortly thereafter tweets, "I invite Bill Barr to say this in front of the Senate Judiciary Committee—under oath."[56] Shortly thereafter, Senator Mark Warner of Virginia, the ranking Democratic member of the Senate Select Committee on Intelligence, publicly calls for Barr's resignation.[57] Barr defends his actions by terming the June 1 protest in D.C. "very serious rioting," a claim contradicted by hours of footage of the event.[58]

The methods Trump and his administration use to quell the protests in D.C. reveal an openness to the domestic deployment of excessive military and paramilitary force that should unnerve all Americans—especially as the nation heads into a historically contentious election season. The weapons the Trump administration brought to bear against the nonviolent demonstrators in Lafayette Square included body-armor-wearing officers with shields and batons, grenadiers, mounted cavalry, OC (oleoresin capsicum or pepper spray) gas canisters, CS (2-chlorobenzalmalononitrile or tear gas) canisters, paint guns loaded with pepper balls, rubber bullets, sting-ball grenades, "flash-bangs," and stun grenades.[59] As troublingly, many of the troops used to disperse protestors were not wearing nameplates, badges, or insignias, and moreover refuse to identify themselves when queried by journalists.[60] As pictures of armed but anonymous government agents on the streets of D.C. go viral, a *Washington Post* column calls "unidentified law enforcement officers" a "dangerous new factor in an uneasy moment" and *HuffPost* decries Barr's "vast, nameless army."[61] In the past, the *Post* notes, DOJ's civil rights division has called "wearing name plates while in uniform" a "basic component of transparency and accountability."[62]

During the course of the protests, the president surrounds the White House with approximately 1.7 miles of what NBC News calls "towering black fencing."[63] The *Washington Post* reports that the fencing turns the People's House into a place where "armed guards and sharpshooters and combat troops are omnipresent" and "the security perimeter . . . keeps expanding," with "[new] fencing . . . going up seemingly by the hour."[64] The White House, writes the *Post*, is now a "veritable fortress—the physical manifestation of President Trump's vision of law-and-order 'domination' over the millions of Americans who have taken to the streets to protest racial injustice."[65] The *New York Times* echoes the *Post*, writing that the White House "increasingly looks like a fortress under siege."[66]

In early June, a leaked government document reveals that Trump has a "1,300-strong force . . . deployed to the south side of White House" that comprises agents and officers from ten federal agencies, including the U.S. Secret Service, U.S. Park Police, U.S. Immigration and Customs Enforcement, National Guard, Customs and Border Protection, Border Patrol, Transportation Security Administration, Coast Guard, Federal Protective Service, and Bureau of Prisons.[67] Yahoo News reports that the White House has provided "scant information" on the scope of authority or chain of command of Trump's massive assemblage of government forces, with the mayor of Washington, D.C., Muriel Bowser, saying, per the digital media outlet, that "she doesn't know which federal law enforcement agenc[ies]" have been "operating in her city."[68] On June 4, Mayor Bowser writes the White House to lodge a formal complaint about "unidentified federal personnel patrolling the streets of Washington," noting that they "pose both safety and national security risks" to the capital's infrastructure and its residents.[69]

The situation beyond the White House grounds is just as dystopian as inside it. A comprehensive *Washington Post* analysis of the June 1 D.C. protest notes that Barr's forces use weapons producing "large explosion[s]" and capable of causing "serious injury or even death," adding that certain Park Police and Bureau of Prisons personnel are videotaped firing into "fleeing" civilians' backs during the effort to move protestors.[70] Also caught on videotape is an Australian cameraman being attacked with a riot shield and an Australian anchor being assaulted by an officer with a baton; the two attackers, both with the U.S. Park Police, are subsequently placed on leave.[71] Even more strikingly, CNN reports that during the early June anti-police-brutality protests in D.C., Minneapolis, and Las Vegas, manned "U.S. government spy planes" were used to "track protesters and perhaps capture cell phone data."[72] On June 5, CNN further reveals that at least one unmanned drone from the Department of Homeland Security was deployed to Minneapolis to surveil protestors there.[73]

On June 1 in D.C., protestors are met, according to *New York Times* homeland security reporter Zolan Kanno-Youngs, by "military helicopters . . . positioned just above rooftops, sending gusts of dust into the air."[74] According to Kanno-Youngs, the result of this extraordinary intervention by U.S. military aircraft was that "a part of a tree fell, nearly hitting passerbys"; the *Times* subsequently reports that the "aggressive" posture of the aircraft—with the "downward blast from their rotor blades sending protesters scurrying for cover and ripping signs from the sides of buildings"—was directly ordered by the Pentagon.[75] Associated Press reporter James LaPorta later reveals that in fact the "aircraft flying over [Washington] . . . in a show of force against George Floyd protesters were ordered by President Trump. U.S. forces in D.C. are operating under an official mission: Operation Themis—[in] Greek mythology, Themis [means] divine law and order."[76] LaPorta notes that many members of the U.S. armed forces were given standard-issue bayonets as part of Operation Themis.[77]

On June 3, *BuzzFeed News* reports that DOJ has given the Drug Enforcement Agency the authority to "'conduct covert surveillance' and collect intelligence on people participating in protests over the police killing of George Floyd," as well as "to enforce any federal crime committed as a result of the protests over the death of George Floyd"; the move follows Barr's repetition of his earlier claim, once again offered without evidence, that scattered violence and looting at several protests were the work of "anarchistic and far left extremists, using Antifa-like tactics."[78] An FBI review of the violence in D.C. during the same twenty-four-hour period as the publication of the *BuzzFeed News* report finds "no intel indicating antifa involvement [in the protests]."[79] The *Daily Beast* does report, however, that "veteran law enforcement officials" are concerned about "the gulf between Barr's treatment of the left-wing protesters and far more violent right-wing elements whom the Justice Department has not prioritized."[80] Barr's seeming irresponsibility in ignoring the danger posed by far-right extremists hoping to use the George Floyd protests as cover for violent, terroristic political action is underscored when CNN reports, on June 3, that in locales besides Nevada "gun-toting members of the Boogaloo [pro-civil-war] movement are showing up at [anti-police-brutality] protests."[81]

In all, the federal response in the nation's capital on June 1 results in multiple injuries and fifty-four arrests in under 120 minutes.[82] Several days after government forces' attack on civilians in Lafayette Square, CNN reports that President Trump has "shared a letter on Twitter that refer[s] to the peaceful protesters who were forcibly dispersed from a park near the White House . . . as 'terrorists.'"[83] Consistent with this startling misnomer, *Politico* reports that at one point during the Floyd protests, secretary of defense Mark Esper referred to "domestic protest areas" as "battle space[s]"—a suggestion that U.S. soil either already is or could soon become a site for military engagements and in-theater scenario planning.[84] According to Bloomberg News reporter Jennifer Jacobs, when Esper, under fire for his comment, thereafter says at a news conference that "he opposes deploying active duty troops to contain protests," Trump considers firing him, "privately ask[ing] advisers if they think Esper can still be an effective defense secretary."[85] Jacobs explains that Esper's remarks about not using the U.S. military against American civilians "anger[ed] White House officials and Trump personally" and were perceived as the secretary "breaking rank . . . [because Trump] didn't want Esper publicly ruling [out]" what by all accounts would be a historic domestic deployment of the U.S. military.[86] Indeed, in order for the deployment to take place, Trump would have to invoke the Insurrection Act of 1807; per the public statement by Esper that drew Trump's ire, "the option to use active-duty forces in a law enforcement role should only be used as a matter of last resort and only in the most urgent and dire situations. We are not in one of those situations now."[87] That the president would contemplate treating widespread anti-police-brutality protests as necessitating military force against Americans on U.S. soil is profoundly troubling.

But it is not merely unsettling militarism that marks the Trump administration's response to the protests; another element is deceit, a longtime touchstone of Trump's handling of both media and voters. After falsely claiming that it did not use capsicum spray (pepper spray) in Lafayette Square, the Secret Service admits that it did, and the U.S. Park Police is thereafter caught by *Vox* in a similar deception; after Trump tells media that federal personnel didn't use either tear gas or rubber bullets on protestors on June 1, evidence uncovered by reporters reveals not only that they did so but also that the use of tear gas was personally ordered by Barr; and after Trump falsely claims that he descended into the White House's underground bunker on May 29 merely to conduct an exceedingly brief daytime inspection of it, an Associated Press report reveals that he in fact went to the bunker for nearly an hour, at night, and (in the view of White House personnel) for his own safety—that is, as part of the Trump administration's seeming overreaction to the largely peaceful demonstrations then happening outside the White House and across the country.[88] Indeed, at one point during the protests the White House is forced to delete a tweet that falsely identifies a Los Angeles synagogue's homemade "rock-filled anti-terrorism barrier" as the work of "Antifa and professional anarchists" who are purportedly "staging bricks" for subsequent looting or acts of violence; the *Washington*

Post deems the "misleading" video in the administration's original tweet a "whopper," attaching to it "four Pinocchios"—the newspaper's highest rating for dishonesty.[89]

On June 4, 2020, CNN reports that most of the crimes occurring in areas with large-scale anti-police-brutality protests are in fact being committed by "caravans" of "well-coordinated," "sophisticated" burglars employing "messaging apps during [their] heists and using both the protests and other tactics to throw police off their trail."[90] Per CNN, police say that the "level of planning" behind the high-yield burglaries they encounter during the late May and early June protests suggests, if not the involvement of "mafia and organized crime," at a minimum teams of professional criminals acting with premeditation and significant "organization."[91]

Reporting from around the country will appear to confirm that much of the violence provoked by Floyd's death emanates from individuals associated with the right wing of American politics. In North Carolina, a man threatens to burn down a black church on June 7, telling two churchgoers, "You n—— need to shut up."[92] In Maryland, a man is arrested for assaulting three people posting Black Lives Matter flyers on a bike path.[93] In Virginia, Harry Rogers, according to local prosecutors an "admitted leader of [the] Ku Klux Klan and a propagandist for Confederate ideology," is arrested and charged with "attempted malicious wounding, felony vandalism, and assault and battery" after he allegedly drives his car into a crowd of protestors.[94]

Disturbingly, many of the most violent and transgressive incidents attendant upon the protests are initiated by police officers. According to a CNN report, six Atlanta police officers are criminally charged after "allegedly using excessive force on two college students" who, while "picking up food" for dinner, "got caught in traffic caused by the protests over the killing of George Floyd."[95] In California, "at least seven Los Angeles police officers . . . [are] removed from field duties after using excessive force" during the protests, according to CNN.[96] A sixteen-year-old in the

Bronx is, per a *New York Times* report, "bruised," "shocked with a stun gun," and given a "bloody laceration from his cheek to his chin" while being arrested during a protest—a case the *Times* reports has become "the most recent focus for critics who charge that the New York police have used unnecessary force" during the protests.[97] The *Times* also reports on a man doctors say may be permanently blind in one eye after being shot by a police-wielded, pepper-spray-loaded paintball gun at a protest in Nebraska.[98] According to CNN, another civilian, journalist Linda Tirado, is permanently blinded by a police-fired foam bullet during the protests in Minneapolis.[99] In California, per the *Los Angeles Daily News*, officers "fired rubber bullets as dozens entered an apartment building seeking refuge with the help of one of the residents . . . One of the hard rubber bullet rounds struck a homeless man in a wheelchair right above his left eye, drawing blood and a large welt."[100] *USA Today* reports on a viral video from Minneapolis in which a large patrol of officers enforcing the city's curfew fired paintball rounds at a group of citizens sitting on their front porch in a residential neighborhood; ten seconds after officers screamed at the residents, "Go inside!" and "Get in your house now!," an order was issued to "light [th]em up!" and the residents were fired upon.[101] In Ohio, Republican governor Mike DeWine removes a member of the Ohio National Guard from his deployment in the nation's capital after it is discovered, per Ana Cabrera of CNN, that he had "expressed white supremacist ideology on the internet . . . prior to [his] assignment."[102] In Philadelphia, a police officer is arrested and charged with aggravated assault "for allegedly beating a Temple University student" during the anti-police-brutality protests.[103] In Chicago, thirteen police officers break into Democratic congressman Bobby Rush's campaign office during the protests, thereafter, according to *Politico*, "loung[ing] on chairs, drink[ing] coffee, and mak[ing] popcorn while looters vandalized nearby businesses."[104]

Yet the most widely discussed incident involving police violence following Floyd's death is assuredly the alleged assault of Martin Gugino by two officers of the Buffalo Police Department. Gugino, a seventy-five-year-old "longtime peace activist," is at the time of his run-in with police unarmed, a cancer patient, and "affiliated with human-rights groups [the Western New York Peace Center and PUSH Buffalo, an affordable-housing advocacy group] and the Catholic Worker movement."[105] As a horrified nation shares images of a seemingly unconscious Gugino bleeding from a head wound on a Buffalo sidewalk while the officers who pushed him and a large number of their peers file past him unconcernedly, Trump takes to Twitter with what the *Washington Post* calls a "deranged" conspiracy theory, falsely suggesting that Gugino is "an ANTIFA provocateur" who "set up" police by deliberately falling and injuring himself.[106] Trump adds, equally falsely, that before falling Gugino "appear[ed] to scan police communications in order to black out the[ir] equipment."[107] As the *New York Times* reports, Trump's conspiracy theory is taken wholesale from the same OAN reporter, Kristian Rouz, who had previously accused Hillary Clinton of funding weapons purchases by antifa activists; according to the *Times*, Rouz "is a Russian native who has also worked for Sputnik, a Kremlin-controlled news outlet . . . [that] has been accused by [U.S.] intelligence services of contributing to Russia's efforts to interfere in American elections."[108]

Trump's would-be defense of their actions notwithstanding, the two Buffalo officers who allegedly injured Gugino are shortly thereafter charged with second-degree assault.[109] Prior to their arrest, RNC national spokeswoman Elizabeth Harrington, apparently seeking to support President Trump's theorizing about Gugino—who now lies in a hospital in serious but stable condition with "a brain injury and a fractured skull"—links to an article claiming that the peace activist was in fact "trying to get punched in the face."[110] Harrington's social media blunder echoes that of Mercedes Schlapp, a senior Trump 2020 campaign adviser, who, per reporting by *Politico* journalist Marc Caputo, during the protests "use[s] her Twitter account . . . to amplify an encouraging tweet of a video of a Texas man yelling about 'fucking n——' as he wield[s] a chainsaw to chase away anti-racism demonstrators."[111]

The murder of George Floyd at the hands of police is of course not the first incident of a black man being killed by law enforcement under circumstances no one in America could countenance, nor is it the hundredth or thousandth such incident. Following Floyd's death, the #SayTheirNames campaign reemerges on Twitter, urging Americans of every demographic to learn, repeat, and honor not just the names but the richly lived lives of the seemingly numberless men, women, and children of color who have been unjustly killed by police. George Floyd's name now joins, in the memories of many Americans of conscience, those of Tamir Rice, Michael Brown, Eric Garner, Philando Castile, Breonna Taylor, Sean Monterrosa, Jamel Floyd, Sandra Bland, Ahmaud Arbery, Walter Scott, Alton Sterling, Stephon Clark, Delrawn Small, Freddie Gray, Ezell Ford, Michelle Cusseaux, Tanisha Anderson, Natasha McKenna, Bettie Jones, Botham Jean, Atatiana Jefferson, Eric Reason, Dominique Clayton, John Crawford III, Dante Parker, Laquan McDonald, Akai Gurley, Rumain Brisbon, Jerame Reid, George Mann, Frank Smart, Matthew Ajibade, Tony Robinson, Anthony Hill, Phillip White, Eric Harris, Mya Hall, William Chapman II, Alexia Christian, Jordan Davis, Brendon Glenn, Trayvon Martin, Victor Manuel Larosa, Jonathan Sanders, Joseph Mann, Salvado Ellswood, Albert Joseph Davis, Darrius Stewart, Billy Ray Davis, Michael Sabbie, Brian Keith Day, Christian Taylor, Troy Robinson, Sean Bell, Felix Kumi, Asshams Pharoah Manley, Keith Harrison McLeod, Junior Prosper, Kenney Watkins, Lamontez Jones, Paterson Brown, Dominic Hutchinson, Anthony Ashford, Alonzo Smith, Tyree Crawford, India Kager, La'Vante Biggs, Michael Lee Marshall, Sterling Higgins, Jamar Clark, Shelly Frey, Richard Perkins, Nathaniel Harris Pickett, Benni Lee Tignor, Miguel Espinal, Michael Noel, Kevin Matthews, Quintonio Legrier, Dreasjon Reed, Keith Childress Jr., Janet Wilson, Randy Nelson, Eula Love, Antronie Scott, Wendell Celestine, David Joseph, Calin Roquemore, Dyzhawn Perkins, Christopher Davis, Marco Loud, Peter Gaines, Torrey Robinson, Kevin Hicks, Christopher McCorvey, Mary Truxillo, Demarcus Semer, Willie Tillman, Terrill Thomas, Sylville Smith, Terence Crutcher, Miriam Carey, Darius Robinson, Paul O'Neal, Alteria Woods, Jordan Edwards, Aaron Bailey, Ronell Foster, Antwon Rose II, Pamela Turner, Christopher Whitfield, Michael Lorenzo Dean, Oscar Grant, Steven Taylor, Korryn

Gaines, Yvette Smith, Redel Jones, Tony McDade, Nicolas Chavez, Freddie Blue, Roy Nelson, Tiara Thomas, Brandon Jones, Bernard Moore, Rayshard Brooks, Danquirs Franklin, Samuel DuBose, Amadou Diallo, and countless others whose names and lives deserve to be discussed and honored with not just a renewed moral commitment to oppose racism and fascism but ardent anti-racist and anti-fascist activism.[112] The families of these men, women, and children deserve to see Americans of every complexion and experience speak out against the protocols, practices, and systemic racism that contributed to the tragedies their loved ones suffered—tragedies that America has too long abided.

Some of these Americans were sitting in their homes when they were killed by police; others were engaged in everyday activities like babysitting, buying groceries, eating out, driving, shopping for gifts, or spending time with friends. Some were sleeping. But all are dishonored when, as Donald Trump did on June 12, a U.S. president says of the "chokehold"—an often prohibited law enforcement maneuver that ended the lives of some of those named above—that "the concept of [the] chokehold sounds so innocent, so perfect," and that "we have some real bad people [in America]. You saw that during the last couple of weeks [of protests]. . . . And you get somebody in a chokehold. And what [are] you going to do now? Let go and say, 'Oh, let's start all over again. I'm not allowed to have you in a chokehold'? It's a tough situation [for the police]."[113] The dignity of the families of those killed in incidents of police brutality is likewise assailed when the president reverently, almost gleefully, describes the Minnesota National Guard dispersing Minneapolis protestors as being like "a knife cutting butter—right through . . . and yes, there was probably some tear gas and some other things, [but] the crowd dispersed and they [the Guard] went through . . . and everything was fine and you didn't hear too much about that location having problems anymore"; Trump adds that such "easy" methods should be used all over the country, pointing to ongoing protests in Seattle as an example.[114] And George Floyd's family in particular is disrespected when, almost unthinkably, President Trump seeks to rewrite their loved one's last words at a public event celebrating the U.S. economy. Praising himself over a slightly better-than-expected jobs report on June 5, the president calls it a "great day" for the recently murdered Floyd—even as protests over his death are still taking place in hundreds of cities and towns across America. "Hopefully, George is looking down right now and saying 'this is a great thing that's happening for our country,'" the president muses. "This is a great day for him, it's a great day for everybody. This is a great day for everybody. This is a great, great day in terms of equality."[115] Hours later, according to a *New York Times* report, Trump retweets a video of one of his most vocal supporters, far-right conservative commentator Candace Owens, calling Floyd "not a good person."[116] The *Times* further notes that on the day Trump touted Great Depression–like unemployment data as a "great day for everybody" and for the cause of "equality," black unemployment—according to the very report Trump was then heralding—was on the rise.[117]

Some of the president's comments about race may remain permanently inexplicable as well as inexcusable. During an interview with Harris Faulkner, a black journalist from Fox News, Trump says of President Abraham Lincoln's actions while in office, which included issuing the Emancipation Proclamation, that "it's always questionable, you know, in other words, the end result"—such a startling comment that Faulkner feels compelled to remind the sitting president that African Americans "are free" because of Lincoln's deeds.[118] Trump subsequently declares that he "will not even consider" renaming U.S. military bases presently named after Confederate military officers, contending, seemingly without irony, that the names of these self-confessed (often slave-holding) traitors to the Union are part of America's "history of Winning, Victory, and Freedom."[119] Trump will further disrespect black Americans when—just hours after calling positive economic news and the deployment of the National Guard to disperse anti-police-brutality protestors a "great day" for police brutality victim George Floyd—he retweets a post, according to *New York Times* chief White House correspondent Peter Baker, "quoting [a] conservative commentator saying of Floyd, 'The fact that he has been held up as a martyr sickens me.'"[120] The damage done by the president's retweet is compounded when he seeks to justify his earlier quotation of Walter Headley, a civil rights era–Miami police chief the *New York Times* reports "was unconcerned with complaints of police brutality," by contending that the phrase "when the looting starts, the shooting starts" has two meanings. Per Trump, the infamous utterance can mean either "if there's looting, there's probably going to be shooting," or "if there's looting, there's going to be shooting."[121] The president, who falsely says the phrase has been used "many times," insists that these are two "very different meanings"—and makes no apology for using the phrase on Twitter, despite the social media platform quickly determining that it "glorifie[s] violence" and hiding it behind a warning message.[122]

Trump's methods and rhetoric during the anti-police-brutality protests are considered so extreme that in extraordinary, even historic statements to the press, some of America's top military officials and veterans must distance themselves from the sentiments expressed publicly by their commander in chief. The chairman of the Joint Chiefs of Staff, Gen. Mark Milley, says of his appearance with Trump at St. John's immediately following the attack on peaceful protestors in Lafayette Square, "I should not have been there" and "it was a mistake."[123] Milley further issues a letter to the Joint Force underscoring that both he and the whole of the U.S. military will "stay true" to their "oath to the American people," an unsettling preelection reminder that Trump has in the past demanded absolute loyalty from his subordinates—not loyalty to the country or to their sworn duties, but to him personally.[124] Echoing Milley, retired four-star general Richard Myers, the chairman of the Joint Chiefs of Staff under Republican president George W. Bush, calls Trump's actions in Lafayette Square "not right," "unconstitutional," and something "that should not happen in America."[125] As for the White House, it issues a statement more than a week after the attack on civilians in Lafayette Square saying that the president has "no regrets" about his or his administration's actions.[126]

On June 11, CNN reports on "a coalition of several hundred West Point alumni from six decades of graduating classes 'who collectively served across ten presidential administrations'" and have now decried, in a public letter, "leaders [who] betray public faith through deceitful rhetoric, quibbling, or the appearance of unethical behavior," an "erod[ing] [of] public trust" the letter appears to lay at the doorstep of both Trump and the military commanders who enabled him during the civil unrest following George Floyd's death.[127] As the letter opines, "We, a diverse group of West Point graduates, are concerned. We are concerned that fellow graduates serving in senior-level, public positions are failing to uphold their oath of office and their commitment to Duty, Honor, Country. Their actions threaten the credibility of an apolitical military."[128] The letter echoes some of the sentiments found in a *New York Times* investigative report following the events in Lafayette Square; according to the *Times*, some members of the D.C. National Guard who participated in the government action in D.C. on June 1 "say they feel demoralized and exhausted. . . . [They] were so ashamed in taking part against the protests that they have kept it from family members."[129] Expressing similar sentiments, hundreds of former senior U.S. officials—including at least 315 former ambassadors and 25 former generals—issue a public statement via the website *Just Security* entitled "The Strength of America's Apolitical Military," in which they announce that they "are alarmed by calls from the President and some political leaders for the use of U.S. military personnel to end legitimate protests in cities and towns across America."[130]

Former Trump secretary of defense Jim Mattis—long silent on the president whose administration he resigned from in December 2018—likewise makes an extraordinary public statement as the protests continue, writing in *The Atlantic* that "Donald Trump is the first president in my lifetime who does not try to unite the American people—does not even pretend to try. Instead he tries to divide us."[131] Mattis adds that the dismal state of America in mid-2020 is the "consequence[] of three years without mature leadership."[132]

As to both the domestic and foreign policy of the Trump administration, there are questions that remain to be asked whose answers may be determinative of the election results in November 2020. For instance, why were nearly 7,500 Twitter accounts run by Turkish president Recep Erdogan's ruling party—accounts that tweeted a total of 37 million times—deemed violative of Twitter's terms of service, and what sort of election-related activities had these accounts executed or been planning prior to their deactivation?[133] Likewise, after Twitter deactivated 1,000 Twitter accounts traced to the Chinese government in August 2019, how were more than 170,000 new accounts linked to Beijing able to appear almost immediately, and what election-year activities had these accounts participated in before finally being removed in June 2020?[134] Why, according to NPR, did "hackers backed by China target[] Biden's campaign staff" with phishing attacks in a manner similar to Russian cyberattacks on Clinton staffers during the 2016 presidential campaign?[135] Were they seeking to honor Trump's public request in October 2019 for aid from the Chinese Communist Party—a request that mirrored a similar one Trump made to the Kremlin in 2016? These events raise a further question: given his prior public support for Trump's efforts to seek dirt on Biden from the Chinese government, what subjects will Secretary of State Pompeo be privately discussing with Chinese government officials when he meets with them in Hawaii in the summer of 2020?[136]

Reports of an upcoming Pompeo-Beijing Pacific summit come as OAN is boasting, according to a report in *The Atlantic*, that "it has obtained several hours of secret recordings of then–Vice President Biden's conversations with Ukrainian officials"; the magazine notes that if these audio recordings indeed exist and are authentic, they are, according to "two former U.S. ambassadors to Ukraine and a former ambassador to Russia," "likely linked to pro-Russian interests in Ukraine and a Russian intelligence operation."[137] That this material should be provided to OAN as Donald Trump Jr. is involved in an effort to purchase OAN raises the specter of the president's son again being involved, as he was in June 2016, in the receipt of valuable political interference offered to his father by hostile foreign interests. *The Atlantic* notes that Giuliani associate Andriy Derkach has already been linked to the release of several such Biden tapes, and that "the person now claiming to have more tapes is OAN's Chanel Rion, the on-air personality who went with Rudy Giuliani, the president's personal lawyer, on his December trip to Ukraine in part to find information on Biden to help Trump."[138] In the past, some such evidence has been received by Giuliani allies from a website with "Russian links," Nabu Leaks, which appears to be the 2020 version of WikiLeaks—but this time focused on smearing Joe Biden with bogus intelligence rather than Hillary Clinton.[139]

As revelations reach American media that the Trump family is linked to the Miss Ukraine Universe pageant through the now-arrested Oleksandr Onyshchenko and Trump friend Phil Ruffin's Ukrainian wife Oleksandra Nikolayenko—a course of connection that includes Eric Trump serving as an unpaid judge for the pageant in Kyiv as far back as 2009—it remains unclear what may be revealed, perhaps even before the election, about the family's long-term ties to corruption and pro-Kremlin figures in Ukraine.[140] Indeed, in a brief excerpt from John Bolton's book *The Room Where It Happened: A White House Memoir,* released in mid-June, Trump's former top national security official reports that he is "hard-pressed to identify any significant Trump decision during my tenure that wasn't driven by reelection calculations," a stunning revelation of systemic corruption that Bolton's publisher immediately augments by confirming that, per the book, "Trump's Ukraine-like transgressions existed across the full range of his foreign policy."[141]

American voters cannot yet know whether the president's domestic transgressions—including systemic meddling in federal investigations involving his associates—will likewise continue unabated in the latter half of 2020, though the odds of a Michael Flynn pardon seem to rise nearly daily. Yet an independent review of DOJ's efforts to dismiss the Flynn case, authored by longtime mafia prosecutor and former federal judge John Gleeson, has now found that the DOJ campaign to invalidate Flynn's guilty plea is a "gross abuse [of prosecutorial power]," "corrupt," "highly irregular," and "riddled with inexplicable and elementary errors of law and fact"; moreover, it "depart[s] from positions that the government has taken in other cases" and therefore appears to be aimed solely at "benefit[ting] a political ally of the President."[142]

Whatever the result of the Onyshchenko and Flynn cases, Trump's political team has certainly never been further from establishing any connection between the Bidens and corruption in Ukraine—and it is more probable than ever before that Trump and his agents' advancement of corrupt interests in Kyiv may yet become public. On June 14, 2020, the National Anti-Corruption Bureau, the entity whose acronym gives the website Nabu Leaks its name, reveals that it has intercepted a $6 million bribe intended to halt the investigation and prosecution of Mykola Zlochevsky—precisely the ambition would-be Trump and Giuliani political instrument Viktor Shokin, as well as Trump business associate Onyshchenko, have in the past pursued.[143] The revelation by NABU of a bribery plot to achieve the ends of Trump's allies in Ukraine is accompanied, according to the *Washington Post*, by an unambiguous declaration by NABU that it has "ruled out involvement by Democratic presidential candidate Joe Biden or his son, Hunter," and an audit of "the many outstanding case files looking into Burisma . . . found no evidence of wrongdoing by the Bidens."[144] Notably, given that a December 2016 video of a Trump transition event featured Ukrainian fiscal service chief Roman Nasirov, NABU also announces that—besides Zlochevsky, former Burisma employee Andrii Kicha, and former tax official Olena Mazurenko—the former deputy head of Kyiv's tax office, Mykola Ilyashenko, has been implicated in the bribery scheme.[145] While NABU does not accuse Nasirov of wrongdoing, the fact that the former fiscal service chief's pending criminal case involves the alleged facilitation of a tax evasion scheme by Zlochevsky ally (and Trump associate) Onyshchenko moves Trump and his clandestine political team one step closer to Ukraine's highest-profile ongoing corruption scandal.[146]

That the Senate Judiciary Committee votes along party lines, on June 11, to subpoena fifty Obama administration officials as part of "efforts to scrutinize the origins of the FBI's investigation into Russia and President Donald Trump's team" confirms that preelection attempts to advance Kremlin propaganda will emanate not just from pro-Trump media organs but from the halls of Congress.[147] When, in early June, the Senate

Select Committee on Intelligence votes on a bipartisan basis (8–7, with Sen. Susan Collins joining the Democrats) to "require presidential campaigns to report offers of foreign election influence to federal authorities," Senate Republicans "prepar[e] to remove the provision of the bill when it heads to the Senate floor"—perhaps because public evidence suggests the Trump 2020 reelection campaign has already crossed the bill's ignominious reporting threshold.[148]

Nor is DOJ aloof from Trump's efforts to remake the history of the 2016 presidential election and tip the scales of the 2020 election. In late May, Dana Boente—the FBI's top lawyer, and a participant in the successful prosecution of Michael Flynn—is "asked to resign," per NBC News, by individuals at "high levels of the Justice Department rather than . . . FBI Director Christopher Wray."[149] Notably, this attack on one of the federal law enforcement officers who investigated and prosecuted Flynn comes as DOJ is set to release, at the prompting of a federal lawsuit brought by the Electronic Privacy Information Center and *BuzzFeed News* reporter Jason Leopold, a new version of the Mueller Report that contains previously redacted information from the Roger Stone investigation. A preview of the redacted material, published by *Politico*, reveals a heretofore obscure nexus between Stone, Flynn, and Trump's autocratic allies in Israel and Turkey, Netanyahu and Erdogan: during the same period in summer 2016 that Stone was seeking election aid from Israel and Turkey in the form of Clinton dirt, Michael Flynn's Flynn Intel Group, an entity with innumerable ties to Israeli and Turkish nationals, was allegedly discussing the possibility of kidnapping U.S.-dwelling Turkish cleric Fethullah Gulen for $15 million and the gratitude of President Erdogan.[150] This confluence of events raises the possibility of previously undisclosed preelection Trump-Israel and Trump-Turkey collusion—collusion potentially involving criminal conduct, illicit payoffs, and "intelligence" intended, per the now-public search warrant applications in the Stone case, as an anti-Clinton "October Surprise." Given Rudy Giuliani's history of cybersecurity and lobbying work connected to both the Israeli and Turkish governments, these developments may also presage the eventual discovery of a Ukraine-like conspiracy to defeat Clinton that matches the one that has apparently been unfolding against Biden since 2018.

On June 4, Trump, per the *Washington Post*, "strongly hints" that he will pardon Stone to ensure that his friend and adviser serves no federal prison time—tweeting to his more than 80 million followers that, as to the matter of a pre-sentence presidential pardon, Stone can "sleep well at night."[151] *Politico* reports the tweet is a "promise" that Stone will not be incarcerated for his actions in 2016, a pledge that the digital media outlet calls merely Trump's "latest intervention" in Stone's federal criminal case.[152]

The prospect of more such dramatic deviations from convention in 2020 and beyond may give Americans the sense that the guardrails for political campaigning have been permanently dismantled, along with so much else the nation long took for granted. Even far-right media organ Fox News—which by summer 2020 is nevertheless considered well to the left of OAN—seems no longer bound by even the most minuscule strictures within its sphere of activity, as the cable news outlet is caught, per a CNN report in June, "publish[ing] digitally altered and misleading images" of the anti-police-brutality protests that dovetail with Trump's campaign rhetoric by erroneously making "Black Lives Matter protesters . . . appear violent and dangerous."[153]

Meanwhile, irregularities in the governance of the nation seem to be appearing at an ever faster clip. For instance, given that the president has in the past appeared to synchronize his administration's pandemic response to demands made by his mega-donors, it is deeply concerning that the Treasury Department has declared that it will not release to the public any information—not even recipient names—related to its distribution of $660 billion in pandemic relief funds for small businesses.[154] At the local level, the ongoing pandemic continues to pose questions the president increasingly does not deign to acknowledge, such as why Texas, Florida, and California are continuing their reopening plans in mid-June 2020 despite, per the *New York Times*, seeing "their highest daily tallies of new virus cases."[155] Even as the Associated Press is reporting a rise in new COVID-19 cases in nearly half of U.S. states and CNN is reporting that hospitalizations are increasing in at least a quarter of the states, the president has turned his attention away from the pandemic entirely, speaking of it in the past tense in a June Fox News interview, ceasing to hold press conferences about his administration's response to the crisis, refusing to hold the 2020 Republican National Convention in North Carolina because the state is insisting on adhering to CDC guidelines regarding social distancing, and meeting with Dr. Anthony Fauci so infrequently that by the beginning of June it has been at least two weeks since the two men have spoken.[156] Trump's inability or unwillingness to meet with the nation's top infectious disease expert stands in contrast to his decision to make the time to order U.S. Military Academy graduates back to West Point so he can give them a commencement address. The result, the AP reports, is that seventeen graduating cadets asymptomatically infected with the novel coronavirus are reintroduced to the West Point community.[157]

It is, by all accounts, due in significant part to his handling of both the pandemic and the Floyd protests that by mid-June, Trump's average approval rating across a number of recent approval polls is at 41 percent.[158] The question is what such polling might drive the president to do in late summer and early fall 2020. So it is not without reason that, on June 10, Senator Cory Booker (D-NJ) indicates that he is "concerned," much as Trump attorney Michael Cohen had expressed concern more than a year earlier, that Trump will refuse to concede if he loses the November 2020 election.[159] Booker's concerns could only have been exacerbated by the Democratic primary in Georgia—a state long plagued by voting problems that its Republican legislators and executive branch officials seem consistently to exacerbate rather than alleviate—with CNN reporting hours-long lines to vote in many majority-minority precincts and concluding that the June 9 election in the Peach State constituted a "meltdown of the voting system" that has "sparked widespread concerns about voter disenfranchisement."[160] As many of the voting restrictions in Georgia and elsewhere that have caused widespread voter disenfranchisement were passed under the guise of anti-voter-fraud efforts, it is particularly startling when, just days before the Georgia primary, *Slate* reports, building off reporting from the *Washington Post*, that "Trump appears to have committed felony voter fraud" by trying "to register to vote under an out-of-state address that is not, in fact, his legal residence."[161] Shortly after the *Slate* report is published, *HuffPost* reveals that Trump's press secretary, Kayleigh McEnany, "cast Florida ballots in 2018 using her parents' address in Tampa, even though she lived in Washington, D.C., and held a New Jersey driver's license."[162] Ciara Torres-Spelliscy, a fellow at the Brennan Center and a law professor at Stetson University in DeLand, Florida, tells the digital media outlet that "if Florida is not really your primary residence, then it's inappropriate for you to be registered as a voter in Florida."[163]

This uncertainty and faithlessness at home are matched by uncertainty and faithlessness abroad. On June 5, the *Wall Street Journal* reports that Trump will withdraw, by September 2020, 9,500 of the United States' 34,500 permanently assigned troops in Germany—a presidential edict, the newspaper opines, that will "dramatically reshape the U.S. military posture in Europe" and, according to "former senior defense officials and lawmakers," "further weaken a key alliance and empower U.S. adversaries. Moscow is likely to welcome the open display of differences between two key North Atlantic Treaty Organization allies."[164] CNN military analyst Mark Hertling, a retired lieutenant general who formerly commanded the U.S. Army in Europe, calls Trump's announcement "dangerous, short-sighted, and . . . an additional gift to Russia [that] will further harm our alliances [abroad]."[165]

Meanwhile, in North Korea, according to the *New York Times*, "two years after President Trump enthusiastically declared that 'there is no longer a Nuclear Threat from North Korea,' classified assessments and experts conclude that the North's nuclear arsenal is far larger than it was in 2018"—a revelation that signals the failure of Trump's "maximum pressure campaign" on North Korean dictator Kim Jong Un, which had variously seen the president taunt the young autocrat on Twitter and receive letters from him that, per Trump, caused the two men to "fall in love."[166]

The president's personal, administrative, and diplomatic recklessness—during the course of the COVID-19 pandemic, the nation's ongoing civil unrest, an election season already marred by significant malfeasance by both Trump and his campaign, and a systemic weakening of democratic governments across the globe—sends America into the 2020 general election more concerned about its continued coherence as a nation than at any other time in modern American history. According to the *Washington Post*, Gail Helt, "a former CIA analyst responsible for tracking developments in China and Southeast Asia," says the Trump administration's crackdowns on peaceful protestors mirror "what autocrats do" and "what happens in countries before a collapse."[167] This in part explains why, by June 7, 80 percent of Americans are telling NBC News/*Wall Street Journal* pollsters that the country is "out of control," and indicating "by a 2-to-1 margin" that they are more troubled by the actions of government agents in response to the George Floyd protests than the violence perpetrated by a small percentage of anti-police-brutality protestors.[168] This extraordinary state of affairs reminds us that the November 2020 presidential election may be not just a critical opportunity but perhaps even one of the nation's last opportunities to right itself before substantially more damage, perhaps even irreversible damage, is done to America's rule of law and American democracy. *Politico* notes, ominously, that "the president and his supporters have a range of mechanisms at their disposal—particularly amidst a pandemic—to restrict voting in person, change voting rules, hobble the postal service, or just intimidate or discourage voters, all of which could have an impact on election results."[169]

Proof of Collusion, *Proof of Conspiracy*, and *Proof of Corruption* together form a three-act play with a surprisingly conventional structure: the inciting incident of Russian interference in the 2016 presidential election, accompanied by clandestine pre-election Trump campaign collusion with America's enemies; the clash between Trump's already compromised pre-election foreign policy and the reality of rising geopolitical instability from Russia to the Middle East; and the inevitable denouement of an impeachment trial, a global pandemic worsened by Trump's incompetence and venality, and a historically ugly reelection campaign that Trump seeks to win by returning to the same sort of transnational collusion with which he launched his political career.

And yet, just as the end of the Trump presidency—whether it comes in 2021 or 2025—will likely not be the end of Trump as an insidious presence at the heart of American life, the eventual end of Trump at some point in the future will not be the end of Trumpism. Whatever happens in fall 2020, Donald Trump's time in the Oval Office has been an inflection point in U.S. history that will still be worthy of historical consideration centuries hence. Future historians will surely marvel at the same incomprehensible disloyalties, tribal fidelities, and inchoate decompositions of our national character that we contemplate now. They will wonder—as we do—how so many of us let any of this happen.

This trilogy of the Trump era, now over 2,400 pages in length—with 12,000 citations to our era's very best journalism—is therefore only a first pass at the dystopian script of this period. It has been rendered, as in this author's view was necessary, via the lens of the "curatorial journalism" demanded by our present surfeit of high-quality digitized information. What comes next, however—whether a dramatic salvation or further flagrant degradation—is likely to unfold faster than any curation can adequately record. All that is left to say is this: given the sacrifices that those Americans who came before us made to preserve our democracy, and that so many are making right now to carry us through the variously grand and esoteric trials of the Trump era, there is nothing we cannot dare to ensure that our descendants look back on our actions with admiration and even—we hope—pride.

ACKNOWLEDGMENTS

Several days after I finished writing this book, my father, Bob Abramson, passed away unexpectedly. My dad's lucky, love-filled life spanned nine decades of American history—from a century-defining world war in the 1940s to a century-defining coronavirus pandemic in the 2020s, from the swing era to vocaloids, from the golden age of television to the age of ubiquitous internet, 5G, and XR.

Because of the COVID-19 outbreak, when my father was rushed to the hospital in late April I could only speak to him by phone. He had hoped to read the manuscript of this book while in quarantine at home; he never got the chance to do so, though as a lifelong avid news-watcher he knew with as much precision as anyone the danger posed to America by this president. And because he was gently, generously, and lovingly attentive to the lives of his children, he not only had digested *Proof of Collusion* and *Proof of Conspiracy* but already knew the narrative strokes— the venality, perfidy, and scandal—that would interweave in this book.

When I was a boy, I believed that what a father passes to his son, if it is to mean anything at all, must be a series of hard skills that help the boy demonstrate the masculine publicly. When my father couldn't play catch with me or teach me to paddle a canoe expertly, I believed he had failed me somehow, deeding me a life in which I would constantly fail myself. I don't know how I came to believe such a foolish thing when I was eight, though it was probably from television. In any case, when my father suffered his first cardiac event in 1984, I became even more convinced that he and I had something wrong with us on the inside—a weakness. I thought about that every day for decades, and it drove me in ways both good and ill.

But as my father, within sight of eighty after a first heart attack a little past forty, lay alone in cardiac distress in the "clean" wing of a hospital in coronavirus-riddled Massachusetts, I thought tearfully about his long life—which he was wise enough to know had been blessed. And what I found, with an alacrity I had never imagined possible, was that everything my dad taught me was everything that mattered: that the world isn't always logical, and doesn't often bend to our logic; that *process* matters; that a life, like an idea, can evolve and self-amend; that a strong heart finds the honorable path; that tears are not an evil; that hard choices are best faced by fearlessly considering every angle; that one can be intelligent and witty without being mean-spirited, decent and generous without being naive, a listener and good-humored without being a follower. That we abide in values, not rituals. My father taught me to attend to the world, even as he grew better and better able, as the years passed, to attend to those closest to him. Most of all, my father taught me to be a reader, curator, and editor of both my own perceptions and the wisdom of others. And with this lesson—a steady but invisible hand—he served as the co-author of this 2,400-page trilogy of books. He spent a patient lifetime helping me reach its completion.

In our last conversation, my father told me that one of the great joys of his life was simply sitting—doing anything or nothing—alongside my mother, the woman he never stopped thanking his lucky stars loved him back. I told him I feel just the same about my wife. My father and mother were married for fifty-three years; he proposed to her within seventy-two hours of meeting her at a summer camp in Connecticut, and she said "yes" four days later. My wife and I have been married only six years, but not a day goes by that I don't count my blessings. She knows the trials, setbacks, and genuinely scary moments that accompanied the creation of this trilogy, all of which she experienced firsthand alongside me. She knows—because she's smart and because I've said it often—that these books would not exist without her love. If my father co-wrote this trilogy, my wife's signature is on every page and in every margin.

My father and I spent our many decades of knowing each other with more in common than I ever fully took in—though the fact that we were both introverts was clear. As an introvert, I know that to have been joined on the journey of this trilogy by someone I count a friend, my agent Jeff Silberman, has been a godsend the same way a bridge over a chasm is. Jeff's wisdom, patience, and temperance during what has been as hectic a span of researching, writing, and proofing as one could imagine—the twenty-one months between beginning *Proof of Collusion* and finishing *Proof of Corruption*, with another sprawling affair, *Proof of Conspiracy*, in the middle—has been a miracle I don't deserve.

On every trip worth taking, you encounter strangers who soon become essential companions. In the arduous fact-checking of *Proof of Corruption*, I was aided by an assiduous team of professionals: Liz Mazucci, Penelope Lin, Janet Byrne, Barbara Clark, Morgan Blue, and Elizabeth Blackford. At Macmillan, my publisher, Jennifer Enderlin, and my editor, Michael Flamini, exhibited great vision and dexterity in shepherding a project of significant scope and complexity, as did the members of the marketing, editorial, and publicity teams at St. Martin's Press: Hannah Phillips, Martin Quinn, Alan Bradshaw, Rebecca Lang, and Laura Clark. I offer special thanks, as well, to Robert Petkoff, who narrated all three audiobooks in the *Proof* trilogy and did so with an aplomb that not only do I admire and envy but will say belies the extraordinary difficulty of the task this somewhat unusual project set for him.

I hope this trilogy does justice to the faith, patience, and friendship of not only the many people behind it but also, as important, its readers. I hope it honors my wife's encompassing wisdom, the nourishing support of my mother and two sisters, and the lifelong model of my wonderful father—a man who will remain in the company of his loved ones always.

INDEX